LAROUSSE

WORLD MYTHOLOGY

EDITED BY PIERRE GRIMAL

GALLERY BOOKS
An Imprint of W. H. Smith Publishers Inc.
112 Madison Avenue
New York City 10016

Larousse World Mythology translated from
Mythologies de la Méditerranée au Gange and
Mythologies des Steppes, des Iles et des Forêts by
Patricia Beardsworth

First published in Great Britain in 1965 by
The Hamlyn Publishing Group Limited

This edition published in 1989 by Gallery Books
An imprint of W. H. Smith Publishers Inc.
112 Madison Avenue
New York City 10016

ISBN 0-8317-5421-4

Printed in Yugoslavia

CONTENTS

COLOUR PLATES

The god Gou of Dahomey. In the fetish worship of Dahomey Gou is the moon, one of the trinity of gods including Maou, the sun, and Lissa, his wife and the mother-goddess, the chameleon. *Musée de l'Homme*

Preceding page: The Sarcophagus of King Nectanebos, third century B.C. The hieroglyphics are from the funerary *Book of Am Duat* and these, with the carved figures, describe the passing of the soul through the underworld in the solar barque. *British Museum*

INTRODUCTION:
MAN AND MYTH

At the beginning of this century the specialist mythologists were fond of assuring us that myth was related to a specific state of primitive human thought: the human mind, they said, before it became sensible to reason, saw the world as a stage for a dramatic conflict between capricious wills, and they stated dogmatically that every human society in the course of its historical evolution was forced to go through a prelogical period in which myth was a normal mode of thought. After this stage came the 'age of the philosophers', followed by the 'age of scholars', discoverers of rational and objective truths.

This, then, was common and official doctrine, the outcome of Positivism and, more distantly, of the Enlightenment. To study myths, it was believed, was to review the errors and follies of man, at times a distracting business, at times mournful, like leafing through an album of pictures of a bygone age.

In the last generation or two, historians of human thought have ceased to be content with this scheme of things: today the myth is no longer considered a mode of thought reserved for primitive societies. If each one of us considers the matter carefully and honestly, he will be forced to recognise that myth is far from foreign to our daily thought, and, what is more, that it is far from opposed in essence to scientific thought.

It is the object of the myth, as of science, to explain the world, to make its phenomena intelligible. Like science too, its purpose is to supply man with a means of influencing the universe, of making sure of spiritual and material possession of it. Given a universe full of uncertainties and mysteries, the myth intervenes to introduce the human element: clouds in the sky, sunlight, storms at sea, all extra-human factors such as these lose much of their power to terrify as soon as they are given the sensibility, intentions, and motivation that every individual experiences daily. But it could be argued that the proposed 'explanations' are puerile and false. Yet if myth is error, is it not the same with scientific 'truths', which are destined to be constantly superseded? Myth and the provisional truths of science are only different approximations to Truth, that enigma of enigmas, which even after so many achievements and discoveries, still remains closed to us. If it is true that scientific progress is a march which has led scientists from error to error, then the same natural affinity exists between primitive explanations of myths and the most modern theories, which, as we now know, are only working hypotheses destined one day to be abandoned. In a certain sense the scientific conception of the atom at the beginning of the twentieth century was a myth, which has proved its truth only in so far as it has been surpassed.

The myth really answers a fundamental need of the human mind, and to grasp this fact we do not need artificially to invent the idea of primitive thought; we need only recall our own childhood impressions—after all, scientific truths play only a very slight part in our most intimate daily life, and what we *know* completely rationally is little compared with what we believe or suppose. Everything in us that is not transfused by rational knowledge belongs to myth, which is the spontaneous defence of the human mind faced with an unintelligible or hostile world. To a child cut off from its mother's reassuring presence the universe takes on a menacing shape; moonbeams and the rattling wind conjure up evil beings. To picture them, give a name to them and call them angels or fairies, is a way of making them favourable from the start and of gaining influence over them by drawing them close. Even at this elementary stage, as it is spontaneously born in the infant mind, the myth is not fundamentally religious: the spirits of woods, light and water are not divinities, only presences capable of influence in spheres over which we have no hold. The relationship that we suppose them to have with ourselves allows us to influence them by persuasion, prayer and magical constraint, and that is how we extend and protract our influence over the world. It is very rare for myth to be a chance dream; on the whole it is essentially a working hypothesis, an attempt to escape from the powerlessness that is our fate.

These myths, which might be called prayer myths, abound in every sphere. They are to be found in particular in the rites of Roman religion. The personality of Jupiter Elicius (He Who Attracts), for instance, has a primary connection with the prayer for fire from the sky to descend safely upon the earth, thus harmlessly ridding the storm clouds of their fearful anger. The myth starts to take shape at the

A two-headed Hermes from the sanctuary of La Roquepertuse (Bouches-du-Rhône). Third to second centuries B.C. Borély Museum, Marseilles. *Suquet*

very moment when someone supposes (this being a veritable scientific hypothesis) a Jupiter who will comply with the demands made in a rite. Then episodes and details accumulate, based on this first hypothesis, and the story will then be told of the rite that failed, the misadventure of the king who did not observe certain sacred rules, and so brought down upon himself the anger of the god and was struck to death by lightning. If one is Roman and careful to subject the universe to the divisions of Law, one will imagine a whole casuistry of thunder; King Jupiter will be portrayed in the midst of his council, examining with the aid of the *dii consentes* (the god councillors) the advisability of striking one place rather than another with heavenly fire, and the best way of doing it. And this mythical product of the imagination, once it has become coherent, complex and consolidated by a whole body of sacred literature, may then be put to the test, just as scientific hypotheses were in a later era. Naturally some minds will be sceptical, but others (the greater number) will refuse to take the risk of incredulity, and the myth will continue to play its part of reassuring, relieving the soul of the weight of crushing anxiety and freeing the mind for other tasks by guaranteeing it the aid of truth.

Bit by bit the mythical universe comes to rule all aspects of life. There are in fact societies which regard myth as reality itself, more real than the objective universe. We find it difficult to understand such an attitude, which seems pathological in origin—or what is called pathological, although it is often nothing but an aggravation of the normal. So when an individual is possessed by myth, we are apt to say that he is ill; when entire societies are affected, we tend, like the philosophers of old, to shrug our shoulders and speak of prelogical mentality. However, this submission to myth is viable; with the help of myth many people resolve a thousand and one everyday problems and

attain moral equilibrium and even wisdom. The 'absurd' rites and beliefs of Roman religion did not prevent the race that believed implicitly in them from building the greatest empire in the world—and Plato, great lover of myths, was none the less one of the most authentic philosophers of all time.

In Dahomey, if a man wants to see into the future in order to determine his actions, he visits the sorcerer, who 'draws the Fa'. The Fa is both a god—the greatest of gods at that, the father of a thousand voodoo demons, the personal genie of the individual consulting him—and a game by which the omniscience of the god is made clear. To 'draw the Fa' a string of date stones or the stones of other fruit is thrown on to a table, falling sometimes on the convex, sometimes on the concave side. For each position there is a corresponding numeral; by reading off the number so obtained against a reference table, it is revealed which minor demon is appearing; the particular problem motivating the consultation must be solved through him. Now there is a myth corresponding to each god, and though the connection between the myth thus evoked and the real situation is often very tenuous, careful reflection will usually produce a link between them and at the same time show the relevance of the myth: this, then, produces a certain state of mind in the consulter, which puts an end to uncertainty and allows him to take action. Detailed knowledge of the myths and their meanings is the special province of the sorcerer, who acquires it in the course of long study in veritable closed colleges. These studies are intended to reveal to him the supernatural half of the real world; thus myth turns into magic. (See René Trautmann's *La Divination à la Côte des Esclaves et à Madagascar*, Paris, 1939.)

The question is not whether the supernatural universe exists or not: this problem does not arise, for it is as meaningless as the material representation

Monolithic head from Easter Island. Nothing is known of the purpose of these huge figures raised by an unknown people at an unknown period in history. *Herbert Stevens*

of the atom or the molecule for the rationalist scientist, who must accept their existence because he adheres to a certain system of laws and hypotheses. Like the most orthodox science (in our view) the validity of the Dahomey sorcerer's magic is proved by its effectiveness. Effective it is, or appears to be; no more is needed to make the mythical world that it postulates quite true.

This fundamental, but for modern man somewhat disconcerting, characteristic of mythical thought has been well described by Carl Kerényi in his book *The Antike Religion*. He tells of the experiences of Sir George Grey, who was appointed Governor of New Zealand in 1845. Sir George soon saw that it was impossible for him to understand the way of thinking of 'subjects unworthy of Her Majesty'. This way of thinking seemed to be on a plane that neither he nor his interpreters could reach: the plane of mythical thought, which imposed on reality structures quite unlike those familiar to the excellent governor. In order to accomplish the mission with which he had been entrusted, Sir George was led to compile a collection of myths, which he published in 1855 under the title *Polynesian Mythology and Ancient Traditional History of the New Zealand Race*. In the Preface he says: 'To my surprise, however, I found that these chiefs, either in their speeches to me, or in their letters, frequently quoted, in explanation of their views and intentions, fragments of ancient poems or proverbs, or made allusions which rested on an ancient system of mythology; and although it was clear that the most important parts of their communications were embodied in these figurative forms, the interpreters were quite at fault—they could then rarely (if ever) translate the poems or explain the allusions.' [What Sir George had discovered was a living mythology, still playing its part of mediator between past and present, and taking from the past the spiritual elements that would

give form to the present, make it more intelligible and consequently make action possible.]

For myth—and here is another of its fundamental characteristics—is an established link between the past and the present. Bronislaw Malinowski described it thus: 'Myth as it exists in a savage community, that is, in its living primitive form, is not merely a story told but a reality lived. It is not of the nature of fiction, such as we read today in a novel, but it is a living reality, believed to have once happened in primeval times, and continuing ever since to influence the world and human destinies . . . . These stories live not by idle interest, not as fictitious or even as true narratives; but are to the natives a statement of a primeval, greater, and more relevant reality, by which the present life, fates, and activities of mankind are determined, the knowledge of which supplies man with the motive for ritual and moral actions, as well as with indications as to how to perform them.' (*Myth in Primitive Psychology*, London, 1926, pp. 21, 39.)

It is easy to illustrate these statements made by Malinowski. In point of fact, the myth most often relates an ancient memorable act attributed, as the case may be, to a god, hero or even ordinary mortal, but always destined to have never-ending consequences. In its simplest form it is the breach opened in the mountain by Roland's sword, or the hill covering the giant's tomb: the landscape, stable as it is, is there to indicate the event in question, which helps create order in the world. There are also more subtle myths, which report a renewable creative act and make it possible, by means of rite, to commence a part of creation all over again in present time. For example, if a certain society acknowledges that the fertilisation of the earth by rain was in primordial times brought about by the union of a god and goddess, the rite will consist of miming each year or each season the form this union took. A priest and a priestess, who are the god and goddess, wearing the costume and adopting the attributes of the deities, imitate their gestures and couple solemnly before the assembled people or in the secret of the sanctuary 'so that creation may continue'. Or perhaps, if two Polynesian societies conclude an alliance, two men, representing the two peoples, in the course of a ritual dance go through a new birth to make them brothers; the rite, in this case, is not only a dramatisation of the abstract notion of fraternity, it is the renewal of a creative act, like that postulated by the myth. The celebrant is absorbed into the universe of myth, and it is he who finally governs reality. In many societies it is from this source that festivals, theatre and literature spring—all that goes to make the life of cities, and allows individuals to experience collective emotions, and enables them to appreciate the values of the city, moral values as well as a sense of beauty.

Trying to define this spiritual quality of the myth, Carl Kerényi recalls the expression that Thomas

Basalt figure of an Aztec god, probably Xochipilli, which means 'Flower Prince'. He was the god of pleasure. *British Museum*

The bull was the symbol of various gods in the ancient Near East. This bull's head was found in the royal tombs of Ur at Tello and dates from the third millennium B.C. *Tel-Vigneau*

Mann used with reference to Freudian experience: 'corresponding to the language of quotations there is a "life in quotations"'. (Thomas Mann, *Freud und die Zukunft*, Vienna, 1936, p. 53.) Myth is both an inspiration and protection for anyone who lives like this; it is a model for present action and a justification of it. But the words that we are forced to use to describe this fundamental experience, life according to myth (which has its being in the obscure zone preceding the emergence itself), are dangerous and deceptive. Myth is not chosen after intellectual deliberation because it can be adapted to action; it is an instinctive choice, accepted with all one's being, and it is compounded more of faith than reasoning. Myth is one of the elements of consciousness; in the collective consciousness it exists as a reality, which finds an echo in the individual consciousness as language sometimes does. Each subject has the impression that he has become part of the myth, that he is reliving it—especially in the course of festivals—and he discovers it to be unfolding for him in the present.

The place of myth, at the very root of thought, when thought is still only an outline plan of action, explains why all races without exception have possessed a mythology—because, without myth, action becomes impossible. It also explains why even the most advanced moderns, the most enlightened, are not without it. In our time, as in the past, political myths exist which have only loose connections with objective historical reality: what contemporary French historian has not been led to evaluate the (still perceptible) influence of a myth like that of the Bastille? The image of Epinal is a form of myth. The Tennis Court Oath and Heracles' pyre are two myths that rely little on authenticity for their effectiveness. But, like the sun's light or the air we breathe, myth reveals itself only indirectly, and each individual must make a personal effort to discover its presence at the basis of his own thinking. It suffuses our consciousness and, what is more, our subconsciousness; it is *our* truth, a truth which it is sacrilegious, at times fatal, to question. And this applies to every sphere of personal life, for there is none exempt from myths, particularly at moments of decisive choice. The heroes one admires give forth myths spontaneously, and we know that without Achilles and without the *Iliad* Alexander would not have undertaken the conquest of the East. Youth has always adopted myths and sometimes in maturity has had the courage to realise them.

And what is true of individuals is true of societies. There is a Homeric society whose vitality, perpetuated by the epics, animates to a large extent the soul of the Ancients. It matters little that perhaps there never was a Trojan War.

But, like everything human, like language and laws, myths become spent and lose their efficacy. There comes a time when myths play a lesser part in the lives of individuals. But myths do not die; they are transformed. Being detached from collective consciousness, which they occupy no longer, they acquire an objective reality, which allows them to be reviewed and exposed to criticism.

Usually a thinker then emerges who collects and classifies them, so formulating a mythology. This happened in Greece in the sixth century B.C. and earlier. It happened too, in different ways, in all those countries where poets shaped mythology into sagas or epics, and where priests incorporated its substance in holy books to nourish religion. Elsewhere, in a humbler capacity, myth became a tale told by the elders, and, thus debased, belongs to the realm of folk-lore.

When mythology ceases in this way to be a living thing, it becomes enveloped in mystery; its inner truth and efficacy are no longer apparent, and its meaning is questioned—unthinkable as long as it was alive! Greek mythology has not escaped this fate; by the time it had taken on the form known to us it was already a mystery to the Greeks themselves. Philosophers, fascinated by what was for them no more than a tissue of absurdities, examined the matter, and the theories that they evolved still govern our modern conception of the myth.

Anxious to lose nothing of the tradition bequeathed them by the past, Greek philosophers imagined that myths, beneath their puerile appearance, concealed secret teachings which they in their wisdom might fathom. But they could not agree about the nature of this teaching. Some said positively that legends were only distorted history; and this theory has often been expounded by the moderns. It calls to mind the celebrated and oft-repeated adage: 'The epic is the form given to history by primitive peoples.' For example, the explanation given of Heracles' labours was that they were a disguise for the exploits of a powerful king, great destroyer of monsters and benefactor of humanity. Each episode was reduced to human proportions; the monsters, it was claimed, were in reality natural phenomena, over which Heracles triumphed by completely non-mysterious means. Thus the Hydra of Lerna was interpreted as a swamp fed by eternal springs, and when Heracles cut off the heads of the monster, he had, according to this theory, diverted the streams supplying water to the marsh. And so it was with all the great legends, all of which received an historical interpretation. This theory, called Evhemerism after its proposer, the philosopher, Evhémère, had wide success among 'reasonable' people (who were not being reasonable at all in this respect) in spite of the difficulties it raises. Yet it had the advantage of being reassuring, and of satisfying the narrowest type of good sense, and perhaps, in fact, it may contain an infinitesimal particle of truth, in so far as myths rely perceptibly at times on historic events, conferring on them eminent and exemplary merit.

Other, less down-to-earth, philosophers affirmed that myths were the popular cloak over a divine revelation. If their message could be deciphered, the mystery of the world would be revealed. This theory found its followers, particularly among Egyptian mythologists. Alexandrian thinkers, analysing side by side myths of every possible origin, built up a complex system, which they placed under the protection of the god of knowledge, Hermes the Thrice Greatest (Hermes Trismegistus), and thus it came to be called Hermetism. For them the myth of Isis, for instance, is a parable of creation, and from it they deduce a complete physical and metaphysical doctrine of the universe.

The moderns, too, have followed the same path; they have often admitted the fundamental postulate of Hermetism, that myth is a symbol, a mask for abstract truth which the exegetist has to discover. Accordingly the cycle of Heracles has long been explained as a solar myth: it would appear that the inventors of the legend had found this way of conserving the result of their astronomical observations —by telling the people a fine story and proposing to initiates a physical doctrine.

It was accepted, for example, that the hero's twelve labours described in picturesque fashion the path of the sun through the twelve celestial signs. But, even supposing Heracles were a solar hero (though such is not the case), this fact in itself would not suffice to explain the myth and would in no way exhaust its meaning. The essential factor, the reason for this astronomical information taking on such a strange disguise, would still be unaccounted for. But, in point of fact, and we can now see this more clearly, the object of the myth, whatever its place or time, is rarely to formulate a physical or astronomical theory, and myth is never—and never has been—a gratuitous physical theory. Its domain is spiritual and moral reality, the inward world. The important thing is that Heracles was strong, patient, heroic, that he came up against Fate, and that he was involved in liturgical dramas that have their echo in the consciousness and activity of men. For this reason the attempts of Max Müller and his school to discover in the name of Greek and Indian divinities proof of their naturalistic symbolism were destined to failure from the very beginning.

Mythologies, as we see them today, appear to be evidence or, if you will, somewhat defaced traces of an ancient state. They are the spiritual prehistory of a society. In this respect they are quite like languages: these too, both those in common use and those confined to literary texts, tell us something about the very ancient past.

The term 'comparative mythology' is fairly old, but it must not lead us into error. In the first place it stood for something quite different from the genetics of myths, which is in itself a very recent science. Previously it was applied to what we sometimes call the ethnographic method, which rests on entirely different postulates. From the middle of the nine-teenth century, in fact, specialists in mythology and folk-lore were struck by similarities between myths of widely varying periods and backgrounds. Ethnologists particularly noted among the primitives myths resembling those of classical mythology, which, being better known, served as a yardstick: universal floods, succession of divine generations, engendering of the human race from the earth and so on, all this gave rise to mythical explanations constructed on similar lines.

Having formally brought together certain myths, the temptation was to establish systematic comparisons, and to suppose that a universal mythical language did exist, and that the differences noted were the result of chance circumstance, or usage, or phase of evolution of a particular mythology. So it became commonplace to explain such and such a Roman myth by a Surinam custom, or a Greek legend by a Polynesian or African rite.

This method gave birth to such important works as Sir George Frazer's *The Golden Bough*, in which certain mythical schemes are studied because they are thought to be fundamental and, in consequence, likely to occur in fields far apart. Thus there was a mythology of royalty (in itself), another of the immortality of the soul, a cycle of vegetation, of death, and so on. But at length it was perceived that this method had a major drawback; it led to neglect of what is the very essence of the myth, its character of social reality, that is, reality specific to a given social group. So comparisons unjustified by historical or geographical possibilities came to be considered illegitimate. Formal resemblances, however striking, did not authorise the establishment of complete identification between myths and beliefs—thus it was decided—where the domains proper to them were separated by centuries or thousands of miles.

What may be called the new comparative mythology, which made its first postulates in the early years of this century, was founded in response to this need for method. Its object is to discover what historically controllable connections may exist between given mythological systems. Just as linguists, by studying various known languages and comparing them with each other, have succeeded in distinguishing the families of languages and in reconstructing anterior linguistic states from which attested languages have emerged, so it has seemed possible to discover, for example, an Indo-European legendry and a proto-Semitic mythology. If the linguists have set an example for the mythologists, they have certainly not done so by chance: comparative linguistics and comparative mythology go together, since language is the mainstay of myth (myths, after all, can exist only through words) and since language is, inversely, informed by myth, which imposes on it a thousand and one traditional ways of viewing the world.

There again, just as the object of linguistics is not to discover the origin of language, so comparative

Leather mask from Novgorod. Masks were worn by worshippers in many places in the ancient world during religious or magic rites. The wearer of the mask usually assumed the role of a god or devil. Eleventh or twelfth century.

Megaliths such as this one in Minorca are found in several European countries, those forming Stonehenge (c. 1500 B.C.) in England being among the most famous. It is believed that they were used in religious rituals. *Viollet*

mythology does not claim to explain the origin of myths. It simply claims to chart their evolution, over as long a period as possible, and to discover the transformations that they have undergone in the course of their existence before crystallising into the form we know. It is thought that in this way it will become possible to discern—underlying the particular mythical form—extremely ancient schemes of thought, the instinctive moulds, as it were, into which the thought of a society flows.

In France, the works of Georges Dumézil have done much to further and disseminate research of this kind. They have shown, beyond any possible doubt, that forms of mythical thought encountered in Rome, for instance, appear—in a perfectly recognisable form—in epics of the Indo-Iranian world, in Germanic sagas, in Celtic tales, that is to say throughout the length and breadth of the Indo-European world. Only Greek mythology is left out, and here the results are not so clear—which implies that it borrows a great deal from Oriental fields, Semitic and pre-Semitic perhaps, and that it is the result of a more complex synthesis.

There, then, one can see outlined the prehistory of Aryan thought; there the secret laws, the postulates determining it, stand revealed. Dumézil lays particular emphasis on the pre-eminent value of certain concepts, like that of tripartition: there is in existence a whole series of myths that presume a society divided into three groups with complementary functions— the sacerdotal class, the warriors, the agriculturalists —and it becomes possible to follow the development of this social system, as migrations separated the different branches of the Aryan race and imposed on them different living conditions. From that point myths came to be as gratuitous as they seem to be at first; they conform visibly to a profound logic—briefly, the comparative method in the hands of its modern masters introduces order where, before them, the most complete confusion appeared to reign.

Naturally the present work owes little to the researches of the comparativists; it aims to bring together some of the principles from which one may hope to gain a fairly exact idea of what was, historically speaking, mythical thought in the majority of great human societies. It will become clear to the reader that this thought is extremely diverse; the differences may indeed appear more marked than the similarities. But the contributors had to remind themselves when beginning to compile this book that myths are not the deplorable product of human folly, or even a necessary precursor of rational thought. They are inseparable from all thought, forming an essential and vital element in its make-up. Without them human consciousness is mutilated, wounded to death. Trying to know them better, even if only from the outside, is not only surrender to the (very legitimate) pleasure of reading and rereading a collection of fine stories, it is a way of probing deeper into men's thoughts.

This painting at Tassili N'Ajjer seems to show a ritual scene, the meaning of which is obscure. Women seem to be the chief cele-brants, leading a procession of men and women. *J. D. Lajoux, from Merveilles du Tassili N'Ajjer*

Prehistoric rock painting from Tanzoumaitak. The female figures are probably engaged in some ritual. From *Les Merveilles du Tassili N'Ajjer* (*J. D. Lajoux*).

Prehistoric rock painting, probably depicting a horned goddess of some agricultural religion. From Aounrhet, Tassili. *H. Lhote*

THE PROBLEM OF PREHISTORIC RELIGIONS

The science of prehistory has brought to light two great revolutionary facts: the enormous, the prodigious antiquity of human lineage, and the existence of a many-sided prehistoric art, which has produced many works as beautiful as those created by historic civilisations.

Lascaux, authenticated by Abbé Breuil from its first discovery, is regarded as one of the landmarks in the history of art. But is it only a gigantic aesthetic creation? Or is it—and this is probable—something more? Is it evidence of a religion? Or were these striking drawings intended only to perform magic? Did the painters mean to encourage the hunters? Or were they already in search of beauty for its own sake?

We must take particular care not to project our own ideas, our own philosophies on this too-distant past, where our conception of things is irrelevant. Our point of departure should be in prehistory itself, though it is very sparing of information on the subject.

However, one preliminary fact is certain: the Mousterian strata contain some unquestionable burial places. They belong to Neanderthal man, who flourished in the Middle Palaeolithic period (between 140,000 and 40,000 years before our era). These creatures, more bestial in features than any other primitive man, used to bury some of their dead. So they had some idea of survival after death, which is one of the psychological preconditions of religion.

The other fundamental precondition is the notion of the divine. We have no direct evidence that such a notion existed in prehistoric times. We must examine various indications one by one. By considering material conditions of existence within these societies, and some of their customs, it is possible to draw some inferences as to their spiritual life.

Examination of the remains of bones in various strata has proved how short the life of the prehistoric man was. Infant mortality was high. Considering the prevalence of famine and epidemics, the main chance for survival for these small groups must have lain in the repeated fertility of the women. So it is possible that the human statuettes, mainly feminine, of the Perigordian and Gravettian cultures of Eurasia (between 27,000 B.C. and 20,000 B.C.) are related to some cult of fertility. They often exaggerate sexual features. Early prehistorians thought of them as portraits in miniature, and from them drew conclusions about the anthropological characteristics of the populations of the period. But the statuettes often have aesthetically conceived deformities (as in the Venus of Lespugue and the Menton statuettes), which testify to their nature as artistic creations. There is therefore no argument against supposing that they represented some divine incarnation of procreation, very early precursors of the mother-goddesses.

But the desire to perpetuate the race was not the only imperative need: prehistoric men were preoccupied with the need to defend themselves and to hunt game. We find it difficult to imagine how tragic these obsessions must have been, considering the prodigious inadequacy of their arms. Right up to the Upper Palaeolithic Age, that is, until the invention of perforating projectiles—first assegais, then arrows—big-game hunting was an exhausting and heroic adventure. Without killing some great beast the tribe was destined to death by famine within a few weeks. They had to hunt! What means were there?

Up to the time of the Mesolithic culture, humanity had at its disposal for attack on its physical surroundings no sources of energy other than fire (flaming brands and forest fires), weight (ditch-traps and precipices) and individual human muscle. Forest fire could be utilised only by many hunters armed with assegais or bows: so it must have been used very

The fertility of plants, animals and women of the tribe was of prime importance to prehistoric man, so he carved figures of women with exaggerated female characteristics who were the precursors of the fertility or mother-goddesses of later time. These were probably intended to perform magical functions — to ensure that life continued and multiplied.

A Neolithic goddess carved in an artificial sepulchral cave at Coizard (Marne). *Musée de l'Homme*

Venus of Willendorf. *Naturhistorisches Museum, Vienna*

little before the Upper Palaeolithic Age (from about 40,000 to 10,000 B.C.). Before that, our ancestors had to be content with ditch-traps, slings, bolas and sticks, which gave a minimal return for effort.

There is evidence that Neanderthal men hunted the mammoth with the lance, scrambling under the beast to pierce its stomach: one can imagine the danger. (A lance, made entirely of yew, was found in the position of the abdomen in the skeleton of a mammoth at Lehringen in Lower Saxony.) Even when the introduction of the assegai made hunting large ruminants possible, returns must still have been fairly low, as the wounds inflicted were rarely mortal, except when poison was used.

From these few facts it is clear that success was a matter of luck, and must have seemed something of a miracle to the hunter. So great was the element of skill, human strength and chance that it must have seemed essential to galvanise the hunter's energy by inducing advanced states of exaltation. He had to imagine the desired success in advance. He also had to try to obtain the consent of the animals, as ethnographic evidence had shown, just as wood-cutters of old used to ask consent of the tree they were about to chop down. [K. Rasmussen, in *The Alaskan Eskimos* (Report of the Fifth Thule Expedition 1921–4, vol. x, No. 3, Copenhagen, 1952, pp. 25–26) describes the Eskimo method of persuading the whale to consent to his own death.] The result seemed so hazardous that preparation became a first necessity: so actual events were forecast, thus ineluctably guided, by negotiations between human desire and the spirit of the victim. Hence the anxious wait, the systematic search for omens, dreams, visions, telepathy — in short, all exceptional, unverifiable states of mind, which our civilisation rejects as such and declares unreal.

Let us be quite clear about this. Through science and modern equipment we have at our disposal

Female menhir statue. First half of second millennium.
Musée de St Germain

Prehistoric figurine carved in limestone. Senorbi. Musée de
Cagliari. *Yan*

The Venus of Lespugue, an Aurignacian ivory statuette
Musée de l'Homme

This doe may been depicted in order to give the wearer of the amulet – the hunter – power over his quarry. *Vertut*

'Procession with bison', carved on a pendant, shows the head, feet and spine of the conquered animal with a line of figures on either side. This may have been a representation of a familiar scene, or perhaps the carver hoped to bring about this desired event by depicting it. Périgueux Museum. *Vertut*

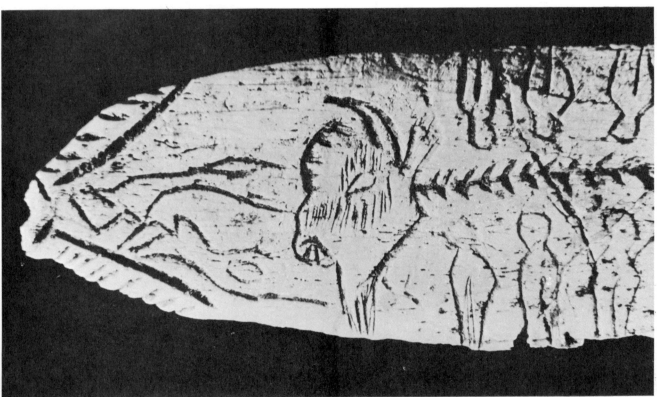

increasing sources of energy, whose exploitation depends only on things we can verify: prehistoric and archaic societies, on the contrary, desperately lacking all forms of energy, sought both the stimulation of muscular energy and 'second states'; the latter aims at developing uncommon perceptions, which cannot be reproduced at will, such as the ability to recognise invisible presences (similar to animal instinct), a sense of direction or even premonitions.

The constant and primitive demands on these prehistoric men resulted in a dependence on perceptions that modern man does not need: thanks to these perceptions the savage lives in a world in which spiritual forces appear to be essential reality, and in this way the spirit becomes more important, almost more real than the physical body. This spirit world, which is peopled and ruled by invisible forces, prepares the mind for religious beliefs.

We have seen that, from this time onwards,

concern for the continuance of the race might give rise to certain anthropomorphic cults: but the divine came to be pictured in other, inevitably animal, forms because of the importance of defence and hunting. For six hundred thousand years, men had to kill to eat. And there were, too, the great wild beasts that stalked man. The animal world was the great obsession night and day, just as corn, barley and rye have, more recently, been the obsession of the peasant. So prehistoric societies probably had animal cults. We can even go so far as to say that these cults may have found expression in cave drawings, in which the human figure is a rare exception and seems deliberately misshapen when it does occur. Painted or carved bison, horses, reindeer, as well as some felines, rhinoceros, mammoths and bears are seen on the walls and ceilings of many caves.

Prehistorians believed at first that these were

Masked woman carrying an object that looks like a bowl. It is possible that she is engaged in a religious ceremony. *J. D. Lajoux*, from *Merveilles du Tassili N'Ajjer*

Some of the figures in this painting seem to have animal characteristics. One on the left has horns and three are almost proceeding on all fours. *J. D. Lajoux*, from *Merveilles du Tassili N'Ajjer*

simple, representational paintings: man depicting, for pleasure, the creatures that were part of his life. The striking verisimilitude of most of these works seemed to support this interpretation. A later theory supposed that these animals were sexual symbols — the horse symbolising the male sex, the bison the female sex. Such theories still belong to the realm of pure hypothesis. But it is within the bounds of possibility that paintings and carvings portrayed not so much the animal as such, as the animal-spirit, the animal as seen by the visionary — a prophetic symbol.

It is worth noting that this last hypothesis would help to explain one of the great curiosities of prehistoric art: the practice of superimposing one painting on top of another. If the painted animal represented not so much an actual creature as the subject of a vision, then it lost value in the course of time: a new vision required representation in place (literally) of the old. This is one possible explanation

Prehistoric man not only painted the animals he wished to hunt, but from time to time he had to paint them again to renew his power over them. This may be the explanation of this scene in the cave of the Trois Frères in which drawings of animals are seen overlapping other, earlier drawings. Copy by Breuil

A prehistoric sorcerer has disguised himself as an animal —
probably to take part in a magic rite.

Rock carving at Tassili, in the Sahara, showing a man with a
dog's head and a dog. *Musée de l'Homme. R. Perret*

of the extraordinary repainting and overlapping of
figures, which is such a prominent feature, for
instance, at Lascaux.

But people will point out that to exert an influence
over beasts is magic, and therefore the opposite of
religion.

However, we must be on our guard against projecting the classifications of modern philosophers on
primitive mentality. As history and the human mind
have progressed, so everything has become particularised, specialised, distinct. The archaic mentality,
on the other hand, blended one thing into another
in a kind of fierce nebula. For instance, a particular
popular festival may have had a dozen meanings at
one and the same time. And each of these meanings
was true to some degree. The question may arise
whether such and such a ceremony held by a savage
tribe was basically magical or religious. It was probably both. The invisible spirit must be revered and, if
possible, influenced, even compelled.

In prehistoric times hunting was carried out under
conditions conducive to magic, and magic, after all,
is but the remote projection of an individual's will.
Fascination is probably the most elementary form of
it. Numerous flesh-eating species practise it regularly
in the form of frightening behaviour, fixed staring
and shrieking. Palaeolithic hunters could not help
resorting to such a technique as this as they tried to
summon up muscular strength, their only source
of energy. Hence the frenetic dances, that entire
school of combative fury which transformed men into
madmen, beginning as soon as childhood ended. For
months on end young boys received their initiation,
being subjected to a brutal and exhausting discipline:
by the time it was over the hallucinated adolescent
had seen visions and was instructed about the world
of spirits to which he addressed himself ever after,
either directly or through a sorcerer.

So it is quite probable that in prehistoric times
magic and religion were not entirely unconnected. It
is equally probable that myths, divulged in the course
of successive initiations, came to dominate ceremonies
that took place in more and more remote parts of
ornate caves. The Cave of Felines at Lascaux is tiny
and very hard to reach; the Combarelles form a
narrow tunnel. Space is so restricted in these spots
that we cannot imagine large assemblies of worshippers; it is much more probable that a very small
number of celebrants gathered there and passed on
the artistic traditions. Besides, the comparative
originality of the scenes depicted on the walls — each
cave having its own style or successive styles — indicates
that they were used by small, relatively closed tribal
sects.

Religion and magic, closely interconnected, inseparable, animal-religion and animal-magic, for *and*
against the beasts themselves — this seems to be the
obscure legacy of all prehistoric art. This age-old
worship of animals has left its mark on the most
ancient religions known to history, both in Egypt and
among Indo-Europeans. For example, according to
Suidas, the tenth-century Greek lexicographer — and
this is indirectly confirmed by Ovid — the woodpecker
was none other than the future Zeus.

We know these prehistoric myths only through
their picture forms: we have no other knowledge of
them. Without Greek texts a metope showing a
woman seated on a bull leaping over dolphins would
never suggest the theme of Europa's abduction. But
who can tell whether the Lascaux bulls were not later
echoed in that far-away incarnation of thunder and
of Zeus?

The rites of some peoples in modern times —
especially some in Africa and Oceania — may be a
clearer echo of the religions that were practised by
our ancestors of prehistoric times.

A deeply incised rock carving at Bardai, North Africa, shows a bull with long horns. Late Pastoral period. *Emil Schulthess (Conzett and Huber)*

Since hunting was one of the chief occupations of prehistoric man many cave paintings show hunting scenes. In this exceptionally fine painting the figures seem almost to be dancing. *J. D. Lajoux*, from *Merveilles du Tassili N'Ajjer*

The cliffs of Deir el-Bahri at the foot of which lie the tomb and temples of Queen Hatshepsut. The pharaohs and their consorts were buried in tombs hidden in pyramids or in the cliffs of the Nile valley. Inside the tombs corridors led to rooms in which were stored all the necessities and luxuries of the pharaoh's earthly life that he wished to enjoy in the world of the dead. *Roger Viollet*

EGYPT: SYNCRETISM AND STATE RELIGION

Ancient Egypt is the country most famous for its cults of gods and the dead. This preoccupation is reflected in the number of temples, tombs, statues and other works of art connected in one way or another with the local religion. The Egyptians were the most devout of men, for the whole atmosphere of their life was imbued with the presence of the divine. Even in modern times most of their sacred monuments still stand in the valley of the Nile, and precious bas-reliefs, statues and porphyry are carefully preserved in the world's museums.

With such a wealth of material to hand, dating from different periods of Egyptian civilisation, the student of Egyptian religion would appear to be at a great advantage, and he should, one feels, have a clear and complete knowledge of its mythology and doctrines. But this is not the case, for although there are many monuments representing certain relatively recent periods, for earlier times they are rare, especially in some transition periods, when beliefs were subject to important transformation.

There is little material surviving from the earliest times, when the essential features of the religion were undoubtedly determined: although certain archaeological remains from the end of prehistory have come down to us, they bear no inscriptions and therefore furnish only very vague indications of the customs and beliefs of this period. The inscriptions that date from the first few dynasties are still fairly laconic, being limited in most cases to indications of names and titles.

By the Fifth Dynasty more sources are available: the *Pyramid Texts* (thus named because they were engraved in the burial chambers of the royal pyramids of the Fifth and Sixth dynasties) provide much fuller information. These texts, on the subject of ritual and magic, convey more precise details of Egyptian beliefs during the period of the Old Kingdom. It should be noted, however, that although they contain elements that were in existence long before the date at which they were copied down, the primitive concepts they reveal are already relatively developed and often differ from their original form.

Another difficulty lies in the very nature of Egyptian religion. Although the inhabitants of the Nile valley were all faithful to the same fundamental concepts (hence their religion affords a measure of psychological unity) theologians did not think it necessary to co-ordinate their beliefs in a really rational system, and they laid even less claim to the foundation of a unified doctrine applicable to the country as a whole. Mythological concepts varied from place to place, and to a certain degree, from period to period. Egyptian religion actually consists of a powdering of local religions. In addition, the Egyptians, being conservative by nature, were reluctant to abandon ancient concepts, even when the concepts themselves evolved, or contact with neighbouring cult-centres led to the introduction of new doctrines: apparently untroubled by the different and often contradictory implications of the various innovations, they always managed to juxtapose or blend them together. The forms of mythological thought were many and various, and appealed to Egyptians as just so many different ways of expressing the same fundamental beliefs.

If a unifying principle exists in this diversity of beliefs, it is to be found in the unitary organisation of the cult of local gods. For the Egyptians, the pharaoh, as son of the gods, was responsible for the standard practice of a cult. In the final analysis, the essence of Egyptian religion for its worshippers lay not in the acceptance of a dogma, but in the ritual practice of a cult.

Little material survives to tell us of the early religious beliefs of the Egyptians. This scene of the sacrifice of an ibex comes from the tomb of Atet at Medum. This technique of limestone painting is a very rare one, found only in this period. It consists of cutting back the surface of the figures and filling the space with solid pigment. Fourth dynasty: *c.* twenty-sixth century B.C. *Fitzwilliam Museum, Cambridge*

The Battlefield Palette shows a lion, probably representing a king, seizing his enemies. This palette dates from the Late Pre-dynastic Period when Egypt was divided into two kingdoms. *British Museum*

In very early times the territory that later became Egypt was divided into a series of principalities, each of which enjoyed complete autonomy under the aegis of a particular god, who had his sanctuary there. In this remote past many local cults probably grew up, and these continued to be practised in spite of political and religious changes: the provinces or nomes of Egypt under the pharaohs, with their chief towns and tutelary gods, were later to provide a reminder of this former state of affairs. In that very early age of antiquity each god had his own particular attributes and appearance, and later Egyptians continued to picture him in the same way.

From the very beginning some of these gods were given typical human attributes; this was the case, for instance, with Min of Coptos, Atum of Heliopolis, Ptah of Memphis, Osiris of Busiris, and several others who can be recognised only by their physical attitude, headdress and emblems. Others took the form of a plant or of some rather bizarre totem—a pillar, obelisk or similar significant symbol. However, in most cases the gods took the shape of some animal, which was regarded as the soul (*Ba*) of the god. This predilection for zoolatrical forms, which so impressed Greek and Latin authors, has been explained in various ways by ethnologists.

It undoubtedly corresponds to practices quite common among primitive peoples regarding animals: believing them to be endowed with certain specific powers, these early men went in healthy fear of them, and this, in the natural course of things, led to veneration. Anubis, an early god of the dead, is depicted as a jackal: Sobk, a god particularly venerated in Faiyum, is depicted as a crocodile; Horus, the god of the sky, appears as a falcon; Thoth, god of the moon and patron of writing, learning and the sciences, is shown either as an ibis with pointed beak or as a dog-faced baboon; Hathor, one of the main figures in the pantheon, takes the shape of a cow; Bastet (or more accurately Oubastet) appears in the form of a cat. Most deities had, at least from time to time, an animal equivalent.

Furthermore, this manifestation in animal form went beyond the purely theoretical. It seems highly likely that from the very earliest times Egyptians had bred one particular member of an animal species and looked on it as sacred. As the years went by this custom was extended until in later periods the whole species was thought sacred. One result of this were necropoles (graveyards) of animals, such as those containing crocodiles, cats or ibis. It is also known that in important cult-centres, such as Memphis, Heliopolis or Hermonthis, a sacred bull was kept in an annex of the temple, and was thought to be the living soul of the local god.

Classical authors, such as Herodotus and Strabo, have remarked on the conditions governing the choice of animal, and excavations have revealed sumptuous necropoles in which bulls were buried

Djed-column surmounted by a crown. The djed-column, symbol of stability, is thought to have originated from the form of a column of bound papyrus. As an amulet placed on the mummy, it later acquired false associations as the backbone of Osiris — here suggested by the god's crown. Probably Late Period: c. fifth to first centuries B. C. *Fitzwilliam Museum, Cambridge*

Composite deity with body of Ptah-Seker (Ptah-Sokaris), ram's head of Amun or Khnum, and hawk's back of Horus. Saite or Late Period: c. sixth to fourth centuries B. C. *Fitzwilliam Museum, Cambridge*

Ptah-Seker. Glazed faience amulet. Saite Period: seventh to sixth centuries B.C. *Fitzwilliam Museum, Cambridge*

Ram of Amun. Fragment from the limestone relief stele of a certain Neferaabet from Deir el-Medina. Thirteenth to twelfth centuries B.C. *Fitzwilliam Museum, Cambridge*

Cults of animals were common in Egypt. Some animals were considered sacred, and gods were frequently depicted with animal heads. One of these was Bastet, shown as a cat or with a human body and cat head. This early drawing on limestone may depict an early cat-god. Later New Kingdom: *c.* thirteenth to tenth centuries B.C. *Fitzwilliam Museum, Cambridge*

In the Late Period the animal cults were largely revived and large necropoles or animal cemeteries testify to the popularity of this cult. This figure of an Apis bull dates, from this period. *British Museum*

with divine honours. For example, in the Serapeum of Memphis the sarcophogi of the Apis bulls are found in lines along deep galleries, the most ancient going back to the Nineteenth Dynasty.

However, the Egyptians very soon conferred human personalities and conduct on the divinities they worshipped, no matter what they had been originally. Creating their gods in their own image, they made them think and act according to human standards. Furthermore, they most often depicted them in therianthropic form, giving them a human body, but affixing to it the head of the animal with which they were previously identified.

As soon as the god came to be regarded as having a human character of a superior kind, he had to live in a temple, like a prince in his palace, surrounded by his family and servants. The temple was the house or domain of the god, and included, as well as his place of residence, workshops and gardens. In the temple proper there was first a monumental gate (the most perfect example of this is to be found in the pylons built in the period of the New Kingdom), then came a courtyard into which those privileged among the faithful were admitted, a stateroom (which later became the hypostyle hall) and finally the private apartments, of which the *cella* or sanctuary was the main one: this is where the god himself was enshrined, undoubtedly in the form of an idol.

Both the meaning and economy of the sacred liturgy can be explained with reference to this conception of the divinity. The god had to be treated like a man of elevated rank. Each day at fixed times he was the centre of ritual—purification ritual, toilet ritual and ceremonial offerings—performed by the highest dignitaries among the priests, who accompanied their gestures and movements with formulas and hymns, which they recited to illustrate the meaning of each rite and to give it a mythological significance.

At festival times, either calendar festivals or local affairs, there were more solemn ceremonies as well as the daily ritual: offerings would be increased, and special liturgies would be used to emphasise the particular character of the festival. Thus it became customary on certain occasions for priests to carry in solemn procession the image of the god in a shrine, often in the shape of a boat with a cabin in the centre. They would take it from the sanctuary, through the public parts of the temple, and even through the town, stopping in wayside chapels as they went. Such processions as these came to be known as the 'great outings' of the god and gave rise to popular celebrations.

According to the Egyptian way of thinking, the pharaoh was the supreme officiating priest of the gods. Being almost of divine origin himself, his filial duties consisted of ensuring the preservation of the gods and executing in their honour the previously described rites. As successor to the former chiefs of principalities, he had to carry out his liturgical duties

Baboon-headed ape. Relief in the temple of Ramesses II at Abydos. Nineteenth Dynasty. *Roger Wood*

in all the cult-centres in the country. This idea was so firmly anchored in Egyptian minds that in the reliefs on temple walls sacred functions are always depicted with the pharaoh officiating as priest. But even supposing that under special circumstances the king did in fact officiate in person at the rites (when, for instance, the Residence Festivals took place), none the less it must be admitted that under normal conditions he delegated his sacerdotal offices to the local high priest and the clergy under him. The sacerdotal hierarchy became very much extended as time went by, especially during the period of the New Kingdom, and in so doing it acquired great power: in addition to the regular clergy, who were divided into several classes with highly specialised functions, there were also lay priests, bound by temporary vows, and an administrative staff connected with the temples and its surrounding estate.

The entire economy of the temples depended on royal generosity. The pharaohs took it upon themselves to restore the sacred building or to build new ones; again, it was through their largesse that divine offerings were made, and they maintained the clergy. If they wanted to show their attachment and gratitude to the gods—perhaps on the occasion of a thirtieth anniversary (the *heb-sed*) or following a victory over long-standing enemies of Egypt—they would frequently establish a new type of offering to the benefit of the temple as well as those serving it. As a result

of this generosity, which increased with each succeeding generation, the great Egyptian temples enjoyed enormous wealth, especially the temple of the tutelary god of the dynasty.

Divine families and myths

At each cult-centre the local god was considered to be the universal god: he had been in existence since time began, and he had, it was thought, organised the world and created all living beings. This fundamental concept, common to all interpretations of the origin of things, is clothed in mythological tales, which vary from place to place and betray the Egyptian genius for invention. The divine legends, with their essential characteristics rooted in the very distant past, tended both to explain how the universe came to be created and to expound the role played by the principal god and those around him. The great local god was endowed with a divine family, or, to be more precise, a circle of followers, who intervened severally in the realisation of the plan of creation and the organisation of the cosmos.

These divine families often followed the pattern of the simplest social groups. A triad was quite common (consisting of the god-father, goddess-mother and divine son). The triad of Memphis consisted of Ptah, the principal god, Sakhmet, the goddess with the head of a lioness, and Nefertum, the young god who

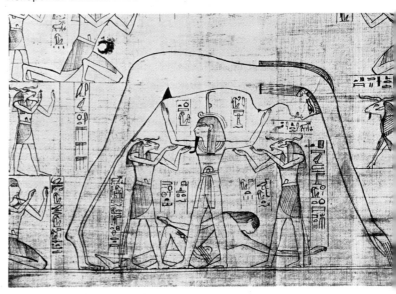

wore the lotus flower on his head; more will be said later about the Theban triad.

Before the principal myths are recounted, it is worth noting that these tales have rarely come down in a complete or coherent version. The only uninterrupted accounts we have of certain myths date from fairly late periods, and these were furnished with details that certainly did not form part of the original myth.

In reconstructing them, one can only refer to other religious and magical texts for allusions to certain features and then develop from them a coherent account. Furthermore, it must be taken into account that myths, like all tales that are passed on by word of mouth, are quite fluid in their development and in their sequence of episodes. Certain features undoubtedly belong to the original, while others were borrowed from allied myths or even from completely different mythical sources. These borrowings often changed or blurred the theme of the original myth.

Of the divine legends of ancient Egypt, several acquired the significance of true cosmogonic and theological systems and became very widespread, thus ensuring great popularity for the chief actors in this divine drama.

A god could owe his prestige to the principle that he represented. This was particularly true in the case of cosmic deities, who embodied the forces of nature. All polytheistic races have held the sun to be an important god, if not the main god, because of the leading part played by the solar star in the economy of the universe.

The popularity of a deity may equally result from his beneficent role. Particular favour was accorded to the gods of fertility, who were at the same time agrarian gods, or mother-goddesses, and, of course, to the funeral gods.

Finally, some gods owed their ascendency to political contingencies. In Egypt, where the royal house was always the foundation stone of the country's social, political and religious structure, the god of the residence tended to become the dynastic god, and had every chance of heading the divine hierarchy. So the god of the king tended to become the king of the gods. Thus Ptah, worshipped at Memphis, became an important god in the Old Kingdom, and later, when the capital transferred to Thebes, for reasons not known to us, Amun rose to the rank of king of the gods.

In the following account every effort will be made to present the myths that permeated Egyptian religious thought as simply as possible. The first to be discussed will be the great cosmogonic myths, which form, so to speak, a foundation for theological concepts; then will follow myths that, though lesser in doctrinal scope, nevertheless fed the faith and imagination of believers.

The Heliopolitan system

The town of Heliopolis, situated not far from the head of the Delta, was a highly important religious centre from very early times. Here, at some indefinite time, certainly earlier than the Third Dynasty, a theological system was developed in which the local god, Atum, played the part of the primeval god.

This system laid down that in the beginning there was nothing but immense chaos, Nun, thought to be an ocean or shapeless magma containing, none the less, potential life. In this chaos there had been a conscious principle in existence since antiquity began, the god Atum, whose name, meaning 'the Whole', 'the Complete', emphasised his abstract and somewhat metaphysical nature.

This god was the first of a divine line, and each ensuing generation represented one aspect or element of the universe. Alone and unaided by any feminine counterpart, Atum succeeded in fertilising himself

and in producing the first divine couple, Shu and
Tefnut. Shu was the personification of the air, in the
sense of the void, and also in the sense of life-giving
substance, whereas his consort, Tefnut, whose role
was less clearly defined, represented the moisture in
the atmosphere.

A second divine couple derived from the first, and
consisted of Geb, the earth-god, and Nut, the sky-
goddess. At this point Shu came between Geb and Nut
and raised the body of the sky-goddess above that of
the earth-god, henceforth playing his part as the
atmosphere.

Finally, two other couples were born of the union of
Geb and Nut; Osiris and Isis, and Seth and Nephthys,
who were in part complementary, in part antagonistic,
and seemed to represent the passage from the cosmological to the terrestrial order of things.

The gods in this system were nine in number, and
so formed a divine ennead (*psedjet*).

The system of the Heliopolitan ennead met with
such favour that variants were later introduced by
artificial means into cult-centres. It was adapted
to local conditions by simply taking Atum, its primary
deity, and making him one with the principal god in
that locality; or else the local god and eventually his
consorts too were placed at the head of the hierarchy
without altering the latter at all.

This is how the doctrine of the ennead must have
appeared in its original simple state. But, however far
back texts go, they show the Heliopolitan system
already transformed and enriched by the addition of
solar elements. Very early on Atum was associated on
the one hand with the cosmic god Re (whose name
merely denotes the sun), and on the other hand with
the falcon-god Horus in his guise of Harakhty, and
thus became Re-Harakhty, Horus of the Horizon.
Horus was one of the most prominent figures in the
Egyptian pantheon: as celestial and solar god his

cosmic role was apparent from a very early date.
Impressed, no doubt, by the falcon's powerful flight,
the Egyptians saw Horus as the god who personified
the sky, and in consequence they came to think of the
eye of the falcon as the morning sun and the evening
sun, or, according to a later explanation, as the sun
and the moon. Horus was particularly prominent in
his role of sun-god, and it was in this capacity that he
is often encountered in Egyptian mythology. The
Horus worshipped at Heliopolis in association with
Atum was known as Horus of the Horizon because
he was thought of, characteristically, as appearing
over the chain of mountains to climb triumphantly in
the sky.

With the navigation of the terrestrial Nile in mind,
the Egyptians associated the sun in its course with
Re's barque crossing the ocean of the sky. They even
imagined that two boats existed, distinguishing
between a day boat (*mandjet*) and a night boat (*mesek-
tet*), the sun-god passing from one to the other at the
critical point in his daily journey.

Yet with a facility for introducing variety, frequently
seen in mythology, the Egyptians also looked on the
sun's daily revolution as an uninterrupted cycle of
transformations. So, at the end of its course each
evening, the sun was thought to be swallowed up by
the sky-goddess Nut, then recreated during the night
and born again in the early hours of morning.

The sun-god was also found in many other forms,
including that of the scarab, which has numerous
implications. The connection between this insect and
the sun appears to reside in a play on words: the word
for scarab (*khoprer*) has the same pronunciation as the
verb meaning 'to become, to be transformed' (*khoper*).
In addition, the Egyptians would appear to have
cogitated on the fact that the scarab encloses its egg in
a ball of dung and rolls it in front of itself. By a natural
process of thought they connected this operation with

the daily transformations of the sun. There is also a hymn which alludes to the various phases of the solar star, and in it the morning sun is referred to by the name of Khepri (the sun as it is reborn), the midday sun as Re (the star in its zenith) and the evening sun as Atum (the sun completing its run).

The sun-god was also connected with certain totems, the most characteristic being the obelisk, a big stone needle considered by certain experts to be a stylised form of the raised stone (known as the *benben* of Heliopolis), and by others to be a permanent image of a ray of sunlight.

Some outstanding aspects of Heliopolitan doctrine can thus be analysed, and its influence must have been considerable during the period of the Old Kingdom. Its prestige went on increasing in the Fifth Dynasty, for the pharaohs of this dynasty came originally from Heliopolis and appear to have held the gods of this city in particular veneration; they even went so far as to build small-scale replicas of the great sanctuary at Heliopolis close to their own pyramids and solar temples. There the god took the form of an obelisk of imposing dimensions, rising in the midst of a vast esplanade.

The Hermopolitan system

Another system, as original as that just described, came into being at Hermopolis, a town in Middle Egypt, the seat of Thoth, the god of writing and the sciences.

Hermopolitan theology must also have originated at a fairly early date, for the *Pyramid Texts* refer to it more than once. It is, however, advisable to recognise the fact that most texts that throw light on the structure of the Hermopolitan system and on the character of the gods essential to it, date from a period at which the initial doctrine had already become contaminated by external influences.

The distinctive feature of this system is its relatively abstract character. Whereas Heliopolitan cosmogony can be formulated as an account of the gradual formation of the universe in a series of episodes, the Hermopolitan system on the other hand emerges as a theory about the four elements of chaos. These elements represent aspects, one might almost say attributes, of chaos itself. On the primeval hillock, which texts refer to as the Island of Flame, four gods appeared simultaneously, each accompanied by his feminine counterpart: they were Nun and his consort, Naunet, the god and goddess of the primeval ocean, which is already familiar thanks to the Heliopolitan system; Heh and Hehet, god and goddess of the immeasurable, whose mission was to raise the sun; Kek and Keket, god and goddess of darkness, producing the gloom of night in which light would shine forth; and, lastly, Amun and Amunet, god and goddess of mystery, the hidden, also known as Niu and Niut, or nothingness, who represented the invisible but active breath of the life-giving air. By their combined action these elementary principles brought into existence the solar star. They were 'the fathers and mothers who created light'. They raised the sun in the sky, so that it, in turn, could create and sustain all the beings in the universe. The four primary gods with their consorts constituted the ogdoad of eight gods; the male gods were depicted with the heads of frogs (referring to the fact that the frog arises from the mud, seemingly self-created), while the corresponding goddesses had the heads of serpents (which likewise have affinities with the depths of the earth).

Because of this system, the city of Hermopolis was called in Egyptian 'the (city) of the Eight' (Khmoun). Hermopolis was also responsible for a myth according to which the sun took shape above a lotus flower emerging from the waters of the ocean. This idea enjoyed great popularity throughout Egypt. It recurred in Memphite theology, and the god in question was given the name of Nefertum.

The Memphite system

Some Egyptian theological systems owed their existence to political factors, and their relatively recent date is evident from the elements they borrowed from pre-existing doctrines.

In this category the most remarkable system is unquestionably that of Memphis, which, as far as one can see, was developed just when the new city was springing to life as a royal residence. The main features of Memphite theology have been preserved by being carved on a slab of basalt—now known as the Shabaka Stone—at the command of King Shabaka (Twenty-fifth Dynasty, eighth century B.C.). Unfortunate gaps in the text, archaic language and disconcerting stylistic features make transcription and translation difficult. But, such as it is, this account enables us to discern the main lines of the doctrine, which were undoubtedly formulated by Memphite theologians about the time of the Third Dynasty.

The system centres round Ptah, the god of Memphis, in his role of demiurge or maker of the universe. Ptah originally existed before everything else and had his being in Nun, the primeval ocean found in other cosmogonies. The primeval god manifested his creative activity through the intermediary of eight forms 'which existed in him', veritable personifications of his own divine essence.

Of these personifications one in particular was involved in the work of creation: this was the god Ur (meaning 'the Great'), who was more or less equated with Atum. This universal god, who, according to Memphite theology, was Ptah himself, accomplished his work of creation by use of two faculties that were part of his essential nature: these were the heart and the tongue, representing thought and speech, the former being the means by which things are conceived, and the latter the organ of command, which utters the creative word. The Egyptians, who disliked the abstract, personified these two faculties,

and deified them as Horus (the heart-cum-intellect) and Thoth (the tongue-cum-will expressed in speech).

By his thought and speech Ur-Atum, local form of the demiurge, brought all living things into existence, starting with the divine college (an idea borrowed from Heliopolis) and the other gods, and then going on to men, animals, plants and minerals, in short everything that is. Having created the forces that provide life and food, he completed his task by founding the principles of law and justice.

The Memphite theology presented a cosmogony that, beneath a mythical and vaguely pantheistic appearance, harboured a doctrine of almost philosophical appeal and reflected the efforts theologians made to give some rational explanation of the task of creation. The priests of Ptah tried to incorporate the principal elements of Heliopolitan doctrine into their own cosmogony, but so as to emphasise the primacy of the god of their own city.

The Theban system

If, as there is every reason to believe, the prestige of Ptah was due to the rise of Memphis as capital city during the Old Kingdom, then the rapid ascent to power of the Theban god Amun during the Middle Kingdom was almost certainly the result of political contingencies.

To begin with, Amun was only one of the gods in the Hermopolitan ogdoad, representing the breath that infuses life into the universe. For reasons unknown to us, the princes of the Eleventh Dynasty, after re-establishing a united Egypt, adopted Amun as god of their royal residence. Once installed in Thebes alongside the former local god, Month, Amun became identified with Min, a fertility god worshipped in those parts, and from that point he rapidly rose to being king of the gods and, in addition, god of the empire. Having no proper mythology, Amun acquired a divine family on the pattern of the triad: as consort he was given the goddess Mut, meaning 'mother', and his son was Khons, who often appeared as a moon-god.

He was also associated with the god Re — and this explains why he took the name Amun-Re — and was even accorded a divine college of thirteen members similar to the Heliopolitan ennead and the Hermopolitan ogdoad, and including some of the members of each.

It is not difficult to imagine the complications that must have arisen in the Theban pantheon as a result of associations and assimilations of this nature. But such subtleties offered no problem to theologians, who were quite used to accepting similar mythological combinations.

In actual fact the god of the dynasty was usually spoken of officially as Amun-Re, King of the Gods, Master of Thebes, titles that indicate his indisputable primacy as head of the pantheon and god of the empire. This pre-eminent position was to remain his

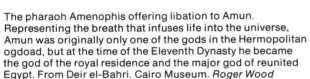

The pharaoh Amenophis offering libation to Amun. Representing the breath that infuses life into the universe, Amun was originally only one of the gods in the Hermopolitan ogdoad, but at the time of the Eleventh Dynasty he became the god of the royal residence and the major god of reunited Egypt. From Deir el-Bahri. Cairo Museum. *Roger Wood*

Amun, the great god of Thebes. His origin is uncertain, but his cult became very powerful. He was always shown as a man, sometimes ithyphallic. His sacred animals were the ram and the goose. Louvre. *Giraudon*

until the pagan period ended, so that the Greeks automatically recognised him as the equivalent of Zeus, and referred to Thebes by the name of Diospolis, the city of Zeus.

Popular myths

In addition to myths illustrating the origin of the universe, there were others that dealt with themes related to problems of everyday life. Of these, none occupied the minds of ancient Egyptians more persistently than the problem of death and the after-life. In the conviction that man lives beyond the grave, they created a fairly detailed picture of the after-life, though this varied according to the period in which they lived and their social status while on earth. But if mere mortals could hope only for a form of survival reflecting the pattern of their life on earth, the pharaohs, on the other hand, could lay claim to a far more sublime destiny on the strength of their divine connections, as is shown in the *Pyramid Texts*. In short, the pharaoh had the right to celestial survival: after purification in the life-giving waters of a mythical lake, the dead pharaoh took his place in the solar barque by the side of Re, and journeyed each day across the ocean sky. He became one with the sun-god, and received the homage of the gods and demons who dwelt up above.

The dead pharaoh also had the special protection of the god Osiris, who at an early stage was looked upon as the prototype of dead pharaohs and raised to the rank of sovereign of the land of the blessed. The role that Osiris played with regard to death was certainly of ancient origin: his popularity as god of the dead increased with time, along with the development of the myth that revealed this aspect of him.

The legend of Osiris must have taken shape during

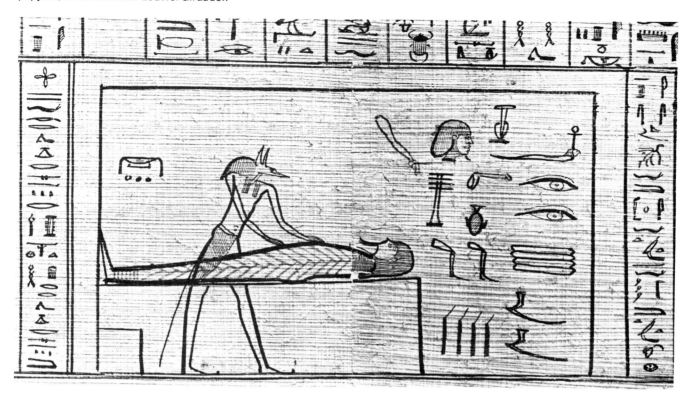

Anubis, the jackal god, patron of embalmers, mummifies the body of Osiris after it has been pieced together again. Jumilhac papyrus, of Roman date. Louvre. *Giraudon*

Osiris, the god of the dead, of the flood and of vegetation, was usually represented as a mummified king. His name means 'The Seat of the Eye'. *Roger Wood*

the Old Kingdom, as is proved by frequent allusions to it in the *Pyramid Texts* and in hymns dating from all epochs. Nevertheless, our knowledge of the origins of Osiris is far from complete. His name, which perhaps means 'the Seat of the Eye', and must contain some mythological allusion, presents an enigma. It is generally accepted that the cult of Osiris, like so many other ancient cults, started in the Delta. Osiris became equated with a local divinity in the town of Busiris, which, of course, echoes the sound of the god's name. This local deity was Anzety, who appeared in the guise of a god-king and had all the attributes of sovereignty. During the period of the Old Kingdom the cult of Osiris spread in Upper Egypt, and the town of Abydos became its centre, for a very ancient royal necropolis existed there, its patron being Khentimentiu, the Chief of the Occidentals—in other words, the god who presided over the destiny of the dead. Gradually the personality of Osiris became fused with that of the local god until Abydos was eventually the principal seat of the Osirian cult, and from that point he was regarded as the supreme god of the dead. The myth of Osiris took shape and developed until it became that touching legend handed down by Plutarch in a somewhat romanticised version. The myth will be reconstructed as fully as possible, using for the most part details given in Egyptian documents, but inserting them into the framework of Plutarch's narrative.

The god Geb, who often appears as the most typical representative of the royal establishment founded by Atum, and is himself the bearer of the double crown, has transferred his powers to his son Osiris. The latter with the help of his sister-wife, Isis, commences his reign under the finest auspices; he takes to his heart the cause of humanity and their well-being, spreading most useful knowledge among them—knowledge of agriculture, vine-growing and

the arts. However, his brother, Seth (Typhon), who is married to Nephthys, becomes jealous of the young king's success and power, and seeks to destroy him. At a feast to which Osiris is invited, his brother succeeds in shutting him up in a chest, which he then casts into the river. Informed of the treachery, Isis at once institutes a search for the chest and finally finds it at Byblos in Phoenicia, hidden inside the trunk of a sycamore-tree, which has been made into a pillar for the king's palace. Isis has the chest returned to her and brings it back to Egypt. But once again Seth manages to get hold of the body of Osiris: he cuts it up into fourteen pieces, which he scatters throughout the land. Isis knows no rest till she has found the various parts of her husband's body, and, having put it together, with the exception of the phallus, she enlists the aid of Anubis, Nephthys and other like deities in order to create the first mummy. Shortly after the death of her husband, Isis takes refuge in the marshes of the Delta and there gives birth to a son, Horus, who is brought up in the greatest secrecy to protect him from the machinations of Seth. Horus grows to manhood and devotes himself to avenging his father: in the hand-to-hand fight between Horus and Seth the former emasculates his adversary and himself loses an eye. Thoth then intervenes to nurse the wounds of the stricken god and his opponent, and heals them both. The gods thereupon decide to put an end to this fratricidal conflict and summon the two adversaries to appear before them. The divine court declares Horus to be in the right, and orders Seth to restore his eye. Once it is returned to him, Horus gives this eye to his father Osiris, and replaces it by the uraeus, or divine serpent, which thenceforth is one of the emblems of royalty. As for Osiris, he transfers his earthly powers to Horus, and retires for ever to the kingdom of the blessed.

In strict fact, no single document gives such a complete and detailed version of the legend of Osiris. This has been drawn up by taking odd elements from myths that originally had an entirely independent existence. Analysis of the legend of Osiris brings to light several themes, of which these are the main ones: death of the god-king Osiris and his replacement by his son Horus: cosmic struggle between Horus, god of the sky and the light, and Seth, god of the wild elements, for this reason associated in Plutarch's mind with Typhon: finally, the myth of the eye of Horus, which is seized and then replaced by the divine serpent, the uraeus.

In addition to its own particular interest and savour, the myth, in the brief description given here, has the merit of explaining the various virtues and qualities ascribed to Osiris by the Egyptians.

Together with Horus, Osiris appears first and foremost to represent one aspect of royalty and to account for the continuity of the monarchy. Osiris is the prototype of the dead king who, having accomplished his task on earth, dies conferring his titles on his son, then comes to life again in a beatified form. Every pharaoh went through the same transformation: invested with the dignity of Horus for the duration of his reign, he was changed into Osiris at the end of his earthly career, and was worshipped as such by his sons and successors.

From the very beginning Osiris was also taken to be one of the very great vegetation gods. His death and immersion in the waters of the Nile, followed by his glorious resurrection, evoked on a mythical level the cycle of nature and its periodic renewal. Osiris, then, is the seed, which dies when buried in the ground, only to be born again a few months later when the shoot comes through bursting with new life. The Egyptians used to give concrete form to this idea by performing a rite (which they believed to be very efficacious) at the end of the flood season in the

Models of objects that had been used by a dead man in his lifetime were placed in his tomb, symbolic of the objects he wished for in the after-life. This model of a funerary boat shows a mummy and figures representing mourners, possibly making the pilgrimage to Abydos, the cult-centre of Osiris, god of the underworld. Middle Kingdom: *c.* 2000 B.C. *British Museum*

Head of Nefertari, from her tomb at Thebes. She wears as part of her headdress the uraeus, a symbol of royalty. *Roger Wood*

month of Khoiakh. They used to trace the outline of Osiris on a net or piece of cloth, and then cover it with a layer of mud on which they would sow seed. As the soil was waterlogged, the seed soon began to shoot up in the shape of the god, forming an Osiris of vegetation, which in their eyes both symbolised and stimulated the renewal of nature.

The rite just described was normally performed in temples, but it also played a part in the funeral liturgy, as is proved by the presence of an Osiris of vegetation in several royal tombs dating from the time of the New Kingdom.

After further consideration of features of the Osirian myth, the Egyptians made him the protector of the dead. The royal funeral rites, although they had their own special significance, soon came to be associated with the chief features of the myth concerning the death and resurrection of Osiris.

The form for the funeral ritual, which is to be found in the *Pyramid Texts* in its most ancient version, emphasises at every turn the connection between the dead pharaoh and the god Osiris into whom the sovereign is transformed. When, towards the end of the Old Kingdom, the prestige of the throne was shaken by political and social trends, the funeral rites of Osiris, which had previously been regarded as the prerogative of dead pharaohs, were usurped more and more often by ordinary people. By the time of the Middle Kingdom, an appreciable number of Egyptians belonging to the leisured classes were being mummified and buried in accordance with Osirian ritual; from the period of the New Kingdom onwards, the popularisation of funeral rites was so commonly accepted that any dead person who had had them performed over him was simply spoken of as the Osiris So-and-So. All that was needed for a corpse to achieve Osirian survival was for his body to receive the rites that had brought the god back to life and to have the appropriate formula recited over it. The famous *Book of the Dead*, which was commonly placed near the mummy, contained among other beneficial formulas a choice of hymns and prayers which enabled the occupant of the tomb to secure the benevolence of Osiris and the deities in his cycle.

The celestial eye

Incidental reference has been made to the eye of Horus, which was plucked out and then restored on the order of a court of the gods. This is an example of a myth built round two themes that were originally quite separate: the theme of the solar eye and the theme of the eye of Horus. In the Osirian cycle of legends there is an episode in which the eye of Horus, on being returned to its owner after his struggle with Seth, is replaced by or is transformed into a royal uraeus.

But the god of Heliopolis, associated with the sun, also possessed an eye, the eye of Re. This eye, which was initially the morning star, was subsequently connected with Osiris after he had been brought back to life by his son. It was not until later that the two forms of the eye were regarded as the sun on some occasions, on others as the moon. Of course the theft and restitution of the eye of Horus was naturally connected with the two most important phases of the moon. As for the eye of Re, it was often identified with the cult of Maat, daughter of Re.

The goddess Maat, who is here closely connected with Re, was the personification of one of the fundamental concepts of Egyptian philosophical thought. Essentially she represented the principle of order ruling the cosmos and giving it its necessary balance. But her role also embraced social and moral order, and in this respect she stood for conformity with the laws of gods and men, or the concept of justice and truth. As goddess of justice, Maat took part in the weighing of the soul of a dead man in the presence of Osiris and his tribunal; the heart, as the seat of the intelligence, should exactly counterbalance justice, as embodied in the goddess.

To return to the theme of the divine eye, and more particularly to the eye of the sun, one version is perhaps worth noting, as it became quite widespread. This, a town in Middle Egypt, where the First Dynasty originated, was the home of a god called Onuris (or more correctly Ini-herit), meaning 'He who brings back the Distant One'. This title referred to the legend that follows, which existed only in later versions, although its theme must have been known during the period of the Middle Kingdom, if not before.

The eye of the sun-god, which at times adopted the shape of Tefnut, the lioness, became violently angry with its master. The goddess (the word 'eye' is feminine in Egyptian) seized the sun-god and withdrew to the depths of Nubia meaning to stay there. After argument Onuris sought her and, having calmed her

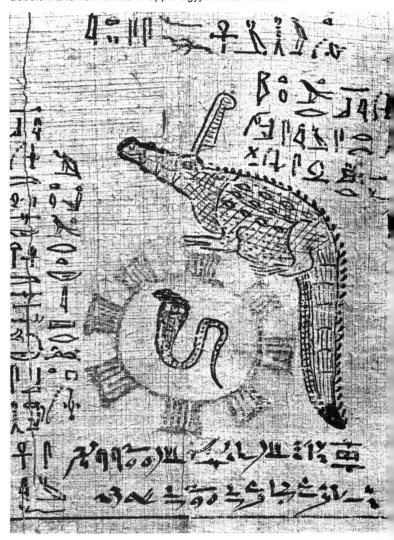

Detail from a magical papyrus, which was a guide for the owner on his journey through the underworld. The crocodile was the emblem of Sobk, worshipped specially at Faiyum, and at Gebelein and Kom Ombo in Upper Egypt. *British Museum*

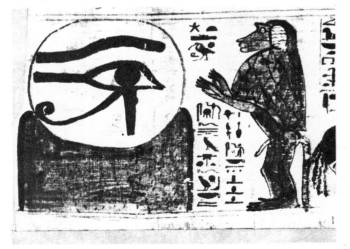

Detail from the papyrus of Hent-Taui, a musician-priestess of Amen-Re. An ape worships the sun-disc which contains the eye of Re as it rises above the eastern mountain. Twenty-first Dynasty. *British Museum*

with promises, brought her back triumphantly to This, where the eye returned to its proper place. This legend illustrates at best the alternating phases of the moon; but, like the other myths quoted above, it has also been connected with the eye of Horus. As in the myth of Horus and Seth, the celestial eye, after going through a phase of absence or disappearance, was restored to its former state.

An attempt has also been made to connect the theme of *udjat* (the healthy eye) with these other ideas. The usual explanation is that *udjat* was the eye of Horus restored to its normal condition through the good offices of Thoth, after it had been removed by Seth. This explanation was undoubtedly acceptable to the Egyptians themselves on occasions, though they were confusing different mythological themes; however, if one accepts the evidence of the *Pyramid Texts*, it would appear that initially the 'healthy eye' referred to Horus' other eye.

The theme of the eye of Horus was much exploited in ritual: in the formulas for the presentation of offerings, the latter are most often identified with the divine eye, which is given or returned to its master. This association of ideas was supposed to make the rite more effective.

Apophis

The theme implicit in both forms of the myth of the eye is that of alternation between two phases: the phase in which the eye functions normally, and that in which it is unable to fulfil its natural role. In the myth of Apophis the theme is that of the struggle between the star of light and the powers of darkness.

The elements of this myth are already present in the embryo in the very earliest texts; but the hostile factors involved do not assume the definite shape of the monstrous serpent Apophis until the beginning of the Middle Kingdom. *The Book of the Dead* and the literature on magic dating from later periods continually made reference to Apophis as the instrument of evil, given to aggressiveness and perfidy.

In the beginning Apophis was the demon of darkness who might at any moment threaten the sun-god; he would do anything to impede the god on his journey, even to the extent of trying to drain the celestial Nile on which Re's barque sailed. Every morning and evening the sun-god, aided by his divine followers, succeeded in circumventing his enemy's manoeuvres and continuing victoriously on his way. Equilibrium in the universe was achieved as a result of the perpetual struggle between these two powers, which opposed and complemented one another.

The secret name of Re

Solar mythology, which was responsible for the major themes just analysed, also found expression in a number of tales that are rather more anecdotal in character, and concentrate on definite episodes in the career of Re: one may well be inclined to see in these

Maat, the goddess of truth, represented the principle of order ruling the cosmos and the principle of social and moral order. As goddess of justice Maat took part in the weighing of the souls of the dead in the presence of Osiris and his tribunal. Bas-relief from the tomb of Sethos I. Nineteenth Dynasty. Archaeological Museum, Florence. *Alinari*

stories a connection with the body of legend involving the sun-god. These texts are to be found in works on magic, which link the adventures and misadventures of the gods with similar human situations requiring the intervention of a magician.

The following is an account taken from a treatise on magic written in the period of the New Kingdom. It relates how Isis contrived to discover the mysterious and all-powerful name of Re.

Isis, who was thought to be a great magician, had knowledge of everything that existed in heaven and on earth. There was only one thing that she did not know—the secret name of Re; once she knew this, the goddess would be in a position to grasp some of the powers held by the master of the universe.

Desirous of these powers, Isis invented a stratagem, which depended for its success on her ability as a magician. She obtained a little of the ageing god's saliva, and after moulding it with soil made a serpent of it and placed it in the path that Re usually took in his daily walk. As she had foreseen, the god walked on the serpent, which bit his foot and caused him great pain. On hearing his calls his followers rushed to his aid; naturally Isis, the instigator of the affair, was among them. Feigning astonishment, she questioned Re, and told him that if her spells were to be really efficacious she would have to know his name—the mysterious name that the god refused to reveal to anyone. Isis was so insistent that Re, beside himself with agony, finally disclosed his secret. He was cured, but from that moment the magic powers of the goddess were vastly increased, so much so that they tended to eclipse those of the sun-god himself.

The myth of the cow

Another myth that is related and sometimes illustrated in several royal tombs dating from the New Kingdom was again about Re in his old age, when he was reaching the end of his career on earth.

When Re, king of the gods and men, felt the advance of age, and knew his body to be changed into gold, silver and lapis-lazuli, he became aware that the men of the valley and desert were adopting an arrogant attitude towards him and were even contemplating revolt against him. Much disturbed, he called a secret council of the gods, attended, as was their right, by Shu and Tefnut, Geb and Nut, and also Nun and the eye of Re. On the advice of these gods he resolved to send his eye (which for this occasion would adopt the shape of Hathor-Sakhmet) to spread destruction among humanity. The cruel goddess immediately began her task, and, having accomplished part of her mission, set out joyfully to rejoin her master. But at that very moment the god repented of his radical decision and desired to spare the rest of humanity. But there was the difficulty of appeasing the goddess' thirst for blood, which was roused by her earlier exploits. Re decided to dupe Hathor-Sakhmet; so during the night he had the entire land covered with a fermented red liquid, which he intended the goddess to mistake for blood. The artifice was immensely successful: the goddess drank such quantities of this liquid that she could not see clearly, even those who were within reach; and so a part of the human race was saved from massacre.

However, Re had taken a dislike to humanity and wished to leave the confines of the earth. So the god Nun urged him to be seated on the cow Nut. When morning came, and men were again displaying their quarrelsome instincts, the cow ascended with the god on her back and was then transformed into the sky. Re was delighted at being raised so high; but the cow was fearful and trembled in every limb. So Re ordered eight demons to act as supports, placing themselves in twos at each of the animal's feet. He also commanded Shu, the god of atmosphere, to get under the stomach of the cow so as to support her body with his outstretched arms.

As we can see, this tale is a variation of the myth explaining the formation and structure of the universe. In the accompanying illustration each of the characters is seen in his prescribed role; but the sun, instead of being enthroned on the back of the cow, is shown to be in the solar barque, sailing alongside the constellated body of the divine animal.

This illustration provides a typical example of the ease with which Egyptians combined more or less parallel mythological conceptions (here the concept of the sky as the ocean and as the ceiling of the universe) without troubling about the contradiction or illogicality implicit in such combinations.

The myth of the destruction of humanity shows Hathor in her least attractive aspect, of a murdering goddess mad for blood, a manifestation that she shared with ferocious Sakhmet, who had the head of a lioness.

But the goddess Hathor, who occupied a prominent position in the Egyptian pantheon, could adopt less sanguinary guises. Hathor, whose name means 'the house of Horus', was frequently depicted as a cow, or as a woman with a cow's horns. Although perhaps nothing more than a local goddess at first, she soon rose to the rank of cosmic deity, identified with the sky and thus with Nut, whom we have just encountered in the same guise of a cow. The question arises as to whether it was by reason of her cosmic nature that she became 'the Mistress of Foreign Lands', or whether it was because of her association with the solar eye. In any case, from the time of the Old Kingdom her patronage was extended to most of the remote regions to which the pharaohs sent expeditions, whether it was Byblos, the main Egyptian trading settlement in Phoenicia, or the turquoise mines of the nearby peninsula of Sinai, or even the mysterious land of Punt, situated in the vicinity of Somalia. Nevertheless, her principal sanctuaries were in Egypt itself. At Dendera, where her temple is still in existence, she was closely connected with Horus,

The sun-god Re is here shown on the solar barque accompanied by Hathor, shown as a cow. Relief from the Nineteenth Dynasty. Louvre. *Giraudon*

The head of Hathor, with sheep's ears, decorates a column in Nefertari's tomb at Abu Simbel. Originally a local goddess, Hathor rose to the rank of a cosmic deity, a sky-goddess, and often appeared in the guise of a cow. Hathor was also the goddess of music and dancing and love and the protector of infants. *Roger Wood*

Re, the sun-god of Heliopolis, presided over the Heliopolitan ennead. Himself absorbing Atum, an earlier sun-god, he was later identified with other gods when their cults became powerful. Here Re is shown with a solar disc on his head and a papyrus sceptre on his knees. Bronze. British Museum. *Mansell*

whom she joined once a year on the occasion of the great festival of Edfu. At Thebes her primary role was that of the protectress of the necropolis: she welcomed and consoled the dead and brought them happiness.

Hathor was above all else a good and helpful goddess. She was the patron of music and dancing and also of love, which was why the Greeks identified her with Aphrodite. She was also the protectress of infants in arms, and had under her command a group of seven goddesses created in her image; they assisted her in her nursing activities and played the part of fairies round the cradle of the newborn babe. It was in this role that Hathor and her followers were present at the divine birth of the pharaoh.

The divine birth of the pharaoh

Several allusions have already been made here to the divine nature and descent of the pharaoh. We may now do well to inquire further into the Egyptian concept of the divine origin of the pharaohs, and it may be appropriate to describe here the mythological meaning and structure that they imposed on this concept.

From the outset of history the Egyptians held that the pharaoh was a superior being, on a higher plane than that of ordinary mortals: to them, the pharaoh was the earthly embodiment of Horus, the god-king, and he was also the protector of the original tutelary goddesses of the kingdoms: Nekhbet, the vulture-goddess of Upper Egypt, and Uadjit (Edjo), the cobra-goddess of Lower Egypt.

However, from the Fifth Dynasty onwards, undoubtedly under the influence of Heliopolitan doctrine, the pharaohs laid special emphasis on their solar origin. Without renouncing their former titles, they adopted the new title of Son of Re, in other

words they styled themselves Son of the Sun.

Furthermore, the legend of Cheops and the Magicians, which may have been composed as far back as the Middle Kingdom, tells how the pharaohs of the Fifth Dynasty came into existence. These princes, who were called upon to inaugurate a new royal line, were said to be born of the union of the sun-god and the wife of one of Re's priests, the master of Sakhebou (a district near Heliopolis). They were brought into the world by goddesses skilled in the art of confinement led by the god Khnum, the potter-god. As the divine obstetricians received the triplets they gave each a name inspired by the particular circumstances of his birth.

The tale, here seen in its simplest popular form, was soon to develop a particular slant. The revised version tells how the princely heir was born of the union of the sun-god, as embodied in the reigning pharaoh and the queen, his wife, thereby making him the genuine flesh-and-blood son of Re. Special note should perhaps be taken of two particular versions of this story, both dating from the Eighteenth Dynasty; here the illustrations of the episodes involved are accompanied by a fairly full text, which reproduces the words exchanged by the characters in this type of religious drama. One of these versions, found under the central portico of the temple at Deir el-Bahri, deals with the birth of the queen Hatshepsut; the other, sculpted in one of the apartments of the temple of Luxor, illustrates the birth of Amenophis III; but to judge by a fragment of inscription from the Twelfth Dynasty, the text must have been composed as far back as the Middle Kingdom.

By the time of the Eighteenth Dynasty, it was not, in fact, the god Re who played the part of the procreator, but Amun. Not that there is anything astonishing about this substitution, for, as we have seen, in the later stages of Theban theology Amun had taken

Columns decorated with leaf motifs and hieroglyphics in the temple of Ptah at Karnak, built in the Ptolemaic period.

Relief panel showing Horus and Seth, who were sometimes rivals, tying up the heraldic plants of the kingdoms of Upper and Lower Egypt during a period of reconciliation. Twelfth Dynasty. Cairo Museum. *Giraudon*

over most of the functions and attributes of the sun-god, including that of father to the pharaoh. When Amun is mentioned in the following legend, his name can be replaced by that of Re if one wants to reconstruct the original situation.

In the first scene Amun announces to the divine college his intention of begetting a prince who will one day ascend the throne.

Thoth plays the part of divine messenger and brings the queen to the nuptial chamber in which her divine husband awaits her. During their theogonic meeting Amun acquaints the queen with his plan and determines in advance the name and fate of the prince who is to be born. Amun then goes to Khnum, the potter-god, whose functions include that of modelling bodies and breathing life into them; he begs Khnum to give. his offspring a body of more than divine beauty. The god sets to work at once; seated at his potter's wheel, he fashions both the body of the child and its *Ka* (its material soul, which in appearance is a replica of its physical body). As the moment of birth approaches the queen, after being congratulated by the god Thoth on her sublime mission, is led by Khnum and Heqet, the frog-headed goddess who attends at births, towards the confinement chamber where the happy event soon takes place.

The queen, seated on a bed of state, holds the child affectionately. Around her throng goddesses and guardian spirits who are her protectors. Bes and Theoris are with this group—they are the accredited protectors of women in childbirth. Hathor, the primary mother-goddess, then makes her entrance: she takes the newborn babe in her arms and presents him to Amun, his father, who looks on his progeny with satisfaction, predicting a glorious future for him.

Then the child is brought back to the queen's apartments. The nurses, known as the Hathors, take charge of him at once, together with the fourteen hypostases

of his *Ka* (in other words the personifications of his various faculties). However, Amun continues to watch over the fate of his son. In the course of another conversation with Thoth, at which the infant and his inseparable *Ka* are present, he gives further instructions. As Thoth is the god of writing and science, Amun no doubt makes arrangements for the education and future of the prince who will one day be ruler of Egypt. In a final scene, in which Anubis and Khnum are in attendance, as well as the goddess of the annals, it seems that the destiny of the young prince is discussed in more detail.

This example shows how a distinct event in a royal career was successfully transposed to a divine plane. It is beyond question that the Egyptians knew that the birth of a king was subject to the same conditions as that of any other child; but, aware of the superhuman nature of the royal prince and the sublime destiny promised him, they succumbed to the temptation of seeing things in mythological perspective because the simple truth of the matter failed to satisfy their imagination. In other myths the gods are often made to behave as human beings behave; but in this case a decisive episode in the royal career is deliberately presented as a divine event.

Horus against the adversaries of Re

The fact that unbroken expositions of myths and divine legends are rarely found is undoubtedly because they were passed on by word of mouth or written down on papyrus rolls, which were kept in the libraries of temples or in the adjoining *scriptoria*. Only in comparatively recent times did someone occasionally show initiative and engrave texts of this kind on the temple walls, to make more certain of their being preserved and also, no doubt, to enable worshippers to learn about the doughty deeds of the local god. Thus there is a naos (the inner cell of a temple) that

Isis, the divine mother. She wears the Hathor crown and
holds a sistrum, a jingling rattle used especially in her rites.
Temple of Sethos I at Abydos. *Roger Wood*

44

comes from a temple in Lower Egypt and was found at El-Arish, which has on its walls an account of the outstanding events in the divine reigns of Shu and Geb. This account includes a description of the struggles of these gods against Apophis and his myrmidons, lingering particularly over episodes that took place in the locality of the temple for which the naos was intended.

But the most typical example of mythological exposition is found in the Ptolemaic temple at Edfu. On the inside face of the sanctuary wall is an account of the wars which Horus Behdeti, the local god, appears to have waged against the adversaries of the sun-god; this account is illustrated, at intervals, with bas-reliefs, showing the principal episodes of the struggle. The text, which covers the entire height of the wall, relates in detail the vicissitudes of this divine war, in the redundant style that contemporary men of letters then affected. To give this text the appearance of an historic document the author used a style suited to official annals.

The events are said to have taken place in the year 363 in the reign of Re-Harakhty. While the god-king was making a tour of inspection by boat in Nubia, he learned that his enemies had raised the flag of revolt against him. This group of conspirators naturally included the myrmidons of Apophis, who tried in every way to oppose Re, the sun-god, who directed the course of the universe.

Re immediately warned his son Horus Behdeti, in other words Horus of Edfu, and ordered him to bring the enemy to his senses. Horus carried off a preliminary victory, thus delighting his father. But the confederates fell back into Egypt, and Horus had to pursue them into their hide-outs all along the Nile valley. This was Horus' opportunity to inflict defeat after defeat upon them. Each time the enemy appeared in a different guise, either that of Seth and Apophis, or as a creature, such as a hippopotamus or crocodile. Wherever he went, Horus accomplished some act of prowess, of which Re was immediately informed by Thoth. He continued his triumphal progress towards Lower Egypt, and in the end forced the confederates back beyond the Red Sea into Asia. With Egypt thus freed from the forces of evil, the two gods returned in the solar barque; Re-Harakhty went back to Nubia, and Horus to his temple at Edfu.

For the modern reader this account, written in a monotonous style and larded with mythological references, is quite hard going; but in the eyes of the temple clergy it must unquestionably have been of interest. First of all it made clear the part that the god of Edfu had played both in the work of organisation and pacification carried out by the god of the universe, and also in his fight against the powers of evil. It also contained—and this had a particular appeal for Egyptians—an explanation of a large number of place-names (toponyms). In fact, the slightest action on the part of Horus and his companions was a pre-

text for a play on words, explaining the name of the place or sanctuary near which the action took place. These puns, which are often only approximate and very artificially contrived, follow one another with such frequency that they make the reading of the myth of Horus a somewhat tedious business for those who do not understand the finer points of these allusions.

Another purpose of this account was to explain the origin of some of the emblems that formed part of the sacred themes, such as the symbol of the winged disc. This was one of the forms that the falcon-god, 'with gaudy plumage', assumed during his expeditions; when, after his final victory, he returned in that shape to Edfu, Re decided that in future the motif of the winged disc would be erected wherever he happened to stop, as an apotropaic and protective emblem. And that is why in all Egyptian temples this motif decorates the cornice above the gates. The origin of this myth may go farther back than the version preserved in the temple of Edfu. One theory put forward is that it is a mythological interpretation of the pharaoh's victory over the barbarians, and this being so, the Asiatics are depicted as Typhon's demons, the enemies of the sun-god. In the Ptolemaic version there has even been an attempt to see a veiled allusion to the feeling of xenophobia that the Egyptians entertained towards the Persians and Greeks, succeeding occupiers of their country. According to this thesis, the enslaved Egyptians were referring in this mythological narrative to the belief that their gods were capable of driving out the foreign rulers one day.

The adventures of Horus and Seth

The tales that have been briefly recounted above contain episodes in which even the most eminent gods display very human weaknesses and get involved in ill-advised adventures. Elements of this nature are not absent from the most canonical myths; so there is nothing astonishing about their discovery in divine legends that grew up alongside official mythology.

A papyrus published about thirty years ago by Sir Alan Gardiner, the Chester Beatty I papyrus, now enables us to conclude that the Egyptians cultivated a type of narrative that borrowed its subject matter from orthodox mythology and yet exploited it very casually, presenting the gods in a somewhat unexpected light. This story, which dates from the end of the New Kingdom, and is full of down-to-earth zest, recounts in racy detail the adventures of brave Horus and wicked Seth, the two rival deities already familiar to the reader.

The fact that it is a folk tale is apparent both from the style and from the use of Neo-Egyptian, a vulgar language dating from the period of the New Kingdom. Yet the non-canonical nature of the account is even more obvious from the constant mingling of elements taken from official myths with facetious

The serpent Apophis was a manifestation of Seth, the brother of Osiris, god of the dead, and his murderer. The deceased tries, with the help of his three sons (lower panel), to placate Seth. *British Museum.*

episodes belonging to folk-lore. It is perhaps worth mentioning that experts have pointed out the quite unrelated sources of mythological themes used in this work, which are sometimes welded together so arbitrarily that the story is lacking clarity and logic. This is what happened, at least to a certain extent, in the following brief version of the story.

When Osiris left the earthly world to go and reign over the Land of the Blessed, two gods laid claim to the throne of Egypt; the first, Seth, was the violent and perfidious deity who had assassinated his brother in order to seize power; the other, Horus, was the posthumous son of Osiris, whom his mother, Isis, had brought up in a remote corner of the Delta in the hope that, when he was a man, he would avenge his father and reign in his stead.

But the dispute between the two claimants had to be settled by the divine tribunal. This tribunal is referred to here under its conventional title of the ennead, but, in fact, it consisted of a number of gods who had but little connection with the ennead of Heliopolis. It was presided over by the Master of the Universe, a divine being corresponding to both Atum and Re-Harakhty, the deities who form the basis of the Heliopolitan system. At the point where the story begins, the proceedings involving Horus and Seth have already been dragging on for eighty years. The majority of gods in the tribunal are in favour of Horus and do not hesitate to recognise the validity of his claims; but the Master of the Universe, who appears throughout this story as an odd, biased creature, dares not concur with the opinion of his peers for fear of bringing down on his own head the wrath of Seth; the latter's power terrifies him, especially as Seth is the accredited protector of the solar barque.

On the suggestion of one of its members, the tribunal, which is loath to face its responsibilities, decided to ask Neith, the goddess of Sais, for a judicial consultation, since she is universally renowned for wisdom. In reply to the letter that Thoth, the secretary of the gods, sends to her, Neith gives Horus her full support. At the same time she proposes to the tribunal that they should make reparation to Seth in the form of two Asiatic goddesses, Anat and Astarte, whom he should take to wife.

The deities signify their approval, but the Master of the Universe points out that Horus is still rather young and frail to assume the heavy burden of royalty.

At this precise moment Bab, a somewhat roguish god, who seems to have been in league with Seth, has the unfortunate idea of addressing the president of the tribunal in blasphemous fashion, so provoking a general tumult in the assembly. The Master of the Universe, cut to the quick by these words, retires in discomforture, but he soon recovers, thanks to the offices of the goddess Hathor, who has the gift of restoring him to good humour. The session is resumed, and Seth and Horus make their entrance and defend their respective positions. Various gods plead the cause of Horus, and Isis proposes to 'place these words before Atum, the powerful prince who is in Heliopolis, and before Khepri, who resides in his barque'.

This interruption on the part of Horus' mother, the exact significance of which escapes us, puts Seth into such a rage that he refuses to continue the discussion as long as Isis, by her presence and insinuations, continues to influence the tribunal of the gods. The Master of the Universe grants Seth's request and decrees that the proceedings shall continue on a remote island, from which Isis shall be barred; furthermore he gives strict instructions to Anti, the ferryman-god, to forbid the goddess access to the island, as her presence is deemed undesirable.

But the astute Isis immediately thinks of a trick that will enable her to overcome the Master of the

Isis, here shown with the head of a lioness, was the divine mother, faithful wife of Osiris and devoted mother of Horus. She was a popular goddess throughout Egypt, and in later times she had priests, temples and festivals throughout the Roman Empire. Relief on temple at Kom Ombo. *Roger Wood*

Isis and Horus. After the murder of her husband, Osiris, the goddess Isis brought up Horus in secret so that he could eventually avenge his father's death and succeed to his kingdom. Bronze statuette. Thirtieth Dynasty to Ptolemaic: fourth to second centuries B.C. *Fitzwilliam Museum, Cambridge*

Universe's decree: she disguises herself as an old woman, and, having bargained with Anti, she persuades him to get her across to the island in return for a gold ring. She then turns into a charming young girl and succeeds in attracting Seth's attention. Failing to recognise her and captivated by her charms, Seth begins to court her. Isis takes advantage of the situation and in the course of conversation cleverly traps Seth, so that he admits that a direct descendant has a greater right to the throne than any other claimant. Delighted at having extracted this declaration from her son's rival, Isis flies off in the shape of a kite, mocking his naïveté.

The latter, realising the trap into which he has fallen, hastens to complain of the duplicity of the goddess to the Master of the Universe, who has to admit that Seth has condemned himself.

The Master of the Universe now convenes the tribunal on the eastern shore and acquaints it with Seth's imprudent declarations relevant to the case, then confers the crown of Egypt upon Horus with the approval of the gods.

But Seth will not let Horus enjoy his victory, and he proposes a competition in which he hopes to gain his revenge: the idea is that they should transform themselves into hippopotami and plunge into the water; the one who remains longest under water will be the victor. And this they do. But Isis, who is present, is terror-stricken on her son's behalf. Meaning to come to his aid and to handicap his opponent, she flings a harpoon, which, instead of striking Seth, wounds Horus. Only when she repeats her manoeuvre does she maim Seth. Then, with one of those inconsistencies of which this narrative contains several examples, she allows herself to be moved by the laments of the wounded rival and removes the harpoon from his back. This gesture of pity makes Horus indignant, and he immediately cuts off his mother's

head and carries it away to the mountains. Isis turns herself into a flint statue without a head.

The Master of the Universe, greatly angered at the news, bids Seth seek out Horus and bring him back. Seth, instead of confining himself to the orders he has received, tears out Horus' eyes and buries them on the mountain to illumine the earth; but they become bulbs and grow into lotuses. Hathor, who has discovered Horus in this pitiful state, pours gazelle's milk into the sockets of his eyes to restore his sight.

However, Seth does not abandon his sinister projects. Pretending to be sincerely reconciled with his former enemy, he invites him to set the seal on their friendship by sharing a banquet with him; but this overture on the part of Seth also ends in treachery. Horus, with the aid of his mother, is quick to avenge himself by playing the same sort of trick in return. Then, when the tribunal is next summoned, he is able to cover Seth with confusion in front of the entire assembly of the gods.

Although the gods confirm their judgment in favour of Horus with greater conviction than ever, Seth delivers his young rival a final challenge in the form of another competition. They are to row a race in boats made of stone, and the winner's prize will be the throne of Egypt. Horus, who has seen through the trap, builds a boat of wood without Seth's knowledge and is careful to camouflage it to look like a stone boat. Naturally his boat is able to stay afloat, while Seth's sinks immediately.

Seth then turns into a hippopotamus again and capsizes his adversary's craft. Yet Horus is able to reach the shore, and he hastens to Neith to complain that the decision made and confirmed by the gods is still not implemented, as Seth persists in refusing to acknowledge it. Since the tribunal is still not sufficiently informed on the subject of the respective rights of the two plaintiffs, the Master of the Universe asks

48

Left: A steatite cippus of Horus with mythological reliefs. The cippi (small stelae) incorporated the god as a child standing on a crocodile and holding snakes and scorpions. They are often inscribed with magical texts. Egypt. British Museum

Above: A faience amulet of the head of the goddess Nut, wearing the headdress of Hathor. Egypt. British Museum

Below: A faience sow, emblem of Isis. Egypt. British Museum

Bes, a dwarf deity, a helper of women in childbirth and a protector against snakes and other terrors. He holds the symbols of life and power. Eighteenth Dynasty. *British Museum*

Selkis, a scorpion goddess, identified with the scorching heat of the sun, was one of the four protector-goddesses (the other three were Neith, Nephthys and Isis) who guarded coffins and canopic jars. Here she guards a corner of the shrine of Tutan-khamun (1361–1352 B.C.). *Roger Wood*

Horus' real father, Osiris, for a written consultation. In his reply Osiris declares indignantly that he cannot see why there is still delay in investing Horus with the cloak of royalty since his claims are incontestable. He lets it be understood that if Horus' rights are not recognised, he, as god of vegetation, will cut off Egypt's food supplies and, as god of the dead, he will send to earth emissaries of death to disrupt the rule of a false claimant. This letter has the desired effect; for the gods, feeling that Osiris' anger is directed at them, hasten to return a definite verdict in favour of Horus. The Master of the Universe has Seth brought before him in chains and forces him to admit Horus' exclusive rights to the royal crown. Thereupon Horus is solemnly installed on his father's throne, to the great joy of Isis and the acclamations of the tribunal. As for Seth, his consolation is to be allowed to howl in the sky as god of storms.

This is a brief resumé of the contents of this long narrative, which has episodes that would not disgrace a comic story by Lucian.

There are experts who have seen, in this product of the Ramesses period, evidence of a weakening of faith in certain sectors of the population. But if one construes the story in this sense (particularly in view of the fact that it was written to amuse its readers) there is always the risk of judging subjectively the state of mind of a society very different from our own, and one not likely to take offence at the improprieties committed by members of its pantheon. In fact the Egyptians created the gods in their own image, with human imperfections and vices, as well as their indifferent virtues.

Personifications and spirits

The deities who have been our concern so far belong to the category of major gods who had recognised cults, whose images are very prominent in the great temples. But outside these primary cults there were lesser cults concerned with minor deities, who, for that very reason, had a more direct appeal to ordinary people. In the minds of their followers these gods had benign functions, rather like popular saints. Cults of this sort probably existed throughout antiquity, but there was an appreciable increase in their number during the New Kingdom and in the following periods, judging by the number of amulets and votive offerings that have survived. One of these deities was Bes, who was generally depicted as a deformed and grimacing dwarf, with feathers instead of hair. His frightening and grotesque appearance kept off dangers, such as snakes. He was the protector of women in childbirth, and he supervised toilet rites and sleep. He was also patron of music and dancing.

Also in this category of protective deities is the goddess Thoeris, meaning 'the Great'. She was portrayed as a female hippopotamus, large and rounded, squatting on her haunches. This goddess was supposed to come to the aid of babes in arms; she also presided over toilet rites. She was sometimes identified with Hathor in her role of protectress of women and mothers.

Finally, mention should be made of the serpent-goddess Renenutet (Thermuthis), whose chief function was to ensure abundant harvests.

Popular divinities and cults

The Egyptians tended to give some real form to deities and spirits, who, by their nature, essentially existed only in the abstract.

Mention has already been made of some of these divine personifications—Maat, for instance, the basic order of the universe; Hu, creative will; Sia, perceptiveness. Magic, power, sight and hearing could equally well be given tangible forms and personalities.

Similarly, any geographical entity could be endowed

with a personality—for example, the sea, the fields, or a feature of the landscape. This is perhaps an appropriate point to mention the spirits known as nils. Portrayed as chubby creatures bearing at arm's length a stiff mat laden with food and vases, they represented either the food-giving river, or the two parts of Egypt (Upper and Lower Egypt) or even the individual provinces in the land. Their identity was indicated simply by placing the appropriate plant or heraldic emblem crestlike on their heads. Long processions of nils were often drawn on plinths in the temples, showing them bringing the local god the products of their districts.

Foreign divinities

When the pharaohs of the Eighteenth Dynasty extended their lands as far as the boundaries of Mesopotamia, the Egyptians came into closer contact with the peoples to the east of Egypt. They learned about the customs and beliefs of the Canaanites and Syrians, and even adopted some of their gods. The spread of Asiatic cults was further favoured by the introduction into Egypt of foreigners brought back as prisoners or engaged as mercenaries by the pharaohs. In Egypt the Canaanite gods were never the object of an official cult, and it may be supposed that their devotees were recruited chiefly among the lower classes of the population. Nevertheless, from the middle of the Seventeenth Dynasty, some Asiatic gods were generally recognised in Thebes and Memphis.

In the texts of that period references to deities from Canaan—for example, Baal, Reshef, Astarte and Anat—were not unusual. The popularity of these gods is shown by a certain number of votive images or steles, where they appear looking characteristically exotic. Reshef, 'master of vigour', for instance, is depicted with a headdress resembling the crown of

Egypt, but decorated with the head of a gazelle; in his capacity of god of war he holds the mace in one hand and the shield in the other. Astarte was worshipped in the district near Memphis where a Phoenician colony had settled. As a goddess of battle she was often portrayed armed and on horseback. This did not prevent her being at the same time the goddess of love, so that she was sometimes confused with Hathor and even with Isis.

The deification of men

In classical times the distinction between the human condition and the divine condition was so clear-cut that any reference to the divine nature of the pharaoh was immediately modified, lest he be confused with the true gods: in his lifetime he was the reincarnation of the god-king Horus; but when he was dead he was identified with the god of the dead, Osiris.

The idea of eminent human personalities acquiring divine rank is a relatively recent one. Such was the case with Imhotep, chief minister of Djoser, a pharaoh of the Third Dynasty (about 2670 B.C.), who was long remembered by Egyptians. We now know, from recent discoveries, that Imhotep was responsible for public works during Djoser's reign, his major achievement being the building of the first step pyramid. But legend later attributed to this historic personage a measure of wisdom and a knowledge of medicine and magic greater than that of even superior mortals, so that he was elevated to the rank of god in the Graeco-Roman period. Sanctuaries were dedicated to him, and the Greeks identified him with Asclepius, the god of medicine.

Amenophis, the son of Hapu, who in his lifetime was a confidant of the pharaoh Amenophis III (fourteenth century B.C.), had a similar posthumous destiny, and was also deified. His name is found in several temples of the Late Period.

Religious syncretism

It is obvious from the preceding exposition that myths and theological systems are never handed down and preserved in their initial simplicity. As soon as the principalities of pre-dynastic Egypt had been united to form one realm, the individual cult-centres emerged from their isolation, and their beliefs were modified by those of neighbouring cities. Thus the process known as 'religious syncretism' began — that is, deities having some affinity to one another were amalgamated, and theological systems, which were originally separate and distinct, borrowed from each other. As far as Egyptian mythology was concerned, syncretism was justified by the fact that several gods looked alike or engaged in similar activities. In a country under the authority of one sovereign, unification had the added advantage of encouraging a greater unity of mythological concepts, even if it was only relative. The tendency towards syncretism was already apparent in the time of the Old Kingdom; but it gathered strength as time went on.

Syncretism was most common with gods who represented the forces of nature or the principal functions of life. By the very fact of their universality such gods are recognisable at all times to all peoples, so that, whatever the variants of personality, they were readily identified with each other. Amalgamation was natural in the case of fertility and vegetation gods and mother-goddesses. So the goddess Isis, who in Osirian myth is the mother of Horus, was linked with Hathor, the cow-goddess, with Nekhbet the tutelary goddess of EL-Kab, and also with Mut, the Theban goddess, whose name in fact means 'the mother'.

But the two gods who were most frequently adopted and identified with others were Re, the sun-god, and Osiris, god of the dead. The sun-god, vested with the supreme virtue of universality, was soon incorporated with all the primary local gods. We have seen already how Re came to be identified with Atum, and how Re and Horus together assumed a new form — Re-Harakhty or Horus of the Horizon. By the same process the crocodile-god of Faiyum was called Sobk-Re, the falcon-god Month, of Theban origin, was known as Month-Re, the ram-god Khnum of Elephantine became Khnum-Re, and so forth.

As for Osiris, once raised to the rank of god of the dead he was soon widely accepted as the chief of the funeral gods. At Abydos he to some extent supplanted Khentimentiu, the Chief of the Occidentals; at Memphis he was later identified with Sokaris, the ancient god of the local necropolis.

Sometimes a mere similarity of appearance resulted in two gods being associated with each other. The most striking example is provided by the falcon-gods, as almost all of them took on the name of Horus. In the same way the cow-goddesses were equated with Hathor. This type of association was perfectly acceptable to the Egyptian mind, which preferred to think in images rather than according to logic.

In actual fact, one of the consequences of syncretism

Month-Re. Month, originally a local deity of Hermonthis, was one of the gods identified with Re. He was a war-god and was usually shown with a falcon head. *Mansell*

Akhenaten and his queen, Nefertiti, embrace their children while the rays of the pharaoh's special deity, Aten, descend to them. Berlin Museum. *Bildarchiv Foto Marburg*

was the inextricable tangle of mythological concepts. Once a similarity between two divine personalities had been accepted, the other characteristics of the gods concerned were reconciled – however different they might be. The result, needless to say, was that the divine legends and even the theological systems often became inconsistent or even incoherent. Egyptologists have had great difficulty in unravelling the tangle and discovering the various elements that went into the composition of the myths.

The doctrine of Aten

If syncretism did not clarify or rationalise beliefs, it did at least help to emphasise the pre-eminent part played by certain gods. In so doing it opened the way to one of the most astounding religious revolutions staged in the ancient Orient; this was the Atenian revolution, which happened in the eleventh century B.C. through the inspiration and guidance of Amenophis IV – Akhenaten.

In the middle of the Eighteenth Dynasty a strong movement in favour of the sun-cult became evident in Egyptian religious thought. There is a series of hymns dating from this period, which, although dedicated to Amun the god of the Kingdom, are in fact really addressed to Re-Harakhty, exalting his work of creation. In these compositions, which reveal a profound feeling for nature, mythological allusions become less frequent and are gradually replaced by factors bearing on the providential influence of the sun-god; he is seen showing solicitude for all the things he has created; he is particularly concerned for all living beings – man, animals and plants – for he is responsible for their preservation and well-being. These concepts, which fitted in so well with the aspirations of men of the time, seem to have created an atmosphere favourable to the birth of the new doctrine, which bears the name of its founder.

Even in his childhood the future Amenophis IV was already attracted to the revived ideal of the sun-cult; it seemed more rational and closer to the natural order of things than the traditional theological systems. It is certainly true to say that from the very beginning of his reign Amenophis IV, while conforming to the ritual of traditional religion, already showed his predilection for the sun-god, either in the form of Re-Harakhty (Horus of the Horizon) or, perhaps, already in the form of Aten. This name in contemporary terminology referred to the sun-disc.

For several years the young king continued to tolerate the established cults; but as the new doctrine took shape in his mind he showed himself more and more disposed towards Aten, even going so far as to build temples to him near to the sanctuaries of Amun and other Theban gods. Not surprisingly, Amenophis IV met a certain amount of opposition in conservative sections of society, and especially among members of Amun's high clergy: the latter saw the power and prestige of their god menaced by the rise of a rival god with claims to universality. Aten's temples, for instance, were piled high with gifts, to the detriment of the ancient sanctuaries.

In circumstances about which little is known, Amenophis IV broke completely with the Theban clergy: he closed Amun's temples and defaced the images and inscriptions that referred to the god whose very memory he wished to efface. He decided to make this rupture with the traditional cults final by moving with his court and adepts to a new city, which was to become his capital as well as the centre of the cult of his god. This town, which he called the Horizon of Aten (its ruins have been found on the site of Tell el-Amarna), developed rapidly and acquired solar temples, palaces and residential districts. There the royal visionary was able to live for twelve years with the illusion that he had instituted a new order under the aegis of the sun-disc. Although it was revolutionary in spirit, Atenian doctrine took certain things from Heliopolitan theology. The founder-god was the sun-god, who had the characteristics and at first the name of his Heliopolitan equivalent, Re-Harakhty, although he was normally known as Aten. But the new doctrine was a purified and rationalised version of the system that inspired it. Rejecting polytheism with its densely interwoven mythology, Amenophis IV recognised only one god. Aten was the source of all light and all life; he acquired the virtues and qualities that were personified in divine hypostases: above all he was the possessor of *maat,* a fairly wide concept simultaneously implying cosmic order, justice and truth.

Aten is portrayed as a disc from which rays fan out towards the earth and end in open hands – they scatter the gifts of the god among all his creatures.

In accordance with concepts that had developed in preceding generations Aten became the god of providence; he ensured the well-being of Egyptians

Akhenaten presents offerings to Aten, who is represented by a sun-disc. The pharaoh tried to destroy the power of the Theban priests of Amun and founded a new capital which was to be the centre of the new cult. Stele. Cairo. Eighteenth Dynasty: 1580–1530 B.C.

and foreign races and united them in his love. By his radiant light he daily renewed the life potential of all creatures on earth, and combined his influence with that of the Nile in order to fertilise the soil. Thus he provided a means of subsistence for men, animals and the vegetable world.

This doctrine is suffused with a love of nature; and the god communicated directly with his creatures, not through any supernatural intermediaries. An ideal such as this was bound to give rise to poetic outpourings, like those contained in the admirable hymns in honour of Aten, some of which have been preserved. If these hymns were not composed by the pharaoh himself, they were inspired by him, and they shed light on the outstanding features of the doctrine.

Akhenaten (He who is devoted to Aten) really considered himself to be the confidant and prophet of his god. Living in intimate communion with Aten, he received from him the revelation of a new order, and his task was to spread the precepts among men. In the inscriptions on their tombs the votaries of Aten made more than one allusion to the teaching they had received at the hands of the pharaoh — from which they had greatly profited.

But this sublime doctrine, founded on the principle of monotheism and proclaiming love of one's fellow men, did not have time to take root during the relatively short reign of the pharaoh who initiated it. Sincere belief was probably restricted to a relatively small circle of followers, while the mass of the population remained secretly attached to the religion of their ancestors. When Akhenaten died, his opponents reappeared and forced the reformer's weak successors to reinstate Amun and the other banished gods. Horemheb, the usurper, headed the counter-reform movement and devoted himself to effacing from the whole of Egypt traces of Aten-cult, henceforth condemned as execrable.

The ancient cults soon regained any ground they may have lost, although they suffered certain transformations under the pressure of new ideas. The ancient Egyptian gods continued to receive the homage of their faithful followers until the early centuries of the Christian era. The Ptolemies, in their desire to unite their Egyptian and Greek subjects, attempted to spread the cult of Sarapis in both countries. He was a god whose name seems to have derived from Osiris and Apis, the sacred bull of Memphis. Sarapis certainly enjoyed a vogue in Hellenised centres. Nevertheless, under the Greek dynasties, as under Roman domination, the Egyptians clung to their national traditions and continued to build luxurious temples for their gods. The reliefs and inscriptions they contained constitute one of the most important sources for the reconstruction of ancient myths. Egyptian religion did not succumb until it felt the irresistible pressure of Christianity. And even then some popular deities were worshipped in remote parts of Egypt until the sixth century.

A group of worshippers with their hands clasped in the attitude
of prayer. 3500 B.C. *Oriental Institute, University of Chicago*

EMPIRES OF THE ANCIENT NEAR EAST: THE HYMNS OF CREATION

In terms of geography the territory covered in this section includes most of the ancient Near East, from Mesopotamia to Anatolia. Ethnographically, it is concerned with populations as different in language and race as the Sumerians (the first socially and politically organised group to appear on this geographical horizon), their Semitic successors of Babylonian and Assyrian origin (who were Mesopotamian in the true sense of the word), the Hurrites, who cannot yet be clearly defined, and, finally, the Hittites, Indo-Europeans superimposed on the native Asian population.

Chronologically this section must, by its very nature, rely solely on written sources, and therefore cannot begin until myth first appears in writing. With the exception of a few vague allusions found for the most part in the texts of Gudea, Prince of Lagash, at the beginning of the Third Dynasty (approximately 2050 B.C.), there are no myths or legends before those revealed in texts dating from the Babylonian dynasties of Isin and Larsa (roughly between 1969 and 1732 B.C.). Even if it is obvious that most go back to a much earlier period, one must take into consideration the question of religious—and literary—evolution, and also bear in mind the influence of certain Semitic concepts on these 'Sumerian' texts, for it is known that the Semites entered Mesopotamia and settled there no later than the Sumerians themselves. To speak of 'the earliest examples' of individual myths, relying on texts written in Sumerian, but dating from the beginning of the second millennium, is an outrageous over-simplification. Granted that Sumerian myths are known to us only through later accounts, it is impossible at the present time to determine what part of them is in fact Sumerian, and what derives from Semitic influences, which might have affected the forms just as much as their content. This is an important reservation.

Goddess smelling a flower. Stone bas-relief. Middle Euphrates. Mari. Eighteenth century B.C. Louvre. *Musées Nationaux*

Sumer

Sumerian myth conforms to the patterns set by mythological archetypes throughout the world, both in civilisations contemporary with that of Sumer (or, at least, of ancient date), and equally in so-called primitive cultures of modern times. Thus Sumer has cosmological myths and myths of origin, which, like myths everywhere, are in this case both a reflection on the cosmos they are meant to explain, and at the same time a justification of the particular type of society from which they proceed. The myth that tells how cosmic order arose out of the primeval state of things explains this evolution in terms that reflect the natural, material and social conditions particular to Sumer. It must be remembered that this mythology, being of a subjective nature, represents the earliest stage in human thought that we know. Here within our grasp are the most ancient origins of myth as well as the very beginnings of human society. The primitive or traditional societies of our own time in which myth is still current as a statement of sacred realities merely produce myths that, when all is said and done, are the end-product of an evolution of several thousands of years. Sumer, by reason of its very anteriority, constitutes one of the most important sources for the study of myth.

Major themes

The cosmogonic myths implied chaos or the void preceding creation and told of the separation of the elements that had been fused together until divine energy began to operate, releasing these different elements and giving them their particular identity; and myths of origin stated how and why a particular phenomenon came into being, whether the subject in question was the creation of man, the institution of royalty, the birth of plants, or the organisation of human activities.

Sumerian mythology drew its material from the permanent principles of Sumerian culture relating to landownership and family life. Its myth attempted to account for the organisation of the cosmos by projecting human and social experience onto a divine plane. The myth and the forms that it adopted were a function of the society from which it stemmed. It told of creation in terms of human experience. Its very elements were those at the basis of Sumerian society: that which moved as opposed to that which was firm, the stable as opposed to the unstable, fresh waters as against bitter waters.

So Sumerian mythology can be explained by reference to the nature of the soil on which this civilisation grew up. In a primeval countryside, still damp with the waters of the flood, on mud brought down by huge wild rivers, in a lacustrine setting with land slowly gaining over water and yet subject to its repeated incursions, man took up his abode. His reactions to this struggle against the elements are

A goddess, probably Inanna, later Ishtar (whose symbol is a star), is shown dominating the forces of nature and fertility. Khafaje. 3000–2750 B.C. *British Museum*

only too apparent in the cosmological myths, which show that the first task of the gods on earth was to give 'canals and ditches their proper course', and to 'establish the banks of the Tigris and the Euphrates'.

Whereas Sumerian myths deliberately ignored all myths relative to the discovery and use of metals, they gave the divine origins of the vegetable world. Lastly, the Sumerian pantheon was organised on the pattern of human families forming one social group. It was a divine group, which in its organisation was a replica of urban Sumerian society, with a 'leader' who could take decisions only in accordance with the advice of the eminent in the land or of the assembly of warriors. This assembly of equals, which played such a large part in Mesopotamian society, played no less part in Heaven, where the assembled gods made decisions.

Myth and ritual became integrated, and symbolic acts reproduced the successive stages of the myth. In this way the rite was realised in action. That was why, in Mesopotamia as elsewhere, myth had its place in such solemn rituals as the Babylonian New Year Festival, in the course of which—because the rite was seeking to establish the renewal of nature, to go back to the beginning of things and to ensure the perennial survival of cosmic order—the *Poem of Creation* was recited, recounting the work of the gods in primordial times. But the myth was equally applicable to human tasks, making them one with the cosmic operation, and were part of the rituals applied to such different concerns as the construction of temples, births and medical practice. And this quality, which promoted the work of men to a plane on which it participated in the divine, and through the intermediary of myth related their work to that of the gods, existed equally in Sumer and Babylon, in the Hittite as in the Hurrite empire.

Neither in Sumer, nor, *ipso facto*, in Babylon, nor Assyria was there any theology or canon of writing. Concepts were fluid. Here, the gods themselves 'constructed', they 'made' heaven and earth, and the *apsu*, the primeval abyss. According to other schools of thought, heaven, earth and the *apsu* existed before all else. Any attempt to reconcile the various views that were acceptable to Mesopotamians would be useless.

At first there appeared to be few elements in this particular sphere that can be compared with the great mythological themes found in other parts of the world. There were two, however: the idea of the cosmic tree and the idea of the primeval monster, conquered by the demiurge, whose dismembered body was made into heaven and earth.

The cosmic tree

A fundamental concept that was common to many ancient and primary cosmogonies—that of the cosmic tree uniting the world below with the divine world of the heavens above—undoubtedly played a part in the most ancient mythical concepts of the Sumerians, but at a very early date it seems to have disappeared—at least in that particular form. It is mentioned in the texts of Gudea, Prince of Lagash, which are of great importance as they form the basis of our present knowledge, and were written to celebrate the erection of a temple to the local god, Ningirsu.

The cosmic tree also figured in some hymns of the Neo-Sumerian period, which date from the dynasty of Isin (1969–1732 B.C.). In one of these texts Gudea referred to the temple of Ningirsu, which, 'like the *gish-gana* tree of *apsu* (the primeval abyss) stretches up above all lands'. This most certainly referred to the mythological archetype of the tree or stake joining the world below to the world above. Although the temple itself was here the symbol of the cosmic tree, at the temple gate another symbol stood, a pole or

Figures such as this one of a god driving an enormous nail are known as foundation-gods. Their function was to protect the foundations of a house or temple against evil spirits or natural disasters. End of third millennium B.C. *Giraudon*

mast 'which reaches right to the sky'. Here again reference was being made to the cosmic tree. The King of Isin, Ishme-Dagan, later referred to the temple of Lagash as 'the great mast in the land of Sumer'. So here we have one of the crowning points in Sumerian religion, where the cosmic tree of Sumer rose in the symbolic form.

This mode of expressing and symbolising a mythological concept was destined to disappear, but right to the end of Sumerian civilisation the idea remained a bond between heaven and earth on one particular sacred spot in Sumer. At Nippur, the holy town in Sumer, which was the residence of Enlil, the great god of the land, the platformed tower, in itself a cosmic symbol, was given the name of Dur-an-ki, 'bond between Heaven and Earth', again using the concept of the bond-pole.

Sumer organised its pantheon around three high gods: An, heaven-god; Enlil, air-god; and a goddess, Ninhursag, the Lady of the Mountain, known by various other names as well. But the connections between these three deities were not clearly defined. Alongside them a god appeared from time to time like an intruder, Enki ('earth-lord?'). The cosmos was divided between them: for An, the sky; for Enlil, the air and the earth; for Enki, sometimes thought of as the son of Enlil, and also called 'little Enlil', the fresh waters of *apsu*; Ninhursag was the prototype of the goddess-mother and appeared, according to tradition, under the name of Nintue, Ninmah or Aruru.

Since traditions differed about their respective roles, it is difficult to reconcile these various factors. It would appear from the mythical texts that Sumerian thought did not seek to proceed in logical or even chronological order. It is only from allusions scattered here and there that conclusions can be drawn. If they are not always compatible with one another, it is probably because they represent different traditions current in different religious centres.

Sea, earth and skies

In a list of Sumerian gods a goddess Nammu, whose name was expressed by the ideogram for 'sea', was described as 'the mother who gave birth to heaven and earth'. Elsewhere she was called 'mother of all the gods', and, more specifically, 'mother of Enki', the god who 'will organise' the world of men. The idea of the cosmos originating in a stretch of water—a concept similar to one expressed in the Bible—was echoed in the Babylonian myth of creation. There, the sea, personified by a female deity, Tiamat, was conquered by the demiurge and her body turned into the earth and the sky. But in Sumer quite a different idea seems to have been current, according to which the creation of the world was effected by successive or concomitant emanations: from the primordial sea come forth the earth and the skies.

These two elements, earth and sky, which were appropriately called 'the twins' in certain texts, as a reminder of the way in which they came into being, were still undivided at this point; this idea occurred again, notably in Egypt. They were separated by a god, Enlil, and this accounts for his name of 'air-god', since air filters between sky and earth.

In the poem that told how the pick-axe, the most valued agricultural instrument, was created, the following passage refers to the separation of the elements. The context provides adequate indication of the fact that this act was only the first in a series of divine acts that gave the world its final shape:

> The lord (Enlil) in order to bring forth what was
> useful,
> The lord whose decisions are unalterable,
> Enlil, who brings up the seed of the 'land' from
> the earth,
> Planned to move away heaven from earth,
> Planned to move away earth from heaven.

Another poem envisaged this separation as the work of two deities, An and Enlil:

> After heaven had been moved away from earth,
> After earth had been separated from heaven,
> After the name of man had been fixed,
> After (the heaven-god) An carried off the heaven,
> After (the air-god) Enlil carried off the earth . . .

A third tradition told of the separation of the primeval elements without going into details as to the identity of the demiurge. Perhaps it was not necessary to do so, but it is permissible for us to think of a natural separation of the fused elements at this particular point in time, and this would have led to the emergence of the cosmos. There is evidence of this tradition in the introduction to the *Hymn to the Locust-tree*, which told of Enki's arrival in Sumer:

> After heaven had been moved far from the earth,
> After earth had been separated from heaven,
> After mankind had come into being (?),
> After the god An was established in heaven,
> After (Enlil) was established on earth,
> And the goddess Erishkigal had received the under-
> world as her share . . .

Then followed the story of the coming of Enki and the history of the locust-tree, the primeval tree, one alone and unique, which grew on the banks of the Euphrates. This tradition conflicts with those previously mentioned. There was a tripartite division of the cosmos: the sky going to An, the earth to Enlil, and to Erishkigal the 'land from which there is no return'. This was an isolated myth, the pattern of which was not echoed elsewhere.

Everything in this disorderly theology was interconnected and interwoven. It is useless to seek order in it. The stages of creation varied according to different traditions. Nevertheless the primary fact emerged

as the separation of the sky and heaven. As to what happened next the myths did not entirely agree.

The myth of paradise

A long text—known by the name of *Myth of Paradise* or *Myth of Dilmun* from the name of a country that almost certainly existed only in mythology, and which was the setting for the story—recalled the time when the god Enki and his wife, 'the pure Virgin', were the 'only couple' asleep in the virgin and clear world of Dilmun. In this country life had not yet appeared.

> In Dilmun the raven utters no cry,
> The *ittidu*-bird utters not the cry of the *ittidu*-bird,
> The lion kills not,
> The wolf snatches not the lamb,
>
> Unknown is the kid-devouring wild dog . . .
> The sick-eyed says not 'I am sick-eyed,'
> The sick-headed says not 'I am sick-headed,'
> The old woman says not 'I am an old woman,'
> The old man says not 'I am an old man . . .'

Undoubtedly this narrative was emphasising that nothing in the familiar world of men had yet begun to exist in Dilmun. Dilmun was the mythical country destined to witness the birth of life when it was created by the god Enki and 'the Virgin', his wife. Until then nothing existed, not even water. It was the task of 'the Virgin' to ask the god to create the life-giving waters:

> Father Enki answers Ninsikilla, his daughter:
> 'Let the Sun-god "in a day . . .",
> From the mouth whence issues the water of the
> earth,
> Bring sweet water from the earth . . .'

And the Sun did so. Dilmun received the water that enabled her 'to drink the waters of plenty'.

> Let thy well of bitter water become a well of sweet
> water,
> Let thy furrowed fields (and) farms bear thee grain,
> Let thy city become the bank-quay house of the
> land . . .

The divine marriage

The next episode told of the divine union and the birth of the gods. This episode was preceded by an act of creation performed alone and unaided by Enki, when, in the presence of the Lady of the Land, Nintu (a name assumed by 'the Virgin' at the moment of conception), he fertilised the swampy land with his own seed. Then followed his union with his wife, who took the name of Ninhursag when she was about to give birth to a child.

The first child of the divine couple was the goddess Ninmu, by whom Enki then had another daughter,

Statue of a goddess worshipped at a street-shrine of Ur.
c. 1750 B.C. British Museum. *Paul Popper*

Bas-relief of man with plumed head-dress. Telloh (Lagash).
Early third century B.C. Louvre. *Musées Nationaux*

A woman's head, sometimes identified with Ninagal, the
Babylonian sun-goddess. Marble. Ur. 2200-2100 B.C.
University Museum, Philadelphia

the goddess Nindurra, by whom in turn he had the
goddess Uttu. At this point Ninhursag intervened and
advised Uttu to repel the god's advances until she had
received the marriage gifts: 'cucumbers, apples and
grapes'. When Enki had brought these gifts, Uttu had
no further reason for rejecting him. However, this
union did not follow quite the same pattern as the
previous ones. The sequence was broken, for Ninhursag next appeared to create eight different plants
from her husband's seed, and Enki saw them growing
in the marshes. He approached and ate them. Then
Ninhursag cursed Enki and departed. The disappearance of the goddess plunged the Anunnaki, the assembly of the high gods, into a state of consternation.
The fox offered to bring Ninhursag back to Enlil in
return for a reward, and Enlil agreed to this.

If thou wilt bring Ninhursag before me,
In my city I will plant trees (and) fields
     for thee, verily thy name will be uttered.

Unfortunately, there is a break in the narrative
here, and the sequence of events is interrupted, but
when the story is resumed Ninhursag was hurrying to
the dying Enki, to whom she addressed these words:

'My brother, what hurts you?'

The god named eight parts of his body, and the re-
pentant goddess told him that she had given birth to a
number of gods in order to cure him. Finally, Enki
'decrees the fate' of these new gods, the last of whom,
Enshag, was to be the tutelary god of Dilmun.

This myth does not fit in with the concepts previously outlined. Its primary purpose was undoubtedly to glorify Enki—for there were numerous indications that he was a deity foreign to Sumer proper—
and, like several other myths in the same cycle, the

Fragment of a perforated limestone plaque with an engraved design showing worship of the goddess Nina, the daughter of Ea. Sargonid period, from Nippur. *University Museum. Philadelphia*

purpose of this one was to establish Enki as the organiser of the world and the founder of divine and human institutions; it was he who ensured order in the world and regulated earthly activities from irrigation to ploughing, from weaving to cattle-raising, for these were all cultural concepts, which Sumerians referred to by one name, 'me', and they were the tangible symbols of civilisation conferred by the gods.

The *Myth of Dilmun* attempted to provide a rational explanation of the birth of vegetation, starting from the fertilisation of the earth by the sweet waters. The earth was Nintu or Ninhursag. The sweet waters were Enki. First of all water welled up from the depths of the earth as the rivers rose and fell and fertilised the soil; this, in turn, gave birth to plants and to the principle of vegetation symbolised by the birth of the goddess Ninmu, 'the Lady who makes things grow'; then (in another version of the text) came Ninsig, 'the Lady who makes things turn green'. Then came the plants raised from the seed of Enki, doubtless without his knowledge, and scattered over the earth by Ninhursag. Finally it was the turn of the plants created by the goddess to heal Enki, and these have names that evoke the sick parts of the god's body, for each is an untranslatable play on words.

This was an agrarian myth, but the actual moment of history at which it was supposed it took place was not revealed. Enlil was certainly present, seated in the midst of the other gods. But neither he nor the Anunnaki played a direct part in the myth. This was the period after the creation of the world, when the gods delegated to Enki and his spouse the task of organisation before man made his entrance into the world.

Sumerian myth was not consistent with geographical fact. Did Sumerians really believe that the historic cities of Sumer had existed ever since the gods first appeared on earth? Dilmun was said to have existed before the appearance of men. It was peopled by gods, and, like Nippur, which was the setting for a myth about Enlil and Ninlil that tells how and why certain gods of the underworld were born, Dilmun naturally did exist in the real world. That suggests that important cities were already in existence in lower Mesopotamia when the Sumerians got there, and this would explain why many place-names in the land of Sumer were not Sumerian.

The Flood

This mythical geography appeared again in the Sumerian myth of the Flood. Although the introduction is fragmentary, it nevertheless tells, in a rather obscure context, of the origins of mankind and of royalty, and of the foundation of five antediluvian royal cities. The beginning of the introduction is missing: it starts where a god speaks—of primeval times:

> After An, Enlil, Enki and Ninhursag
> Had fashioned the black-headed (people),
> Vegetation luxuriated the earth,
> Animals, four-legged (creatures) of the plain,
>   were brought artfully into existence.

So we have here a new tradition in which the goddess-mother, Ninhursag, and a great male triad, consisting of An, Enlil and Enki, created men, then vegetation and, finally, animals.

Then, in terms very similar to the official list of Sumerian royal dynasties, the myth set forth the origins of royalty with its symbols, which came down from heaven to earth, and the foundation of the five primeval cities where this royalty was first established: Eridu, Badtibira, Larak, Sippar and Shuruppak. After a long gap came a Sumerian account of the Flood: 'To destroy humanity, such is the decision, the "word" of the Assembly of the gods', although no reason for it is given in the text. A god informed

Sumerian priest with libation vase. *British Museum*

Plaque in low relief showing Sumerian sacrificial ceremonies.
Upper register: a priest accompanied by female attendants
pours a libation to a seated god. Lower register: a priest pours a
libation before the door of a temple or chapel. A male attendant,
flanked by two female attendants, carries a kid for sacrifice.
In early times Sumerian priests usually offered sacrifices naked.
Limestone. From the temple of Ningal at Ur. Early Dynastic
period: c. 2500 B.C. *British Museum*

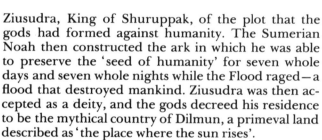

Ziusudra, King of Shuruppak, of the plot that the gods had formed against humanity. The Sumerian Noah then constructed the ark in which he was able to preserve the 'seed of humanity' for seven whole days and seven whole nights while the Flood raged—a flood that destroyed mankind. Ziusudra was then accepted as a deity, and the gods decreed his residence to be the mythical country of Dilmun, a primeval land described as 'the place where the sun rises'.

The Babylonian epic of Gilgamesh, which adopted the Sumerian account of the Flood with little modification, made the hero reside 'far away, at the mouth of the rivers', undoubtedly the Tigris and Euphrates, to the east of Mesopotamia, on the very spot where Dilmun stood, on the edge of the world, as it were, on pure and virgin earth.

The reason for man

Just as the Old Testament states that God put man in the Garden of Eden to replenish the earth and subdue it, so Sumer, in the dawn of time, sets forth the tasks incumbent on humanity, and the arduous fate it has to bear, and says that men were created by the gods to serve them. Thus the creation of mankind was made to appear necessary, in the sense that the gods raised these new beings to relieve them of tasks that they previously performed themselves; furthermore, men were necessary so that the gods might at last enjoy eternal life to the full, for it was this that distinguished gods from human beings.

All this comes from the myth known by the name of *Myth of Cattle and Grain;* it contains a reference to the time when the Anunnaki could not eat or drink their fill, because the human race had not yet been created to see to their needs. It describes the period when the god An had already created the Anunnaki 'on the mountain of Heaven and Earth', but nothing was yet possible in the world because there were no functional gods, for they had not yet been created.

Because the name of Ashnan (the grain-goddess) had not been born, had not been fashioned, because Uttu (the goddess of clothing) had not been fashioned, there was no ewe, no lamb.

Because the names of Ashnan and Lahar (the cattle-god) . . . were not known, grain did not exist.

This myth contains a striking example of the Sumerian concept (later adopted in Babylon) of the supremacy of the 'name', the mere pronunciation of which was equivalent to an act of creation; and there is some connection between this myth and ideas reflected in the *Myth of Dilmun,* which also tells how and why the gods of plants and the functional gods were born. Before these gods came into existence, the Anunnaki 'like mankind in the moment of creation, had no knowledge of bread for nourishment, no knowledge of clothing to clothe themselves, they ate plants as do sheep, drank water from ditches . . .'. Here is a reminder of the wretched and difficult start made by mankind (which undoubtedly remained vivid in Sumerian minds).

So the gods created Ashnan and Lahar: crops and cattle were raised, but 'the gods remain unappeased' —an allusion to some unfinished organisation of the cosmos. 'In order that he might look after their holy sheep-folds, man then received the breath of life.'

From that point onwards everything was in its place in that cosmos, not by reason of a gratuitous act, but from sheer necessity. The world created by the gods of Sumer was entirely for their own advantage. The men they put on earth had no other reason for existence than to till the soil for the greater glory of the gods, and, especially, to see to their needs, so that they could be relieved of unwelcome tasks that they had had to assume themselves in the dawn of time.

Babylon

The Semitic dynasties of Isin and Larsa brought to
an end the political hegemony of the Sumerians over
Lower Babylonia, and the Third Dynasty of Ur, which
disappeared about 1955 B.C., captured the final
brilliance of this hegemony.

Political upheavals produced no 'revolution' in the
field of religion, since in fact the scribes and priests
of Isin and Larsa—who were perhaps authentic
Sumerians—were those responsible for copying and
handing down Sumerian literature.

In the Babylonian myths, which gradually replaced
ancient Sumerian myths, it is almost impossible to
determine how much is of Semitic religious origin.
There is nothing to show that a Babylonian myth is
not simply a translation or adaptation of a hitherto
unknown Sumerian theme. It is now known that
before the Semites made a vast epic poem of the
episodes of the legendary life of Gilgamesh, these
episodes were already recounted in Sumerian legends,
just as it is known that the Babylonian account of the
Flood was only an adaptation of the 'historic' tradition regarding the origins of Sumer. And the same is
true of many literary works. On the other hand, certain Babylonian myths are quite clearly adaptations,
if not simple translations, of Sumerian myths.

This Semitic world, which, politically, was vastly
different from the Sumerian world, was strangely
dependent on it to judge by the results of religious
speculation. One has the impression that the Semites
adapted Sumerian ideas wholesale, and that they
contributed very little in this field to the development
of religious thought—with one exception. This exception—the Babylonian *Poem of Creation*—affords
evidence of a remarkable effort of adaptation, and
it shows how cosmological themes that were the
common property of Occidental Semites were integrated with concepts of Sumerian origin, and finally
it makes a political and religious statement.

The symbol of Marduk, chief god in the Babylonian pantheon, set above a composite creature, the *mushrushu*. Neo-Babylonian (612-539 B.C.) Agate. *British Museum*

Naked goddess, possibly Astarte. Terracotta statuette. North Syrian. Second millennium B.C. *Fitzwilliam Museum, Cambridge*

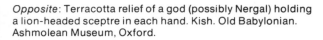

Opposite: Terracotta relief of a god (possibly Nergal) holding a lion-headed sceptre in each hand. Kish. Old Babylonian. Ashmolean Museum, Oxford.

In another connection myth in the Semitic religion of Babylon was much more closely integrated with rite than in Sumerian thought. In fact, although the *Poem of Creation* was essentially part of the ritual of the New Year Festival in Babylon, the truth is that there was not a single Semitic myth—whether of Sumerian origin or not—which did not likewise form an integral part of a specific ritual. This fact is important and should be continually borne in mind.

The *Poem of Creation*

This long poem, in seven tablets, which was known to Babylonians by its opening words, *Enuma elish,* 'When on high', has been handed down more or less intact in copies that, at the very earliest, date from the ninth century B.C. and some also survive from the second century B.C. These texts come from most of the great religious centres in Mesopotamia, from Assyria and Babylonia alike, from Ashur and Nineveh, as well as Sippur, Kish and perhaps even from Babylon itself (certain versions are based on texts from Babylon and Nippur). This alone shows the importance of the poem in the Babylonian scheme of religious thought. It was written in a special language, a dialect form of Babylonian. This fact and certain other indications lend weight to the supposition that it was originally composed in the period of the First Dynasty in Babylon, somewhere between the nineteenth and seventeenth centuries B.C., though it is impossible to be precise.

Besides being a religious testimony, the *Poem of Creation* is a political document, which can be explained by reference to the origins and political success of the First Dynasty in Babylon. Until the day when the founder of the dynasty seized Babylon, it was a mere village with a local god; under the impetus of energetic kings (the most famous of whom was Hammurabi) this god became the nucleus of a vast centralised empire, and held together under his own divine aegis the principalities of Lower Mesopotamia, some of which possessed well-known sanctuaries. The imperial doctrine in process of formulation had its counterpart in a religious doctrine, which was to effect the same revolution in the spiritual field as the sovereigns of Babylon had accomplished in a temporal sphere. So the essential purpose of the *Poem of Creation* was the glorification of the god of Babylon, Marduk, who became the head of the Babylonian pantheon.

Of course, the ancient cults continued: Nippur remained the centre of the cult of Enlil; Ur, that of Sin, the moon-god; Uruk, the centre for the god of the sky, Anu. But in the case of Babylon, henceforth 'city of royalty', the local god was elevated to high god in the strict clerical hierarchy; he became the demiurge. Every effort was made to exalt Marduk, and everything in Sumerian mythology that might fit this purpose was emphasised.

That there was an attempt to create synthesis and

Ishtar, Babylonian goddess of fertility, whose cult spread throughout the ancient Near East and to Greece. Terracotta plaque. Mesopotamian. Ninth to eighth centuries B.C. *Fitzwilliam Museum, Cambridge*

syncretism is clear to anyone studying the poem. The original myth can be discerned in the background; it cast Enlil in the role that priests in Babylon subsequently gave to Marduk. The use of different traditions can be detected, some of them stemming directly from Sumerian mythology, others, like that of the primeval creature here called Tiamat, seemingly of Semitic religious origin. Tiamat's role was to be conquered by the demiurge and to give her own body to be used for the sky and the earth.

The early part of the poem describes the time when 'up above the skies were not named, below the earth had no name', when the waters of the primeval *apsu* 'procreator (of the gods) and Tiamat who gave birth to them' mingled their waters. Nothing existed: 'No god had yet appeared, nor received a name or fate.'

In the beginning were the waters, the sweet water, *apsu,* and the salt water, Tiamat, the sea, as yet unseparated and with nothing to disturb them. The waters contained in themselves the seeds of life. They brought into existence, one after another, divine couples (or divine generations) between each of which aeons of time passed, and each succeeding one was more powerful than its predecessor:

> Then it was that the gods were formed within them.
> Lahmu and Lahamu were brought forth, by name
>   they were called.
> Before they had grown in age and stature
> Anshar and Kishar were formed, surpassing the
>   others.
> They prolonged the days, added on the years,
> Anu was their heir, of his fathers the rival;
> Yea, Anshar's first-born, Anu, was his equal.
> Anu begot in his image Nudimmud.
> This Nudimmud was of his fathers the master . . .

These were the first divine generations. Begotten of the primeval waters, increasingly powerful deities succeeded one another in couples: Lahmu-Lahamu, Anshar and Kishar, then Anu by himself, and finally Ea, whose spouse Damkina appeared later. One particular interpretation is indicated. Although the nature of the first divine couple remains mysterious, after this the names seem to embody cosmic concepts. Anshar and Kishar represented 'the things above' of the sky (*an*), and 'the things below' of the earth (*ki*), and in addition there was a new factor in this active universe—a chaos animated by principles that led to the definitive formation of the cosmos. Then Anu, the sky-god, followed, and, finally, his son, Enki-Ea, and they reigned over what was, in this order of things, the equivalent of the primeval sky and the cosmic abyss that supported the earth.

Tiamat and Apsu were disturbed by the noise made by the gods. 'Their behaviour pains me,' Apsu says. 'By day I cannot rest, by night I cannot sleep. I want to destroy them, put an end to their comings and goings.'

It would be difficult to go into detail about the problems raised by the *Poem of Creation,* but it is nevertheless worth noting that the reason given by Apsu for destroying the gods—their noisiness—was exactly the same as those that the gods gave when they eventually decided to destroy mankind by the Flood. An inconsistency can be seen here too: Day and Night are mentioned, though their birth does not occur till the fifth tablet, when Marduk organises the cosmos.

Tiamat was reluctant to destroy her offspring. Yet on the advice of his vizier Mummu, Apsu would not renounce his plan. But Ea was mysteriously informed of the plot and 'poured sleep' over Apsu, put him in chains and slew him; then he bound Mummu and established his residence in the *apsu.* 'Ea and Damkina, his spouse, rest there in majesty.'

Here in the deep waters of *apsu* Marduk was born. Anu made the winds rise and created the waves, which were a source of disturbance to Tiamat. So on the advice of 'the gods deprived of rest' she prepared for a fresh attack, this time on the younger gods.

'The Abyss-Mother, who shaped everything' chose one of her first-born gods, Kingu, and made him her husband. Then he led the forces of chaos into battle against the demiurge, champion of the gods.

The second and third tablets tell of the preparations for combat and of the monsters created by Tiamat to aid her in the forthcoming struggle. The gods in fear and trembling instructed Ea and Anu in turn to confront the monsters. They refused. Anshar summoned an assembly of the gods and they instructed Marduk to defend them. He accepted on condition that he was given supreme power. This was granted: the gods 'speak the destiny' of Marduk, and he prepared for combat (fourth tablet).

The account of the theogony, the struggle between the demiurge and the forces of chaos, takes up the remainder of the fourth tablet. The divine drama was presented in twofold aspect: opposing natural forces and deities personifying them. Tiamat was the sea; Anu created the winds, which disturbed her. Marduk was the sun and the power of renewal, which in spring—both the primeval spring in the dawn of time and the springtime of each year—wakened the earth from torpor and gave it life.

Combat began, as in the *Iliad,* with the opponents challenging one another:

Then joined issue Tiamat and Marduk, wisest of
    gods,
They strove in single combat, locked in battle,
The lord spread out his net to enfold her,
The Evil Wind, which followed behind, he let loose
    in her face.
When Tiamat opened her mouth to consume him,
He drove in the Evil Wind that she close not her
    lips.
As the fierce winds charged her belly,
Her body was distended and her mouth was wide
    open.
He released the arrow, it tore her belly,
It cut through her insides, splitting the heart.
Having thus subdued her, he extinguished her life.
He cast down her carcass to stand upon it.

Marduk defeated 'Tiamat's band', her army of demons. He bound them and imprisoned them. Their leader, Kingu, was bound, and 'put in the ranks of dead gods'. Having conquered his enemies, Marduk went back to Tiamat's body. Then the work of the demiurge and the organisation of the cosmos began; having overcome the forces of chaos, the god created the world:

With his unsparing mace he crushed her skull,
When the arteries of her blood he had severed,

Boundary stone with bas-relief showing King Melishipak II presenting his daughter to the goddess Nanai. End of third millennium B.C. Louvre. *Archives photographiques*

The North Wind bore (it) to places undisclosed.
On seeing this, his fathers were joyful and jubilant,
They brought gifts of homage, they to him.
Then the lord paused to view her dead body,
That he might divide the monster and do artful works.
He split like a shellfish into two parts:
Half of her he set up and ceiled it as sky,
Pulled down the bar and posted guards.
He bade them to allow not her waters to escape,
He crossed the heavens and surveyed the regions.
He squared Apsu's quarter, the abode of Nudimmud,
As the lord measured the dimensions of Apsu,
The Great Abode, its likeness, he fixed as Esharra,
The Great Abode, Esharra, which he made as the firmament.
Anu, Enlil and Ea he made occupy their places.

This last line is a reference to the tripartite division of the heavens, and to the 'three paths' of the stars, which were placed under the invocation of the great triad.

The fifth tablet is an astrological treatise, explaining the placing of the stars, the length of the years, the divisions and signs of the zodiac and the birth of the moon, 'adornment of the night'. All of these were the work of Marduk. This is the most fragmentary tablet of the poem. There is no description of the cosmos. However, about the middle of the tablet, with serious gaps on either side, there is a description of the formation of the world, for which the second half of Tiamat's body was used; a mountain towered upwards on her head, from her eyes emerged and flowed the Tigris and Euphrates and on her breasts rose rich hills. With part of her curly tail Marduk joined heaven to earth, and her back supported the heavens. The monsters brought to life by Tiamat to help her in her fight against the gods were changed into statues and support the gates of *apsu*.

In the sixth tablet we have the description of the creation of man, which, curiously enough, is not said to be the work of Marduk, but of Ea. No doubt the Babylonian priests dared not go too far when it came to contradicting fundamental concepts of a theology that, although often betrayed, had from the remotest periods of Sumerian civilisation quoted Anu, Enlil and Enki (Ea) as the creators of humanity.

Marduk, then,

Is resolved to fashion artful works.
Opening his mouth, he addresses Ea
To impart the plan he had conceived in his heart:
'Blood I will mass and cause bones to be.
I will establish a savage, "man" shall be his name,
Verily, savage-man I will create.'

And the demiurge says in words that Sumerians and Babylonians never ceased to repeat in the course of their long history:

He shall be charged with the service of the gods, that they might be at ease!

In his reply Ea returned to one of the favourite themes of Mesopotamian theology: that of the creation of mankind from the blood of a god who had been sacrificed, a theme that will be found again and again in numerous independent myths in the *Poem of Creation*. In this case one of the gods conquered by the demiurge was sacrificed. The assembled gods have decided that Kingu shall die:

They bound him, holding him before Ea.
They imposed on him his guilt and severed his blood (vessels)

The sun-god, whose rays spring from his shoulder, holds up his symbol, the saw, as he rises between two mountains. Ea, the god of the Deep (indicated by flowing water in which fish swim), steps over a bull and holds a bird in his hand. Usmu, his two-faced attendant, stands behind him. On the mountain to the left of the sun-god stands Ishtar, the winged war-goddess. Akkadian. *c.* 2250 B.C. *British Museum*

Out of his blood they fashioned mankind.
He imposed the service and let free the gods.
After Ea, the wise, had created mankind,
Had imposed upon it the service of the gods—
That work was beyond comprehension;
As artfully planned by Marduk, did Nudimmud
   create it . . .

When this work was done and the task of the demiurge finally accomplished, Marduk conferred on the gods their respective places in heaven and on earth. Then the gods in gratitude built a temple for Marduk with their own hands, the great Esagila temple. The tablet ends with the mention of Marduk's various names. It seems likely that, originally, this was the final tablet of the poem, but the version that has come down to us has a seventh tablet entirely devoted to the enumeration and explanation of the fifty names of Marduk.

The myth in ritual

In the *Poem of Creation* Marduk symbolised both cosmic order and also the sun (one of the first epithets conferred upon him emphasises this fact) and his warmth dispersed the mists of the sea, represented by Tiamat. In his capacity of sun-god Marduk also symbolised the forces of spring. Now this renewal of nature at the end of winter and the victory of the spring sun over the forces of death (winter) were among the basic concepts of Babylonian religion, which remained a naturistic religion until it eventually died out.

The holy time for Babylonians began at the spring equinox, which marks the rebirth of the year. At this period there is conflict between the sun and winter, and this is a repetition of the conflict that took place at the dawn of time between the demiurge and chaos. Thus the New Year in Babylon was the most solemn moment in Babylonian religious life, and the ritual for it has been preserved. Because one of the acts sanctified in the work of the demiurge was re-enacted at this time of year, the *Poem of Creation* was recited in the course of the festival; and because the poem expresses a concrete reality and tells of the victory of Marduk—and to *tell* in the eyes of Mesopotamians was to make a thing become real—it thus ensured a new victory for the demiurge and the renewal of nature, sanctifying the continuity and conservation of the ordered world.

A certain number of traditions from various Sumerian cosmologies were included and assimilated into the *Poem of Creation*. It superimposed a new theme on a primitive story, in which Ea and Enlil had played leading parts. Only the theme of the sea-monster—symbol of chaos—which appeared in the very beginning, was of Semitic origin.

The theme of the god who was sacrificed that man might be born—the sixth tablet—and the reason for the creation of man were Sumerian concepts. A myth known as the *Cosmology of Assur* took up these major Sumerian themes:

When the sky had been separated from the earth
   (the two)
Constant and remote twins,
When the mother of the gods had been created,
When the earth was created and fashioned,
And the destinies of the sky and the earth fixed,
When ditches and canals had received their proper
   course,
And the banks of the Tigris and Euphrates had
   been established

the high gods asked themselves: 'What are we going to do now, what are we going to create?' Thereupon they decided to create humanity. They said to Enlil:

Cylinder seal showing Zu, an Assyrian storm-god, in the form of a bird, appearing before his judge Ea. Two gods guard him on either side and a third, with a plough over his shoulder brings up the rear. Akkadian (2340–2180 B.C.) *British Museum*

Terracotta head of a Babylonian demon. 7th–6th centuries B.C. *British Museum*

In Ouzoumoua, the place of the earth and the sky,
We shall sacrifice (both of (?)) the gods Lamga.
From their blood we shall create mankind
And the service of the gods will be its lot for ever.

And so it was done. Two beings were born: Ulligarra and Zalgarra, the ancestors of mankind.

A few other Babylonian myths have been preserved, but merely repeat with certain variations these major themes. It is interesting to note that the majority of them formed an integral part of rituals, rather like the concept that was outlined with reference to the New Year Festival in Babylon. Thus it came about that a myth giving the origins of man was connected with a ritual destined to facilitate births. The text in question has been preserved in several versions from a very early date in Babylonian and Assyrian history. Unfortunately the text is incomplete. The first column and the beginning of the second are missing. The gods have decided to create man 'to bear the burden of creation':

The goddess they called . . . the mother,
The most helpful of the goddesses, the wise Mami:
'Thou art the mother-womb,
The one who creates mankind.
Create, then, Lullu and let him bear the yoke!'
This idea was taken up again in the *Poem of Creation*, where the name of the first man was Lullu as before:

Let him be made of clay, animated (?) by blood.

Enki (Ea) took part in the work, as in the *Poem of Creation*, making the suggestion that a god should be sacrificed, and his blood should endow man with life:

Let them slay one god,
And let the gods be purified in the judgment (?)

With his flesh and his blood
Let Ninhursag mix clay,
God and man
Shall . . . benefit (?) jointly by the clay!

One might refer again at this point to the myth which formed part of the ritual for the construction of temples, a ritual that hails from Babylon. Once the initial ceremonies of preparation were over, when the first brick of the new temple was put in place, one of the priests recited over it a prayer representing a tradition very similar to the preceding one, since the task of creation was almost entirely attributed to Ea:

When the god Anu created heaven,
(When) the god Nudimmud created the *apsu*-ocean,
  his dwelling,
The god Ea pinched off a piece of clay in the *apsu*-
  ocean,
Created the god Kulla for the restoration of
  temples,
Created the reed marsh and the forest for the work
  of their construction,
Created the gods Ninildu, Nimsimug, and Arazu
  to be the completers of their construction,
Created mountains and oceans for everything . . .
Created the deities Gushkinbanda, Ninagal, Nin-
  zadim and Ninkurra for their work,
(Created) the abundant products (of mountain and
  ocean) to be offerings . . .
Created the deities Ashnan, Lahar, Siris, Ningiz-
  zida, Ninsar,
For making their revenues abundant . . .
Created the deities Umunmutamku and Umun-
  mutamnag to be presenters of offerings,
Created the god Kusug, high-priest of the great
  gods, to be the one who completes their rites and
  ceremonies,
Created the king to be the provider . . .
Created men to be the makers . . . .

When Babylonian civilisation came to an end the religious concepts were still those that had been formulated at the beginning of Sumerian history. The above myth, in which Ea appeared as the organiser of the world, is fundamentally the same as the ancient Sumerian myth quoted at the beginning of this section, which told of the creation of the functional gods—the gods of vegetation and the gods presiding over various operations implicit in the organised life of society. Just as it was about to die out, the static civilisation of Babylon made an attempt at survival on the basis of outworn principles in a world that was in full religious evolution.

The hero Gilgamesh holding a lion. His adventurous life was the subject of a vast epic poem. Louvre. *Bulloz*

Hurrites
and
Hittites

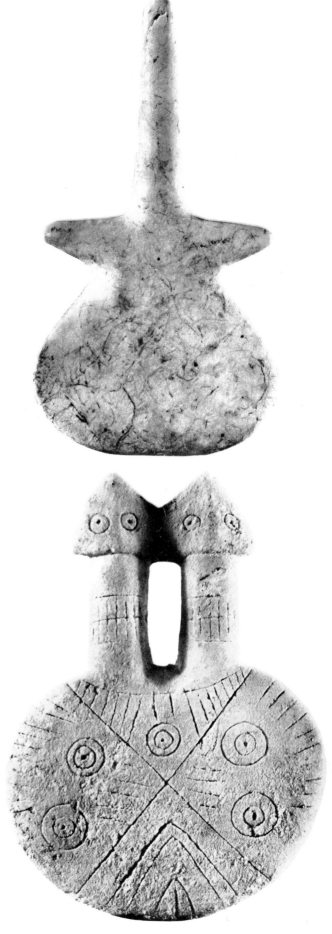

The influence of Mesopotamia exerted beyond her own boundaries in cultural and religious spheres cannot yet be estimated. How and why this influence spread particularly in Northern Syria and Anatolia is unknown. Its extent can often be marked on the map; but the intermediary factors by which it made itself felt are only too often missing, even though one can blaze a trail—already faintly suggested by archaeology and historical research—from the alluvial plains of Mesopotamia, up the Euphrates and finally to Upper Syria and the plateau of Anatolia. In addition to deities who seem purely Hittite in origin—and there were very few of these—and gods belonging to some obscure Asian pantheon, the Hittites had a vast number of deities of Mesopotamian origin. An all-embracing transference of Mesopotamian cults occurred here, and this phenomenon requires some historical explanation.

The Hittites were Indo-European invaders who settled in Asia Minor before the eighteenth century B.C. and came into contact with the major civilisations of the ancient Orient: on the one hand there was Mesopotamia, and on the other that vast cultural area, which as yet defies definition though it is known to stretch as far as northern Syria. However, these contacts alone do not account for all the phenomena that constituted Hittite civilisation.

For instance, the cuneiform script that was later used by the Hittites was not borrowed from Assyrian settlers, although shortly after the Hittites settled in Asia Minor—after the end of the Third Ur Dynasty in Lower Mesopotamia, that is some time after 1955 B.C.—they were in close contact with the particular type of Mesopotamian civilisation brought across by Assyrians. Yet the fact is that the Hittite script was a development of the one used by the scribes of the Third Ur Dynasty. This creates a certain problem.

About 1650 B.C., during military campaigns in the

Two idols or gods of the third millennium B.C. At this time the Hittites only suggested the human form, though the double-headed figure has circles representing the eyes. *Salchow*

Hittite divine couple. The god, wearing a belted tunic with a fringe, carries a bunch of grapes, a symbol of his divinity. The goddess, wearing a more decorated tunic, carries a mirror, also a sign of divinity. Marash. Eighth century B.C. *Arts Council*

A bas-relief showing the head of a Hittite goddess wearing a high polos surmounted by a veil. She carries a pomegranate. Karchemish. Eighth century B.C. *Arts Council*

region of the Euphrates, the Hittites came into contact with an ethnic group whose political and cultural influence at the time was preponderant in Upper Syria—these people were the Hurrites.

The Hurrites appeared on the historical horizon of Mesopotamia at a very early date—before 2300 B.C.— for by then they had settled to the east of the Tigris. They were already an important political factor in the time of Naram-Sin, King of Agadea (2270—2233 B.C.), but very little is known about them in the centuries during which they rose to power. An Aryan dynasty in the fifteenth century made the small Hurrite states into one vast empire stretching from the Tigris to the Mediterranean.

Since there is a total lack of historical data, the only possible course is to attempt to reconstruct a 'history', taking into account, as far as the limited means available will permit, religious and cultural facts given in contemporary documents. For, even if these do not shed much light on the question, they do at least put it in a compelling form.

The Hittites never had the sort of direct and constant contact with Babylonia that alone would account for the predominant influence of Babylonian ideas on the development of Hittite religious culture. So there must have been an intermediary factor. Historical circumstances all point to the Hurrites as the link. As we know from the annals of the Hittite king Hattusil I (c. 1650—1620 B.C.) the Hittites brought back prisoners and spoil from their campaigns against the Hurrite states; these included priests and statues of gods stolen from temples. This seems to have been the beginning of the religious influence of the Hurrites over the Hittites. From this time onwards, and finally when the great Hurrite centre at Cilicia, the Kizzuwatna, came within the reach of the Hittites at the time of Suppiluliuma (c. 1350 B.C.), Hittite civilisation acquired a pronounced Hurrite colouring, both in the social and in the religious field.

Over the centuries, and as their political organisation was taking shape, the Hurrites were in immediate contact with Mesopotamia—for them the source of all civilisation. Undoubtedly their greatest glory, to which they owe their place in the evolution of the ancient Near East, was to have had some obscure intuition of the realities and beliefs contained in the alien Mesopotamian culture; and they can also be esteemed for having followed this school of thought in spite of the fact thay they themselves were initially barbarian. The structure of Hurrite society, particularly of its social, judicial and military aspects, can only be guessed. But in the case of its religious ideas the opposite is true. While apparently preserving intact a number of alien concepts the Hurrites developed an extremely original idea of 'divine setting'. (It may be mentioned in passing that this ability to take alien ideas and made them one's own is the sterling test of any race destined to act as 'a carrier of civilisation'.) Although they were scattered throughout the ancient

Orient, transcending frontiers and nationalities, in the political field they were successful in creating a vast empire out of a confederation of nations and races, and in conferring a certain, if temporary, cohesion on that vast, inarticulate land mass situated between the Tigris and the Mediterranean. What is more, they realised that some religious unity could and should correspond to political unity. So in their system of thought the union of races had its counterpart in a regrouping of separate religions, a vast synthesis of the most varied religious concepts. Thus religious syncretism developed, and an attempt was made to create order out of the different religious beliefs of the ancient Near East, and to make a single and unique theology prevail, in which Hurrite, Sumerian and Canaanite deities all had their place.

This explains the development of the two great Hurrite myths, the *Royalty in the Skies* and the *Song of Ullikummis*.

A considerable number of Hurrite texts have been found in the Near East in the region between the Tigris and the Euphrates, and the Tigris and the Mediterranean. The majority of these documents—which are texts of a religious or magic nature—come from the royal archives of the Hittite kings of Hattusas (now known as Bogaz-koy, in Turkey).

These texts are written in a language composed of several dialects, which is not yet fully understood; it is of the type known as 'agglutinative' and does not stem from either Indo-European or Semitic languages. The texts are therefore difficult to decipher.

Fortunately, many Hurrite texts were translated into Hittite, a known language, and these include religious documents that are of primary interest to us: in a word, Hurrite myths.

Hurrite theogony

Hurrite theogony, which implied the existence of a cosmogony of which only traces have been preserved, is known to us through a certain number of fragmentary texts found in the Hittite royal archives at Bogazkoy. These texts are Hittite translations of Hurrite originals, which are either lost or as yet unpublished. On the whole and in the version handed down to us these translations date from the last years of the Hittite empire, that is to say, about the year 1300 B.C.

It would be impossible to try to estimate at present the importance of Hurrite theogony in relation to the development of Hittite religious thought. In itself it is certainly not original: it appears, in fact, to represent the final stage of syncretist and religious thought, developed probably in Upper Mesopotamia from the beginning of the second millennium onwards when Hurrite circles were reacting to religious ideas from Sumer and northern Syria.

So it is not surprising to find an echo of Sumerian myths in Hurrite theogony, or to discover some of the high gods of the pantheon of Sumer. However, there is nothing in Sumerian religious literature or in the corresponding Mesopotamian myths of Babylon and Assyria that sheds any light on the strange adventures of the deities involved here.

The Hurrite concept of successive divine groups appears entirely foreign to the ordered concepts of Sumerian theology, which was certainly aware of divine hierarchies, but did not consider perfection in world order to require a theogony in the Hurrite sense of the word. The Hurrite theological framework was imposed on basic Sumerian ideas, and this clearly limited the amount borrowed from Sumer as well as from the myths of northern Syria. In fact the great universal gods of the Sumerian pantheon were those who played a part in Hurrite theogony, not the local gods, even when the latter usurped pride of place as a result of their devotees' political success. The Hurrite texts of the *Kumarbis* and the *Song of Ullikummis* undoubtedly disregarded the Babylonian god Marduk in a fairly deliberate fashion, because most Hurrite borrowings from Babylonian sources occurred before the time of the First Dynasty. Moreover, the setting of Hurrite myths in northern Syria clearly had a historical reason and can be accounted for by the pre-existence of cults and myths and holy places of pre-Hurrite origin, such as Mount Casius (the Khazzi of the myths) near Antioch.

Of course Babylon and Assur, and perhaps Sumer too, stipulated the existence of a 'gigantomachy' before creation; it was known as the *Enuma elish*. It is no mere chance that the archives of Bogaz-koy, which provide plenty of evidence of works translated or copied from Babylonian originals (notably the epic of Gilgamesh), show no trace of the Babylonian *Poem of Creation*: there is conflict here between fundamental religious concepts. Yet on the other hand, if one bears in mind the fact that Hurrite influence—notably in the religious field—gains in strength from the reign of Hattusil I till the end of the empire, by which time it is predominant, then it is not surprising to find many traces and much evidence of Hurrite myths at Bogaz-koy.

The texts themselves, which were the vehicles for Hurrite myths about divine hierarchies and theogony were often mere fragments, and the order in which they occurred is not always known. They form, however, a cycle of stories with a Hurrite deity as principal protoganist: the god Kumarbis, 'father of the gods'. There are too few texts available for a valid assessment of his true nature. From the texts we have it is clear that Kumarbis was not considered to be a creator and organiser of the world. The primeval gods of the Hurrite pantheon belong to preceding divine generations. Those same texts, notably the *Song of Ullikummis*, refer to a primitive creature, Upelluris, on whose shoulders (as with Atlas) 'they'—'they' doubtless being the gods of ancient days mentioned in certain texts—'raised the sky and the earth'.

Rock relief at Gavur Kalesi showing two gods. *A. Perissinotto*

Thus the act of creation occurred long before the episodes of the *Royalty in the Skies* and of *Ullikummis*. In the very beginning there were the 'fathers of the gods', and 'ancient gods', quaint deities who were then forgotten and displaced, and, like the Titans, lived in the 'dark earth' once the young gods had emerged: in other words, dethroned and hunted from the sky, they too were cast into the underworld.

Nevertheless, creation was not perfect from the very beginning. Certain legends that were perhaps of proto-Hittite origin referred to the chaotic state of things that followed the creation of the universe, and recalled that one day the moon 'fell from the skies'. The allusion in the myth of the *Royalty in the Skies* to the birth of the Tigris was also characteristic of this type of creation in that it was brought about gradually.

Background to the myths

The gods who took part in the divine drama were those generally associated with the Hurrites; they frequently appeared in Hurrite ritual and also in Hittite ritual of Hurrite origin, and especially in texts by priests or magicians of the Kizzuwatna: they included Kumarbis; Teshup, the storm-god; Khepat, his consort; the bulls of the storm-god, Sheri and Khurri; and Ishtar of Nineveh. Then, in addition, there were the high gods of the Sumerian pantheon. In fact there were not only the divine couples of Sumer—Anu-Antu, Enlil-Ninlil and Ea—but its holy places were adopted too: Nippur, centre of the Enlil cult; and the *apsu*, the abode of Ea, which according to the geography of myth was the town of Eridu.

The setting for the myth of the *Royalty in the Skies* was the sky, but there was continual coming and going between heaven and earth. The divine seed fell on Mount Kanzuras (which has not been identified, but was undoubtedly an actual place). Nippur was already in existence, and the Sumerians told the story of its divine origins on the very border of time. The problem becomes complicated when the scene of the myth shifts from Sumer to the Occident and the Mediterranean, by way of Urkish, the historic city of Kumarbis, and Nineveh, unquestionably a Hurrite centre even before Mitanni laid hands on Assyria; added complication results from a role being given to the sea in a personified form—this is a Canaanite concept—and another of particular importance to Mount Khazzi; this is the Casius of the Syrian coast, the holy mountain in the texts of Ras-Shamra, the Sapon, and the abode of a deity whose cult continued right up to Roman times. (The Jupiter Casius was the *interpretatio latina* of the Baal Sapon, who invites comparison with the Baal of Mount Carmel from the point of view of aniconic cult and nature.)

So the problem surrounding the origin of Hurrite myths in the Kumarbis cycle arises under particularly difficult conditions due to our almost total ignorance of Hurrite modes of thought. In the face of this strange amalgamation of Sumerian concepts and oddly contradictory factors, which—within the framework of the same myth—transfer the reader to a different setting, the tendency is to regard these myths as expressing an attempt—the first in time—at religious syncretism with Canaanite myths occupying as important a position as Sumerian ideas.

Historical and geographical facts lend weight to this interpretation of the problem. The Canaanite contribution to the development of the myth cannot be over-emphasised. Only the future will tell whether this contribution can be assessed accurately, and whether Ras Shamra in particular—but also Bogazkoy which has brought to light Hittite translations of Canaanite myths—will enable us to come to grips with this problem of origins, which is of primary importance with regard to the effect of Kumarbis on the *Theogony* of Hesiod.

A Hurrite god, Sharma or Sharruma, son of the storm-god, Teshup, and Hebat holds King Tudhaliyas IV in his protective embrace. Rock relief at Yazilikaya. 1400–1200 B.C. *A. Perissinotto*

One of the sphinxes guarding the gateway to the Hittite city of Alaja Huyuk. *A. Perissinotto*

'The Divine Royalty'

The remaining fragments of this myth provide no indication as to its title, but the colophon of one of the tablets containing this document bears the words: 'First tablet of the song of . . .', which immediately raises the question of a possible connection between the myth and a Hittite ritual festival (compare the myth of Illuyanka associated with the Purulli Festival, festival of spring?). The text starts with an exordium inviting the gods to lend an ear:

[Let there listen the gods who are in heaven] and in the dark earth! Let there listen the mighty gods [. . .] Naras, [Napsaras, Min]kis, Ammunkis! Let there listen Ammezadus [and the ancient gods], fathers and mothers [of the gods]!

Let there listen [Anus and Antus], Isharas, the fathers and mothers. Let there listen Enlil [Ninlil] and the mighty and firmly established gods! In the olden days Alalus was king in heaven. As long [as] Alalus was seated on the throne, the mighty Anus, first among the gods, was standing before him; he would sink at his feet and set the drinking cup in his hand.

For nine years, Alalus was king in heaven. In the ninth year Anus gave battle to Alalus and vanquished him. Alalus fled before him and went down to the dark earth. Down he went to the dark earth and Anus took his seat on the throne. The mighty Kumarbis would give him his food; he would sink at his feet and set the drinking cup in his hand.

For nine years Anus was king in heaven. In the ninth year Anus gave battle to Kumarbis, and [like?] Alalus Kumarbis gave battle to Anus. [When] he could no longer withstand Kumarbis' eyes, [Anus] struggled forth from his hands. He fled, Anus, [like] a bird soaring up to heaven. Kumarbis rushed after him. He seized [him] Anus by his feet and dragged him down from the sky. He [Kumarbis] bit his 'knees' and his manhood went down into his inside. When it was there, when Kumarbis had swallowed Anus' manhood, he rejoiced and laughed. Anus turned to him. He spoke these words to Kumarbis: 'Thou rejoicest over what thou has inside thee, because thou has swallowed my manhood. Rejoice not over what thou hast inside thee. I have planted a heavy burden there. I have impregnated thee with three mighty gods. I have impregnated thee with the mighty storm-god, with the river Aranzahas and with the great god Tasmisus, three terrible gods [whose] seed I have planted in thee.' Having spoken these words, Anus went up to Heaven and hid himself. [Kumarbis], the wise king, spat out what he had in his mouth . . . What he spat out [fell] on Mount Kanzuras. . . . Filled with fury, Kumarbis went to Nipp[ur] . . . .

A long break occurs in the text at this point (the final third of the first column of the tablet is missing; the second and third columns are incomplete). It seems that the storm-god stayed inside Kumarbis. There follows a dialogue between Anu and the storm-god. The latter seems to speak of his great future. Anu advises him and tells him how to leave Kumarbis' body at the end of his period of gestation. Then Kumarbis goes to the god Ea, 'king of wisdom': 'Give me my son, I want to devour (my son?)' he tells him. And in fact it seems that Kumarbis then receives something to eat which has a disagreeable effect, for Ea advises him to have recourse to a magician called 'the poor'. By dint of magic practices and sacrifices, he brings about the birth of the storm-god, who is taken to Anu. There follows a break in the text.

With the aid of the storm-god Anu plots the ruin of Kumarbis. Then there are preparations for combat. Zaba, god of war, appears, with the Bull Sheri, 'the Day', one of the sacred bulls of the storm-god. The story of the battle is missing due to a gap in the text. The fourth column tells of the birth of two deities fathered by Anu on the Earth:

Ea, [the king of] wisdom [. . .] counted: the first month, the [second] month, the third month passed; the fourth month, the fifth month, the sixth month went by. The [seventh month], the eighth month, the ninth month went by. The tenth month [arrived]. At the tenth month, the Earth began (to) groan. When the Earth groaned [. . . . she gave birth to [two (?)] children [probably 'two sons'].

A messenger goes to announce the birth to Ea (?): 'The Earth (has) given birth to two children . . .'

These two children, the Tigris and the god Tasmisus fight with the storm-god in the final struggle against Kumarbis, who is ultimately defeated and cast out, and the storm-god is installed as 'king of the sky'.

The *Song of Ullikummis*

The *Song of Ullikummis*, which belongs to the Kumarbis cycle, follows after the *Royalty in the Skies*. It relates the following episode in the great divine drama—Kumarbis' attempt to retrieve divine royalty from the storm-god who has robbed him of it.

As in the preceding song, the *Song of Ullikummis* begins with a prelude: the bard announces his intention of singing of the great feats of Kumarbis:

First tablet:

Of the god who [. . .] thinks wise thoughts in his mind, of Kumarbis, the father of the gods, I want to sing. Kumarbis thinks wise thoughts in his mind. He nurses the thought of [creating] misfortune and of raising up an evil being. He plots evil against the storm-god. He contemplates [creating] a rival for the storm-god. Kumarbis dwells on wise thoughts in his mind: he strings them together like pearls.

When Kumarbis had thought out these thoughts in his mind, he instantly rose from his seat. He took his staff in his hand, fastened the winds to his feet as swift sandals. He set forth from Urkis, his city, and betook himself to the [. . .] where there was a great stone. The stone was three (?) miles long and [. . .] miles and a half wide. At the bottom it had (?) . . . . His desire was aroused and he slept with the stone. Into her . . . his manhood. He took her five times, he took her ten times.

(Then follows a gap of thirty to thirty-five lines.)

The birth of Ullikummis

At night [. . .]. [When came] the [middle] watch [. . .] stone [. . .] stone. [They (?)] br[ought] in the world [. . .] the stone [. . .] son of Kumarbis [. . .]. The [. . .] women brought him into the world and the goddesses Gul-shesh and Makh placed him on Kumarbis' lap. Kumarbis rejoiced over his son. He pressed him against his heart(?), he fondled him. He decided to give him a propitious name. Kumarbis said to himself: 'What name [shall I give] to this child which the goddesses Gul-shesh and Makh have presented to me and which [. . .] shot forth from her body like an arrow? Now then [. . .] let his name be Ullikummis. Let him ascend to heaven and [assume] kingship. Let him vanquish Kummiya, the [beaut]iful (?) city. Let him strike down the storm-god. Let him crush him like salt (?) [. . .] and let him trample him underfoot like an ant(?). Let him break (?) the god Tasmisus like a reed [. . .]. Let him shoot down the gods of heaven like birds. Let him break them [like] empty pots!'

When Kumarbis had spoken these words, he said to himself in his soul: 'To whom shall I entrust my son? Who [. . .] and [will bring] him [up] in the dark earth. The sun-god [of the sky] and the [moon]-god will not see him. The storm-god of Kummiya, the mighty king, will not see him and

Head of a god, found at Karchemish. *Giraudon*

A Hittite king wearing his priestly robes and carrying the *lituus*, a sacred crook, pours a libation to the storm-god, who is brandishing a thunderbolt and wearing the typical conical headdress of the gods. From Malatya, now in Ankara Museum.
A. Perissinotto

shall not kill him. Ishtar, the goddess of Nineveh, the [. . .] shall not [break (?)] him like a reed [. . .].'

Kumarbis speaks to Impaluris: 'Impaluris, give ear to the words that I am going to say to thee. Take thy staff in thy hand, fasten the winds to thy feet as swift sandals, and go to the Irsirra deities . . . .

'Come! Kumarbis, father of the gods, summons you to "the house of the gods . . . ." [The Irsirra] will take the child and will [convey] him to the [dark] earth . . . .'

[When] Impaluris [heard these words, he took] his staff, put on [his sandals] and set forth. He betook himself to the Irsirra. He spoke these words to the Irsirra deities: 'Come! Kumarbis, the father of the gods, [summons] you. But [you are not to know] his motive in calling upon you. Hasten, come!'

When the Irsirra heard these words, [they hastened] they hurried. [They set] forth and covered distance without stopping once. They presented themselves to Kumarbis and Kumarbis spoke to them: 'Take this child and take it away with you. Bring him down to the dark Earth! Be quick! Place him, like an arrow, on the right (?) shoulder of Upelluris. In one day he shall increase a cubit, in one month he shall increase one acre . . . .' When the Irsirra heard these words, they took [the child] from Kumarbis' lap. They took him in their arms and pressed him to their breasts like a garment. They took him and placed him on Enlil's lap. The

[god(?)] raised his eyes and saw the child as it stood in his divine presence. His body was made of diorite. Enlil said to himself in his soul: 'Who is he? Are they really the goddesses of fate who have reared him? Is it he who shall see (?) the fierce battles of the great gods? By none other than Kumarbis is this vileness done. Just as he raised the storm-god, so he has now [raised] this terrible diorite-man as his rival.'

Enlil [having spoken] these words, [the Irsirra took the child] and placed it like an arrow on the right (?) shoulder of Upelluris. The stone grew. The mighty [waters (?)] made him grow. In one day he increased a cubit, in one month he increased an acre . . . . The fifteenth day arrived: the stone had increased . . . . He [Ullikummis] [was standing] in the sea; his knees like an arrow (?). It stood above the water, the stone, like [a pillar]. The sea reached up to its belt, like a loincloth. Like a tower (?) the stone rose. It was as high as temples and the *kuntarra* house in heaven.

Ullikummis and the sun-god

The sun-god of the sky looked down from heavenly heights and saw Ullikummis. Ullikummis [too] saw the sun-god. The sun-god [said] to [himself]: 'What mighty (?) god [is standing there] in the sea? . . . He laid his hand to his forehead [. . .]. In wrath [. . .]. When the [sun]-god had seen [the stone], [...] he betook himself to the storm-god [...]. (When) he saw the sun-god arrive, Tasmisus said: 'Now why does the sun-god come here? [...] The reason for his coming must be a very important reason which cannot be put aside. It must be a very serious matter [which forebodes] a hard battle, a revolution in heaven and famine and death on earth.'

The storm-god spoke to Tasmisus in these terms: 'Let them prepare a seat for the sun-god. Let them set a table that he may recover his strength.'

No sooner had they spoken than the sun-god arrived. They brought forward a seat on which to sit down, but he would not [be seated]. They brought forward a table, but he did not serve himself. They gave him a cup, but he refused to put it to his lips.

The storm-god spoke to the sun-god: 'Who is the bad chamberlain who set up a seat for thee and thou dost refuse to sit on it? Who is the bad serving-man who prepared a table from which thou dost refuse to eat? Who is the bad cup-bearer who offered thee [the cup (?)] from which thou dost refuse to drink?'

So the first tablet of the Song of Ullikummis ends.

The second tablet, which is incomplete in the beginning, opens with a dialogue between the sun-god and the storm-god, which should follow the missing account of the sun's visit to Ullikummis. The storm-god is angered by the tale he has been told and calms the fears of the sun-god:

'Eat and satisfy thy hunger, drink beer and quench thy thirst [...]. Return thou to heaven.' At these words, the sun-god rejoiced [...] he ate [...] he ate [...] he drank [...] he rose and set forth to the sky. Left alone, the storm-god takes counsel with himself.

The storm-god and Tasmisus took each other by the hands. They set forth from the *kuntarra*, the temple. Ishtar came down from the sky [...] and said to herself again in her own mind: 'Where are the two brothers hurrying thus?' and she got up swiftly, Ishtar, and she went (?) to meet (?) the two brothers. They took one another by the hands and ascended Mount Hazzi. The king of Kummiya [*i.e.*, the storm-god] watched: he set his eye on the awesome (?) diorite man. He looked at the awesome (?) diorite man: his arms fell to his sides. The storm-god sat down on the ground. Tears flowed [from his eyes] like rivers. With tears in his eyes, the storm-god spoke: 'Who can bear [such a sight]? Who will dare go and battle [against the diorite man]? Who can bear [the sight] of his terrible (?).' Ishtar replied to the storm-god 'My brother [...] does not know. His bravery has been decupled [...]. The child whom they have brought into the world [...]. Dost thou not know? [...] [when (?)] we were in the house of Ea [...]. If I were a man [...] [I should fight him myself]!'

This stele shows Teshup, the storm-god. In his right hand he carries an axe and in his left hand forked lightning. He wears a dagger in his belt. Babylon. Eighth century B.C. *Arts Council*

(Then follows a gap of about twenty-five lines.)

Ishtar apparently tries to charm the monster by her songs. She sits by the sea and sings:

Ishtar [took?] a harp and *galgaltouri* instrument. She took [...] and [began to sing] a song [...]. She put [her clothes] down on the ground. She sang, Ishtar. She leaned against (?) a rock and the stone from the Sea. There came a great wave from the sea. The great wave spoke to Ishtar: 'For whom dost thou sing? For whom dost thou fill thy mouth [with songs]? Man is deaf: he does not hear.. He is blind: he does not see and has no [perception (?)]. Go then Ishtar, find thy brother [*i.e.,* Ullikummis] while he has not yet become all-powerful, while [his] appearance has not yet become terrifying (?).' When Ishtar heard these words, she abandoned [her projects (?)]. She threw away the harp and the *galgaltouri* [...]. She lamented ...

After a break which may or may not be important, the text continues with a discourse by the storm-god:

'Let them mix fat, let them (bring) pure oil! Let them anoint the horns of Serisu the bull! Let them plate with gold the tail of Tella the bull [...]. Let them [...] the powerful rocks! Let them summon the storm, the rain and the winds [...]. Let them bring forth the flashing lightning from its sleeping-chamber. Let them prepare the heavy wagons as best they can and let them bring me back word!'

When Tasmisus heard these words, he hastened and brought (?) Serisu the bull from the (?) pasture [...] and Tella the bull from Mount Imgarra. [...] Before the great gate [of the *kuntarra* (?)] [he led them (?)]. He brought pure oil. [With it he anointed] the horns of Serisu the bull. He [plated with gold] the tail of Tella the bull.

(There is here a gap extending to the fourth column of the tablet.)

Third tablet: a gap of about thirty lines.

When the gods heard [the tale of the defeat of the storm-god], they made ready their wagons and handed [to Astabis (?) ...] Astabis leaped on to his wagon like a [...] and drove the wagon towards [...]. He gathered the chariots together. He thundered and amid a noise of thunder he [went down (?)] towards the sea.

The text then mentions seventy gods who accompany Astabis in his expedition against Ullikummis, which is to end in failure:

He cannot [...] Astabis and the seventy gods fell (?) into the sea.

The attack made by Astabis and the seventy gods leaves Ullikummis unharmed; he continues to grow: He made the heavens tremble and [the earth ...] [like a tower], he grew and reached *kuntarra*. The height of the diorite man was 9,000 leagues and his girth 9,000 leagues. He towered in front of the gate of the city of Kummiya like a [...]. He made Khepat leave her temple, so she could no longer receive the messages of the gods, so that she could no longer see either the storm-god or Suwaliyattas. Khepat spoke to Takitis: 'Listen! O Takitis! Take thy staff in thy hand, put on thy swift sandals. Go and summon the assembly of the gods. The diorite man has assuredly killed my husband, the noble king.' Takitis tries in vain to carry out Khepat's command: there is no longer a road.

A carved ivory plaque depicting a ruler or god enthroned.
Assyrian. Ninth or eighth century B.C. Ashmolean Museum.

Two bull-men flanked by two lion-men. Relief from
Karchemish. 1050–850 B.C. Ankara Museum. *A. Perissinotto*

The defeat of the storm-god

Here we should have the story of the struggle and
defeat of the storm-god in the course of his fight
against Ullikummis, and these events have already
been referred to at the end of the second tablet. When
the text does in fact continue we find Tasmisus, the
god's messenger telling Khepat of the fate of the
storm-god:

'In a lowly place my lord will have to stay until the
years have passed away which have been assigned
When to him.' Khepat saw Tasmisus, she almost
fell from the roof. If she had taken a step she would
have fallen, but her women restrained her and did
not let her go. When Tasmisus had spoken these
words, he descended from the tower and went to
the storm-god: 'Where shall we sit down? On
Mount Kandurna? While we are on Mount Kandurna, someone else will go and be seated on
Mount Lalapaduwa. [If] we go [. . .] there will no
longer be a king in heaven.'

Tasmisus advises the storm-god to go to Ea, the
god of wisdom, in his city of Apsuwa, the abode of
the primeval waters. (Extremely fragmentary text.)

The assembly of the gods

The divine conflict threatens world order. Ullikummis is not content just to slay the storm-god: he wants
to destroy the whole of mankind. Ea addresses the
assembled gods:

'Why will you destroy [humanity]? Do not men
offer sacrifices to the gods? . . . [If] you destroy
mankind, no-one [will pay heed] to the gods, no-
one will offer them sacrificial loaves or libations.
The storm-god, the powerful king of Kummiya,

Rock relief at Ivriz showing a king (? Warpalawa) paying
homage to a god. 1750 B.C. *A. Perissinotto*

will (himself) have to put his hand to the plough, and Ishtar and Khepat will have to grind the corn.'

Ea is offended particularly with Kumarbis: 'Why dost thou wish to harm mankind? . . . do they not offer thee their sacrifices joyfully in thy temple, O Kumarbis, father of the gods?'

Very incomplete dialogue between Ea and Enlil, then Ea goes to Upelluris. He addresses him:

'Knowest thou not, O Upelluris, knowest-thou not the news? Dost thou not know him, this power-ful (?) god whom Kumarbis has fashioned to oppose the gods, to plot the death of the storm-god. He towers up in the sea like a diorite rock. Dost thou not know him? Like a tower (?) he has risen. he has blocked off the heavens, the holy house of the gods and Khepat [. . .].' Upelluris replied to Ea: 'When they built heaven and earth upon me, I did not know anything. When they came and separated heaven from earth with a cleaver (?), I knew nothing of that either. Now my right shoulder hurts me a little, but I do not know which god it is.' When Ea heard these words, he turned Upelluris' shoulder: the diorite man was standing on Upelluris' right shoulder like an arrow. Ea spoke these words to the olden gods: 'Listen, olden gods, you who know the words of yore! Open the ancient storehouses of the fathers and fore-fathers! Let them bring the ancient seals of the an-cestors and let them seal them again afterwards. Let them bring the ancient copper cleaver (?) with which they separated heaven from earth. Let them cut (?) the feet of Ullikummis whom Kumarbis has fashioned as a rival to the gods!'

The last lines of the text are, once again, extremely broken. Ea directs Tasmisus to inform the gods that he has made Ullikummis infirm: 'Go and fight him again!' The gods reassemble. They have regained courage. All together.

They begin to bellow like cattle against Ullikum-mis. The storm-god leaped upon his chariot . . . . With thunder he went down to the sea and en-gaged the diorite man in battle.

Ullikummis invites him to measure his strength against him. He boasts of carrying out his projects:

'[In the heavens] I shall assume the kingship. [I shall destroy] Kummiya. I shall take over the kun-tarra. [I] shall [drive] the gods [from the heav]ens.'

The last lines of the text, again very broken, should refer to Ullikummis' defeat.

Other Hittite myths

Two other Hittite myths are worthy of mention: the myth of the serpent Illuyanka and the myth of the

Stone relief of shepherd from the monumental gate of Prince Asitavad in Karatepe. Eighth century B.C. *J. Powell*

Part of a stele found in Karchemish showing the hieroglyphic script which the Hittites inherited from an earlier culture. Syro-Hittite period (1000–700 B.C.) National Museum, Ankara. *J. Powell*

god Telepinus. The first forms part of the ritual 'of the Purulli festival [New Year Festival?] of the storm-god of Nerik', one of the cult-centres of the Hittite empire. It is extremely interesting to note that the text of this myth specifically states the role the myth played in the celebration of the festival. This same point has been emphasised in connection with certain Mesopotamian myths, but the remarkable thing here is that the text gives two versions of this myth, noting that the first is 'the one no longer told'.

This myth tells of the storm-god's fight against the great serpent, Illuyanka. Although overcome at first the god slays his rival in the end with the aid of a human being. In form and detail this myth is nearer to folk-lore than actual myth, but it is directly connected with those universal myths that tell of the struggle of a deity against a primeval monster. Here, as in most myths from Hittite and Hurrite Asia Minor, gods and men lived side by side on earth.

The *Myth of Telepinus* (a very similar myth exists with the storm-god as protagonist) relates the disappearance of the god of vegetation: 'Telepinus, my son, grew angry and took away all good things . . . .' The gods go and seek him, but without success. Finally the bee finds him resting 'in a meadow by the wood near the town of Lhizina'. She rouses him from sleep by stinging him. After various episodes that reawaken his anger, Telepinus is appeased and returns to his temple, when life becomes normal again. This myth also formed part of a ritual, undoubtedly celebrated in Hittite country when drought or prolonged dry weather occurred. This themes of the myth — disappearance of the vegetation god, the bee's sting that awakens him (folk-lore theme, the bee's sting being regarded as a cure for paralysis) — are found everywhere. There is a particularly close, but not unexpected, analogy with the Sumero-Babylonian myths, which tell of Ishtar's descent into hell — when she disappears all reproduction ceases on earth — and, naturally, also with those Canaanite and Syrian myths belonging to the cycle of Tammus-Adonis, myths in which the disappearance of the young god brings about a cessation of life.

For most Sumerian texts, as a general rule S.N. Kramer and T. Jacobsen have been taken as guides, and it would be impossible to overestimate the enormous progress made in the comprehension of Sumerian religious texts owing to the work of these scholars. The following books are well worth consulting: *Ancient Near Eastern Texts Relating to the Old Testament*, edited by James B. Pritchard (Princeton University Press, 1950, p. 37 ff.), and another work by the same author, published under the title *History Begins at Sumer* (Thames and Hudson, 1962) contains interesting theories. The relevant chapters in T. Jacobsen's *Before Philosophy* (London, Penguin Books, 1949, p.137 ff.) are beyond doubt the most evocative of the Mesopotamian world of any that have yet appeared.

Phoenician goddess of fertility with two caprids to which she offers plants. There are many similar compositions in which two caprids feed from the Tree of Life, symbolising the goddess Ashera. The flounced skirt indicates Minoan influence, and this goddess may have had characteristics borrowed from a Cretan goddess. Louvre. *Giraudon*

WESTERN SEMITIC LANDS:
THE IDEA OF THE SUPREME GOD

'The Semites never had a mythology. Their clear and simple conception of a god set apart from the world precluded those great divine poems in which India, Persia and Greece developed their imaginative ideas.' In formulating this judgment in 1855 Ernest Renan was thinking of the Semitic origin of the great monotheistic religions—Judaism, Christianity, Islam—and of the absence of myths in the literature of the pre-Islamic Arabs, who were the last representatives of the ancient nomads and, to judge by their mode of life and civilisation, were also the founders of monotheism. Shortly after this cuneiform scripts were deciphered and revealed the existence of a rich mythology among Oriental Semites, Assyrians and Babylonians, and thus scholars had to reject Renan's statement. But the myths and legends contained in Assyro-Babylonian tablets are not the original product of Semitic genius, they are translations or adaptations from the Sumerian. Until 1930 our knowledge of Occidental Semitic religions did not justify the use of the term 'mythology' in connection with Phoenicia or Syria.

Indigenous documents take the form of inscriptions—dedications, funerary steles, international treaties—which are usually quite brief. They contain the names of very many deities invoked by the worshipper or appealed to for protection. Now the gods' names vary so much from one region and one town to another, that any reconstruction of a pantheon common to the Occidental Semites remains open to criticism. From the most remote times the Phoenicians of Byblos—as Egyptian documents prove—worshipped a goddess who concealed her real name and merely bore the title Baalat, or 'lady' of Byblos; royal inscriptions of the first half of the first millennium B.C. connect her with a Baal, or 'master' of the city. In the fifth century B.C. in Sidon the national god bears the name of Eshmun (the Greek Asclepius) and the goddess is called Astarte. A few miles south of Sidon the people of Tyre had as the head of their pantheon the god Melqart, literally 'king of the city' (Heracles in Greek), while in Carthage, a North African colony belonging to Tyre, thousands of dedications bear witness to the favours of a divine couple, Baal Hammon and the mysterious Tanit, whose name, if nothing else, seems of African origin. The same diversity is characteristic of Aramean pantheons, starting with the pantheon revealed in the great inscription of King Zakir de Hama (eighth century B.C.)— this is dominated by Baalshamin, the 'Master of the Skies', followed by the astral deities Shamash, the sun, and Shahr, the moon, and coming right up to those of Palmyra, Dura-Europas and Hatra (when the Roman Empire dominated the Orient), in which the most heteroclite influences come to light: Occidental Semitic, Babylonian, Arab, Hellenic, Iranian.

Such diversity may result from the fact that, in an area that was geographically divided and had no political unity except that imposed from outside, religion was primarily a matter for each individual city. Each town with its suburbs formed an actual state, anxious to express its individuality on both the religious and political planes. The fact that they all shared a common tongue and were of common descent gave rise to the supposition that dissimilar names concealed deities of identical form and function. This is an untenable supposition, for in almost every sphere we know nothing of the connections that existed between deities in the minds of their devotees. In other words we have no knowledge of their mythology.

The Ras Shamra Texts

The discovery of poems at Ras Shamra, the Ugarit of
the ancient world, proved that the Semites were not
incapable of creating myths. These texts merit some
attention, not only because of their antiquity—they
were composed in the thirteenth century B.C.—but
especially because they furnish the only known examples of accounts that include all the various
members of a complex pantheon. They do not present Semitic mythology in its archaic or primary
state, but rather give a sample of Semitic mythology,
and it is possible that in the other city-states of Phoenicia or Syria the local clergy developed analogous
mythologies, of which only fragments have survived
in the works of Greek authors.

The site of Ras Shamra, which was excavated from
1929 onwards by C. Schaeffer and G. Chenet, was
found to contain clay tablets inscribed in a hitherto
unknown cuneiform script. As there were thirty
signs it was in fact an alphabet and not a spelling-
book like that used by the Assyro-Babylonians. Although there was no bilingual inscription, it was soon
deciphered and the working hypothesis of the first
interpreters was fully verified: the texts were written
in an Occidental Semitic language related to Phoenician and to the 'language of Canaan' adopted by
the Israelites. The tablets taken from the Baal temple
between 1929 and 1938, edited and translated by C.
Virolleaud, are largely mythological in content.
They are poetic in form and, like the poetry of the
Old Testament, obey the principle of parallel lines.
Here is an example:

(*a*) No enemy shall rise against Baal,
(*b*) no adversary against the Rider of the Clouds.

Nabuaplaiddin is presented to the sun-god Shamash, who is enthroned within his shrine. Abu Habbah. Middle of the ninth century. *British Museum*

Unfortunately the texts in our possession are too often mutilated: of the 400 lines that should go to make a poem, only a hundred have survived on an average, and even then the existing fragments are not consecutive. The difficulties encountered in interpreting the undamaged parts are sometimes insuperable: Ugaritic script does not indicate vowels at all, and a negative particle appears exactly the same as an affirmative particle; the translation of many terms can only be conjectured, either according to context, or by having recourse to occasionally doubtful etymologies. Bearing in mind these internal difficulties, we must be content with a partial and temporary idea of Ugaritic mythology until such time as new discoveries emerge.

Ugarit was the meeting-point of many influences: Semitic, Sumero-Babylonian, Hurrite, Egyptian, Aegean, as is shown by its composite art and the documents in different languages which have been collected on the spot. But the myths are copied down in the Semitic idiom, and the gods involved have Semitic names. So the Semites knew how to create myths. Perhaps it is necessary to add that they did not do so for the pure pleasure of story-telling. Certain texts carry indications of a liturgical nature, and show that the poems were to be recited or sung at festivals celebrated in the temple. The myths related and justified successive stages of ritual, and led the faithful to relive the exploits of the gods.

The god El

The Ugaritic pantheon was presided over by El, and his name, which was common to almost all Semitic languages, means 'the supreme god'. His title of 'bull' gave him irresistible power, he was the father of innumerable gods, the 'father of men' and the 'creator of created things'. He was an old man and was called 'the father of the years', just as the God of Israel in the dream of Daniel (VII, 9) received the title of 'ancient of days'. El had the hoary beard, infinite wisdom and kindness of an old man. He was the 'Favourable', the 'Merciful', and we are reminded of these epithets by the 'beautiful names' that the Koran confers on Allah.

However, this creator seems strangely alienated from his creation. He dwelt in a mysterious and faraway place: 'at the source of the rivers, in the hollow of the abysses'; this reference was probably to the conflux of the two branches of the cosmic river, which enclosed the visible universe with its waters (the 'waters above' and the 'waters below' separated by the firmament, according to Genesis, I, 6–7). The gods came there to present their complaints to El, but, in the epic narratives that follow, he remains in the background. One wonders whether he was an idle god, a creator who had retired from his creation. It seems more likely, however, that he was a majestic guarantor of cosmic order, supervising from above the play of forces that were embodied by other gods, nearer to men and adored, perhaps, with greater fervour.

Perhaps it was not always so. The poem entitled *Birth of the Gracious Gods* appears to be the only mythological cycle in which the god El plays a more active part himself. El is seen standing by the sea, where he charms two women because of the size of his 'hand' (*membrum virilum*). While a bird is being roasted, the two women become his wives. They give birth to the 'gracious gods', Shahar, 'Dawn', and Shalim, 'Peace' or 'Twilight', who are suckled by the goddess Athirat, the Merciful, and the official wife of the father of the gods. The new-born have large appetites and El counsels them to spend seven years among the crops and pasture lands while food is accumulating in the barns. The text is constantly interspersed with instructions, which either tell how certain rites should

A stele from Ras Shamra shows Baal in a warlike attitude. A pair of horns, which project from his headdress, are a reminder that he was sometimes shown as a bull. The club he is wielding may have been forged for him by Kathar, the artisan-god. The waves at the foot of the stele indicate that he is master of the sea. Fourteenth century B.C. *Giraudon*

A horned goddess with a worshipper holding a lotus flower. Stele from Beth-Shan. Thirteenth century B.C. *University Museum*, Pennsylvania.

be performed or remain enigmatic. One of them: 'Cook a kid in milk' supplies the reason behind the instruction given to the Israelites in Exodus, XXIII,19: 'Thou shalt not seethe a kid in his mother's milk. The poem was meant to accompany the celebration of a sacred marriage destined to promote the fertility of the fields and the fecundity of the flocks. An agrarian myth, the poem of the *Birth of the Gracious Gods* contrasts with other Ugaritic texts because El plays an important role in it. It is astonishing that there is no myth telling how 'this creator of created things' carried out his work of demiurge. Perhaps, in fact, the head of the Ras Shamra pantheon was eclipsed by a new god, or more recently promoted to eminent dignity by the Semites of Ugarit as the god Baal.

Baal and the Prince of the Sea

According to the Old Testament Baal was the usual way of describing the 'false gods'. Etymologically he is the 'Master', and this title alone indicates his extensive attributes. In Ugaritic literature Baal is a distinct divine personality with many facets. He had the epithet 'calf' or 'young bullock', and a similar figure may be recognised in the 'calf of gold' whose image was raised and adored by the infidel Israelites (Exodus, XXXII, 4; I Kings, XII, 28). Living on the heights of Tsaphon — which perhaps means 'the dark cloud' — he was a storm-god, like the Aramean god Hadad, and like the Yahweh of the Israelites. He, or a similar figure of the same name, was invoked in vain on top of Mount Carmel (I Kings, XVIII) by the prophets opposing Elijah, who prayed to him to end the drought. Since he directed or embodied atmospheric phenomena and rainstorms, he was responsible for the good harvest. Armed with the thunderbolt, he was in the last resort a god of war, who rose to the rank of champion of the gods and in an almighty struggle conquered the place of honour among the gods of Ugarit.

The Prince Yamm — his name means 'the Sea', and he was also called the 'River Judge' — has decided to build a house for Baal. He asks the assistance of the architect and artisan god Kathar, the 'Clever', who symbolises the wondrous civilisations beyond the sea, for 'Crete is his dwelling-place, Egypt his patrimony'. This is the news they bring to El. He seems to approve his son's plan and is ready to recognise Yamm as king among gods, disregarding the protests of Astar, who is a pretender to the divine throne and has been constantly evicted. But Yamm becomes arrogant. One presumes that Baal has refused to pay his tribute, for the prince of the sea sends his envoys to the council of the gods to demand the surrender of Baal. On learning of the approach of the mission, the gods are seized with fear, and in consternation 'bow their heads upon their knees'. Baal makes them ashamed of such cowardice and begs them to raise their heads. Yamm's envoys greet El respectfully, and he tells them, not without irony perhaps, that he is ready to hand Baal over to them, but he warns them that they will be up against a strong man. However, Baal is to be helped by the goddess Anat, his warlike sister, and Astarte. When the account continues, Baal is being armed for combat against the prince of the sea. The obliging Kathar has forged two clubs for him, which, like the swords of the valiant knights of old in tales of chivalry, have symbolic names, endowed perhaps with magic powers: 'Chaser' and 'Driver', they are called, and they 'fly to Baal's hand like eagles'. With them Baal crushes his enemy's head, and Astarte (?) proclaims: 'For sure, Yamm is dead and Baal is our king.'

The myth about Baal and the prince of the sea has been given two different interpretations. One of them, historic in nature, sees Yamm as a personification of the 'peoples of the sea' attacking the Phoenician coast and driven back by the national god of Ugarit. The other interpretation depends on a comparison between this myth and the Babylonian *Poem of Creation* in which Marduk, the champion of the gods, flays the body of Tiamat, the power of the sea, and creates the world out of it; but the references that could lend weight to this hypothesis are not very clear, and it is impossible to speculate on the considerable gaps in the text. Even if Baal does not appear to be a demiurge, he may at least be regarded as an organiser of the cosmos menaced by the attacks of the surrounding waters.

The palace of Baal. The goddess Anat

It is impossible to be dogmatic about the exact order of the texts that have Baal as their hero. It cannot, for instance, be stated with certainty that the two tablets that seem principally concerned with the construction of Baal's palace come immediately after the episode of his victory over Yamm. Indeed the first of these two tablets starts with a curious scene: there is, to begin with, some question of preparations for a banquet in honour of Baal, then we see his sister Anat fighting and massacring warriors, up to her knees in blood as she adds to the pile of heads. This bellicose fury of hers explains why the Egyptians portrayed her as they did, and why she enjoyed such favour with the victorious pharaohs of the Nineteenth Dynasty, as did another Semitic goddess who greatly resembled her, the horsewoman Astarte. When the massacre is over, Anat receives a message from Baal ordering her to return to more peaceful tasks, which seem to be connected with the fertility of the soil, for the warrior virgin was also a fertility goddess and goddess of life. Her name is connected with the Semitic word for 'source', *ayn*. Baal calls his sister to him. Anat shows astonishment: has she not slain all her brother's enemies, the prince of the sea, the dragon Tannin and also Loran, 'the tortuous serpent, the beast with seven heads?' Presumably Baal asks his sister to intercede in his favour, for we next see her again in the presence of El declaring to him: 'The puissant Baal is our king, our judge, there is none above him . . .yet he has not a house like the gods, he has no court like the sons of Athirat.' Yielding either to her blandishments or threats, the father of the gods acquiesces, and sends to Egypt for the architect-god, Kathar. In the second tablet Athirat herself, mother of the gods, recognises Baal as king, and asks El to have a magnificent palace built for him of gold, silver and lapis-lazuli, so that Baal may provide abundant rain. Next we see Kathar at work, lighting the fires for his forges in the palace under construction, but Baal views Kathar's plans with concern, for the architect wants to have openings in the house he is building. However, Baal's thoughts are soon with the sumptuous banquet he is going to offer the gods and goddesses, and he goes off to visit the cities in his kingdom. On his return he accepts Kathar's plan, one window shall remain open. Suddenly the tone changes. No sooner has his kingship been consecrated by the building of the palace than it is threatened by the god Mot, who dwells in a subterranean and evil-smelling abode. Mot challenges Baal.

Baal's palace seems to be both the celestial abode of the god, and its terrestrial reflection, the temple of Baal at Ugarit. The poem was intended for recitation at inauguration ceremonies (compare the account of the dedication of the temple at Jerusalem by Solomon in I Kings, VIII) or at Baal's periodic enthronement. As master of storms Baal is responsible for the food required by men and gods, but in order to spread his blessings he has to leave his dwelling-place and fall to earth in the form of rain. This is shown in the following episode.

Baal and Mot

Mot, whose name appears to mean 'Death', summons Baal to descend into his avid jaws. He stretches 'his lips to the skies, his tongue to the stars'. Baal offers no resistance and declares himself Mot's slave. Before giving himself up to his adversary, Baal couples with a heifer—perhaps Anat in disguise—and she bears him a son. This episode seems to indicate that Baal presided over the reproduction of livestock before his disappearance. When the account continues, the death of Baal, 'Prince of the Earth', is announced to El, and the father of the gods is chief mourner. Anat weeps and beats her breast. However, Athirat tries to make Astar sit on the throne that Baal has left, but the claimant is not the right size. Anat, who has gone to look for her brother with the aid of the sun-goddess, Shapash, and who knows every corner of the universe, finds Mot and makes him vomit: 'She reaps him, sifts him, burns him with fire, scatters his flesh over the fields and the birds devour it.' Then El is warned in a dream, and knows that Baal is to come back to life: in anticipation he sees 'the skies dripping oil, and streams running with honey'. He orders Anat and Shapash to go and seek Baal, and a broken

A gold Phoenician mask from Byblos. First millennium B.C. Louvre. *Giraudon*

portion of the tablet relates how the two goddesses carry the dead god to the top of Tsaphon where, it may be presumed, he will resume his glorious reign.

What we have here is clearly an agrarian myth, the basis for a fertility ritual. Baal is the personification of the rain needed by the earth to produce its fruit. Mot is the incarnation of the grain, which must swallow great quantities of water from the sky. When the showers are over, Baal is dead, he has given his substance to the ripening corn. But at the very moment when Baal's throne stands empty, at the height of summer, Anat and the sun-goddess, devoutly collecting the god's remains, prepare for the regathering of the clouds. The treatment that Anat metes out to Mot is understandable if one thinks of the ritual of the 'last sheaf of corn': the spirit of fertility is liberated from the corn so as to obtain a new crop the following year. The rite is evident behind this episode in the myth. In much the same way Anat's mourning is a model of the tears shed by the faithful, of the flagellations that they inflicted on themselves when overwhelmed by the thought of Baal's pathetic fate; for he sacrificed himself to ensure their preservation, and gave himself of his own free will — since his choice was made when he allowed Kathar to make an opening in his celestial palace, a window through which he was to descend to earth and be scattered over the land. Agrarian cults often generate emotive and fervent piety; the myth of Baal and Mot indicates that the Semites of Ugarit knew the intense emotions of these cults, and shows how Baal could and did become the first and dearest of their gods.

Royal legends

In the poems of *Keret* and *Danel* we are no longer in the world of gods, but that of men. However, as in the Homeric epic, the scene constantly shifts between heaven and earth.

King Keret has lost all his family, wife and children, and now has no heir. El, who is his father, as Yahweh is the father of the king of Israel (Psalms, II, 7; LXXXIX, 27) appears to him in a dream and orders him to go with his army to the land of Udum to King Pabil, whose daughter he is to marry — she is Huriya, 'as charming as Anat, as lovable as Astarte'. Keret carries out the god's instructions. Once he is with Pabil he refuses all presents, asking only the hand of his daughter. In the council of the gods Baal intercedes and asks El to bless Keret. The benediction is granted: Keret will have seven, eight children, one of whom will be suckled by the goddesses Anat and Astarte. Keret's reign is prosperous, and he offers a banquet to the great ones in his kingdom. At this point there is a gap, and when we hear of Keret again he is surrounded by growing children and is gravely ill. 'Father! Are you going to die like men? Do gods die?' asks one of his sons. Yet the whole territory over which Keret reigns appears to lament him already, and, perhaps nostalgically, one column is given to evoking the fertility of the soil, the abundance of crops and the wine-harvest, all the forms of prosperity that Psalm LXXII attributes to a just king. After a council of the gods in which El asks who can cure Keret, he recovers his health and curses the too-hasty son who wanted to profit from his weakness so that he might rule in his stead.

Danel, one of the kings in western Semitis myth claimed as a just and wise man of long ago, is another king who has no descendants. He has no son to assist him in the cult and to fight his enemies. Baal takes pity on him, intercedes with El on his behalf, and a son is born to Danel and called Aqhat. One day Danel is

91

Shadrapha, 'Shed the Healer', standing on a lion. This probably represents the triumph of the god-healer over the forces of evil. Amrith, Phoenicia. Fifth century B.C. *Giraudon*

seated at his gate 'to judge the cause of the widow and the orphan' and he sees Kathar approach. Danel gives him something to eat and drink, as did Abraham to his three divine visitors from Mamre (Genesis, XVIII, 1). Kathar gives Danel a bow and arrows, which he entrusts to Aqhat, sending him off to hunt. Aqhat meets Anat, and she covets Kathar's bow. She offers him gold, then silver, and finally promises to give him immortality if Aqhat will agree to give her the bow. The young man eludes her: he knows only too well that all men are doomed to die and discreetly mocks the huntress. In her frustration she goes to complain to El and prepares her revenge. With the aid of a certain Yatpan, Anat wheels among the eagles above Aqhat and crushes his head. Danel gives vent to grief when he hears of his son's death and puts a seven-year curse on the earth. Many of the details of the poem remain obscure; it seems that Aqhat's sister undertakes to punish Yatpan, it also seems that Anat states her intention of bringing Aqhat back to life, and the accomplishment of certain rites by Danel have perhaps the same purpose.

These legends give details of the physiognomy and the role of the high gods of Ugarit: El, Baal, Anat. But they are not so much religious texts as poems of wisdom, full of teachings about man's condition, about the attitude that he must take towards the gods. Their central and common theme seems to be kingship and its divine origin, as the poem of *Keret* illustrates. Not only does the king ensure order and justice in his kingdom, but in addition his blessing produces prosperity, his curse sterility. Finally, *Keret* and *Danel* emphasise the misery of the king deprived of offspring: the grace of the gods is needed to remedy this. Old Testament accounts of kings and patriarchs likewise stress the importance of posterity blessed by God.

The Old Testament

The Israelites have little mythology. At the beginning of the century it was fashionable to interpret patriarchal legends in terms of astral mythology; this fashion is now over. It is certain that since Yahweh is an exclusive figure, his cult is not conducive to epic accounts having the gods for heroes as in the Ugaritic poems. The absence of myths, in this sense of the word, does not, however, mean that the Bible is without mythical themes. When the nomadic Israelites from the steppe settled in Palestine, they came into contact with urban populations whose superior level of civilisation could not fail to impress them. The Palestinians were organised into city-states, their religion was polytheistic, and the example of Ras Shamra leads one to the conclusion that mythology was not entirely foreign to them. These 'pagans' were, first of all, enemies in the sight of Israel, destined to succumb in the holy war of Yahweh, but some of them became allies and adopted the religion of their conquerors, especially when, about the year 1000 B.C., David and Solomon turned the Canaanite city of Jerusalem, which had been peaceably occupied, into the capital of a kingdom and the site of the Temple. The institutions that then appeared—royalty, organised clergy, certain festivals, the Temple itself—have no basis in the nomadic past of Israel. All the evidence indicates that the most ancient of Hebrew Psalms were composed in Jerusalem: they are documents about the cult of Zion. The prophets, of course, condemned the cult of the false gods with singular vigour, but the forms of their cult, the hymns that were sung to them, the exploits attributed to them have surely survived in the praise of Yahweh, who was described to Canaanite allies and to Israelites won over to Canaanite civilisation as the true Baal, the true El.

The Psalms and prophets such as Isaiah, who is highly influenced by the lyric of the Temple, transpose the old theme of Yahweh's victories into terms recalling the combats of Baal. So, in Psalm LXXIV, 13–14:

> Thou didst divide the sea by thy strength: thou brakest the heads of the dragons in the waters.
> Thou brakest the heads of leviathan in pieces....

Leviathan, the piercing and crooked serpent Isaiah speaks of (XXVII, 1) is none other than Lotan in Ugaritic mythology. Like Baal, Yahweh 'rideth upon the heavens' (Psalms, LXVIII, 4); like Baal, Yahweh is he who gives corn and wine and oil (Hosea, II, 10).

The Ras Shamra texts mention several times the council of gods presided over by El. The image reappears in the Old Testament; Yahweh is enthroned amid the 'sons of god' and judges the world from the midst of this divine court:

> God standeth in the congregation of the mighty;
> he judgeth among the gods.
>
> (Psalms, LXXXII, 1.)

And the prologue in the sky of the Book of Job presents this court in session deciding on the fate of the hero.

This is not a concession to ambient polytheism. For the Israelites the 'gods' were foreign powers that the people of Yahweh had brought into subjection or must subject to their god and their law. Semitic mythology has furnished the lyric with an arsenal of lofty themes exalting Yahweh, the greatest of the gods, the king of the gods, who gives Israel victory over her enemies.

In Jerusalem, likewise, Hebrew traditions acquired the form in which they are now known. There, too, old myths could be adapted to the glory of the god of Israel. That is why the creation of man as related in Genesis II and III provides reminders of Sumero-Babylonian mythological accounts. It is an open question whether the Biblical account was directly

A silver Syrian statuette of a goddess. Twentieth to nineteenth centuries B.C. *Giraudon*

influenced by Mesopotamia or whether it echoes a lost Canaanite myth. But in the case of the Biblical account of the Flood it is possible to come to some conclusion. Many details recall the episode of Utnapishtim in the Gilgamesh epic; however, according to Genesis, VIII, 4, Noah's ark ran aground on the mountains of Ararat, not mentioned in the Babylonian text. Ararat is what Mesopotamians knew as Uruarti. So it can be seen that the Biblical account must have been inspired by Hurrite mythological tradition. The Hurrites originally came from the lands neighbouring on Armenia and settled in Palestine in the second millennium (Genesis, XIV, 6).

Subsequent Jewish literature produced similar mythical themes. The Book of Enoch contains the celebrated account of the fall of the angels, the final transposition of the condemnation of the pagan gods by Yahweh. The scene of this episode is Hermon, terrestrial image of the mythical mountain, where the supreme god of the Canaanites exercised his royal prerogative and judgment.

Traces of Semitic myths in classical texts

It seems likely that a certain number of elements of Semitic origin may have been absorbed into the great body of mythological literature written in Greek. In the legend of Heracles, for instance, the death of the hero on the pyre of Mount Oita is perhaps a transposed version of the ritual observed at Tyre of Melqart's regeneration through fire. Classical texts, in any case, are our only source of information regarding an incontestably Semitic deity in mythological literature.

The deity in question is Adonis, whose name is a Hellenised form of the Phoenician *adoni*, 'my Lord'. Greek and Latin poets and mythographers recounting the legend quote his father as being either a Syrian king called Theias or Cinyras, king of Cyprus, and his mother as Myrrha. According to legend she was changed into a tree and gave birth to a child of radiant beauty. Aphrodite took charge of the child and entrusted it to the care of Persephone, who became fond of it and refused to give it up. To cut short the ensuing argument Zeus decided that Adonis would spend a third of the year with Aphrodite, another third with Persephone, and could dispose of the rest of his time as he wished. Adonis chose to give these four months to Aphrodite. The story also told how Adonis died when out hunting, struck in the thigh by a wild boar.

The cult of Adonis was known to Greeks in the sixth century B.C., unquestionably through contact with Cyprus. At the same period Ezekiel (VIII, 14) notes his existence in Jerusalem under the Babylonian name of Tammuz. Later on numerous classical and patristic proofs exist of the diffusion throughout the Mediterranean world of this touching cult, in which the joy of Adonis' and Aphrodite's reunion was succeeded by the grief of his sudden death and the women's funeral lament. Ephemeral gardens symbolised the grace and prompt decline of the deity. Adonis was certainly a Semitic fertility god, representing the spirit of vegetation, perhaps an avatar of the Ugaritic Baal, but the myth that has just been summarised shows that the Greeks must have embroidered on this legend, given it a romantic twist, and enriched it with details borrowed from the myths of other non-Semitic agrarian deities, such as that of Core.

It is not possible to attach firm belief to the evidence concerning Semitic mythology left by an author of the second century A.D., Philo of Byblos, who provided information under the title of *Phoenician History*, although he in fact claimed to be transcribing the teaching of a Phoenician sage, Sanchoniathon, 'previous to the Trojan war'. Fragments from Philo of Byblos, which Eusebius of Caesarea left in his *Evangelical Preparation*, consist of three quite separate accounts.

The first part is a cosmogony, less religious in character than scientific, and in it the physical elements obtrude, not the gods. The doctrine in question brings to mind the Orphic cosmogonies.

The second part, a history of the progress of humanity, attributes the civilising inventions to great men whose names sometimes form part of Semitic vocabulary: these are abstractions, like Misor (Hebrew *mishor*, 'rectitude') inventor of salt, or deities like Khusor, inventor of incantations and navigation, behind whom it is easy to recognise the Ugaritic Kathar. The Evhemerist attitude taken by Philo is incompatible with the exposition of a mythology. Probably all that here survives of Phoenician religious tradition is the names of a few deities.

Finally, a *History of the Uranides*, of war between the generations of deities: in the beginning was Elyun, the Most High, succeeded by Uranus. He is dethroned and emasculated by his son Cronus, who is Elos, but he has an avenger in the person of Zeus, who is Adados, now king of the gods. There too we find the names of Semitic deities: Elyun is Elyon, who is named in an Aramean inscription and his is the title of the god of Israel in the Psalms; Cronus-Elos is El; Zeus-Adados is Hadad, the name of the Aramean storm-god coupled with Zeus in the Hellenic period. But the scheme of things in which these names of gods occur is not Semitic: it implies a theogony like that of Hesiod, but it is even more comparable to the Hurrite myth of Kumarbis, which involves four generations of gods, and not three as in Hesiod. A Ras Shamra tablet provides evidence of the combination El-Kumarbis and shows that this myth was known in Ugarit where so many influences first saw the light of day. However, the conclusion that it is therefore a Semitic myth cannot necessarily be drawn.

When the Phoenicians founded their colony of Carthage, they adopted Tanit, virgin goddess of the heavens and the moon, as the protectress of the city. Tanit was derived from Astarte, known to the Hebrews as Ashtaroth. In the Old Testament the Hebrews were frequently exhorted to forsake the worship of Baal and Ashtaroth. Mosaic at Carthage. *Roger Wood*

Head in ivory encrusted with gold from the palace of Ras Shamra. This may have been a king or queen of Ugarit, or it may represent Baal. *Musselmany and Kurmly*

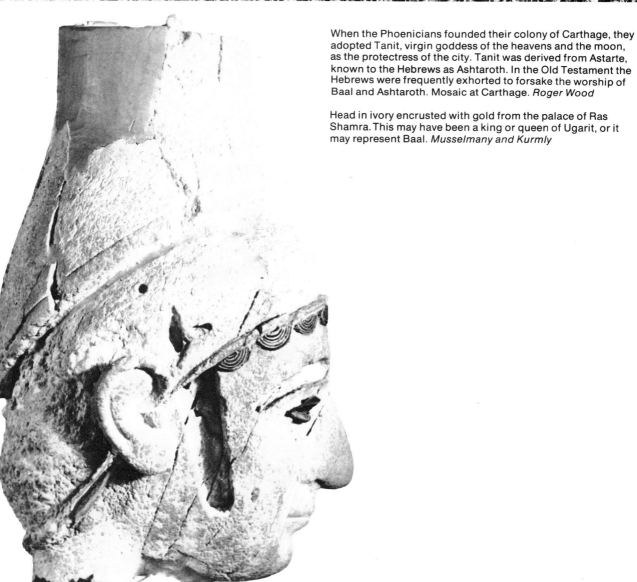

GREECE: MYTH AND LOGIC

To the Hellenic mind *logos* and *mythos*, 'reasoning' and 'myth', are two antithetic modes of thought. The former includes everything that can be stated in rational terms, all that attains to objective truth, and appears the same to all minds. The latter includes all that concerns the imagination, all that cannot be subject to verification, but contains its truth in itself or, and this amounts to the same thing, in powers of persuasion arising out of its own beauty.

The whole of Greek thought moves back and forth between these two poles of *logos* and myth, and people have often found it astonishing that the race considered the most rational of all races believed, and may even have invented, the most absurd fables. But it is pointless to wonder whether the Greeks believed in myths. One might just as well wonder whether the sculpture of Zeus by Phidias is a faithful representation of the Olympian god. The question is meaningless. Phidias' Zeus is beautiful, and he induced in the contemplative soul a sort of intuition of the divine through beauty. To that degree, and that degree only, the statue represented the god. So it is with myths; each individual could believe in them or doubt their veracity as he pleased. They were never articles of faith imposed on the people by a religious authority. The comic poets treated them with absolute disrespect; but, at a deeper level, every man had the right to modify these myths, and there was not one poet in the whole history of Hellenic literature who did not deal with the traditions of legend according to his whim, modifying them, adapting them, or giving them some particular moral significance. Mythology, being a fluid concept, free from the constraints of reason, is like the clay that Greek artists used as they pleased to model hundreds of different images. This is the most important characteristic of mythology, and it explains why it has proved fertile for the history of human thought; since time began

it has provided material for poetic or philosophical creation; and yet it has never constituted an immutable principle, accepted once and for all, nor has it ever been a revelation granted by a theology.

This is so palpably true that Plato could create a new myth in order to describe the nature of love. In *The Symposium* Plato imagines that the Creator originally intended human beings to be much stronger and better-endowed than they are now. And he so fashioned men that they had two heads, four arms and four legs and were of such terrifying strength that the master of the gods, alarmed at his own creation, decided to make them weaker; for this purpose he divided them into two halves, each of which became autonomous. And this, Plato says, is how mankind came into existence. But these half-beings, subconsciously sensing that they are incomplete, desperately seek their other half so that they might be made whole. This instinctive feeling, this inclination towards another, is the very essence of love.

What Plato did in *The Symposium* other writers had done before him; and others were to do after him. In mythology there is a whole series of legends invented to illustrate an argument or explain a moral principle; the only difficulty is to distinguish between this type and the other, and the Greeks could not always do so. They even attempted to find deep meanings in myths that had never any.

Allegorical myths are neither the more numerous nor the more important. It is simply not true that all Greek myths at a given moment in their history were the repositories of secret truths. Some Greek and certain modern thinkers have believed this, but they are wrong. The myths recounted by philosophers or those told by poets like Hesiod, who were moralists and thus philosophers after a fashion, belong to a particular category, and came into being only because the mythical mode of thought was familiar in their

The temple of Poseidon, Cape Sunion. *Toni Schneiders*

Cycladic idols. Abstract figures of this kind were common in the Ancient World. Third millennium B.C. *Giraudon and M. Chuzeville*

times. A mythology did exist prior to the allegorical myths; it was a way of thought, as has been said before, which in practice proved capable of creating a universe endowed with its own laws, as we know through literature: first came the epic, then the lyric and tragedy, and finally the philosophers added their contribution.

We still know nothing about the origins of this mythical thought. Undoubtedly, in the very beginning, Hellenic mythology was the result of a function inherent in the human mind—the faculty of creating imaginary realities—and it is certain that this faculty was originally exercised from preference in the field of religion. So Greek myth was closely connected with religion, but it was not one with religion. It might even be called anti-religious in that it tended to desecrate deities by introducing them into fables, giving them a past history and associating them with adventures that have frequently scandalised truly religious spirits. In Crete there was a 'tomb of Zeus': Pindar alludes to this Cretan myth, only to reject it resolutely, giving as the reason for this impiety the Cretans' innate taste for gratuitous lies!

The essential function of mythology is to bring the divine down to earth, in fact to minimise the differences between the immortals and mortals. So Zeus was seen to be in love, Apollo was the slave of a Thessalian king, Aphrodite was wounded with a spear and Hephaestus was lame. The gods have biographies like those of human beings. They were born, they loved, betrayed anger, fought and sometimes died. Moreover, they willingly descended to earth, moved about among men and took physical shape without any metaphysical consequences. It is obvious that this type of fable must be distinguished from true religious thought. In the sanctuaries priests meditated on the nature of the gods: sometimes their teaching came in the form of a myth—in this case a sacred allegory—but they were careful not to confuse deity with the image that poets and simple followers of the faith had of it. Mythology owed much to the sanctuaries but it did not develop entirely in their shadow.

In the complete body of myths there are many that have a popular air about them, or, to be more precise, a quality of folk-lore, and perhaps this is where we should look for the solution to the problem of origins. These are all myths that appear to derive from rites and images foreign to primitive Hellenic tradition. When the Hellenes came to the shores of the Mediterranean, they were confronted with deities and cults that they could not understand. They already had gods with distinct individual personalities, and they instinctively sought to 'recognise' these gods in the new religious world around them. The differences that they noted could be explained away by using the enormous possibilities of myth.

For example, in the Aegean there was a female deity, the Lady with the Wild Beasts, who was shown standing between two wild animals. The religious significance of the image naturally escaped the

Seated goddess, perhaps Demeter or Persephone. Yellow ochre clay. Boeotia *c.* 580 B.C. British Museum. *Edwin Smith,* in *Art Treasures of the British Museum (Thames and Hudson)*

Gold funeral mask, found at Mycenae, and popularly known as the mask of Agamemnon, though recent research has disproved this. 1650–1450 B.C. National Museum, Athens. *J. Powell*

invaders, and they, for their part, thought that they could see their own goddess Artemis, in her. The concept of the huntress-goddess, which later came to be widely recognised, was born of this confrontation of ideas. Perhaps the innumerable legends of divine metamorphoses arose in the same way too—it was a convenient means of accounting for the hundreds of different forms with which one and the same deified personality came to be associated. Zeus was the principal beneficiary of these inventions, and this gave rise to an exceptionally rich cycle of myths.

This abundance of mythical material, created by the spontaneous reaction of the Hellenic mind to the complex religion with which it was faced, remained formless, independent of any sacerdotal authority, and at the same time capable of evincing considerable variations from one part of Greece to another. There were deities common to all the Greeks, but the myths, for their part, did not exhibit this characteristic of universality till much later, and they always had local variations, which indicate that, in the beginning, they occurred here and there after the waves of invaders had already split up and become scattered in different territories on the continent and the islands.

The great Greek myths appear to have taken shape before the date of the oldest texts we have in Greek—the Homeric poems. Homer, of course, does not relate any myths (or hardly any, for at times myths have been introduced into episodes in the *Iliad* and the *Odyssey*), but numerous references to divine genealogies demonstrate the existence of a previously constituted mythology. The Homeric poems include not only myths relating to divine persons, but also legendary traditions concerning heroes who were half-human, half-divine beings fathered by a god on a mortal woman or beings of entirely mortal parentage who had succeeded in winning the favour of the gods. There is a vague zone in which heroes and divine creatures tend to become confused, and certain heroes must have been gods at one time, one suspects, then lost part of their prerogative for various historical reasons. There were also heroes who were historical characters, kings or thaumaturges who had, with time, become the central characters in legends. Their tombs had become holy places, and their names were linked with tales of wonder. The two phenomena may even concur, and in that case a deified human being received the cultural and mythical heritage of an ancient local god who had practically disappeared. We suspect that this happened fairly frequently in the case of Heracles, the most invasive of the heroes, and it is highly likely that in the traditions relating to the kings of Mycenae and Argos, or to the early sovereigns of Attica, history and myth are inextricably confused.

However, in spite of all the confusion that prevailed over the elements of Greek mythology, this huge body of material was classified and put in order. Myths tended to become international, and mythology

Rhyton or drinking vessel from Crete, the top register showing a bull-fighting scene. *Roger Viollet*

emerged as the common vehicle of Hellenic thought due to literary outpourings that spread beyond the narrow framework of cities, to colonisation with its attendant swarms, to the development of commercial relations with all the lands bordering along the eastern Mediterranean, and, lastly, to the renown of some great sanctuaries, such as Delphi and Olympus in Greece and Miletus in Asia. At this point in time myth gained currency beyond the city; it no longer arose out of a local tradition, it was imported from outside — or rather it returned, adorned, embellished, reinforced by all the elements it had acquired from comparison with the myths of other cities and even other peoples. Now, at last, mythology came into its own and played its essential part, which was to be a system of thought destined to explain the things that defy reason. For instance, in the case of Egyptian religion, with its countless figures of monsters and animals; instead of being disconcerted by their alien aspect the Greeks explained them away by referring them back to a time when, in terror of the giant Typhoeus, the gods disguised themselves in the most varied shapes and sought shelter even in the sands of the Libyan desert. Thus order was restored: the unknown, the unusual appeared again in a reassuring guise.

At this stage Hellenic mythology branched into several separate cycles, which formed the general basic framework for later myths. First of all came the theogonies, that is, the story of the birth and genealogy of the gods, as well as the story of creation. We suspect that this was foreign to the most ancient Hellenic mythology, and that the idea came to the Greeks from outside, probably from Asia Minor. From this time each of the great gods was endowed with legends of different origins. This gave rise to what may be called the cycle of the Olympians. Ancient features belonging to the religion of the Indo-European conquerors survived here, but there were also other foreign factors, which were Asiatic, Aegean and, generally speaking, pre-Hellenic in origin.

Besides the cycle of the Olympians heroic cycles also appeared, and these seemed more closely linked to history. The legends of the loves of Zeus, for example, could be situated in any epoch. But the birth of a hero, or the Trojan War, or the founding of a town were connected with traditions of definite date, which, as far as possible, had to be respected. This second type of myth was less free than the other, for the different cycles affected one another. For instance, it became necessary to explain why Heracles never met Theseus, although they were supposed to have lived at the same time. And why the same Heracles did not go and fight against Troy, although he had known Nestor, who took part in the expedition, and was consequently his contemporary. All these considerations, carefully weighed by the first 'historians' of Greece, led to revisions that were intended to reconcile the different legendary traditions and place them in an acceptable chronological sequence.

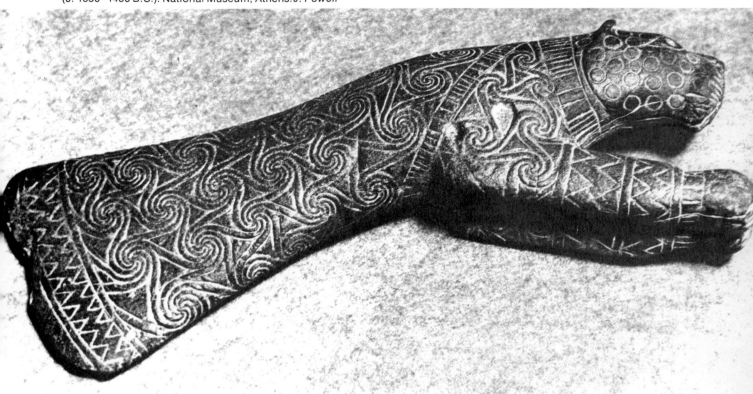

Finally, these same heroic cycles, as used by epic poets, gave rise to narratives of a more literary nature than the legends considered so far. The most famous example of these creative works is the *Iliad*; but we know that there were others in existence, and that not only Troy, but Thebes, Corinth, Athens, to mention only a few, became centres of whole bodies of mythical literature of which only a very small part has come down to us.

This classification, which came about as mythology evolved, can be conveniently used today; it will be followed in the account given here. These four major categories (theogonies, cycle of Olympians, heroic cycles, legendary romances) are completed by a fifth group, consisting of isolated legends, which, though few in number, remain as evidence of what was the great flowering of myths in Greece prior to classicism and the standardisation it brought.

The theogonic systems

The poem of Hesiod

Hesiod, a poet who came from Ascra in Boeotia, composed the most famous *Theogony* in the course of the eighth century B.C. Hesiod's family came from Cyme in Aeolis, and he was probably influenced by Oriental thought, and thus came to choose the history of the creation of the world and the divine generations as the subject for an epic and didactic poem.

Hesiod's *Theogony* showed a religious synthesis of a highly complex nature, in which deities from all over the Oriental world were intermingled and organised in a quasi-historic system. Of course, purely 'Hellenic' gods were found in it too, for they were introduced by Aryan invaders. These formed the majority of the great Olympian gods, thus called

because by tradition their palace was located on the summit of Mount Olympus (just as the great feudal nobles of the Mycenaean era, whose exploits were sung by Homer, had their citadels on the summits of hills). But in addition to the major deities—Zeus, Apollo, Hephaestus and the rest—Hesiod conferred a place of honour and an important role on numerous divine persons who are often hard to distinguish and vague of feature, and these sometimes represented forces of nature, astral bodies or sea-demons, or spirits of vegetation, and sometimes they were simple moral abstractions with transparently obvious names, such as Force or Discord.

The beginning of things

In the beginning, Hesiod said, was chaos—that is to say a state of being in which there is nothing but space, pure expanse, nothing organic, nothing that can be described. Then in this void the first of the realities took shape, and so limited it and gave it a meaning: the Earth (Gaea in Hesiod's language, Ge in classical Greek), 'the sure foundation of all that is'. At the same time the universe was divided into compartments in the following way: there was henceforth a chaos, 'under the earth'—and this chaos gave rise to Erebus, that vast underlying space in which hell later found a place—and a void above the earth: there Earth installed her first-born, the Sky, who was an emanation of herself. While this organic division of the universe was taking place, Eros, Love, was born—the abstract principle of desire, not the perverse and cunning little winged god whose insolent exploits were recounted with pleasure by the poets of the Hellenic period. It was absolutely necessary to bring Love into being at the very outset of creation, for he was, as it were, the 'motor' of the universe: Love brought about monstrous unions of cosmic principles. What it begat defies the imagination and

Minoan seal, showing goddess with attendants.

This early terracotta figure from Tanagra, Boeotia, is thought to be Gaea (Earth) one of the first generation of Greek gods. Louvre. *Schneider-Lengyel*

these unions were aspects of the immense dialectic of creation.

Chaos produced two offspring: Erebus and Night. Earth, meanwhile, having formed Heaven, then gave birth to mountains and nymphs, who at this point were mountain spirits, that is to say the vital principle animating the secret life of the mountain. Earth was also made responsible for the creation of the Sea (Pontus, a masculine principle, referring to the powerful and brutal waves surrounding Earth, who created them all by herself without any intervention on the part of Love). Thus the stage was set for creation: earth provided a solid base, with mountains rising right up into the sky, and the luminous vault of the heavens was reflected in the sterile expanse of the sea; day and night were already alternating, for the goddess Night had produced two children of light, Aether and Day. The first-mentioned was the pure, clear light that one imagines to be in the highest reaches of the atmosphere—the light of the gods. Day, on the other hand, brought light to mortals, and alternated with its mother, Night. It is worth noting that the major stars, the sun and the moon, do not figure explicitly in this first creation. They were not primordial gods, but elements of the 'starry Sky', and their birth, under the names of Helius and Selene, is not mentioned until we come to the third generation of deities.

The generation of Titans

Soon Heaven and Earth reign supreme, Uranus and Gaea, and this particular couple produced twelve children, the Titans and the Titanesses. There were six Titans: Oceanus, the eldest, then Coeus, Crius, Hyperion, Iapetus and finally Cronus. They had six sisters, the Titanesses: Theia, Rhea, Themis, Mnemosyne, Phoebe and Tethys. Only a few of the deities named in this list were associated with definite

Helius, god of the sun, rising at dawn from the sea. The boys diving into the sea before his chariot represent the fading stars. *British Museum*

Eos, the dawn, and Cephalus or Astreus, the dawn wind. From their union was born the morning star.

functions. Themis was Justice; Mnemosyne, Memory, or, more usually, Remembrance, as monuments go to show and, indeed, the impression left by the name in the minds of men. They were abstract principles and their presence among the primeval deities was in itself some indication of the conditions essential to the establishment of order in the world—for the continuity of this world was guaranteed by Mnemosyne, as there was no god of time at this stage in the theogony. Time in its material form was expressed by the alternation of day and night, and in the spiritual sense by Mnemosyne herself. Tethys (who should not be confused with her quasi-namesake, Thetis, the nereid, mother of Achilles) was a goddess of the sea; she seems to have personified the feminine attribute of fertility with regard to the sea. She became the wife of Oceanus, her eldest brother, and she bore him more than three thousand children, all the waves in the world; her abode was far away in the west, in the red land of evening, which the sun visited each day when it descended in the sky.

The meaning of the Titans' names is not so obvious—apart from that of Oceanus. One astral spirit is recognisable, Hyperion, 'dweller on high', who married his sister Theia and begat the sun and moon, Helius and Selene. The majority of the Titans are important only because of their descendants: Coeus, for example, coupled with his sister Phoebe (the Brilliant) to produce Leto, who later became the mother of Artemis and Apollo. Crius fathered several children on Eurybia, one of the daughters of Earth and of Pontus—these were Astraeus (later one of the partners of the dawn-goddess, Eos), the giant Pallas (who must be carefully distinguished from the goddess Pallas Athena, daughter of Zeus), and finally Perses, who was the father of the goddess Hecate. The latter was known as the Lady of the Night, goddess of abundance and eloquence, but she was also a redoubtable magician, who could skilfully change into a dog, a she-wolf or mare, and her three-headed statue frequently stood at crossroads. Iapetus, for his part, espoused Clymene, a daughter of Oceanus and Tethys, who bore him four children: these were Atlas, the giant who is later forced to carry the sky on his shoulders, Menoetius, who was one of the conspirators in the revolt against Zeus and, by way of punishment, was struck by a thunderbolt and sent to Tartarus, and finally Prometheus and Epimetheus, whose legend will be discussed at greater length on page 112.

However, the Titan whose descendants acquired particular importance was the last-born, Cronus. He it was who set in motion the fates, which proceeded inexorably towards the point in time when the divine generation of Olympians was established in power.

Uranus and Gaea brought many other beings into the world apart from the Titans: the Cyclopes (Arges, Steropes and Brontes, three storm-spirits,

Hypnos, god of sleep. 450–300 B.C. Possibly a Roman copy. British Museum. *Edwin Smith* in *Art Treasures of the British Museum (Thames and Hudson)*

whose names indicate lightning, storm-clouds and thunder, respectively), then the Hecatoncheires, the hundred-handed giants Cottus, Briareus and Gyges. Uranus hated the Hecatoncheires and refused to let them see the light of day; he kept them shut away in the depths of the Earth, to the latter's extreme discontent. Moreover, she was weary of the continual child-bearing imposed on her by her partner. Secretly she asked her eldest sons, the Titans, to help her be revenged on Uranus. Only the youngest, Cronus, consented, for he hated his father—for reasons largely unknown. Gaea then gave him a very hard, sharp flint sickle, and then, one night, when Uranus came again to Gaea, Cronus was lying in wait and castrated his father. Drops of blood from his wounds rained down on the earth and the sea and other deities were thus begotten.

The Erinnyes were born when his blood fertilised the earth (they were also called the Eumenides, the Kindly Ones, by way of conciliation); their names are Alecto, Tisiphone and Megara, the three Furies, cruel spirits who dwelt in the depths of the underworld where they tortured criminals; giants also sprang from Uranus' blood, and a new generation of nymphs, the Meliae or ash-nymphs. A girl was also created when the blood and seed of the god fell on the sea, and she went first to the island of Cythera, then to Cyprus. This was how Aphrodite's life began (the Greeks connected her name with the word for foam).

'And with her went Eros,' Hesiod goes on to say, and comely Desire followed her at her birth at the first and as she went into the assembly of the gods. This honour she has from the beginning, and this is the portion allotted to her amongst men and undying gods—the whisperings of maidens, and smiles and deceits with sweet delight and love and graciousness.' (*Theogony*, v. 201 and following, translated by H. G. Evelyn-White.)

The primeval deities

So Cronus, the youngest Titan, was left alone to reign over the world in process of formation. However, other divine generations were arising all around him. Night gave birth to Fate, Destiny (Ker) and Death (Thanatos, regarded by Greeks as a masculine spirit); she also bore Sleep and the whole race of Dreams, as well as Momos, the god of sarcasm, and Pain, and Nemesis, who was divine vengeance; the latter punished any immoderate action, or even feeling, anything pertaining to the 'sin of pride', any refusal to respect the existing order. Night also brought forth the Hesperides, the nymphs of evening, still without the aid of a masculine partner. There were three of these nymphs: Aegle, Erytheia and Hespera. They lived in the far west, beside Oceanus, not far from the Islands of the Blessed, where happy souls dwelt, and there they kept eternal guard over a magic orchard with fruits of gold.

Night also produced many cruel spirits: Deceit, Tenderness, Old Age, and Strife, who in turn begot other scourges: Forgetfulness, Famine, Sorrows, Battles, Murders, Quarrels, Lying Words, Lawlessness, Ruin and, finally, Oath, who was the worst of evils if one committed perjury and thus invited his fearful curse. The world was slowly preparing to receive men and held hundreds of causes of suffering in readiness for them. We may be sure that in these pages of the *Theogony* Hesiod gave free rein to his own pessimism, which is so evident in the rest of his work. But it is by no means certain that this feeling was shared by all Greeks, whom one imagines to be more carefree than he, and more enamoured of the world's charms.

Sea-demons

As far as Nature's smiles are concerned, one must look to the descendants of Pontus to provide them;

Votive chariot in terracotta from Cyprus

his first-born was Nereus, 'who is true and lies not', called the Old Man of the Sea, 'because he is trusty and gentle and does not forget the laws of righteousness, but thinks just and kindly thoughts'. (*Ibid.* v. 233 and following, translated by H. G. Evelyn-White.)

Thaumas was another child of Pontus and Mother Earth, and he later became the father of Iris, the goddess of the rainbow and messenger of the gods; then there was Phorcys, sometimes thought to have been the father of the sea-monster Scylla; finally, two daughters, Ceto and Eurybia. Nereus and Doris, one of the daughters of Oceanus, became the parents of the nereids. The number of nereids varied according to tradition; usually there were fifty of them, but sometimes there were twice that number. Only a few of the nereids, who for the most part are only names, have their own legend: Thetis was one of these, the mother of Achilles; also Amphitrite, who became the wife of Poseidon, the Olympian god of the sea; and Galatea, who was Sicilian by birth, was another mythical figure. The young and beautiful nereids spent their time spinning and singing in their father's palace of gold; they formed a chorus of compassionate witnesses to the dramas and mysteries of sea life amid the tritons and dolphins.

The spirits of the deep were not always as benevolent as this. Thaumas, another of Pontus' sons, father of the gracious Iris, had more daughters, called the Harpies and known individually as Aello and Ocypete (Storm-foot and Swift-wing); sometimes a third sister was also included, Celaeno (the Dark One, she who makes overcast the sky before a storm at sea). These Harpies (Snatchers) were evil spirits; when they alighted on the sea, with all speed, nothing could prevail against them; wherever they went they seized all before them. They were depicted as birds of prey, with sharp claws, and were said to live in the

Strophade Islands in the middle of the Ionian Sea.

The Graeae, the three Old Women of the Sea, were the offspring of Phorcys, and bore the names of Enyo, Pemphredo and Dino; they lived in the far west, in a misty land where the sun never shone. Between them they possessed only one eye and one tooth, which they used in turn. The three Graeae had three other monsters for sisters, the Gorgons. They were called Sthenno, Euryale and Medusa. Of these three only Medusa was mortal. These hideous creatures had huge tusks like those of a boar; they had glaring eyes, which turned to stone anyone who dared to meet their gaze. They had serpents for hair and gold wings to enable them to fly. Like the Graeae they lived on the edge of the world, objects of horror to gods and men. Medusa, one of the Gorgons, and Poseidon became the parents of two children who sprang from their mother's body after she had been slain by Perseus: they were Pegasus, the winged horse, and Chrysaor, the hero with the golden sword, who in his turn became the father both of Geryon, the three-bodied giant vanquished by Heracles, and also of the Viper (Echidna); this terrifying monster produced three children fathered by Typhon: the monstrous dog Orthrus, Geryon's companion, the Hydra of Lerna, who also fell victim to Heracles, and the Chimaera, who was later to fight Bellerophon.

It was also believed that Orthrus lay with his own mother, Echidne, and two other famous monsters were born of the incestuous union, the Sphinx of Thebes and the Nemean Lion. This is an explanation dreamed up by poets desirous of providing a background to the nightmare figures in the heroic cycles.

Birth of the Olympians
Cronus also wanted heirs. His sister Rhea had three daughters by him, Hestia, Demeter and Hera, and three sons, Hades, Poseidon and Zeus. But there was

Zeus with thunderbolt. Bronze figure from Dodona. *c.* 470 B.C. State Museum, Berlin

In Greek mythology Mount Olympus was believed to be the abode of the gods. *Boissonas*

a curse on Cronus. Being of a knavish and violent nature, he refused to placate Gaea after he had turned his father off the throne. Instead of freeing his brothers, condemned by Uranus never to see the light of day, he kept them shut away in their subterranean prison, thus inviting Gaea's wrath. She made a vow that he would himself know the dire fate that he had inflicted on his own father, and that he would be dethroned by his own children. And so, to protect himself from this threat, he devoured the children that Rhea bore him the moment they came into the world. The first five he swallowed up, but when the time came for the birth of Zeus, Rhea decided to save this child. With Gaea's help she found shelter in a Cretan cave and was there delivered of her infant. Then she took a stone and wrapped it in swaddling clothes and then took it to Cronus saying that this was her child. Without further question he seized the stone and swallowed it. Zeus was saved, and by the same stroke Cronus' own fate was sealed.

Zeus grew up in a cave in Crete where he was nursed by the nymph Amalthea and young warriors armed with spears and shields, the Curetes. The Curetes (which means 'Young men') kept up an unceasing war-dance round the grotto where the infant lay; they made as much noise as possible, clashing their weapons together and uttering warlike cries. The point of all this was to drown the noise of wailing, lest Cronus should discover the ruse and devour his son. It would appear that in this case that myth, as it so often did, grew out of a rite: a ritual war-dance was practised in Crete and many other Hellenised countries by individuals imitating the spirits of the storm and acting as these spirits were thought to act in the mountains and the sky; such dancing as this probably gave rise to the story of Rhea's ruse.

Thus Zeus was protected and so grew to manhood and acquired all his divine powers. The time came for Gaea's prophecy to be fulfilled. Zeus' consort at this time was Metis, a daughter of Oceanus, whose name means 'Prudence', or more often 'Perfidy'. She gave him a drug, which would make his father vomit and bring up the children he had previously devoured and still carried inside him. They all emerged, and with these allies Zeus attacked Cronus and his comrades, the Titans. They joined battle, and this war lasted ten years. Finally, Gaea's oracle promised Zeus victory if he would accept help from the monsters that Cronus had imprisoned in Tartarus. Zeus obeyed, thus realising Gaea's wish, which Cronus himself had always disregarded. Zeus delivered the monsters and was victorious. Cronus and the Titans were then confined to the depths of the underworld and so took the place of the monsters, who became their guards.

During the struggle against Cronus and the Titans the monsters had given the young gods powerful weapons, which were to figure in future among their emblems. Thus the Cyclopes forged the thunderbolt

A three-bodied monster, possibly Typhon, one of the giants Zeus had to defeat after he became king of the gods. Acropolis Museum, Athens. *Boudot-Lamotte*

The war between the gods and the giants. Before he could feel secure as the king of the gods, Zeus, with the aid of the Olympians and Heracles, had to defeat the giants. Amphora. Fifth century B.C. *Giraudon*

Rhea, mother of Zeus and wife of Cronus, was one of the Titanesses. Cronus, fearing that one of his children would supplant him, swallowed them as soon as they were born. Determined to save the youngest, Zeus, Rhea presented her husband with a stone wrapped in swaddling clothes to swallow, and Zeus was brought up secretly until he could take revenge on his father. Villa Albani, Rome. *Alinari-Giraudon*

Battle between Athena and the giant Enceladus. The giant is armed in the manner of an Athenian hoplite, with round shield, short sword, and lance. Bibliothèque Nationale. *Giraudon*

and lightning for Zeus—and ever after that Zeus was regarded as the god of the stormy sky. Again it was the Cyclopes who gave Hades a magic helmet, which made the wearer invisible. Poseidon for his part received a magic trident, which could make the earth and sea shake. And, whereas Hades became the god of the invisible world and reigned over the souls of the dead, Poseidon acquired the power of troubling the waves and provoking tempests and earthquakes, which were so frequently experienced in the basin of the Aegean Sea.

The victorious Olympians divided the universe between them. Although he was the youngest, Zeus obtained the highest position and reigned over the sky. Hades had to be satisfied with the part of the world situated beneath the earth—the underworld. Poseidon became lord of the sea.

The battles waged by Zeus

However, the reign of the new gods was far from safely established. Gaea was still discontented. Although some of her children, the Hecatoncheires and the Cyclopes, had regained their freedom, the Titans were now imprisoned in their place, and Gaea felt no less maternal towards them than towards the others. She decided to pursue her intrigues, and this time she had recourse to the giants, those monsters she had produced when Uranus' blood fell upon her. She persuaded them to revolt against the new masters of the world. The giants were protected by all manner of magic devices. Not only did they have considerable strength, but, although they were mortal, Fate had decreed that they would not die until a mortal and a god slew them at one and the same time. There was also a magic herb that could make them invulnerable to mortal blows. Under these conditions a victory on the part of the Olympians was more than doubtful. As soon as Zeus discovered that the giants were going

to revolt (doubtless informed by Metis) his first thought was to obtain the magic herb. He instructed the Sun, Moon and Dawn to give forth no light, so that no-one could see clearly until he himself had found the precious herb. The two opposing sides joined battle at Pallene, an island off the Thracian coast where the giants were born. The giants threatened heaven by hurling up firebrands and enormous boulders. Each god retaliated with his chosen weapon: Zeus hurled his thunderbolt, Poseidon intervened with his trident, and Athena, a daughter of Zeus under the protection of his aegis, the goatskin breastplate, which was also her emblem, sent thunderbolts to strike the enemy monsters. Fighting on the side of the Olympians was one mortal, Heracles. The presence of this Argive hero is highly surprising, since Heracles was born some time after the war of the giants; up to that point, indeed, there was no mention of the creation of man—regarding which, as we shall see, only vague and contradictory traditions existed in Greek mythology. Hesiod does not mention the story of the war of the giants, which became particularly popular in the Hellenistic period, and probably Heracles was a later addition to the legend, although gigantomachy was certainly not invented by poets of the post-Alexandrian period, and the early versions date back to remote times.

Typhon

Hesiod told of another occasion in which Zeus fought a monster; and this formed a further episode in the battle waged by Olympus against the primeval gods, which classical philosophers liked to construe as the triumph of order and reason over disorderly violence and brute force. The duel with Typhon in the *Theogony* provided the subject for a long exposition, but its authenticity has been contested by modern editors with perhaps excessive severity. However, the episode was well known in the time of Pindar and Aeschylus, and it abounds in bizarre details that indicate an ancient, probably Asiatic, origin. According to Hesiod (or the pseudo-Hesiod), Typhon was the youngest son of Gaea and Tartarus. Gigantic in height, he was taller than any mountain, and his head reached the stars; his hands had a hundred dragons' heads instead of fingers; from waist to toe he was nothing but vipers; he had wings; and his eyes flashed fire. As soon as Zeus saw this monster he was afraid, and he hurled a thunderbolt at him. In the *Theogony* that was the end of the fight. Typhon was struck by a thunderbolt, and, breathless and broken, he was soon imprisoned in Tartarus. In other traditional versions the struggle was prolonged and extended. These relate that when the gods saw Typhon attack Heaven they were afraid and so fled to Egypt, where they took to the desert and disguised themselves as different animals to avoid recognition. Apollo was said to have become a kite, Ares a fish, Dionysus a goat, and Hephaestus a bull. These

Poseidon slaying the giant Polybutes. As a reward for his support in the wars Zeus gave Poseidon the sea as his kingdom. Bibliothèque Nationale. *Giraudon*

strange metamorphoses were obviously invented by the Greeks to account for the zoolatry in Egyptian religion, because they were anxious to rediscover their own national deities behind the strange facade of the Egyptian gods; so they represent a later addition to the legend. While the rest of the Olympians were in full flight, Zeus and his daughter Athena stood their ground. Finally, Zeus grappled with the monster on Mount Casius, on the boundary between Egypt and Arabia. Typhon was first wounded by Zeus' sword, but he managed to get hold of it and to gain the upper hand. He severed the sinews of Zeus' arms and legs to curtail his movements, then he hoisted him on his back and carried him off to Cilicia where he imprisoned him in a cave. He hid the sinews and nerves of the god in a bearskin, and Delphyne, a dragon, stood guard over them. In their own private world Zeus' fellow Olympians tried in vain to think of a way of delivering their master. Finally, Hermes and Pan thought of a trick and succeeded in stealing the nerves and sinews, which they replaced in Zeus' limbs, and once more the fight against Typhon was resumed. Zeus rode up to the sky on a chariot and from there he hurled thunderbolts at his enemy. He pursued Typhon for a long time all over the earth. Traces of this pursuit could be seen almost everywhere, particularly on Mount Haimos in Thrace. The combat was ultimately brought to an end in Sicily, where Typhon had taken refuge, Zeus hurled Mount Etna upon him, and thus he was made prisoner for ever.

The fumes and flames belching forth are evidence of the monster's powerlessness and anger and of the might and intelligence of Zeus in inflicting such a defeat as this upon him.

However, there is in existence one other myth concerning the god's battle against the monster, and this is the legend of the Aloadae. Iphimedeia, a daughter of Triopas and the wife of Aloeus, had fallen in love with Poseidon. She bore him two children, Otus and Ephialtes, who grew one cubit in breadth and one fathom in height every year. When they were nine years old, being then nine fathoms high, they declared war on Olympus, and soon their insolence spread throughout the world. They began by piling Mount Pelion on top of Mount Ossa, then proclaimed their intention of throwing the mountains into the sea until the latter became dry land. Moreover, they declared that they each wanted to marry a goddess. Ephialtes claimed Hera as his wife, and Otus chose Artemis. And then, in order to prove their might, they imprisoned Ares in a brazen vessel to punish him for having caused the death of Adonis, and there he remained for thirteen months. His eventual release was due solely to Hermes, and he emerged half-dead from this experience. Tired of such outrages, Zeus hurled his thunderbolt at the Aloadae and condemned them to eternal torture in the underworld.

The second generation of Olympians

The six children of Cronus, who were henceforth sole masters of the universe, almost complete the world of gods. Not entirely, however, for the Olympians themselves had descendants who shared their privileges.

Following the tradition set by Cronus, Zeus soon took to himself a divine wife. Hesiod quotes Metis as his first companion. This union came to an unfortunate end, for Gaea and Uranus, the holders of divine secrets, revealed to Zeus what Fate had in store for the children born to Metis and himself: the first was to be a very wise and valiant daughter, but the second would be a violent youth destined to dethrone his father. Faced with this danger, Zeus swallowed Metis before she could give birth to her first child. When the time had come for the birth, Zeus summoned the god of the forge, Hephaestus, and ordered him to take an axe and split his head in two. And straightway from the head of Zeus emerged a girl fully armed: this was the goddess Athena, who was wisdom and courage personified.

Zeus' second wife was Themis, the incarnation of law or equity. The first offspring of this union were the deities known as the Horae (the Hours or the Seasons). The Horae were three in number, and Hesiod called them Eunomia, Dice and Eirene—Order, Justice and Peace—but Athenians knew them as Thallo, Auxo and Carpo; these names evoke the three principal stages of vegetation: the sprouting of the plant, its growth and its fructification. The naturalist aspect of these cults was soon complicated by the addition of social concepts, and the spirits who presided over the fertility of the land were transformed into abstract principles pertaining to city life. Zeus fathered three other daughters on Themis, known as the Fates, or Moerae: Clotho, Lachesis and Atropos, who determined the destiny of every human being. This destiny was symbolised by a thread, which the first of the Fates drew from her distaff, the second wound, and the third cut when the span of life that it represented was over.

Zeus' third wife was Eurynome, the sea-nymph, who also bore him three daughters, the Graces (*Charites*) Aglaia, Euphrosyne and Thalia. Like the Horae the Graces were vegetation spirits; they spread joy in the world of nature and in the hearts of men. They lived on Olympus, together with the Muses, with whom they loved to sing and dance. Like the Muses they were companions of Athena and presided with her over feminine tasks.

For a time Zeus' companion was his own sister Demeter, on whom he fathered a daughter, Persephone, whose legend will be related later. Then he became attached to Mnemosyne, and they had nine daughters, the Muses, 'who take pleasure in festivals and in the joy of singing'. Another tradition concerning the origin of the Muses says that they were the daughters of Zeus and Harmonia, a goddess descended from Atlas. The Muses were not only divine singers, destined to entertain the immortals, they were the patrons of all intellectual activities, including the highest, everything that freed man from physical reality and gave him access to eternal truths. Eloquence, persuasion, wisdom, knowledge of the past and the laws of the world, mathematics, astronomy, all came within their province, as well as poetry and music proper and dancing. They knew the secret of lessening men's anguish, and they were an inspiration to kings when they addressed their subjects with persuasive words. The first song sung by the Muses, the most ancient, was the hymn of victory in honour of the Olympians' victory over the Titans. The number of Muses, given as nine according to the canons, was probably not immutable. There seem to have been only three of them at Delphi, and

there was a cult in existence at Lesbos dedicated to seven Muses. From the classical period onwards it became general to think in terms of the traditional list, which included Calliope, Clio, Polyhymnia, Euterpe, Terpsichore, Erato, Melpomene, Thalia and Urania. Prior to this time they were not rigorously differentiated, and any one of them could undertake any given function. In classical times Calliope came to be considered as the muse of epic poetry; Clio, of history; Polyhymnia, of the mimic art; Euterpe, of the flute; Terpsichore, of lyric poetry and dancing; Erato, of lyric poetry and hymns; Melpomene, of tragedy; Thalia, of comedy; and Urania, of astronomy—and these are the somewhat conventional spheres assigned to them by the moderns.

After Mnemosyne, Zeus fathered two children on Leto, the daughter of the Titans Coeus and Phoebe. These were Artemis and Apollo, who were immediately drawn into the group of major deities. Then the god Hermes was born to Maia, daughter of Atlas. The last in line of the divine wives of Zeus was his sister Hera, who bore him a son, Ares, the god of war, and two daughters: Hebe, who personified youthfulness, and whose task for a long time was to serve nectar at celestial banquets, until at length she became the wife of Heracles; and Eileithyia, the female spirit who presided over childbirth.

But even after his marriage with Hera, Zeus, as we shall see, was not a faithful husband, and he loved many mortals, including Alcmene, who bore him a son, Heracles, and a daughter, Semele, on whom he fathered Dionysus, the god of wine. Furious at her abandonment, Hera alone created and produced a son without the help of Zeus; this was the god Hephaestus, who presided over the work of smiths and the arts of the forge.

And thus the group of great deities, the twelve Olympians, was practically complete: Zeus, Poseidon, Hephaestus, Hermes, Ares, Apollo, Hera, Athena, Artemis, Hestia, Aphrodite and Demeter. Two major deities are missing from this list, Hades and Persephone, who lived in the underworld and did not belong to the light half of the universe. Dionysus, a newcomer—his cult was introduced long after the establishment of the great canonical myths—was accepted only as guest of honour.

Nature-demons

The other gods lived a separate existence. Some—for example, Helius, Selene, Eos (sun, moon and dawn, respectively)—were circumscribed by their particular activities; each had a palace, which he left every day at the appointed time to ride on his chariot across the sky and so bring light to men. Others were scattered about the world, such as Amphitrite, Poseidon's wife, mother of the sea-god Triton; it was her pleasure to live in the far west, hidden in a gold palace, in the depths of the obscure waters of Oceanus. There was also Pan, who listened to the prayers of Arcadian

Daughters of Zeus, by either Mnemosyne or Harmonia, the muses were patrons of intellectual activities. Detail of Attic red-figured kylix. c. 420 B.C. *Fitzwilliam Museum, Cambridge*

Pan, half man, half goat, was the herdsman god, an early divinity of Arcadia. Terracotta statuette. Attic. Early fourth century B.C. *Fitzwilliam Museum, Cambridge*

shepherds and wandered the mountains, particularly Mount Cyllene; he was therianthropic—half man and half animal—with a hairy body and the lower limbs of a goat, and he also had the goat's prodigious agility and bestial passions. For his pleasure he pursued nymphs and young boys indiscriminately. His portraits show him wearing a crown made from a pine branch, and playing the syrinx (or 'pipes of Pan'), an instrument composed of reeds of different lengths. The poets did not agree about his origins: some said he was the son of Zeus; others, the son of Hermes or some other god.

Throughout the world there were nymphs—in the streams, beneath the bark of trees, in the waves of the sea. Each river also had its own god. Hellenistic art happily depicted them as men in the prime of life, with beards and horns on their brows (the symbol of power), sometimes resting against an urn from which the river flows. But even before this conventional imagery came into being, the river-gods were the object of a cult, and many legends were told about them: how they loved such and such a nymph, had children by her, and how they could change themselves into all kinds of beings. River-gods, as we shall see, played a part in the heroic cycles. Achelous, for instance, entered into the adventures of Heracles.

No desert was too terrible to have spirits, and their whims were loved and feared. All were active in their own field, conceived passions like those of men, loved and suffered although they were immortal. There were deities of this kind not only in the world of nature, but also in cities, where they presided over public and family life. They were often referred to vaguely as *daemones*—a word made infamous by the Christian religion, but it originally conveyed overtones of respect and often of affection.

The position held by Mortals

In this vast fresco of creation there remains the task of determining the place held by the human race. On this point Greek mythology, caring less about logic and coherence than certain other mythologies, affords only fragmentary and often contradictory indications. In most myths, everything happens as if men were 'given, existed in principle', as if their presence was self-evident; traditional stories told of origins of certain noble families, but there were no stories about ordinary people. Greek mythology was unquestionably aristocratic in tendency and spirit. If the great were descended from the gods on high, then the populace was born of the earth, in the manner of plant or animal species. The story of Zeus creating hoards of ants to people the island of Aegina is characteristic in this respect.

Each part of Greece had its own traditions regarding the origin of its people. The Argives for instance, spoke of a 'first man', Phoroneus, saying that he was the son of Inachus, the river-god, and the nymph

Melia (whose name shows that she was an ash-nymph). This union of a river-god and tree-spirit resulting in the birth of a mortal expresses a complete view of humanity; it was considered both to be divine and to resemble all living things, such as plants and life-giving waters, and, like the whole of nature, it was subject to the rhythm of the seasons, being born of Mother Earth and destined to return to her.

In Arcadia the first man was said to be Pelasgos, and to be 'born of the earth', long, long ago, even before the moon shone in the sky. In other lands mortals were said to be the descendants of nymphs and deities. Thus in Greek thought there was not the continuity observed elsewhere between the divine and the human. For the Hellenes, the human was only one degree less than the divine, and the two conditions partook of the same nature. There was greater power, a longer expectation of life in the deities (the major gods were immortal, but the lesser deities, like nymphs, were sometimes regarded as mortal, subject to death after a very long life), but gods and men spoke one and the same tongue, were aware of the same sort of beauty and the same desires, and, above all, gods and men were both in the grip of Fate, and the decrees of Fate were as immutable for Zeus as for the most humble and wretched of men.

Prometheus

There was, however, one myth about the creation of man that in the end gained particular fame in Greek mythology: this was the story of Prometheus. Prometheus and his brother Epimetheus were the sons of the Titan Iapetus. So they were 'cousins' of Zeus. They were an antithetic pair. Prometheus was as clever and farseeing as Epimetheus was blundering and slow-witted. Their mother was a nymph, sometimes called Asia and sometimes Clymene, and she bore Iapetus two other sons, Atlas and Menoetius, who

took part in the war against Zeus and were killed with a thunderbolt and sent down to Tartarus. At first Prometheus and Epimetheus were not on the side of the rebels: they did not fight against Olympus, but at the same time Prometheus did not intend to submit completely to its law. And his independence of the new masters was shown in his relationship with men.

There was a tradition, which gained recognition during the classical period, that claimed that Prometheus fashioned mankind out of clay. But this version of the legend came into existence after Hesiod. In the eyes of this author Prometheus was simply the bene-factor of humans, taking their side against Zeus, a tyrant heedless of mortal happiness. One day, Hesiod recounts, during a sacrifice at Mecone, Prometheus flayed and jointed a bull; in one half of the hide he put the flesh and entrails of the animal, concealing them beneath the stomach; in the other half he put the bones of the bull, hiding them beneath a layer of rich fat. Then he told Zeus to choose between them—what was left being the allotted portion of mankind. Zeus gluttonously chose the fat, but on looking closer saw that he had been tricked, for there were only bones underneath. He flew into a terrible rage, and in his resentment against Prometheus and humanity, who had got the flesh he himself desired, he withheld fire from them by way of punishment. Once again, Prometheus intervened; he went up to Olympus and stole some sparks from the 'wheel of the sun'; then he brought them back to earth, hidden inside a giant fennel (a pithy stalk sometimes used as a kind of tinder). Then the anger of Zeus knew no bounds. He seized Prometheus and chained him to a pillar in the Caucasian mountains; a mon-strous eagle, the issue of Echidna and Typhon, tore at his liver unceasingly, but it always grew whole again, for Prometheus was immortal. A more subtle and severe punishment was invented for humans;

A relief from Tarentum showing the twelve Olympians: Hestia, Hephaestus, Aphrodite, Ares, Demeter. Hermes, Hera. Poseidon, Athena, Zeus, Artemis and Apollo. *Bruckmann*

theirs was irreparable, whereas Prometheus was destined to be freed by Heracles.

Pandora

Zeus planned to punish mortals, and so he asked Hephaestus and Athena to create a new being of great beauty, on whom each of the gods would confer an attribute. The result of the collaboration between Hephaestus and the goddess was the birth of woman. And as she had received gifts from all the gods, she was called Pandora (from two Greek words meaning 'all' and 'gift'). She possessed beauty, grace, manual dexterity and persuasion, but Hermes had also implanted deceit and trickery in her heart. When this was done, Zeus offered her to Epimetheus and asked him if he wished to marry her. Now, before the god made his apparently ingenuous offer, Prometheus had warned his brother about the ruses adopted by Zeus and had forbidden him to accept any present from the god under any circumstances whatsoever. But Epimetheus did not stop to think; charmed by Pandora, he wanted to make her his wife at once, and Pandora came down to earth to live with him. At that time men led happy lives, free from care and ill. All the plagues had been enclosed in a jar by some farsighted god. No sooner had Pandora arrived on earth than she began to pry everywhere, and before long she came upon the jar. Her curiosity was awakened, and she could not resist the temptation of raising the lid, whereupon all the plagues escaped and spread among mankind; in alarm Pandora closed the jar; but one spirit had remained within, and this was Hope, which failed to escape.

Another version relates that the jar was given to Pandora as a wedding present, containing every imaginable good quality. But Pandora carelessly opened the lid, and they all escaped and went back to the abode of the immortals. Only Hope remained among men to be their sad lot, a derisory compensation for their ills.

Deucalion and the flood

There is every indication that this myth is a folk story invented by a misogynic poet, who contrived more or less to connect it with the legend of Prometheus, the demiurge—but it is also found elsewhere, particularly in Thessaly, where Deucalion, son of Prometheus, figures in a story about the creation of humanity.

The story goes that Deucalion married Pyrrha (the red-haired), daughter of Epimetheus and Pandora. At this period the earth was inhabited by a violent and vicious race of men, called by Hesiod 'the men of bronze'. They incurred the anger of Zeus, and he decided to punish them by letting loose a great flood on the earth to drown them. But he decided to spare 'two just people', and these were Deucalion and Pyrrha. On his advice they built an 'ark', a large chest, and got into it. For nine days and nine nights they floated about on the swollen waters, then they came to rest on a mountain in Thessaly. There they disembarked and waited for the waters to recede. Zeus then sent them Hermes, his messenger, to inquire what their wishes were. As the world was deserted Deucalion chose to have companions. Thereupon Zeus commanded Pyrrha and Deucalion to throw over their shoulders 'the bones of their mother'. Such impiety scandalised Pyrrha, but Deucalion realised that the reference was to 'the bones of Mother Earth', and he picked up rocks and threw them behind him. Pyrrha followed his example, and at once men arose from the stones thrown by Deucalion and women from those thrown by Pyrrha. After this Deucalion and Pyrrha lived a long time and produced children in the normal fashion. These children were the ancestors of the different branches

113

of the Hellenic race. Their eldest son bore the name of Hellen, and he himself had three sons called Dorus, Xuthus and Aeolus. The first and last are the ancestors of the Dorians and Aeolians respectively. As for Xuthus, two of his children were Achaeus and Ion, who were the ancestors of the Achaeans and the Ionians. At this point the theogony ends.

The cycle of the great gods

Who were the great gods of Greece? Tradition recognises twelve Olympians, but several other deities whose cults were officially accepted in all the great Hellenic cities may also be included. And that brings us to the only acceptable definition of great deities: those who were the object of a cult in most Greek-speaking states. For this reason they became the object of universally recognised myths, the common patrimony of Greek thought. The majority of these deities were of Indo-European origin, but, as they assimilated several indigenous cults along the way, their myths tended to absorb heterogeneous elements from their surroundings, and these in turn affected the emergent image of each deity. And so local variations arose, which gratified the particularism prevalent in cities and sanctuaries. Thus the Apollo of Delphi was not identical with that of Delos: the two myths are not interchangeable, at times they are even contradictory. All the ingenuity of priests and poets was needed to try to 'impose' a relatively coherent version of the myth, one that all the faithful would find acceptable.

Thus at a fairly early date each deity acquired a cycle of legend of complex origins, in which myths, half-historic traditions and folk inventions were inextricably mingled. The first tended to express the profound religious nature of the god, the second reflected the avatars of his cult, and the last named translated the dreams of an anonymous imagination or the aspirations of popular piety. This complex body of legends relating to the great gods prevented any one trend of theological thought from emerging clearly. Neither the attributes, nor the functions, nor the adventures of the deities led to coherent religious concepts, and any attempt at interpretation—the moderns have proposed very many—may well be suspected of being arbitrary.

The great deities divided the universe among themselves: in each case their power was exercised within a relatively well-defined field. Zeus was obviously god of the sky, light, storm and rain. When it rained the peasants believed that the beneficial water that fertilised their fields came from Zeus. Poseidon reigned over the sea, Hephaestus was the god of fire, and so forth. But, on looking closely, one discovers curious overlapping. In the gigantomachy, for instance, Athena possessed a thunderbolt, as did her father. She was armed with spear and shield like Ares, the god of war. She was also invoked as the patroness of artisans, and in this capacity she resembled

Zeus, the chief god in the Greek pantheon. His wife was his sister, Hera, but he had many love affairs with goddesses and humans in which he used a variety of ingenious disguises. Louvre. *Giraudon*

Hephaestus. He, in turn, as god of fire, was in competition with the Cyclopes, the smiths of Zeus. And one could go on quoting examples. Apollo was considered to be the sun-god, at least from the fifth century B.C. onwards, but he was not identical with Helius, who was the star itself, the sun, adored on the island of Rhodes. Artemis, his sister, was and yet was not Selene (the moon). This accounts for the failure of explanatory theories, which were long in vogue and claimed to deduce the myths relating to each of the gods from a naturalistic principle. Once more it must be confessed that 'myth' is not 'reason', that it is not 'the rational in a lower form', but an autonomous reality, obedient to subtle laws and pure contingencies.

Zeus

Zeus was the master of the gods. The poets were wont to address him also as 'father of men' — but, as we have tried to show, this title was not entirely merited; it applied only to the Zeus of the philosophers, regarded as supreme god, sovereign sculptor of the universe. This was by no means a primitive notion. Zeus was the master of men as Agamemnon was the half-imposed, half-elected king of the Achaeans. In this capacity, he was the guarantor of contracts, oaths, the protector of guests. Social life unfolded beneath his vigilant gaze. At the same time, as we have said, Zeus was god of the sky, the master of celestial fire. From the time of the Homeric poems onwards this was the side of his personality that was most apparent. As 'king' of heaven he exercised a kind of providence; but his will was held in check by the immutable laws of fate, and his role was often limited to making these laws known and respected. Except for this restriction he could govern and follow a policy; his decisions were rarely arbitrary or dictated by passion. They corresponded to hidden intentions, the wisdom of which was ultimately revealed. He was the sovereign dispenser of good and evil to mortals.

In the *Iliad* mention is made of two jars, which stood at the gate of Zeus' palace, one containing good qualities and the other evil features, and usually Zeus drew in turn from each when he created the character of human beings. On occasion he drew exclusively from one or the other jar, and so created the happy and unhappy people in the world.

This concept of Zeus as master of individual destinies, developed from the time of Homer down to that of the philosophers, helped to establish the notion of a divine providence, which was the precursor of the idea of a single god. For the stoics Zeus was the pre-eminent god, identified with the soul of the world; his thoughts were nothing less than eternal laws, and the aim of knowledge for man was quite simply the perception of this divine thought.

The *Theogony* of Hesiod relates the most accepted tradition regarding the birth and childhood of Zeus. But there were others; Arcadia in particular prided itself on having been the cradle of the god. It is easy to deduce that the pan-Hellenic Zeus was formed by absorbing many local 'great gods'. In Crete itself Zeus probably took the place of a vegetation god, since Cretans exhibited a 'tomb of Zeus', and few but vegetation deities were believed to be subject to periodic deaths and rebirths.

The various marriages Zeus made with goddesses have been outlined. His unions with mortal women were, on the other hand, too many to enumerate, and poets have told these tales again and again. The vanity of great families certainly accounted for some increase in their number, for they would pride themselves on having an ancestor who was in direct line of descent from the king of the gods. It was claimed that Zeus was the first ancestor of the Heraclids, since Zeus and Alcmene were the parents of Heracles. Aeacus was also the offspring of Zeus, by the nymph Aegina, the daughter of the river-god Asopus. The story goes that this very beautiful nymph was carried off by Zeus. In fury Asopus searched throughout Greece for his daughter, but failed to find her, until Zeus was eventually betrayed by Sisyphus who wanted Asopus in return to give him a stream for the acropolis of Corinth. Asopus gave him the stream Pirena by way of payment for the information he had received, but both of them were cruelly punished. Asopus was killed by a thunderbolt, and Sisyphus sent to the underworld, where he had to remain for ever, rolling an enormous rock up a steep slope. Zeus took Aegina to the island of Oenone 'Wine island', and she bore him a son, Aeacus. Aeacus in turn married Endeis and had two sons, Telamon, father of Aias (Ajax), and Peleus, father of Achilles.

Io

The love of Zeus for Io was also highly important as far as royal genealogy is concerned. Io was a young girl from Argos, a priestess of the goddess Hera. Versions vary, but according to one interpretation she was the daughter of Iasos, or alternatively the natural daughter of the river-god Inachus. One night Io had a dream. She was ordered by a god to go to the edge of the lake of Lerna and there to allow Zeus to embrace her. Io obeyed after consulting her father, who for his part asked the oracle at Delphi for advice. The god replied that the girl should accept Zeus' love, unless she was prepared to bring celestial wrath upon herself and her family. So Zeus and Io were brought together, but soon Hera suspected what had happened and was jealous. Zeus then turned Io into a superb white heifer, so that she would escape his wife's anger. And he was able to swear calmly to Hera, when she asked him, that he had never loved this animal. Hera was not deceived and asked for it to be handed over to her; then she gave it for safe keeping to a monster, Argos, who had a hundred eyes and closed only fifty of them at any one time.

So began a life of trial and hardship for Io; she journeyed the whole world over, wandering here and there without finding a place of rest; for a long time she stayed near to Mycenae, then in Euboea, and the earth grew the most succulent plants for her. Finally, Zeus took pity on her; he sent Hermes to her, and he put Argos to sleep with a wave of his magic wand and then slew him. But even then Io was not free from torment. Hera sent a gadfly to torment her. In her fury at this Io began to roam wildly. She set off along the sea coasts, which were later called the Ionian Sea after her; then she crossed the straits between Europe and Asia (the Bosporus, or 'passage of the cow'). She spent a long while wandering in Asia, then finally she came to Egypt, where she gave birth to a child, her son by Zeus. Then she was changed into a constellation.

Epaphus, the son of Zeus and Io, was immediately seized by Hera, who placed him in the care of the Curetes; but they were killed by Zeus, and the young man was brought up in Egypt, where he married Memphis, the daughter of Nil, the river-god, who bore him a daughter, Libye. She became the mother, by Poseidon, of two sons, Agenor and Belus, who were the fountainheads of two royal lines, those of Syria and Egypt. A later descendant of the Syrian royal house was Cadmus, the founder of Thebes. The house of Danaus, one of the royal houses of Argos, was similarly connected with the Egyptian throne.

Europa

The alliance between Zeus and the descendants of Io was renewed later. The son of Libye, Agenor, had a daughter called Europa, whom Zeus happened to see one day as she was playing with her companions on the seashore at Sidon (or Tyre). He fell in love with her at once. Disguising himself as a snow-white bull, he came to lie at Europa's feet. The other girls fled, but Europa was quite unafraid; she even ventured to climb on the animal's back. Immediately it got up, entered the water and swam rapidly out to sea. In this way Zeus and his burden reached the island of Crete, where he ravished her beside a spring not far from Gortyn. And the plane-trees that shaded them were granted a concession and thereafter never lost their leaves. Three sons were born to Europa and Zeus—Minos, Sarpedon and Rhadamanthys. Then the god gave her in marriage to the king of Crete, Asterius, who adopted the children. After his death Europa received divine honours and was transformed into a constellation.

The Trojans

Zeus was also the ancestor of the Trojans, and of their adversaries, the Atreids. This is the story of the love of Zeus for Electra, a daughter of Atlas, who bore him a son, Dardanus. Dardanus lived on the island of Samothrace. A flood forced him to leave the island on a raft, and he came to the coast of Asia, where he was received with kindness by King Teucer, the son of the river Scamander and the nymph Ida

Europa, the sister of Cadmus, founder of Thebes, was
abducted by Zeus in the guise of a snow-white bull.

(the deity of Mount Ida). Dardanus married Teucer's daughter and built the citadel of Troy. He was the founder of the line of Trojan kings, and in the fourth generation his descendant was Laomedon, the father of Priam.

Certain amorous episodes in the life of Zeus have become famous because of the strange circumstances in which they were supposed to have happened. The two adventures most frequently recounted in antiquity were unquestionably his unions with Danaë and Leda.

Danae

Danaë was a descendant of a daughter of Danaus, Hypermnestra, the only daughter to refuse to obey her father's command to kill her husband. She had twins, Proetus and Acrisius, by Lynceus, and after a long struggle they finally divided Argolis between them, Proetus reigning at Tiryns and Acrisius in Argos itself. Acrisius had one daughter, Danaë, but he dearly wanted a son. He questioned the oracle, who told him that Danaë might give him a grandson, but the latter would be certain to kill him. To prevent the oracle from being fulfilled, Acrisius built an underground chamber with walls of bronze and imprisoned his daughter there, far from any contact with human beings. But this precaution proved useless. Zeus entered the prison in a shower of gold and seduced Danaë. She gave birth to a boy. But Acrisius refused to believe in the divine origin of the child, and he placed mother and child in a coffer, which he cast into the sea, so that he would not soil his hands with the blood of his own daughter and grandson. Zeus saw to the safety of the improvised boat, which arrived safely on the shores of the island of Seriphos. And later the child, Perseus, accomplished many exploits that proved that he was of divine birth. Heracles, a later hero who performed feats of even more spectacular valour, was one of his descendants.

Leda and the Dioscuri

The love of Zeus for Leda was less dramatic. Leda was the daughter of Thestius, king of Aetolia, and Eurythemis; through Dorus, she was a direct descendant of Deucalion. When Tyndareus was expelled from Lacedaemon by his half-brother Hippocoon and the latter's sons, he took refuge at the court of Thestius, who gave him the hand of his daughter. But Leda aroused the love of Zeus, and he came to her disguised as a swan.

Leda bore two pairs of twins, each pair enclosed in an egg. One of the eggs contained Polydeuces (better known by his Latin name, Pollux) and Clytemnestra; the other, Castor and Helen. Polydeuces and Helen were the offspring of the god, while Clytemnestra and Castor were the children of Tyndareus, who had lain with his wife on the same night as she was visited by Zeus. Castor and Polydeuces, who were called the Dioscuri (*Dios kouroi*, 'sons of Zeus'), had a widespread cult, especially in the Dorian cities.

Leda was wooed by Zeus in the guise of a swan. Two of her children were Castor and Pollux, who, among their other adventures, joined the Argonauts in their search for the Golden Fleece. Uffizi Gallery, Florence. *Mansell*

Because it had been prophesied that the son of Danaë would kill his grandfather, Acrisius, Danae was confined to an underground room. Zeus entered her prison in the guise of a shower of gold, and Perseus was born from this union. (After Harrison and MacColl.)

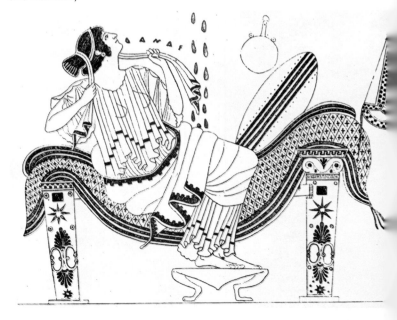

They were depicted as two young athletes, travelling the world on horseback; Castor was pre-eminently a warrior, while Polydeuces was a boxer who liked to fight with a cestus.

Castor and Polydeuces also joined the expedition of the Argonauts, and it was said that Polydeuces distinguished himself in a fight against Amycus, King of the Bebryces, who forced strangers to fight him and then vanquished them and put them to death; but Polydeuces was the victor. The Dioscuri also took part in the hunt at Calydon with Meleager. However, they always remained somewhat apart from the great cycles. They were not involved in the Trojan War, an anomaly that was explained by saying they were engaged elsewhere at the time in a dreadful adventure that cost Castor his life.

This is the dire tale: Tyndareus, the human father of Castor and Polydeuces, had two brothers, Aphareus and Leucippus. Aphareus had two boys, Idas and Lynceus, who were cousins of the Dioscuri, and Leucippus had two daughters, the Leucippides, Phoebe and Hilaeira. Now Idas and Lynceus were to marry the Leucippides, but on their wedding day Castor and Polydeuces, who had been invited, abducted the two girls. This abduction marked the beginning of a long period of hatred between the cousins, and Castor was killed by Idas in an ambush, while Polydeuces killed Lynceus. Idas thus incurred the wrath of Zeus, who killed him with a thunderbolt. Polydeuces was taken to Olympus, where Zeus offered him immortality. But Polydeuces refused to accept it if Castor had to remain in the underworld. Moved by his plea, Zeus allowed them to spend every alternate day together in the underworld and the other days with the gods. Finally, they were both deified and became the constellation of the Twins. They were the originators of Saint Elmo's fire, which sailors regard as a good omen.

Not all the stories about Zeus are of an amorous nature. In the *Iliad* a curious tale is told of a revolt stirred up against him by Hera, Athena, Apollo and Poseidon, who were preparing to put him in chains and thus hold him prisoner. But the goddess Thetis got wind of the plot and summoned the Hecatoncheir Aegaeon (or Briareus) to his aid; the mere sight of the monster was enough to deter the four rebels. On another occasion, when Hephaestus had taken Hera's part in a quarrel with her husband, Zeus seized the god's foot and tossed him into space. In the same way he kept order everywhere, intervening as arbiter among the gods, punishing the major criminals, such as Ixion or Sisyphus. Similarly, he was instrumental in saving Heracles from many a false move, and to a certain extent the hero himself may be regarded as the tool of Zeus, who created him to purge the world of monsters that terrified the human race.

Accepted as the chief of the gods by all the Greeks, Zeus was adored in his sanctuary at Dodona, where he had his oracle. He also presided over the Olympic games, at which the famous statue wrought by Phidias portrayed the god as a terrible 'gatherer of clouds', repository of the secrets of the universe, a harmonious combination of will, power, wisdom and reflection. He was a symbol of virility in the mature man—the ideal point of equilibrium at which the unquenched passions of youth are dominated by the power of reason.

Hera

Hera was the wife of Zeus; she was the last of his divine companions, the daughter of Cronus and Rhea. Her mother entrusted her to Tethys, who brought her up on the very edge of the world in the palace of Oceanus during the struggle between Zeus and the Titans. But Zeus and his sister were said to have had a long betrothal, which dated back to the time when Cronus was still ruling the world. There were numerous and diverse traditions relating to the union of Zeus and Hera. One version, reported by Pausanias, tells how the youthful Hera found a cuckoo stiff with cold on a wintry day and held it to her breast to warm it. Now this bird was none other than Zeus himself, who had disguised himself thus to overcome his sister's refusal to satisfy his desire for her. But Hera did not yield to him until he had promised to make her his legal wife. The story was also told how each year the goddess bathed in a sacred stream at Nauplia, and thus recovered her virginity.

The marriage of Zeus and Hera took on a very great religious significance; as may be imagined, at times it amounted to an act of worship on which the fertility of the world depended. Homer, in Book XIV of the *Iliad*, gives a very human version of this union of the god and goddess, but almost everywhere in Greece rites persisted that were intended to commemorate (or more probably to 'provoke' by magic) their marriage. On these occasions the statue of the goddess was decked in the apparel of a young bride and was carried in procession through the city to a sanctuary where a marriage bed was proffered. This rite was also observed at Alalcomenæ, where it was said to have been invented by the local hero, Alalcomeneus. The latter, it would appear, had heard the goddess's complaints about the perpetual infidelities of Zeus and advised her to have a wooden statue made of herself to be taken in solemn procession as to a true marriage ceremony. Hera followed this advice and won back her husband's love.

A similar legend developed at Plataea. There the hero of the story was the local king, Cithaeron (eponym of the mountain of that name). During his reign, so the story went, Zeus and Hera had been quarrelling; Hera had rejected her husband and escaped to Euboea. Zeus lamented the fact to Cithaeron and was advised to fashion the statue of a woman, and then wrap it in a greatcoat and place it on an ox-drawn cart. When Hera saw this, she was fascinated and asked about it. In accordance with the rumours that King Cithaeron had already spread about it, she was told that Zeus was abducting the daughter of the river-god Asopus to make her his wife. Hera hurried forward, pulled the coat from the statue and saw that she had been teased. She laughed and was reconciled with her husband. A ceremony was held every year at Plataea as a reminder of this event. In this way an old rite based on sympathetic magic received an interpretation acceptable to village folk-lore. Poets usually set the scene of the marriage of Zeus and Hera in the garden of the Hesperides in the far west. Other sources put forward the idea that the golden apples ripening in this garden were a wedding present from Gaea to the goddess, who thought them so beautiful that she planted them in her garden by the sea.

This marriage was blessed with three children, Ares, Eileithyia and Hebe. As for Hephaestus, Hera's fourth infant, his paternity is not usually attributed to Zeus. Hera, the goddess who protected wives and legal marriages, was very jealous of Zeus, whose innumerable infidelities she found hard to forgive, and she was particularly ardent in her hatred and pursuit of the illegitimate children fathered by her husband. Heracles, in particular, was victimised by Hera, and it was due to her that he had to enter Eurystheus' service. Sometimes Zeus punished Hera for her acts of violence. For example, when Heracles was returning to Greece, after taking the city of Troy, the goddess raised a terrible storm to wreck his boat. Zeus in displeasure then literally suspended the goddess from Olympus, having attached an anvil to each of her feet. But once Heracles was made a deity, Hera was solemnly reconciled with him and gave him the hand of her daughter Hebe.

Hera was one of the three goddesses who entered the contest of beauty on Mount Ida in Phrygia. As the shepherd Paris was appointed by Zeus as judge and chose Aphrodite, Hera harboured bitter resentment against Troy. In the course of the Trojan War she favoured the Achaeans, protecting Achilles (whose mother, Thetis, was said to have been brought up by Hera) and conferring immortality on Menelaus.

Hera was the principal goddess of the city of Argos, where she possessed a famous temple. Her emblem was the peacock, and its plumage was considered to be the image of the hundred eyes of Argos, the watcher she had set to guard Io. The goddess was often portrayed with a pomegranate in her hand, the symbol of fertility.

Demeter

Demeter, who took her name from Mother Earth, was one of the generation of children born to Cronus and Rhea. Her name provides a link with the Indo-European deities that the Hellenes brought over with them. But her divine personality was gradually enriched with numerous traits undoubtedly borrowed from pre-Hellenic deities. She was never confused with Earth, Gaea, who was thought of as a cosmic element. Her province was cultivated soil, especially land producing corn. And so her legends proliferated wherever fertile plains dominated the scene, and the chosen grounds for her myths were the plain of Eleusis, not far from Athens, and Sicily, which was for long one of the granaries of the ancient world.

Demeter's first husband was probably Poseidon, at the time when the latter was still the horse-god and had not elected to dwell in the sea. The goddess was said to have disguised herself as a mare to escape his ardour, but Poseidon immediately changed himself into a horse and thus her ruse proved useless. Demeter had two children, a horse, called Arion (who later became the mount of Adrastus at the time of the war of the Seven against Thebes, and later still was the property of Heracles), and then a daughter, who was simply called 'the Mistress' as it was forbidden to use her name. In the *Odyssey* mention is made of other loves of Demeter, for Iasion for instance (brother to Dardanus) by whom she had a son, the god Plutus (Wealth). But Zeus saw the lovers from the heights of heaven and killed Iasion with his thunderbolt in dire displeasure.

By the classical period these myths of Demeter were mere survivals, and most of them had been put together in a single narrative with many episodes, which formed the basis of the religion at the sanctuary of Eleusis, where her mysteries were celebrated.

The abduction of Persephone

Demeter was said to have been one of the wives of Zeus before his marriage with Hera, and she, too, bore him a daughter, called Persephone. The latter grew up happily among the nymphs together with the other daughters of Zeus, Athena and Artemis, and was little concerned about marriage. But her uncle Hades fell in love with her at first sight and immediately carried her off. The scene of this abduction varied according to tradition: sometimes it was said to have been the plain of Enna in Sicily, at other times the plain of Eleusis was cited, or the scene was set in Arcadia or in Crete, each country claiming to have been the theatre of this particular drama.

When Demeter realised that her daughter had disappeared, she called her many times and then travelled the entire earth in search of her. But she naturally failed to find the girl, since Hades had taken her to the underworld. For nine days and nine nights Demeter wandered the earth, without taking food, washing or resting. To light her way she held a torch in each hand. On the tenth day she met Hecate, who had heard the cry uttered by Persephone as she was being carried away, but had not managed to see her abductor, for his head was shrouded in darkness. Only the Sun, who was 'the eye of the world', could tell the stricken mother what she wanted to know. Then, in her anger, Demeter decided to refrain from all activity; she would no longer bless the harvest, and, in short, the whole earth was to be afflicted with sterility until her daughter was restored to her. Demeter disguised herself as an old woman and went to Eleusis. There she sat on a stone, which from that time forth bore the name of 'Stone without joy'. Then she went to the threshold of the king's palace, where, as usual, old women were chattering. One of them, Baubo (or Iambe) took pity on this beggar and offered her soup. But Demeter refused it. Then Baubo in anger (or perhaps to amuse the other women) mockingly raised her skirts. Demeter smiled and accepted the soup.

The goddess entered the house of the queen, Metaneira, to nurse her son, Demophoön, or, according to other versions, Triptolemus, the elder brother of Demophoön. But one night the queen witnessed a strange spectacle; she saw the old woman holding the child by one leg and letting him touch the fire. Metaneira was afraid and let out a cry. Demeter dropped the infant and revealed her own identity. She said she had wanted to make the child immortal by burning away the mortal elements of his body, but the mother, by her interruption, had made the operation impossible. Leaving Demophoön (who was said to have survived), she went back to the sky. Previously she had given Triptolemus, Metaneira's other son, the task of making corn known throughout the world. For this she gave him a chariot drawn by winged dragons, ordering him to fly over the fields scattering seed. Later Triptolemus was to become a judge in the underworld, and he was sometimes depicted with Minos, Aeacus and Rhadamanthys.

However, Demeter's voluntary exile had upset world order to such an extent that Zeus (who had secretly given his consent to the abduction of Persephone) ordered Hades to give the girl back to her mother. Hades replied that this was no longer possible. Anyone who had crossed the threshold of Tartarus could return again only if he had observed certain rules, in particular if he had abstained completely from food during his stay in the underworld. Now Persephone, while walking in the garden of Hades, had eaten a pomegranate seed; she had been seen by Ascalaphus, a son of the nymph of the Styx; Ascalaphus had recounted the incident, and Persephone therefore had to remain in the underworld. Demeter's first reaction was to change Ascalaphus into an owl. Meanwhile she continued to demand the return of her daughter. A compromise had to be reached. If Demeter would go back to her occupation of nurse, Persephone need stay only half the year in the underworld, and the other half she could spend with her mother. And that is why the countryside is sterile during the winter, when Persephone is separated from Demeter, her return being accompanied by the coming of spring.

Hundreds of local episodes became connected with this Eleusian myth about the goddess. Many shrines were said to have been founded because Demeter had visited the spot during her search for her daughter.

Zagreus

Together with Demeter and Persephone a third deity, called Iacchus, figured in the mysteries of Eleusis. Originally Iacchus was the shout uttered by the faithful in the course of religious processions, but his personality developed as time went by, and he assumed the task of leading the processions of initiates. Sometimes he was believed to be a son of Demeter, but usually he was considered to be the reincarnation of Zagreus, a son of Persephone and Zeus, and a central character in the Orphic stories.

The legend of Zagreus is one of the most odd in Greek mythology. In order to beget this child Zeus seems to have disguised himself as a serpent and then ravished Persephone. The god wanted to make Zagreus his heir and eventually confer world royalty upon him. But the Fates decided otherwise. So that he might escape Hera's jealousy, Zeus had entrusted the little child to the care of Apollo and the Curetes, who hid him in the forests of Parnassus. But Hera discovered where he was concealed and ordered the Titans to abduct him. Zagreus changed into a bull, but did not succeed in escaping the Titans, who cut him to pieces and devoured him, half raw, half cooked. Athena and Apollo hastened to the scene of disaster, but they were too late; they could save only scattered pieces of the divine child. But these included the heart of Zagreus, which was still beating. Zeus absorbed it and regenerated the child within his own body, and he then took the name of Iacchus. After this he became more or less confused with Dionysus and figured in the mysteries of Eleusis. His previous fate made him ready to act as patron to any religion of rebirth and immortality, for in the Titans' banquet he had lost the whole of his mortal self and in its place obtained divine life.

Apollo

Although Apollo did not appear until the second generation of Olympians, he was the son of Zeus and Leto and was one of the greatest gods in the Hellenic pantheon. Myths concerning him originated in all parts of Greece, and political as well as spiritual life was dominated by his vigorous personality. He certainly represented an amalgam of several deities from every known branch of Hellenism. There was a Dorian Apollo, brought across by the Indo-European invaders, and there is good reason to believe that another Apollo came into Greece via Hittite culture and appeared as an Oriental before he merged with the Dorian god. This double image of the god was reflected in the fact that there were two sanctuaries of Apollo, at Delphi and Delos. It also undoubtedly accounts for the great favour that the god enjoyed among the Greeks in Asia Minor as well as among those on the continent. But in the form in which Apollo's myths are known to us, they had already merged sufficiently for one to speak of a single body of myth on the subject of Apollo.

Corinthian goddesses, possibly Demeter and Persephone. c. 620 B.C. *British Museum*

Persephone (Kore), daughter of Demeter, was abducted by Hades, who made her queen of the underworld. She was permitted by Zeus to spend half the year with her mother, and her return to earth heralded the coming of spring. 480 B.C. Eleusis Museum. *Mansell*

An archaic bronze statuette of Apollo. Seventh century B.C. *Courtesy Museum of Fine Arts, Boston*

Apollo, god of music and medicine (one of his original attributes, which he yielded to his favourite son Asclepius who became solely identified with the science) and Artemis, the huntress-goddess, were twin children of Zeus and Leto. Delos, where they were born, was thereafter sacred to Apollo. Red-figured lekythos, by the Villa Giulia painter. *Ashmolean Museum, Oxford*

Zeus, then, had ravished Leto, and the goddess was about to give birth to his children. But Hera in her jealousy had forbidden Leto to take shelter anywhere on earth. The wretched goddess wandered without ceasing until she was welcomed on a floating island, barren and rocky, called Ortygia (Quail Island) or Asteria, which was so poor a place that it had nothing to fear from Hera. There the children of Zeus were born, first Artemis, then Apollo. In gratitude the god marked the island as the centre of the Greek world and gave it the name of Delos, 'the Brilliant'.

When Apollo came into the world, sacred swans circled the island seven times, for it was the seventh day of the month. Zeus immediately showered gifts upon his son: he gave him a golden mitre, a chariot drawn by swans, and a lyre. And he commanded him to go to Delphi to found his sanctuary there. But, before taking Apollo to Delphi, the swans flew north with him to their own country on the edge of the ocean: that was where the Hyperborean people lived, a supremely happy race for whom life was sweet. When the old people eventually became weary of existence, they accepted voluntary death by throwing themselves into the sea. Apollo was their high god; there he went at fixed times to receive their homage. So, after his birth, he remained there a whole year; then he came back to Greece and reached Delphi in midsummer. Nature had made herself beautiful for him. Each year the arrival of the god was celebrated with solemn ceremony and great slaughter.

When the god first arrived, the site of Delphi was occupied by a monstrous dragon, the guardian of an ancient oracle of Themis. Its name was Python, and it was given to raiding the surrounding countryside. Apollo slew it with his arrows. But, to appease its divine shades after death, he founded expiatory games in its honour (these became the Pythic games, the great games of Delphi), and he decided to perpetuate the oracle by adopting it himself. In token of this decision one of his own emblems, a stool, was consecrated in the sanctuary at Delphi. In addition, he instituted a priesthood and decided that a priestess called Pythia would tell his prophecies seated on the holy stool. Then Apollo went to Thessaly in the valley of Tempe to purify himself after the murder of the dragon. From this time onwards a festival was celebrated at Delphi once every eight years to commemorate the death of Python and the purification of Apollo.

However, the god's reign at Delphi met with some resistance. He had to defend his privilege against Heracles, who, so the story goes, came to consult the oracle, and, when the priestess refused to answer him, made to seize the stool so as to found an oracle of his own elsewhere. Apollo came to the aid of the Pythia and fought Heracles for possession of the stool. But Zeus intervened and made peace between his two sons by hurling a thunderbolt between them. And the oracle remained at Delphi.

The loves of Apollo

Apollo was portrayed as a beautiful youth with long, blue-tinged curls, and naturally his name was quoted in connection with many amorous adventures. On one occasion he fell in love with the nymph Daphne, a daughter of the river Peneius in Thessaly; but Daphne would not give herself to him and fled into the mountains. Apollo pursued her and was about to overtake her when Daphne begged her father to save her. She was changed into a laurel-tree, which afterwards became Apollo's tree and emblem.

Apollo also loved the nymph Cyrene, on whom he fathered the demi-god Aristaeus. As musician and god of the lyre, he directed the choir of the Muses, and, inevitably, adventures with them were imputed to him. On Thalia he fathered the Corybantes, turbulent demons rather like the Curetes. On Urania he fathered Linus and Orpheus, two famous musicians.

Asclepius

The birth of Apollo's favourite son, Asclepius, the god of medicine (whom the Romans called Aesculapius) was heralded by a dramatic adventure. Apollo had loved Coronis, the daughter of Phlegyas, the the king of Thessaly, and she was with child by him. But even before its birth Coronis had yielded to a mortal, Ischys, the son of Elatus. Apollo was told of the infidelity of his mistress by a raven (who as a result of this indiscretion was changed from her original white to the now familiar black). In his anger the god killed Coronis; then, just as her body on the pyre was about to be consumed by flames, he drew the living child from her corpse. This child, Asclepius, was taken by his father to Chiron, the centaur, who taught him medicine.

Asclepius soon made great progress and even discovered means of raising the dead. For this purpose Athena had given him blood from Medusa's wounds. The blood from the veins on her left side was a strong poison, but that which flowed from her right side could bring the dead back to life. Asclepius put his knowledge to liberal use, to the extent of occasioning complaints from Hades; this made Zeus afraid lest the art of Asclepius should upset world order, and so he killed the god of medicine with his thunderbolt. Apollo was seized with violent rage, and, taking his arrows, he killed the Cyclopes who had forged Zeus' thunderbolt.

Zeus considered punishing this crime by sending Apollo to Tartarus, but, on Leto's request, he consented to ease the punishment, and instead he ordered his son to become the slave of a mortal for one year. Apollo then went to Thessaly, where he served as herdsman to King Admetus.

Apollo had another adventure, which, although it did not end as tragically as his love for Coronis, none the less showed the god in a similar predicament. Apollo loved Marpessa, the daughter of the king of

Aetolia, Evenus. But she was abducted by Idas, the son of Aphareus, in a winged chariot that Poseidon had given to the young man. Apollo set off in pursuit of them and caught up with them at Messenia. The two rivals began to fight for the girl, but here again Zeus intervened and separated them, giving Marpessa the right to choose whom she preferred. Marpessa chose Idas, the mortal, and gave as her reason that she was afraid of choosing the god lest he should abandon her when she was old and ugly.

With Cassandra, one of the daughters of Priam, Apollo was no more fortunate. He was in love with her, and in his endeavour to seduce her he promised to teach her the art of divination. Cassandra agreed to these lessons, but when she felt she had learned enough she then refused to yield to the god. He was outraged and yet quite incapable of depriving her of the newly acquired knowledge, but he did at least take from her the power to make others believe what she said. So Cassandra prophesied accurately, but in vain, for there was no-one who trusted her word. But tradition states that though Cassandra herself may have rejected the god, he nevertheless obtained the favours of Hecuba, wife of Priam and mother of Cassandra, who bore him a son, the young Troilus.

Hyacinthus and Cyparissus

Apollo also loved young boys, in accordance with a time-honoured custom among the Dorian people. His adventures with Hyacinthus and Cyparissus, however, did not end happily. The former was a young Lacedaemonian prince of great beauty, and Apollo fell in love with him. One day when they were both throwing the discus in the gymnasium, either the wind caught the projectile or else it hit a rock and rebounded to strike Hyacinthus on the head and kill him. Apollo was distraught; to make his friend immortal he transformed his body into a flower, the hyacinth, and its petals were said to be marked with the initial of Hyacinthus' name.

The legend of Cyparissus resembled the previous one quite closely. He was the son of Telephus, who was himself the son of Heracles, and he became the object of Apollo's love. His favourite companion was a magnificent stag, which followed him everywhere. But one summer day, when the stag was asleep in the shade, Cyparissus unintentionally struck it with his javelin and killed it. In his despair the young man longed for death. So Apollo transformed him into a cypress, which became a symbol of sadness.

Apollo was obviously not unconnected with the spirits of vegetation. It is all the more remarkable that he was sometimes regarded as a pastoral god. His period in the service of Admetus has been mentioned. There he watched over the herds and made the cows calve twice a year. On another occasion, after Poseidon, Hera, Athena and Apollo himself had conspired against Zeus, he was sentenced to slavery, together with Poseidon, and was sent to Laomedon, king of Troy. While Poseidon built the city wall, Apollo watched over their master's herds on Mount Ida. Apollo was said to enjoy watching herds — especially those that young Hermes stole from him when Hermes was still in his cradle.

Perhaps his pastoral activities were not unconnected with one of his principal functions, that of god of music. Apollo liked to prophesy in verse, and he was the god invoked by poets. But he was also a terrifying god, a pitiless archer who inflicted rapid death. He was the god of epidemics — as indicated by the one that he inflicted on the Achaean army at the beginning of the *Iliad*, and with his sister Artemis he took part in the murder of the children of Niobe. Certain animals, such as the wolf, the squirrel and the doe, were specially dedicated to Apollo, also certain types of birds, such as the swan, kite and crow, as well as a sea-animal, the dolphin, whose name in Greek, *delphis*, recalls that of the sanctuary at Delphi.

Artemis

Artemis was the sister of Apollo, and like him she was born at Delos. As soon as she was born, she used her skill in midwifery to help her mother, Leto, who was about to give birth to a second child, Apollo. Although a virgin she was the protectress of women in labour, and they frequently called upon her in dire distress, since she could, with her arrows, send them to a swift death. Deaths in childbirth were attributed to her.

She was a huntress and travelled the woods, happy in the company of dogs, wild animals and mountain nymphs. She it was who brought about Orion's death, that unfortunate hunter, who either insolently defied the goddess in a discus contest, or else tried to seduce one of her companions, the virgin Opis, or perhaps attempted to ravish her in person. Artemis sent a scorpion to sting his heel, and thus killed him. But when Orion was subsequently turned into a constellation, Artemis made sure that the scorpion received the same honour.

Another hunter, Actaeon, met his death because of the curse of the goddess. Actaeon was the son of Aristaeus and, on his father's side, the grandson of Apollo. One day, when out hunting with his dogs in the mountains, he came across the goddess bathing naked in a stream. The goddess turned him into a stag, and the young man's dogs, no longer recognising their master, threw themselves upon him and tore him to pieces.

Oeneus, the king of Calydon, once forgot to sacrifice his first crops to Artemis, as custom dictated. This provoked her wrath, and she sent a monstrous boar to ravage his fields; a great hunt had to be organised and in it the hero Meleager lost his life. The same theme appeared again in the legend of Agamemnon. One day, while waiting at Aulis with the entire Achaean army for favourable winds to set sail for Troy, he happened to kill a stag so expertly that

Gold ear-ring showing Artemis, the huntress-goddess, grasping two lions. From Camirus, Rhodes. Late seventh century B.C. *Ashmolean Museum, Oxford*

In the legend of Actaeon, the hunter surprised the goddess Artemis bathing. She changed him into a stag and he was torn to pieces by his dogs. Actaeon was a sacred king of the pre-Hellenic stag cult, who was torn to pieces after his fifty months' reign. Palermo Museum. *Anderson*

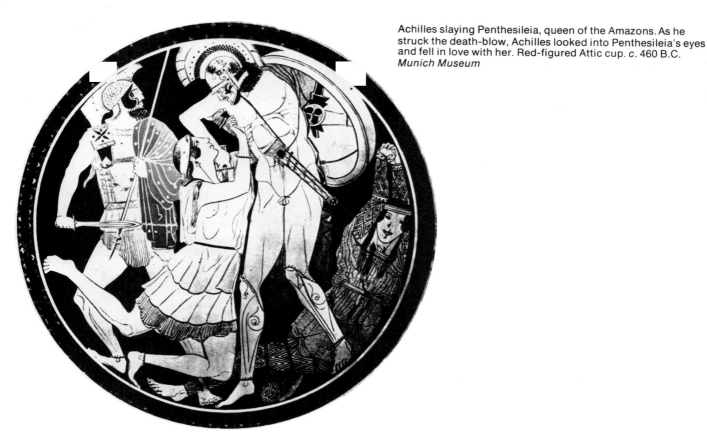

Achilles slaying Penthesileia, queen of the Amazons. As he struck the death-blow, Achilles looked into Penthesileia's eyes and fell in love with her. Red-figured Attic cup. *c.* 460 B.C. *Munich Museum*

he cried: 'Artemis herself could have done no better.' Artemis resented this and becalmed the whole fleet. Teiresias, the soothsayer, discovered the cause of this setback, and told Agamemnon that the goddess required him to sacrifice Iphigeneia, his own daughter, and in return she would remove the difficulties in his path. But at the last moment, on the sacrificial altar itself, she substituted a hind in place of Iphigeneia and took the girl to the country of the Tauri (Crimea), where she made her a priestess of the cult practised there in her honour.

Niobe

Another famous anecdote tells how Artemis took revenge on the children of Niobe. Niobe was the daughter of Tantalus, and she had borne Amphion of Thebes seven sons and seven daughters. In her happiness and pride she said one day that she was better than Leto, who had but one son and one daughter. Leto took offence and asked her children to punish the insolent mother. Apollo killed the seven boys with his arrows, and Artemis likewise slew the seven girls. Niobe in despair fled to her father on Mount Siplyon in Asia Minor and was turned into a rock; from the rock issued a stream formed by her ceaseless tears.

The Amazons

In Asia Minor Artemis was the object of a cult very different from that of the mainland. A sanctuary was dedicated to her at Ephesus, where her temple was regarded as one of the seven wonders of the world. Sometimes it was said to be the work of the Amazons, a race of warlike women who lived, so the story went, beside the river Thermodon. The Amazons refused to acknowledge the existence of men except in the capacity of servile workers; according to some traditions they mutilated their male children or even

killed them, and ensured the continuation of their race by chance contact with strangers. As for their daughters, each had her right breast burned off so that she could handle bow or lance more easily. The principal passion of the Amazons was war. They fought against several Greek heroes: Bellerophon, Heracles, Theseus and even Achilles (for the Amazons sent a contingent against Troy, under the leadership of their queen, Penthesileia, who appears to have met her death at the hand of Achilles, and, with her dying glance, inspired inexpressible love in her slayer). Artemis the virgin huntress was naturally the patron of the Amazons. On the other hand, Artemis of Ephesus seems to have been a fertility goddess—Mistress of the Wild Beasts, as she was known throughout the eastern Mediterranean before the arrival of the Greeks.

Hermes

Hermes, also, was a son of Zeus. His mother was Maia, the youngest of the Pleiades. He was born in a cave on Mount Cyllene in Arcadia. From the moment his life began his inventiveness was apparent. Following the usual custom, his mother wrapped the newborn child in swaddling-clothes and put him in a winnowing basket, which served as a cradle. Then she went away. But the child managed to wriggle and loosen his wrappings, and he set off for Thessaly where his brother Apollo was watching over the herds of Admetus. At that time Apollo was in love with a local youth, and while he neglected his herds, Hermes stole from him twelve cows and a hundred heifers. Then he fastened a leafy branch to the tail of each animal and went on his way to Cyllene. When he got back to the cave where he was born, he discovered a tortoise there. From this he detached the shell and stretched over it cords made from the intestines of sacrificial bulls; this was the first lyre.

Hermes speeding across the waves carrying the lyre, which he invented, and the caduceus Apollo gave him. Red-figured cup. *British Museum*

Hephaestus, the god of fire and of the forge, was the son of Hera and husband of Aphrodite. 400–350 B.C. *British Museum*

Opposite: Terracotta goddess or female votary. Marble. Probably early Minoan. Cnossus. Fitzwilliam Museum.

Meanwhile Apollo was looking everywhere for his animals. Thanks to his powers of divination he soon knew the whole story, and complained to Maia on Mount Cyllene. But she simply pointed to young Hermes carefully wrapped in his swaddling-clothes. Apollo had recourse to Zeus, who commanded Hermes to return his brother's property. However, Apollo had by then seen the lyre in the grotto on Cyllene and heard the strains that Hermes drew from it and he exchanged his herd for the instrument.

Shortly after this Hermes invented the pipes of Pan, which Apollo bought from him; in exchange he gave him the golden rod that he had used in minding his cattle. This is the origin of the caduceus, Hermes' particular emblem. Zeus was so charmed by the young god's exploits that he made him his herald. That is why Hermes acted as messenger to the gods, and his special task was to conduct the souls of the dead to the underworld. Hermes protected travellers, merchants and thieves. Perhaps in the beginning he was simply the spirit of the piles of stone placed along the roadside as landmarks. Then his personality developed, incorporating other deities, notably a shepherd-god from the Arcadian mountains and also a god who protected markets and village squares. That is why he was the patron of both merchants and orators and also, curious though this may seem, the god of the palaestra (wrestling-school). Perhaps this last function derived from the fact that he was the bringer of luck.

The loves of Hermes

Several amorous adventures were imputed to this god. He fathered a son on Chione, and Autolycus, as he was called, showed a particular gift for stealing whatever he wanted without being discovered. He also took part in the Argonauts' expedition. Autolycus tricked his own daughter Anticleia into a union with Sisyphus at the same time as he gave her in marriage to Laertes. This is why Odysseus, the official son of Laertes and Anticleia, was sometimes regarded as the son of Sisyphus, another known for knavish tricks.

At Athens Hermes was thought to have loved Herse, one of the daughters of Cecrops, and she bore him the hero Cephalus; and he was also said to have fathered on Aglauros, another daughter of Cecrops, a son named Ceryx, the herald and first high priest of Eleusis. This same place, Eleusis, was the scene of another adventure, which Hermes shared with Deianeira (a name that seems to be a ritual epithet for Persephone), and which resulted in the birth of the eponymous hero, Eleusis himself. An obscure tradition also cited him as the father of the god Pan, borne him by Penelope, either when she was unfaithful to Odysseus or before her marriage to the latter.

Usually, Hermes was simply the interpreter of divine will. He bestowed arms on heroes—for example, when he gave Perseus the helmet of Hades, and Phrixus and Helle the ram with the golden fleece,

which was to carry them through the air. Zeus commissioned him to kill Argos, Io's gaoler, and to accompany the three goddesses to the contest of beauty on Mount Ida. Zeus was, moreover, indebted to him for his victory over Typhoeus, and Ares owed his freedom to him.

Hephaestus

Hephaestus was the god of fire—not, like Hestia, the deity of the domestic fire and hearth (for she remained an eternal virgin, the image of family stability, and for this reason entirely devoid of myth)—but the fire of the forge, the creative flame, which is the foundation for all metal work; and undoubtedly at first he was not very different from the innumerable spirits of metallurgy and mines found in different corners of the Hellenic world; for instance, the Dactyls of Ida, the Cabeiri of Samothrace, perhaps even the Telchines of Rhodes, and also, of course, the Cyclopes, who forged the first thunderbolt.

The birth of Hephaestus has already been described, also the story of his ejection from Olympus at the hands of Zeus, after which he came down to the island of Lemnos; as a result of this adventure Hephaestus was lame and so incurred the hatred of his mother, Hera. Another version claimed that the god was lame from birth, and that Hera herself chased him from the sky. In his desire to have his revenge on her, he secretly made a gold throne, which held prisoner anyone who sat on it. This he sent to his mother, who was held captive by it. Before he would consent to free her, he demanded a place on Olympus, and obtained his seat among the gods.

He was also portrayed as one of the combatants of the gigantomachy, and killed the giant Clytius with a branding iron. He also appeared at the time of the Trojan war with flame and fire. But he did not scorn to work with his hands, and Thetis requested him to make armour for Achilles. He had his workshop in the volcanoes, and there he was aided by the Cyclopes.

Curiously enough, this luckless creature was said to have won the favours of the most beautiful goddesses: Aglaia, the youngest of the Graces, and Charis (grace personified). He was married to Aphrodite, but she was unfaithful to him with Ares. The adventure was told in the *Odyssey* as follows: Aphrodite had become the mistress of Ares, and so the Sun, who can see everything, reported it to Hephaestus, who decided to have his revenge. He placed an invisible net around his wife's bed, which closed over the guilty pair and made them completely helpless. Then Hephaestus invited all the gods to come and see them. As soon as she was freed Aphrodite fled, while the gods gave themselves up to helpless laughter.

Hephaestus had several sons, including the Argonaut Palaemon, the legendary Ardalus and also the brigand Periphetes, who was killed by Theseus.

The Parthenon, dedicated to Athena Parthenos (Athena the Virgin), was built at the instigation of Pericles and under the supervision of Phidias. Begun in 447 B.C., the building was completed in 438 B.C., and enriched with carvings and statuary. *Roger Viollet*

Athena

Athena was another daughter of Zeus, and, like Artemis, she was committed to eternal chastity. Metis, her mother, was said to have been swallowed by Zeus, and then to have given birth to this daughter. Again like Artemis, Athena was a fierce warrior and enjoyed the clash of arms. But instead of a bow she carried a lance, and wore a goatskin breastplate (the aegis). So it is not surprising to find that she took part in the war against the giants; she even killed Pallas and Enceladus with her own hands. The *Iliad* says she fought on the side of the Greeks—perhaps because Paris chose Aphrodite in preference to herself in the contest of beauty between the three goddesses. She also helped Heracles and gave him arms. She was Odysseus' self-appointed protectress, and constantly intervened in the *Odyssey* to get him out of his endless difficulties. She was not so much a goddess of violence as a deity of resolute courage, and she was guided and enlightened by reason. She was said to have invented the war-chariot, and ships too, since she presided over the building of the *Argo*. But she was no less skilled in the arts of peace—as is shown in the story of a famous quarrel which brought her into conflict with Poseidon.

The quarrel arose because both claimed to be patron of Attica. The gods were called on to be arbiters, and they decided that the country should belong to the god who gave it the finest gift. Striking the earth with his trident, Poseidon brought forth a salt spring. But Athena simply planted an olive-tree, and all the gods judged that the olive, tree of peace and long patience, was preferable to the murky stream, and granted Athena the patronage of Attica.

Erichthonius

Another very strange myth spoke of Athena in connection with the Acropolis of Athens. Athena wished to remain a virgin, but she could not prevent Hephaestus falling in love with her one day when she visited him in his forge. She fled from him, but Hephaestus set off in pursuit, and, although he was lame, he caught up with her on the Acropolis of Athens and took her in his arms. Athena defended herself, but in his desire the god brushed against her. In disgust she rubbed herself with a piece of cloth and threw it on the ground. The earth was thus fertilised and produced Erichthonius, whom the goddess accepted and regarded as her own son with a curious tenderness. She enclosed him in a chest, so as to bring him up without the knowledge of the other gods, and entrusted the chest to the three daughters of Cecrops, king of Athens. But Aglauros, one of the three daughters, could not contain her curiosity and opened the basket. What she saw filled her with terror: the little child, guarded by two serpents, appeared to her so terrible that she went mad and hurled herself from the top of the rocks on the Acropolis. Athena herself brought up the child at her sanctuary in Athens, and later King Cecrops handed over to him his royal powers. Erichthonius was the founder of that dynasty of kings of Attica from which Theseus was descended.

The Palladium

The epithet Pallas, which often preceded the goddess' name, probably means 'young girl' but this epithet was misunderstood and so gave rise to another myth. It was said that the young goddess had been entrusted by her father to the god Triton, who brought her up with his own daughter, who was called Pallas. The two children both practised the arts of war, and Athena accidentally wounded and killed her friend. To make amends for this Athena made a statue in her likeness and called it the Palladium, and meanwhile she herself took the name of

Athena, goddess of war and wisdom, was the protectress of Athens. Her name indicates that she was of pre-Hellenic origin. Athens Museum. *Alinari*

the dead girl. The Palladium was placed on Olympus by Zeus, where it remained for a long time. But one day Zeus tried to violate the goddess Electra, one of the Pleiades, and when Electra took refuge near the Palladium Zeus threw it from the heights of Olympus. The statue fell near Troy, at the time when the city was being founded. So the statue from the sky was placed in the temple of Athena, which was under construction on the citadel, and this fetish was regarded as a pledge of the city's safety. Later the Palladium was stolen by Odysseus with Diomedes' help. But traditions differ greatly as to the later fate of the miraculous statue; traces of it were found in Arcadia, Samothrace, Argos, Athens and even in Italy, where it would appear to have been taken by Diomedes, or even by Aeneas himself, and finally it would seem to have found its place among the household gods of the Roman people, in the sanctuary of Vesta. This archaic type of statue (it is a *xoanon*, a wooden idol, showing the goddess stiff and upright) perhaps goes back to a pre-Hellenic cult, like many of the characteristics of Athena herself.

Arachne

Athena presided over the activities of women artisans; she was the patron of spinners, weavers and embroiderers. A story was told about Athena and Arachne, the Lydian daughter of Idmon of Colophon, a dyer. Arachne was exceptionally skilled at weaving and embroidery and was said to have been the pupil of Athena, though this displeased the girl, who claimed that she owed her skill to herself alone. She went so far as to challenge the goddess to a competition and Athena accepted, but appeared first in the guise of an old woman and invited the presumptuous creature to be more modest. Arachne's only reply was to insult the goddess further, so the latter revealed who she was and the contest began. Arachne's tapestry was perfect; and Athena was roused to such wild passion that she destroyed her rival's work. Then the goddess struck the girl with her shuttle, and Arachne was immediately changed into a spider. Athena's wrath was, in fact, well known and this was not the only story revealing that side of her nature.

Aphrodite

In Hesiod's *Theogony* Aphrodite rose from the sea when it was made fertile by the blood of Uranus. In spite of these early origins she was not to be found in the most ancient Greek pantheon, although her birth preceded that of Zeus. She was an Oriental who entered the Hellenic world by way of Cyprus, where she had her principal sanctuary at Paphos. From there she went to Cythera, before settling in Corinth.

Aphrodite was the goddess of the act of love. She was portrayed, according to the period, as a naked or a draped figure, holding in her hand a dove, her favourite bird. Around her were her servants, especially the Graces and the Horae, who were

seen together in her retinue, particularly from the Hellenistic period onwards. She was depicted as floating on the sea surrounded by nereids and all the minor deities embodying grace.

Aphrodite was naturally the heroine of numerous love stories. Her guilty passion for Ares has been mentioned. Their love resulted in the birth of several deities: Eros (Love) and Anteros (Reciprocal or Answering Love), Deimus and Phobus (Terror and Fear), and also Harmonia, who was later to become the wife of Cadmus of Thebes.

Adonis

From her early Oriental period Aphrodite retained another lover, the Syrian god Adonis, who was adopted by Greek mythology. His myth was usually told as follows: the king of Syria, Theias, had a daughter called Myrrha or Smyrna, who was cursed by Aphrodite and forced to commit incest with her father; with the complicity of her nurse she succeeded in deceiving him for eleven nights, but on the twelfth Theias discovered who she was and prepared to kill her. Myrrha fled, and the gods, taking pity on her, turned her into a tree, the myrrh-tree. Ten months later the bark peeled off and an infant emerged and was given the name of Adonis. Aphrodite was moved by the beauty of this child, and she took it and gave it to Persephone to bring up. But Persephone became infatuated with the beautiful child and refused to give him back to Aphrodite. The arbiter in the dispute between the two goddesses was Zeus, and it was decided that the young Adonis should live a third of the year with Aphrodite, a third with Persephone and a third with whichever he pleased. Adonis preferred to spend two-thirds of the year with Aphrodite, and only one-third of it in the underworld.

Some years later, when Adonis was out hunting, a boar, sent to harm him either by Artemis (it is not really known why) or by Ares (who was jealous of the young man), gored the youth in the thigh and killed him. As Aphrodite hastened to his aid she scratched her foot on a thorn, and the rose, which until that moment had always been white, became a deep red. From the blood of Adonis rose the anemone flower, which is so often seen in spring in the eastern Mediterranean lands.

In honour of Adonis Aphrodite founded a funeral cult, which was celebrated each spring by Syrian women, and it then spread throughout the ancient world. Seed was planted in vases and watered with warm water; these plants sprouted quickly, but died soon: they were known as 'gardens of Adonis'.

Anchises and Aeneas

On one occasion Aphrodite was seized with a violent passion for Anchises, a Trojan prince who looked after his herds on Ida. She wished him to fall in love with her, and so she came to him, claiming to be the

Aphrodite, the goddess of love, beauty and fertility. Probably of non-Hellenic origin, she became popular throughout Greece. Bronze. *c.* 200 B.C. British Museum. *Edwin Smith* in *Art Treasures of the British Museum (Thames and Hudson)*

daughter of the king of Phrygia, and to have been abducted and left on the mountainside by Hermes. Anchises was troubled by her beauty and lay with her. Then she revealed who she really was and told him that she would bear him a son who would have a very great destiny. This son was Aeneas. She forbade Anchises to say anything to anyone of their love, but one feast-day, after much wine, Anchises could keep his secret no longer. So Zeus punished him, either, according to some, by making him lame or, alternatively, by depriving him of his sight.

Paris

The famous contest of beauty also took place on Ida, and it was destined to spark off the Trojan war. One day, Discord (Eris) threw an apple on to Olympus during an assembly of the gods. It was to be given 'to the most beautiful'. Three goddesses laid claim to this title. Zeus had them taken by Hermes to the mountain near Troy where one of the sons of Priam, Paris, was watching over his herds. Each goddess tried to persuade the judge to decide in her favour. Hera offered to make him lord of Asia, Athene to make him invincible in war; Aphrodite for her part promised him only the hand of Helen. Paris awarded the apple to Aphrodite. It was also stated that she removed her clothing to show the young man the perfection of her form. So Aphrodite was, in a way, responsible for the Trojan war; and throughout the siege of the city she protected Paris, saving him from danger during his duel with Menelaus. She also saved Aeneas when Diomedes was about to kill him. After the fall of Troy she made certain of the survival of the Trojan race by permitting Aeneas to escape, carrying Anchises on his back.

Although Aphrodite's protection could be effective, her rages and curses were renowned. She inspired in Eos (Dawn) an insurmountable love for Orion. She chastised the women of Lemnos, who failed to worship her, by sending an unbearable smell to plague them. Finally, she forced the daughters of King Cinyras of Paphos to give themselves to strangers. Philosophers gave much thought to the nature of Aphrodite, and like Plato they made a distinction between two aspects of the goddess, one Uranian, 'celestial', as the goddess of pure love, and the other Pandemian, or 'popular', as the goddess who presided over ordinary love affairs.

Ares

Ares, god of war and lover of Aphrodite, was the son of Zeus and Hera. From the time of the Homeric epic onwards, he appeared as the spirit of carnage. In the Trojan war he helped the Trojans, but did not refuse aid to the Greeks either, since his only real interest was to fight. On the battlefield he was accompanied by secondary spirits, Deimus and Phobus (Terror and Fear), who were his sons, and by Enyo with the bloodstained face.

Hermes brings three goddesses — Hera, Athena and Aphrodite — to Paris, son of King Priam of Troy, to judge which is the most beautiful. Aphrodite promises him the hand of Helen, wife of Menelaus of Sparta, and wins the contest.

An incised bronze mirror-cover shows Aphrodite, the goddess of love and beauty, playing dice with Pan, an ancient Arcadian god, who is shown as half man and half goat. Fourth century B.C. *British Museum*

Ares was thought to prefer Thrace as his country of residence, for it was a horsebreeding country traversed by warring peoples. Some traditions made him the father of the Amazons, with Harmonia as their mother. His legend was also found at Thebes. He was said to possess a stream on the Cadmea, the citadel of the town, and this stream was guarded by a dragon whom he had fathered. When Cadmus came to found the town, the dragon denied him access to the stream, but Cadmus killed it and, to expiate this murder, he had to serve as Ares' slave for eight months. However, when this period had expired, the gods married Cadmus to Harmonia, his daughter of Aphrodite.

The misfortunes of Ares

Although he was god of war, Ares was not invincible on the field of battle. At Troy Diomedes inflicted a wound on him with the aid of Athena, and Ares escaped to Olympus where Zeus had his wound tended. On another occasion, when Heracles fought Cycnus, one of the sons of Ares, the latter refused to accept the fate awaiting his son — that he would be killed by Heracles — and joined the fight himself, only to be wounded in the thigh by Heracles and forced to leave the battlefield. Ares in his brute strength was often victim of his own lack of judgment. When the Amazon Penthesileia, his daughter, was killed at Troy by Achilles, Ares hastened to avenge her, but failed to take into account the will of the Fates, so Zeus used his thunderbolt to intervene.

The hill of the Areopagus in Athens owed its name to one of the god's misadventures. There was a stream at the foot of the hill. There, one day, Ares caught sight of Halirrhothius, the son of Poseidon and the nymph Euryte, as he was attempting to ravish Alcippe, a daughter Ares had fathered on Aglauros. Ares hurried forward to protect his daughter and killed

Ares, the god of war, was the son of Zeus and Hera. Unlike Athena, who represented courage and honour in war, Ares was a bloodthirsty god who delighted in slaughter. However, this marble statue from the Museo delle Terme, Rome, shows him in a gentler aspect with Eros playing at his feet. *Mansell*

Athena and Poseidon competed for the patronage of Athens. Poseidon caused a salt spring to issue from a rock, but Athena produced an olive-tree and so became protectress of the city. From an amphora by Amasis. Cabinet des Médailles, Paris.

Halirrhothius. But Poseidon made him appear before a tribunal, consisting of all the Olympians, on the very hill at the foot of which the murder had taken place. The gods acquitted Ares. In memory of this event a very ancient tribunal used to be convened at Athens on the Areopagus or 'hill of Ares' and it originally sat in judgment on all murderers and, ultimately, on all crimes of a religious nature.

Ares loved many women. Apart from his famous adventure with Aphrodite, he loved many mortals and had children by them. These usually turned out to be men of violence and attacked travellers. In this way he begot three sons on Pyrene—Cycnus, Diomedes the Thracian and Lycaon. All three were eventually killed by Heracles. He was also the father of Oenomaus, the king of Pisa in the region of Elis, whose story is connected with the institution of the Olympic Games. Oenomaus had a daughter, Hippodameia, whose hand he systematically refused to the numerous suitors who presented themselves. Anyone who asked to marry Hippodameia had to engage in a chariot race against him. Oenomaus was the constant victor, for his horses had been given him by Ares and were divine. Then he would kill his unhappy rival and nail his head to the gate of his palace. One day Pelops, the son of Tantalus, made his appearance. Hippodameia fell in love with him and helped him bribe Myrtilus, her father's charioteer. Myrtilus replaced the bronze bolt that held the wheel to the axle of the king's chariot with a wax bolt. During the race, Oenomaus was flung off and perished as he was dragged along by his horses.

Poseidon

Poseidon was the son of Cronus and Rhea, and he reigned over the sea, which was bestowed on him by Fate. In his infancy he was said to have been raised by the Telchines, the magic spirits of Rhodes who specialised in metallurgy and were equally skilful at sculpting images of the gods and at conjuring up rain or snow. In his adolescence Poseidon married Halia, the sister of the Telchines, on whom he begot six sons and one daughter, called Rhodus, an eponym of the island of Rhodes.

Poseidon reigned not only over the sea itself, but also over the shores; he made rocks and islands tremble and drew forth streams. He was armed with a trident, the three-pronged implement of tunny fishers, and he was drawn along in a chariot by monstrous creatures—half horse, half serpent. Around him was an entire retinue of sea creatures, dolphins, nereids and different spirits of the sea, such as Proteus, the shepherd who watched over Poseidon's seals and could change himself into any shape he pleased, or Glaucus, who was mortal-born and earned his living as a fisherman until, by chance, he tasted a magic herb and became a sea-god—and there were many others besides.

Poseidon had taken part in Hera's conspiracy against Zeus. He was punished for this, and had to enter the service of Laomedon, king of Troy, for whom he built the city walls with Aeacus. But when the work was finished Laomedon refused to pay the agreed sum. Poseidon had his revenge by sending a monster to ravage the countryside, which had to be killed by Heracles after the king had been forced to sacrifice to it his own daughter Hesione. The god was always hostile to the Trojans, and during the war he fought on the side of the Greeks.

Poseidon was avid for the praise of mortals, and wanted to become the patron of several cities. Consequently, he came into conflict with several other deities and usually did not realise his wishes. His quarrel with Athena on the subject of Attica has been mentioned. He was Helius' rival for Corinth, but the giant Briareus was appointed judge and conferred

the town on Helius. At Aegina he was supplanted by
Zeus; at Naxos, by Dionysus; at Delphi, by Apollo;
at Trezena, by Athena. At Argos Phoroneus was appointed to resolve the conflict between the god and
Hera, and he found in favour of the latter. Poseidon
inflicted drought on the Argive plain and made all
the streams in the land run dry. At this point Danaus
and his daughters arrived in the region of Argos.
Poseidon fell in love with one of the Danaids, Amymone, and withdrew his curse. The hero Nauplius
was born of the god's love for Amymone.

The sons of Poseidon

Poseidon usually had children by the women he
loved, but his progeny, like the turbulent offspring
of Ares, were violent wrongdoers. He fathered
Polyphemus on Thoösa; the former was one of the
Cyclopes mentioned in the *Odyssey* (not to be confused
with the Uranian Cyclopes). With Medusa he had
the giant Chrysaor and the horse Pegasus. On
Iphimedeia he begot the Aloadae, Cercyon and the
bandit Sciron, both of whom perished at the hand of
Theseus. Lamos, king of the Laestrygones, whom the
Odyssey made out to be a cannibal, and the unfortunate
hunter Orion were his sons.

Like Zeus Poseidon was the mythical ancestor of
a great number of families; his union with Libye,
granddaughter of Io, resulted in the birth of Agenor,
king of Sidon, and Belus, the father of Danaus and
Aegyptus. He was also the grandfather of Sicyon and
Corinth. He is regarded as one of the ancestors of
the king of Pylos, Nestor, and of Pelias, as well as the
Theban heroes Amphion and Zethus.

Poseidon had a legitimate wife, Amphitrite, a
nereid, but she did not bear him any children.

Hades and Persephone

The underworld

The realm of Hades was often described by poets,
but the idea people had of it varied according to the
period. It was usually imagined to be a territory
surrounded by flowing waters, a vast marsh crossed
by rivers with sinister names; the Acheron (a name
significantly connected with the word 'pain'), the
Cocytus (or 'river of groans'), the Styx, the Phlegethon
(or 'river of fire') and Lethe (or 'river of forgetfulness'). Acheron and Cocytus were, in actual fact, two
rivers in Epirus which crossed desolate landscape in
which there were 'mouths of hell'. The other three
were purely mythical. There was a story that Acheron,
son of Gaea, had been sentenced to remain under the
earth for part of his course because of some ancient
misdeed. During the gigantomachy he had, it was
said, consented to provide water for the giants.

The Styx

Styx was the son of Night; he had fought on the side
of the Olympians and, for this reason, Zeus accorded

him the privilege of being the guarantor of vows
made by the gods. Whenever a god wanted to bind
himself by a vow, Iris would go and draw a ewer of
water from the Styx and take it back to Olympus as
witness to the vow. If the god perjured himself, he
was deprived of breath for an entire year, then for
nine years he lived away from divine assemblies. The
name of Styx was also given to a stream in Arcadia
whose waters were said to have harmful properties;
it was a strong poison and broke up metals that were
plunged into it. This stream was considered to be a
resurgence of the underworld river.

Charon

When the dead arrived in the underworld the first
thing they had to do was to cross Acheron's swamp
in a boat rowed by a ferryman called Charon, a sinister
old man, who had to be paid an *obolos* (farthing) for
the crossing. Hence the custom of placing a coin in
the mouth of a dead man. If they were unable to pay
the price of their crossing, the dead became lost souls,
condemned to wander alongside the Acheron without
ever finding rest. That was also the fate of the
unburied dead.

The judgment of souls

Once they had reached the kingdom of Hades, the
dead were judged by a tribunal composed (so it was
believed in the classical period) of three judges:
Minos, Aeacus and Rhadamanthys, whose reputation
for piety was their qualification for this office after
their deaths. Rhadamanthys, in particular, a brother
of Minos and Sarpedon, and the son of Zeus and
Europa, was regarded as having compiled the code
of Cretan laws during his lifetime, and this had been
taken as a model of its kind in many Greek cities. The
guilty were punished in Tartarus. The 'elect' souls
were sent to the Elysian Fields, a miraculous place
of sojourn, where they continued to live a slower
mode of life, still full of pleasures, in meadows bedecked with asphodels. At least, this was the belief
that finally prevailed. But in ancient times the idea
of moral judgment was almost unknown. The damned
were those who had incurred the wrath of the gods,
and were thus subject to divine vengeance.

The damned

Among the damned were Sisyphus, Tantalus, Ixion
and the Danaids. Sisyphus, who founded the city of
Corinth, was a descendant of Deucalion. He witnessed
the abduction of young Aegina, daughter of Asopus,
at the hand of Zeus, and revealed the name of the
abductor to the girl's father. Zeus then sent the spirit
of death, Thanatos, to seize him. But Sisyphus
managed to lay hands on Thanatos and put him in
chains, with the result that there were no further
deaths for some time. Finally, Sisyphus agreed to set
him free. But when Thanatos was ready to take him
away, Sisyphus prevailed upon his wife to leave his

Charon, the ferryman of the underworld, who carried the souls of the dead over the river Styx. Attic white-ground lekythos. 455–400 B.C. *National Museum, Athens*

Dionysus, god of wine, son of Zeus and Semele. His followers were satyrs, Sileni and Bacchantes, whose revels were notorious. Bronze. From Gela. *Ashmolean Museum, Oxford*

body unburied. In the underworld he then asked permission to return to the world and punish his impious wife. Hades let him go back, and naturally Sisyphus made no attempt to return to the underworld. When at last he died at a great age, the gods made haste to give him a task that would hold him prisoner. He had to roll an enormous rock up a slope, and, when it reached the top, the rock rolled down to the bottom and Sisyphus' task began at the beginning again.

Tantalus was a son of Zeus, and he reigned in Lydia. His children were Pelops, an ancestor of the Atreids, and Niobe. He was said to have perjured himself to avoid having to return Hermes' dog, which had been entrusted to him. In the underworld Tantalus was confined in a lake; when thirst overcame him he would attempt to moisten his lips, but each time the water receded. Fainting from hunger, he would attempt to reach a fruit-laden branch that hung just above his head, but the branch would rise out of reach.

Ixion, who was guilty of attempting to violate Hera, was fastened to a wheel of fire that turned in the air.

As for the Danaids, the fifty daughters of Danaus, they had fled from the latter's brother Aegyptus and his fifty sons and taken refuge in the Argive plain. When the fifty sons of Aegyptus had succeeded in finding Danaus, they demanded their cousins in marriage; Danaus consented, but on their wedding-night he gave his daughters swords and ordered them to kill their husbands. Only Hypermnestra had the courage to disobey. Her sisters did nothing to redeem their guilt and were punished in the underworld. They were condemned to pour water continually into a bottomless vase, which never filled.

Cerberus

The entrance to the underworld was guarded by a dog, Cerberus, with three heads, three serpents' tails and a body bristling with vipers. It was the son of Echidna and Typhon. As Cerberus was fastened to a chain, he merely barked at the souls of the dead, allowing them to enter, but forbidding them to leave. He was, however, vanquished by Heracles, who brought him back to earth, but, not knowing what to do with him, sent him back to Hades again. Later, Cerberus was charmed by the music of Orpheus and fell asleep, and in this way Orpheus eluded him to gain entry into the palace of Hades in search of Eurydice.

Dionysus

Dionysus was the last of the gods to become an Olympian. He was the son of Zeus and Semele, who was the daughter of Cadmus and Harmonia. Zeus' wife, Hera, was jealous of Semele when she became the object of her husband's affections and perfidiously suggested that Semele should ask her lover to show himself to her in all his splendour. Zeus reluctantly agreed, and Semele was killed by a thunderbolt.

Cybele, often identified with Rhea, the mother of the gods. She assisted Dionysus after Hera had sent him mad. The cults of Cybele and Dionysus were similar. From Camirus, Rhodes. Terracotta. *c.* 480 B.C. *British Museum*

Dionysus, the god of wine, rescued and married Ariadne after she had been abandoned by Theseus on the island of Naxos. The satyrs, shown here, were constant companions of Dionysus. Attic black-figured amphora, by the Ryecroft painter. Late sixth century B.C. *Ashmolean Museum, Oxford*

However, Zeus seized the child from its mother's body, stitched it into his thigh, and at the right time the infant emerged perfectly formed. The young Dionysus, or twice-born as he was known, was then entrusted to the care of nurses. The first person to take him was Ino, the second wife of King Athamas of Orchomenus. Hoping to divert Hera's jealousy, Zeus suggested dressing the child in female clothing; but Hera was not duped and sent both Athamas and Ino mad. Athamas killed his younger son, Learchus, by throwing him into a cauldron of boiling water, and Ino committed suicide with the elder boy, Melicertes. She threw herself into the sea with him — but she was transformed into a sea deity, Leucothea (white goddess), and the child became the little god Palaemon. After this tragedy Zeus gave Dionysus to the nymphs of Mount Nysa to bring up (this was often claimed to be in upper Armenia), and disguised him as a kid for this purpose—which may account for the epithet of 'kid' later applied to the god in ritual.

Dionysus grew up and discovered the vine and its uses in the country around Mount Nysa. But Hera sent him mad, and he began to wander about the entire East. He was purified in Phrygia by the goddess Cybele (the great goddess of the land, whom the Greeks often identified with Rhea and called the mother of the gods; her cult was orgiastic, finding expression in violence, and was therefore vaguely connected with the cult of Dionysus). When he had regained his sanity Dionysus went to Thrace, but Lycurgus, the ruler, gave him a poor welcome. The king was about to take him prisoner, but Dionysus fled to Thetis, the nereid. However, Lycurgus succeeded in capturing the Bacchantes—women who followed the god and celebrated his rites. Thereupon Dionysus sent the king mad, and, in the belief that he was cutting down a vine, Lycurgus severed his own leg with an axe. Then his kingdom was beset by total sterility. When the oracle was consulted, it declared that the king should be put to death; so his subjects tore his body to pieces.

The triumph of Dionysus

From Thrace Dionysus went to India, which he conquered with the armed troops he mustered on the way with the aid of his own spells. Then he returned to Greece accompanied by a triumphal procession in a chariot decorated with vine-leaves and drawn by panthers; his escorts were the Sileni, Bacchantes, satyrs and other fertility demons, such as the god Priapus.

Dionysus eventually reached Boeotia in Greece, which was his mother's region. His wish was to introduce the Bacchanalia into Thebes, where Pentheus reigned as king. During these revels, the populace, especially the women, fell into a kind of mystic delirium, and ran about the mountainsides shouting and oblivious to all decorum. Pentheus forbade these rites. But he received his punishment, for his own mother, Agave, in a state of religious fervour, tore him apart with her own hands, mistaking him for a fawn.

Dionysus demonstrated his powers in Argos in a similar way; there he drove the two daughters of King Proetus to madness, and they wandered about the countryside in the belief that they had been turned into cows. They were cured by the seer Malampus, who obtained for himself and his brother Bias two-thirds of the kingdom of Argos. Another tradition attributed the delirium of Praetus' daughters to the wrath of Hera.

Then Dionysus attempted to gain access to Naxos and hired the services of pirates. These tried to sell him as a slave, so Dionysus changed their oars into serpents and filled their vessel with clinging ivy. The

Sicilian coin showing Silenus at an altar and (*left*) in a chariot. A wise satyr, gifted with prophecy, he was entrusted with the education of Dionysus. *c.* 460—450 B.C. *Fitzwilliam Museum, Cambridge*

pirates were afraid and threw themselves into the sea, where they were transformed into dolphins.

As the final episode in his travels Dionysus went down to the underworld to look for his mother, Semele. Hades agreed to give her back to him, and Semele was welcomed to the sky, where she took the name of Thyone. Before returning to Olympus himself, the god abducted the young Ariadne, who had been abandoned by Theseus on the island of Naxos, and made her his wife.

The companions of Dionysus

The satyrs (Satyroi) were to be found among Dionysus' regular escorts; they were demons of the countryside and were portrayed in different ways in different regions. Sometimes the satyr was depicted with the torso of a human being and the lower part of a horse, and sometimes it had the hairy legs and rear part of a goat attached to a human bust.

Satyrs were generally thought of as creatures who pursued nymphs, lived well, and slept in the sunshine or in the cool air of caves. Their lubricity is evident from their portraits.

There was a literary genre, the satire, which depicted them as the companions of Dionysus, patron of dramatic poetry. Marsyas, the unfortunate flautist who ventured to challenge Apollo and was flayed as punishment, was one of the satyrs, but myths rarely cite by name these half-divine, half-bestial creatures.

Silenus

In Dionysus' immediate circle an old satyr, Silenus, had particular authority. He was said to have been entrusted with the education of the god. He was the son of Pan or perhaps of Hermes, or he may have been the offspring of Uranus when he was mutilated by Cronus. Silenus was a wise and profound spirit whose appearance was deceptively grotesque. More-

over, he would consent to reveal his prophecies only under extreme pressure. One day Silenus was led in chains to the king of Phrygia, Midas. The latter recognised the satyr, set him free and treated him with courtesy. In reward Silenus granted the king's request that everything he touched should turn to gold. But this power proved to be so disastrous that the king hastened to beg Dionysus to take from him the gift that had proved to be a curse.

The Centaurs

The centaurs (Centauroi) may also have some connection with the retinue of Dionysus. They were monstrous creatures—half horse, half man. There was a belief that they were the result of the mating of Ixion and the cloud that Zeus had made to resemble Hera in order to frustrate the unlawful desires of this Thessalian king. The centaurs lived in the mountains and forests and ate raw flesh. They were brutish in their habits and liked to abduct young girls. This was how they got involved in a famous fight against Theseus and his friend Peirithous, the Lapith prince, who had invited the centaurs to his wedding. They were closely related to him, as he was also a son of Ixion. At the marriage celebration the centaurs soon became drunk, and one of them tried to violate Hippodameia, the bride. There was a tremendous uproar; finally Theseus and the prince forced the centaurs to leave Thessaly.

There were, however, two centaurs who had a different genealogy and gentler habits: Chiron, the child of Cronus and Philyra, and Pholus, son of Silenus and an ash-nymph. Chiron was friendly towards men and did good; in particular he was the protector of Peleus, the father of Achilles, and when Peleus, who had been slandered in the presence of King Acastus, was abandoned unarmed in the mountains by the latter at the mercy of the centaurs, they

Man and centaur. The centaur was a brutish creature, half man, half horse, who lived in the mountains and forests. Metalwork. Eighth century B.C. *The Metropolitan Museum of Art, Gift of J. Pierpont Morgan, 1917*

The revels of the Sileni. The Sileni resembled satyrs in their habitat and bestial habits. Satyrs were usually shown with some of the physical attributes of goats, the Sileni with the ears and tails of horses. Vase painting.

would have killed him if Chiron had not wakened him in time and given him his sword. Chiron brought up Achilles, Jason and Asclepius and taught them morals, music and medicine. Chiron was immortal; but he was accidentally wounded by one of Heracles' shafts, and was in such pain that he exchanged his immortality for the mortality of Prometheus and was thus able to find rest.

The cycles of the heroes

Heracles

The typical hero was Heracles. His name was significant in itself, since it means 'the Glory of Hera'. It was not the name of a god, but perhaps a ritual name, deliberately adopted by a votary of the goddess or assigned by sacerdotal tradition to a 'consort' of the great goddess of Argos. Modern scholars are unable to give a definitive explanation of either the origin or true character of Heracles. It seems unlikely that he was a 'fallen god' or a historic figure magnified to epic proportions. It seems more probable that he was the result of a vast mythical synthesis in which mingle and blend local legends, sacerdotal traditions from Hera's sanctuary at Argos and pre-Hellenic elements of every kind—some perhaps from Syria, if it is true that Heracles was similar to Melqart in certain ways (though in fewer than have been claimed).

The stories relating to Heracles are extremely complex. Even ancient mythologists are known to have found it very difficult to establish a coherent biography for the hero. Following their example, his career will be divided here into the 'canonical' cycle of the twelve labours, exploits independent of this cycle and adventures of secondary importance connected, with a greater or lesser degree of skill, with the twelve labours.

The origins of Heracles

Ancient mythologists declared that the real name of the hero is not Heracles, but Alceides. The name of Heracles would appear to have been bestowed on him by Apollo when he became Hera's servant. Through his mother, Alcmene, and his father, Amphitryon, Heracles was descended from Perseus, for his two grandfathers, Alcaeus and Electryon, were both sons of Perseus and Andromeda. So he is of pure Argive blood, and it was by accident that his birth took place at Thebes. Most of his adventures took place in the Peloponnesus, and his descendants returned and settled there much later on. Amphitryon had had to leave Argolis and settle in Thebes as a result of an accidental murder. Taking advantage of his absence (he was away on an expedition against the Teleboans) Zeus seduced Alcmene, but could do so only by disguising himself as Amphitryon and taking his place for one night—thereby fathering Heracles. In the morning Amphitryon returned, and the result of their union was another son, Iphicles.

Even before Heracles' birth Hera's jealousy found outward expression. Zeus had unwisely stated that 'the next child to be born a descendant of the Perseidae would rule Argos'. Hera then managed to retard the birth of Heracles and to arrange that another descendant of Perseus should be born first; this was Eurystheus, who came into the world after only seven months, thus qualifying by virtue of Zeus' sacred word for the title of king of Argos and master of Heracles.

The childhood of Heracles

When he was eight months old, Hera sent two serpents to Heracles' room to suffocate and choke him in his cradle. There he lay with his twin, Iphicles.

Heracles at sea in a golden jar. Perhaps the best known of the Greek heroes, Heracles travelled the world and overcame a variety of forces of evil.

Heracles breaking off the horns of the hind of Ceryneia. He is watched by Athena and Artemis. *British Museum*

But Heracles seized the serpents by the throat and strangled them.

He was brought up as an ordinary Greek child. Linus, the musician, taught him the rudiments of music and the arts, but his pupil lacked self-control, and one day, when his master was attempting to correct him, Heracles struck him with a stool and killed him. The child was then sent into the country, where he became a shepherd. There he was taught to be a skilled archer by Teutarus, the Scythian. When at last he stopped growing Heracles was four cubits and one foot tall, and at the age of eighteen he had his first success in the face of danger, when he killed a lion that was ravaging the countryside around Mount Cithaeron. In reward the local king, Thespius, gave him his fifty daughters, for he wanted grandsons by the hero. These fifty sons of Heracles later colonised Sardinia.

As he was returning from hunting this lion, Heracles met the envoys of King Erginus of Orchomenus, who were coming to claim the tribute paid to their master by the Thebans at that time. Heracles cut off the noses and ears of the members of this embassy; then later, when Erginus marched against Thebes with his army, he challenged him and imposed on him twice the tribute that Erginus had previously demanded from Thebes.

The labours of Heracles

Creon, the king of Thebes, then gave the hero the hand of his daughter, Megara, who bore him five children, but Hera sent Heracles mad and he killed all the children. This was Hera's way of reminding Heracles that he was to enter the service of Eurystheus. Heracles obeyed, and this was when the twelve labours began. These twelve exploits, performed by order of Eurystheus, were sometimes regarded as expiation for the murder of the children borne him

by Megara. At this time Heracles either made or was given his special weapons: he fashioned his club in the valley of Nemea from the trunk of a wild olive; Hermes gave him a sword; and Apollo gave him a bow and arrows. According to other traditions he received everything from his protectress Athena.

The Nemean lion

The first labour was to hunt the Nemean Lion—a prodigious animal, son of Orthrus and brother to the Sphinx of Thebes. This lion lived in a double-mouthed cave; Heracles stopped up one entrance to the cave, and wrestled with the monster until he choked it to death. When the lion was dead, Heracles used the animal's own claws to remove the pelt, which became his armour, and its head served as his helmet.

The hydra of Lerna

The second labour was the destruction of the Hydra of Lerna, the daughter of Echidna and Typhon, who had been reared by Hera herself. The Hydra was a hundred-headed serpent, and its very breath was so venomous that it could destroy life. Heracles cut off these hideous heads, but they grew again at once. So he commanded his nephew Iolaus, who was with him, to seal each wound with a flaming brand. Then he dipped his arrows into the Hydra's blood to make them poisonous.

The boar of Erymanthus

On Mount Erymanthus lived a monstrous boar. Heracles forced the animal to come out of its lair and pushed it into the deep snow that covered the entire countryside. Then, when the animal was tired, he captured it and carried it alive on his shoulders to Eurystheus, who was so afraid that he took refuge in a sunken jar.

The hind of Ceryneia

At Oenoe, near the Hill of Ceryneia, a gigantic hind was destroying crops; she was sacred to Artemis, and it was sacrilege to touch her. Heracles hunted her for the whole of one year. When she was exhausted, he wounded her slightly with an arrow and carried her across his shoulders. As he was crossing Arcadia he met Artemis and Apollo, who wanted the hind back and accused him of intending to kill the sacred animal. But he extricated himself by saying that the affair was the responsibility of Eurystheus, for he himself acted merely on the king's command.

The birds of Stymphalus

In the region of the lake of Stymphalus in Arcadia a dense forest sheltered countless birds, which had originally flocked there when frightened by wolves. They devoured all the fruit and even attacked passers-by. Eurystheus ordered Heracles to destroy them. He could not get them to leave their forest until he had recourse to bronze castanets given to him by Athena and made by Hephaestus. When the birds heard the castanets, they soared upwards, and Heracles killed them with his arrows.

According to another version these birds were vultures that devoured men, and they used their steel feathers to pierce their victims.

The stables of Augeias

At Elis in the Peleponnesus there was a king called Augeias, who was a son of the Sun. He inherited a great fortune in flocks and herds from his father, but he never had the dung removed from his stables, and eventually it spread and made the country sterile. Heracles was given the task of cleansing these stables. First he made the king promise that he would give him a certain sum if he did it in one day. Heracles succeeded by dint of diverting two rivers, Alpheius and Peneius, through the palace yard. But Augeias refused to pay the agreed sum and banished Heracles.

The Cretan bull

The seventh labour took place in Crete, where a monstrous bull was running wild. Who or what it was is not certain. Perhaps Zeus had disguised himself as this bull when he abducted Europa. Perhaps it was the animal that Pasiphaë fell in love with. Perhaps it was a present from Poseidon that Minos had kept in his herd instead of sacrificing it to the god as agreed. The bull had to be brought back alive to Eurystheus. Heracles went to Crete, obtained permission from Minos and captured the bull on the run. Then he brought it back to Greece (some say that he swam back with it) and presented it to his master. Eurystheus offered it to Hera, but the goddess refused to accept the gift and set it free. This was the bull that Theseus had later to conquer on the plain of Marathon as a task set him by Medusa.

The horses of Diomedes

Diomedes, king of Thrace and son of Ares, possessed four mares that fed on human flesh. Heracles went to Thrace and set Diomedes himself before the mares, and they devoured him.

The girdle of the Amazon

Eurystheus had a daughter, Admete, who wanted the girdle of Hippolyta, the queen of the Amazons. This girdle had been given to the queen by Ares himself. Heracles set off with some companions and reached the Amazons. Hippolyta willingly agreed to give him her girdle, but Hera provoked a quarrel between the Amazons and Heracles' followers. A battle followed. Heracles, thinking that he had been betrayed by Hippolyta, killed her.

The cattle of Geryon

The last three labours took Heracles far from the known world. Eurystheus sent him first to seek the cattle of Geryon, the son of Chrysaor. The cattle were guarded by the herdsman Eurytion and his dog Orthrus on the island of Eurytheia. This island lay in the far west, beyond Oceanus. To cross the ocean, Heracles borrowed the 'goblet of the Sun', in which the solar star sailed back to his palace every evening on the other side of the world. Heracles had to threaten the Sun with his arrows before he was offered the loan of the goblet. In the same way he had to intimidate Oceanus to avoid being pitched about violently on the waves during his crossing. Finally, he reached the sacred island, where he struck Orthrus, the 'sheep-dog', with his club and killed him. In the end Geryon, the cattle-owner himself, came to the aid of his men, and was slain in the same way. Then Heracles returned as he had come, disembarking at Tartarus Tartessus. There he set up two pillars, which mark the edge of Oceanus (the 'Pillars of Oceanus', which nowadays are called the Rock of Gibraltar and Cape Ceuta). Then he set out on a long journey through Spain and Gaul on his way back to Greece. He was attacked on the way by innumerable brigands, particularly in the region of Liguria, in the plain of Crau, where he stoned his enemies with boulders given him by Zeus, and which even today still bestrew the countryside. At Rome he had to fight Cacus, the brigand of the Aventine Forest. When he finally got back to Argos he offered the rest of Geryon's herd in sacrifice to Hera.

The dog Cerberus

The eleventh labour took Heracles to the underworld to seek the dog Cerberus. Before his departure he was initiated into the mysteries of Eleusis, and so learned how to reach the kingdom of Hades and, even more important, how to get back again.

Heracles went through the 'jaws of Hell', which lay off Cape Taenarum. A few spirits of the dead tried to bar his way, notably the Gorgon Medusa, but the hero

When Apollo's oracle at Delphi refused to answer questions put to him by Heracles, the hero tried to steal the sacred stool. Apollo came to the aid of the priestess, Pythia, and the quarrel was eventually settled by Zeus who affirmed Apollo's rights in the case. Amphora of Andodices. c. 530 B.C. *State Museum, Berlin*

While seeking the Apples of the Hesperides Heracles encountered the giant Antaeus, whose strength was renewed every time he touched the ground. Heracles overcame him by lifting him off the ground. Detail of krater of Euphronius. Louvre. *Giraudon*

Busiris, son of Poseidon, and an Egyptian king, slaughtered on the altar of Zeus all foreigners who entered Egypt. Heracles killed the wicked king. Attic red-figured stamnos from Vulci. Manner of Hermonax. c. 470 B.C. *Ashmolean Museum, Oxford*

surmounted the obstacles, and presented himself to Hades. The latter agreed to let him have Cerberus if he could master him with his own hands. This Heracles did. Whereupon he returned with his prisoner to Eurystheus, who in fear and trembling had taken refuge in his sunken jar. Not knowing what to do with the dog, Heracles took it back to Hades.

The apples of the Hesperides

Finally, Eurystheus demanded the 'golden apples' from the garden of the Hesperides. The Hesperides, whose name means 'the nymphs of evening', had set a hundred-headed dragon to watch over their garden; it was the offspring of Echidne and Typhon. Heracles set off. As he was crossing Macedonia he met Cycnus, son of Ares, and killed him. Then he went through Illyria and reached the mouth of Eridanus (the Po), where he was told by nymphs that the only creature who knew the way that he must take was the sea-god Nereus. He gained access to Nereus, took him prisoner, put him in chains and then forced him to speak.

From that point Heracles' itinerary becomes well-nigh impossible to follow. He went to Libya, where he had to combat the giant, Anteus, the son of Earth, who renewed his strength every time he touched the ground. Heracles could defeat him only by raising him in his arms. Then he crossed Egypt, where he killed King Busiris, who offered all strangers in sacrifice to the gods; then he was to be found in Arabia, where he killed Emathion, son of Tithonus. Reaching the Red Sea, he embarked again in the 'goblet of the Sun' and came to the Caucasian Mountains, where he freed Prometheus by killing the eagle that gnawed away perpetually at its unhappy victim's liver. In gratitude Prometheus helped him by divulging that he would not be able to pick the miraculous apples himself, but would have to get Atlas to pick them for him. So he went to find Atlas, who had the task of holding up the sky on his shoulders, and he offered to take his place while he went to pick the desired fruit. Atlas acquiesced, brought back the apples, and then declared that he would go and give them to Eurystheus himself. Heracles pretended to agree, but simply asked Atlas to slip a cushion on his shoulder. The latter made to do so without suspecting a trick, but while he was holding the sky Heracles escaped with the apples, leaving Atlas with his burden.

When Eurystheus was given the marvellous apples, he offered them in sacrifice to Athena, who asked Heracles to return them, for Fate had decreed that they should not be found anywhere else on earth.

Military expeditions

There were many military expeditions accomplished by Heracles with the aid of his numerous companions. In the course of one such expedition he fought against Troy. Heracles had been cheated by King Laomedon, who ruled over the city. He had, in fact, saved the life of Hesione, the king's daughter, when she was about to be devoured by a monster, and, although Laomedon had promised to give him some sacred mares, once Hesione was safe and sound, he refused the agreed reward. This happened on Heracles' return journey after the war against the Amazons. Later Heracles returned with a fleet of eighteen ships and attacked the town. Telamon, one of his most faithful companions, scaled the wall and was first into the city. Laomedon and all his children were killed with the exception of the youngest, Podarces (who later became King Priam), and Hesione, who was later married to Telamon.

On his return from Troy Heracles and his companions captured the island of Cos, where they had been washed up by a storm. The hero lay with Chalciope, the daughter of the king, who bore him a son called Thessalus, the ancestor of the Thessalians.

Then Heracles went to Elis to demand the sum that King Augeias had wrongfully withheld. Augeias raised an army against him, commanded by his nephews, the Molione, giants of superhuman strength. Taking advantage of Heracles' absence, the enemy overthrew his troops and wounded Iphicles mortally. But the hero had his revenge, for he killed the two giants in an ambush, took the town of Elis, massacred Augeias and installed the son of Augeias, Phyleus, on his throne, for the latter had previously pleaded for Heracles in his father's presence. The foundation of the Olympic games is often said to have taken place at this juncture, together with the consecration of the sacred enclosure and the dedication of a sanctuary at Pelops.

Pylus in Messenia was the realm of King Neleus, who had eleven children, the eldest being Periclymenus (actually the son of Poseidon) and the youngest, Nestor. Heracles had a longstanding and somewhat vague grudge against Neleus. So, after defeating Augeias, he turned his attention in his direction. Heracles and Periclymenus, who could assume whatever shape he pleased, fought in single combat. The latter disguised himself as a bee, but Athena saw this and told Heracles of the trick; he then crushed the insect between his fingers and Pylus was soon captured. Heracles then went on to kill Neleus. He put young Nestor on this throne and asked him to keep the kingdom intact until his own descendants, the Heraclids, should be ready to rule over the Peloponnesus. Nestor himself, when advanced in years, took part in the Trojan war.

Heracles' final attack in the Peloponnesus was made against Hippocoön and his many sons, who were then rulers of Sparta, as they had driven out the legitimate masters, Icarius and Tyndareus, fathers of Penelope and Helen respectively.

A final expedition took Heracles to Thessaly where he had formed an alliance with Aegimius, a son of Dorus and king of the Dorian people. He first of all delivered Aegimius from the threat that the Lapiths were holding over his head. Then he put to rights a longstanding quarrel which had brought him into opposition with the Dryopes, a race who lived in the mountains of Parnassus. On a previous occasion, when Heracles was crossing their territory with Deianeira and their son Hyllus, they had come across Theiodamas, king of the Dryopes, ploughing his land and had asked him for something to eat. The king had refused. So Heracles unyoked an ox from the plough, slaughtered it, cut it to pieces and ate it. Theiodamas fled, but returned with a band of men who caught Heracles unprepared. Deianeira was wounded. Finally Heracles was able to retire after killing Theiodamas. When he returned with an army, he had no difficulty in seizing the kingdom, and the Dryopes dispersed, some going to Euboea, others to Cyprus, and the remainder to Argolis.

Various adventures

The cycle of Heracles included a great many other adventures, and those mentioned here are simply some of the main ones. For instance, during the hunt for the boar of Erymanthus, Heracles happened one day to be the guest of the centaur Pholus, to whom Dionysus had made a gift of a sealed jar, recommending him to open it only in the presence of Heracles. After the meal Heracles and Pholus opened the jar and began to drink from it. The smell of wine immediately drew a host of centaurs armed with firebrands and whole trees. A terrible fight ensued. Ten centaurs were killed, and Pholus was accidentally but fatally wounded with one of Heracles' arrows.

On another occasion, when Heracles stopped at the palace of King Admetus in Thessaly, he found it in mourning. Alcestis, wife of the king, had agreed to die instead of her husband, and her funeral was in progress. Heracles hastened in pursuit of Thanatos, the spirit of the dead, seized Alcestis from him and gave her back to her husband.

Heracles was connected with the death or capture of a great number of brigands, one of whom was the giant Alcyoneus, who attacked passers-by with stones on the isthmus of Corinth. In the same way he was associated with the Cecropes, two clever thieves. Their mother, the sea-nymph Theia, had warned them against a certain hero called Melampygus (Black Bottom). They attacked Heracles while he slept, but he overcame them and put them over his shoulder, fastened to the opposite ends of a pole, rather as though they were young goats. In this position one of them noticed that Heracles possessed the striking feature for which Melampygus was famed. Their pleasantries on this subject amused Heracles so much that he agreed to let them go. But later Zeus changed them into monkeys and removed them to the island of Ischia. Heracles then went on to kill Syleus and Lityerses, the accursed vine-grower and reaper, who used to force passers-by to work in their fields and then massacre them.

Above: Bellerophon, mounted on Pegasus, slaying the Chimera.
Terracotta relief from the island of Melos. Painted, gilded,
and pierced for attaching to wooden furniture. British Museum.

Left: Terracotta statuette of Ephesian Artemis.
a fertility goddess worshipped at Ephesus, Asia Minor. Though
the two cults were of independent origin, she was often,
wrongly, identified with the Greek goddess of the same name.
Second to first centuries B.C. British Museum.

Deianeira

After this the adventures of the hero show no coherence until we come to the final period of his life. On his earlier visit to the underworld Heracles had met his friend Meleager, who asked him to marry his sister, Deianeira, when he returned to earth. Heracles agreed, won the girl after a fight against the river-god Achelous, who wanted to marry her, and remained some while at Calydon with his father-in-law, King Oeneus. But he accidently killed a young relative of the king and thought it best to go into exile. So he set off with Deianeira and their son Hyllus. A centaur called Nessus took travellers across the river Evenus. Heracles crossed first. When Nessus had Deianeira in his boat he attempted to violate her. She called for help, and Heracles killed the centaur with an arrow. In his dying moments the latter advised Deianeira to soak a piece of cloth in his blood and make a tunic with it; if her husband should ever cease to love her, she was to dress him in this garment.

Omphale

Writers have been inclined to portray Heracles as an attendant of Omphale, waiting on her, exchanging costume with her and spinning at her feet—echoes perhaps of some Lydian myth in which a goddess was waited on by an effeminate consort. The enslavement lasted three years. On his return, Heracles, who had asked the hand of Iole, youngest daughter of Eurytus, made her his concubine. Then Deianeira remembered the love-charm that Nessus had given her and decided to make use of it.

Death of Heracles

Fresh from his victory over Eurytus, Heracles wanted to consecrate an altar to Zeus, and for this purpose sent to Deianeira asking for a new garment. She sent him the tunic impregnated with the blood of Nessus.

Heracles defeats the river-god Achelous in order to win the hand of Deianeira. Vase painting. *British Museum*

Heracles and the Cecropes. The latter were the sons of the sea-nymph Thea, and they were very clever thieves. After he had defeated them, Heracles tied one at each end of a pole. Attic black-figured lekythos. *Ashmolean Museum, Oxford*

Heracles put it on and the poison blood burnt him unbearably. He tried to tear it off, but hurt himself all the more as it was so firmly stuck to his skin. So he was taken to Deianeira at Trachis. When she saw what she had done, she committed suicide. Heracles entrusted Iole to his son Hyllus, asking him to marry her. Then he climbed Mount Oeta, built a high pyre and mounted it. He commanded his servants to set fire to it, but all refused except Philoctetes, who resigned himself to the task and was given Heracles' bow and arrows as a reward. The pyre was still burning when a clap of thunder was heard, and the hero, freed from his mortal self, was taken up into the sky. He became reconciled with Hera when he reached Olympus. A ceremony was enacted portraying his birth (that is his emergence from the bosom of the goddess) and he married Hebe, the personification of youth.

Historical and legendary events begun by Heracles did not cease with his death. Immediately afterwards all his children were persecuted by Eurystheus. They took refuge in Athens, where Theseus (or his son) welcomed them. Eurystheus declared war on Athens, but was killed in the fight by Hyllus. Then the Heraclids wanted to return to the Peloponnesus, the country of their ancestors. Under the leadership of Hyllus they had no difficulty in seizing the country, but after a year it was ravaged by a plague, and an oracle stated that the Heraclids had come back too soon. So they left and settled in the plain of Marathon. From time to time they questioned the oracle, which gave them ambiguous answers. The Heraclids then renewed their attempts, and again they failed to take the Peloponnesus. Only when the third generation under the leadership of Temenus attacked by sea did they succeed in conquering the country.

Theseus

Theseus was, in some ways, the Attic Heracles. He was thought to have lived one generation earlier than the Trojan war, but he belonged to one generation later than Heracles. The legendary Theseus was undoubtedly based on a historical personage. Purely religious elements were rare in his cycle of legends.

Through his father, Aegeus, Theseus was descended from Erichthonius and the kings of Attica. Aegeus, who had been unable to have children by his successive wives, went to consult the oracle at Delphi, and was told not to 'untie the mouth of your wine-skin until you reach the citadel of Athens'. Aegeus, who did not understand that he was being advised to be continent until he reached home, left in despair. He went and asked Pittheus, the king of Troezen, one of the sons of Pelops, what he thought it meant. Pittheus understood at once. He managed to make Aegeus drunk and during the night put his daughter Aethra beside him. Aegeus lay with her, and she bore him a son, Theseus. Another version tells that the same night Aethra was told in a dream to

Cretan sacrificial procession, from the sarcophagus of Haghia Triada. A priestess, leading the procession, pours red liquid, possibly blood, into a large vase between two pillars, each surmounted by a double axe and a bird. She is followed by a woman (bearing an offering) and a musician. *Samivel*

Theseus slaying his wife Antiope. When Theseus abandoned Antiope so as to marry Phaedra, the Amazons attacked Athens to avenge their sister, but Antiope perished in the battle. Etruscan mirror case.

Theseus slaying the Minotaur, watched by Ariadne and perhaps by Daedalus, the architect of the labyrinth. Attic amphora. Bibliothèque Nationale. *Giraudon*

GREECE: MYTH AND LOGIC

go and offer a sacrifice on an island, and there she was violated by Poseidon. Theseus in that case would be the son of a god.

The child spent his early years at Troezen, as Aegeus did not want to take his son to Attica because his nephews, the Pallantids, were trying to provoke disorder. Before he left Troezen, he hid a sword and a pair of sandals beneath a rock, advising Aethra to keep the secret of their son's birth from him until he was big enough to move the rock and recover the tokens himself. The time came when Theseus was sixteen, and he took the sword and sandals and decided to go to Athens.

At this time the isthmus of Corinth was ridden with bandits. Heracles was waiting on Omphale at the time, and the bandits had regained their courage. At Epidaurus Theseus had to kill Periphetes, who put travellers to death with his bronze crutch. Then at Cenchria he put an end to the giant Sinis, who used to fasten his prisoners to a pine-tree, which he bent right over so they were torn apart as he released the branches. He also put to death the sow of Crommyon, a wild beast that attacked human beings. After this he killed the giant Sciron, who forced travellers to wash his feet and then flung them into the sea, where they were devoured by an enormous tortoise. Finally, he prevailed over Damastes, whose surname was Procrustes. Procrustes possessed two beds, a large and a small, and he made his tall prisoners lie on the small bed and cut off their feet; the short ones he put on the big bed and stretched them violently.

Eventually, Theseus reached Athens. Aegeus was in the power of the magician Medea, who had promised to cure his sterility. Medea immediately guessed the identity of the young man, whose fame had preceded him. Aegeus was at first afraid of the unknown arrival, and before he had even seen him he allowed himself to be persuaded by Medea to invite him to a banquet with the intention of poisoning him. Theseus accepted the invitation, but when he appeared with the sword and sandals once hidden beneath the rock, Aegeus realised that it was his own son. He sent Medea into exile and acknowledged Theseus in the presence of all his citizens.

There was a tale that Medea imposed a test on Theseus before attempting to poison him or, rather, persuading his father to do so: he was to fight the Marathonian bull, a wild animal that was devastating the countryside. Perhaps it was none other than the Cretan bull brought back by Heracles. Theseus overpowered it and offered it in sacrifice to Apollo.

Theseus' first act after his official recognition as the king's son was to fight the Pallantids. They were nephews of Aegeus, angered that his heritage would not be handed down to them and therefore resolved on violence. They divided into two groups and laid an ambush for Theseus, but he was warned about it by a herald called Leos and so frustrated the plot and massacred his enemies.

The minotaur

However, there was a curse on Attica. Its inhabitants had previously and most falsely taken the life of Androgeus, the son of Minos. Minos demanded retribution in the form of seven youths and seven girls who were to be sacrificed to him once every nine years. When this tribute was about to be paid for the third time, Theseus asked to be chosen as one of the victims. They were to be fed to the Minotaur, the monster that Pasiphaë bore after coupling with a bull. As he set off Theseus was given two sets of sails: black for the outward journey as it was an occasion for grief; white for the return journey if he succeeded in killing the Minotaur.

Once in Crete, Theseus was imprisoned in the labyrinth that housed the monster. But, before this, he had been noticed by Ariadne, daughter of Minos, and she fell in love with him and gave him a ball of thread so he could find his way about the complicated corridors of the labyrinth. Theseus promised to marry her on his return. In the labyrinth Theseus felled the Minotaur with blows; then he set off on the return journey with Ariadne and the young people he had saved.

On the way the ship put in at Naxos. Ariadne fell asleep on the shore, and the next day, when she woke up, she found that she was alone. Theseus' ship had sailed without her. It is said that Theseus loved another woman, or again that he had received orders from Dionysus to abandon Ariadne, whom the god wanted to marry. Soon after the ship had sailed Dionysus arrived in his triumphal chariot and took the girl to Olympus.

Meanwhile, Theseus, who was grief-stricken at his abandonment of Ariadne, forgot to change the sails of the ship. Aegeus was watching for him on the shore and thought that he must have perished; in despair he threw himself into the sea, which from that time on was known as the Aegean Sea. Theseus was made king. His first task was to take the scattered villagers and farmers and bring them within the city of Athens. He built the main monuments, organised a constitution, minted coinage: this was his historical contribution.

Several events happened in the course of his reign: the war of the Seven against Thebes and the expedition of the Amazons. Theseus was said to have gone to fight the Amazons and perfidiously abducted one of them, Antiope. The warrior-women then marched on Athens to free their sister. A decisive battle took place near the Pnyx. The Amazons were defeated and signed a peace pact. The cause of the war was also recounted as follows: Theseus married Antiope with her consent, but, after she bore him a son, Hippolytus, he repudiated her in order to marry Phaedra, a sister of Ariadne. The Amazons then came to demand justice for Antiope, who, however, perished in the battle.

Peirithous

There is a group of legends relating the friendship between Theseus and the Lapith prince, Peirithous. The latter was jealous of Theseus' reputation, so stole his cattle and was preparing to fight him when he was suddenly struck with admiration for his adversary and offered him his friendship instead. It was Theseus and Peirithous who fought together against the centaurs.

One day the two friends decided that they would both marry daughters of Zeus. They first abducted Helen for Theseus. Helen was not yet of marriageable age and was taken in complete secret to Aphidna, where she was guarded by Aethra. But the Dioscuri, her brothers, went at once to free her during Theseus' absence. Then the two companions set off for the underworld to win Persephone. Hades received them amiably and invited them to be seated at his table. But their seats had magic properties and the two men were held captive until the day when Heracles, passing through the underworld, obtained permission to deliver Theseus. Peirithous, for his part, remained rooted for ever on the 'chair of forgetfulness' to which he had been committed by Hades.

Phaedra and Hippolytus

When he returned to the light of day, Theseus found a very troubled situation both in his palace and in the city. His wife Phaedra had in his absence fallen in love with Hippolytus, the son whom the Amazon had borne him, and had told the boy of her love. Hippolytus was utterly hostile to such passion and refused her with indignation. When Theseus returned, Phaedra tore her clothes, put on mourning and pretended to be distraught because, she said, Hippolytus had attempted to violate her. Theseus became violently angry. He remembered that Poseidon had previously promised that he would make any three wishes that Theseus formed come true. Not daring to kill his son himself, Theseus asked the god to send a monster to put him to death. In response to the hero's plea a monster rose from the sea as the young Hippolytus was driving his chariot in the region of Troezen, and so frightened the horses that they broke loose and dragged Hippolytus to his death. Phaedra hanged herself in remorse.

Death of Theseus

The situation was no better in the city. Power was shared by different factions, and Theseus was king only in name. Feeling that he would never gain real control of his kingdom, he went into exile cursing Athens. He retired to the island of Scyrus, where King Lycomedes pretended to welcome him favourably, but took him up on to a mountainside and cast him into the sea. At the time this death passed unnoticed, but after the Medic wars the oracle of Delphi ordered the Athenians to bring the ashes of Theseus back to their own country.

Jason and the Argonauts

The exploits of Theseus and Heracles are in each case about one single hero. The enterprise undertaken by Jason (Iason) and the Argonauts was a collective venture that stirred the heroic world profoundly.

Jason was a Thessalian hero. Aeson, his father, was the son of Cretheus and Tyro (the latter was the object of Poseidon's affections). He was robbed of his kingdom, the land of Iolcus, by his half-brother Pelias, son of Tyro and Poseidon. However, he gave his son Jason to the centaur Chiron to bring up. When he reached manhood, Jason left Pelion and made his appearance at Iolcus wearing a panther-skin, holding a lance in each hand and having no sandal on his left foot. Pelias was in the act of offering a sacrifice; at the sight of this man he was afraid, for an oracle had told him 'to beware of the man who had no shoe'. Jason walked up to the king and demanded the kingdom from him, saying that it was his by legal right. Pelias dared not openly refuse him, but asked him first to bring him back the Golden Fleece of the ram which, in earlier days, Phrixus and Helle of Greece had taken to Colchis. It was well known that this fleece was in a wood sacred to Ares at Colchis, and the king of the land, Aeëtes, son of the Sun and the sea-nymph Perseis, had a most fearsome dragon mounting guard over it. Pelias believed Jason would never return.

Jason accepted the mission, then went to seek the advice of Argos, son of Phrixus. Prompted by Athena, Argos built the first longship, the *Argo*, which was capable of taking Jason and his chosen companions to Colchis, which was on the far shore of the Black Sea. The ship was soon built in the port of Pagasae in Thessaly, with wood from Mount Pelion; but the prow was made of a piece of oak from Dodona (where Zeus had an oracle); it was provided by Athena, and this piece of wood was endowed with powers of speech and prophecy.

The voyage

Before long companions flocked to Jason's side, and he chose about fifty of them. Many different lists of the Argonauts, as they were known, have been compiled. However, certain names are always included: Orpheus, the musician who was to provide the rhythm for the rowers; Tiphys, the helmsman, who had been trained by Athena; the soothsayer Idmon; the two sons of Boreas the North Wind, Calais and Zetes; then Castor and Polydeuces, and their two cousins, Idas and Lynceus. Heracles is sometimes named, but fate decreed that he would not reach Colchis.

The journey started off well. The omens were favourable; the first stopping-place was Lemnos, where there were only women, for they had killed all the men for being unfaithful to them after Aphrodite had put a curse on them. The women of the island were kind to the navigators; they bore them

The building of the *Argo*. Jason, sent to seek the Golden Fleece in Colchis, chose fifty companions, known as the Argonauts, to accompany him on his adventure. From a Roman roof-tile. British Museum. *Alinari-Giraudon*

Phaedra, the wife of Theseus, fell in love with her stepson, Hippolytus. When he refused her advances, she accused him of having attempted to violate her. Theseus then prayed to Poseidon to slay his son. *British Museum*

sons, the founders of a new race. At Samothrace, where they put in, the Argonauts were initiated into the mysteries of the Cabeiri, which were celebrated on the island. Then they entered the Hellespont and were favourably received by the Doliones and their king, Cyzicus. They set sail, but the wind changed during the night and before dawn they were back again on Dolionian territory, where they were not recognised, but taken for pirates and attacked. In the course of the fight King Cyzicus was killed. When day came, the opposing sides recognised one another, and in his grief Jason founded the funeral games in honour of Cyzicus.

The Argonauts then set sail for the Mysian coast. Here young Hylas wandered away and was kidnapped by water-nymphs. Heracles went to look for him and did not rejoin the ship. Then the *Argo* went to the island of the Bebrycos, ruled by King Amycus, who used to challenge travellers to a boxing-match. Polydeuces took up the challenge and killed the king or, according to other sources, made him promise to behave better in future. The next day a storm washed the *Argo* up on the coast of Thrace, where Phineus ruled. He was a blind seer, a son of Poseidon, and the gods had set a singular curse upon him. Whenever he wanted to eat, the Harpies, winged demons, flew down and snatched dishes from the table and befouled the rest. The sons of the North Wind, Calais and Zetes, had wings, and they rose in pursuit of the Harpies, caught up with them and made them promise by the Styx never to torment Phineus again.

In gratitude Phineus prophesied the future of the Argonauts: he advised them to beware of the Symplegades (Blue Rocks). These were reefs guarding the entrance to the Bosporus, and when a ship wanted to pass, they came together to bar the way. Phineus told the Argonauts to try an experiment before going through the straits; they should send a dove between the reefs, and if it got through, the boat was to follow, but if it failed there was no point in going ahead. The Argonauts took this advice. The dove succeeded in flying between the rocks, which caught only one of its tail feathers. When the reefs were once again well apart, the *Argo* went forward with all speed; it cut through the straits and left only one plank from its stern behind. From this moment onwards the Blue Rocks remained motionless, and the way into the Bosporus was open for ever.

After visiting Mariandyne, where the soothsayer Idmon (who had foreseen his death from the beginning) was killed while out hunting by a boar, the *Argo* entered the mouth of the Thermodon and reached Colchis. The helmsman Tiphys died shortly before this and was replaced by the hero Ancaeus.

Medea

When Jason explained to King Aeëtes of Colchis the purpose of their visit, the king did not refuse to give them the Golden Fleece. But he imposed certain conditions: Jason must yoke a pair of fire-breathing bulls with brazen feet, presents from Hephaestus. Then, with their aid, he must plough a field and sow it with dragon's teeth—from the dragon of Thebes. Jason would never have fulfilled these conditions if the daughter of Aeëtes, Medea, who had conceived a violent passion for him, had not come to his aid. First she made him promise to make her his wife and to take her to Greece with him, then, as she was a magician (like Circe, her aunt), she gave him a balm with which he was to anoint himself before facing the bulls and she taught him how to manage them. Jason, thus prepared, successfully mastered the bulls and ploughed the field, but when he had sown the dragon's teeth a group of hostile armed men sprang out of the ploughed soil. Jason hid himself,

Many tales were told of Jason and the Argonauts. One was of Jason's search for a treasure guarded by a sea-monster. He is shown here being ejected by the sea-monster and watched over by Athena, the protectress of the Argonauts. Red-figured kylix. Vatican Museum, Rome.

then threw a stone into their midst. The warriors all accused one another of throwing it and fought until they killed each other.

The return voyage

However, Aeëtes did not keep his promise; he even tried to set fire to the *Argo*. But Medea, by her witchcraft, put to sleep the dragon that guarded the Fleece so Jason could take it from the sacred oak on which it hung. Then Medea fled with Jason, taking with her her young brother, Apsyrtus. Aeëtes set off in their pursuit. In order to delay him Medea killed her brother and cast his severed limbs on the sea. Aeëtes lost precious time picking them up; then it was too late to continue the pursuit.

The *Argo* entered the mouth of the Danube (the Istrus) and sailed up-river. By this route they reached the Adriatic (the geography in the legend is somewhat vague), where Zeus raised a violent storm against them. The prow of the ship began to speak and revealed that the Argonauts bore the responsibility for the murder of Apsyrtus, and that they must go and be purified by Circe. The *Argo* sailed up the Po (Eridanus), then entered the Rhine and sailed down as far as the island of Aeaea, the abode of Circe. Circe purified Medea, but refused to receive Jason, so the ship sailed away again. Guided by Thetis herself, on Hera's orders, it crossed the sea of the Sirens without difficulty. Orpheus sang to prevent the sailors being tempted to listen to the song of these evil birds, but one of his companions, Butes, preferred the Sirens and jumped into the sea. Aphrodite saved him and took him to Sicily.

Continuing on its way, and crossing the straits between Scylla and Charybdis safely, the *Argo* reached the island of Phaealcia. There the Argonauts met a band of men from Colchis, whom Aeëtes had sent in pursuit of them. The *Argo* had only just left Phaealcia

when a violent storm washed it up on the Syrtis. Carrying their ship on their backs, they crossed the sands and reached Lake Tritonis, where its god, Triton, showed them a way of getting back to the sea.

When they tried to approach Crete, they were prevented from landing by a giant called Talos, a robot, the work of Hephaestus, who guarded the island for Minos. Three times a day he went round the island and hurled enormous rocks at approaching ships. Talos was invulnerable, except that, in his ankle, under very thick skin, he had a vein on which his life depended. Medea bewitched him (lured him by false visions) and contrived to make him graze his ankle on the rocks—and thus he died. The Argonauts were able to disembark, spend a night on the shore and set off again the next day. But in the sea off Crete they were suddenly surrounded by thick cloud. On hearing Jason's prayer, Apollo sent them a flash of light, which showed them a little island near by where they could beach the ship. They gave this island the name of Anaphe (the Revelation). Then, sailing past the coast of Euboea, the ship reached Iolcus, after only four months' voyage, bringing back the Golden Fleece. Then Jason went to make an offering of the ship to Poseidon at Corinth.

Jason's exploits were over. As Pelias refused to hand over his kingdom to the young man, Medea persuaded his daughters to attempt to renew their father's youth by magic means, which she promised to reveal to them. But she gave them false instructions and they only succeeded in killing their father. As a result of this murder Jason and Medea had to take refuge in Corinth, where they lived for ten years. Then Jason wearied of Medea and became betrothed to Creusa, the daughter of King Creon. Medea sent the girl a nuptial gown, which gave forth violent flames when she put it on and consumed the entire royal palace together with Creusa and Creon. Then Medea killed the two children she had had by Jason and fled on a winged chariot. After all these adventures Jason returned to Iolcus and regained his kingdom from Acastus, the son of Pelias, who had succeeded his father.

Medea led a wandering life for some time. She remained for a while at Athens with Aegeus until the coming of Theseus (whom she tried to trick Aegeus into poisoning) forced her to leave the region. She found refuge in Asia, in the land of Media, which took its name from her. Then she returned to her father, and restored his kingdom to him, for it had meanwhile been seized by Perses, Aeëtes' own brother. One tradition about Medea was that she never died, but was carried off to the underworld to be the wife of Achilles.

Meleager

Aetolia had its own hero, Meleager, round whom a whole cycle of legends grew up. He was the son of Oeneus, the king of Calydon, and Althaea, a daughter of Leda. His father's name, Oeneus, was derived from *oinos* (wine). The story was told of Dionysus presenting himself at his court and falling in love with Althaea. Oeneus became aware of this and looked on the god's love with favour. To repay him the latter gave him the first vine-plant in Greece. Deianeira was the offspring of Dionysus and Althaea. Meleager, for his part, although he had a human father, Oeneus, was said to be the love-child of Ares and Althaea.

Seven days after the birth of Meleager the Fates appeared to Althaea and predicted that the destiny of the tiny child was linked with a certain brand burning in the hearth. If the brand burned away, Meleager would die. Althaea hastened to remove and extinguish the brand. Then she carefully hid it.

When Meleager was a man, it so happened that Oeneus had forgotten to include Artemis in a sacrifice he had offered to all deities after the harvest. Artemis sent an enormous boar to ravage the land around Calydon. Meleager decided to rid the kingdom of this scourge. He called together a great number of hunters, a list of whose names has been compiled by mythologists. This list includes many names found among the Argonauts: Idas and Lynceus, Castor and Polydeuces, Theseus, Admetus of Pherae (the husband of Alcestis), Jason himself, Peirithous, Telamon, son of Aeacus and king of Salamis, Peleus, the father of Achilles, Amphiaraus the Argive, the sons of Thestius, who were brothers of Althaea and consequently uncles of Meleager, and finally a huntress, Atalanta, daughter of Schoeneus from Arcadia. Atalanta, it was said, had been exposed on Mount Parthenion at birth by her father, who wanted male heirs. She was suckled by a bear until some hunters found and reared her. When she grew up, Atalanta refused to marry; she was devoted to

Artemis, and on one occasion had killed with her arrows two centaurs who had attempted to ravish her. It was also said that she refused to marry because an oracle had told her that if she married she would one day be changed into an animal. And so, as she was a very swift runner, she declared that she would wed only the man who could run faster than she. When a suitor came to race against her, she would give him a slight lead, then pursue him with a lance in one hand. When she caught up with him, she would kill him. Now a certain Melanion came to ask for her hand, and the usual test began. Melanion, however, had brought some golden apples, given him by Aphrodite. Each time he was about to be overtaken he let one apple fall. Atalanta stopped to pick them up, and so Melanion won the race. One day, after their marriage, Atalanta and Melanion went hunting. They entered a temple (belonging to either Zeus or Cybele), and Melanion lay with her there. In vexation Zeus changed them both into lions—because it was thought that lions did not couple with lionesses, but with leopards. So this was the story of Atalanta, who was to play such a major role in the hunt at Calydon.

For nine days Oeneus feasted the hunters. On the tenth day they made for the open in spite of the reluctance of some of them to have a woman in their midst. But Meleager was in love with Atalanta, and he persuaded them to accept her presence. The boar was soon flushed; when hard pressed, it killed two of the hunters. Atalanta was the first to wound the animal with an arrow. Amphiaraus inflicted a second wound on it, and Meleager finished it off. He immediately presented the corpse to Atalanta, which aroused the indignation of the sons of Thestius. In his rage Meleager killed his uncles. As soon as she learned of this murder, Althaea threw into the fire the brand that was linked with the life of her son, and Meleager expired. But when she came to her senses and realised what she had done, Althaea hanged herself. The sisters of Meleager—Gorge, Eurymede, Deianeira and Melanippe—so bemoaned the death of their brother that Artemis turned them into birds; they became guinea-hens. But Dionysus gave Deianeira back her human shape, and Meleager in the underworld spoke to Heracles of her, and this led to their marriage.

Meleager had a half-brother, Tydeus, son of Oeneus and Periboea, who figured in the war of the Seven against Thebes, and who was the father of Diomedes.

One or several heroes were worshipped in each city or by each separate race in Greece, but the intermingling and intermarriage among princely families in the heroic period makes it difficult to limit the legendary cycle of any one of them to a particular country. The extraordinary mixture of customs, beliefs and races that existed in pre-classical Greece is seen nowhere more clearly than in its mythology.

The Calydonian boar-hunt. Because Oeneus, father of Meleager, forgot to sacrifice to Artemis, she sent a boar to ravage the countryside. With the assistance of Atalanta and a group of Greek heroes, Meleager succeeded in killing the boar. Sarcophagus lid. Late second century A.D. *Ashmolean Museum, Oxford*

Atalanta, who refused to marry unless a suitor could defeat her in a foot-race, also took part in the Calydonian boar-hunt organised by Meleager. Roman mosaic from Carthage. Fourth century A.D. *British Museum*

Incidents in the legendary cycles take place beyond the Hellenic world, and gods and heroes of other lands are introduced—usually in a modified form—into them. Gradually, behind the legendary account, the main human currents of what is called protohistory are seen to take shape.

Bellerophon, for example, was a hero of Corinth, but most of his exploits unfold in Lycia, where he foreshadows those Greek adventurers who in the historical period play such a major part in the affairs of Asia. Bellerophon was a son of Poseidon; his human father was Glaucus, son of Sisyphus, who was famous only for the manner of his death. Beaten in the funeral games in honour of Pelias, Glaucus was trampled by the horses of his own quadriga and devoured by them. They were mares which he refused to have coupled lest they should lose their turn of speed. Aphrodite extorted the ultimate penalty from him for this offence against her divinity.

Bellerophon, Glaucus' son, had accidently killed a citizen of Corinth (who might have been called Bellerus—thus providing a popular etymology for the hero's name). He had to leave the land and take refuge in Tiryns with King Proetus, who cleansed him of his crime. But Stheneboea, his wife, fell in love with Bellerophon and asked him to meet her. He refused. She then complained to her husband and accused the young man of wishing to seduce her. Not wanting to kill his own guest, Proetus sent Bellerophon to his wife's father, Iobates, with a letter asking Iobates to put the bearer to death. Iobates was king of Lycia.

Iobates began by imposing a most perilous labour on Bellerophon: to combat the Chimaera. This was a troublesome monster, with a fire-breathing goat's head, the fore-quarters of a lion and the hind part of a dragon. Iobates was of the opinion that the young man would never vanquish it alone. But Bellerophon had a valuable aid, the winged horse Pegasus, which had been created from the blood of Medusa and given him by Poseidon (or Athena). Mounted on Pegasus Bellerophon plunged down on the Chimaera from a great height and killed it. Iobates then sent him to fight the warlike Solymi who dwelt near by. He routed them with the aid of Pegasus. Iobates sent him to fight the Amazons and Bellerophon again carried off the victory. Then he had an ambush laid for him, but Bellerophon massacred those who had intended to murder him. Iobates, by now convinced that the hero was of divine descent, renounced the idea of killing him. He showed Bellerophon the letter from Proetus and gave him his daughter's hand in marriage. On his death his kingdom was bequeathed to Bellerophon.

Later, the hero returned to Tiryns. On learning of his return Stheneboea killed herself. Another version said that she tried to escape on Pegasus, but was unseated in the air and fell to her death. Bellerophon's life ended unhappily. In his pride he presumed to fly to Olympus on Pegasus. But Zeus flung him back to

The Corinthian hero Bellerophon and his winged horse, Pegasus, which helped him to carry out the tasks set him by Iobates, king of Lycia. Palazzo Spada, Rome. *Anderson-Giraudon*

earth, where he either died or was so badly wounded that he remained infirm until his death.

Bellerophon and the daughter of Iobates had a daughter, Laodameia, whom Zeus made the mother of the hero Sarpedon. Sarpedon makes an honourable appearance in the *Iliad* and must not be confused with the Sarpedon who was brother to Minos and Rhadamanthys and a son of Zeus by Europa. The confusion is all the easier because the son of Europa is presented as a king of Lycia and founder of Miletus, while the son of Bellerophon commanded a detachment of Lycians of Troy.

Perseus and Andromeda

Reminders of bygone migrations are to be found in the legends of the land of Argos. Mention has been made of the way in which Danaus, who was descended from Io, came there with his fifty daughters. Danaus did not take long to supplant the reigning king, Gelanor, and he founded the citadel of Argos. He also brought with him the cult of the Lycian Apollo (Apollo the Wolf), seemingly of Oriental origin. When his nephews, the sons of Aegyptus, arrived, they were assassinated, as has already been described, by his daughters. But one of them, Hypermnestra, spared her husband, Lynceus, and was banished by Danaus. Danaus was later reconciled with his son-in-law, who succeeded him, and the line of Argive kings stemmed from him.

The two grandsons of Lynceus and Hypermnestra, Proetus and Acrisius, were twins and hated one another. They were said to have fought from the moment of their birth. When they grew up they declared war on one another over who should inherit the throne. Acrisius won and Proetus went into exile in Lycia, where King Iobates received him. The latter provided him with an army, having given him his daughter Stheneboea in marriage, and re-established him in his own country. Proetus decided to leave Argos to Acrisius, and he founded a new town, Tiryns. And so the kingdom of Argolis was divided into two equal parts.

However, Acrisius had no heir. The story has already been told of the way in which the oracle dissuaded him from allowing his daughter, Danaë, to marry by foretelling that his grandson would kill him. Zeus outwitted Acrisius and we left Danaë and her son, Perseus, in a coffer, approaching the shore of Seriphos. They were received by a fisherman called Dictys, who was the father of the tyrannical ruler of the island, Polydectes. The latter fell in love with Danaë, but Perseus, older now, took good care of his mother. One day the tyrant invited Perseus and his friends to a banquet, and in the course of the meal he asked them what wedding presents they would give him. Perseus replied that the only present fit for a king was the head of one of the Gorgons. Polydectes took him at his word and sent him for it.

Athena and Hermes provided the hero with the

Perseus fleeing after cutting off Medusa's head. Equipped with winged sandals, a magic wallet, Hades' helmet of invisibility, and Hermes *harpe*, Perseus succeeded in cutting off the head of the gorgon Medusa in fulfilment of his promise to the tyrannical Polydectes. Clay pitcher, by the Pan painter. 470–460 B.C. *British Museum*

means of fulfilling his imprudent promise. First of all he went to find the three daughters of Phorcys, who told him how to find the nymphs in charge of the winged sandals, magic wallet (*kibisis*) and the helmet of invisibility, which belonged to Hades. The nymphs gave all these objects to Perseus, and Hermes added a *harpe*, a sword shaped like a reaping hook. Perseus at last sought out the three Gorgons, Sthenno, Euryale and Medusa, whom he found asleep. Only Medusa was mortal. Thanks to his sandals Perseus rose up in the air, and while Athena held above him a polished bronze shield to act as a mirror, he decapitated the monster. These precautions were necessary, for anyone who looked a Gorgon in the face was turned to stone. Perseus put Medusa's head in the wallet and started back. Medusa's sisters pursued him in vain, for he wore the helmet of invisibility.

On his way home Perseus passed through Ethiopia. There he saw a girl, fastened to some rocks on the shore, and a monster emerging from the sea to devour her. This young creature was called Andromeda, and her mother, Cassiopeia, was the cause of the entire tragedy, for she had claimed to be more beautiful than the nereids. They asked Poseidon to send a monster to devastate the land of Ethiopia. An oracle then told the king, Cepheus, that the scourge would cease only when he gave his daughter Andromeda to the monster. Perseus, moved to compassion, asked Cepheus for the hand of his daughter if he should succeed in setting her free. Cepheus consented, and Perseus, thanks to his magic weapons, obtained an easy victory. He was about to marry Andromeda when her uncle formed a conspiracy against him, intending to kill him. Perseus showed the head of Medusa to the conspirators, who were changed at once into stone statues. Then he set off again for Seriphos with Andromeda.

At Seriphos a dramatic situation awaited him. Polydectes had indicated his intention of ravishing Danaë, and she had taken refuge as a suppliant among the altars of the gods. Perseus changed the tyrant and his allies into statues and so set his mother free. He returned the magic weapons to Hermes and gave Medusa's head to Athena, who put it on her shield.

Perseus decided to return to Argos to see his grandfather. But when Acrisius knew that his grandson was approaching, he fled, fearing the fulfilment of the oracle. He took refuge at Larissa. Now it so happened that Perseus came to Larissa to take part in the games. He threw a discus, which struck Acrisius in the foot and killed him. Perseus' despair knew no bounds when he found out whom he had unintentionally killed, and though he gave Acrisius funeral honours he did not dare return to Argos to claim the throne. So he went to Tiryns and exchanged the kingdom of Argos for that of Tiryns with his cousin, Megapenthes, son of Proetus, who was then ruler. Later on another dynasty, that of the Pelopidae, was to succeed the descendants of Perseus in Argolis.

Cadmus

The legend about the origins of Thebes is similar to the preceding legends. Like Danaus, the founder of the city was of Oriental origin; like him he was descended from Io, through Epaphus, Libye and Agenor. His brothers were Phoenix, Cilix, Thasus (the eponyms of Phoenicia, Cilicia and the island of Thasus); their sister was Europa. When Europa was abducted by Zeus in the guise of a bull, Agenor sent his sons to look for her, telling them not to return without her. Cadmus, accompanied by his mother, Telephassa, went to Thrace. After the death of Telephassa he went to consult the oracle at Delphi, which advised him to abandon the search for Europa and to found a city. He was to follow a cow and to choose as his site the spot on which the animal collapsed with fatigue. As he was going towards Phocis from Delphi, he noticed a magnificent cow with a moon on each of its flanks (that is to say, a white ring). He followed it, and the cow led him to Boeotia. Finally, it lay down, and Cadmus knew that the oracle had been fulfilled. He wanted to offer the cow as a sacrifice to Athena, and with this in mind sent some of his companions to draw water from a nearby stream, called the Stream of Ares. But it was guarded by a dragon, which killed most of Cadmus' men. He made haste to slay the monster. Immediately, Athena appeared unto him and advised him to sow the teeth of the dragon in the ground. Cadmus did so; at once a human crop of armed warriors sprang from the earth. They looked threatening, so Cadmus threw a stone into their midst from a distance, and the warriors then all accused one another and began to fight. Only five survived, and these became the ancestors of the noble Theban families.

Cadmus was Ares' slave for eight years by way of expiation for the murder of the dragon. After this, thanks to Athena, he founded the kingdom of Thebes, and Zeus gave him Harmonia, daughter of Ares and Aphrodite. The wedding was celebrated with great pomp. The gods were there and the Muses sang. The Fates gave the bride a gown that they had woven, and Hephaestus gave her a gold necklace of his own workmanship. This necklace and gown were to play a major part in the war of the Seven. Harmonia bore Cadmus several children: Autonoë, Ino, Agave (mother of Pentheus) and Semele (the mother of Dionysus) and a son, Polydorus.

Towards the end of their life, Cadmus and Harmonia went to Illyria; there they were changed into serpents and reached the Elysian Fields. The dynasty of the Labdacidae to which Orpheus belongs was founded by their son, Polydorus. Labdacus, grandfather of Oedipus, was Polydorus' son. But a change of dynasty occurred before Labdacus' reign.

Antiope

As Labdacus was only a year old when Polydorus died, the regency was entrusted to the Theban

Cadmus slaying a 'dragon'. Advised by the Delphic oracle, Cadmus looked for a site for a city in Boeotia. He planted the teeth of the slain 'dragon' and from these sprang armed warriors, five of whom became the ancestors of the Theban noble families. Detail from Laconian kylix. Louvre. *Roger Viollet*

Nycteus, a descendant of Zeus and Pleione. Then, on the death of Nycteus, it was held by his brother, Lycus. Now Nycteus had a daughter called Antiope, who was so beautiful that Zeus fell in love and lay with her in the guise of a satyr. Because she feared the anger of her father, Antiope fled from home before the birth of her children and found refuge at the palace of King Epopeus. Nycteus in his despair committed suicide, after charging Lycus to avenge him. Lycus attacked Sicyon, killed Epopeus and brought back Antiope as his prisoner. Two children were born to Antiope as she was being dragged from Sicyon to Thebes: Lycus left the children, Amphion and Zethus, on the mountainside, where they were found and raised by shepherds. At Thebes Lycus and his wife Dirce ill-treated Antiope. But one night her chains fell off, and she fled towards the cottage where her children were being brought up. She made herself known, and they had their revenge on Dirce by fastening her to the tail of a furious bull. Lycus was also killed.

Amphion and Zethus reigned jointly at Thebes. Amphion, who was a musician, constructed the city walls and attracted stones by playing his lyre. Zethus, who was a man of action, carried them on his back. The people of Thebes used to draw visitors' attention to certain stones that gave a musical sound when struck. These were said to mark the spot where Amphion put down his lyre. Labdacus did not regain Cadmus' throne until the death of the two brothers.

The great literary sagas

With the arrival of the heroic cycles legends begin to become divorced from myth and to inspire complex works in which the first lineaments of a 'history' of the Hellenes can be detected. Continuing their evolution, these same legends formed, as it were, an immense source from which first Greek poets, from the time of Homer onwards, then Roman poets, drew their material, and thus these legends helped express throughout the years the basis of moral and spiritual experience in the ancient civilisation.

Generally speaking the theogonic myths appear but seldom in literary elaborations. Occasionally the 'lyrical' writers, in the widest sense (including the authors of so-called Homeric hymns), had recourse to them. But, in contrast to what happened in India and ancient Persia, the theogonic myths are not usually a subject for poetry. They occur in literary works as an episode or ornaments, or passing reference is made to them. Greek literature on the whole is on the human, as opposed to the divine, level; it deals with history rather than with myths. And this was perhaps one of the chief reasons for the fecundity of Hellenic mythology—that it tended from the beginning to inspire sculptors and painters to portray the human form in their work, and poets to express themselves in dithyrambs, tragedies and dramas permeated with human truth.

The *Iliad* and the cycle of Troy

The *Iliad*, in the eyes of the Ancients, was an essentially historic poem. Nowadays we believe that there was a historic core, but this was extended to include a great deal of legendary material borrowed from the heroic cycles and arranged in a different order. The *Iliad* was an attempt (largely collective, no doubt) to construct a work with a pan-Hellenic significance. It tells the story of a pact between the races living in Greece in Achaean times (before the Dorian invasion —which legends call the Return of the Heraclids) and how in accordance with this pact they went to claim reparation for the abduction of a woman from a

Fragment of a terracotta vase showing part of a 'heroic' army.
A fully armed soldier is ready to mount each of the chariots.
Acropolis Museum, Athens. *Alinari*

barbarous race, the Trojans, who dwelt in Phrygia. But as it happened, they had no feeling of racial hatred for the enemy, or of being profoundly different from them. Greek patriotism and hostility towards Asia did not appear (and even then it was only sporadic) until after the Medic wars. The gods simply chose one side or another to suit their personal whims, and sometimes passed from one camp to another. What was in question was not the destiny of a people or a race, but that of a noble family, often of a single hero. And the reasons given for events could be found in the history of this family or that individual. That is where legend comes in, faithful to its purpose of explaining the world.

The Atreidai

The *Iliad* tells of one short episode in a long drama that began several generations before the war of Troy. The story of Pelops' wooing of Hippodameia has already been told. Two sons were born of this marriage, Atreus and Thyestes. These two had a violent hatred for one another, the result of a curse that Pelops laid on them. Atreus and Thyestes had killed their half-brother, Chrysippus, so their father cursed them and sent them into exile. They took refuge at Mycenae with Eurystheus, who was their cousin german, or, according to other versions, they went to their uncle Sthenelus. They were given the task of governing the town and territory of Media.

After the death of Eurystheus, who was killed by the Heraclids, an oracle advised the people of Mycenae to make a son of Pelops their king. Atreus and Thyestes each began to plead his own cause. Some time before this Atreus had found a lamb with a golden fleece in his own flock. Although he had made Artemis a vow that he would sacrifice the finest product of his flock to her that year, he had kept the fleece for himself and shut it up in a chest. How-

ever, without his knowledge, Aerope, his wife, had given the magic fleece to her lover, and this lover was none other than Thyestes. In the presence of the Mycenaeans, Thyestes proposed that they should elect as king the candidate who could produce a golden fleece. Atreus accepted, for he felt sure of winning. Then Thyestes produced the stolen fleece and was elected.

At Zeus' command, however, there was a second test. It was agreed that if the sun changed course Atreus would reign over Mycenae; if not, it would be Thyestes. Thyestes accepted the trial, and at once the sun set in the east. So Atreus became king of Mycenae, and he immediately banished his brother. But when he learned at a later time of Thyestes' intrigue with Aerope, he pretended to become reconciled with him and had him recalled. When Thyestes returned to Mycenae, Atreus secretly killed three children that Thyestes had had by a naiad and served them up to their father, who unknowingly ate of their flesh. When Thyestes had eaten this frightful meal, Atreus revealed the nature of the meat he had consumed and presented him with the heads of his three children.

Thyestes took refuge in Silcyon and gave himself up to thoughts of revenge. On the advice of the oracle he begat a son, Aegisthus, on his own daughter Pelopia (concealing his true identity) and so arranged matters that Pelopia married her uncle, Atreus. The latter raised his wife's son without knowing who the real father was. When the child was grown up, he imposed on him the task of killing Thyestes, but Aegisthus discovered in time that Thyestes was, in fact, his father, and so he returned to Mycenae, killed Atreus instead, and put Thyestes on the throne. But the role of Aegisthus was not the finish there, and the interplay of successive acts of vengeance was to continue from one line of descendants to the other.

The Trojan war was a favourite subject for Greek artists; it is
interesting to compare this treatment of Paris' abduction of
Helen with that on page 96. Bas-relief: Lateran Museum, Rome
Giraudon. Vase painting. *British Museum*

Atreus and Aerope had two sons, Agamemnon and
Menelaus. Agamemnon married Clytemnestra, the
daughter of Tyndareus and Leda, but this marriage
too was marred by violence, for Clytemnestra's first
husband was a son of Thyestes called Tantalus.
Agamemnon killed this first husband to obtain the
young woman for himself. She was loath to agree to
marriage: three daughters, Chrysothemis, Laodice,
brothers, the Dioscuri, so threatened Agamemnon
at one point that he had to take refuge at the court
of Sparta with Tyndareus. Castor and Polydeuces
became reconciled with their new brother-in-law,
but the union of Agamemnon and Clytemnestra was
doomed, as the rest of the legend shows.

However, several children were born of this
marriage: three daughters, Chrysothemis, Laodice,
and Iphianassa, and a son, the last-born, Orestes.
A more recent tradition (found in the tragic poets)
speaks of two daughters, Iphigeneia and Electra, and
hardly any mention is made of the other daughters.

Helen

After Aegisthus had killed Atreus, Agamemnon and
Menelaus had to leave Mycenae; they sought shelter
in Sparta with Tyndareus. It was the time when all
the princes of Greece were assembled in Sparta to
demand the hand of Helen. Tyndareus was highly
embarrassed, for in choosing one he feared to dis-
please the others and so risk war. He was therefore
glad to listen to the advice given him by Odysseus,
prince of Ithaca, one of the poorest of the suitors.
Odysseus advised him to bind them all by an oath
to accept Helen's own choice, and he added that
they should promise to give their aid to the chosen
husband if anyone should dispute his rights. Tyndareus thought this an excellent idea; the oath was
sworn, and Helen chose Menelaus.

For several years the couple lived happily in Sparta.

When he died, Tyndareus left his kingdom to them,
while Agamemnon reigned at Mycenae (or Argos,
traditions vary). Then Paris arrived on the scene.
He was the Trojan to whom Aphrodite had promised
the hand of Helen, most beautiful of mortal women.
There came a time when Menelaus had to leave
Sparta to go to the funeral of his grandfather Cat-
reus in Crete. So it was easy for Paris to seduce Helen
and to take her to Troy. For his sake Helen abandoned
her daughter by Menelaus, Hermione.

The Greek army assembles

Menelaus was warned of his misfortune by Iris, the
messenger of the gods, and hastened to return to
Sparta, where he called together all those who had
previously given Tyndareus their oath.

It was not easy to win the aid of Odysseus. Palamedes, the son of Nauplius, was sent to Ithaca to
fetch Odysseus, but he had just had a son by his
beloved wife, Penelope, and was not inclined for
adventure. Palamedes found him busy ploughing
his fields with a plough drawn by an ox and an ass.
When a furrow was complete, Odysseus would sow
salt in it. It appeared that he had gone mad. But
Palamedes took little Telemachus, the son of Odysseus, and put him on the ground in front of the
plough. Odysseus then stopped his team and,
abandoning his pretence of insanity, agreed to keep
the oath he had given Tyndareus.

Odysseus was sent to the harem of King Lycomedes
at Scyros, where Achilles had been concealed by his
mother, the nereid Thetis, because she knew that
the young man was destined to perish if he went to
Troy. And so Achilles was living there among young
girls, his identity effectively concealed by his youthfulness and long, blond hair. But his presence was
known to be essential at Troy. So Odysseus, disguised as a merchant, gained entrance to Lycomedes'

palace; then he offered his wares for sale, and whereas the women chose fabrics and jewels, Achilles took up the weapons. Odysseus thus recognised him and persuaded him to join the expedition.

At last the army was assembled. Each of the princes had provided a contingent, and Agamemnon was chosen as the supreme chief. The troops assembled at Aulis. Calchas, the official soothsayer, offered a sacrifice, and a favourable omen was sent by Zeus: a serpent darted from the altar towards a nearby tree, devoured eight little birds that were in a nest, together with their mother, and was then turned to stone. Calchas concluded from this that the war would last ten years, and that the town would be captured.

The expedition to Mysia

According to one tradition, not included in the *Iliad*, when the army first embarked it set the wrong course and had to disembark at Mysia in the kingdom of Telephus, a son of Heracles. The Mysians repelled the invaders, and recognising their error the Greeks returned to their own country—although Telephus was quite seriously injured by Achilles' lance. Telephus had later to come to Aulis and ask Achilles for the appropriate cure. The remedy was a little rust from the same lance, which alone was capable of healing the wounds it caused. The adventure involving Telephus was the subject of a tragedy by Euripides that has not survived.

Eight years after this first unfortunate expedition the Greeks assembled again at Aulis, but they had to wait for favourable winds. Total calm lay over the sea. Calchas was consulted, and he said that it was due to the anger of Artemis, and that Iphigeneia must be sacrificed to appease her. Unknown to the Greeks Artemis substituted a hind at the last moment and took the young girl to serve her as a priestess in Taurus.

At last the fleet was able to set sail. At Lemnos they had to abandon Philoctetes, Heracles' former companion, who carried the hero's arms. Philoctetes had wounded himself with one of his own arrows, and this incurable wound gave off a foul stench.

Achilles' anger

For the first nine years of the siege of Troy there were few notable events. Achilles and Agamemnon took part in several pirate raids on coastal towns. At Chryse and Lyrnessus, they took prisoner two girls, two cousins called Chryseis and Briseis, and brought them back to camp. Achilles' share of the plunder was the young Briseis. Agamemnon obtained Chryseis, the daughter of a priest of Apollo called Chryses, who complained to his god. Apollo at once sent a plague upon the Achaeans, although he was otherwise favourable to them. Calchas, on examining the omens, knew why the god was annoyed—Chryseis must be sent back to her father.

This is the point at which the *Iliad* begins. It was assumed that all the preceding events would be known to the reader. They form an unwritten saga on which the epic was based and were used in other poems that are no longer in existence. The subject of the *Iliad* is only one episode in the Trojan war: the quarrel between Agamemnon and Achilles, which almost caused the downfall of the Achaean army.

At the beginning of the poem, the assembled soldiers have learned what has caused the plague and force Agamemnon to send Chryseis back. Agamemnon demands Briseis by way of compensation. Achilles, who loves the girl, or perhaps is simply obstinate, refuses to give her up. Agamemnon, by virtue of his authority as supreme leader, obliges him to do so. Achilles has to obey, but he refuses—and this he has the right to do—to take any further part in the war.

Soon fighting begins around Troy. Agamemnon is the victim of a dream, which leads him to believe that he can obtain victory without Achilles. But the successes of the Trojans soon disillusion him. The camp is attacked by Hector, the son of Priam, king of Troy, the main hero on the Trojan side. Agamemnon realises that he must effect a reconciliation with Achilles. He sends Briseis with costly gifts and promises Achilles the hand of one of his daughters. From this point Achilles has the initiative. Achilles has already allowed Patroclus, his faithful friend and cousin, to attack the walls of Troy. Patroclus was killed by Hector, and his armour (which belonged to Achilles) was removed by the Trojan as a trophy of his victory. Thetis has new armour made by Hephaestus and Achilles rejoins the battle. From now on the poem devotes itself almost entirely to recounting Achilles' victories — for the shadow of death is already hovering over him. His horse Xanthus (the Chestnut) is endowed for the moment with powers of speech and predicts his early death. But Achilles pays no heed; in the past all sorts of signs have been given him of his destiny; each time he has neglected the warnings. Although he could have lived a long and peaceful life at Phthia, where his father, Peleus, rules, he has chosen of his own free will a short and glorious existence. No-one can resist the prowess of Achilles; the adversaries fall one by one. Finally, all the Trojans return to the town, and Achilles and Hector are left face to face alone outside the walls. For the first time in his life Hector is afraid. He flees with Achilles in pursuit. In Olympus Zeus is watching the fight with all the gods around him, and he weighs the fates of Achilles and Hector in gigantic scales.

The death of Hector

Once their fates are known to Zeus, nothing can stop the drama from unfolding. Athena, disguised as

The fight for the body of Patroclus, friend of Achilles. Gods fought on behalf of the Achaeans and the Trojans in the course of the Trojan war.

Athena stands between Achilles and Agamemnon, perhaps in the role of peacemaker during their quarrel at Troy. Terracotta, From Tanagra. *Giraudon*

Hector, prince of Troy, is slain by Achilles, watched over by Athena. Vase painting. *Alinari-Giraudon*

Deiphobus, Hector's brother, comes to his side. Hector thinks he has support, so he stops and turns to face Achilles. But then Athena disappears. Hector knows that this is the end, and he is killed by Achilles. With his dying breath Hector predicts the imminent death of Achilles.

The *Iliad* ends with the ambassadors of Priam coming to claim from Achilles the body of Hector. It does not continue with what would seem to be the natural end of the story—the death of Achilles.

It is possible to reconstruct the later events of the Trojan war through allusions found in other works of literature—the *Odyssey*, for instance, references made by tragic dramatists, the notes of ancient commentators and the surviving fragments of lost epics.

The saga of Achilles includes numerous episodes. First of all the fight against Penthesileia, the queen of the Amazons, who came to the rescue of the city when Hector's funeral was taking place. At first she had some success, driving the Greeks back as far as their own camp, but Achilles mortally wounded her; then, just as she was about to die, he looked into her eyes and fell desperately in love with her. Achilles also had to fight Memnon, the son of Dawn, and eventually killed him.

The story of the death of Achilles was told in various ways. Some traditions state that Achilles fell in love with one of the daughters of Priam, Polyxena, whom he had seen when Hector's body was weighed to decide the ransom Achilles was to accept for it. It would appear that Achilles secretly offered to betray the Greeks to Priam at this point if he would give him his daughter. Priam seemingly accepted, and the treaty was to be signed in the temple of Apollo, not far from the gates of Troy. Achilles went there alone and unarmed, but Paris was hiding behind a pillar and struck him down with an arrow.

The most generally accepted legend said that Achilles died fighting, killed by Apollo's shaft, which struck him in the heel, the only vulnerable part of his body; for in his childhood his mother had plunged him into the waters of the Styx to make him invulnerable, but a leaf was stuck to one heel and this prevented the magic water from touching the child's weak spot.

Achilles was lamented by the nymphs and Muses in Thetis' retinue, and the Greeks raised a tomb to him on the shore, which was shown to travellers in antiquity. Alexander and Caesar visited it. But Thetis took her son to the White Island in the mouth of the Danube, and there he continued to live the life he preferred. Sailors passing close to the island heard the continual clash of arms by day and by night, the clink of glasses and the gay sounds of an eternal banquet. Achilles' ghost was said to have had companions after death: Polyxena, Medea, Iphigeneia and even Helen.

The capture of Troy

The deaths of Hector and Achilles did not mean the end of the Trojan war. It was soon known that the gods would grant the Greeks victory only if certain conditions were fulfilled. The young son of Priam, Helenus, had to be captured, for he had received the gift of prophecy from Apollo. He alone knew the secrets of the gods. After the death of Paris, Priam had refused Helenus the hand of Helen and had given her to another son, Deiphobus, whom Hector favoured. In disappointment Helenus had taken refuge in the mountains, where Odysseus found him by an equal measure of force and persistence. Helenus foretold that Troy would be taken on three conditions: if Neoptolemus, the son of Achilles, came to fight on the Achaean side; if the bones of Pelops were brought back to Asia; and if the Palladium (the divine image made by Athena, which

Sarpedon, slain by Patroclus during the Trojan war, is carried away by Hypnos (Sleep) and Thanatos (Death). Vase painting. *British Museum*

One of the conditions that had to be fulfilled before Troy could be taken by the Achaeans was the theft of the Palladium (a sacred image made by Athena) from the temple of Athena on the citadel of Troy. Odysseus and Diomedes succeeded in fulfilling this condition. Here Diomedes is shown with the statue. Attic red-figured cup (interior), by the Diomedes painter. Early fourth century B.C. *Ashmolean Museum, Oxford*

had fallen from Olympus) was taken from the Trojans. Helenus also said that Philoctetes was to lend the Achaeans the aid of Heracles' arms. All these conditions Odysseus contrived to fulfil.

It was not difficult to seek the bones of Pelops, which were interred at Pisa, in Elis, where he had previously lived with Hippodameia. Neoptolemus, the son that Achilles had fathered on one of the daughters of King Lycomedes at Scyros (who is often called Pyrrhus, the Red One, on account of the colour of his hair) was living with his grandfather. Odysseus, Phoenix and Diomedes went as ambassadors to him. Lycomedes tried to prevent his leaving, but faithful to the warring tradition of his father Neoptolemus followed Agamemnon's envoys.

Stealing the Palladium was more difficult, as it was closely guarded in the temple of Athena on the citadel of Troy. Odysseus and Diomedes undertook to steal it. They entered the town (some say by a sewer) and Odysseus gained access to the citadel. On his way he appears to have been recognised by Helen, who did not denounce him, but, on the contrary, helped him, thus acquiring some claim to his gratitude. Then Odysseus set off with his plunder, after massacring several guards. The only condition still to be fulfilled was to persuade Philoctetes to come to Troy. He had been abandoned at Lemnos and was leading a miserable life. He bore a profound hatred for the Achaean chiefs, who had left him without proper care after he had been wounded. Once again Odysseus accepted the mission. With his powers of persuasion he successfully explained away the Achaeans' conduct, and promised that Philoctetes would be cared for by the sons of Asclepius, Podaleirius and Machaon, who were at Troy, and thus he could not fail to get well again. Philoctetes was prevailed upon to follow Odysseus. Moreover, he was cured, as Odysseus had promised.

The Trojan horse

So all the conditions were fulfilled, and Troy must inevitably be captured. But the Greeks had to have recourse to a final ruse—half stratagem of war, half magic rite—the idea of which seems to have come from Helenus once again. A huge wooden horse was built, in which the best of the warriors hid. Then the Achaeans razed their camp, embarked on their ships and sailed away. But they sailed only as far as Tenedos, an island not far from Troy. One man was left behind, Sinon, cousin german to Odysseus, another grandson of the resourceful Autolycus. Sinon was captured by Trojan shepherds while he was pretending to hide and taken to Priam. There he put on an act, pretending that he had been persecuted by the Greeks, who, he said, had intended to sacrifice him to the gods. He then allowed the Trojans to extract false statements from him about the intentions of the Greek leaders with regard to the wooden horse.

This horse, according to Sinon, was an offering intended for Pallas Athena in reparation for the sacrilege committed by Odysseus when he stole the Palladium. The Greeks, he said, had been alarmed by various omens, and Calchas had told them that the goddess required them to devote a cult to her in the form of a horse. So the Greeks built a wooden horse, so big that the Trojans would not be able to get into their town, for they knew that if the Trojans worshipped the horse within their city walls they would have supremacy over Greece. Sinon had just finished these false revelations when an omen, equally false, was sent by Apollo. Laocoön, Apollo's priest, was the victim. When he heard Sinon's discourse, Laocoön accused him of lying, and he formally opposed the idea of making a breach in the wall to let the horse in, as the majority of the Trojan leaders were proposing. But just when Laocoön was about to offer a sacrifice on the shore, two monstrous serpents came out of the sea and strangled him and his sons. This was a punishment sent by Apollo for an act of sacrilege committed much earlier in his temple, but the Trojans thought that the gods were punishing him for opposing Sinon's advice, and so the decision was taken to pull down part of the walls of Troy and bring the horse into the city.

The following night Sinon freed the warriors who were inside the horse and gave the agreed torch signal to the Greek ships. The warriors from the horse massacred the Trojans and opened the gates of the town to the rest of the army. Troy was taken.

The fate of the captives

Menelaus hastened to the house of Deiphobus, where he knew Helen was living. He badly mutilated Deiphobus and seized his unfaithful wife. Traditions differ in the account of their meeting. Either Helen betrayed Deiphobus, concealed his arms and allowed Menelaus to take possession of the house, so as to gain pardon for herself; or Odysseus interceded for her; or else Helen quite simply took refuge before the domestic altar, and in her disordered state of dress presented such a moving spectacle to Menelaus that he had not the courage to put her to death.

Meanwhile, on the shore, the Greeks were sharing out the Trojan spoils with frequent quarrels. The most famous quarrel—a subject often treated by tragic poets—was that between Odysseus and the 'great Aias' (Ajax), son of Telamon. Thetis had promised to give Achilles' arms to the most valiant Greek, he who had inspired most fear in the Trojans. Ajax and Odysseus both claimed the prize. Trojan prisoners were questioned to help them reach a decision, and they designated Odysseus, some say in spite. Odysseus obtained the arms, but during the night Ajax went mad, massacred the herds that were to provide food for the Greeks, and in the morning, when he saw what he had done, he committed suicide.

The fate of Trojan captives was determined in various ways. Cassandra, the prophetess, was given to Agamemnon. Polyxena was slaughtered on the tomb of Achilles. Andromache, the wife of Hector, fell to the lot of Neoptolemus, the son of Achilles, but Odysseus demanded that Astyanax, the son of Hector, be killed. He was thrown from the top of the city walls. The old queen, Hecuba, who had been present at the murder of her husband, killed by Neoptolemus before the domestic altar, avenged herself in the most terrible manner on one of her sons-in-law, King Polymnestor. He had massacred the youngest son of Priam, who had been entrusted to Hecuba so that at least one representative of the royal dynasty would survive if disaster befell the Trojans. For this crime Hecuba had Polymnestor brought to her on some false pretext and tore his eyes out. The Achaean leaders decided that she should be stoned. But later, instead of her corpse under the pile of stones, they found a fiery-eyed bitch, which ran away.

The return journeys

The long tale of Troy was not finished, even when the town was captured. The destinies that were set in motion on the day when Dardanus founded the first citadel on the hill, significantly named 'hill of Error' (Hill of Ate), continued to unfold almost for ever and to have their effect on the world.

For the majority of Achaean leaders there was the drama of the return journeys (*Returns* was the name of a lost epic). Some, like Menelaus, who had a legitimate reason for fighting against Troy, escaped misfortune. The majority were victims of a curse, and for a number of years they knew no rest.

The greater part of the fleet came within sight of Greece with most contingents aboard. But off the coasts of Euboea at night they were led astray by a fire burning on the reefs, and most of the ships were wrecked. This fire had been lit by Nauplius, the grandson of the other Nauplius begotten of

The Trojan horse, in which were concealed Achaean soldiers ready to open the gates of the city to Agamemnon's army. Bibliothèque Nationale. *Giraudon*

After the fall of Troy the Achaeans exacted a fearful vengeance on the Trojans, the survivors of the war being murdered or enslaved. This painting shows Trojans being sacrificed on the funeral pyre of Patroclus.

Poseidon and Amymone. Nauplius was a remarkable helmsman; it was sometimes claimed that he replaced Tiphys at the helm of the *Argo*. His son was Palamedes, who persuaded Odysseus to join the Trojan expedition. Odysseus was so incensed against Palamedes that he arranged to have him wrongfully accused of sacrilegious theft at Troy, and the Achaeans who heard the case declared that he should be stoned. Nauplius decided to avenge himself on the Achaeans and for this reason he brought about the shipwreck of their fleet in Euboea.

Agamemnon

Agamemnon, who had remained at Troy rather longer than the others, was not shipwrecked with the rest of the fleet, but was, none the less, victim of another form of revenge, which was awaiting him in his own palace. In his absence he had entrusted his wife Clytemnestra to the care of an old bard, Demodocus. But Clytemnestra, whose feelings of rancour towards her husband had not abated, arranged to get rid of this inconvenient chaperone and lived openly with Aegisthus, the son of Thyestes. The curse of Pelops had not yet worked itself out. Aegisthus knew that Agamemnon's return was imminent and posted watchers so that he might welcome the king on the shore with great protestations of joy. He offered him a banquet, in the course of which he killed him. This is the simplest version of the story. But this is not the version found in the tragic plays, notably those of Aeschylus. They depicted Clytemnestra as the murderess of her husband. She was driven to it by Aegisthus, but also by her own rancour, and another reason was supplied by the news of the liaison between Agamemnon and Cassandra. When Agamemnon returned, she greeted him smilingly and gave him a tunic to put on, the sleeves of which were sewn up. Agamemnon took a bath, and unsuspectingly

This Argive vase shows a naval battle in which foot soldiers prepare to fight with spears and shield. Below, Odysseus and his companions blind the giant Polyphemus who had made them captive. *Mansell*

Odysseus tied to the mast of his ship, while his sailors' ears are stopped with wax as they sail past the island of the Sirens. Mosaic. House of Dionysus and Odysseus at Dougga. Third to fourth centuries A.D. Bardo Museum, Tunis. *Roger Wood*

began to put on the garment, but naturally met with some difficulty. When Clytemnestra saw him in this plight, she took a sword and killed him.

Aegisthus and Clytemnestra remained sole rulers at Mycenae. But Electra, one of Agamemnon's daughters, succeeded in removing secretly her young brother, little Orestes, thus saving him from certain death. Orestes was brought up in Phocis by Strophius, together with the king's son, Pylades. When he grew to manhood Orestes was ordered by Apollo to avenge his father by killing Aegisthus and Clytemnestra. Orestes obeyed. He presented himself at the palace in the guise of a traveller and struck Aegisthus. The latter cried out, and Clytemnestra came hastening to him. She recognised her son and begged him to have pity on her, but Orestes was obdurate, and she was slain.

As the assassin of his own mother Orestes was pursued by the Erinnyes—the Furies—who allowed him not one moment's repose. Accompanied by Pylades he sought refuge at Delphi, where Apollo absolved him of his murder. But the Erinnyes continued to pursue him relentlessly. Finally, he was arraigned before the tribunal of the Areopagus in Athens, and the judges were equally divided between condemnation and acquittal. But Athena, who presided over the tribunal, voted for clemency and Orestes was set free. Thenceforth the curse of Pelops ceased to take effect.

The return of Odysseus

The most famous of all return journeys is that of Odysseus. It formed the subject of the *Odyssey*, and stories about Odysseus eventually came to form a heroic cycle, which was particularly popular in Italy and Etruria.

After the fall of Troy, Odysseus quarrelled with the other leaders and followed Agamemnon. But he soon separated from him and sailed to Thrace, where he took and ravaged the town of Ismarus. He spared only Apollo's priest, Maron, who made him a gift of twelve jars of precious wine, both sweet and strong. Then he sailed south and after some days he landed in the country of the Lotophagi, people who lived on a wonderful fruit, the lotus-fruit, which was so superb that whoever tasted it was unwilling to leave the place again. Odysseus had to use force to get his men away from this delicacy.

Turning north again Odysseus came to Sicily, to the land of the Cyclopes. He went ashore with twelve men, and they entered a cave owned by the Cyclops Polyphemus, a fearful giant who had only one eye, which was set in the middle of his forehead. Polyphemus took them prisoner and prepared to devour them two by two. Odysseus succeeded in making him drink some of Maron's wine, which they had brought with them, and the monster sank into a profound sleep. Taking advantage of this, the hero blinded the giant, and he and his men made good

Odysseus pursued by Boreas, the North Wind. From a burlesque vase. *Ashmolean Museum, Oxford*

their escape hidden in the fleece of the giant's sheep. Poseidon, who was the father of Polyphemus, conceived a violent hatred of Odysseus from this moment.

After he had escaped from the Cyclopes, Odysseus arrived at the island of Aeolus, the master of the winds, who gave him a sack containing all the winds—except a favourable breeze to take them home to Ithaca. But his companions opened the sack when Odysseus was asleep; a storm was let loose, and drove them back to the island of Aeolus, who refused to receive them. Odysseus set off again, trusting to chance, but the Laestrygonians, a cannibal race, deprived him of all his boats, save one, and in this craft he got to the island of Aeaea, where Circe the magician lived.

Circe was the daughter of the Sun and the sea-nymph Perse, and the sister of the king of Colchis, Aeëtes. She lived alone with her servants and turned any travellers who came to her palace into animals. Ignorant of what was awaiting them, Odysseus sent ahead a group of sailors; the magician received them kindly, gave them a magic drink and turned them into wolves, dogs and other animals. When his companions did not return, Odysseus went alone to find them. In the wood Hermes approached him and told him the secret of resisting Circe's spells. If he put a herb known as *moly* in the drink, the sorceress would be at his mercy. Armed with the magic plant, Odysseus resisted the spells; he drew his sword and forced Circe to turn his friends back into men. Then he spent a month (or a year) of delight with her, and she bore him a son, Telegonus. When the time came for him to leave, Circe advised Odysseus to consult the ghost of the seer Teiresias in the land of the Cimmerians.

Teiresias was duly evoked, and revealed his future to Odysseus, who indefatigably set forth again. He sailed by the Isle of the Sirens, daughters of the muse Melpomene and the river-god Achelous. These monsters were half woman and half bird, and their music attracted sailors, who were then wrecked on the island's reefs and devoured by these creatures. On the advice of Circe, Odysseus stopped the ears of the sailors with wax, then had them tie him to the mast of the ship. Only Odysseus could hear the divine singing, so they got through the dangerous straits. Then he had to sail through the straits guarded by Scylla and Charybdis, one a six-headed monster who devoured sailors, and the other a terrifying whirlpool.

Odysseus then landed on the island of Thrinacia, where white oxen grazed that were sacred to the Sun. There the travellers were becalmed and had to stay longer than they intended, so that, prompted by hunger, Odysseus' companions could not resist killing an ox while he was asleep. The Sun then went to complain to Zeus. When the ship set off again, the god sent a terrible storm, the ship foundered and all were drowned except Odysseus, who was fastened to the mast. He was tossed on the sea for nine days and nine nights; then, on the tenth day, he landed on the island of Calypso, a nymph who kept him there for several years. But Athena persuaded Zeus to send Hermes with instructions that Calypso should let him go. And thus, after building himself a raft, and surviving a tempest sent by Poseidon, he came, exhausted but alive, to the island of the Phaeacians.

Odysseus' journeys were now almost finished. The Phaeacians received him with kindness, and bestowing many gifts upon him had him conveyed as far as Ithaca, his own kingdom. But this Odysseus had to reconquer, for it was in the hands of a group of young princes, suitors of Penelope, who had taken possession of the entire palace and laid down the laws of Ithaca. Disguised as a beggar, Odysseus succeeded in entering his palace, recognised by only one or two faithful thralls. Now in the palace Odysseus had left a bow, which only he was able to bend. On the night of his return each of the suitors attempted to bend the bow, but failed. Then Odysseus took the bow and shot down the suitors. At last Odysseus had regained his kingdom.

And so the *Odyssey* ends, but the saga of Odysseus was not quite over. A story was told of how the hero took to the sea again, went fighting in Epirus, or to establish towns in Etruscan territory among the Tyrrhenians, until, finally, he was accidentally killed by Telegonus, the son that Circe had borne him.

The birth of tragedy

The Trojan war and the postscript to it—the stories of the homeward voyages—were subjects very dear to poets, especially tragic poets. They endured for many centuries, and with time the material grew richer, for it tended to attract and to assimilate local legends. But other cycles also provided subject-matter for poets, in particular the Theban cycle.

The Theban cycle

Oedipus, the supreme tragic hero, was a descendant of Cadmus. His father was Laius, son of Labdacus; the last-mentioned was the son of Polydorus, the son of Cadmus and Harmonia. In the *Odyssey* Oedipus' mother was called Epicaste; the tragic poets call her Iocaste, and she was generally connected with Pentheus and therefore with Echion, who was one of the Spartoi (men who sprang from the dragon's teeth sown by Cadmus). Iocaste is the name she has retained, for Sophocles uses it in the Oedipus tragedies.

The birth of Oedipus

Oedipus was born with a curse upon him. Traditions vary as to its nature. Sometimes it was said that an oracle prophesied that the child born of Iocaste and Laius would kill its own father. In other versions an oracle forbade Laius to have children; if he disobeyed, not only would the child in question kill its

167

The heroic cycles became the subjects of Greek drama, in which masks were worn by the actor. This bas-relief in stone shows how one of these masks must have appeared. *Ashmolean Museum, Oxford*

The Greek Sphinx, unlike the Egyptian, was a creature to be feared. Oedipus saved Thebes from the Sphinx and so became king. 550–500 B.C. *British Museum*

father, but it would bring a frightful succession of misfortunes upon its own house. Another version, which seems anxious to provide moral justification for this divine decree against Laius, related that at the time when Lycus was ruler of Thebes, Laius had sought shelter at the court of King Pelops at Pisa. There he fell in love with young Chrysippus, son of the king, and corrupted him; he was even said to have been the first to have felt and practised unnatural love. For this reason Pelops put a curse upon him, and the gods, sanctioning this curse, intended to deprive him of male heirs.

Laius took no heed of the warning of the gods, and he had a son. But, out of prudence, he had the child removed and left out on the mountainside. He also had the child's ankles pierced and a strap put through them, and the swelling caused by this wound was the origin of the name Oedipus, which means 'Swell-Foot'. The baby boy was found by Corinthian shepherds, who took him to their king, Polybus. Periboea, his wife, thought the child very beautiful and brought him up with the greatest care. She was all the more charmed with the gift made by the shepherds as she passionately wanted a child, but was unable to bear children.

Throughout his childhood and adolescence, Oedipus remained at the court of Polybus, who looked on him as his own son. But when he grew to manhood, he left Polybus and went to seek his fortune in the world at large. Various reasons for this are given. The simplest version, perhaps the oldest, was that Oedipus went to look for some horses stolen from Polybus. Other traditions state that in the course of a quarrel with a Corinthian he was taxed with being a foundling. He questioned Polybus about it in some anxiety of mind and was told that in fact he was not the king's own son. Oedipus then decided to go off and look for his real father.

Whatever the reason, this journey was to be decisive for Oedipus as it led to his meeting with Laius, which was generally said to have taken place in Phocis. They met on a narrow road; and when Laius' herald ordered Oedipus to allow the king to pass and killed one of his horses because he was slow to obey, Oedipus in anger killed both the herald and Laius.

And yet Oedipus had been warned by the gods. When he had met Laius he was returning from Delphi where Apollo's oracle had told him that he would kill his father and marry his mother. In spite of this warning he could not escape his destiny.

After the death of Laius Oedipus went on his way, unaware of what he had done, until he reached the gates of Thebes. There he met the Sphinx, a monster half woman, half lion. This monster asked riddles of passers-by and devoured those who could not answer.

The Sphinx

The riddles of the Sphinx were always the same: 'What being walks sometimes on two feet, sometimes on three and sometimes on four, and is weakest when it has most?' 'Who are the two sisters who give birth to one another?' The answers are obvious: to the first question, 'man'; and to the second, 'Day and Night' (both words being feminine in Greek). But the Thebans could not answer them. Oedipus solved the riddles, and the mortified Sphinx leaped into a ravine and was dashed to pieces on the rocks. The grateful Thebans wanted Oedipus to be their king. After the death of Laius, Creon, Iocaste's brother, had taken office, but he stood down in favour of the stranger, who then married Iocaste, his mother.

The drama

Soon, however, the secret of Oedipus' birth was to be revealed. In an ancient version Iocaste recognised him by the scars on his heels. But Sophocles invented (or followed) a much more dramatic tradition. When Oedipus became king of Thebes, a plague befell the city. Creon was sent to Delphi to ask the cause of it, and he came back with a very clear reply: the plague would cease only when the death of Laius was avenged. Then there began a long official inquiry, conducted by Oedipus himself, who had already sworn a terrible oath against the murderer, whoever he might be. Eventually, the truth was uncovered: Oedipus was indeed the son of Iocaste and his father's assassin. When Iocaste heard the dreadful facts she went into the palace and hanged herself. Oedipus put out his own eyes with Iocaste's brooch and left Thebes for voluntary exile. He went forth from the town with his daughter Antigone. His two sons, Eteocles and Polyneices, turned from him in horror, and he cursed them.

When the legend was in its epic stage of evolution, the death of Iocaste did not interrupt the reign, for Oedipus continued to direct the affairs of Thebes, and died in the course of an expedition against the neighbouring people, the Minyans of Erginus. But Sophocles with his great art produced an image of Oedipus wandering blind, then seeking shelter in Attica, where Theseus welcomed him with kindness. Oedipus died in the grove of Colonus in Attica, and an oracle declared that the country where he was buried would be blessed by the gods. When they learned of this, Eteocles and Polyneices asked Theseus to give them his mortal remains, but were refused.

The War of the Seven

But the curse on Oedipus, and the 'original sin' implicit in his very birth, continued to have their effect on the next generation. Eteocles and Polyneices inherited the throne of Thebes, and to avoid argument they decided to reign in alternate years. Eteocles was king first. Polyneices went away. But when the year was over and he returned, his brother refused to hand over the throne to him. So Polyneices decided to organise an expedition and use force to establish his rights.

Now at this time a prince called Adrastus ruled over Argos, sharing the land with Amphiaraus and Iphis. This had been the position since Proetus shared his kingdom with the seer Melampus and his brother Bias, in order that his daughters might be cured. After Polyneices was hounded from Thebes by Eteocles, he arrived at Adrastus' palace one stormy night. By coincidence Tydeus, the son of Oeneus, king of Calydon, arrived at the same time, having been sent into exile by his father because of a murder. They met in the forecourt and started to quarrel. Adrastus was wakened by the noise, had them both brought in, and absolved Tydeus of the stigma of murder. Then he noticed that one youth had a lion on his shield and the other a boar, and he remembered an oracle telling him that he was to marry his daughters to a lion and a boar. He gave

Polyneices the hand of the elder girl, Argeia, and to Tydeus he gave the younger, Deipyle. Furthermore, he promised both men to return with them to their respective countries and re-establish them in their kingdoms. This is how the war of the Seven against Thebes began. Descendants of Bias, Melampus and Proetus took part in the expedition as well as Arcadian and Messenian troops. The Atreids, who ruled at that time over Sparta and Mycenae, abstained from fighting. One commander was needed for each of the seven gates of Thebes, and these were the Seven; Adrastus (the supreme commander), Amphiaraus, Capaneus (descendant of Proetus), Hippomedon (a nephew of Adrastus), Parthenopaeus (often thought to be the brother of Adrastus), Tydeus and Polyneices. The army set out; as it passed through Nemea, it founded the Nemean games. The Seven had their first victory against the Thebans on Ismenos, and forced them to retire to their city. But when the army of the Seven attacked the city, it was wiped out. Eteocles and Polyneices fought in single combat and killed one another. Of the seven leaders only one survived — Adrastus — and his horse, Arion, galloped away with him, far from the field of battle.

The Epigoni

Not discouraged by this failure, Adrastus undertook another expedition some ten years later with the sons of those who had died in the previous battle — this was called the war of the Epigoni. This expedition succeeded, and consequently Thersander, son of Polyneices, was installed on the throne of Thebes. But Adrastus lost his own son, Aegialeus, killed by Laodamas, the son of Eteocles, and, in his grief, Adrastus threw himself on to a funeral pyre and thereby fulfilled a prophecy made by Apollo.

One episode from the war of the Seven became particularly famous as it was the theme of Sophocles' tragedy *Antigone*. After the death of her father at Colonus Antigone returned to Thebes, where Creon was in power (this is Sophocles' version). When the Seven attacked, Antigone watched the battle and saw her two brothers kill one another. Creon granted funeral honours to Eteocles, who had been fighting for the Thebans, but decreed that Polyneices should not be given burial, as he had brought a foreign host to attack his own city. Antigone, however, disregarded Creon's decree, believing that it was a sacred duty, superior to all human laws, to bury one's kin. So, according to the appropriate and essential ritual, she scattered the requisite handful of dust over the mutilated body of her brother. For this she was condemned to death by Creon and buried alive in the vault of the Ladbacidae. She hanged herself in this prison, and Haemon, the son of Creon, who loved her, followed her to her death.

Oedipus, crushed by a fate that he did not deserve, has become the supreme tragic figure, epitomising

Initially a fortress, the Acropolis of Athens became the centre of the religious life of the city-state, containing its chief temples: the Parthenon, dedicated to Athena; the Erechtheum, named for Erechtheus, legendary founder of the city; the Propylaea; and the temple of Athena Nike. Largely destroyed during the Persian wars, the buildings on the Acropolis were not only an offering of gratitude to the gods for the preservation of the city; they are monuments to the beauty of classical architecture and sculpture. *Camera Press*

a dreadful conception of the universe in which liberty is only a mockery. Antigone, by comparison, is a symbol of piety and love, mercilessly broken by an arbitrary and iniquitous decree. In both cases human consciousness entered into conflict with crushing forces, which are quite powerless, none the less, to make it deny itself.

So about the time that Phidias was sculpting the Olympian *Zeus*, in which the majesty of the father of the gods was expressed, myth in the hands of the tragic poets stayed faithful to its primary function: that is, to form a language, a method of thought, capable of grasping realities, which would otherwise remain inaccessible if reason alone were the only means of attaining such truths.

Other legends

The great legendary cycles were an inexhaustible source of inspiration for poets and artists. They helped to create a national spirit among the Greeks; but the unyielding particularism of cities and races persisted and led to the preservation of local myths never entirely absorbed into the common store.

Cecrops

Attic legends, in particular, formed a group with original characteristics, which were independent of the major cycles dominated by Argive traditions. It seems probable that Attica, where an especially brilliant civilisation flourished from the fifth century B.C., existed for a long time somewhat apart from the rest of the Achaean world. Moreover, it was a relatively late period before the Athenians succeeded in introducing one of their own contingents into the list of nations and peoples taking part in the Trojan war—a list that in the *Iliad* goes by the name of the 'Catalogue of Vessels'.

The first king of Attica was Cecrops, according to tradition. He appears to have risen from the very soil of his native land, which then took the name of Cecropia, whereas previously it had been called quite simply Actaea (the Promontory). He married Aglauros, daughter of Actaeus, the mythical eponym of Actaea, a purely imaginary figure invented to provide the first 'queen' of the land with a father. Cecrops and Aglauros had four children: a son, Erysichthon, and three daughters called Aglauros II, Herse and Pandrosos. But Erysichthon (whose name evokes the domain proper to Poseidon—that of earthquakes) died in his youth without heirs, and this is the moment when little Erichthonius, son of Hephaestus and—morally at least—of Athena, was born. Mention has been made of the way in which the three daughters of Cecrops caused their own downfall through indiscretion, whilst Erichthonius was reared by Athena herself.

Erechtheus, Philomela and Procne. Oreithyia

Erichthonius married a naiad, Praxithea, and they had a son, Pandion, who succeeded him as king of Attica. Pandion also married a naiad, called Zeuxippe, and they had two boys, Erechtheus and Butes, and two girls, Philomela and Procne. During Pandion's reign the king of Thebes was Labdacus, and, as often happened in historical times, war broke out between the people of Attica and the Boeotians. Pandion negotiated an alliance with a king of Thrace, Tereus, who was a son of Ares, and to seal the alliance gave him his eldest daughter, Procne, in marriage. Soon she bore her husband a son, called Itys. But Procne was unhappy in Thrace and wanted to have her sister, Philomela, brought to her. Tereus agreed and went to fetch the girl. But during the journey he fell in love with her and ravished her. Then, to

Oreithyia, daughter of King Erechtheus of Attica, was abducted by Boreas, the North Wind. She later bore him two sons, Calais and Zetes, who joined the Argonauts. Jug. 480–460 B.C. *British Museum*

The bull played a prominent part in the myths of the ancient world. One of the most famous legends was that of the Minotaur of Crete. This painted bull figure, with a gentler aspect, is from the Late Minoan III period. *Ashmolean Museum, Oxford*

prevent her making complaint to her sister, he cut out her tongue. But Philomela thought up a way of making herself understood; she embroidered in tapestry the story of the rape. Procne decided to avenge her. This she did by killing Itys, her own son, and serving Tereus a meal of the flesh of his own child. After this she fled with her sister.

When he knew what his wife had done, Tereus seized an axe and rushed in pursuit of the two sisters. He caught up with them in Phocis. Philomela and Procne saw him following them and prayed to the gods, who had pity on them and changed them into birds. Philomela became a nightingale and Procne a swallow. Tereus was turned into a hoopoe.

Erechtheus and his wife, called Praxithea, like the wife of Erichthonius, had a great number of children, boys and girls. The story of one of them, Oreithyia, is one of the most original of the Attic myths. One day the girl was walking with her companions on the banks of Ilissus, the river at Athens, when the god of the North Wind, Boreas, a Thracian like Tereus, but also a member of the race of Titans—since he was supposed to be the son of Eos (Dawn) and Astraeus—abducted her and took her away to his distant land. According to another tradition, the abduction took place during a Panathenaic festival, while the procession was going up towards the Acropolis and Athena's temple. Oreithyia lived with Boreas and bore him two sons, Calais and Zetes.

The other daughters of Erechtheus knew no kinder fate. During a war between the Athenians and the people of Eleusis the king asked the Delphic oracle how he could achieve victory, and the god answered that he must sacrifice one of his daughters. Erechtheus unflinchingly acceded to the oracle's demand and slew one of his daughters, but the other daughters vowed that they would not outlive their sister, and they all committed suicide.

Daedalus and Minos

Another Attic legend, which also formed part of the *geste* of the legendary kings, takes us once again back to the land of Crete. This is the legend of Daedalus, which on the mythical plane posed the problem of the birth (or rather the rebirth) of the practical arts.

Daedalus was an Athenian, a descendant of Cecrops. He was usually taken to be the son of Alcippe, a daughter of Aglauros II (one of the daughters of Cecrops) and the god Ares. So Daedalus was descended from the first royal dynasty of Athens. He was a typical example of the universal inventor—sculptor, architect and mechanic by turns. He was even connected with the construction of robots, animated statues that were able to perform most of the actions of living beings. Daedalus worked at Athens, and studying under him he had his nephew Talos. Talos proved so clever that Daedalus became jealous of him; so much so that when Talos invented the saw (taking his inspiration from a serpent's jaw), Daedalus threw him from the heights of the Acropolis. But the murder was discovered, and Daedalus was tried by the Areopagus and found guilty. He was sent into exile, and fled to Crete to the court of King Minos, where he became sculptor and architect extraordinary to that sovereign. The wife of King Minos was Pasiphaë, the sister of Perseus and Aeëtes, the sons of Helius, and, like them, a fine magician. She had fallen in love with a bull, so Daedalus made a wooden cow in which the queen could conceal herself and so be able to satisfy her passion. The Minotaur was the offspring of this love. Daedalus then built the labyrinth, a palace with complex corridors in which Minos imprisoned the Minotaur to conceal his wife's shame. Then, when Theseus came to fight the monster and Ariadne desired to save him, it was once again Daedalus who

Disc with ancient Near Eastern pictographs. From Phaestus. Herakleion Museum, Crete. *Toni Schneiders*

Orpheus singing, surrounded by Thracians. Krater by the Orpheus painter. *c.* 450 B.C. *State Museum, Berlin*

saved the situation. On his advice Ariadne gave Theseus a ball of thread, which he unwound as he went farther and farther into the labyrinth; in this way he was able to retrace his path.

When Minos discovered how Theseus had managed to escape, he flew into a violent passion and had Daedalus himself imprisoned in the accursed labyrinth with young Icarus, his son. In this way the king felt sure his architect would never escape. But Daedalus made two pairs of wings out of the feathers of fowl previously devoured by the Minotaur, and he held them together with some wax that he found. So Icarus and he got out of the labyrinth by taking to flight like birds. But Icarus was young; he was so happy in flight that he went too high and imprudently got too close to the Sun, so that the wax that held his wings together melted, and he fell into the sea—a sea that has ever since been called the Icarian Sea. Daedalus, however, went on his way and landed at Cumae.

When he learned of his prisoner's escape, Minos decided to pursue him. Guessing which direction he would take, he went to Sicily and there inquired from town to town if Daedalus was in the locality. Now Daedalus had in fact taken refuge in Sicily, at the court of King Cocalus. Minos, who knew Daedalus' weakness for subtle inventions, had devised the following stratagem for discovering where he was. Wherever he stayed he showed his host the shell of a snail and a thread and challenged him to pass the thread through the shell without breaking it. When Cocalus received Minos, he could not resist the temptation to solve the problem. He went secretly to Daedalus, who was hiding in his apartment, and asked him how he should set about it. Daedalus fastened the thread to an ant, which went through the shell, taking the path of the spirals, then came out again still trailing the thread. When Cocalus in

triumph brought the threaded shell back to Minos, the latter was no longer in any doubt—he knew that Daedalus was near by. Cocalus had to admit it, and promised to give him up to Minos. But Daedalus, who suspected the presence of Minos, installed a system of pipes in the palace bathroom down which he poured boiling pitch on Minos, and so killed him.

Orpheus

There is one very unusual figure in legendary tradition, and that is Orpheus, who became the focus of various currents of religious, sometimes of mystical, thought, which we are still far from fully understanding.

Orpheus was the son of Oeagrus, a river-god, the supposed son of Ares. His mother was one of the Muses—perhaps Polyhymnia, or Clio, or Calliope. In other versions, genealogists connected Orpheus with the family of the mythical musician, Thamyris; in this case his mother was quoted as being Menippe, the daughter of Thamyris. The Thracian origins of Orpheus were never forgotten; in portraits of the Roman period he was dressed in the national costume of Thrace. His whole story took place in this land of vast, wind-swept plains, where a large part of the myth of Dionysus also had its setting. Orpheus seems to have been the king of some Thracian tribes. He was the incomparable singer, musician and poet. He played the lyre and was sometimes said to have invented it, sometimes to have perfected it, increasing the number of strings from seven to nine, 'on account of the number of the Muses'. Orpheus' songs had a magic power; they were so beautiful that the whole of nature was affected by them; wild animals followed him, trees and plants leaned towards him and, above all, the souls of even the most fierce men grew gentle at the sound of his music.

Orpheus took part in the Argonauts' expedition,

but he did not row, for he did not possess the physical strength of ordinary heroes; he gave the oarsmen the rhythm, and when a storm arose, he calmed the external elements and gave the sailors back their serenity. He persuaded the Argonauts to become initiated into the mysteries of the Cabeiri when they called at Samothrace. The Cabeiri were strange gods, pure demons with immense power, who could be :.amed only with extreme caution. Orpheus had been initiated into this secret religion and wanted to obtain the protection of these barbarous gods for the expedition. The songs of Orpheus were even lovelier than those of the Sirens, and he saved the lives of the Argonauts by singing to them as the ship sailed alongside the reefs of the Sirens.

Orpheus in the underworld

The most famous episode in the Orpheus legend is that of his descent into the underworld, and this was undoubtedly a mythical version of the powers of deliverance that were attributed to his rites. Virgil was responsible for the finest version of the myth, which is to be found at the end of the *Georgics,* but this is certainly not an early version, and a trace of the Alexandrian style of approach is discernible. Orpheus, we are told, had married Eurydice, daughter of a wood-nymph and Apollo, or perhaps a nymph herself. One day, when the young woman was walking by a river in Thrace, she was pursued by Aristaeus, the son of the nymph Cyrene and a river-god; she ran off, but she was bitten by a serpent lurking in the grass and died. Orpheus, inconsolable, determined to find his way to the underworld and bring Eurydice back to earth. The sound of his lyre charmed not only the monsters guarding the approaches to the infernal world, but the gods of the dead themselves, and for an instant the damned were relieved of their torment. Hades and Persephone agreed to surrender Eurydice, but on one condition: that Orpheus must go back to the world of light, followed by his wife, without once turning round to look at her before he left the kingdom of the dead. Orpheus agreed and set out on his return journey. However, just as he was about to step into the light, he was afflicted with terrible doubt: had Persephone tricked him, he wondered, was Eurydice really behind him? He could not resist turning round, and saw Eurydice fade away, dying for a second time. This time the underworld remained obstinately closed to him. Orpheus returned alone and inconsolable to the world of men.

Death of Orpheus

The death of Orpheus was told in various ways. It was generally agreed that he was killed—torn apart by Thracian women. But the reason varies. It was sometimes said that his countrywomen, jealous of his fidelity to the memory of Eurydice, felt insulted and punished him by death; or that Orpheus surrounded himself with youths, so that he should have no further relationships with women, and that he was punished by women for his perverted passions; or that Orpheus on his return from the underworld had founded mysteries in the course of which he revealed to men the secrets that he had discovered there. But he forbade women access to them. One evening, when the men were all with him, having left their arms at his gate, the women kept watch, then took the arms and massacred Orpheus and his faithful followers.

When the Thracian women had torn Orpheus' body apart, they cast the pieces into the river, and these were carried out to sea. In this way the head and lyre of the poet floated as far as Lesbos, where the inhabitants built a tomb for them.

The theology known as Orphic grew out of these legends. This was concerned with the mysteries of death, and taught the rites necessary to ensure entrance to the Land of the Blessed.

Eros and Psyche

Several centuries after Plato, in the work of a Platonist, Apuleius, there appeared a myth which has enjoyed great popularity, although its nature and meaning are still obscure. The story of Psyche (Soul) and her love for Eros (Love), are told at length in *Metamorphoses,* the novel written by Apuleius about the middle of the second century A.D. While making very pleasant reading, the story is nevertheless fraught with philosophical symbolism.

Psyche was the daughter of a king, and she had two sisters. All three were great beauties, but Psyche outshone her sisters; her radiant charms seemed more than human, and people came from far and wide to admire her, and then they began to worship her as though she were a new Aphrodite. Psyche's sisters had no difficulty in finding husbands, but Psyche remained sadly in her father's house without suitors. The king despaired of ever finding a husband for her, and he consulted the oracle, which gave a sinister reply. It said to adorn the girl as though for her wedding and to lead her in procession to the mountainside, where she was to be abandoned on top of a rock. There a monster would come for her and take her away with him. Psyche's parents were in despair. Yet they had to obey this decree, which was evidently the will of the gods.

Now what had happened was this: Aphrodite, jealous of the divine honours being paid to Psyche, had decided to have her revenge. She sought out her son Eros and commanded him to inspire in Psyche irrational love for some abject creature, the most humble, poor and ugly of mortals. But Eros, when he saw the girl, fell in love with her and made plans to win her love. And so Psyche, abandoned by her parents and the accompanying crowd on top of the rocks, was spared the approach of the horrible monster with which she had been threatened. Instead, Zephyrus, the West Wind, lifted her gently and carried her to a valley, where, with infinite care, he put her down on a flowery bank. Emotionally exhausted by this time, the girl fell asleep, and when she awoke, she saw that she was in a wonderful garden, and that in front of her rose a palace with walls decorated with gold. The gates of the palace were open; there was no-one about, but curiosity made her go in. She was greeted not by creatures of flesh and blood, but by voices, which bade her welcome, invited her to take a bath, then to sit down at a table that was set with the most delicious dishes. Moreover, other voices were singing and instruments were playing in concert. The banquet over, she was led, still by disembodied voices, to a room where a bed was already prepared. Psyche lay down, and when the room was in complete darkness she sensed a presence beside her: it was the husband of whom the oracle had spoken, but he did not seem to Psyche either as monstrous or as terrible as she had feared, although she could not see him.

The next day, before dawn broke, the husband flew away, and when day came the miracle began again. Invisible servants saw to Psyche's needs, offered her endless distractions, and in the evening her husband returned. Several days passed in this way, and Psyche was gently becoming accustomed to the novelties that had so astonished her at first. She was happy. But then she began to miss her family, and especially her sisters whom she loved dearly. She told her husband, who began by warning her of the danger into which this nostalgia might lead her. He foretold that the presence of her sisters would be fatal to her. But Psyche was so obstinate, her husband so tender, so desirous of pleasing her, that in the end he agreed. Zephyrus brought Psyche's two sisters to the wonderful palace, and they were immediately afflicted with the most bitter jealousy of their sister's happiness. Eros repeated his warnings: Psyche should not attempt to see him, she should be content with her happiness and not yield to curiosity, and then this happiness would last. If she did not pay heed, she could expect the most dire catastrophies to befall her.

The sisters returned; they asked her endless questions, and finally pretended to have fears for her that they were unable to conceal from her any longer; this mysterious husband was none other than a frightful dragon, they said, who was fattening her up to prey on her later. So she must act while there was still time, and to this end, they gave her some terrible advice: the following night, before her husband arrived, she was to conceal a lamp in her room; she should also have a sharp blade ready, and when her mysterious husband was fast asleep, she was to take out the lamp and by its light kill the monster.

Psyche obeyed, but, when she had the lamp in her hand, instead of a monster, she beheld the most perfectly beautiful adolescent with two folded wings of quivering down. She recognised Eros. Her hand began to tremble, so that a drop of boiling oil fell on

Eros, son of Aphrodite and god of love, inspired grand passions by smiting with a whip or an axe or by inflicting wounds with an arrow. Instructed by his mother to inspire love for a fearful creature in the beautiful Psyche, he became enamoured of her. Red-figured lekythos c. 470 B.C. *Ashmolean Museum, Oxford*

the body of the sleeper. Eros woke with a start, saw
that he had been betrayed, and in a flash he flew
away out of reach. 'Psyche,' he told her, 'you wished
to see me. You know who I am. Now I must leave
you; you will never see me again.' Poor Psyche wept
and fainted, but her husband was already far away.

Psyche decided to seek her husband. But first of
all she punished her two sisters by telling them that
Eros was asking to see them, so they threw themselves
headlong from the top of the rock where Zephyrus
usually came to get them and were dashed to pieces
in the ravine below. Then Psyche travelled the whole
world, asking for Eros. But no deity was willing to
brave the wrath of Aphrodite; none would agree
to help her, so the poor girl had no alternative but
to surrender herself to her enemy. Aphrodite began
by torturing her, then she imposed different tasks
on her, including that of descending to the underworld to ask Persephone for a small box containing
a beauty ointment. Aphrodite specified that she was
not, under any circumstances, to open it. But Psyche's
curiosity prevailed, she opened the box, a vapour of
sleep escaped and she lost consciousness.

However, Eros himself was desperate, for he loved
Psyche. When he saw her deep in magic sleep, he
flew towards her, wakened her, then went up to
Olympus to ask Zeus for permission to marry this
mortal. Zeus willingly gave his consent, and Psyche
and Aphrodite were reconciled. Eros and Psyche
later had a child, who was called Voluptuousness.

This is an allegorical myth; Apuleius might have
been considered the inventor of it if the figure of
Psyche had not appeared in Alexandrian painting
and reliefs, which have no connection with Apuleius'
narrative. There she is depicted as a young girl with
butterfly's wings playing with Eros. But even if Apuleius did not invent the characters in his myth, he
undoubtedly thought up their adventures himself,
using an old folk theme, that of Beauty and the Beast,
and introducing several episodes from legends of
classical mythology. This was his way of describing
the adventure of the Soul, which was to him the reflection of pure Beauty chained to earth by its low
passions, especially curiosity. The Soul cannot bear
the sight of divine Beauty before it has undergone
the necessary preparation and tests. It must be
helped in its ascent by Love, which in the end will
give it access to the divine world of Ideas.

However artificial this myth of Psyche may be, it
has too many links with Hellenic mythology to be
entirely divorced from it. It shows that this mythology was still a living, creative force in the world of
philosophers and novelists in the second century
A.D. Although Apuleius did not believe in the actual
existence of the creatures he portrayed (often with
a measure of irony), none the less, in his eyes, myth
could still be used to show the most secret truths, and
to give them the only expression compatible with the
restricted range of the human spirit when confronted
with the divine.

A Roman sculptured decoration on an altar in the Old Forum at Djemila, Algeria. The bull, cock and ram are the sacrificial victims. The altar fire is surrounded by cult instruments (possibly Mithraic). *Roger Wood*

ROME: GODS BY CONQUEST

Alongside Greek mythology with its wealth of charming and dramatic legends, Roman mythology cuts a poor figure. The contrast is the more striking as the poetry and religion of Rome developed in an atmosphere permeated with Hellenism, and at first sight it may seem that the Romans managed only to plagiarise what the Greek world handed on to them. And somewhat clumsily at that. The Roman gods, in the classical period at least, are simply the Hellenic gods with different names. Zeus has become Jupiter, Hera is called Juno, and so on for all the Olympians. The Roman poets made completely free with the traditional myths, and sculptors and painters from Greece and the Orient emulated and copied the divine types fixed by tradition since the fourth and third centuries B.C. Legendary scenes from the epics and Greek tragedy were reproduced in the same way. And so there are certain difficulties surrounding the definition of what is truly Roman mythology, and only recently the scholars were content to state that there was no national mythology in Rome, and that the conquerors had simply appropriated the inventions of the races they had overcome.

But today the tendency is to modify that judgment; to admit that there is a Roman mythology but that it is not to be found in the most obvious place, and has neither the same origins nor the same functions as Greek mythology. Whilst the latter grew up essentially around divine and heroic figures and moved towards historical reality only by degrees, Roman myths are more intimately connected with city life and frequently appear in the guise of history. Furthermore, Roman deities rarely possess a 'cycle' of autonomous myths, whereas the Greek legend of Apollo or Hermes, for example, presents a portrait of the god, with each episode adding successive touches to support his personality. Roman legends, on the other hand, are much less complex and have an obvious unity, as if they never passed through a stage of elaboration; they are concerned not with a god, but rather with a social function or rite, which they interpret. Finally, it seems that Rome managed to preserve with remarkable persistence very ancient legends, mythical forms relating to social and religious structures current long before Indo-European immigrants reached Italy, thus forming the chief component of the 'Latin' people. This important aspect of the origins of Roman mythology has been mainly revealed by the work of M. Georges Dumézil, who devoted himself to the task of determining the connections between mythical thought as revealed in classical Roman texts and that of other Indo-European peoples who, at different periods, were cut off from the common cultural stem.

Jupiter

Jupiter, or Jove, was the supreme god of the Roman pantheon. He was probably an Etruscan god originally, but his name and the major aspects of his character indicate a close identification with the Greek Zeus. He was a sky-god, Jupiter Lucetius, the light-bringer—and the days of the full moon, the Ides, were sacred to him. Like Zeus he was associated with rain and thunder, and his oldest temple, at Rome, contained the *lapides silices*, believed to be his thunderbolts. Throughout Italy temples were built in his honour on the summits of hills and at places that had been struck by lightning.

Jupiter was not only the protective deity of the race, but the guardian of public morality, being concerned with oaths, treaties, alliances and wars. He was also associated with the moral duty of a citizen towards the gods, the state, and the family. His dedication festival was held annually on the thirteenth of September, the day on which the consuls of the republic took office.

Venus, goddess of love, with her attendants. Venus was the Roman equivalent of the Greek Aphrodite. This silver medallion was probably a mirror cover. From Tarentum. First century A.D. *British Museum*

Janus, the god of beginnings, was always shown facing two different directions. Roman coin. Bibliothèque Nationale. *Giraudon*

The genius of Mars, god of war. After Jupiter Mars was the most important of the Roman gods. Bibliothèque Nationale. *Giraudon*

He later became the protective deity of the emperors, and as such he was worshipped throughout the Roman empire.

Juno

Juno, the sister and wife of Jupiter, was the special protector of women. Just as every man had his genius, so every woman had her juno, who presided over all aspects of her womanly life—especially marriage and childbirth. She was guardian of the bride's girdle, the protector of the newly married woman as she entered her new home, presided over the ritual of marriage, helped women in childbirth, and enabled the newly born child to see. Women who were sterile prayed to her for fertility, and once a year—on the first of March, the *matronalia*—the matrons of the city made special offerings at her temple in a grove on the Esquiline.

As the moon was supposed to control the sexual life of women, Juno was a moon-goddess, and was worshipped on the Kalends or days of the full moon.

By historical times Juno was not only a domestic goddess, but Juno Regina, the queen of all junos and of heaven. In this role particularly she assumed many of the characteristics of Hera.

Janus

Janus seems to have been a uniquely Roman god, and it was believed that his worship, which had been a minor local cult before the founding of Rome, was introduced to the new city by Romulus himself.

Janus was the god of beginnings. He presided over doors and gateways, and over the first hour of the day, the first day of the month and the first month of the year (January). He was represented as having two heads looking in opposite directions, and his symbols were keys and a doorkeeper's staff.

The *Ianus geminus*, his gateway to the north-east

Vesta, goddess of the hearth, one of the most popular of the Roman gods. She is shown here as the tutelary goddess of the bakers' guild. Marble relief. *c.* A.D. 140. *State Museum, Berlin*

Vulcan, an ancient Italian god of destructive fire. His cult was propitiatory, and his shrines most frequent in places where fire was most feared. *Luxembourg Museum*

of the Roman forum, was shut in times of peace (four times only before the Christian era) and open in times of war.

Mars

After Jupiter, Mars was the most important of the Roman deities, and he was worshipped throughout central and southern Italy. As god of war many of his festivals were held in the spring, the beginning of the campaigning season—and so his name was given to the first month of the old Roman year.

In one of the temples of Mars in the heart of the city were kept the sacred spears and shields (*ancilia*) of Mars. On the outbreak of war the consul had to shake these spears and say 'Mars vigila!' (Mars, wake up!) If the spears moved by themselves this was a bad omen. In March and October (the beginning and end of the campaigning season) the *ancilia* were carried in procession by his priests, who also performed war-dances. One of his special festivals involved a horse-race and the sacrifice of one of the horses, whose head was cut off and decorated with cakes. His sacred animals were the wolf and the woodpecker, and various plants—for example, the fig-tree and the laurel—were associated with him.

Mars seems also to have been an agricultural god— the protector of the fields not only in times of war, but against disease and unfavourable weather.

Mars held a special place in the Roman pantheon, partly as the father of Romulus and partly because of the importance of military achievement in the republic of Rome and the Roman empire.

Vesta

Vesta was the goddess of the hearth, her name being the etymological equivalent of Hestia, whose cult was similar—though Vesta held a much higher position in the Roman pantheon than Hestia in the Greek. In the earliest days of the Romans the necessity of keeping a fire always alight became a sacred obligation for which the king was originally responsible. This duty devolved on to the young daughters of the king, since it was too important, and later too sacred, to be entrusted to slaves.

So, in later days, not only were fires kept permanently alight in Roman homes as an act of devotion, but a public cult existed in which a sacred royal hearth was tended by young, well-born girls known as the Vestal Virgins. These were chosen, in republican days, by the *pontifex maximus*, who to this extent took on the task of the former kings.

The Vestal Virgins entered the service of the goddess at six to ten years old. There were initially two of them, later six, and the term of service varied from five years in the early days to thirty in later years. In addition to tending the sacred fire their duties included fetching water from a sacred spring, the preparation of sacred foods, the guardianship of sacred objects, and the daily ritual at the shrine of Vesta.

The *pontifex maximus* had absolute control over the daily lives of the Virgins and could inflict punishment on them for any offences, including ordering that they should be buried alive for breaking their vow of chastity.

Vesta's shrine stood near the Regia, or Palace of King. Images of her are rare, but those that do exist show a woman fully draped and accompanied by an ass—her favourite animal.

Vulcan

Vulcan was an ancient Italian fire-god, particularly associated with destructive fire. He was worshipped as a means of averting fires, and his shrines were most numerous where fires were most feared, such as the areas near volcanoes and where grain was stored – notably at the port of Ostia. It is interesting that his shrines always stood outside the walls of the cities.

Vulcan was associated with several primary goddesses – namely, Maia (the Earth Mother) and Vesta in her role of earth goddess. To him was attributed the paternity of Servius Tullius, one of the kings of Rome, who proved his parentage by the useful talent of being able to make fire descend on his enemies.

Perhaps the most curious custom associated with Vulcan was the sacrifice of live fish, which were thrown on to fires lit on the banks of the Tiber in order to persuade the god to spare more vulnerable objects.

Until the classical period Vulcan had little in common with Hephaestus, and it was only in these later times that he was depicted as a smith, wearing a bonnet and a tunic that left his right arm and shoulder free, and with the anvil, tongs and hammer.

Saturn

Saturn was an ancient god of agriculture, associated with the sowing of the seed and with plenty. His name may have been derived from *sator* (a sower) or with *satur* (stuffed or gouged). In early times his cult-partner was the fire-goddess Lua (*lues*, plague or destruction), and later, when he became identified, for reasons that are not altogether clear, with Cronus, he was associated with Rhea.

The temple of Saturn stood on the Capitoline Hill and contained the treasury as well as the standards of the legions when they were not campaigning. The statue of the god had woollen bands about its feet to prevent it from running away. An unusual feature of the cult of Saturn was that he was sacrificed to by worshippers with uncovered heads.

The greatest festival of this god was the Saturnalia. This took place in December, and may have been associated with the winter sowing. Originally a rural festival, it naturally became very popular in cities also, and was extended to last for seven days. During this time all public and private business came to a standstill. Law courts and schools were closed and executions and military exercises were suspended. Slaves were temporarily freed, and were permitted to say and do as they pleased. Gifts, especially of clay or wax dolls, were exchanged, and the citizens sat at table feasting and drinking all day. The custom of electing a mock king for a day may have been derived from Greece or the Near East.

Saturn is usually depicted with a sickle or with ears of corn.

Minerva

Originally a domestic goddess, particularly associated with handicrafts, Minerva (*mens*, mind) was one (with Jupiter and Juno) of an Etruscan trilogy. She presided over the guilds of craftsmen, dramatic poets and actors. At an early period she became closely identified with Athena, the Greek goddess of wisdom and war, and her cult spread at the expense of the hitherto popularly venerated Mars, the god of war. The *quinquatrus*, became much more her festival than his.

Minerva's cult was popular throughout the empire. Her symbol was the screech-owl.

Mercury

Mercury, the god of trade, appears to have been a direct importation of the Greek god Hermes. He was introduced towards the end of the fifth century, after Rome had expelled the Tarquins and felt the need of deities who would assure good harvests and prosperous trading. The temple of Mercury on the Aventine Hill became a focus of the corn trade, and later of trade in general. His festival was celebrated on the Ides of May and he was usually shown with the symbols of Hermes – the caduceus, winged sandals and a purse.

Minor deities of Rome

The minor gods of Rome included agricultural gods, gods of the underworld, of the city, of the family, and deified heroes.

It seems certain that most of the deities of the Roman pantheon existed in Italy in pre-Roman times or from very early Roman times, and that they then had distinct characters and functions. Later identification with Greek deities, reinforced by the Greek influence in the arts, particularly sculpture, obscured these early characteristics.

Faunus

Of ancient Italian origin, Faunus ('the kindly one', from *favere*), was the god of fruitfulness of the fields and of animals. He was especially worshipped by herdsmen and belonged to the forests. The son of Picus (a minor god) and grandson of Saturn, he was believed to have been one of the early kings of Rome. He had prophetic powers, and his rites were purificatory, animals being sacrificed in his honour.

He was associated with Fauna (Bona Dea), his daughter or his wife, who was worshipped exclusively by women, and with Ops, an ancient Sabine goddess of agricultural fertility.

Consus

An ancient Roman god, Consus presided over sowing, and was closely associated with Ops. His festivals were celebrated after the autumn harvest and after the winter sowing.

Pales

Initially a male god, Pales took on feminine form and became the protectress of flocks. Her festival, the Palilia, was celebrated on 21 April, the day of the foundation of Rome, during which the animals under her care were purified.

Minerva, one of the most popular of the Roman goddesses. Although she eventually acquired many of the attributes of Athena, her origins were Etruscan. Bronze. Early Etruscan. Sixth century B.C. British Museum. *Edwin Smith* in *Art Treasures of the British Museum (Thames and Hudson)*

Liber Pater

A god of the fertility of the fields, Liber Pater acquired some of the characteristics of Dionysus, and his festivals were held mainly in the countryside and were merry rather than formal. His festival, the Liberalia, came to be the favourite day for Roman boys to don the *toga virilis*.

Silvanus

The god of uncultivated land, Silvanus was a god of uncertain character. Although he presided over the clearing and tilling of land, it was necessary to propitiate him before embarking on such tasks.

Gods of the Underworld

The Roman concept of the underworld and its deities was borrowed initially from the Etruscans, and later modified by Greek myths.

The underworld was presided over by Eita or Ade and his wife, Persipnei. There are few myths associated with the king of the underworld, and he was pictured as being grim and pitiless. Two other figures were Charon and Tuchulcha, the latter being a demon with ferocious eyes, the ears of an ass and a beak, with two serpents twined round her head and a third round her arm. Two groups of genii, one representing good, the other evil, escorted the dead to the underworld.

Dis Pater, the richest of the gods, Orcus, the god of death who carried off the living to the underworld, Februus, probably of Etruscan origin, who gave his name to the month February, the month of the dead, Libitina, goddess of funerals, the Lemunes or Larvae, ghosts of the dead, who returned to the world to torment the living, were other underworld gods who were feared, and they received few sacrifices.

The Manes, the 'good ones', could be propitiated. Sacrifices were offered to them, and it is possible that the gladiatorial combats were originally held in their honour. Their festivals, the Parentalia and the Feralia, were celebrated in February.

The Romans believed that the underworld was literally under the earth and that certain openings — caves, lakes, marshes — led to it.

Fortuna

The goddess Fortuna was of very ancient origin, and she was worshipped in many parts of Italy. She was a protective deity and was represented with a cornucopia as a symbol of plenty, a ship's rudder to indicate that she could control destiny, and a ball, which may have indicated the uncertainty of fortune.

Genii

The genii were not restricted in number, and there seems to have been a genius for each district, tribe, colony, street, house and gate, as for each man. In early times the genius of a man and the juno of a woman seem to have been associated with their roles as heads of the household and family. In later times a genius seemed to have been a manifestation or the determining factor of the character of a man — good or bad — and later still he assumed a protective role. A genius was born and died with each man, and was worshipped only by the individual to whom he belonged.

Lares and Penates

The Lares were originally deities of the farm-land, particularly of farm boundaries. From this they developed into guardians of the cross-roads, in the city as well as the country, and protectors of travellers; then they became guardians of the city itself.

Closely associated with the Lares were the Penates, the 'dwellers in the store-cupboard' — or guardians of the family larder. The Lares, the Penates and Vesta were associated with the hearth, which formed their altar, and together they were the chief guardians of the household.

Gods of the Waters

Tiberinus, the god of the river Tiber, was naturally very important in Rome. He was propitiated to prevent him from flooding, and festivals were held in his honour.

There was a god for each stretch of water, spring and river. Nymphs were usually associated with water, though some had other functions, notably those of prophecy.

Legends in history

When Livy produced an account of the earliest Roman times, he admitted that the events that he retraced seemed more like legends than historical facts. This and other early 'histories' do, in fact, bear the imprint of the magical, and many episodes undeniably reflect the strong influence of folklore. So, the legend of Rome's founder, Romulus, begins like a folk story: a beautiful princess had been imprisoned by her uncle, a usurper, lest she might provide the senior branch of the family with an heir (the crown by right belonged to it). The girl, however, gave birth to a child in spite of his precautions and under the most mysterious conditions. Her seducer was said to be none other than the god Mars. When the uncle learned that the princess had given birth to twins, he hastened to order that they should be abandoned in open country to be devoured by wild animals, or to perish of cold or hunger. But his orders were disobeyed and the infants left in a basket on the floodwaters of the Tiber, where they were miraculously saved; their frail craft was washed up at the foot of the Palatine, and as the water receded a she-wolf (the animal sacred to Mars) came out of the thickets, and lay down beside the two children; she warmed them and fed them on her own milk. When a shepherd came by, the beast departed, her mission accomplished. The astonished shepherd took the infants home and handed them over to his wife to care for,

so that the designs of the usurper were thwarted and Romulus and Remus grew up in the shepherd's hut. On attaining manhood they dethroned their uncle, avenged their mother, and taking with them a handful of volunteers, founded Rome in the very place where they had spent their infancy.

If the birth and childhood of Romulus were miraculous, his death was no less magical. The story runs that one day when he had assembled the senators on the field of Mars to review the entire populace, a very violent storm suddenly broke; for a few moments there was total darkness, and when light returned, Romulus had disappeared. The senators were suspected by the people of having assassinated him, but the following day a man named Julius told how he had seen Romulus on a roadway at the very moment when the storm broke, and Romulus had revealed to him that Jupiter himself, the god of thunder, had snatched him away under cover of the momentary darkness to take him to Olympus. Romulus added that he had become a god, and asked that he should be worshipped under the name of Quirinus. The common people unquestioningly accepted the fact that the first king of Rome had become a god and duly observed his wishes.

Equally miraculous tales were told of Romulus' successors. It was said, for example, that Numa, the third king of Rome, was in direct communication with the gods, and that he was advised by a certain nymph called Aegereia whom he consulted in a grotto. Servius Tullius, the son of a slave and a god of the domestic hearth, had appeared in the form of a phallus rising from the embers. In short, the whole tradition regarding Roman kings was characterised by episodes of a popular nature which render it suspect.

It is possible that some of the episodes are poetic and literary elaborations inspired by themes from the Greek poets, especially the tragedians. For instance, the miraculous birth of the divine twins recalls similar situations in Greek legend; the story of Romulus is known to have provided a theme for Roman poets, who at the end of the third century B.C. might well have introduced in Rome embellishments which they found in their Greek models. But it is probable that the essential principle of the legends is in fact Roman, and that Romulus, Numa and Servius were not inventions of the poets.

The legendary elements are, in fact, only a cloak, and one can and must enquire whether the accounts of the early days of Rome contain a historic reality, or whether their substance is perhaps the material of myth; if, for example, the succession of early kings or the account of the building of Rome by the united efforts of the 'Latin' settlers (installed on the Palatine by Romulus) and the Sabines from the Tiber valley and the region to the immediate north of the town are anything other than the historical projection of the old mythical themes found in another form in other Indo-European communities.

Tradition has it that the companions of Romulus were in dire straits once they had established their town, for they had no women and the neighbouring villagers obstinately refused to allow marriage with their daughters. Then Romulus conceived the idea of inviting all the inhabitants of the nearby towns to a great feast in the course of which there would be horse-racing. While attention was held by this spectacle, the young Romans were to take advantage of the moment and abduct the daughters of their guests. Following this outrage the fathers—they were nearly all Sabines—demanded their return, but were refused. They immediately appealed to the Sabine ruler, King Tatius, and persuaded him to march on Rome. Battle was joined in the Forum. There were victories and losses on both sides, then suddenly in the midst of the slaughter the Sabine daughters intervened and threw themselves between the combatants. They had decided that they were far from sorry to have these men as husbands, and so they begged them and their own fathers not to pursue a needless course that could only make them widows and orphans. So Romans and Sabines agreed to conclude a peace, and united to form one people.

These are the facts which Roman tradition presents as historical reality. But Dumézil has drawn attention to a similarity between Romans and Sabines, on the one hand, and, on the other, two groups or races of gods who appear, for example, in German mythology as the Aesir and Vanir. Like the Aesir, the Romans are essentially warriors; the Sabines resemble the Vanir in that they too are essentially peasants and cattle-raisers. And the legend of the war between Sabines and Latins likewise appears to conform to a very ancient pattern. In the beginning, or so it would seem, the war between the Aesir and Vanir (or, at least, the prototype which prompted this Germanic version of the legend) was essentially a myth which had a particular purpose—it was intended to account for an unusual structural characteristic inherent in Indo-European society. This was the juxtaposition of three functional groups: a class of lawyer-priests, a class of warriors and a class of peasants and cattle-raisers. According to Dumézil, the Aesir in Scandinavia and Romulus and his companions in Rome represented the union of the first two classes against the third. The Sabines, of course, were not a mythical people; there is historical proof of their existence, but Roman tradition makes them play a part which would appear to have no connection with historical fact. 'When republican Rome created an "early history" for itself,' writes Dumézil (*Naissance de Rome*, Paris, 1944, p. 161), 'the first people responsible for the annals (that is, the first "historians") retained the ancestral mythology handed on from generation to generation.... The myths at their disposal included one which accounted somewhat crudely for the functional hierarchy of Indo-European societies...', and this is the myth used to reconstruct in a completely arbitrary manner the forgotten events of the period when the city was founded.

The detail found in interpretations of Rome's earliest history, seen in the light of the great Indo-European mythical schemas, is often highly complex and leaves much room for doubt. But it is quite probable that archaic traditions of an even earlier date than the foundations of Rome helped to form the image handed on by historians. Sometimes this influence can be seen quite clearly, as in the legend of the Horatii and Curiatii.

The legend is well known: in the reign of King Tullus Hostilius (673–642 B.C.), Rome was at war with Alba Longa, and it was agreed to let the struggle between the two cities be decided by two groups of three champions. Representing the army of Alba were three young men, triplets, called the Curiatii, and from the Roman ranks three warriors, also triplets, the Horatii. The two groups confronted one another in the presence of the two armies and the fight began. At the first encounter two of the Horatii were killed and the three Curiatii wounded. The Romans were already in despair. It was feared that their surviving champion – already in flight – would be outnumbered. But by feigning flight the single Horatii forced the three Curatii to separate because of the limitations of their different wounds. When he considered the moment ripe, the lone warrior turned about and with no great difficulty killed the three dispersed warriors in turn. In triumph he returned to Rome at the head of the army. At the city gates he was met by his sister, betrothed to one of the Curiatii. She immediately recognised his coat hanging over her brother's shoulder, for she had woven it herself. Lamenting loudly, she began to call upon death to take her also; greatly angered, Horatius, considering his sister's mourning to be an insult to his own victory, drew his sword and took her life. For this he stood trial, and the tribunal was about to condemn him for the murder when, the story goes, his father's prayers prompted the people to acquit him.

This legend seems to reproduce the schema of a myth dealing with an initiation rite into the arts of war. Comparison with an Irish story involving the hero Cuchulainn is highly relevant in this respect. In both tales we have a drama with a warrior hero who, in the course of a three-fold fight, proves his supremacy, then on his return to normal life must forfeit this supremacy because he is anarchistic by nature and dangerous to a city at peace. This dramatisation of an initiation rite (the admission of the adolescent into the group of warriors) became a heroic story in Rome; in Ireland it acquired miraculous epic proportions.

The myths and the city

In the light of the analysis made by Dumézil, the legend of the Horatii adds to our knowledge of fundamental notions of the 'Roman consciousness'. It reveals a true 'theology of war' and shows the con-

nections between the world of war and the world of peace. It is probably no mere accident that the legend affords the first example of the right of appeal to the people, which is the prerogative of a man accused of a capital crime. The problem that it raises is, of course, concerned with the right to kill, the legitimacy or legitimisation of violence, the enforced or accepted limits placed on man's fury in war. And, finally, Horatius' trial by the people is the chief precedent for a whole body of legislation.

The Roman mind, which was anxious to organise social life and in some measure to explain as well as to justify the judicial institutions for the preservation of order and stability, happily used myths as a source of reference, conferring upon them the authority associated with history. In this way the legend of the Sabines was made to account for many details of conjugal life. For example, the status of a woman in the Roman household, the honours she received, her absolute certainty that she would be required to do no menial tasks, but simply to 'spin wool' and direct the servants, all this was said to have been solemnly promised the Sabines in the treaty that put an end to that particular war. In the same way, the rite or custom of carrying the bride over her husband's threshold was considered to be a symbol and a reminder of the legendary abduction.

Even if many things in very early Roman history were invented so that they would fit in with the mythical patterns that existed prior to the city itself, nevertheless it must be remembered that the mythical imagination of the Romans acted at times in retrospect, inventing legends to justify rites and customs, and then projecting them into the past. The ability to construct myths is not the privilege of a by-gone age. The mid-nineteenth century school of historians who embarked on a critical analysis of Roman history insisted that certain narratives were already prefigured in classical institutions with such accuracy that there could be no question of fortuitousness.

Kings in legend are, for example, often associated in pairs: Romulus and his Sabine contemporary, Tatius, and , in an even more distant past, Saturn and that most obscure king, Camus, then Saturn and Janus. It is impossible to ignore the implication that this pattern – a 'college' of two kings – prefigures the college of two consuls, and, at an even deeper level, that it corresponds to what was apparently a permanent requisite of Roman political thought – mistrust of power in the hands of any one person, an instinctive, even unhealthy, fear of 'tyranny'. Finally, this trait reappears in the Roman empire, when supreme power is very often shared.

Likewise indigenous to Rome are myths concerned with the rise to power of the *plebs*: first the revolutions described by ancient historians, then the secession of the common people on the Aventine and the Sacred Mount (when the patricians in their egoism refused to grant them the smallest rights, although they were

numerically superior, and constituted the biggest force in the city). These events are presented more like dramatic ritual than acts of sedition. Historians insist on the absence of violence, on the controlled and rational nature of the demands, as if under such circumstances human passion had played no part. One has the inescapable impression that here too we are dealing with legends of valour, and, therefore, with true myths.

Naturally, religious rites have also given rise to legends intended to account for existing reality. For example, there was a goddess called Bona Dea, the Good Goddess, worshipped by Roman matrons. Every year they celebrated the 'mysteries' of the goddess, and men were not allowed to take part. The presence of a man at these ceremonies was considered to be a grave sacrilege. It was forbidden to bring a myrtle branch into the temple of Bona Dea and to pronounce the word 'wine' during ceremonies. Wine libations were called 'libations of milk'. The legend of Bona Dea, however, explained away these oddities. It was said that when she was married to the god Faunus, she became drunk on one occasion, and to punish her he had beaten her so cruelly with myrtle switches that she died. Hence the double taboo on myrtle and wine. In addition, there were variations on this legend. It was told that Bona Dea was not the wife but the daughter of Faunus, and that the god had conceived an incestuous passion for her; to satisfy his lust, he had made her drunk and as she still resisted him he beat her with myrtle. The diversity of accounts suggests that the rite came first, and that popular imagination subsequently ran riot.

This is only one of a body of legends connected with the thousand and one sanctuaries all over Rome, ancient statues portraying obscure subjects, chapels with bizarre names, and endless other relics. At the foot of the Palatine a god was worshipped called Aius

Locutius, in other words 'sayer and speaker'. His precise functions are unknown, but he was said to have demonstrated his powers once, shortly before the invasion by the Gauls, when he made a prophecy which should have put the Romans on their guard had they attached the proper importance to it.

The countless legends tended, naturally, to be connected with great episodes in the nation's history which caught the imagination, or else with the great myths of the city. Several sites near the Forum or the citadel on the Capitol were supposed to have been the scene of particular events during the war against the Sabines, which had attracted a whole cycle of 'etiological' anecdotes. The most famous is undoubtedly the legend of Tarpeia, intended to explain the presence on the Citadel of an ancient statue, showing a female figure half-hidden by a pile of shields. The origin of this odd work of art is, of course, unknown. It may well be a goddess of war with a cult dating from pre-Hellenic times and imported into Rome. But this is a debatable point. The story runs that Tarpeia, a girl who lived on the Citadel at the time when King Tatius was threatening Rome and had his troops posted all round the Forum, had caught sight of the young king and fallen in love with him. Tarpeia did not hesitate to acquire merit in his eyes by offering him the keys of the citadel. Tatius accepted but, far from responding to the young girl's love, once he had occupied the citadel he had her smothered beneath his soldiers' shields. According to another version, Tarpeia acted out of cupidity not love; as her reward for treason she asked for 'what the Sabines carried on their left arms'; by this she meant the gold bracelets which warriors wore by way of ornament; Tatius took her at her word and she perished beneath the shields which were also carried on the soldiers' left arms.

Similarly, there was once a swampy hollow in the Forum called the Curtius Lake, and the story went that a Sabine horseman of this name had been drowned there. An alternative version claimed the origin of the name to be associated with a young Roman who had deliberately thrown himself into a chasm which had mysteriously opened there, and would not close again until Curtius, realising that the gods wanted a sacrifice, surrendered himself to the powers of darkness that his country might benefit from his act.

Roman religion, which has a great wealth of picturesque rites and popular festivals, was an admirable subject for legendary exegesis, and the *Annals* of Ovid and Plutarch have preserved a good deal of it for us. For example, to quote but one, on the fifth of July (the anniversary of Romulus' death) a curious festival took place, called the *Nones caprotines* or 'nones of the wild fig'. On that day everyone went into the country and the women formed little groups under improvised huts made of fig branches. Servant-girls ran here and there, threw stones at one another and struck one another, but without malice, and in the end everyone drank and made merry. The explanation of all this was that it commemorated an event which had taken place when the Gauls occupied Rome and left the Roman state considerably weaker on their withdrawal. The Latin cities, under the sole command of the dictator Livius Postumius, had taken advantage of this and attacked the town. They sent a deputation demanding that the Romans surrender virgins and widows—in short, this was their revenge for the abduction of the Sabine women—and the Romans were well aware that the Latins wanted only an easy way of getting slaves. However, depleted as they were, they could not contemplate open resistance. A servant-girl called Philotis (or Tutola) got them out of their difficulty. She proposed a stratagem: the Romans were to pretend to accept, and when evening came Philotis and other servant-girls, dressed as free women, should be taken to the Latin camp. This was done, and in the middle of the night, while the abductors slept, Philotis sent an agreed signal from the top of a wild fig-tree, and Roman soldiers attacked the enemy while they lay helpless.

Foreign legends

From the very beginning Rome was highly receptive to spiritual influences, and at an early stage her mode of thought showed the stamp of foreign intervention. And so it is possible to find in Roman legend not only Hellenic, but Etruscan and, generally speaking, Italic elements. Certain ways of envisaging the life and activities of the major gods in Rome are certainly of Etruscan origin. For example, the Jupiter adored on the Capitol is not identical with the Greek Zeus, nor with the 'Indo-European' Jupiter from whom, of course, he had inherited many features. This Jupiter is considered to be the president of an assembly of celestial gods, the *Dii consentes*, who form his council and whom he consults before revealing his presence in a flash of lightning, and he owes a great deal to the Etruscan god Tin. The Etruscan world also provided certain legendary traditions relating to the art of divination, for example, the tradition involving the little demon Tages, who rose one day from a furrow traced by a ploughman and began to predict the future as soon as he saw the light of day. In the village where he lived for some time, he instructed men in the art of interpreting signs sent by the gods, and his carefully noted precepts were said to form the nucleus of books of prophecies which circulated in Etruscan territory.

The Etruscans had an excellent knowledge of Greek myths, and paintings found on the walls of their tombs, engravings on Etruscan mirrors, reliefs on funeral steles or urns, and designs on vases of Etruscan workmanship, usually represent scenes from Hellenic mythology, although it is not always easy to know whether the versions shown are exactly

the same as those we have directly from Greek sources. Sometimes it seems possible to detect some signs of a local adaptation, and there were certainly many demons in Etruscan belief virtually unknown in Greek legend. But our ignorance of the Etruscan language (what can be deciphered is still fragmentary and uncertain) prevents access to the myths themselves, though we imagine they exist. Above all, it prevents assessment of their effect on Rome. However, from a certain date the constant recurrence of the theme of life in the underworld or in the afterworld gives grounds for thinking that Roman popular beliefs concerning the beyond were affected as much by Etruscan influence as they were by Greek. The character of Charon, who to the Greeks is a simple ferryman with the task of taking souls across the infernal river, becomes in Etruria (and perhaps also in Rome) a demon whose much more sinister role consisted in felling the dying man with an enormous mallet when he was on the point of surrendering his soul.

But it is still Greek mythology which at a very early stage puts its particular imprint on Roman mythical thought from the very beginning. Nor could it be otherwise, since Rome grew up on the border of the Etruscan world, which was itself entirely permeated with Hellenism. This early Hellenisation of Roman legend is far in advance of the literary borrowings which had only just begun in the second half of the third century B.C. Portraits and legends of the Greek gods were present in Rome from the end of the sixth century B.C., and Rome acquired new traditions or modified her old, to some extent at least, because she adhered to Greek legends: for example, Heracles, whom the Romans called Hercules, undoubtedly because the name had come to them via an Etruscan intermediary, Hercle, is at an early stage involved in rites celebrated at the 'Ox Market' between the Aventine and the Tiber. The story is that the hero on his return from victory over the oxen of Geryon in the far west, had passed through Rome with his herd. There he would appear to have been attacked by a giant called Cacus, a local demon on the Aventine, who stole some of his beasts. In an attempt to regain his property, he gave battle to the terrible Cacus, whom he overcame and killed in spite of the monster's strength and wiles. In memory of this, Hercules was said to have founded a great altar on the very soil of victory and to have established a cult of Jupiter, the Conqueror. This cult has many connections with the national rite that celebrated triumph in war.

The Roman cult of Castor and Pollux, the Dioscuri, grew up in this same Hellenistic atmosphere, and at a very early date they had their temple in the Forum. Even if divine twins are found in the most ancient Aryan tradition, it is apparent that their cult was of minor importance until the influence of the Greek couple gave it definite shape and life.

Finally, there is another Greek legend, that of Aeneas, that played an extremely important role at a turning-point in Roman history. This legend existed in the Etruscan world, just as did those in the Trojan cycle. But for various reasons Rome adopted it and the idea that the early origins of its founder, Romulus, were Trojan. This legend satisfied the Roman sense of *pietas* (piety), one of their most profound moral values, since it told how Aeneas fled when Troy was captured, taking with him his father and his household gods, for he cared nothing for his own safety if that which he held most dear had to be sacrificed to it. For centuries this legend inspired poets but its potentiality was not fully revealed until Virgil made it the theme of his *Aeneid* and built a national epic round it. On that day the imperial regime established by Augustus found its justification and reason for existence.

The investiture of Ardashir I (left) by Ahura Mazda. The king's horse rests its foot on the body of the previous king, a customary pose, while the god's horse rests its foot on the evil spirit Ahriman. Sassanian rock-carving at Naksh-i-Rustam. Sixth century B.C. *Roger Wood*

PERSIA: COSMIC DUALISM

Mazdaism

The mythology of ancient Persia (Iran) has one strange characteristic: there is little painting or sculpture to illustrate it. The wealth of sculpture that constantly illustrates and clarifies the written or spoken Indian myth, for example, is absent here, not because it has been accidentally lost in the course of history, but seemingly because its absence is a principle in itself. Herodotus, the first historian to give an outsider's view of Iran, does not fail to remark on its absence. This is not a mythology devoid of imagery, which would be a contradiction in terms, but a mythology devoid of sculpted or painted imagery: the myths are found in written texts. And even here there are difficulties, for the texts are not very numerous, the most ancient are fragmentary, and the most recent are of very late date, when Iran was already Musulman. But these relatively recent syntheses have the advantage of expressing an old tradition that developed in a very different way from that of its sister nation, India, in the course of centuries. Indeed, in the beginning India and Iran formed a single branch of the old Indo-European tree. Although the Indo-European origins of Persian religion are highly important to the understanding of its pantheon (for it is difficult to grasp at first sight the differences between the gods, and one is left with the impression that the parts they play are very much alike), comparison of the two throws very little light on Iranian myth once it has taken shape and become, so to speak, set in its own mould. So this study will attempt to 'synchronise' myths as far as possible, since a study of the genesis or history of the myth would, in any case, be an impossible task, continually posing insoluble problems of chronology.

There will be constant reference to books written in Pahlavi (Middle Iranian) as late as the ninth and tenth centuries A.D. because these are living traditions although they were copied down in the time of the Sassanids, and they give us a more coherent picture than Avestic texts (the *Avesta* is the sacred book of Zoroastrians) in the pre-Christian era. As these latter were intended for the liturgy or religious law, they present only small fragments of the myths at one time. Here we shall deal in turn with theological myths (the gods, their genesis and order), cosmological myths (the world created under pressure of evil and the time of cosmic struggle), soteriological myths (which clarify the essential role of the priest and, above all, of Zarathustra, and follow the movement of the world towards purification and its own end), and finally the sacred 'institutional' myth.

Major deities

The god of ancient Iran, Ahura Mazda (Wise Lord), is a supreme god, lord and creator, who would fall outside the bounds of myth altogether if it were not necessary to explain his connection with a group of entities, the Amesha Spentas (Powerful Immortals) who have surrounded him since the writing of the *Gatha* ('hymns' or 'songs' believed to be the work of Zarathustra himself). Scholars found that they had to explain this relationship in the very early stages of their research, and they showed that the Amesha Spentas were ancient Indo-European gods who shared with Ahura Mazda (Ohrmazd) the function of sovereign gods, though the parts they played were not allotted in quite the way as in India. But their subordinate character — the fact that they are created — which is a point made perfectly clear in later theology, does not make them like any other creatures, nor are they merely superior to other creatures though of the same order. This is where Iranian theology enters the sphere of myth; the Amesha Spentas are gods without being God, they are created without being creatures and preside over

189

great natural features without becoming identified with them. These entities, called *Yazata* (venerables), are six in number: Vohu Manah, Asha, Kshathra, Haurvatat, Armati, and Ameretat.

Vohu Manah (in Pahlavi: Vohuman) or Good Spirit, ensures the presence of God in the souls of the just, and takes them to paradise after death.

That Ahura Mazda is not first in rank and is both outside the group of six and at the same time the first of the seven, is proved by the fact that his 'worldly' equivalent is the 'just' man, over whom this god presides as his own particular domain, while the equivalent for Vohu Manah is bovine (the bull or cow, which provides sacred urine or milk to be mixed with the *homa* of the sacrifice).

Asha (Right), the second entity, called Arta to begin with—the Indian Rita—and later Ashavahisht (the better Asha), is the protector of fire: and this at once reveals his nature. He is the guarantor of moral and physical order in the world, and his principal adversary is the demon world. The essential part played by the element fire in Iran is well known; oaths are sworn by it, it is an effective protector against demons and the supreme object of the religious cult. To their neighbours the Persians were 'fire-worshippers', and until the Musulman domination wherever there was a sufficient number of Mazdeans in one town, there was at least one temple of fire. Undoubtedly the exclusivity of this cult preserved Mazdaism from any other, less abstract religious faith. However, although Vohu Manah is of superior rank, Asha is more closely concerned with cosmic order than with human order: convincing evidence of this emerges when one considers their terrestrial antitypes, the cosmic bull and fire, the latter being far more universal and, in a sense, more abstract.

Kshathra or Shatrevar (Power), the third in the hierarchy, would appear to be concerned with war since he protects metals, but according to the *Bundahishn*, he plays the part of the defender of the poor. The mythology of war did in fact undergo a radical change in Zoroastrian Persia, and the warrior was reduced to the function of protector of the unfortunate. This entire subject is the subject of an epic in the *Book of Kings* (*Shah Nama*), in which the emphasis is on heroes, champions who give the whole of their long lives to waging war, without any connection, however remote, with the 'gods'. At most, Kshathra is predisposed to defend royalty, and uses arms to maintain peace and promote religion.

The first three of the Amesha Spentas must certainly seem an ill-assorted trio: yet they fit in for the historian, for in their prehistory he encounters the normal order he would expect: the first two sovereign gods and the god of war. They also interest the student of myth in its final form, who contrasts the later arrangement.

The second group consists of a very ancient feminine deity, Spenta Armati, accompanied by a couple called Haurvatat and Ameretat (prosperity or health, and immortality), in other words the Harut and Marut of Islam. Spenta Armati (in Pahlavi, Spendarmat) is patroness of Earth, and symbolises submission, devotion and adoration. Her two aides, with their highly indicative names, preside over the waters (which are purifying and healing) and over plants (which in principle have medicinal qualities).

This, then, is the basic 'framework' of the Mazdean pantheon, but many other gods have been drawn into a comparatively close group around the Six. Some of those most frequently encountered are described below.

A curved and decorated goddess with a gold ear-ring in one ear. Female deities were rare in Persian mythology and Spenta Armati is the only goddess among the Amesha Spentas. Amlash. 900 B.C. Teheran Museum. *Paul Popper*

Two scorpion men standing under the symbol of Ahura Mazda. Persian impression of a cornelian cylinder seal. *Louvre*

The System of Minor Gods

It is worth noting a certain characteristic that confirms the mythical nature traditionally attributed to the Amesha Spentas: the *Bundahishn* expressly states and repeats several times that Ohrmazd (Ahura Mazda) is the first of spiritual beings and after him come the Amesha Spentas. Ohrmazd is thus the first of the series of seven, since he is the creator of the Six, and he is at the same time the seventh who closes the series. And so theologians who tell us that the Six are created, that they retain some recollection of the time when they were gods, and that this ambiguity persists, and do so in vain. Moreover, the Six contrast strongly with the host of other gods who make up the Mazdean pantheon, and the regroupings in which they are presented merely betray this difference in origin.

The two groups of the Six are usually placed to the left and right of Ohrmazd and opposite him is Sraosh or Srosh (genius of hearing and mediator between god and man), who presides over the *geteh* (material) world just as Ohrmazd presides over the *menok* (spiritual) world. Sraosh also acts as psychopomp to the dying, and the cult observed for three nights following a death is dedicated to him. In the *Shah Nama*, Sraosh is the divine messenger who is most often mentioned.

When it comes to listing the other gods, the simplest pattern is that of the *Bundahishn*, for this has the advantage of grouping them around the Amesha Spentas.

Ohrmazd (Ahura Mazda) is unquestionably a god apart, but one of the first things we are told about him is that he created the *khwarenah*, a concept of fortune or destiny of primary importance in Persian mythology, and without equivalent in related mythologies. Scholars were too hasty to use the word 'glory' to translate this term, which was compared to the *kabod* of the Old Testament. The *khwarenah* is neither a manifestation nor an epiphany, but more in the nature of a charism enabling all social categories to fulfil their particular functions in a privileged and exclusive manner. In the final analysis every man has his *khwarenah* or final cause, but it is mainly an attribute of sovereigns of the Kayanide dynasty (a mythical dynasty that appears in the *Shah Nama* and other epics), of Persians or Persia, and, lastly, of priests whose functions were essential to the preservation of civil society. The mythology of the *khwarenah* is difficult to follow, because it dwells in water although it appears to be a fire deity (fire rather than light); the contradiction is removed when one remembers that fire comes originally from plants whose growth depends on the water they receive, that is, from wood which ignites under friction.

Charismatic fire is what gives the early heroes of Iranian myth their strength and prosperity. Yima is one such hero; the first man—and not, as in India, king of the dead—he is in the beginning wondrously endowed with *khwarenah* and then loses it through his own fault and thereby automatically loses his kingship. As multiple and changing as fire, the *khwarenah* appears in various forms and in the *Chronicle of Ardashir*, which tells the story of the accession and exploits of the founder of the Sassanid dynasty, it is symbolised by a goat which accompanies Ardashir in his flight for freedom towards the sea: only then, when he reaches the coast, does he feel certain of being in true possession of his *khwarenah* and of supplanting the last sovereign in the Arsacid dynasty.

The national *khwarenah* of Persia is as important as that of the heroes, for this it is that gives the nation its superiority over others. The *khwarenah* of the Kayanids and the *khwarenah* of the Iranian nation helped to promote an extremely strong sense of possessing hereditary gifts, and is certainly a reason for Iranian Islam's doctrine of imams, and its ultra-sharp sense

Fire played such an important part in Mazda ritual that the Mazdeans were known as fire-worshippers. This Achaemenian fire altar is at Pasargades. *A. Perissinotto*

of Mohammedan succession. Both royal *khwarenah* and sacerdotal *khwarenah* stem from Ohrmazd and are his most lofty and characteristic creation.

The assistants of Vohu Manah are Mah, the Moon, who presides over phases of time and the movements of the waters (tides); Geush Urvan, the soul of the primeval bull—or bovine—venerated in Mazdaism as highly as in Indian religion, and protected on earth, according to the principal prayer of Mazdaism, by Zarathustra (Zoroaster) himself; and finally Vayu (or Ram), who plays a specific part after death, helping the soul of the just man to surmount obstacles on his journey after death. Vayu is also an aspect of time.

In fact the *Bundahishn* refers now to Vayu, now to Zurvan, applying the same epithets and the same distinctions to both. 'Zurvan undivided' and 'Zurvan of the long rule' are two aspects of time—and of Vayu too. Being privileged, Vayu inherits two separate roles from them, one transcendent and with no attribute other than limitless duration, the other founded on the succession of seconds which will make him fit to be the instrument of Ohrmazd. Ohrmazd, essentially a creator god, gives duration and limit to the world just as he does to evil. Though evil in no way depends on him, he is superior to it and master over it precisely because his control of time enables him to limit it. Time serves to 'exhaust' evil and therefore has the measure of it: this will be seen later with reference to creation.

The assistants of Ashavahisht are Atar, the god of fire or transcendent fire, Sraosh, whom we have seen to be a sort of complement to the Amesha Spenta group, and Vahram. Fire is directly linked to the social classes over which it presides: the fire of the priests is Farnbag fire; Gushnasp fire is the fire of warriors, and Burzin Mihr fire is the fire of peasants. This classification has continued to operate

without prejudicing that based on the different material sources of fire in use, and it is of capital significance precisely because mythology is largely moulded according to social divisions. But the 'physical' classifications of 'fires' emphasises how widespread they are in the universe, even to the extent of forming, as it were, its very substance: the 'physical' types include Berezi-Savang fire which rises before Ohrmazd, Bohu-fryan fire which dwells in plants and in wood, Vazisht fire which is the lightning lodged in the clouds, Spenisht fire which is common fire, and finally—beyond compare—Vrahran fire, the most sacred fire, which man lights to be especially venerated. Vrahran fire consists of a combination of fifteen or sixteen special fires, most of them belonging to guilds connected with metal-work, but also concerned with disreputable trades or occupations. This would seem to suggest that the sacred fire redeems and purifies the perverse uses to which man puts this element. One text (*Zatspram*) tells how, when the world was being created, fire was compounded with each of the six elements of which it is made: sky, water, earth, plants, cattle, man. Although fire plays a major role in Mazdean cult, the god of fire (he who bears its name, Atar) plays a very modest part in its theology. It is Verethraghna, a martial god and the patron of Vrahran fire, who plays a much more important role here. An explanation of this anomaly can, in part, be found in the Armenian legend (Armenia was, of course, Mazdean before turning Christian) of a god of fire who bore the same name, Vahagn.

If the mythology of fire is rarely represented in the fragments of extant Mazdean texts, there is still sufficient external evidence, some of an archaeological nature, to prove the importance of this cult, and to account for the epithet 'fire-worshippers' which the Mazdeans acquired. The essential part of the cult, the

Worshippers at a fire altar (*left*) and before a shrine (*right*). Persian minature. *c.* 1600 A.D. *Victoria and Albert Museum*

A Sassanian clay tablet found at Takht-i Suleiman in 1963. It bears a Pahlavi inscription indicating that a sanctuary of the fire of the warriors, Gushnasp, was situated there. *Deutsches Archaologishes Institut (Istanbul)*

sacrifice of the *Yasna* (sacramental liturgy), takes place in the presence of fire; the judicial oath is sworn by fire; shining in the night, fire hunts and destroys demons; and by the evidence of ancient geographers and archaeology Iran was studded with fire temples. The sacred nature of fire is also revealed in the myth of Keresaspa, a hero of many exploits, who has the greatest difficulty getting into heaven because he once 'struck' or extinguished the (sacred) fire, who complained of this insult.

Vahram (the Avestic Verethraghna) is a deity who can assume the shape of a bull, a white horse, a camel, a boar, a handsome youth, a bird, a ram, a wild goat, a warrior (all symbols of strength in war and sexual vigour) and yet he survived in mythology because of his igneous origin. This explains also why he, together with Atar, is the companion of Arta.

Among Kshathra's assistants are the Sun, Mithra, the Sky and the Celestial Luminaries; this combination is all the more interesting for showing Mithra associated with the sidereal deities on the one hand, and on the other with the god of metal and weapons. So Mithra, who will be seen again when his cult spreads under the Roman Empire in the wake of the legions, already has a military aspect, though in this context arms maintain order and discipline, not war. A military career presumes asceticism, restraint, respect, and the restoration of justice, and its practice therefore implies a superior knowledge of human actions that comes from an omnipresent deity, the Sun. This, it would seem, is the explanation of the sidereal character of Mithra, which stands out so clearly in the *Yasht* (sacrificial hymn) dedicated to him, and in the Roman monuments of Mithras, which emphasise the relationship between god and planet. It is also known that in the languages of central Asia to which Mazdaism has made some contribution the name of Mithra refers unambiguously to the sun. As to his identification

with justice, this can be seen in his role of judge of the dead in Mazdean mythology, even though he has completely abandoned the function of sovereign god that is Ohrmazd's alone.

The assistants of Spenta Armati (Spendarmat), are a group of female deities. The first is called, quite simply the Waters (Ardvi Sura Anahita), to whom a complete *Yasht* is dedicated. This deity played an important but somewhat mysterious role in Iran. Whereas in India the rivers are physically and mythologically of great importance, Iran (in the broad sense) has only one great river, the Oxus (Amu Daria), which forms its northern boundary. So Indian river mythology had little place here, and in a way was ill at ease, and at first sight there might appear doubt whether a'genuinely Iranian water goddess ever existed. *Yasht 5*, one of the earliest texts, proves that she did, but there is some foundation for the idea that Anahita tended to lose prestige in Iran, whereas under the Hellenic name of Anaitis she acquired importance in Asia Minor and generally throughout the Occident, where she was worshipped, if not as a river deity, at least as a female goddess. She is even found in Jewish and Musulman legend, where she becomes confused with Spenta Armati and is flanked by her 'dioscuri', Hordat and Amurdat. She presides over the waters and extends her patronage to seminal fluids and, in consequence, to animal and human fecundity. In addition she is usually associated with a sacred liquid of a different type, the *Haoma*, for in Iran the *Haoma* (like the *Soma* in India) is pressed for its intoxicating juice, the elixir of immortality, and its ritual consumption and libation is the principal act of sacrifice. In both countries, *Haoma* is sacrificial plant and god, daily sacrifice and prelude to the eschatological sacrifice which brings about the transfiguration of the world. The ritual involved, the *Yasna*, though less complex than in India, is still fairly rich and the most important part of Avestic liturgy.

Among the minor deities is the female Daena (*dên*). She is the 'knowledge' or 'religion' of Ohrmazd, in other words, according to the texts, she is just discernment between gods and demons. She is the revelation of Ohrmazd to his first 'creature', Vohu Manah, a revelation that includes the good rites as well as the virtuous acts to be accomplished and indeed all the features that mark the principal differences between gods and demons, between *ahuras* and *daevas*. This revelation, which is both knowledge and practice, is the realisation of 'religion' for the Mazdean. This is so marked that some scholars have felt it necessary to distinguish between daena-revelation and daena-religious consciousness. The two notions form one, as can be clearly seen from the eschatological image of the *dên*. It is worth noting, too, that the word *dên* passed into Musulman Arabic as the current term for 'religion'... at the moment in Mazdaism when 'religion' paired off with 'sovereignty' without becoming fused. There can be union and harmony between civil and religious powers, never unity and fusion.

Khordat's collaborators are Tishtrya, Vat and Fravartin. The first two, Tishtrya (the star Sirius) and Vat the Wind, are both connected with atmospheric phenomena accompanying rain, and are only vaguely defined in Mazdaism, but Fravartin is an entirely original concept which must have played an even more important role than texts suggest. Fravartin is really a plural concept; the holy Fravashis are pre-existent souls of all living creatures, those who are already born and those not yet born, and at the same time include a constituent part of man as well as his soul, strength and body. The Fravashi is both tutelary spirit and that part of the human mind which separates from the soul after death to join its sisters and form a sort of troop, returning to earth once a year on the days known as Fravartikan. The role of the Fravashi is to assist man in all that concerns his growth and the propagation of his race, notably in the fight against demons who seek to impede him.

The function of the Fravashis is to defend living creatures, men or gods. Hence the somewhat military character which has led them to be compared not unjustly with the Valkyries of Germanic mythology, and with both individual and collective 'vitalising' functions. In fact, they ensure fertility and thereby the solidarity of the tribal and ethnic group. This is an aspect that the philosophic speculation of later Mazdaism abandons in favour of the more individual concept of the Fravashis as part of the human compound.

In contrast, looking not towards the past as something protective and life-giving, but towards the future as a renewal and 'correction' of the past— there is the Saoshyans (Saviour), who is in a way an eschatological champion, hence a perfect man, the 'just' man who appears to be the prime cause of

the world, and its saviour. The *Bundahishn* merely mentions him in connection with the Fravahr (final rehabilitation), but he appears again in the myth of Zarathustra.

And just as entities with a social or eschatological role are grouped about Khordat, so there is around Amurdat, his inseparable companion, a group consisting of Rashnu, a judge in the infernal region who helps Mithra, and Ashtat, a sort of psychopomp who is aided by Zam, a spirit of Earth and therefore in touch with the beyond.

This is the principal pattern formulated by Mazdaism in its attempt to organise its pantheon and integrate the highly dissimilar elements surrounding the original heptad of the Amesha Spentas into a more or less functional harmony.

Mazdean dualism

The chapter from the *Bundahishn* describing the gods just listed is itself followed by a counterpart, of obvious artificiality. Corresponding to each god is a *dev*, or demon, and corresponding to each virtue a vice. This is the form which Iranian dualism takes in its final state, the counterpoise of good and evil. But its earlier aspects are those to be reviewed here. First —and this is the most characteristic thing about Iranian religion—moral dualism, that of good and evil, is found almost from the beginning: two primeval spirits fight and these spirits undoubtedly depend on Ohrmazd. The Good Spirit identifies himself with Ohrmazd, while the Evil Spirit acquires a sort of self-sufficiency. His dependence will show itself only in so far as the Good Spirit knows his perverse plans in advance, knows how to contain him and determines freely and with judgment the moment of his ultimate defeat.

In the *Gathas* ('hymns' or 'songs' considered to be the work of Zarathustra himself) moral dualism primarily expresses the opposition between good and evil in the ritual order, but preoccupation with the ritual does not exclude moral preoccupation as such. Above all, it *represents* this moral aspect, and because the rite is graphic, symbolic and concrete by its nature, preoccupation with ritual permeates the moral aspects of Iranian mythology until the myth, repressed by the presence of ambient Islam, is so strongly 'moralised' that it coincides with absolute monotheism. The aniconic nature of Mazdaism contributed much to this transformation, which boasted much ritual but little theology.

So in the beginning, Ahriman (Angra Mainyu), the Evil Spirit, widely separated from the Good, is seized with curiosity and envy, and tries to invade the domain of Good, which is luminous and pure. He is repulsed and the victory is attributed to the infallible effect of the prayer (the Ahuna Vairya) preferred by Ohrmazd, who meanwhile decides to allow Ahriman a period of semi-victory, the better to conquer him once and for all in the end.

The investiture of King Narseh (left) by the goddess Anahita. As her cult spread it grew in importance and in Achaemenian times the King was initiated in her sanctuary. Relief at Naksh-i-Rustam. Third to fourth centuries A.D. *A. Perissinotto*

Time: the myth of Zurvan

In both Iran and India time represents not only the succession of events (infinite time), but the wearing away of beings, their transformation and their death, their greater or lesser renewal according to the prevailing concept of time as cyclic or linear (finite time). It is a philosophic concept, but one which is clothed in two harmoniously linked kinds of myth. First there is the notion that the ages of the world are articulated according to three phases: universal creation of good and evil, the intermingling of these two forces, and the separation and final victory of good. Then there is the concept that the ages following the coming of Zarathustra are divided into epochs which tend towards corruption and which are successively 'turned back' with the coming of each of the three sons of Zarathustra, conceived (long after his death) of his seed (preserved in a lake) by a young girl who came to bathe there. The first schema stems from a moral concept and the second from a more physical conception of history as a wearing away and degeneration, but their fusion is completely normal and, whereas in India it is the second that dominates, in Iran it is the first that colours the second. But, from that point onwards, Iran has to explain not so much the pattern of creation in time (for creation arises out of eternity) as the existence of evil in the world before the creation of the world.

So, in the margin of the official theology of Mazdaism, in which Ahriman is from the first in conflict with Ohrmazd and the question of his origin is unsolved, a more esoteric mythology shows them both to be begotten of the same father, Zurvan (Time) who, though supreme god, has been offering sacrifices for a thousand years in order to obtain a son, and in the end doubts the efficacy of his own acts. Ahriman is conceived as a result of this doubt, while Ohrmazd springs from the merit of the sacrifices. When they

are still in their mother's womb (or their androgynous progenitor) Ahriman, realising that the first-born will enjoy the privileges of kingship, hastens to enter the world before Ohrmazd. With his plans thus thwarted, Zurvan can but divide time between them, with the assurance that in the end the god of good will prevail.

This is an ancient myth persisting right up to the Musulman period, connected in a curious way from earliest Indo-European times with a ritualistic concern, one might almost say 'scruple': when ritual acts are performed, there must not be the slightest doubt about their efficacy lest they become invalid, or, as here, congenitally ambivalent. The myth of the devil begotten of doubt remains apart from the official religion, but there is too much evidence of it for its authenticity to be questioned. It is even thought that it may have some connection with a quasi-metaphysical myth of the Indian *Rig-Veda*, which shows the gods of creation emanating from a sort of formless being on a totally different plane, and who, in any case, is not a creator. The idea of the world appearing out of a 'sacrifice', a sacred act of ritual, is, on the other hand, current among the Brahmans. So, the thing that is proper to Iran in the transformation and utilisation of these mythical elements is the dualism, the simultaneous birth of the principles of good and evil, which are so clearly differentiated and opposed that they are already in conflict before the creation of the world, which only serves to consolidate the ultimate victory of good and make it definitive.

But how are the two worlds articulated, that of creation and that of creation before creation, which consists chiefly of the Amesha Spentas and the spiritual beings. At this point we are not concerned with matter as opposed to the abstract or spiritual, but with a tangible, perceptible world, a real world confronting another world no less real but transcendent. The second creation—what Mazdaism calls the *geteh*

The androgynous Zurvan giving birth to Ohrmazd and Ahriman, flanked by figures representing the ages of life. Silver plaque from Luristan. *Cincinnati Art Museum*

The alliance between throne and altar was a characteristic Iranian concept. It is illustrated in this relief at Taq-i-Bustan where King Ardashir II is seen receiving his crown from Ahura Mazda while Mithra stands behind him on a lotus flower. *c.* 325 B.C. *Paul Popper*

(material) as opposed to the *menok* (primal matter) world—appears to be summoned into existence by the action and incursion of the evil that precedes it. Dualism in moral order and dualism in social degrees and categories of being are inseparable. Before formulating these notions in philosophic terms, as in the text of *The Decisive Resolution of Doubts,* Mazdaism directed them into myths where they expressed a presentiment of reality. What was clearest was the pre-existence of evil and the final victory of good. At the very beginning the good god proposes a pact to the devil, an offer of surrender which the latter is swift to refuse, thereby declaring war although it was already begun: all that the good god then has to do is to regulate the interplay of operations, to assign a length of time for the conflict. So, the prologue in the sky leads to the prologue on earth.

It was natural that the interplay between the two worlds should lead to the concept of a correspondence between microcosm (man) and macrocosm (endless form), or, at least, should tend to annex a myth known elsewhere. It is found in Mazdaism in a fairly common form. The world is first created, according to one text, in the 'body' of Ohrmazd, who makes it grow there and unfolds the elements, the sky coming from his head, the earth from his feet, water from his tears, vegetation from his hair, the bull from his right hand, and finally fire from his intelligence (if that is the best transcription of a word that refers to one of the faculties of the soul). Two things are indicated by this formula—that creation, even that of the material world, first takes place in the *menok* state, and that this world is a likeness of the creator.

Zarathustra's revelation

It is as difficult to pronounce upon the historical traits of Zarathustra, the date of his birth, even the character of his work, as it is simple to find documentation to support his legend, our only interest here. In the *Gathas* he is already to be found as a priest; that is, his function, like that of the Vedic priest, is to offer the sacrificial libation of *Haoma,* and he too expects the sacrifice to bring about 'renewal' of the universe, bound up in some way with the cycle of the year. The hymns show too that Zarathustra is hindered in his work by men and demons, and that he has need of temporal aid, a secular champion who appears in the form of King Vishtaspa. Here we have the prototype of the *alliance* between throne and altar that is characteristic of the Iranian concept of kingship and makes clear the fairly restricted degree of the sovereign's sacredness. This legend is developed at length in Pahlavi texts and is also sketched briefly in other, Avestic texts. In these Zarathustra becomes a character whose birth was something of a miracle, whose childhood was full of marvellous exploits and who received a revelation through the intermediary of the Amesha Spentas, who appeared to him in turn. From

this point on he began his task of ousting national Mazdaism with an ascetic monotheism of his own formulation.

This marks the 'coming of religion' into the world, the moment towards which the whole of history has been tending, and from this point another history unfolds, leading through the progressive destruction of demons to the eschatological transfiguration. The doctrine of salvation (soteriology) is thus wedded not only to the world of sacrificial rite but to the 'history' of the central character, so closely that the priest of the *Gathas* is equally founder of religion and prophet. The Musulman heresiologists were not mistaken when they identified Zoroastrianism with 'prophetism' as opposed to Brahmanism, although for the historian both have the same source.

As this revelation is central to the history, the person of Zarathustra is equally related to two figures, initial and final, consisting of primeval man, Gayomart, and the ultimate saviour, Saoshyans. These ties of blood ensure the continuity of the human race. And just as there is a *khwarenah* for heroes (*kavi*), so there is a sacerdotal and prophetic *khwarenah*, which is an integral part of the person of Zarathustra and dwells in him in plenitude. Finally, the *Haoma*, the object of sacrifice, is intimately bound up with the priest who performs the sacrifice and it, too, becomes part of his nature. From being a simple priest Zarathustra in the myth becomes a cosmic character, and the questions that he asks of the Amesha Spentas in the *Gathas* (which at this level are given the style of hymns) are transformed in the myth into 'discourses' which he has with each of them, spread out over some ten years. This is an endogenous development, not at any rate the result of Islamic influence (since the texts are certainly prior to the seventh century) and even less the result of Hebrew prophetism, for it shares none of the latter's characteristics.

One of the principal charisms of Zarathustran legendary is his power against demons, which enables him to frustrate their scheming and paralyse their acts. But the episode that acquires the most meaning in the legendary tale is the conversion of King Vishtaspa, when Zarathustra visits his court performing miracles before winning him over to the Good Religion. Vishtaspa resists so long and so effectively that finally Ohrmazd sends two angels to reveal Zarathustra's mission to him in a vision: when Vishtaspa regains consciousness he proclaims himself to be converted. This begins a long series of wars against neighbouring kings who refuse to accept Mazdaism or try to prevent Vishtaspa from following it.

For Zoroastrians the whole of history evolves from these holy wars according to a pattern of alternating decadence and renewal. This is a feature of the Purana of India too, although the latter has cycles which are never closed but infinite, while Iran conceives of time as moving towards a final point. The lack of relief and individuality in the champions of each

'strong time' suggests that the Iranian concept is the earlier of the two. From the point of view of myth, it has a certain originality to be seen again in the eschatology.

Eschatology

This divides very sharply into individual eschatology and general eschatology. The soul after death has a definitive fate, which depends on its actions during life, but it will not rejoin its body until the final resurrection, which will also be the transfiguration of creatures rediscovering their state prior to the *geteh* creation. For the individual, the decisive moment comes after the three days that the soul spends near the body from which death has separated it. When the fourth day dawns, the soul goes to the Bridge of the Separator (Chinvat Bridge), accompanied by auxiliary gods, Sraosh, Vayu the Good and Vrahran, and there the demons enter into dispute with them. The judgment is revealed when the bridge admits or bars the passage of the soul. But first Mihr, Sraosh and Rashnu must weigh the soul, or to be more precise, its actions during life. Once the bridge is crossed, the soul judged good sees a charming young girl who proves to be its virtuous actions and reminds it of the good it has done. Then it smells a wonderfully perfumed breeze blowing from paradise, and the celestial journey commences, leading to the infinite light where it will enjoy beatitude. The sinful soul, in contrast, falls into the gulf, where demons torment it and where it is visited by a ghoul representing its sins. It then goes on its way to hell. In this fairly classical portrayal of the final judgment, it is worth noting the original appearance of the figure symbolising the virtuous personality, or its counterpart the sinful personality, which goes unrecognised by the soul at first: this is the soul's *dên*, both its own consciousness (hence itself) and the effects of this consciousness. The content of a life is presented here as a plenitude rather than a retreat or a parting, which is the opposite of the Indian concept.

General eschatology is a combination of a reversal of the myth of creation and a number of the 'heroic' myths, which extend the concept of the Saoshyans. The chief aim of creation, as we have seen, is to destroy evil: this done, it has but to be absorbed into its original state. Time 'runs out' in three millennia which correspond to the appearance of the three posthumous sons of Zarathustra: Oshetar, Oshetar-mah and Saoshyans. The beginning of the fourth millennium in the history of the world is regarded as future time; the preceding period is that of the last Iranian kings and of the Arab and Turkish invasions. In it calamities will disappear and an era of generosity and peace begin. It will be followed by a disaster due to torrential rains caused by the fateful Malkos, a descendant of the Turi Bratroresh, who is believed guilty of the death of Zarathustra. Then beasts and humans will leave the enclosure built by

Yima in the beginning (*see* p. 200) and, as they spread,
maladies will disappear. Thus the end corresponds to
the beginning, and the myth expresses this by a
repetition of events and duplication of characters.

The second period, that of Oshetarmah (Uxshyat-
nemah) also includes an initial moment of prosperity
and peace followed by the liberation of the terrible
Dahaka, symbol of tyranny. This leads to the arrival
of the third champion, bearing the Gathic name of
Saoshyans, 'he who makes to prosper'. It is during his
reign that the final transfiguration and resurrection
of the body will take place.

The *Bundahishn*, briefly summarised above,
emphasises the cyclic structure of the history of 'salvation': it does not stop there, but, like many other
Pahlavi texts, shows that in the final struggle numerous heroes or kings are involved. Many of them are
found in the text of the later *Shah nama*.

The first to be summoned by man, fire, water, and
plants to oppose Dahaka is Thraetona (Feridoun).
Dahaka (later Zohak), a tyrannical king on whose
shoulders grow two voracious serpents, is the symbol
of violent, orgiastic kingship destroying the 'elements'.
Thraetona does not prevail and recourse is taken to
another hero, Sâm Kersasp, son of Nariman, who
puts Dahaka to death. Then, after a long period of
ruling over the world, Kersasp hands over to Kay
Husroy, who governs with Saoshyans (representing
religious tradition) as his great *mobed* (chief of the
ecclesiastical hierarchy). Kay Husroy is succeeded by
the first Mazdean king, Vishtasp, and Saoshyans by
the founder of the religion, Zarathustra.

Yet Saoshyans is also quoted elsewhere as playing
the part of sacrificer at the resurrection of bodies
when the bull Hadayans is put to death, and a drink
that will confer immortality on all men is prepared
from the fat of the animal mixed with *Haoma*. This
suggests that the primeval creative sacrifice of the
bull, which will recur in the cult of Mithra, is the
prototype of the ritual sacrifice today restricted to
Haoma, and also the prototype of the ultimate re-
creative sacrifice which gives back life and re-estab-
lishes creation in its original state. By it men will
acquire perfect dimensions and be endowed with anything they lack, including spouse and offspring. They
will take their place in paradise in the presence of
Ohrmazd, but whether it is a beatifying vision or not
is not known. A flood of molten metal will cover earth,
in which the just will take no harm and the impious
will be immediately purified and released from hell
where they have been waiting since death.

'Human' mythology

Between these two great mythical compositions, that
of the beginning and that of the end, is a no less
cosmic yet human mythology, which reflects even
more clearly the social organisation and the spirit
of Iranian society. This is the point at which the whole
relevance of Dumézil's researches into Indo-European
ideology appears, and also into its slightly changed
direction in Iran, which may or may not have been
due to Zoroastrianism but certainly marked it out as
different from the Indian and Celtic 'treatments'. Its
distinctive feature is not the existence of three classes,
sacerdotal, military and 'economic' or productive; it
is their structural composition, found in many different forms, and the way in which they are considered
to constitute a single whole. There is a common structure for men and their classes and for the gods and
their types, which at times makes the business of
separating sociology from theology a delicate affair.
But even where there are 'transfers' from one group
to another, there can be no question of abolishing the
boundaries between the two domains: the passage
from social structure to divine domain, from the
judicial to the transcendent order, with its own

inseparable mythological trappings, demonstrates man's need to find in transcendency the source and security of even the most ephemeral of worldly 'orders'. To what degree this is a legitimate object is a question of metaphysics. The fact remains that for the scholar who describes and analyses myths, 'legendary' history and the rearrangement of 'true' history (where the process can be detected) are indispensable auxiliaries.

The myth of Yima

Yima (twin), son of Vivahvant, according to an early popular belief, was not the first man but the first king. One tradition sets his reign at a thousand years. In the beginning he is offered the role of bearer of the revelation of the Good Religion by Ahura Mazda, but he says he is not fitted for the task and is exonorated without blame. But although he refuses to instruct in religion, he does at least consent to multiply the creatures of Ahura Mazda and to govern them. Here we appear to have the first evidence of the clear-cut distinction made between religious and civil power. Yima's is a golden reign of plenty in which there is no want, no catastrophe, no war. Furnished with a ring (?) and a golden goad, he rules and spares his subjects the perils of foul weather, illness and death, with the result that the human and animal populations outgrow the capacity of the earth. Three times Yima enlarges it with his magic instruments. This is the first solution to the problem of population that myth offers. In *Fargard 2* of the *Videvdat* the second solution follows immediately on the account of the first. Here it is a question of reducing the population of the world, preserving only the finest specimens; this is brought about by a cataclysm which takes its pattern from the icy winters and torrential thaws of central Asia. The golden age cannot last for ever. Ahura Mazda gives Yima warning that hardship will strike at the wickedness on earth and advises him to excavate an underground enclosure *(vara)* and to store there the seed of all species against the wrath to come in cataclysmic storm. All creatures will grow slowly, and men will reproduce themselves only once every forty years. After the cataclysm Yima, god on earth, re-emerges with his elect. To ensure the purely 'temporal' nature of the whole operation the text ends with the brief affirmation that the religion of Mazda was introduced into the *vara* by Karshiptan, the bird.

Zarathustra condemns Yima as a sinner for making animal sacrifices and for eating the flesh of the immolated victim. In the *Avesta* Yima's prosperity lasted just as long as he followed Truth. But when he confessed to lying in his mind then he forfeited his kingly privilege and glory. Pahlavi texts suggest that Yima finally sacrificed to both *daevas* and *ahuras*, and —worse—claimed that he was the creator. His royal fortune was assumed by Mithra, the sun-god with whom legend associates him: Yima the god of light on earth, Mithra the heavenly god of light.

An entirely different aspect of the Yima myth emerges after his death: after a long, prosperous reign he succumbs to the attacks of Azhi Dahaka, who saws him in two with the aid of Spityura. Later tradition infers that he was guilty of pride, and that this was the cause of his downfall. And when the *Book of Kings* takes up the legend of Yima it retains this tradition, which fits in very well with the character of the 'hero-civiliser' finally laid low by his wish for power. Indian tradition gives him quite different treatment, for here Yama is not only king of the dead, but the hero of a curious poem, the *Rig-Veda* (X 10), in which he defends himself against the incestuous advances of his sister Yami.

The myth of Gayomart

This is not the myth of a king or hero who wants to civilise the world, but of Primal Man: according to Zoroastrian tradition Gayomart is created by Ohrmazd immediately after the Primal Bull who is to supply him with food and help him. The two primal beings stand on the two banks of the river that flows from the centre of the world, the good Daiti. Here they are attacked by Ahriman, for they alone have withstood his attempts to spread evil. Ohrmazd, foreseeing the Bull's death, administers a soporific to lessen the pain of death. First the Bull is killed and then Gayomart, who announces as he dies that the human race will, regardless of his imminent death, none the less be born of him.

Ahriman's triumph over Ohrmazd would appear to be complete but the latter has subtler plans for Ahriman's ultimate destruction. The death of the Bull and Gayomart ensure the fertility of life on earth. From the Bull's blood later springs forth vegetation; from its seed (carried to the Moon) come all animals. And where Gayomart's seed fertilises the earth where he was slain, there forty years later springs a plant that splits into two human beings, a male and a female, Mashye and Mashyane, who are the father and mother of humanity.

This myth is probably a very early one, as is the role of the demon, for it is quite common to find a 'deceitful' creature involved in myths concerning the origin of humanity. (This does not imply that the whole of etiology is permeated with dualism, as in Iran.) Similarly, two sexes is a theme found elsewhere. What is peculiarly Iranian, and at the same time totally opposed to Mazdean doctrine (which postulates that good cannot come of evil) is the fact that the demon is called Ahriman. Equally Iranian is the use made of the ultimate fertilisation of the earth by Gayomart to found on this myth the practice of consanguineous marriage, which antiquity regarded as an Iranian custom. Many civilisations which knew of the fertilisation of earth by man, or of the myth of the first incestuous act between brother and sister that gave birth to the whole human race, looked no further than the myth itself.

One final feature should be noted: the connection between the Bull and the moon as revealed in texts. The seed of the Bull is preserved in the moon, and the latter's crescent shape has an obvious resemblance to the horns of the ox; the Iranian text in this instance is inspired by the same ideas as several Indian texts.

The myth of Thraetona

Thraetona is the conqueror of Dahaka, whom he chains to Mount Demavand to be killed by Kersasp at the end of time; but his main importance is in his role of universal king. When he proceeds to divide the world between his three sons, Salm, Toz and Erji, he grants them wishes: the first asks for wealth, the second valiance, and the third for law and religion, for the *khwarenah* of the *kavi* (religious leader) lay upon him. So Erji receives the better part of the world, Iran and India, while Salm obtains the lands of the West, and Toz those of the East. The preferential treatment accorded to the youngest brother excited the jealousy of the two others and was the cause of his death. This myth is all the more interesting as it combines an Indo-European theme (that of three closely bound social orders represented by the different wishes of three brothers) and the theme of dividing the world.

The myth of Kay Us

Although Kay Us is merely a name mentioned in passing in the fragments of the *Avesta*, he is the grandson of Kay Kavat, ancestor and eponym of the Kayanid dynasty which plays an important role in the legendary history of Iran. Precious information about this dynasty is available in Pahlavi books; the later *Book of Kings* affords more plentiful references. Kay Us is ruler of the world, and builds on Mount Elbruz palaces of gold, silver, steel and crystal, which have the magic property of restoring youth to the old and to the sick who walk round them. But the king's pride is to deprive him of immortality, for his ambition is to conquer the sky and the abode of the Amesha Spentas. His attempt to do so brings about his downfall. During his reign there has already been evidence of his pride in a dispute about the frontier between Iran and Turan (later identified with the land of the Turks). The boundary has been marked out by an ox of magic powers. Kay Us sends Srit, a warrior, to kill the ox, but the ox succeeds in convincing Srit that this act would precipitate the greatest catastrophes. Srit in terror makes his report to Kay Us and rather than obey his orders he begs that he should be put to death. Kay Us then orders him to go to a forest where a spirit will appear in the guise of a bitch. Srit obeys his master's orders, duly encounters the bitch and strikes it down. The bitch will divide in two an infinite number of times, and Srit will finally succumb to the ravenous pack.

Kay Husrav

The grandson of Kay Us is famed for his destruction of a temple of idols on the edge of Lake Tchechast, a story that is rich in detail Kay Husrav succeeds in this venture thanks to Fire, to whom he then raises a temple near the lake at Tchiz. This is all that is left of an old tale telling of the foundation of fire and especially of the extirpation of false cults. On this account it is important in the history of Iran, where, in spite of the rarity of historical documents, several more are found relating similar events.

Apart from his role of champion of the Good Religion, Kay Husrav lives on in Iranian mythology for his wars against Fraysib (later Afrasyab) whom legend makes the king of the hereditary enemy, the Turks, though they do not play a part until much later.

These references help to explain how the 'human' mythology of Iran proliferated to the point of providing material for the immense heroic epic, the *Book of Kings* by Firdousi. The *Book of Kings* is not of course the only epic to deal with this material; but the study of the minor epics ('minor' as applied to value and not to volume) is in its infancy. It is not surprising that these historic legends should also shed light on 'religious' myths.

It has already been explained that Mazdaism is a religion with no pictorial or sculptural illustration. It has become obvious, furthermore, that it is known to us only through fragments of text that are often grouped artificially: the task then arises of slowly rediscovering, with the aid of analogies and conjecture, their rightful place in the overall structure when this itself has been established.

The cult of Mithra

The cult of Mithra reviled by orthodox Zoroastrians for its part-worship of *daevas* has its roots in ancient Iranian national beliefs and became widespread from the Christian era onwards. Roman Mithras differs from Mithra of the *Avesta*. The essential role of the former is as slayer of the bull as a ritual act of re-creation. In Iranian texts Mithra is the god of contracts and, with Sraosh and Rashnu, a judge of the dead. He is also a sun-god driving a chariot drawn by white horses, and god of war. Before the reform of the national religion by Zarathustra he is held in highest regard along with Ahura, though his dispensation of justice is harsh to 'followers of the lie'. In the period following the reform he suffered an eclipse and was dissociated from Ahura, only to be re-established and restored to the Zoroastrian pantheon after Zarathustra's death, with the introduction of newly formulated rites involving self-mortification and purity. The pattern of Mithra's decline, fall and ultimate restoration reflects the need to introduce less ascetic, less intolerant elements into primitive Zoroastrian monotheism, to seek a medium of common worship with the worshippers earlier condemned by the prophet.

Paradoxically, if the *Avesta* and Pahlavi texts provide written information about Mithra, the later religion which bears his name and his alone offers only monuments in great number—and it seems likely that there are many yet to be discovered. Such monuments carry minimal inscriptions, which are for the most part highly elliptical. Precious evidence provided by early Greek and Roman authors gives a clearer idea of points left vague or equivocal in the works of art. Without the guidance of inscriptions, the historian is obliged to describe the monuments and to attempt his own interpretation of them.

Mithra is the only Iranian deity to be assimilated by the West, and the way in which the cult moved westwards from Iran is unclear. But there can be no doubt that its principal deity is the old Iranian god, depicted as a sort of hero wearing a Phrygian bonnet, and portrayed especially as killing the bull. One particularly well-known relief shows his expression to be neither fierce nor triumphant, but almost reluctant, and this killing is believed to be something very different from an adventurous exploit: it is a sacrifice in pursuit of re-creation, a sacrifice that quickens nature (symbolised by an ear of corn at the end of the bull's tail, by a dog and a serpent that licks his blood, and by a scorpion crushing his testicles). It is the old Indo-Iranian concept (shared by other nations) of sacrifice or, to be more precise, of ritual immolation. This same relief has, on either side of the central motif, twin figures dressed as shepherds each carrying a torch; one is raised high while the other is lowered towards the ground (presumably representing the rising and setting of the sun). Their names, though the etymology is uncertain, are Cautes (representing the dawn) and Cautopates (representing dusk).

The motif of similar reliefs is often complicated by the addition of half-length figures—Sol and Luna, a raven which seems to be taking a message to Mithra from Sol (perhaps the command to slay the bull) and sometimes Neptune—and also by scenes from the life of Mithra (his birth from a rock, his search for the bull he pursues and hunts and the miracle of the water that gushes from a rock when an arrow is thrown). All these scenes are treated freely according to local artistic tradition. Sometimes the stone bearing the central motif of the taurobolium is made to move on a pivot so as to show on the other side another scene of equal importance, portraying the meal that Mithra shares with Sol. This arrangement shows that the second scene follows the first and is, as it were, its climax.

Finally, in certain Mithraea clear portraits of adepts are graded according to their degree of initiation, which votive inscriptions explain. There were in fact seven degrees of initiation. The symbols for the seven degrees and their connection with the seven planets are depicted in mosaics discovered quite recently in the Mithraea at Ostia. They are, in

A mithraic monument found at Vénasque. It shows the head of Mithra, wearing a Phrygian bonnet, surmounting the sun, with which he became identified, and flanked by two lions representing the fourth degree of initiation. *Roger Viollet*

ascending order: Corax (Raven), Nymphus (Husband), Miles (Warrior), Leo (Lion), Perses, Heliodromos and Pater (Father), titles which perhaps acted as masks. The inscriptions also mention the Cryfii, young people or even children who are not yet accepted into the Mithraic community but are being prepared for it, and are already in attendance at ceremonies. On some frescoes, the different orders are indicated by short inscriptions, but we do not know their different functions. There is no actual proof that Corax, for example, was the messenger of Sol, as he appears to be in the reliefs. The word Miles emphasises the highly military nature of the cult of Mithra, while Perses similarly confirms the origin of the cult, though its 'art' is so far removed from it. Heliodromos would appear to be the courier of the Sun, as he is depicted as the driver of the quadriga. The character of Perses (the Persian) is in part revealed in a text by Porphyrus, who tells us that they used to purify his hands with honey, for it is a fruit preservative and he was guardian of fruit. Similarly, Leo receives the same purification, this time to protect from all transgression, all evil, all uncleanliness. The role played by Nymphus or Husband is much less clear; but there is no reason to suppose a (mystic?) marriage with Mithra. Finally, Pater, at the summit of the hierarchy, is responsible for the community and must be adorned with all the gifts that befit the chief of the group. These seven degrees of initiation and hierarchy are often represented by some septenary arrangement on painted walls or mosaic pavements.

Some idea of the mode of initiation can be gained from the paintings in the Mithraeum at Capua, which depict the endurance tests to which the initiate had to submit. We already know that he was bound to secrecy and was held to it by a previous oath. The tests were terrifying, though this is scarcely surprising

when one considers that Mithra's adepts were all men and doubtless soldiers for the most part.

As can be deduced from the many monuments, the cult spread wherever there were Roman legions, and this was certainly the vehicle of the Iranian gods transplanted in the West. The violent aspect of the immolation of the bull—whatever its higher significance might have been—the harshness of the initiation tests, the disguises, the fairly rough nature of sculptures and reliefs, all this indicates a cult which, without being void of nobility, nevertheless retained a certain crudeness.

Another rather fearful feature of the cult of Mithra (and examples have been found in a great number of temples) was the portrayal of a naked deity with the head of a lion and a huge serpent entwined about his chest. For a long time it was accepted that this represented Kronos (Saturn) who had assumed the character of the Iranian god Zurvan and therefore stood for infinite time. Recently the suggestion was made that it depicted not Kronos but Ahriman, because of its frightening appearance and certain dedications 'to the god Ahriman'. The two explanations are probably not incompatible. Connected with death and dissolution, time has all the appearance of an enemy and may be identified with Ahriman, who in certain Mazdean texts is claimed to be the author of old age. But in this particular case, if it were necessary to seek an equivalent of this god or demon in the Mazdean pantheon, preference would have to be given to Zurvan-of-the-long-rule rather than Zurvan-without-limits, who is time undivided, dominating the succeeding ages, particularly as the seven coils of the serpent entwined about the god's chest represent the seven stages connected with those of the purification and the ascent of the soul. It is an entirely temporal process over which only a deity knowing both succession and death can preside. The distinction between the two Zurvans rightly serves to underline the difference between the two aspects of 'time', one being eternal duration, the other succession. Whatever the truth may be, nothing is known of the ritual purpose of the statue of time in the cult. Perhaps it was merely a reminder.

But what of the value and meaning of the myth? Here we have a religion for soldiers, though they were few in number, for the many temples are all very small, and it is still by no means certain that the popular religion of the legionaries reached the populations in whose midst they set up their camps. Military too is the content of the cult; its aim was to develop in its adherents the virtues of strength and endurance, through appropriate symbols and rites: the taurobolium, a bath in the blood of the immolated ox was, as it were, the peak of achievement. To be accurate, one might perhaps question the use of the word 'religion' with regard to Mithra: like other cults in the Roman Empire, this one undoubtedly was grafted on to the official religion without excluding it or any other casual cults.

The cult was foreign: what was retained, apart from peculiarities of initiation, was Mithra's virile, almost brutal nature, which however brought order in the world through prowess and especially through fertile sacrifice. This last feature seems to be easily the most ancient and to emerge from the Indo-Iranian concept of sacrifice: the killing of the primal bull, attributed to Ahriman in later Mazdean texts, was perhaps restored to Mithra and preserved in this isolated branch, which was almost entirely Hellenistic or Roman as to the rest. The statuary and painting, moreover, are occidental, as can be seen by comparison of the Mithraea of Europe with the Mithraeum of Dura-Europos, which is completely Persian. Thus it is not impossible that artists should have taken themes from the legend of Heracles in order to depict that of Mithra. Similarly, in the Balkans the ancient motif of the Thracian horseman interfered with the taurocton. But these are stylistic and, on the whole, superficial influences. The myth itself seems to be essentially Iranian.

Manichaeism

Manichaeism, an ascetic form of dualism of lightness and darkness, spirit and matter, evolved by the prophet Mani, drew on Zoroastrianism, Gnosis, Buddhism and Indaism for its elements. In spite of evident resemblances with Iranian mythology, Manichaeism differs widely from Mazdaism. The fundamental truths which Mani postulated in the third century A.D. were dualism based on the distinction between two principles, one good and spiritual, the other bad and material, and the division of time into three moments: the anterior moment, in which the world does not yet exist; the median moment, in which light, invaded by darkness, puts up a fight and the world (created to defend) fills with light although it is bad; finally the posterior moment, when the mixture is sorted out and light is restored definitively to its true place. There are truths which seem common to both Manichaeism and Mazdaism; indeed for some time one might have taken the Chinese descriptions of Manichaeism (confirmed later by rich discoveries in central Asia which produced so many Iranian, Turkish and Chinese texts of obviously Manichaean origin) to be allusions to Mazdaism, which was not unknown in the Far East.

Manichaeism, like later Mazdaism, is radically dualistic. But from this common principle they rapidly diverge, for the Manichaean considers Evil as a material thing, and Good as a spiritual principle, whereas the Mazdean pre-creation embraces both the material and the spiritual at a transcendent level, interrupted for a moment by creation and struggle, and finally wholly rediscovered. Manichaean 'disengagement', on the contrary, is not complete, and leaves behind a mass of irreducible and eternal

damnation. And, above all, the good that matter (evil) has invaded and subjugated is much more than a creation: it is an emanation, an 'evocation' which, proceeding from the Father of Grandeurs, bears his image and yearns for return to his principle. The part played by matter is not only to divide and disperse the light particles as far as possible, but also to stamp out and extinguish their own awareness of their exile. Revelation, or a series of revelations, will on the contrary recall the soul to its original state, which is also its destiny. This is an awakening commanding the whole of salvation, and has qualified Manichaeism as a religion of the saviour-saved, a corollary of its initial pantheism.

The system is extraordinarily complicated: in the beginning, the Father of Grandeurs and Prince of Darkness dwell in utterly conflicting domains (light, fragrant, spiritual on the one hand, dark, evil-smelling and material on the other) and yet they are contiguous. Mazdaism, being more mythical, separates the two domains from one another physically as well as qualitatively. At the moment that Evil assails the domain of Good, the Father of Grandeurs, whose goodness prevents his using force to defend himself, can but emanate a 'mother of life' who in turn emanates a 'primal man' who arms himself with five more emanations, corresponding to the elements. None of this is of avail, for primal man is defeated and drawn into Evil, who at the same time absorbs his emanations; this means not only that Good is the prisoner of Evil, but that he is also branded by error and illusion, the characteristics of Evil. So primal man must regain consciousness in order to call upon his principal and Father, who sends him a series of saviour-messengers with obscure names and genealogy, who finally succeed in setting him free. This preliminary salvation plays the part of a 'prologue in the sky'; the elements emanated by primal man remain to be saved, but they are of a less perfect substance. The work of salvation now changes its sphere of operations: henceforth its stage will be the world, a world that is predeterminedly evil. So it is Evil, and especially matter, that is to be utilised by some organisation of extreme complexity for grouping the light particles, filtering them and finally extracting them like a metal from its matrix.

The characters involved in this long process are a number of emanations who imprint on this substantially wicked world an impulse which finally works for the benefit of good. But this reveals the basic pessimism of Manichaeism; since matter is evil, the whole of material creation and, finally, the whole of creation is tainted with the original evil. The essential goodness of the Father of Grandeurs has no 'contacts', no radiance. The atmosphere of Manichaeism would be singularly rarified if it were not for Evil, which unfurls its prodigious number of aeons, an idea undoubtedly borrowed, with some modification, from the gnostic cosmogonies described

Bas-relief of a winged genius from Pasargades, Cyrus' capital. Sixth century B.C. *A. Perissinotto*

Two crowned sphinxes sitting under the winged disc, symbol of Ahura Mazda. Glazed brick relief from the central court of the Susa palace. 404–358 B.C. *Louvre*

by Saint Ireneus and Clement of Alexandria.

To return to the basic pantheism thought to exist in Manichaeism, the question is whether it exists only in the mythical formulation which is natural to Manichaeism, and whether it is a misinterpretation to pose it in philosophical terms. This is the particular point on which comparison with Mazdaism is illuminating: just as, in the latter, ancient myths are an object of faith, even when all that remains are fragments intelligible only in the light of reconstructed Indo-Iranian history, so Manichaean myths appear to utilise mythical scraps gleaned from all sides in order to express a philosophic truth. The deployment of images is the result of borrowing (from gnosis, Christianity, Mazdaism, Buddhism) and one might therefore be tempted to see it as second-hand mythology and in consequence of doubtful authenticity. In one of the most brilliant studies of Manichaeism, H. H. Schneider showed that far from being Oriental in its roots, it was a breath of Hellenistic spirit caught up in the mass of old Oriental religions from which it borrowed at will quasi-decorative elements. That would certainly explain the attitude of Saint Augustine, who in his youth chose Manichaeism as more rational, more explanatory, more 'scientific' than Christianity. The systematic yet at the same time incoherent features of the system are not the least surprise that Manichaeism reserves for its students.

It would seem, in short, that one has to recognise in Manichaeism a primary intuition which presents itself as a revelation, and this is indissolubly linked with a philosophic system, the whole being very closely related to gnosis, before vesting itself with myths borrowed from other religions. In fact, the primeval truths of Manichaeism are presented in a form that is very close to the Mazdean myth: this can be explained, or so this writer believes, by the fact

that Mani was born and lived in the Sassanid Empire, and so Mazdaism was a main source from which the Manichaean system borrowed. But it does not have complete priority: the mark of Christianity is clear, especially on the Marcion heresy that is in strict opposition to the 'world' and grace, creation and salvation, and, at a deeper level still, in opposition to the person of Jesus the victim and saviour. The Father of Grandeurs, who lives in an abode of light, cannot protect himself from invasion by the evil principle, consisting of matter and darkness, except by a defence that is at the same time a sort of capitulation. He is too good to defend himself with weapons of war: he emanates aeons which come to his relief, but their action principally adulterates Evil and they allow themselves to be engulfed in it. In other words Good is a parasite of Evil, instead of the contrary, and a second age must come before Good wakes up to his perilous situation of exile, and then, thanks to new emanations and a very complicated interplay of events, so organises the world as to bring together the Good that has been scattered and pulverised by Evil, and makes it escape from its prison at last. Jesus is one of the saviours of this system, but so is Mani, who expounds and preaches it. It might even be said that other prophets before Jesus had their part in the revelation. But it is the Church of Mani which is the true, the definitive Church, just as the holy books of which the prophet Mani is the author are those which contain the whole truth. The Church had a firmly organised hierarchy which undoubtedly helped to bring about the quasi-universal and strangely homogeneous diffusion of the doctrine found everywhere down to the smallest detail. It is the inverse of the myth: that is, it is a system, and so it has only been briefly mentioned, in spite of all that it contains of interest to us both intrinsic and for the light it sheds on Iranian mythology.

Two recurrent Hindu symbols, the wheel representing the cyclic nature of the universe and the couple representing its multiplicity, are shown in this first to second century A.D. stone dish. North-West India. *British Museum*

INDIA: THE ETERNAL CYCLE

The mythologies of India have one principal feature that distinguishes them from most others—India's myths are still very much alive. For the Hindus, for example, the adventures of Rama have the same reality today as scriptural history has for us, and the offerings made to Agni are as important to them as the sacrifice implicit in the Mass is to Roman Catholics. For Indians the history of the gods is not simply the theme of almost all their literature and their plastic arts: it is intimately bound up with their everyday life from morning till night, from birth to death. It is also the source, illustration and means of communication of all the most noble moral, philosophical, religious and spiritual teachings. And even when they are in search of scientific law or artistic convention it is to this history that they turn, and there that they find guidance.

In the same way, for Buddhists and Jains, the lives of Buddha and Mahavira still have as much authenticity as the life of Jesus has for Christians.

And so it would be both impertinent and superficial to attempt to study this 'mythology' only in ancient texts, which are deliberately hermetic, and often badly translated, and in so doing to overlook the present-day authorities who are versed in this wisdom, and for whom myths are a principal means of expression.

Attention should, moreover, be drawn to the fact that although Jainism and the religions belonging to the group known as aboriginal have remained almost exclusively confined to India, Buddhism and Hinduism have swept far beyond its boundaries. Hinduism spread particularly to Cambodia and Java, where some of its finest works in the form of architecture and sculpture are to be found. As for Buddhism, which practically ceased to exist in India numerous centuries ago, it was swift to invade the peninsula of Indo-China, China, Japan and other Asiatic regions and it has remained the predominating religion there. Finally, there are countries like Tibet, where the two religions have become closely interwoven, especially in their Tantrist form.

Parvati, the beautiful wife of Siva. Bronze. *Madras Museum*

Hindu Mythology

Sources and historical evolution

When we study Hindu mythology, we are naturally tempted to apply recent methods of historical criticism; in other words, our inclination is to differentiate and isolate its various sources, to unravel intricate relationships and retrace the development of different beliefs.

At present this type of interpretation is categorically rejected by all members of the faith; so, in so far as we follow recent methods, we become incapable of understanding what the myths mean to Hindus of to-day.

It must be recognised that the theses advanced by our religious historians—though they themselves would admit that they are contradictory—do not, in fact, stand up to serious examination. However, all the sages of the past and also those of our own time unreservedly recognise the fact that those scriptures considered to be the most ancient, the *Rig-Veda* in particular, contain the highest truth in its totality; the rest are merely commentaries.

All these sages, without exception, including those who adhere to the most abstract philosophies, as Sabkara did two thousand years ago, and as Ramana Marharsi does in our own time, admit the existence of the gods as a truth that is actually experienced. And those gods who appear most frequently in the most archaic texts—Agni, Indra and even Varuna and the Maruts—are always the objects of fervent and widespread cults.

Finally, Hindu mythology in its entirety, from its most venerable traditions to its most recent formulations, constitutes, even to the minutest detail, so coherent a whole that the removal of a single factor would destroy the balance.

Instead of looking for some historical evolution, one would do better to reflect on the fact that, in the earliest recorded times, the sages had a direct vision of things unimpaired by mental reasoning, and they were content to make elliptical allusions to the planes of consciousness which they wished to share with their disciples. With progressive emphasis being laid on the mental approach, these teachings had to be made explicit by relating myths in detail and presenting them in a more philosophic form. But their substance remained unchanged.

To seek some social distribution of beliefs and myths would be as fruitless as to impose a history on them. In fact, with very rare exceptions, all the gods have always had fervent worshippers in all castes. To establish this fact all one has to do is glance at the temples and asrams of India.

So in this exposition there will be no arbitrary dissection of the Indian pantheon either in time or space, for in order to consider it in this way one would have to render it lifeless first. We shall observe it just as it is, with its majestic architecture and its teeming life.

The triple nature of god: Brahma the creator reads the Vedas, Vishnu the protector holds a lotus and Siva the destroyer wields an axe. Nineteenth-century painting. *Calyana-Kalpatam*

Vishnu and Lakshmi seated on the serpent Ananta. A lotus grows out of Vishnu's navel on which Brahma is seated. Painted clay group. 1880. *Victoria and Albert Museum*

A mythology as complex as the universe

The majority of students interested in research into Hindu mythology have been alarmed by its complexity. The stories of gods, demi-gods, demons, sages and heroes overlap and form such a tangled web that not only is it almost impossible to isolate one story alone, but none can be understood except in the light of the others. Scholars have almost always beaten a weary retreat, declaring that the texts are foolish and childish in spite of some fine flights of poetry. Yet the complexity of other fields of knowledge does not astound or arouse indignation. But mythology includes both the visible world and all that escapes the senses, as well as the past and the future. It is hardly surprising that a synopsis cannot be made of it. Since Hindu mythology is a close copy of reality and attempts to show it as both static and dynamic, apparent and hidden, individual and generic, human and cosmic, it is at one and the same time infinitely complex, perfectly fluid, and minutely precise. It has millions of gods, each with a variety of functions and bearing many different names, sometimes more than a thousand. And inversely, a number of these functions are assumed, according to circumstance, by different gods. These gods beget one another much as heat produces electricity, and electricity heat. On occasion they are reabsorbed into one another, they stand substitute for one another, triumph over one another and venerate one another. And all this interlocks like the wheels of a high-precision machine; not a word, not a name could be replaced by another in any text whatsoever. But just as it would be impossible to describe the earth and all that is on it in a few pages, so one can do no more here than trace the broad outlines of the vast Indian pantheon and describe certain episodes in its eternal harmony.

The creation of the worlds

The Absolute

It is essential to bear in mind the fact that Hindu mythology is based not only on monotheism, but on monism, or to be more exact, non-dualism — that is to say, the conviction that everything that exists may ultimately be referred to one, the Absolute.

The Absolute, which is given the name of 'That' or Brahman by Hindus, is by its very nature impossible to depict. The closest approximation to it is thought to be the words of the *pranava* (a religious verse of which the most sacred syllable is '*Om*'), and the written symbols that are often used to denote it. These graphic symbols appear either alone or as if encircling the image of the god or gods, through whom the worshipper seeks awareness of the Absolute.

The Absolute (Brahman) is sometimes manifested outwardly ('All that exists is Brahman,' the scriptures say), and is sometimes not made manifest ('Brahman is truth, the world is illusion,' the scriptures say also). In the periods when the Absolute is not manifested this world does not exist, the One has not become multiple, and there is neither nature nor human soul, there is not even as yet a personal god in the accepted Christian sense. The appearance of universes and their disappearance are therefore not unique, but cyclic events.

Birth of the Creator

This static, non-manifest Absolute is frequently represented in Hindu scriptures as well as iconography by Vishnu, the Vishnu who will recur later as one of the countenances of the personal god, that of conservator and protector of the worlds. In his earlier role he protects and conserves the worlds, but, as it were, in reserve, in potentiality. In addition, another myth shows us the sage Markandeya in this period of non-manifestation, moving about in Vishnu's stomach and surveying all these embryo worlds.

Yet another myth shows Vishnu lying motionless on a thousand-headed cobra, which floats on an ocean of milk, infinite and immobile. The ocean represents at one and the same time absolute totality, non-differentiation, uniformity, and non-movement. The serpent is called Ananta, eternity — in other words, absence of time.

When the One multiplies, it first emanates its manifestation (*sakti*), represented in the myth as Lakshmi, wife of Vishnu and obviously goddess of abundance and harmony. This is the primal duality that is essential before any other can appear.

Then from Vishnu's navel a pink lotus-flower emerges on the end of a long stalk which is in the hands of Vayu, vital force, and seated on the flower is the first divine shape with an active role to play in the creation. This is Brahma, the primeval ancestor of the Hindu pantheon; the familiar creator of many myths. He has four arms, each holding a book, and four mouths, each of which recites from one of the books. These are the eternal laws, the Vedas, to which he must conform in the execution of his task. It is therefore understandable that the Vedas, the basic holy scriptures of India, should be considered by Hindus as existing prior to the creation of the world.

But these laws do not suffice the creator. He must understand their origin and purpose, as well as the reason for his own existence. 'Who am I,' he asks, 'who sits on this lotus-flower? Whence comes this lotus which grows in isolation on the waters? Perhaps there is something beneath it which holds it up?' So he climbs into the lotus stem, but abandons his exploration when he finds nothing, and he enters into meditation. Vishnu then appears to him, blesses him and advises him to surrender to fervent austerity. Only the heat he therein engenders enables him to proceed to the work of creation.

For the Hindus, the inward search is the only one that reveals what is important, for knowledge of the external world conveys only a superficial vision. This necessity for meditation, austerity and even sacrifice, particularly before any act of creation, is one of the *leit-motivs* of Indian holy scripture, and the gods are subject to it too.

Be that as it may, the achievement up to this point is the mobilisation both of the basic eternal principles and of creative divine will, which governs the forces involved. The subsequent development is that in which dualities-polarities appear, the opposed forces.

Opposition of gods and demons

This is the substance of the myth in which Indra, king of the gods, and Vairocana, king of the demons, are jointly instructed by Brahma, and from this one lesson each of them absorbs only what he must do in order to play the part assigned to him in the cosmos. It should be firmly established that Vairocana, like many demons, is highly sympathetic. He is a pious creature, respects holy law and the scriptures, and is desirous of performing his mission well.

The churning of the ocean

Once this duality—or rather polarity—of the god and the devil in the world has appeared, multiplicity proper can manifest itself—not as yet the multiplicity of objects, beings and individualised movements, but that of secondary principles that will enable the rest to come to life. This is the myth of the churning of the ocean. The majority of characters who were present at the appearance of the creator, Brahma, are seen again, but here they play different parts.

The ocean of milk, which is still an infinite and undifferentiated mass, has become both proto-matter and proto-energy, in which individualisations will crystallise. Vishnu, who has turned into a tortoise, is now at the heart and in the depths of this ocean, and he provides the stable base on which rises the axis of the world, Mount Mandara. The serpent Ananta (here called Vasuki), principle of omnipresence and extension, coils round Mount Mandara like a rope, whilst the gods of Indra seize his head and the demons of Vairocana hold his tail. It should be noted that both gods and demons co-operate in this way on the express command of the creator, Brahma. Pulling in turns in opposite directions they make Mount Mandara rotate rapidly, thus churning the ocean of milk, with the result that the elements of creation spout forth.

On reflection it is quite normal that the first element to emerge should be immortality. For when the combined action of gods and demons implies mortality—this being characteristic of all that is created—immortality must emerge to act as counterweight, but this must not be confused with eternity. The second element is medicine; the texts do not tell us whether its role is to bring early death or immortality; but basically death is perhaps something that has to be endured before man can triumph over it. Then there appear such elements as beauty, joyous intoxication, gentleness, vitality represented by a horse, the possibility of exercising desire in different fields, physical strength represented by an elephant, the arms that ensure victory, and a poison that has no antidote.

The golden egg and the primeval being

The story of the golden egg then reveals how, in the beginning of the world, individual animate and inanimate objects came into being.

In the beginning, the universe was shrouded in darkness, total, indiscernible, undiscoverable, unknowable, as if it was completely absorbed in sleep. Then the Lord revealed himself, irresistible, self-existent, subtle, eternal, the essence of all beings, indiscernible. Desirous of producing different creatures from his own body, he created the waters and put a seed in them. This seed became a golden egg, Hiranyagarbha, as resplendent as the sun, and he himself was born in it and so was Brahma, the ancestor of all worlds. This Lord, having swelled in the egg for a celestial year, split it in two by mere process of thought. The upper half of the shell became the celestial or divine sphere, the bottom half became the terrestrial or material sphere. Between the two, atmosphere took up its position, with the earth floating on the waters, and on the ten cardinal points.

From this egg came forth the primeval being, with a thousand thighs, a thousand feet, a thousand arms, a thousand eyes, a thousand faces, and a thousand heads. He was, the *Rig-Veda* says, the entire universe, all that has been and all that will be.

This primeval creature, or *purusha*, then offered himself in sacrifice in order to create the world, and each of his limbs and the elements in its composition gave birth to a series of entities which corresponded to one another on the different planes of creation. According to other texts it was the multiplicity of gods in the universe who made a sacrifice of him, but the meaning remains the same. The innumerable descriptions of this sacred act, which are to be found in Hindu scriptures, are far from being identical. There is no single arbitrary account that is mechanically repeated, but versions that complete one another and shed light on one another.

From his mouth issued the Brahman caste, the Word, Agni, and the gods in general, and also goats. From his armpits the seasons were born. From his abdomen spurted demons. From his thighs emerged the merchant caste and cattle. From his feet came earth, the caste of manual workers and horses. The sun came from his eye, the moon from his soul, the atmosphere from his navel, the sky from his head, and so on.

After this, the scriptures say, 'having formed all that exists and the cardinal points, this primeval

The giant Mahesamurti bust in the caves at Elephanta showing Siva as destroyer, creator and preserver. *Almasy*

The churning of the ocean. Vishnu, as Mt. Mandara, stands on the back of a tortoise; the serpent Vasuki is coiled round the mountain and pulled alternately by the *devas* and the *asuras*. Relief from Angkorwat. Musée Indo-Chinois, Paris. *Giraudon*

being, the first-born of sacrifice, entered into himself with himself'. A picturesque way of implying that the divine inhabits and totally impregnates this universe, which he brought forth from his own substance. This is shown even more strikingly in another myth in which a deity, like a huge spider, secretes an interminable thread, weaves a web with it and then lives in this web.

God in the world

The triple countenance of the Divine

A third element is needed to correspond to nature and the human soul: the personal god, capable of relationships denied the Absolute. India usually gives this personal god the general title of Iswara, which is pre-eminently a philosophic term, for in the practice of the cult and in daily life only one of these aspects is usually appealed to at a time. That is why in the scriptures, as in art, he is usually represented as Trimurti, a collection of three faces on one head: Brahma, Vishnu and Siva, who correspond respectively to the creative, conservative and destructive action performed by the one and only divine. These three aspects are as inseparable as the elements of our own activity since, in the framework of this universe, one cannot exist without the others. Germination creates the tree, destroys the seed and preserves the species; the joiner creates the table, destroys the tree and preserves the wood.

The preservative, protective aspect is Vishnu, who, as we have seen, preserves the worlds, even between their periods of manifestation. When the world exists, Vishnu protects it in two ways: on the one hand, from the heights of his supreme paradise; and on the other, by descending periodically to earth.

Vishnu in his paradise

The *Rig-Veda* teaches that Vishnu is 'of wondrous power' (*purudasma*). He is generally represented pictorially as a beautiful adolescent, blue in colour (Ramakrishna explains that if some gods, represented in the forms of men, seem blue, it is because they are immense and far away from us. The dense layer of atmosphere that intervenes colours them in this way). In his four hands Vishnu holds his conch (Panchajanya), the terrible discus (Sudarsana, also called Vajranabha), a mass of arms (Kaumodaki) and a lotus-flower (Padmá). He is dressed like a king, with a jewel-studded crown. On his chest is a tuft of curly hair, the Srivatsa, a particular object of devotion, and the jewel Kaustubha, which rose from the ocean of milk when it was churned up. His mount is the god-bird Garuda.

He bears a thousand different names, of which the following are most frequently found in use: Ananta, meaning 'infinite'; Yajnesvara, lord of sacrifice; Hari, the abductor (who seizes souls in order to save them); Janárdana, who captures the adoration of men; Mukunda, liberator; Mádhava, spouse of Lakshmí; Kesava, hairy (his hair being the rays of the sun); Narayana (source and refuge of beings, or rather 'born on the waters'); Hrishikesha, who is master of the sensory organs; Murari, who triumphs over the *asura* Mura; Padmanabha (with the lotus-flower as his navel); and Purusottama (supreme being).

From his paradise (Vaikuntha), where he is accompanied by his *sakti*, the goddess Lakshmí, Vishnu surveys what is happening in the universe. Thus, one day, he suddenly interrupts a game of dice and prepares to descend to earth. 'One of my worshippers, a launderer,' he says to Lakshmi, 'is being beaten and is calling me to his aid.' But almost immediately he sits down again: 'The launderer has seized a stick and is defending himself single-handed; now I do not need to go to his help!'

The avatars of Vishnu

'Whenever order, justice and morals are in danger' —it is Vishnu himself who puts these words into the mouth of his greatest avatar—'I come down to earth and take human shape.' Westerners, who are so sceptical about other things, have long argued about the correct number of these 'descents' or avatars: some texts list ten, others twenty-two, and others say that they cannot be counted. Perhaps the simple reason is that this direct intervention at human level is more qualitative than quantitative, more cumulative than strictly chronological, and that it can be somewhat arbitrarily subdivided if need be, rather as the sky can be divided into a greater or lesser number of cantons.

Tradition even insists that certain avatars are incomplete or multiple. So, according to various authors, Rama-chandra is only $\frac{8}{16}$ of an avatar, whereas his brother Lakshmana possesses $\frac{4}{16}$ of the complete state, and his two other brothers $\frac{2}{16}$ each, making $\frac{16}{16}$ in all. Similarly, many Hindus consider that it is one and the same avatar who appeared half as Chaitanya in the sixteenth century and half as Ramakrishna in the nineteenth century. Krishna is said to be the only complete avatar (*purna-avatara*).

There is something fairly subjective about all this. To any Hindu seeker of spirituality his master (*guru*) is not only an avatar, but the greatest who has ever been. This is psychologically correct, since his divine inspiration comes to him through this *guru*. A great sage of our times, Swami Ramdas, explains this by saying that the divine in us is unable to make itself understood until we have reached a certain stage of development, and that until then, if it is to exercise its influence, it must take the external form of a person other than ourselves: this is our *guru*, who represents for us the totality of the divine.

The list most often found contains ten avatars, the first three of which take the form of animals; the fourth and tenth are half animal, half human in shape, and the five others appear in human guise.

The avatar of the fish (*matsya-avatara*)

One day when the sage Manu was performing his ablutions, he found in the hollow of his hand a tiny fish which begged him to spare its life. He put it in a jar, but in one day the fish grew so big that he had to put it in a tank; the next day, it needed a lake. Soon the lake was too small: 'Throw me into the sea,' said the fish, 'I shall be better there.' Then he warned Manu of an approaching flood. He sent him a large craft, and ordered him to take on board with him a pair of each living species and the seeds of all plants.

Almost before Manu could obey, the world was flooded; only Vishnu remained visible in the shape of a great sea-unicorn with scales of gold. Manu anchored his vessel to the fish's horn, with the great serpent Vasuki serving as a rope. And thus humanity, animals and plants were saved from destruction.

The tortoise avatar (*kurma-avatara*)

This avatar is connected with the incident of the churning of the sea. So great was the power of Vishnu, so many the forms that he was capable of adopting that, even while he was holding the mountain on his back, he was also present, though invisible, among the gods and demons pulling the rope. His energy was also flowing into Vasuki, the king of the serpents, while everyone could still see him seated in his glory on the top of Mount Mandara.

The boar avatar (*varaha-avatara*)

In this legend the earth under flood has been captured by demons. In the form of a boar Vishnu darts across the sky, plunges deep into the waters and manages to trace the earth by its smell. He kills the demon Hiranyaksha, who holds earth prisoner, raises her from the abyss with his powerful tusks and brings her back to the surface with him. As Varaha, Vishnu is depicted in statues as a giant with a boar's head, carrying in his arms the goddess of the earth.

The man-lion avatar (nrisimha-avatara)

Hiranyakasipu is a very powerful demon-king. As a result of his austerities, he has induced Brahma (or Siva) to confer upon him such power as has enabled him to dethrone Indra (god of storms) and send the gods from the sky into exile. He has proclaimed himself king of the universe, and allows no-one to worship any god other than himself.

His son Prahlada is devoted to Vishnu, for he has been initiated by the latter himself into the secret of his heart. Hiranyakasipu is angered by the sight of his son dedicated to the cult of his mortal enemy, and subjects the young man to a series of tortures to deter him from his vocation. But with redoubled fervour Prahlada begins to preach the religion of Vishnu to men and demons. Hiranyakasipu orders him to be put to death. But, the sword, poison, fire, furious elephants and magic spells all prove powerless, for Prahlada is protected by his god.

Once more Hiranyakasipu calls his son to him; and, while Prahlada with infinite gentleness tries once more to convince his father of the grandeur of Vishnu and his omnipresence, the wrathful demon cries out: 'If Vishnu is everywhere, how is it that I do not see him with my own eyes?' And striking one of the pillars in the audience chamber, 'Is he here for example?' 'He is present in everything, even when invisible,' Prahlada gently replies. Then Hiranyakasipu swears and strikes the foot of the pillar, which falls to the ground. Immediately Vishnu in the form of a man with a lion's head emerges from the column, seizes the demon and tears him apart.

Prahlada then succeeds his father and reigns justly and wisely. His grandson is the demon Bali, who makes another incarnation necessary.

The dwarf avatar (vamana-avatara)

Bali, a demon or *asura* who reigns over the three worlds, withstands all Vishnu's attempts to win him over. So the other gods beg Vishnu to resort to reincarnation in order to reconquer the realm that is theirs by right. Vishnu agrees to be reborn in the form of a Brahman dwarf.

While Bali is engaged in offering a sacrifice on the banks of the sacred river Narmada, the dwarf comes to him. Bali knows his duty: having touched his forehead with the sacred water, which the Brahman had used to cool his feet, he bids him welcome and offers to carry out his wishes. The dwarf modestly replies: 'I ask you only for a little plot of earth, a mere three feet, and I shall measure it exactly pace by pace. I desire nothing more. A wise man should be content to ask for no more than he needs.' Bali knows perfectly well what is happening; Narada, messenger of the gods, has told him. But Bali cannot disregard the

Vishnu as Matsya-avatara, the avatar of the fish, in which he saved the world during the flood. Kalighat painting. *c.* 1860 *Secretary of State, Commonwealth Relations*

Prahlada, attacked by an elephant sent by his father, prays to Vishnu and is saved. Kalighat painting. *c.* 1890 *Victoria and Albert Museum*

Vishnu, in the avatar of the lion, tearing to death the demon Hiranyakasipu for his persecution of Prahlada. *A.S.I.*

Vishnu, in the avatar of the dwarf, covers the world in two strides to establish his authority over the demon Bali. Relief from Mavalipuram. Seventh century A.D. *Goloubew*

laws of hospitality; so he grants the Brahman his gift.

Then Vishnu, suddenly assuming divine stature, crosses the entire universe in two strides. He has still a third step to take. Turning towards Bali he says: '*Asura,* you promised me three feet of land. In two strides I covered the world; where shall I take the third stride? Anyone who does not give a Brahman what he has promised him is destined to fall from his estate. You deceived me, you deserve to go down to the regions of hell.' 'I fear hell less than the loss of renown,' Bali answers, and offers the god his head that he might place his foot upon it.

Then Vishnu gives him the underworld as his kingdom, and he returns the other worlds to the gods. But he has such admiration for Bali's frankness that he becomes the guardian of his gate, and promises him that he will be Indra when he is reincarnated.

Another myth makes Indra responsible for the death of Bali, which is said to take place during the battle between Indra and the demons under the leadership of Jalamdhara. In this myth Bali falls, and a stream of precious stones flows from his mouth. At this Indra approaches in astonishment and severs the body with his thunderbolt. Bali was so pure in his conduct that the different parts of his body then give birth to the seeds of precious stones. From his bones come diamonds, from his eyes sapphires, from his blood rubies, from his marrow emeralds, crystal from his flesh, coral from his tongue and pearls from his teeth.

Rama with the axe (*Parashu-Rama*)

Unlike all those who precede and succeed him, this avatar does not come to fight an individual demon. His aim seems to be to defend and avenge his father, Jamad-Agni, 'he who knows the identity of god and fire'.

For instance, when his mother has impure thoughts, he executes his father's command and decapitates her. Then, when King Kartavirya with the thousand arms has insulted his father, he massacres the caste of the Kshatriya (warrior caste), to which the offender belongs, twenty-one times.

But his activity is not only destructive. When, by way of thanks for his obedience, his father offers to grant him a wish, he asks that his mother should come back to life, this time in all purity, and this request is fulfilled. Each time he destroys the Kshatriya caste, he agrees that the Brahmans, the purest caste, shall lie with the Kshatriya women to produce another warrior caste. This, however, does not prevent him from finally leaving the earth in shame, and taking refuge in austerities. Tradition states that Malabar emerged from the sea so that Varuna might make him a present of it.

Rama-chandra

Rama, the elder son of King Dasaratha of Ayodhya, has to renounce the throne, so the story goes, and go

Rama-chandra, one of the most popular Hindu gods, with his bow in his left hand. Copper. South India. Twelfth century. *Victoria and Albert Museum*

into exile in the forest because of a stepmother's intrigues. As he is about to leave, he advises his wife, the beautiful Sita, to remain in the palace, for forest life would be too harsh and dangerous for her.

But Sita insists; she knows that she has the right to do so, for a wife's first duty is to share the fate of her husband: 'Whatever calls you away, whether it is asceticism, a hermitage or heaven, I want to be with you. I shall never weary of following you. Reeds, grasses and thorn-bushes in my path will seem as soft as lawns and antelope skins when I am with you. The dust blown upon me by the gale, O my dear husband, will seem like precious sandalwood powder. With you, it is heaven; and without you it would be hell. Know this, O Rama, and be perfectly happy with me.'

Rama allows himself to be persuaded and Sita follows him into exile, as does his brother Lakshmana.

But Ravana, king of the Rakshasas, desires Sita; he succeeds in drawing Rama away in pursuit of a magic gazelle, and then forcibly abducts Sita in his aerial chariot. In his kingdom of Lanka (Ceylon) he holds her captive.

Wild with despair, Rama blindly seeks his wife, and swears to slay her abductor. A vulture, Jatayu, shows him the way, and a whole race of monkeys and bears put themselves at his disposal. Hanuman, one of the animals, is clever enough to cross the sea and bring the hero news of Sita, whom he has comforted. Rama is sure of victory, but he has to solve the problem of getting to Lanka with his army. He decides to beg the help of the ocean, and is allowed to build a pier. So all the monkeys and bears, at the command of Nala, a smith, take trees and carry them to the shore, then place them on the sea; others roll enormous boulders. These rocks drop into the sea with a noise of thunder and float on the surface.

There is also a squirrel who wants to help. He rolls over in the dust on the dry land, then runs to the end of the pier and shakes off all that has clung to his fur. The bigger animals laugh at him. But when Rama sees him he comes to stroke him and show his gratitude. And that is why, from that time onwards, Indian squirrels have three long yellow bands on their back, the trace of Rama's fingers.

After five days the bridge is complete, and is wide and firm. Rama and Lakshmana begin to cross with their army. Some monkeys swim across after them; others fling themselves into the air. The noise of this army drowns the roar of the ocean.

Soon Rama arrives beneath the walls of Lanka. A terrible battle begins; by dint of sheer miracles of valour the hero's troops gradually prevail over those of Ravana. Rama himself, once he is purified and has sung the hymn to the sun, has to take up arms, for Ravana advances towards him. They are like two blazing lions. With his murderous arrows, Rama cuts off the ten heads of the monster one after the other, but they grow again. Then he takes an arrow (*astra*), which has been given him by the sage Agastya: the

Hanuman and his army crossing to Lanka on the bridge of rocks thrown across the ocean. Pen and ink drawing. Nineteenth century. *Secretary of State, Commonwealth Relations*

The abduction of Sita by Ravana while her husband and his brother are decoyed away by a magic gazelle. Gold and tempera. Jaipur. Nineteenth century A.D. *Victoria and Albert Museum*

Rama riding to the rescue of Sita, preceded by Hanuman, who carries a mace. Gouache, Kangra. Late eighteenth century A.D. *Secretary of State, Commonwealth Relations*

The battle beneath the walls of Lanka. Moghul school. c. A.D. 1600 New Delhi. *Bulloz*

Krishna, the best-loved of Vishnu's avatars, with his fair-skinned brother Bala-Rama. Kalighat painting. c. 1860. *Victoria and Albert Museum*

god Vayu has endowed its feathers with life, its tip is made of sunlight and fire, and its weight is equivalent to that of Mount Meru and Mount Mandara. Adding *matras* (a secret Vedic formula) to this arrow, Rama puts it in his bow and shoots it; it goes straight home, cleaves Ravana's chest, and, still covered with blood, returns to the hero's quiver. This is how the king of the Rakshasas dies.

The gods then rain down flowers on Rama's chariot, and sing hymns of praise, for the purpose for which Vishnu has taken human form has been fulfilled.

At first Rama refuses to accept Sita as a wife, for he wishes to prove to everyone that she has remained true to him in spite of the time spent with Ravana. So Sita longs only for death, and has a funeral pyre built. Approaching the flames with joined hands, she cries: 'Just as my heart never leaves Rama, O so may thou, Agni, never deprive me of thy protection!' Then she steps into the flames. While all those present are lost in lamentation, Agni is seen to rise with Sita in his lap, as radiant as the morning sun. The judgment of Agni has been given. Rama opens his arms wide to the irreproachable, saying: 'I knew of Sita's virtue, but I wanted her to justify herself in the eyes of the people. Without this trial, some would have said: "The son of Dasharatha yields to desire and scorns traditional laws." Now, everyone will know that she is really mine, like the sunbeams, which belong to the sun, their source.'

Then Rama returns to Ayodhya, where he takes in hand the government of the realm.

Rama-chandra is perhaps the most popular Hindu deity. In almost every Indian tongue there is a vast epic, the *Ramayana*, which recounts his exploits, and any storyteller can make a crowd sob by saying or chanting his name. There is a wealth of popular images of him, and there are innumerable Hindu names of which the word Rama forms part. Gandhi himself devoted at least an hour each day to listening to passages from the *Ramayana*. For the Hindus, who are so enamoured of morals, Rama is the completely moral man, whose virtue cannot be impaired whatever trial is imposed on him. His glory is shared by his wife, Sita, who is to all India the purest feminine ideal. Ramakrishna counted among his most precious spiritual experiences a vision in the course of which Sita entered into him.

This halo also surrounds Bharata, Rama's half-brother, who had to supplant him much against his will and so decided to rule only in his name, and even installed Rama's sandals on the throne. His unimpeachable loyalty is so highly prized that India is still called Bharata-varsha (country of Bharata).

Bala-Rama and Krishna

Krishna is quite different; for him human morality is of somewhat subordinate importance, for he takes a loftier view of things. Whereas, in the eyes of Swami Randas, Jesus represents the perfection of love

Basudev carrying the baby Krishna to the house of Nanda the herdsman for safety. Kalighat painting. c. 1900, *Victoria and Albert Museum*

Krishna as a child with his adopted mother Yasoda. Kalighat painting. c. 1875. *Victoria and Albert Museum*

and Buddha the perfection of renunciation, Krishna corresponds to the perfect deification of life.

Coming a little before him is his brother Bala-Rama, but although he is almost always included in the list of ten avatars, he plays only the part of supernumerary to Krishna, who is by far the most charming and human of Vishnu's incarnations.

He was born at Mathura between Delhi and Agra. His mother Devaki was the sister of King Kamsa, and he destroyed her children as soon as they came into the world because a celestial voice had predicted that he would be assassinated by one of them. Krishna owed his life entirely to a trick, whereby his parents exchanged him for the daughter of a modest herdsman, Nanda. Krishna spent his youth with the shepherds, and in the company of Bala-Rama.

Shortly after his birth, Krishna, who was already energetic and resourceful, began to show his prowess. He could uproot two trees at once, mock and triumph over fearful demons, and at the same time steal butter, play with monkeys, eat soil and so on. One day his mother by adoption, Yasoda, was stupefied to see the whole of the universe when she looked down his throat. (A similar adventure had befallen the crow Bhusandi when it flew into Rama-chandra's mouth.) Krishna on one occasion braved Indra in person. When some shepherds were preparing to give homage to the god, he advised them to worship Mount Go-vardhana instead, for it provided nourishment for their herds, and also to worship the herds themselves, which gave them milk. Then, appearing on top of the mountain, he declared: 'I am the mountain.' And he took for himself the first fruits that were offered. In fury Indra sent cataracts to drown the shepherds and their cattle, but Krishna lifted the mountain and, holding it on one finger, he protected his friends from the storm for seven days and seven nights. Indra was stupefied at this, and went so far as to come down from the sky with his wife, Indrani; and both asked him to befriend their son Arjuna.

One day when the shepherdesses had gone bathing in the Jumna, he stole their clothes and climbed up a nearby tree. When they emerged from the water and could not find their saris the shepherdesses were at a loss what to do; their distress increased when they caught sight of Krishna laughing from the tree. Hiding themselves in the river, they begged him to have pity on them, but he would not agree to give them back their clothing until they came to get it one after the other, with their hands joined above their heads in the attitude of supplication.

The shepherds' daughters and wives, forgetting their usual modesty and reserve, abandoned their work and their homes to follow Krishna into the forest as soon as they heard the sound of his flute. The sage, Bhagavan, sometimes reproached them, but he also told them that Krishna would be the means of their salvation. For whatever manner of approach one makes to him, he offers liberation. Some knew

and sought him as a son or friend, others as a lover, some even as an enemy, but everyone received his blessing and deliverance.

All the shepherdesses in love with Krishna wanted to give him their hand, when he danced with them in the *rasalila*; so he multiplied his hands as many times as was necessary and then each could hold his hand in her own.

The erotic mysticism of the *Gita-govinda*, the Hindu *Song of Songs,* still delights countless people: 'By the sensual pleasures he gives them, Krishna delights all women; at the touch of his limbs, as dark and gentle as a string of lotus-flowers, they know the delights of love, while the beauties in the heifer park kiss him to their hearts' content . . . . May the learned souls, who seek ecstasy in Vishnu, learn from the song of Govinda awareness of what makes the essence of love!'

Once he is adult, Krishna leaves the shepherds, and returns to Mathura, where he kills Kamsa and some other wrongdoers.

Then he plays a decisive part in the war of Mahabharata between the five sons of Pandu and their hundred cousins, the Kurus. Krishna is the friend and counsellor of the Pandavas, and even becomes Arjuna's divine charioteer.

Now Arjuna hesitates to take part in this useless massacre. He can see no reason for killing his friends and relatives. Krishna reminds him that he belongs to the warrior caste and that his *sva-dharma,* his personal moral law, forbids him such cowardice. Besides, it is only in appearance that some kill and others are killed. The soul is eternal. And all those who are on this battlefield have, in fact, always existed and will never cease to be. These observations lead Arjuna to ask Krishna many questions, and their dialogue forms the splendid philosophic poem of the *Bhagavad-gita.*

After numerous harsh fights, the war ends in the total destruction of the two armies. The Kurus have four survivors and the Pandavas seven, counting Krishna, who dies shortly afterwards as he has foretold. As he sits meditating in the forest, with his legs crossed, the balls of his feet are uncovered. A huntsman from afar, taking Krishna for a deer he is pursuing, shoots an arrow, which strikes him in his only vulnerable spot, his left heel. The huntsman approaches and despairs of his mistake, but Krishna tells him neither to be afraid nor to grieve. These words of consolation are the last that he pronounces on earth. In complete radiance he then ascends to the sky, where the gods welcome him. Then darkness invades the earth.

Kalki

To close the series of ten avatars we should mention Kalki, who is yet to come. In the shape of a giant with a horse's head he will close the age of iron and will put an end to the wicked. When his work is done, everything will be reabsorbed into the Absolute, until such time as creation begins again.

When dancing with the shepherdesses Krishna multiplies himself to give a hand to every girl. Painted cotton. *Bildarchiv Foto Marburg*

An incident from the long and very complicated war of Maha-bharata, showing Bhima, on foot, attacking Aswathana. Moghul. 1598. *Victoria and Albert Museum*

The destructive face of the Divine

If the Divine, after creating the world, were content merely to protect it, man would be left in a blind alley. That which had a beginning would then have no end — and that is unacceptable to Hindu logic. The soul would not emerge from its consciousness of multiplicity, it would not return again to the infinite — and that is unacceptable to Hindu spiritual aspiration.

And so, to the countenances of creator and protector, which the Divine already possesses, is added that of destroyer of the multiplicity created by Brahma and protected by Vishnu. This is the role of Siva. Hindu art portrays him in numerous, very different, ways. In his anthropomorphic aspect he usually has four arms; the two upper hands hold a tambourine and a trident, the two others make gestures of giving and reassuring respectively. In the centre of his forehead is a third eye; it is sometimes also scored with three horizontal bands. The god is wrapped in a tiger skin, he wears a serpent as a necklace, another as a sacred cord, and others are wound round his arms. His hair is twisted and often dressed in the high chignon (*jata*) associated with the ascetic and ornamented with a crescent moon. Sometimes the fifth head of Brahma can be seen in the hair, or the goddess Ganga (the Ganges). He is mounted on Nandi, the bull.

The Terrible (Rudra)

In his terrifying aspect Siva is Rudra, the powerful in the sky, whose work begins on earth, the violent, who directs the ascent of the conscious being; his strength is pitted against all evil, striking the sinner and the enemy. Tolerating neither imperfection nor hesitation, he is the most terrible of the gods, the only one of whom the Vedic *rishis* (a group of sages) are really afraid. He is the divine by virtue of being master of our evolution through violence and battle. But he is also the supreme healer. If he is opposed he destroys; if his aid is invoked he heals all wounds and cares for the sick and the suffering. The strength to struggle is his gift, as are also peace and final joy.

The gods fear him almost as much as mortals do. One day, when Prajapati (Brahma) committed incest with his daughter Ushas (dawn) who turned into a gazelle to escape from him, Rudra looked on it as a grave sin. Fear-stricken, Prajapati called out: 'I shall make thee lord of the animals, do not kill me!' From that day on Rudra was called Pashupati, lord of the animals, he who masters the animal nature in human beings. But he shot none the less, prepared later to regret having to shoot at the demiurge himself.

As a destroyer, Siva lives where bodies are burned, in a place haunted by frightening monsters; sometimes a string of skulls bedecks his chest; he is the chief of the *bhutas* and *pisachas*, phantoms and vampires. But the real place of cremation for the Hindu is the heart of the disciple, where the ego and the

Nandi, the bull-mount of Siva. Copper. South India. Eighteenth century. *Victoria and Albert Museum*

fruits of action are consumed, and all that is left is the divine spark in man, the *atma*.

Kama's attempt

Siva is the prince of ascetics, and his worshippers follow an essentially ascetic discipline. As he remains in eternal meditation – the motionless centre of movement, says Tagore – on the no less eternal snows of Mount Kailasa, his wife Parvati often finds time hangs heavy. One day, weary of waiting in vain for her husband to come to her – although she had subjected herself to unbelievable austerities to win his divine favours – in despair she solicited the intervention of Kama, god of desire in general, and sexual desire in particular.

Well aware of the risk involved in such intervention, Kama did his best to escape, but the goddess insisted and he had to obey. He bent his bow with its string made of a chain of humming bees and prepared to shoot his arrow at Siva's heart to remind him of his conjugal duties. The 'great god', Mahesvara, knew of the attack intended upon Siva. As his meditation was not yet complete and had not yet terminated in the total dissolution that is the preliminary condition of all creation, he could not permit such intervention. With his third eye, that of inward vision, he struck the imprudent attacker with his thunderbolt. It should be said in his defence that he later yielded to the supplications of the widow, and brought Kama back to life; and that is why desire continues to play here below the indispensable part incumbent upon it. But Parvati's wish was not granted.

This myth shows that Siva's role of saviour, intended to make man rise above the plane on which he is conscious only of multiplicity, can have no effect on desire once it has taken hold, no matter how divine the object of this desire, nor how pure its influence. Man must first rise to the plane of unity by

pure, untroubled meditation. It is only after this experience has been taken as far as possible that one can return without danger to the plane of multiplicity, for then in everything that comes into view one can see the divine scheme of things in its perfect and total harmony, the great rhythmic dance of the god Siva.

The planner god

Siva plots calamities which threaten the end of the world before it has played out its part. When the ocean was being churned and the gods were first pulling the head, and then the demons the tail of the serpent Vasuki, it spat out such potent poison that the world was about to be destroyed by it. Multiplicity thus revealed the frightful perils that come in its wake. Only one being could conjure up these perils, a being who had made man not the slave, but the master of the universe: none other than Siva. But in fact, Siva receives the poison in his hand and drinks it – this is why in art he is shown as Nilakantha with a throat made blue by this terrible liquid.

The descent of the Ganges

Another myth in which the destroyer shows his supreme powers of protection is that of the descent of the Ganges. In former times the Ganges, which now waters the three worlds, washed the sky only. One day the earth had become so cluttered with the ashes of the dead that there seemed no possible way of cleaning it. A sage, Bhagiratha, whose asceticism had won him wondrous powers, thought of bringing the purifying Ganges down to earth, for its mere proximity was enough to wash away all uncleanliness. But the sacred river was such a size that its descent entailed the risk of shaking and destroying the earth, just as the sudden descent of a dazzling divine light on a man insufficiently prepared can destroy his

physical body. Here again Siva intervened. He invited the Ganges to fall upon his head, and from there the river, after it had meandered for a long time amid the god's hair, divided into seven torrents, then flowed slowly and smoothly over the surface of the terrestrial world.

Moreover, there is an esoteric and close correspondence between the purifying Ganges, which circulates in the universe like the blood in our bodies, and Siva who, like the heart, motionless in its rhythm, provokes and directs this life-giving and purifying circulation in the universe and in the human being.

The god who renews

Precisely because he constantly ensures the destruction of worlds where multiplicity reigns, Siva allows it to be constantly created and recreated. And so he is worshipped everywhere as a principle of continuity and generation in the form of the *linga* (phallus).

Whereas Brahma simply set the universe in motion, Siva enables the indispensable work of continual renewal to take place. And the other gods recognise the capital importance of this, as the following story

in silent immobility, I noticed great Narayana, the soul of the universe, with his thousand omniscient eyes, both being and non-being, lying on the formless waters, supported by the thousand-headed serpent of the infinite. Dazzled by his radiance, I touched the eternal being and asked him: "Who art thou? Speak!" Then, raising his still sleepy lotus-eyes to look at me, he smiled and said: "Thou art welcome, my child, resplendent lord!" Offended, I replied: "How canst thou, god free from sin, treat me as a master would his pupil and call me 'child', I who am the cause of creation and destruction, the creator of a thousand universes, the source of all that exists? Why dost thou

pronounce such foolish words?" Vishnu replied: "Dost thou not know that I am Narayana, creator, preserver and destroyer of worlds, eternal male, immortal source of the universe and its centre also. Even thou wast born of my indestructible body."

'We were both arguing bitterly above the formless sea, when a glorious shimmering *linga* appeared before our eyes, a flamboyant pillar with the brilliance of a hundred fires, capable of consuming the universe, without beginning, without middle, without end, incomparable, indescribable. Then the divine Vishnu, as troubled as I was by these thousands of flames, said to me: "We must look for the source of this fire. I shall go down; thou shalt rise with all thy might." Taking the shape of a mountainous blue boar with sharp tusks, a long snout, sonorous snort, and short feet that were firm, vigorous and irresistible, he plunged into the depths. For a thousand years he kept going down, but he did not touch the base of the *linga*. I, meanwhile, had turned into a swan, white all over, with burning eyes and great wings and my flight was as swift as the wind and as thought. I soared for a thousand years to find the top of the pillar, but was unable to reach it. As I was returning I met the great Vishnu likewise returning weary and disconcerted.

'Then Siva stood before us, and mastered by his *maya*, we bowed before him. On all sides arose the '*Om*', eternal and clear. Vishnu told him: "Our dispute has been blessed, O god of gods, since thou dost appear unto us to put an end to it." Siva replied: "Thou art in truth the creator, preserver and destroyer of worlds; maintain in this world, my child, both inertia and motion. For I, supreme lord, undivided, I am three: Brahma, Vishnu and Siva; I create, I maintain, I destroy." '

The inseparable nature of these different aspects is also emphasised in iconography, not only by the Trimurti, but also by other composite images. Thus

Hari-Hara, who in our day has countless admirers, is a combination of Vishnu and Siva. He is shown to be divided in two by a vertical: the right side bears the attributes of Siva (ascetic's chignon, trident, tiger-skin), the left side those of Vishnu (tiara, discus, garland of flowers, draped garb).

The Master of the Dance (Nataraja)

As destroyer and renewer, Siva determines the rhythm of the worlds. Thousands of years before scientists discovered the similarity of structure between the atomic nucleus and the solar systems, the Hindus asserted that the same rhythm must of necessity be found at all stages of creation and in all domains. That is why ideas about rhythm and density —for rhythm acts first and foremost on density— play a role in Hindu thought comparable to that which we associate with weight and shape, which are merely derived manifestations of them.

Now what in the eyes of man is the purest manifestation of rhythm, if not dancing? So Siva is the supreme dancer, the king of dancing, Nataraja. And he is frequently depicted as such, in a pose of perfect harmony, in the midst of a vast crown on which myriad sparks alternately flare and die again. Even so worlds appear and disappear. Prostrate beneath his feet, Tripurasura, the demon of the three towns, of the three worlds, obligingly offers to act as his stool. And Siva makes use of him, for this triple universe is the entire reason for his dance.

One of the myths leading up to this dance is that of the ten thousand *rishis* whom the god visited in order to make them see the truth. But the *rishis* received him with curses. When these had no effect, they called upon a terrible tiger, which leaped upon Siva to devour him. Smiling, the god removed the monster's pelt with the nail of his little finger and draped it round him like a silken shawl, Then the *rishis* summoned a vicious serpent: Siva hung it round his neck like a garland. Then a devilish dwarf appeared, black all over and armed with a club. But Siva placed his foot on its back and began to dance. The weary hermits watched him in silence, captivated by the splendour and astounding rapidity of the wondrous rhythm. Suddenly, seeing the heavens open and the gods assemble to contemplate Siva, the sages who had resisted his teaching threw themselves at the dancer's feet and adored him.

Better than any words, the dance could in fact evoke the supreme and perfect rhythm of this dynamic and triumphant joy in which the individual is at one with the great 'interplay' of the world (*lila*). 'He whom no sign could describe is made known to us by his mystic dancing,' says a Sivaist poet from Southern India.

The fact that he plays more than one role explains why the same god is sometimes called Rudra 'the terrible', and sometimes Siva 'the benevolent', 'he who is of good augury'. There is no need to argue, as so many experts on India have done, either that there was a historical evolution, which all Hindus energetically deny and which has no foundation in the scriptures, or that it was a naïve ruse on the part of the worshippers who flattered 'the terrible' with euphemisms to win his favour, although they did not believe in them any more than he did.

The Divine Mother

The particular aspect of the Divine, as envisaged by Hindus, which we find most difficult to grasp is that of the divine mother. Both supreme and subordinate, supra-divine and yet possessing material humanity, terrible and more adorable than any other, she is strictly 'one' and of unbounded multiplicity.

The greatest gods, and this remains partly true of many others, can have no direct contact with the tangible elements in the universe. They must first, and this has already been seen in the case of Vishnu and of Siva, emanate of their own accord a power of manifestation, which is their *sakti*, and which myth and iconography depict as their wife or daughter; worshippers call her the divine mother.

As the action of most gods is multiple or in any case complex, the *sakti* of each has several names and as many different appearances. Each of these 'goddesses' is, at the same time, the whole of divine power, yet this does not prevent her being entirely incarnate in the mother of the family of each human household, and in the *kundalini* at the base of the vertebral column in the case of each human being.

Mahasakti is most often mentioned, and she corresponds to the absolute Brahman, and constitutes his power of self-manifestation; then there is also Mahesvari, corresponding to the total personal god Isvara, then Mahasarasvati, Mahalakshmi and Mahakali, who correspond respectively to Brahma, Vishnu and Siva. This is how the writer Aurobindo describes them: 'The Mother (Mahasakti) has three modes of being: the transcendent, supreme, original *sakti*, who is above the worlds and serves as a link between creation and the still unmanifested mystery of the supreme; the universal, cosmic Mahasakti, who creates all beings and contains, penetrates, supports and directs the millions of processes and forces; and, lastly, the individual, who personifies the power of the two most vast aspects of her existence, makes them alive and close to us and interposes herself between human personality and divine nature.

'Four great aspects of the Mother, four of her chief powers and personalities, have been demonstrated in her conduct of the universe and in her relations with terrestrial affairs. One is her personality of calm plenitude, comprehensive wisdom, tranquil kindliness, inexhaustible compassion, sovereign and superior majesty and overmastering grandeur. The second aspect personifies her power of splendid

energy and irresistible passion, her warlike disposition, crushing will, impetuous promptness and her world-shaking force. The third aspect is ardent, gentle and marvellous in the profound secret of her beauty, harmony and delicate rhythm, in her complex and subtle opulence, her irresistible charm and captivating grace. The fourth is provided with a secret and penetrating capacity for intimate knowledge, careful and faultless work and calm precise perfection in all things. Wisdom, energy, harmony and perfection are the attributes which these four aspects or powers bring with them into the world, which they manifest in human disguise and in their *vibhutis* (types of superhuman power attainable by humans), and which they will establish according to the divine measure of their ascension in those who can open their terrestrial nature to the direct and living influence of the Mother. To these four we give the four great names of Mahesvari, Mahakali, Mahalakshmi and Mahasarasvati.'

The wife of Siva

As Uma, the gracious, the Mother practises the most rigorous asceticism on the summits of the Himalayas, to draw Siva's attention and win his good graces.

According to legend, the sudden appearance of Siva's third eye would appear to have been due to a piece of cunning on the part of his wife. While he was meditating in the mountain, Uma, who was observing the same vows in imitation of her lord, one day slipped mischievously behind him and with her gracious hands hid his eyes. At once the life of the universe went out; the sun paled and all creatures trembled in fear. But suddenly the darkness disappeared, for a flaming eye had just opened in Siva's forehead, a third eye like the sun, from which spurted flames which set light to the whole of the Himalayas. Then the daughter of the mountain, with tears and supplication, showed such grief that the god had a kind thought and restored the mountains to their former splendour with their rich vegetation and wild creatures.

As Parvati, daughter of the Himalayas, Siva's wife is depicted as a very beautiful young woman, sitting close by her divine husband, with whom she chats about love and higher metaphysics in turn. Many sacred texts, particularly in the *Tantras*, take the form of dialogues in which Siva instructs Parvati. The story is told, however, that one day the goddess claimed she could dance as well as her master. The assembly of the gods was made the judge of this, and Siva danced for them with Parvati copying each of his steps faithfully and perfectly, until a moment came when Siva raised his leg so high that feminine modesty prevented the goddess from imitating him. She had to admit herself defeated.

When Siva delegates to his wife the task of dancing the cosmic dance (and at this point she takes the name of Ma Kali or black mother), this dance then unfolds on the plane of the human soul (i.e., of the microcosm),

ذکر کیومرث

زشاهان باز و فرهنگ روی	زگفتار دهقان چنین کرد یاد	که تاکرد بنیاد کیتی خدای	سوی که تاریخ دهقان عالم نهاد
بینداخت بر مرد دهقان خراج	جو نشست بر تخت و بنهاد تاج	سرنامداران کیومرث بود	نخستین خدیوی که کشور گشود

جهان را بنام نکو عهد کرد | راویان آثار از آن باد شاه اخبار چنین کرده اند | بداد و دهش خلق را وعده کرد

کیومرث از اسباط مهلائیل بود و زجمله الاسباب فرزند صلبی آدم بوده است و امام محجة الاسلام محمد بن العراقی در کتاب نصیحة الملوک آورده است که کیومرث برادر شیث بود و بعضی کویند بنیاد اولاد نوح است و در رغم طایفه از معنی کیومرث خود مراست علی الجملة تا اختلاف اسباب اتفاق ارند که نخستین باد شاهی است از باد شاهان جهان و معنی کیومرث بلغت سریانی حی ناطق اوست یعنی زنده کویا و بحقیقت اسم او با مسمی مطابقتی دارد باوجود بسط ملک و کثرت سپاه و نفاد امر مشغوف بود بسیاحت و منازل و مراحل درجا قدم اورد و شهادکرد و شکستن و بحر او سواحل کردشتن و جولان تدبیر ملک و مصالح رغبت بیرداختی در رغشان مهاوی مهیب و شعاب شوامخ عظیم ما او ساختی و شبها و روزها بنوحه و عبادت کند اندیشی جز نکرد بکردانی دنکشانش رربقه عهد و پیمان و طوق عبودیت اورد باد و ورد و مرد و و معفارت شیاطین محاربان سلاح او جوب و فلاختی بود و لباس او از بوست بودکه اکثری چنین کویند و بنیدکه دیو وری را در اوبا لبنی آمد مراسکا را اورده و نکدبند کردیادند

دوستی و دشمنی و حرب باد دیوان ظاهر بودی تا وقت نوح بعد از طوفان برخلق نایدید شدند و باد بارکیومرث را لباس آدمیان زجلبود ربوبانات بود و مردمان از دیوان در زحمت بودند و خلایق بور را از ظلم ایشان خلاص داد و دیوان را از آباد انها براند و جناح عدل و احسان بر سرزنی آدم بکشتند و درکشف ظلام متظلمان و قضا حوایج ملهوفان زبا لعنبا نمود و کفت ان ملک الارض رضی الله باد شاه زمین و نکاه دار انج خلقم نفرمان خدای تعالی واقف اوکلشاه نشستنکاه خود نزند بیک دماوندساخت بغایت خوب صورت بود و بافر اورد و فرزند آمد و مشی و مشانه نام نهاد مشی منکر و مشانه مونث و بعضی کویند هیشنک فرزند اوست و مشی بغایت زاهد و متعبد بود و روزی از زبده برسید که از کارها بهتر بنزد بشرکت کم آزاری و برستش خدای عز و جل هیشنک کفت جه ازی شوان بود مکر حب بود از ایشان وطاعت نتوان کرد مکرشها و دین ازخلایق بکراه کرفت و درکه مشتری بودکه در بدر بدبین اورد وقتی و کامی و میساختی و دین بدبین بدآمدی پس آمدی بس کرو می زادن

rather than on that of the universe, the macrocosm. And that is why Kali, while being identical with Siva, remains subordinate to him. In these functions the goddess is depicted looking terrifying; she is naked, dishevelled, wild-eyed, with lolling tongue and she brandishes in her hands a blood-stained knife and a dripping human head. A necklet of human heads lies on her breast. But in this role she has always one foot on Siva, who is lying on the ground like a corpse, although certain anatomical details sometimes emphasise his role as a fertility god.

Without the unbounded strength that the god gives her in her static aspect, Kali's dynamic energy would not exist. But, if one looks more closely at the goddess one sees that she also has a hand that blesses and protects. And initiates know that all the heads are the false personalities which we human beings assume, of sin, weakness and attachment, which she must brutally remove, one after the other, so that we may find our true identity again, divine and perfect. That is why Vivekananda said to his disciples: 'Adore the terrible one!' And even the gentle wife of Ramakrishna had one of the names of Kali, Sarada, and as Sarada she was portrayed as a warrior mounted on a lion.

Going by the name Durga (the inaccessible) Siva's wife answers an appeal made by the gods, and takes it upon herself to destroy a demon, Mahesa, who had dethroned them all. There is a dreadful battle, and the demon changes first into a buffalo, then an elephant and finally a giant with a thousand arms. Durga, however, remains invincible; mounted on a lion, she crushes the monster and kills it by piercing it to the heart with her lance. Durga is portrayed with a beautiful, serene face, but she has ten arms, all carrying weapons; one hand is holding the lance that penetrates to the heart of the crushed monster. Her right foot is on her lion, and the left on the nape of the demon's neck.

She is also Bhairavi, the redoubtable; Ambika, the progenitor; Sati, the perfect wife; Gauri, the brilliant. Her complete identification with Siva is emphasised in iconography by an image of Ardhanarisvara ('the god who is half woman'); the right half of the figure is a man's body and the left half that of a woman.

The wife of Vishnu

Lakshmi, who is usually called Sri, appears as herself in relatively few myths. But she accompanies Vishnu in most of his incarnations.

When the ocean is churned and he is a tortoise, she appears looking radiant seated on the full-blown flower of a lotus; the celestial musicians and great sages begin to sing her praises, the sacred rivers ask her to bathe in their waters, the sea of milk offers her a crown of immortal flowers. And the great sacred elephants who hold up the world pour the sacred water of the Ganges over her out of gold vases. Being Vishnu's wife she sits on his lap and refuses to look at

the demons who desire her as goddess of prosperity.

When she is with Vamana, she becomes Padma (or Kamala), with Parasu-Rama she is Dharani; she is Sita with Rama-chandra, Rukmini with Krishna. She lives with Dattatreya, the essential *guru*, an incarnation common to Brahma, Vishnu and Siva, who comes disguised as a licentious drunkard in the eyes of men.

Goddess of fortune in every sense of the term, she is unstable in her attachments. She herself says that none among the gods, the *gandharvas*, the *asuras*, or the *rakshasas* can sustain her for ever. After living for a long time with Prahlada, she deserts him when he agrees to transfer his purity to Indra. The *asura* Bali also loses her to Indra, when he gives way to pride. And to keep her, Indra had to divide her into four equal parts at her own request; one part was kept by earth, another in the waters, another in fire and another among just men. Her connections with Indra are again confirmed by the fact that when incarnate she becomes Draupadi, the spouse common to the five Pandavas, themselves incarnations of Indra.

She confers various and different benefits according to that part of themselves that her worshippers surrender to her, and she abandons forthwith anyone who puts her on his head, which is exactly what the demons, *daityas* and *danavas*, do whenever they manage to lay hands on her.

Brahma's wife

Sarasvati is not only the Word, as is proper to the power of manifestation of the creator, she is also, though this is less important, goddess of music, wisdom, and science, mother of the Vedas. The *devanagari* alphabet (Sanskrit) was her invention. She is a beautiful young woman with four arms. With one of her right hands she holds out a flower to her hus-band; in the other she holds a book of palm-leaves indicating her love of erudition. In her left hand she has a chaplet and a little drum. Elsewhere she is portrayed sitting on a lotus, with only two arms, playing the *vina*.

A legend concerning the birth of Sarasvati accounts for the four faces of Brahma and the creation of the world:

First of all Brahma formed of his own immaculate substance a goddess known by the name of Satarupa, Sarasvati, Savitri, Gayatri or Brahmani. When he saw this lovely girl who had come from his own body Brahma fell in love with her. Satarupa (she who has a hundred forms) moved to the right to avoid his glance, but immediately a head appeared on that side of the god's body. And as Satarupa turned towards the left and passed behind him, two new heads came forth. She fled up to the sky; so a fifth head took shape, which was later burned up by the fire of Indra's eye. Then Brahma said to his daughter: 'Let us give birth to all sorts of living creatures, men, *suras* and *asuras*.' Hearing these words, Satarupa returned to earth. Brahma married her and they retired to a secret place, where they stayed together for one hundred divine years. That is when Manu was born, who is also called Svayambhuva and Viraj.

The measureless Divine

Beneath the One represented by Brahma, Vishnu, Siva and the divine mother—who is a direct though differentiated emanation of them—there are all the individualised and particularised manifestations of god in the world. These are 'the gods' of India, who number three hundred million, whose adventures and quarrels—among themselves just as much as with the sages, heroes and demons—form the great body

Sri, goddess of fortune and prosperity, in a traditional Hindu pose. Twelfth to thirteenth centuries. *British Museum*

Brahma, mounted on a bird, with the five faces which he grew after the birth of Satarupa. Talc drawing. South India. *Victoria and Albert Museum*

of Hindu mythology and the part that is most difficult to interpret—all the more so as each is capable of innumerable combinations. Far from qualifying for some simplified classification, such as good or evil, god or devil, the Hindu god represents a conjunction of forces and laws whose interplay—like that of the forces of nature—is sometimes favourable, sometimes contrary to the realisation of what we believe to be just, and may represent a factor of progress, or of hindrance, or even of regression, according to the groupings he confronts in this or that episode in his life.

Indra

In the world as we know it, the most highly developed creature is unquestionably man, who is essentially a being of mental abilities. And so it is quite natural that, in this universe, the king of the gods is Indra, who is recognised by Aurobindo as being the 'mind' developed to the highest degree of which it is capable.

All the contradictions and incongruities, which seem to abound in the myths connected with Indra, can easily be explained if this role is remembered. The mental faculty is our most powerful means of action and comprehension; there is a temptation to place all the others under its control and make them dependent on it; it is worshipped by men. But we also know what excess, intolerance, dishonesty and fear can result from the pride man takes in it, and from his obscure but sharpened awareness of his own inborn limitations. All this is to be found in the myths about Indra.

The principal task undertaken by the king of the gods is that of maintaining perpetual domination over the demons Vala and Vritra so as to succeed in obtaining light, force, illumination and *svar* (paradise).

The myth of the Panis

This myth is, in Aurobindo's view, the most important of all, for it discloses the secret of the meaning of the Vedas. The story itself is quite simple: some creatures of darkness, the Panis, steal 'cows' belonging to the gods and hide them in a cave. Sarama, a bitch, gets on to their scent and Indra sets them free with the aid of Brihaspati and the seven Angiras—seven in this case, but sometimes they are nine (*navagvas*) and sometimes ten (*dasagvas*). Historical interpretations (cattle raids by the Dravidians) and meteorological interpretations (return of the sun after the night) would obviously not suffice to explain the fact that for more than fifty centuries one of the most religious and philosophical peoples on earth looked on this story as containing precious teaching.

The Sanskrit word *go*, which is usually translated by 'cow', also means 'ray' or, to be more exact, 'ray of illumination'. And so the ecstasy procured by *soma* 'gives *go*', as does dawn, which is *gomati, gavam janitri*. Similarly the term *asva*, which usually means 'horse', also indicates vital force in sacred Hindu texts. This is why Vedic singers never tire of asking the gods for cows and horses so that the upper worlds (*svar*) and immortality might be made accessible to them. And all gods, in fact, obtain and make gifts of the cow and the horse, light and force. But this is more especially the role of Indra, master of cows (*gopati*), for he milks the cows and even *is* the cows themselves.

Now the Panis (the traffickers, the avaricious, those who retain), with their leader, Vala (he who surrounds, encloses, conceals), have hidden this light deep in the mountain, in its hardest material core. A sacrifice must be offered to set it free. The Angirasas (*rishis* who are both human and divine, for they are the divine flames of Agni whether they are accompanied by Brihaspati or not), these supreme Angiras

must speak the true word, the *mantra*. Indra, 'the seeker of cows' (*gaveshana*), primed with energy from Soma, goes with the Angiras to set free the light. Guided by Samara (intuition), 'who has found the fortified vastness of the *go*, they discover the fortress-cave, break down the walls, triumph over the Panis and lead the lights 'upwards' into a divine dawn.

At times, the work of Indra is accomplished by Agni, or by Soma, or by two of the others, or even by the Asvins 'who rejoice in the mental faculty, and are the first to step over the threshold of the current of the *go*'.

In other texts, it is Brihaspati, father of the Word, who undermines Vala by his cry, and sometimes it is said to be Sarasvati, the inspirer of the Word. Often the Maruts, who chant the Word, and Pushan, one of the forms of the sun, 'He who believes', also collaborate in this great victory. But Indra 'is the leader of all these gods', lord of light, king of the luminous sky called *svar*. All the gods enter into him, for he is luminous or divine mentality, and they take part in the unveiling of the hidden light.

The *asura* Vritra

There is a parallel to the preceding myth in the myth of the *asura* Vritra. Tvashtri the demiurge, who is responsible for assembling the elements of the world like the pieces of a framework, had a son, Trisiras, who had three heads. With one head he read the Vedas, with the second he took nourishment and with the third he stared fixedly at the horizon. He excelled all men in rigorous asceticism as well as in pious humility. These three aspects of the faculty of knowing and deciding, which he personified, seemed to be an 'alternative solution' to the claim made by the mental faculty to be the sole arbiter of everything. And so Indra became alarmed at the day-to-day increase of a force which seemed destined to absorb

the entire universe, and he determined to intervene. The most attractive young women among the *apsaras* were told to charm the young ascetic, but it was all in vain. Indra then struck him with his thunderbolt. But even after death the body of the Brahman filled the world with such glorious radiance that Indra's fears were not set at rest. He then commanded a passing wood-cutter to cut off the three heads of the corpse; the instant this was done great flights of doves and other birds rose from the body.

To avenge his son, Tvashtri conjured into being a fearful demon to whom he gave the name of Vritra, the enveloper, the obstructor. And, in fact, this *asura* held back the waters of *svar*, which are the waves of truth and which take the form of seven rivers — that is, according to Aurobindo, 'the seven principles of being, both divine and human, the sum total of which constitutes the perfect spiritual existence', and refused to let them spread over the world. This demon was immense and his head touched the sky. He challenged Indra to combat. A horrible struggle ensued in which the demon was victorious. He seized the king of the gods, stuffed him into his mouth and swallowed him. The other gods were terrified and at a loss what to do next. Then they hit upon the idea of making the demon yawn. As soon as he opened its mouth, Indra curled up and sprang out of the gaping jaws, and the battle began afresh. But the god was put to flight. In his humiliation he went to consult the *rishis* and they, together with the gods, went to invoke the god Vishnu, who advised them to make peace, mysteriously adding that he would one day become incarnate in the form of a weapon which would kill Vritra.

The *rishis* succeeded in persuading Vritra to become reconciled with his enemy, but he laid down a single condition: 'Give me,' he said, 'your solemn

promise that Indra will not attack me with a weapon made of wood, or stone or iron, or with anything dry, or with anything wet; promise me also that he will not attack me by day or by night.' The pact was thus concluded.

However, Indra was secretly meditating his revenge. One evening when he was on the shore, he caught sight of his enemy; and suddenly he thought: 'The sun is sinking on the horizon, darkness is approaching, night has not yet come, nor is it daylight now. If I could kill the demon now, between day and night, I would not have broken my promise.' While he was reflecting, a huge column of foam rose from the sea, and Indra realised that it was neither dry nor wet, nor made of wood, stone or iron. (It might be presumed that the mental faculty had renounced rigid, exclusive categories.) He seized the foam and dashed it down on the demon; he fell lifeless on the shingle, for Vishnu, keeping his strange promise, had given rise to this strange weapon, and no-one could withstand it. The gods rejoiced, and all nature too; the sky filled with light and a gentle breeze began to blow; even the beasts in the fields rejoiced.

Indra felt, however, that he bore the weight of great sins, for he had killed the Brahman Trishiras, and he had lied to Vritra.

Nahusha

'Knowing the nature of virtue', Indra fled to the confines of the world and hid in a lotus stem. Naturally without its king the universe was a prey to the most dire disasters. So *rishis* and gods decided to enthrone King Nahusha in Indra's place, for this king was endowed with all the virtues. Nahusha, whose name more or less denotes the idea of proximity, probably represents the quantitative intellect, in contrast to his predecessor who was pre-eminently qualitative. But in the legend he gradually succumbs to sensuality, and finally, as might have been foreseen, he desires Sachi, Indra's wife—in other words, he wishes to appropriate all Indra's power of manifestation. After long and laborious negotiations, in the course of which they send several unsuccessful delegations to Indra, gods and *rishis* persuade the pure and virtuous Sachi to simulate acceptance. She will receive Nahusha provided that he comes in a chariot drawn by *rishis,* a thing that no god has ever dared to do. Blinded by pride, Nahusha then engages in discussion with these sages on the subject of the authenticity of the Vedas and in the heat of argument he touches the head of one of them, Agastya, with his foot, and in the latter's hair is hidden another *rishi,* Bhrigu. Agastya curses Nahusha and sentences him to exile; he must wander the earth for ten thousand years in the guise of an enormous serpent—with whom, later, Bhima and Yudhishthira have long conversations on the noblest of topics. In this way the myths are interminably linked together.

In the texts, Indra or Mahendra (the great Indra) is also called Sakra (the powerful), Satakratu (he who has celebrated a hundred sacrifices), Pakasasana (he who has punished the *asura* Paka) and Puramdara (the destroyer of fortresses). He is mounted on the elephant Airavata. His chariot, Vimana, is driven by Matali. He dwells on Mount Meru.

The sun

The sun (Surya) has unquestionably the most complex mythology, resulting from the variety of personalities associated with it, each of which has a special and well-defined part to play, both from the point of view of cosmogony and on the level of psychology or yoga. A passage in the *Brahma-purana* gives Surya twelve names, each of which is followed by special epithets, as if twelve distinct deities were involved. Here is a literal translation, which does not take into account the deeper meaning:

'The first form of the sun is Indra, lord of the gods and destroyer of their enemies; the second, Dhatri, creator of all things; the third, Parjanya, who lives in the clouds, and causes water to rain down on the earth by its rays; the fourth, Tvashtri, who lives in all corporeal forms; the fifth, Pushan, who procures food for all beings; the sixth, Aryaman, who enables sacrifices to be accomplished; the seventh derives its name from alms and makes beggars rejoice over his presents; the eighth is called Vivasvat, and takes care of digestion; the ninth is Vishnu, who is constantly taking shape in order to destroy the enemy of the gods; the tenth, Amshuman, maintains the organs in good health; the eleventh, Varuna, dwells in the depths of the waters and gives life to the universe; the twelfth, Mitra, lives in the orb of the moon to further the well-being of the three worlds. These are the twelve splendours of the sun, the supreme spirit, who, by means of them, permeates the universe and radiates as far as the secret soul of men.'

Perhaps his most complete name is Suryasavitri, lord of light and truth, creator of all forms, because he represents causal truth. The luminous 'cows' that set Indra free are his creation. Mitra and Varuna are powers emanated from him.

Surya

As far as his principal functions are concerned one must distinguish between Surya the illuminator, Savitri the creator, and Pushan the enhancer.

Surya is *vipra*, the enlightened, for he throws the light of truth on the mental faculty and on thoughts; he is *brihat*, the vast, for he sets man free from the limited awareness of the ego and from his surroundings, and thus gives him wider scope; he is *vipashchit*, of clear perception, for he possesses lucid discernment regarding things in their entirety, their parts and their relevance; he reveals their truth, their meaning, purpose, reason for existing and their proper use. By following Surya in his progress all the other gods attain his amplitude. He is portrayed as a dark red man with three eyes and four arms. In two of his hands he holds water-lilies, with a third he confers blessings, and with the fourth he encourages his worshippers. He is sometimes seated on a red lotus-flower, and rays of glory radiate from his body.

In his guise of Bhaga, Surya is, more precisely, the lord of enjoyment, of the sort that results from right action and right creation, and takes its proper place in the divine rhythm through knowledge that heeds and informs the Word; because of this, Bhaga is also Savitri, the creator, fulfilled in the divine purpose of his creation.

Savitri

This 'brilliant god Savitri, who by his might and grandeur has traced out our terrestrial worlds in light', is the creator of the true and the just. It is he who creates immortality and the highest form of enjoyment of the gods. And so he is 'the soul of all beings with a body' (*atma sarvasaririnam*), 'he who rules time'. To him and to his power of creation, 'not in the sense of fabrication, or the mechanical formation of things', the most famous and sacred verse of the Vedas is addressed; this verse is the *Gayatri*, which the Hindu intones a great many times each morning.

He has golden eyes, golden hands, golden tongues. He rides in a chariot drawn by dazzling chargers with white hooves; his golden arms stretch right across the sky with gestures of benediction.

Pushan

Pushan, the prosperer, our comrade, the companion of our enlightened mental faculty (Indra), has a threefold role. He helps us to conserve what we already possess in the way of strength, knowledge and enlightenment; he takes care to see that we are neither attacked nor diminished. Furthermore he restores to us what we have lost; he is asked to soften the hearts of the Panis and make them change their mind, so that they will give up their prey of their own free will. And, finally, he is the lord of growth; he makes us reach our full stature, he achieves plenitude for us. He cherishes thought as it develops, much as a lover cherishes his betrothed. He is the master of the way, and knows all its various stages, and he also removes obstacles and enemies from our path.

Ushas

Considering the importance attached to the sun, it is not surprising to find that dawn plays a correspondingly large part, and uses the same sort of metaphor. 'In the whole *Veda*,' says Aurobindo, 'Ushas, daughter of the sky, has always the same function. She makes the other gods waken from sleep, act and develop. She is not only the mother of the rays (*go*) of illumination, she is also the mother of the gods.' Her influence is felt equally among men. 'Through her increasing illumination, the entire nature of man is enlightened; through her, he arrives at truth, through her he enjoys beatitude.' As a human goddess among mortals (*devi martyeshu manushi*), she awakens, prompts and leads men towards both right action and happiness (*suvitaya*), for she is not only 'vast with truth' (*brihatim ritena*), full of truth (*ritavari*), she is also the mother of truths and she is even truth itself (*sunrita*). In both of the last cases 'she is both a worker towards great victory, and the luminous result of this victory when she appears in her fullness.'

Ushas rides in a brilliant chariot drawn by cows or horses that are reddish in colour. Poets compare her either to a charming young girl adorned with a mother's care, or to a dancer covered in jewels, a beautiful adolescent emerging from her bath, or a bride sumptuously attired appearing before her husband.

Always smiling, sure of the irresistible power of her charms, she advances, half-opening her veils. She dispels darkness and reveals the treasures hidden in its folds. She lights up the world to the farthest horizon. She is the life and health of all things. If birds rise on the wing each morning, it is due to her.

Like a young matron she awakens her whole household, and sends them about their various tasks. She performs a service for the gods by waking up those who will worship them and light the sacrificial fires. They beseech her to awaken only the good and generous, and to let the wicked sleep.

She is young, since she is born anew each morning; and yet she is old, since she is immortal. While successive generations disappear one after the other, the life of dawn goes on for ever.

Agni

The importance of this god emerges clearly from the fact that eight of the ten books of the *Rig-Veda* begin with hymns addressed to him. According to Aurobindo he is 'divine will or conscious power, and as such is the master of the universe'. As far as Hindus are

A graceful goddess in the Gandhara style. Terracotta from Afghanistan. Seventh century. *Musée Guimet*

concerned, nothing can happen without divine will, Agni, being involved as inspiration, motive power, actor, instrument and end. And so he can scarcely be identified with one single form or name to the exclusion of all others. 'Agni is in the earth, in plants; the waters contain Agni; Agni is in stones; Agni is within men; Agnis are in cows and horses; Agni shines from the heavens; the atmosphere belongs to the god Agni. Mortals set fire to Agni, the bearer of oblations who loves clarified butter. The dark-kneed earth, clad in Agni, will make me alert and brilliant.' So says a hymn in the *Atharva-Veda* addressed to the earth. In the sky he is the sun, in the air he is lightning and on earth fire, but being Matarisvan (as Vayu is too) he has the divine faculty of 'scattering things in the Mother' and can therefore penetrate to the deepest layers of matter. 'This divine will governs and guides us, knows the meaning of our blindness, the aim of our aberration, and from the tortuous interplay within us of cosmic untruth, it draws forth the gradual manifestation of cosmic truth.'

Agni will serve as guide to anyone who approaches him; he is the divine workman, the hope of men, the surest, gentlest and nearest of the gods, the immutable light placed in us so that we may see, and he is also the swiftest apprehension of swiftly moving things.

Like Ushas he plays an important part *vis-à-vis* the gods; all are contained in him, he is the 'I' of all gods, he is their father and yet their son, for he introduces into creation the powers destined to bring about evolution as and when conditions are ripe for the realisation of a new phase. And these powers are, in actual fact, the gods. Therefore, on the plane of the human soul, Agni creates the gods in us and is the prime cause of their complex action.

According to Hindu concepts, the sacrifice *yajna* is the essential act in life. Gandhi declared it to be 'a principle which was created at the same time as humanity', and added that 'a life of sacrifice is the supreme summit of art'. Now in this supreme act Agni plays every part: he is at once the offering, the priest, he for whom the sacrifice is celebrated, the flame, the messenger and the one to whom the sacrifice is offered, 'the fire of divine will, which receives the sacrifice and becomes its priest'. And so Agni's constant symbol is the sacrificial fire. He is described as being a red man with three legs and seven arms. He has black hair and eyes. His jaws are sharp and flames spurt from his mouth. He is born in the waters. And he rides on the back of a ram.

His most usual appellations are Pavaka (the purifier), Dhumaketu (he who has smoke for a standard), Jatavedas (authority on all births), Anala (mystic name for the letter 'R' and basic sound corresponding to Agni) and various names commencing with Havya- or Huta-, as a reminder that he bears (or burns) offerings.

When man refuses to submit to divine will (in other

words, will not agree to offer sacrifice), Agni seeks to charm rather than to chastise him.

Soma

Soma has several very different aspects in Hindu mythology: on the one hand, he is creator and father of the gods, the supreme being created before the three Vedas, on the other hand he is the moon, and he is also a plant, as well as the liquor that is distilled from the plant and the intoxication produced by the liquor. Essentially he corresponds both to beatitude (*ananda*) and to the possibility of enjoying this beatitude, which without the possibility of enjoyment would not exist. Soma, 'the supreme dappled bull', is the father of the diversity of existences.

As the enjoyment of *ananda* is in Hindu cosmogony the final cause of creation, it is normal to consider the possibility of this enjoyment as existing not only prior to the worlds, but to the laws (Vedas) which have to rule this creation. This role is confirmed by a myth in which divine will (Agni) and beatitude (Soma) melt together to become one and the same substance 'and for this reason it impregnates the entire universe'. He is the essence of gold, the unalterable metal, the most sacred of all substances, which may indeed replace fire in sacrifices.

In the framework of individual life 'Soma, lord of *ananda*, is,' so Aurobindo tells us, 'the true creator who possesses the soul and extracts from it a true creation. For him the enlightened intellect and heart have been fashioned in a purifying element; freed from all narrowness and all duality, the consciousness has been extended to receive the whole flood of sensory life and mental life, and to change it into pure enjoyment of the true existence in the divine and immortal *ananda*.'

But this absolute beatitude cannot exist on the plane of multiplicity and relativity to which the gods are confined. The thing that makes the transposition possible is the intoxication of ecstasy. And that is what the gods seek. And so worshippers offer them *soma*, the sacred drink, which 'in ascending waves of honey' produces this drunkenness. Only when the gods, especially Indra, have drunk of it, and thus cast off the inherent limits of their specific nature, can they accomplish the highest missions with which they are charged: to triumph over demons, conquer paradise, undermine Vala and Vritra, win back from the Panis the hidden *go*, and so on. When it is the turn of Arjuna and Krishna to conquer Indra, they have to have Soma's weapons in order to succeed.

But as this ecstasy is not the true *ananda* it cannot be eternal. This is why in all sacrifices new offerings of *soma* must be repeatedly made to the gods if their intervention is sought. This is one of the reasons why the god Soma is associated with the moon, because its light also waxes and wanes unceasingly.

The phenomenon of the periodic waning of the moon is also sometimes explained by the fact that,

during its periods of regular rotation, the gods drink the *soma* that it contains in turn; however, it is usually attributed to a curse uttered by Daksha. The latter considered that Soma was showing too much affection for one of his daughters, Rohini, and sentenced his son-in-law to death by consumption; but, thanks to his wives who interceded on his behalf, Soma's punishment became periodic instead of eternal.

When the bird-god Garuda, spiritual aspiration, puts the pious *asura* Bali in chains, he can only do so with Soma's help, that is with the ecstatic intoxication of love for the divine, who is Vishnu.

Of the ten books of hymns which make the *Rig-Veda*, there is one entirely devoted to the glory of Soma.

Soma, in mythology, is very rarely treated anthropomorphically. However, mention might perhaps be made in passing to the tale of his relationship with Tara, the wife of Brihaspati, which will be referred to later on.

Aditi

Aditi is supreme nature, mother of worlds, which take shape on the seven planes of her cosmic action in the form of energy in the conscious being; she is also infinite light, which nothing can prevent, the divine world itself being one of its formations. She is also supreme and infinite consciousness, which is vast and blessed and is hidden in the subconscious, and she is infinite existence to which the gods owe their birth, and source of all cosmic forms of consciousness, physical consciousness as well as the superior forms.

In the cosmos she is indivisible consciousness, the undivided and infinite unity of things, in which there is no duality (*advaya*), whilst her sister and rival, Diti, also called Danu, is the divided consciousness, which separates and dualises.

As a good protectress and leader, she realises herself in human form in the birth and interplay of her glorious children, the gods, whereas Diti, who is ignorance or obstruction, is mother of Vritra and the other *danavas*, enemies of the gods and of man in his progression. Aditi corresponds to that which is universal and divine in man, Diti to that which is individual and human in him.

Aditi, who is perhaps the source of divine attributes rather than of the gods themselves, is symbolised by the cow that nothing can kill; it is both the food-giving cow (*dhenu*), from which flow the seven rivers, and the cow of light (*go*), which gives birth to the dawns, the primeval and supreme light made manifest in seven rays (*go*), which are her seven names and seven seats (*dhaman*), and which are also the goddess herself.

She is sometimes portrayed as Vishnu's wife, and if one takes into account certain aspects of her influence, it would appear that she might have made a second marriage with her son Surya. Ushas the dawn, as mother of gods and illuminations, is but a form or power (*anika*) of Aditi.

The Adityas

The Adityas, sons of Aditi and Kasyapa, vary in number from two to fifteen, and texts even speak of the supreme Aditya, who would be Varuna the sun, or Vishnu, or Siva. Usually, however, there are eight or twelve Adityas. The list generally includes a high proportion of aspects of the sun: Surya, Savitri, Vivasvat, Bhaga, Pushan and Martanda (the hidden, lost or dark sun). Other gods often mentioned in this connection include Amsha, a feeling of uninterrupted unity with the divine essence, the ever young and dazzling Aryaman with numerous chariots, the Asvins, Chandramas (the moon), Dhatri, who forms the embryo, Jaya, or victory won by self-refinement, Kubera, Mrityu (death), Rudra, Sakra (Indra), Skanda, Tvashtri, Vishnu in his incarnation of Vamana, Yama and especially Mitra and Varuna. They are usually born in pairs as twins — for example, Dhatri and Aryaman, Mitra and Varuna, Amsa and Bhaga, Indra and Vivasvat.

The children of Aditi, begotten of her in just law (*rita*) and manifested in this active life of her movement, protect the world against chaos and ignorance. They maintain the invincible interplay of truth in the universe, and construct the worlds in the image of truth. They are brilliant, golden, pure, immaculate, impeccable, holy, strong, irresistible, vast, profound; they are kings who never sleep, see far, have numerous eyes and whom nothing can undermine.

Their worshippers are protected by them as a warrior is by his armour.

Varuna

Varuna is the spiritual image of an infinity that embraces and illumines. All space is his, all infinity is his province. 'The two oceans (of air and earth) are the stomachs of Varuna,' said the *Atharva-Veda*, 'and he also resides in this little pool of water.'

The witness of all action, present 'in the third person' at every gathering, he knows what has been done and what remains to be done. He contemplates from on high the varying truths, and his abode is in mortal consciousness. He is constantly referred to as *svarat* or *samrat*, master of himself and of the world.

He destroys all that may hinder our growth. When he is present in man, all that limits and affects nature, by leading it into error and sin, is destroyed at his touch. He brings us 'the ethereal purity and oceanic vastness of infinite truth', for in us he is 'the oceanic upsurge of the divine'. He envelops us in light; by his vastness and ample vision he makes our own limits recede.

He helps us embark on the immaculate and well-rigged divine craft, which does not founder and conveys us beyond the reach of evil and sin. This is a place where brilliant dawns are seen, rivers flow, and the sun unharnesses the horses that draw his chariot. Varuna contains, sees and governs all this in his immense being, by his unlimited knowledge.

Remaining in us as a thinker endowed with knowledge, he is the purifier, the guardian of the truth. By his royal power, he frees us from the triple bond, and he pays for us the debts contracted by our ignorance. And so the *rishis* implore: 'Free us from the sin that we have committed, for if we have acted against the law it is from lack of will.' But he is also the destination, for the 'rivers flow towards the truth Varuna'. In addition he rules over the physical as well as the moral world; his commands determine celestial movements and the circulation of waters. The wind is his breath, the stars are his eyes. He traces the sun's path.

Iconography shows him to be a white man, clad in gold armour, mounted on a sea-monster, the *makara*. He is holding a noose, 'knot in which all wisdom rises and collects'. His abode is the hill of Pushpagiri 'on which rests the original and unimpaired activity of the gods'.

At one time Varuna and Mitra were both in love with the *apsara* Urvasi, and they contrived to have two sons, Agastya and Vasishtha, whom Varuna turned into a *rishi*.

Mitra

If the purity, infinitude and strong royalty of Varuna form the splendid framework and majestic substance of the divine being, Mitra (his twin brother) is its beauty and perfection, for the divine is a plenitude as well as an infinite. Using Varuna's purity as his raw material and bringing this purity to bear on understanding, he enables understanding to dispense with all discord and confusion, and he thus establishes the right movement to be made by the strong and luminous intellect. The opulent Mitra brings us this particular light and harmony, this just distinction, this right relation, this amicable concord, the happy laws of the free soul in accord with itself and with the

truth in all its richness of thought, its brilliant actions and its thousandfold enjoyment. Its law of action is happiness in complete accord with truth, for this harmony and perfect temperament are founded on truth and divine knowledge. His *maya* forms part of an infinite creative wisdom, supreme and faultless; he constructs and joins together in illuminated harmony every one of the numerous planes, the successive stages and the progressive seats of our being. It is said of Mitra that absolutely perfect souls adhere to 'the felicity of this beloved in whom there is no wound', or that they are firmly fixed to him, for in him is no sin, no crack, no scar.

Mitra fashions in gods and men impulses which spontaneously bring about all the aspirations of the soul. He is the principle of harmony by which the multiple mechanisms of truth harmonise in a perfectly sealed union. 'The adorable Mitra is born in us as the blessed organiser of things and as all-powerful king.'

Mitra and Varuna are perhaps states rather than forces or entities, and that is undoubtedly why, in a hymn, the *rishi* Varusruta says to Agni: 'O Agni, when thou art born, thou art Varuna; when thou art perfectly illumined thou dost become Mitra.' That is, when he is entirely liberated and fulfilled, freed from the enveloping perversity of the world, this god of flame and force proves to be the solar deity of love, harmony and light, Mitra, who leads men towards the truth. The many-roomed abode of our being, contained in Varuna, must be ordered by Mitra in just harmony of its utility and equipment. Mitra is the harmoniser, the constructor, the constituent light, the god who effects a just unity, of which Varuna is the substance and the periphery that increases without end.

Tvashtri

Tvashtri, or Visvakarman, divine power of construction in the world, is the carpenter, for as the fashioner of the world he adapts and assembles the pieces, moulds the forms, creates and gives all forms; and so it is he who has given to the earth and sky and all things the variety of their forms. He is always continuing and perfecting his work, sometimes with the aid of his disciples, the Ribhus. He fashions husband and wife for one another as soon as they emerge from the womb.

He takes his plane and shaves off seven-eighths or fifteen-sixteenths of the brilliance of Surya, and with the shavings he forms 'the three worlds' and in addition the weapons of the gods, especially Indra's thunderbolt — though this does not stop him being at times in a state of open hostility with this god. His daughter Saranyu weds the sun Vivasvat and, according to the *Rig-Veda*, 'the whole world gathers' for the occasion.

His weapon, Parvata, bears a name normally used for a mountain but which in the beginning meant

Varuna, the god of the oceans, mounted on a sea monster. Tempera and water colour. South India. *c.* 1820 *Victoria and Albert Museum*

'that which is composed of knots and ruptures'. What better description could one give of him than that supplied by Aurobindo, who calls him 'the principle of infinite division and aggregation'?

The Asvins

These twin gods, who are the colour of gold or honey, are also counted at times as two of the Adityas. They are the sons of the sun (Vivasvat) or of the sky, or again of the ocean, or of the undersea fire (Badava), and they are handsome young horsemen, as agile and swift as falcons, who take on many different shapes. Their wife is Surya, the daughter of Savitri. They are also called Nasatyas, the true ones, or the saviours, and they prepare the way for dawn by bringing the morning light into the sky. Their three-wheeled chariot was constructed by the triad of the Ribhus, and their whip spreads the dew.

They are sometimes thought to be the sky and earth, sometimes the evening star and the morning star, or life and death, or intellect and action. They are so inseparable that they have hardly any individual names and when a mortal woman (Madri) begs them to let her bear a child, together they grant her twins (Nakula and Sahadeva).

This duality, unlike some others, is useful and helpful. The Asvins, to whom very many hymns are addressed, are the friends of the sick and those in disgrace. They are doctors, they give cures and more particularly give back life, as the following story testifies:

The old *rishi* Chyavana had a young and beautiful wife, Sukanya. The twins caught sight of her while she was bathing and said to her: 'Why, O adorable figure of a woman, did your father give you to so elderly a man who is approaching death? You are as radiant as summer lightning; in the sky itself we have met no-one to equal you; even unadorned you

grace the forest. How much more beautiful still you would be with sumptuous robes and splendid jewels! Abandon your aged husband and choose one of us, for youth does not last for ever.' She replied: 'I am devoted to my husband Chyavana.' They insisted: 'We shall make your husband young and handsome. Then you can choose whom you wish to be your lord from the three of us.' Sukanya reported these words to her husband, who consented. Like the Asvins he bathed in the stream, and all three emerged young and radiant. Seeing them look so much alike, Sukanya hesitated long over her choice. Once she recognised her husband, however, she refused anyone else. Then Chyavana, in his joy at having regained not only his wife but also youth and beauty, obtained Indra's consent that the two horsemen should take part in the offerings made to the gods and consume the *soma* with them. For until that moment they had not had the right to do so. And it is said of them that thanks to the ecstatic illumination granted them by Soma, they can dissolve all mental structures, traverse celestial waves, and go beyond the mental sphere.

Ganesa and Karttikeya

These are the children of Siva and Parvati. Ganesa represents the call to spiritual power and Karttikeya trust in material power. The difference between the two brothers comes out clearly in one particular myth. Their parents wished to 'marry' them one day, in other words to confer upon them the power of self-manifestation. But Siva wished to put them to a test to determine which of the two children would have priority of manifestation, or, in mythological terms, would marry first. By way of a test, he invited them both to make 'a circle round the earth' (to embrace terrestrial manifestations in their entirety and dominate them) as quickly as they could. Karttikeya, otherwise Skanda, made off at

Ganesa does not appear in the most ancient Vedic pantheons, but seems rather to be an epithet applied first to Vishnu and then to Siva. He lost his human head soon after his birth *A.S.I.*

once with all speed, while Ganesa, taking his time about it, respectfully made a circle round his parents. When Siva asked him why he did this, he replied: 'It is said in the Vedas that he who honours his parents by circling round them seven times has as much merit as he who circles the earth seven times.' And so he was acknowledged to be the victor.

Ganesa, who is also called Ganapati, is one of the most popular Hindu gods. Parvati found him in her hand when she was wiping perspiration from her body after her bath. He is shown with a corpulent human body surmounted by an elephant's head. The holy scriptures give several explanations of this last-mentioned detail. The most generally accepted is the following:

At the time of his birth, all the gods in the Hindu pantheon were invited to come and salute the new-born and bring him their good wishes. All accepted the invitation except Sani (Saturn) who, in both Indian and Western astrology, symbolises obstacles, difficulties and delays. Although Parvati was well aware of why Sani was afraid of influencing the child, she insisted on his being present. She did not want the infant to be deprived of the stimulus to rapid growth provided by obstacles in his path. So Sani came and one glance from him was enough to reduce the head of the babe to ashes. At the mother's request Vishnu set off to look for another head and he brought back the head of Indra's elephant, Airavata, which was placed without further ado on the shoulders of the young Ganesa. And the latter came to be called Vighnesa, Vighnesvara, 'the lord of obstacles', and his particular role was to help his worshippers surmount every difficulty.

His mount, or standard, which is the same thing, is a rat, a symbol in Hindu fable of the sagacity of this world, of trickery and political resourcefulness, like the fox in Aesop's fables. The rat is the creature who produces the most perfect maxims on the way to behave towards one's friends, enemies, and others. And it is natural that he should first be conquered, then subdued and employed by the being who represents spiritual strength, whom he was bound to recognise as his superior, since his own cunning would tell him that Ganesa would prove a better guide than even his own perspicacity.

Ganesa enjoyed food, especially the cakes given as offerings and called *mandana*, meaning 'that which gives joy'. One day when he had partaken of a great number of these cakes, his mount was frightened by a serpent—the rat's age-old enemy. He reared and threw his rider, who fell so awkwardly that his excessively inflated stomach burst. Ganesa hastened to pick up the spilled confectionery, replaced it in his stomach, which he closed again and, to make certain no further ill would result, he girded himself with the serpent. At the sight of this, the moon and constellations burst out laughing. In fury Ganesa seized one of his tusks and threw it at them. It is also said

that if he has only one tusk it is because he used the other to write the *Maha-bharata* at the dictation of the sage Vyasa.

As patron of letters he procures wealth and ensures the success of all enterprises. Nothing must be undertaken, not even the cult of another god, without first worshipping Ganesa. He is particularly revered by the merchant class.

Karttikeya (or Skanda)

He is the god of war created by Siva at the request of the gods that they might be delivered from a demon. Directing the flame from his third eye into the depths of a lake, Siva brought forth six children, which were suckled by the wives of the *rishis*. But one day Parvati, hugging them all together, clasped them so hard that they came to form a single body, though the six heads remained and are depicted in most statues of Karttikeya. The god of war is mounted on a peacock and carries a cock on his standard.

Hanuman

The monkey-god Hanuman is the son of Vayu. Perhaps it is because of this relationship that he enjoys almost unlimited physical strength. When his master Rama wishes it, he takes one leap across the stretch of the sea between India and Ceylon and even repeats this performance with a whole mountain in his outstretched arm. One day, when his half-brother Bhima insisted on seeing him in his divine form, he grew as big as a forest, as high as the Vindhya mountains, and in his brilliance, which rivalled that of the sun, he forced Bhima to close his eyes. And he said to Bhima, 'O thou without sin, thou art only capable of seeing me when I am this size, but I can grow as great as I wish.'

Strength, however, was not the reason for his fame, but the combination of powerful virility and total chastity, which makes him a model servant of Rama, a perfect worshipper.

Most mythological incidents connected with him are found in the epic of Rama, to whose service he is entirely devoted. Following a great victory, Rama distributed prodigious wealth among his collaborators. And to Hanuman he gave a magnificent necklace of fine pearls. Lakshmana, Rama's brother, showed anger at this: 'How could a monkey appreciate those pearls?' 'Follow him,' Rama replied, 'and watch what he does with them.' Now Hanuman took a pearl between his teeth, broke it, looked at the pieces carefully, and threw it away. He did the same with a second and a third. More and more outraged, Lakshmana came to tell his brother. 'Ask him why he is doing this,' replied Rama, showing no concern. When Lakshmana put the question, Hanuman answered: 'These pearls have no value.' 'Why?' asked Lakshmana. 'Because they do not contain the name of lord Rama.' 'And you,' said Lakshmana, now quite beside himself with anger, 'have you my brother's name within you?' 'Look!' came Hanuman's simple answer. With his nails he tore open his chest and bared his heart. There the holy name of Rama stood out in letters of flame.

Garuda and the serpents

The sage Kasyapa had two beautiful wives, Kadru and Vinata, both daughters of Prajapati. When the sage offered to give them heirs, Kadru chose a thousand serpents for sons, all equal in splendour. Vinata wanted only two sons, but their strength, energy, manly form and prowess were to surpass those of the sons of Kadru. Once he had lain with his wives, Kasyapa withdrew into the forest, with the recommendation that they should take great care of his unborn heirs. Much later, Vinata laid two eggs and Kadru a thousand. Their servants put them in receptacles, which were kept very warm. After five hundred years, the thousand serpents broke their shells, but still the twins expected by Vinata did not appear. Jealous and impatient, Vinata broke one of the two eggs; she found an embryo with only the upper half developed. This was Aruna, the red glow of dawn, who cursed his mother, predicted a glorious fate for his brother, and went up into the sky, where ever since he has driven the sun's chariot each morning.

Another five hundred years went by; then from out of the other egg came Garuda, the 'eater of serpents'.

The significance of these myths becomes apparent when one knows that serpents are the guardians of spiritual truths on the terrestrial and material plane, while Garuda represents the aspiration to spiritual truth and to strength on higher planes. Garuda naturally feels hatred for serpents, for, being what he is, he cannot accept the fact that visions of spiritual truths should remain limited to their effects on lower planes. This struggle is illustrated by numerous myths, including the following:

Garuda's mother had brought upon herself another curse, and to free herself from it she had to procure for her nephews, the serpents, the ambrosia that confers immortality. She entrusted the task to her son, and after an epic struggle against all the gods, he took the precious beverage from them. As he had promised he put it in the midst of the serpents, but he also explained to them that before they could taste of it they had to purify themselves in every way, by ablutions, fasts and meditations. And the devout serpents, whose fear of Garuda did not lessen their absolute confidence in him, went to perform all these ceremonies. When they returned, Indra had already gone off with the ambrosia, for Garuda had made a secret pact with him. The inference is that the more we purify our spiritual concepts on the material plane, the less chance they have of staying there, all the more so as our mental faculty, as represented by Indra, is greatly opposed to their development.

Garuda is obviously the mount chosen by Vishnu, the protector and conserver of the universe, for if men did not have in them this aspiration which he represents, how could Vishnu conserve the world? Having no further purpose, no possibility of going beyond its present stage of development, the world would disintegrate.

The serpents

The serpents, usually called Nagas and Naginis, have a triple mission on the terrestrial plane: in the first place, they forbid access to spiritual truths to those who are not worthy of them; in the second place, they confer them upon those who deserve them, and, finally, they strive to prevent these truths from going beyond the material plane. This last-mentioned factor explains why the names they bear, Bhujagas, Pannagas, Uragas, emphasise the fact that they crawl on their stomachs, that they are flat on the ground, incapable of rising, and so on.

We have already seen that when Ganesa risks losing the very pure material offerings stored in his stomach, he subjects them to imprisonment with the aid of a serpent.

In their first two roles, the serpents are powerful, redoubtable and endowed with surprising powers. The countless statues of them, generally found under trees—especially in southern India—are always the object of a fervent cult. Certain royal dynasties cite the Nagas as being their ancestors. The queen of the serpents, Manasa, is one of the deities who most willingly grants the wishes of sterile wives when they invoke her and surrender to the appropriate austerities. There are close links between the serpents and Siva: even now in our own time, the adepts of certain Sivaist sects are never bitten by serpents.

When the worlds are dissolved, Indra's love of all that Takshaka, the king of the serpents, represents, makes him strive to safeguard the thousands of dualities. When Bhima, poisoned and bound by his enemies, who represent the basest material egoism, is in addition thrown into a river by them, the serpents bite the intruder, and their venom acts as an antidote. They are the heroes of numerous myths, such as this:

A young novice, Utanka, is entrusted with the mission of taking his *guru's* wife a pair of ear-rings given her by the queen. (Ear-rings, in Hindu symbolism, are the things that delimit the activity of the mental faculty, giving it full powers in its own domain and preventing it from going astray. Indra, god of the mental faculty, had to have recourse to almost inadmissible subterfuges to get possession of the ear-rings worn by Karna, son of the sun, at his birth.) However, the queen, wife of King Janamejaya, warns the young man that the Naga Takshaka has long coveted these jewels.

The Brahman sets off, and on his way he catches sight of a naked beggar, who at one minute seems to be approaching, then disappearing from view the next. Shortly afterwards, Utanka stops to perform his ablutions and puts the ear-rings down on the ground. The beggar slips quickly up to the jewels, snatches them and takes to flight. When Utanka discovers the theft, he diligently pursues the culprit, but just when he is about to lay hands on him, the robber throws off his disguise, and in his original serpent form slides away into a crack in the ground. Once back in the serpent world, the crafty Takshaka takes refuge in his palace.

Then Utanka remembers the words spoken by the queen. How can he reach Takshaka now? He prods the hole with the end of his stick, but without success. Seeing him overcome with grief, Indra sends him his thunderbolt: 'Go and help this Brahman!' The thunderbolt comes through the stick and into the crack and blows the hole open. Utanka goes in after it.

Opposite:
Agastya visited in his hermitage by Rama, Sita and Lakshmana.
Tempera and gold on card. Late eighteenth or early nineteenth
century. Victoria and Albert Museum.

Section of a sandstone frieze nymphs (*apsaras*) and
musicians (*gandharvas*). From a Jain temple at Kathiawar.
Eleventh to twelfth centuries A.D. *Victoria and Albert Museum*

Once he is in the limitless world of serpents (Patala), he finds it full of admirable establishments, great and small, devoted to games, and in addition ornamented, even encumbered with hundreds of porticos, towers, palaces and temples in various architectural styles. He declaims a hymn in praise of the Nagas, but this does not make the serpents return the jewels to him.

Utanka meditates. A wondrous symbolic vision of nights and days, of the year and the seasons, unfolds before his eyes; then he sees Indra himself, on horseback. He praises the god in a sacred hymn, and Indra is satisfied and offers him his aid. 'Have the serpents brought under my power,' Utanka begs of him. 'Blow on my horse's croup,' Indra answers. Utanka obeys, and immense flames suddenly leap from the steed and submerge the serpents' world in smoke. Takshaka is terrified and hastens from his palace to return the ear-rings to the young Brahman.

Indra then lends Utanka his marvellous horse, which takes the young man back to his preceptor in an instant. He arrives in time to hand the required jewels to the king's wife at the appointed hour.

'Troops of deities' (*deva-ganas*)

Some categories of gods exist only collectively, and individual personalities do not emerge distinctly from their ranks. The chief ones will be mentioned here.

The Rudras are essentially forces, or specialised individual energies. They are called the impetuous ones, the violent, those who bring about transformations. Varying greatly in number, those in the sky use rain for arrows, those in the air have the wind, those on the earth use food. Sometimes said to be the sons of Vasudeva, or again of Kasyapa and Surabhi, they are usually considered, however, to be aspects, parts or manifestations of the god Rudra.

The two principals are Aja Ekapad, 'the non-born with a single foot', who stands for generative sexual force, and Ahirbudhnya, 'the dragon of the depths, strength of growth and germination'.

The Vasus, latent principles within all things, are bound to the idea of riches and material abundance.

The Maruts, popularly gods of the winds, are mental energies and work for knowledge. Brothers of Indra, they are not, however, properly speaking gods of thought, but gods of energy whose power can be felt in the domain of the mind.

In the singular, Marut, or more frequently Maruta, refers to Vayu (also called Pavana, Vata), who is the god of the wind and vigorous force. He frequently accompanies Indra, and it is this latter, god of the mind, who then drives their chariot, drawn by a thousand horses.

The Visvadevas, gods 'without descendants', seem to correspond to the laws that rule the universe, or to the points of application of forces (Rudras) on matter (Vasus).

The Sadhyas, who became immortal by the celebration of sacrifices, are the means by which individual entities can attain harmony with the great cosmic current and be borne along by it.

Some of these deities are connected more particularly with rhythm; these are the celestial singers and dancers, *gandharvas* and *apsaras*. The *gandharvas* are the link between the various rhythms, just like the melody in music. This is why their anger rises when a sage, such as Narada, or a hero, such as Arjuna behaves in a manner out of harmony with the music of the spheres. Both sexes are represented among them.

As for the *apsaras*, who in fact are rarely seen without the *gandharvas*, they correspond to creation, which is the normal outcome of rhythm. And so the gods often have recourse to them when a sage by his austerities has reached a plane of awareness superior

A dravidian statue of Siva. Represented in many different ways, Siva is sometimes given five faces, sometimes three, but most often only one. Usually he is shown with four hands. Here he has his right foot on the conquered asura Vyadhi *Giraudon*

to the divine, and thus risks, as the scriptures put it, shaking the earth (in other words, endangering the world of multiplicity) and plunging everything into the Absolute. Then the gods dispatch an *apsara* who, in the form of a divinely beautiful young woman, tries to tempt the sage to bring him to create and procreate, that he might descend to man's plane of consciousness.

The Ribhus

Although they do not form part of the *deva-ganas*, the three Ribhus also constitute an indivisible group. As powers of supreme truth symbolised by the sun, they have made their father and mother young again. Joining with the brightness emanating from their father, they rise into the air to supply the sun. They are the sons of the 'good archer', Sudhanvan, and are clever artisans, inhabiting the solar sphere, and it was they who made Indra's chariot and hair, and the chariot of the Asvins.

But their most curious accomplishment consisted of 'dividing' into four goblets a 'bowl' (*chamasa*) given to mankind by their master, Tvashtri, in the beginning of creation—a task which they accomplished at the instigation of Agni and against the wishes of Tvashtri himself. Perhaps one should look on this as a stage in the concretisation of the universe. This goblet, from which the gods could come and drink the libations of sacrifice, would then exist on only one plane (the spiritual?) and the Ribhus may be said to have extended its use to the mental, vital and physical planes.

In the singular the name of Ribhu sometimes refers to Indra, Agni or even the Adityas.

The enemies of the gods

Asuras

The dividing line between gods and demons is not clearly marked; far from being mutually exclusive, they complement one another. The essential task of the gods is to struggle eternally against the demons and to triumph continually over them, but not to demolish them nor eliminate them. If the demons disappear, the gods have no further purpose and they also disappear, and it is the end of the worlds.

The term most generally used in reference to demons, *asura,* is frequently applied to the gods, including the greatest of them, Varuna, for example. And the sun, Surya, is sometimes called 'the *asuric* champion of the *devas*'.

The most powerful weapon of the *asuras* is their piety. In austerities and devotion they are the rivals of the gods, and in recompense are granted powers by the creator that make them almost invincible. Their officiating priest, Usanas (or Sukra), possesses such miraculous holiness that the officiating priest of the gods, Brihaspati, does not hesitate to send him his own son Kacha to receive instruction from him. Their

city was built by the architect of the gods.

The respect Vishnu has for the *asura* Bali has also been mentioned here. And we know that Prahlada and Vibhishana are considered to be models of devotion. Mandodari, the wife of the terrible Ravana, is even today held up as an example to Indian women.

And so it is dangerously deceptive to translate the terms *asuras, rakshasas, daityas, danavas* and even *pisachas* by devils or demons, and the terms *devas, suras* and so on by gods or angels. The *Taittiriya Samhita* classes evil beings in three categories: *asuras* oppose the gods, *rakshasas* oppose men, *pisachas* (almost always vampires) oppose the dead; but these categories are much less clearly demarcated in practice than in theory.

In all these struggles, either between gods or between gods and demons, it is always a higher, more advanced concept that triumphs over another that is less high and less advanced, but no less worthy, and the latter always proves to have been indispensable to the arrival of its successor; it has prepared the way for it, and when conquered it joyously salutes the progress of this successor on the endless road of evolution. It frequently happens that the victorious god absorbs into himself the soul of his enemy, which is the most miraculous recompense. Perhaps it is in the hope and desire for this recompense that great sages ask to be reborn as enemies of god; the way of hatred or love turned the wrong way up, *virodha-bhakti*, is in fact highly prized. This can be explained by the fact that the Hindu considers the uninterrupted thought of the divine to be the quickest and safest road to salvation, and that, psychologically, man is more easily obsessed by what he hates than by what he loves. When, after the terrible battle of Lanka, Rama asks Indra to bring back to life his companions in arms, he does not make the same request on behalf of the *rakshasas* who have perished; but Tulsidas tells us this is because 'in dying they were so absorbed in the thought of Rama that they were freed from all obligation to be reborn'.

Jalamdhara

The story of Jalamdhara is fairly characteristic of the struggles between *devas* and *asuras*. One day Indra and the other gods went to visit Siva on Mount Kailasa, and amused him with songs and dances. Charmed by this, Siva asked his guests to express a wish, and Indra in a tone of defiance immediately asked to become a warrior as powerful as Siva himself. The wish was granted and the gods left. But Siva sat wondering what use Indra was going to make of his new power; while he meditated, a form of anger, black as night, rose before him and made a suggestion: 'Make me resemble thee, and tell me what I can do for thee.' Siva ordered him to go into the river Ganga (Ganges) and marry her to the ocean.

A son was born of this union: the earth trembled and wept, the three worlds rang with the noise of

A group of friendly goddesses. Relief at Angkor Wat. *Almasy*

Head of an *asura*. Khmer style. Twelfth century. Musée Guimet. *Larousse*

thunder. Brahma, contemplating the extraordinary strength of this miraculous infant, called it Jalamdhara and allowed it to conquer the gods and possess the three worlds. His childhood was full of prodigious deeds: carried by the wind, he floated over oceans; he played with lions that he had tamed.

Shortly after his marriage to Vrinda, he declared war on the gods; thousands of warriors were killed in both camps. The gods recovered life and health thanks to the magic herbs picked in the mountains, but Jalamdhara, who had himself received from Brahma the gift of bringing the dead back to life, submerged these mountains. Then Vishnu in person attacked Jalamdhara, but the demon succeeded in overthrowing him, and refrained from killing him only when Lakshmi begged him to desist; Jalamdhara, who had thus conquered the *devas,* chased them from the sky and sought rest and peace.

However, the gods were not resigned to their fate. They consulted Brahma, who took them to Siva, seated on his throne and surrounded by myriads of devoted, curly-haired servants who were all naked, deformed and covered in dust. He advised them to unite their powers to forge a weapon capable of crushing the enemy. So the gods created masses of flames, to which Siva added the burning rays from his third eye and Vishnu contributed the fire of his anger. At last Siva approached this ignited mass, put his heel on it and began to spin at dizzying speed to forge a flaming disc. Its rays reddened Brahma's beard, for the latter wanted to look closer, and the gods were blinded by them. However, Siva hid the weapon under his arm, and soon battle was resumed.

This time the war was complicated by a love intrigue: Jalamdhara lusted after Parvati, the wife of Siva. But she turned into a lotus, and her ladies-in-waiting into a protective swarm of bees. In revenge Vishnu disguised himself as Jalamdhara and succeeded in seducing the latter's wife, Vrinda, but when she discovered the trick she died of grief, cursing her seducer. Jalamdhara, mad with rage, returned to the field of battle and attempted a final assault. Siva and Jalamdhara challenged one another to single combat. Siva, brandishing the discus, cut off the head of his adversary, but the latter had the power to make it grow again. Siva had to call to his aid the goddesses, wives of the gods, who turned into she-ogres and drank the blood of the *asura*; and Siva was able to return to the gods their goods and their realm.

Sisupala

The *asura* Sisupala is a reincarnation of Hiranyakasipu, who destroyed Nrisimha, and also a reincarnation of Ravana, the great enemy of Rama.

He was born the son of a king, but had three eyes and four arms; on this account his royal parents were fearful and were preparing to abandon him when a celestial voice told them: 'Have no fear, cherish the infant; his time is not yet come, but he who will cause his violent death on his day of destiny is already born. Until then he will be blessed with fortune and fame.' Somewhat comforted, the mother took courage. 'Who is it who will cause the death of my son?' she asked. The voice replied: 'You will recognise him by this: when the child is on his lap, his third eye will disappear and you will see his extra arms fall off.'

So the king and queen went to all the monarchs in the neighbouring lands. They asked each one of them to take the child on his lap, but nothing in his appearance changed. They returned home disappointed. Some time later, Bala-Rama and Krishna came to visit them. They played with the child; as soon as Krishna took him on his lap the third eye shrivelled up and disappeared, and his two extra arms vanished. Falling to her knees, the queen cried out: 'O lord, grant me a wish.' 'Speak,' replied the young god.

Vasishtha, one of the ten great sages born of Brahma. He wears
his hair in the ascetic's chignon. Tempera and water colours.
South India. *c.* 1820. *Victoria and Albert Museum*

'Promise me that when my son offends you, you will
pardon him.' 'Certainly, even if he offends me a
hundred times I shall pardon him.'

Many years later, King Yudhishthira offered a
great sacrifice with much celebration. Kings and
heroes were invited to the feasts. Krishna too was
present, and it was to him that the royal family had
decided to render homage first. But Sisupala protested. 'It is,' he said, 'to insult all the monarchs
present to give precedence to someone who has no
right to it.' And others among the guests agreed.

King Yudhishthira did all he could to conciliate
Sisupala. But the latter refused to be appeased. The
elderly great-uncle Bhishma, on being consulted,
replied with a smile, 'Lord Krishna himself will
resolve this conflict. What chance has a dog against a
lion? The king seems to be a lion, until the real lion is
awakened. Let us wait and see!' Sisupala, in his fury
at being compared with a dog, insulted the venerable
old man, who, unperturbed, raised his hand for
silence and told his guests the story of Sisupala.

All eyes turned towards Krishna, who looked with
gentleness on the furious king. But when Sisupala
repeated his mocking insults and his threats, the god
said simply, 'Now, the cup of your misdeeds is full.'
Immediately, the divine weapon, the flaming discus,
rose behind Krishna and, traversing the air, fell on
Sisupala's helmet and cleft him from head to foot.
Then the soul of the wicked king escaped like a mass
of fire, and came to bow before Krishna and to be
absorbed into his feet.

From the demiurge to the sage

In Hindu mythology there is no clear demarcation
between the gods and sages (*rishis*), except that the
latter are less subject to error than most of the gods,
and by their austerities frequently acquire greater
power. The list of avatars, as we have seen, is hardly
limiting; deities marry human beings, and on occasion
even have human children without recourse to
marriage; finally, some characters, the Angiras, for
example, are presented sometimes as secondary
demiurges, sometimes as simple ascetics and sometimes even as pure abstractions, though this does not
prevent each character from remaining perfectly
consistent with itself.

Prajapati and Visvakarman

Prajapati, 'lord of creatures', is a name given to
Brahma, Indra, Savitri, Soma, Siva, Garuda, Krishna,
Manu and many others. This name is also given collectively to ten sages, 'born of Brahma's mental
faculty', from whom humanity is descended: Marichi,
Atri, Angiras, Pulastya, Pulaha, Kratu, Vasishtha,
Daksha (or Prachetas), Bhrigu and Narada. And also
seven great *rishis*: Gotama, Bharadvaja, Visvamitra,
Jamadagni, Kasyapa, Vyasa, Valmiki (the list varies
according to the texts) and they are at the same time
the seven stars in the Great Bear. Sometimes Prajapati is placed opposite Brahma as his subordinate.

Visvakarman, 'he who fabricates all', is also a name
given to Brahma, Siva, Surya, Indra, the *asura* Maya
and others. Great architect of the universe, he has on
all sides eyes, faces, arms and feet; he gives the gods
their names, offers the world in general sacrifice
(*sarva-medha*) and, finally, sacrifices his own life. On
a less elevated plane, he generally identifies himself
with Tvashtri, the great carpenter. He planes the sky
when it is too dazzling, he builds the city of Lanka
for the *asuras* and carves the gigantic statue of
Jagannatha.

If Visvakarman, who has ordained everything, also
sees all and establishes the foundations and distinctions of everything, Prajapati is generator and protector of generation. Gods and *asuras* are his children.
As deities and creatures 'remained confusedly united
he entered them through form. That is why it is said
that Prajapati is form. Then he entered into them by
name. That is why it is said that Prajapati is the name.'
By a higher abstraction he becomes the Absolute,
Brahman, and even the indeterminable absolute,
whose only appropriate name is the interrogative
'Who' (*Ka*).

Brihaspati

Like the previous figures, Brihaspati is god (important
hymns in the *Rig-Veda* are addressed to him) and
great sage. He is above all the master of the creative
word, of inspired speech. His cry, which is the 'thunder of the sky', dispels the darkness, breaks the rocky
mountains (*adri*, the symbol of formal existence, of
rigid and limited physical nature) in which truth has
been enclosed; he kills the enemy with hymns of
illumination (*arkaih*), massacres and makes paradise
(*svar*) visible. This god with seven mouths, of many

births, seven rays, and ecstatic tongue (*mandrajihva*) is the complete thought of truth; he has firmly established the limits and definitions of earth and of material consciousness.

As Brahmanaspati, he creates, that is expresses, through the Word; from the gloom of the unconscious he brings forth all existence, all conscious knowledge, all movement of life, all forms to come; he accelerates in us the progress of conscious formations towards their supreme goal; he makes certain eternal worlds manifest to knowledge.

So he is not without some resemblance to the creator Brahma, and this Aurobindo explains in these terms: 'By the word of truth, Surya, who engenders all, creates; by rhythm, Brahmanaspati evokes the worlds; Tvashtri fashions them.'

He is one of the Angirasas, or even the supreme Angiras, and the officiating priest (*purohita*) of the gods as well as their spiritual guide—and in this respect he resembles Agni. But if Agni is the priest of the oblation, then Brihaspati is more particularly the priest of the Word.

A curious myth gives details of his connections with Soma. One day Soma abducted Tara, the wife of Brihaspati, and she was already pregnant when her husband found her again. When the child, Buddha, was born, there was great discussion as to who the father was. Under pressure from Brahma, Tara in the end confessed that it was Soma.

At the level of spiritual discipline it is natural that the use of the Word, the repetition of the holy name of God (a much honoured technique in India) should give way to ecstatic intoxication (Soma) in which all speech ceases. Once the ecstasy is over, the mental faculty (Brihaspati), regaining its rights, wants to know if the awakening to wisdom (Buddha) is the direct result of its own efforts, or the climax of ecstasy —and is finally constrained to admit this last supposition. Tara, the power of manifestation of her husband, etymologically represents the 'passing to another shore'.

This story has an astrological interest too, for almost all Indian myths have an astrological application which is easy to understand. In fact, Brihaspati corresponds to Jupiter, Soma to the moon, Tara to the fixed star, and Buddha to Mercury.

The Manus

These are fourteen demiurges who succeed one another in the history of the world, each reigning over the earth for one *manvantara*, a period of 4,320,000 years. The first, Svayambhuva, born of Svayambhu, the one who exists without other agency, gave birth to the ten Prajapatis; the famous 'Laws of Manu' are said to come from him. The present Manu, Satyavrata, is also called Vaivasvata, because he is son of the sun (Vivasvat) and of Samjina, daughter of Tvashtri. He is the hero of the story of the flood. He has sixty sons, the most famous of whom, Iksvaku, the original ancestor of the sun dynasty of the Kshatriyas, hands down his teaching.

Atharvans and Bhrigus

The Atharvans complement the activity of the Angirasas, and are the *rishis* of travel, found on the road. 'The Angirasas,' says Aurobindo, 'acquire the richness of illuminations and powers of truth hidden behind the lower life and its devious turns; Atharvan, who is one of their band, forms the path, and then Surya, lord of light, is born to be the guardian of divine law.'

The Bhrigus are also frequently associated with the Angirasas, Krishna in the *Bhagavad-gita* recognises them as the greatest of the *rishis*. They 'discovered the flame of the secret divine force in the growth of terrestrial existence'.

The first to bear the name of Bhrigu, one of the ten patriarchs, in his capacity of holder of sacrificial knowledge, exercises powerful authority over the most august immortals. When various sages could not decide which of the three gods, Brahma, Vishnu or Siva, was the most worthy of the adoration of the Brahmans, Bhrigu was given the task of putting them to the test. Approaching Brahma, he deliberately omitted one of the marks of respect due to him; the god reprimanded him, but accepted his apology and forgave him. Bhrigu then entered Siva's dwelling and did the same thing; he would have been reduced to ashes by the wrathful god if he had not appeased him with humble and gentle words. Thereupon he went to Vishnu, who was asleep, and kicked him in the chest to rouse him; far from becoming angry, the god asked him if he had hurt himself, and gently rubbed his foot. 'Here,' said Bhrigu, 'is the greatest of the gods; he surpasses the others for he has the most powerful weapon of all, goodness and generosity.'

A woman by the name of Puloma was betrothed to a demon, but Bhrigu fell in love with her and married her according to Vedic rite before taking her away with him. With Agni's help, the demon discovered the woman's hiding-place and carried her back to his own dwelling. Bhrigu was filled with wrath against Agni for helping the demon, and cursed him saying: 'Henceforth, thou shalt eat anything.' Agni asked him why he uttered this curse since he had done nothing but tell the truth. Agni reminded him that when one lies deliberately, one is thrown into hell together with the seven preceding and seven ensuing generations, and that he who refuses to give information on request is equally guilty. Agni went on: 'I, too, can be quick to curse, but I respect Brahmans and control my anger. In truth I am the mouth of gods and ancestors. When clarified butter is offered them, they partake of it thanks to me who am their mouth; how then can you say that I eat anything?' So Bhrigu agreed to modify his words: 'Just as the sun by its light and warmth purifies the whole of nature, so Agni shall purify all that enters into his flames.'

Vishnu sleeping on the serpent Ananta. Relief from
Mavalipuram. Seventh century A.D. *Goloubew*

The son of Bhrigu, Dadhicha, had, by his austerities, attained such wisdom that he was the strongest creature in the world, equal in stature to the king of the mountains. When the *asuras* were threatening the gods, Indra, on the advice of Brahma, asked Dadicha for his skeleton. The sage surrendered his body with docility, and with his bones (more powerful than thunder) Indra and the gods were able to massacre 'ninety times nine Vritras'.

Daksha

Daksha, the son of Brahma, is sometimes considered to be the chief of the Prajapatis. He was born of Aditi, and Aditi was born of him. Of his sixty 'fine-eyed' daughters, he gave ten in marriage to Dharma (the law), twenty-seven to Soma (they became the constellations, *nakshatras*), thirteen to Prajapati Kasyapa (they became the mothers of the gods, demons, men, birds, serpents and all living creatures), three to Trakshya (Garuda), two to Agni (or Krisasva), two to Angiras, two to Bhuta, and one, Sati, to Siva. The complete number and their distribution varies from text to text.

Now on one occasion, when he was celebrating a sacrifice, Daksha invited all the gods to it with the exception of his son-in-law Siva, of whose way of life he did not approve. In despair, Sati threw herself into the flames. Siva then sent one of his emanations, Virabhadra, and thousands of demi-gods who smashed everything, trampled on Indra, broke Yama's stick, blinded Bhaga, tore out Bhrigu's beard, broke Pushan's teeth, massacred all present and finally decapitated Daksha and threw his head into the sacrificial fire. After this Sati, brought to life again by Siva, begged that her father should be spared. So Siva brought him back to life but, as the head of the patriarch could not be found anywhere, he was given a ram's head.

Some scholars have regarded this myth as indicating a historic struggle between members of Rudra's sect and other worshippers who refused to admit this god into their pantheon. It is more probable that it conveys a totally different teaching—for example, that sacrifice has no value except when the sacrificer offers himself in a holocaust, or, and this amounts to almost the same thing, that the Sivaist concept (sudden and total emergence from the plane of awareness of multiplicity) has to be accepted even in the framework of other eschatologies.

Narada

Narada is a divine sage, a *devarshi* (*deva-rishi*) the son of Parameshthin (Brahma), an incarnation of Vishnu and fervent worshipper of this same Vishnu. The part he plays seems to consist pre-eminently in revealing to each individual the god's intentions concerning him. Sometimes he provokes divine instructions, which are given either directly, or by the intermediary of other sages, and sometimes he himself gives these instructions, either in abstract terms or in the form of precise advice. He is the champion of individualisation and the total flowering of each creature according to his particular nature—this sometimes leads him to encourage fights and discord, and has won him the name of Kalipriya.

His father, Brahma, the creator of multiplicity, naturally wanted Narada to take a wife and thus help people the world. But Narada, preferring to lead a life of entire devotion to Vishnu, refused, and even went to the extent of cursing his father, who was indiscreet in his insistence, and sentencing him nevermore to be an object of worship and to be plagued with desire for his own daughter. Brahma replied by condemning his rebel son to live a life of sensuality and to be dominated by women. Narada thus became a *gandharva* and lived for 300,000 years surrounded

by fifty magnificent wives; during this time he made himself master of music and invented the most perfect of Hindu instruments, the *vina*. Then he was born as a *paria*, and underwent numerous yogic disciplines one after the other, after which he became the greatest of divine sages, the supreme messenger between the gods and men, and friend and counsellor of Krishna. He is said to be responsible for some of the *Bhakti-sutras*, which is one of the finest manuals of devotion of all time.

Agastya

This great sage, particularly venerated in the south of India, was born of both Mitra and Varuna when they loved the *apsara* Urvasi. His special function seems to be to make anything that might form a major obstacle to the progress of the universe disappear for ever. So when the Vindhya mountains constantly rose in height and were in danger of hiding the sun's light from the earth, the sage, who was their *guru*, begged them to grow lower to let him pass and not reassume their original height until he had returned again. Having exacted this promise, he came back by another route.

When the Kaleyas demons took refuge by day in the ocean to persecute the sages during the night, the gods begged Agastya to intervene. He drank up the ocean so that they could exterminate most of the demons, but when he was begged to fill it up again it was found that he had digested all the water. In the town of Manimati, the demon Ilvala used to transform his brother Vatapi into a ram, cook him and serve him up to the Brahmans; then he would call for Vatapi, who took shape again and destroyed the bodies of his brother's unfortunate guests as he made his way from within them. When Agastya had taken part in one of these banquets, Vatapi failed to respond to his brother's call, for he too had been digested in the sage's stomach.

Agastya's ancestors, who seem more human than divine, required him to have heirs. So he meekly procreated a son, Idhmavaha, who was the equivalent of a thousand other heirs, and who acquired great fame by carrying wood for his father to light the sacred fire. But, in order to have this child, Agastya had first created for himself a wife, Lopamudra, who was a combination of all the most beautiful elements in all creatures and of the merits of the most demanding asceticism.

Durvasas

Another sage with a gigantic appetite is the irascible *rishi* Durvasas, who is not afraid to put the most powerful gods to the test. This is what Krishna himself says of him: 'The Brahman Durvasas, dressed in rags, was travelling round the celestial and human worlds, threatening all those who might accord him hospitality. As no-one paid him any heed, I invited him to be my guest. At times he would eat enough for

several thousand people, at other times next to nothing; he would laugh or cry for no apparent reason; he had lived longer than anyone else at that time; one day he burned all the beds, all the bed-covers and all the pretty girls and went out. Then he asked for rice in milk (*payasa*). As I always kept all kinds of food and drink in readiness for him, I had some brought to him. He ate a little, then ordered me to coat my whole body in the rice, and this I did. Then he rubbed Rukmini with it, had her harnessed to a chariot, which he mounted, and set off goading and whipping her as he went. Then he jumped from the chariot and started to run in a southerly direction with us following. He declared that he was satisfied, because I had mastered my anger, and told me: "As long as men and gods like food, each and every one of them will have just as great a liking for you. You will have glory as long as there are just men in the world. You will be loved by all. All that has been broken, burned or destroyed in your residence will be made new again—only better than it was. Death will not be able to strike you in the parts of your body that you rubbed with rice cooked in milk—but you should have put some on the balls of your feet too!'' And I beheld my whole body transformed to one of dazzling beauty. He also blessed Rukmini, predicted that she would be the foremost of my 60,000 wives, and that after her death she would live in the same world as myself. On returning home, we found that everything that Durvasas had broken or burned had been made whole again.'

The wise animals

It is not only among men that sages are found. As has been seen, there are divine *rishis*, such as Narada. And there are also *danavarsis* (demons), such as Usanas. There are even sages among animals and some of them play a very important part.

For instance, there is the vulture, Jatayu, who saves King Dasaratha when he is thrown from the upper airs by Sani (Saturn) after his attempt to get Sita back again. When he is mortally wounded in a fight against the demon Ravana, he is welcomed by Rama and Lakshmana, who confer upon him pious funeral honours 'to make sure that his soul knows the joys of paradise'.

In the Hindu *Ramayana* of Tulsidas the kite Kakabhushundi, 'whose intelligence knows no limits and who has unceasing devotion for Sri Hari', enlightens and consoles the god Garuda, who is disconcerted by what he has seen, and tells him the story of Rama.

The king of the bears, Jambavat, a relation of Rama, can also be put into this category. When Prince Satrajit had sung to perfection the praises of the sun, the latter made him a gift of the magic stone Syamantaka, which protects its owner or destroys him according to whether he behaves well or badly.

The prince, fearing that Krishna might deprive him of the stone, entrusted it to his brother Prasena, who misbehaved and was killed by a lion. Jambavat in turn killed the lion and robbed him of the stone which he carried in his jaw.

Krishna was then suspected of killing Prasena, and so he set out with a whole army. When at last he came to the bear's cave, he went in alone and a single combat ensued which lasted for twenty-one days. After this Jambavat admitted his defeat and gave the hand of his daughter, Jambavati, to his guest.

The end of the worlds and of man

The individual soul (*jiva*) is never allowed to die, but must constantly be born again in another shape, starting from the lowest of planes (mineral and vegetable), then the lower animals, then the higher animals, and finally reaching human life, which is the highest form of all, because it is the only one that enables the soul to escape from the everlasting round of death and

rebirth (*samsara*) and to recover awareness of its truth, Atman. Between successive incarnations the soul sojourns for varying lengths of time in hells or paradises where the fruits of past actions (*karma*) are meted out, and must be accepted passively whether they are good or bad; the soul may even inhabit the bodies of gods or demons, again temporarily, but such cases are exceptional.

The liberation

The ultimate and final escape from *samsara* is what the Hindus call liberation (*mukti, moksha*), independence (*kaivalya*), supreme happiness (*nihshreyasa*). According to the various sects and schools it is either conceived as the passage to the state of awareness of absolute unity, in which Atman is Brahman, or as total and intimate absorption in the divinity, Vishnu or Krishna, for example. Moreover, this liberation is not necessarily linked with physical death. A soul may well awaken to it, and yet continue for some time to animate the body that it inhabits. This is the case with the *jivan-muktas* (those who are liberated during life). And tradition has it that there are always some of them on the sacred soil of India.

Yama

Since the soul has not completed its long pilgrimage, what becomes of it when it dies? It becomes a *pitri*, or ancestor, under the jurisdiction of Yama, who holds the foremost rank among the dead, just as his twin brother, Manu Vaivasvata, is first among living men. Yama sits in judgment on the dead and assigns them to their respective abodes, bestowing happiness on the virtuous and suffering on sinners.

It is difficult to prevail on Yama when he comes at the appointed hour to seek his victim on earth. However, the gentle and beautiful Savitri, the wife of Satyavan, succeeded in persuading the god of death to give her back her husband by dint of persisting in her conjugal affection for him. As Yama was bearing away Satyavan's soul, Savitri followed obstinately in his footsteps, until the god was moved by this fidelity to offer her the fulfilment of a wish, provided she did not ask to have her husband brought back to life. 'Then give me,' she replied, 'a hundred robust sons fathered by Satyavan to perpetuate our race.' Yama had to honour his promise and to do this was obliged to bring Satyavan back to life.

Yama, who is also called Dharmaraja, the lord of the application of the law, and Dandadhara, the stick-bearer, the punisher, is portrayed riding on a buffalo. He is green in colour, wears red clothing, and has a crown on his head, a flower in his hair and a lasso in his hand.

There are numerous and varied sorts of hell; texts differ, but between 21 and 8,400,000 hells exist, and the tortures endured are described in abundant imaginative detail. They are not to be confused with

Yama, lord of death and hell, on a buffalo. Tempera and water colour. South India. *c.* 1820. *Victoria and Albert Museum*

Siva's wife as Parvati, the gentle mountain goddess, one of her many thousands of forms. Musée Indo-Chinois. *Giraudon*

the lower worlds, *patalas*, the resplendent abodes of the Nagas.

The various paradises are essentially places where the company of God is enjoyed, and therefore there are almost as many of them as there are known aspects of the Divine. The most highly prized seem to be the Brahmaloka, Kailasa, Vaikuntha, Goloka (or Vrindavan), and the Indraloka, which are respectively those of Brahma, Siva, Vishnu, Krishna and Indra.

Here it must be pointed out that the Hindus do not hold these paradises in very high esteem. They are mere halts along the way of the ascent. Sages like Mudgala have refused to enter them. And an *Upanisad* explicitly states: 'In paradise fools reap the fruit of their good actions; and then they drop back into this world, or lower still.'

The two ways

Various *Upanisads* present the two possibilities: *deva-yana* (the divine path) and *pitri-yana* (the path of the ancestors). In the first case, the soul passes in turn through flame, through day, the first two quarters of the moon, and the six months in which the sun moves south. But it does not reach the twelfth month; that is why it then goes to *pitri-loka* (world of the ancestors), then to *akasa* (proto-matter of the worlds), and to the moon (Chandramas), where it becomes the food of the *devas*; when this stage is completed it becomes *akasa* again, then wind (Vayu), smoke, fog, cloud, rain, plants, human food and finally 'fire (Agni) that is man, whence it is reborn in the fire that is woman'. Even Vivekananda declared himself unable to explain this rich symbolism in detail.

Universal dissolution

Evidence has already been given which shows that the life of the worlds is itself cyclic in nature. The explanation given by the great philosopher Samkara

is that a period in which the universe appears in its material, crude and visible shape is regularly succeeded by another in which it exists only at the level of potentiality. The passage from one to the other is what is called in India *pralaya* (universal dissolution) through which 'each thing returns to its immediate cause' and thus the world, in the inverse order of creation, is reabsorbed into *akasa*, then into the Absolute, Brahman. Furthermore, it is not necessarily a question of an event that has a precise situation in time. According to the texts, for example, there may or may not be *pralaya* between the reigns (*man-vantara*) of two successive Manus. One must look upon it as a more or less crude substitute of one plane of consciousness for another. One such transformation is related in the *Maha-bharata* in the famous episode of the forest fire.

Agni has become weary of ritual offerings, however pure they might be, and has decided to consume the 'forest of delight' of the dualities, Khandava, where all living beings enjoy fun and frolic. But it is protected by Indra, king of the gods, and Agni fails. On Brahma's advice Agni then solicits the aid of Krishna and Arjuna, prototypes of the adored-adorer couple. These two then engage in a terrible battle against Indra and all the gods, that is to say, all creatures inhabiting the domain of the dualities. Finally, Indra, who as we have seen stands for intelligence, has to beat a retreat in the face of adoration and faith, as they are more powerful than he. But he applauds their victory; for Arjuna is both his incarnation and his son, who must continue and supersede him. Agni allows nothing to survive in the conflagration except what will be necessary in the next creation. And in this next creation, instead of opposition and struggle, there will be co-operation, and things will complement one another. It is apparent that Hindu mythology paints a resolutely optimistic picture of the next stage.

Mythology of Jainism

Among the Jains, time is depicted as a wheel that makes one complete revolution in two thousand billion oceans of years. The six spokes (*ara*) radiating downwards form half of this period, the half known as *avasarpini*. The six spokes turned upwards are the half known as *utsarpini*. The length of the spokes varies within each half, but the total length remains the same for each; the spokes are placed in inverse order in the two halves.

In addition, each half is divided into thirds, and *sukha* (that which is good, agreeable) and *duhkha* (that which is bad, grievous) reign in varying proportions over the character of these thirds. In the *avasarpini* these are: *ati* (excess, intensity)—*sukha-rupa, sukha-rupa, sukha-kuhkha-rupa*; and in *utsarpini* they are: *duhkha-sukha-rupa, duhkha-rupa, ati-duhkha-rupa*. We are at present at the end of an *avasarpini*.

The *tirthamkaras*

In the course of each *avasarpini* twenty-four great sages appear one after the other called *jinas*, (conquerors), or *tirthamkaras*, who have traced a ford across the torrential and catastrophic current of life in the world (*samsara*). These great instructors of humanity have practised rigorous asceticism and so acquired a clear intuition of what goes to make ignorance and human misery, and they have learned how to go beyond this and gain the total and rich peace of Nirvana. The life of each one is recounted with an abundance of detail in the sacred texts; their

In Jain mythology the wife of Siva is called Ambika. High relief in steatite from a Jain temple. *Victoria and Albert Museum*

Two *tirthamkaras*, Rishaba the first and Mahavira the last of the present era. Stone sculpture. Twelfth to thirteenth centuries. *British Museum*

birthplaces and where they entered Nirvana are, even today, the sacred destination of devout pilgrimages. Their names are constantly adopted and taken by countless Jains.

In iconography, *tirthamkaras* are shown in a state of complete nudity; statues of them are frequently colossal. Each one has its own characteristics in such things as proportions of the limbs, colour, symbols, posture and position of the hands and legs. The *tirthamkara* is frequently framed by his *yaksha* and *yakshini* (or *yogini*) the male and female guardians of his temples, who sometimes correspond to the Hindu deities. In fact, just as in Hindu religion the sages often occupy a more eminent position than the gods, so the *tirthamkaras* of the Jains are 'super-gods', who accompany, venerate and serve ordinary gods, in particular the sixteen *vidya-devis*, goddesses who are much worshipped in order that different kinds of knowledge (*vidya*) may be acquired.

Rishabha

The first *tirthamkara* in this present age was Rishabha (sometimes spelled Vrishabha), who is thought of as the founder of Jainism. His father, Nabhi, was the last of the fourteen Manus; during his reign fruit-trees made their appearance, rain began to fall steadily, and the need arose for laws to be imposed on men. His name derived from the fact that he taught how the umbilical cord (*nabhi*) should be cut, for there was no such thing until this period. Rishabha's mother, Maru Devi, gave birth to him at Ayodhya, the land of Rama-chandra, where four other *tirthamkaras* were also born. In dreams she was warned of the supernatural destiny awaiting her son, and this came in the form of sixteen visions which announce the birth of a *jina*: a white elephant, a white bull, a white lion with red shoulders, the goddess Lakshmi, two scented garlands with black bees humming above, the full moon, the rising sun, two gold vases with gold lotus-flowers in them, fishes in a stream of lotus-flowers, a lake with waters seemingly of liquid gold, the ocean, a throne inset with stones, a celestial palace, the residence of the king of the Nagas, a pile of gems, and finally a smokeless fire.

Indra and Sachi came in person to welcome the *jina*, who from his early days possessed all knowledge and all wisdom. On his father's request, he married two sisters. The eldest was Yasasvati and she was the mother of one hundred sons, including the powerful King Bharata, and she also had one daughter, Brahmi. The younger sister, Sunanda, had a son, the god Kama, and one daughter. Rishabha taught the people agriculture, different trades and the arts, and organised the three castes (at the time there were no Brahmans). After this, he turned into a *samnyasin* (travelling monk), tore out his beard and his hair, and threw away his clothes and his jewels. At the end of six months of uninterrupted meditation (*tapas-charuna*), he destroyed the four *karmas* who did

harm and attained omniscience. He then began his preaching, which lasted a long number of years, then, having destroyed the last ties, he entered Nirvana, between the two peaks of Mount Kailasa.

Rishabha, who is generally accompanied by a zebu (whose image is imprinted on the balls of his feet), is portrayed between his cow-headed *yaksha*, Gomukha, and his *yakshini*, Chakresvari, who has sixteen arms.

Second to twenty-second *tirthamkara*

After Rishabha there appear in turn: Ajitanatha, the unconquered; Sambhavanatha, who opens up possibilities; Abhinandana, feeling of voluptuousness; Sumatinatha, good sense; Padmaprabha, lord of the lotus; Suparsvanatha, crowned by a five-hooded Naga, and with Varanandi and Kali on each side, both armed with tridents; Chandraprabha, lord of the moon; Pushpadanta (or Subidhi), whose emblem is a marine monster; Sitalanatha, free from emotions; Sreyamsa, who was born at Sarnath; Vasupujya, universal adoration; Vimalanatha, purity, who is also found in the preceding *utsarpini*; Anantanatha, eternity; Dharmanatha, just law; Santinatha, peace; Kunthunatha; Aranatha, who triumphs over the enemy; Mallinatha, who was the only woman in the entire list; Munisuvrata, strict observation of monastic vows, who has a tortoise as his emblem; Naminatha and Neminatha (or Aristanemi), first cousin to Krishna.

All of these, with the exception of Vasupujya, reached Nirvana in the Sammeda-shikhara hills (in Bihar), which are now called the mountains of Parsvanatha.

Parsva

The twenty-third *tirthamkara*, Parsvanatha Jinendra, is reputed to have come into the world at Benares, 84,000 years after the death of his predecessor, Neminatha, but only 246 years before the birth of his successor, Mahavira. He is the incarnation of Indra in the thirteenth sky, and the son of King Visvasena, a direct descendant of Iksvaku and of Queen Vama. When he embraced monastic life at the age of thirty, no less than four Indras came to celebrate the event. One day, when he was meditating in the forest, the demon Samvara, who had been his enemy in numerous incarnations, tried to cause his death in a flood. But Dharanendra and Padmavati, king and queen of the Nagas, on whom the sage had once previously taken pity, protected him with their cloaks. And now they frame his statues. When he reached the stage of illumination, he began to preach and counted among his disciples 350 sages versed in the scriptures, 10,000 sages who were history scholars, 1,400 saints endowed with clairvoyance, 1,000 omniscient sages, 1,000 sages endowed with occult powers, 600 logicians, 16,000 ordinary saints, 36,000 nuns, 100,000 men of property, 300,000 faithful wives, numerous gods and goddesses and even animals. When he reached a hundred years of age he entered Nirvana.

Mahavira

The last *tirthamkara*, Mahavira, who was practically a contemporary of Gautama Buddha, was born in 626 B.C. at Kundalapura. According to the scriptures, he took the form of an embryo in the womb of Devananda (the enjoyment of god), wife of the Brahman Rishabhadatta (gift of Rishabha). But, in the sky, the king of the gods, Sakra, deemed that it would be better to convey the embryo of Mahavira from Devananda's womb to that of Trisala Rani, the wife of the Rajah Siddhartha. He summoned the chief of the celestial infantry, Harinagamesi (the man with the antelope's head), and ordered him to effect this change. When Harinagamesi had accomplished his mission, he left Trisala lying on a superb couch, in an ornate, perfumed and flower-bedecked setting. In her turn she too saw the sixteen incomparable manifestations one after the other, just as Devananda had done before her.

From that moment Siddhartha was accompanied by good fortune. His wealth in gold, silver, land and crops increased; his army grew in number and strength; his fame and glory radiated in all directions. And so, once the child was born, he decided he would call it Vardhamana, 'he who brings wealth'. On the thirteenth night of the month of *chaitra* the gods and goddesses came down from the sky to celebrate the birth, and the *asuras* showered flowers and fruit on the palace of Siddhartha, and also gold and silver, pearls, diamonds, nectar and sandalwood.

His childhood was distinguished by miracles. One day, when his young companions were running away from a serpent, he started to struggle with it and made it lose consciousness. This incident earned him the title by which he is usually known — that of Mahavira.

For thirty-two years Mahavira led a secular life. He married Yasoda and they had a daughter Priyadarsana. Then his parents, who followed the doctrines of Parsva, decided to leave this world. They lay down on ground strewn with grass and let themselves die of starvation. So Mahavira found himself no longer bound by the promise he had made in his mother's womb never to cause her any pain. He asked his elder brother and authorities in the kingdom permission to become an ascetic; then he gave all his personal goods to the poor.

The gods came down from the sky, approached and paid him homage. A procession formed comprising men, gods and *asuras* all shouting 'Victory! Victory!' The firmament glowed like a lake covered in lotus-flowers; on earth and in the air the most melodious instruments were heard.

Vardhamana spent twelve years in asceticism. Then one day he sat down near an old temple, under a *saka* tree (a teak); for two and a half days he remained motionless, fasting and deep in the most profound meditation. When he arose on the third day the state of illumination was complete. He was in possession

of supreme and absolute knowledge; he was *kevalin* (omniscient), a perfect sage, blessed, an *arhat*, a *jina*.

When after thirty years of preaching he entered Nirvana, the gods went with him and aided him; he became one of the delivered, *mukta*, the perfect, *siddha*.

The swastika

The Jains make the swastika the first of their eight symbols. To them it is the emblematic representation of a perfect being (*siddha*). In fact, the central point (*bindu*) stands for life (*jiva*), and the four branches stand for the four conditions of future life (that is, to become a god, go down to hell, be reborn in human form, and be reborn in the body of a lower animal). But in fact, in the swastika these four branches are bent back and, as it were, closed up, for the *siddha* is free from any rebirth.

Mythology of Buddhism

Gautama Buddha

Gautama Buddha lived between about 563 and 483 B.C. in north-east India.

The future Buddha, or Bodhisattva, had already passed through thousands of existences by way of preparation for his ultimate transmigration: before coming down to earth for the last time, his abode was in the sky of the Tushitas and he preached the law to the gods.

One day he realised that his hour had come and he became incarnate in a member of the family of a king of the Sakyas, Suddhodana, who ruled at Kapila-vastu, on the borders of Nepal.

It was a miraculous conception: Queen Maya (whose name literally means 'illusion') had a presentiment, and dreamed that she saw the Bodhisattva come down into her womb in the form of a beautiful elephant as white as snow. At that moment, entire creation showed its joy in the form of miracles; musical instruments played without being touched, rivers stopped flowing to contemplate the Bodhisattva, trees and plants were covered with flowers and ponds with lotus-flowers. The next day, Queen Maya's dream was interpreted by sixty-four Brahmans; they predicted the birth of a son who was destined to become either a universal emperor or a Buddha.

When the moment of birth approached, the queen went into the garden of Lumbini, and standing there, holding the branch of a *saka* tree in her right hand, she gave birth to the Bodhisattva, who emerged from her right side without causing her the slightest pain. The child was received by Brahma, and the other gods; but he began to walk immediately, and a lotus appeared wherever his foot touched the ground. He took seven paces in the direction of each of the cardinal points, thus taking possession of the world. On the same day the following were also born: Yasodhara Devi, who was to become his wife;

the horse Kantaka, which he was later to ride when he fled from the palace to seek supreme knowledge; his squire, Chandaka; and his friend and favourite disciple, Ananda; as well as the tree of the Bodhi, beneath which he was to receive illumination.

Five days after his birth the young prince received the name of Siddhartha. On the seventh day Queen Maya died of joy, to be born again among the gods, leaving her sister to take her place and look after the young prince. The perfect devotion of this adopted mother has become legendary. A devout old man who came down from the Himalayas, the *rishi* Asita, predicted the destiny of the child, and recognised in him the eighty signs that are the pledges of high religious vocation. When the child was taken to the temple by its parents, the statues of the gods prostrated themselves before him.

When the young prince was in his twelfth year, the king called together the Brahmans in council. They revealed that the prince would devote himself to asceticism if he cast his eyes on the spectacle of old age, sickness and death, and if afterwards he met a hermit. The king, however, preferred the idea of his son becoming a universal monarch to that of his turning ascetic. The sumptuous palace and the vast and beautiful gardens where the young man was destined to live were therefore surrounded by a triple enclosure and guard. And the use of the words 'death' and 'grief' was forbidden.

A little later the king came to the decision that the surest way of forming a bond between the prince and his kingdom was to see that he got married. To discover which princess would awaken his son's love he had some splendid jewels prepared and announced that Siddhartha would share them out among the neighbouring princesses. When all the presents had been distributed a final girl presented herself, young Yasodhara, daughter

of the minister Mahanama. She asked the prince if he had anything for her, and he, meeting her look, took off the precious ring that he wore on his finger and gave it to her. This exchange of glances, and the strange gift had not gone unnoticed by the king; the girl's hand in marriage was sought.

However, the tradition of the Sakyas allowed their princesses to accept as husband only a true Kshatriya of proven ability in all the arts of his caste. Yasodhara's father was somewhat doubtful of Siddhartha, who had been brought up in the cushioned life of the court. So a tournament was organised; the prince emerged as the winner of all swimming, fencing and fighting events. Furthermore, he was the only one who could string and draw the sacred bow, of enormous size, bequeathed by his ancestors. So he received Princess Yasodhara's hand in marriage and his life flowed along from that point amid the pleasures of the women's apartment.

But soon his divine vocation awoke in him. The music of the various instruments ringing in his ears, the gracious movements of the dancers intended to charm his eyes no longer moved him, but proved, on the contrary, the vanity and instability of all objects of desire, and the impermanence of human life. 'The life of a creature passes like the torrent in the mountain and the lightning in the sky.'

One day the prince called his equerry and said that he wanted to visit the town. The king ordered it to be swept and decorated and any ugly or sad sight to be removed from his son's path. But these precautions were of no avail. While he was going round the streets a trembling old man, bent double over his stick, wrinkled and breathless with age, appeared before the prince. In astonishment the young man learned that decrepitude is the common fate of those who live all their life through. Later, he began to wonder if there might be a way of escaping old age.

Queen Maya's dream of the white elephant, the sign that she had conceived a son who would become Buddha. Stone relief. Gandhara style. *British Museum*

Gautama Buddha preaching his first sermon. Beneath him his disciples are shown surrounding a wheel, which was his symbol in earlier iconography when he himself was never depicted. Sandstone. Gupta style. Fifth century. Sarnath Museum.

Prince Siddhartha taking leave of his sleeping wife and harem to follow a life of meditation. Stone relief. Second to third centuries A.D. *British Museum*

Another day he met an incurable invalid in the same way, then a funeral procession, and he learned of suffering and death.

Finally, heaven placed an ascetic in his path—a beggar who told him that he had left the world to pass beyond suffering and joy to attain peace at heart.

All these experiences, confirmed by meditation, awakened in Siddhartha the idea of abandoning his present life and embracing asceticism. He opened his heart to his father: 'Everything in the world, O king, is changing and transitory. Let me go off alone like the religious beggar!'

Grief-stricken at the idea of losing his son in whom reposed the hopes of the royal line, the father had the guard round the walls doubled and he increased the pleasures and distractions so that the young man would abandon all ideas of leaving.

At this point Yasodhara gave birth to Rahula. However, even the tenderness involved in this new tie could not deter the Bodhisattva from his mission.

His decision was made final when he was unable to sleep one night and came upon the dozing harem: lifeless faces, bodies slumped in the involuntary confession of sleep and unconsciousness, artless abandon in the midst of disorder: 'Some slobber and dribble at the mouth; some grind their teeth; others snore and talk in their sleep. Some women have their mouths wide open . . . .' It was like a foretaste of the horrors of the cemetery.

His mind was made up. However, before he left, Siddhartha wanted to look upon his beautiful wife, Yasodhara, once again. She was asleep, holding the newborn child in her arms. He would have liked to kiss his son, but, being afraid of waking the mother, he left them both, and lifting the curtain that was weighted with precious stones, he went out into the cool night with its countless stars and mounted his

steed, Kantaka, accompanied by his equerry, Chandaka.

The gods, acting as his accomplices, put the guards to sleep and raised the horse's feet so that no-one was roused by the noise of horse's hooves. At the gates of the town, Siddhartha handed his horse over to Chandaka and took leave of his two friends, recommending them to console his father; in silent farewell the horse licked his feet.

With one stroke of his sword the prince cut off his hair and threw it into the air, where it was caught by the gods. A little farther on, meeting a huntsman, he gave him his sumptuous robes in exchange for his rags and, thus transformed in appearance, he went to a hermitage where the Brahmans accepted him as a disciple.

Siddhartha had now and for ever disappeared; he had become the monk Gautama, or, as he is still called, Sakyamuni (the ascetic of the Sakyas). He sought in yoga the apprenticeship to wisdom, living in turn in several hermitages, particularly with Arada Kalama; but these doctrines did not teach him what he was looking for. He pursued his wanderings and stopped in the end at Uruvilva, beside a very beautiful river. There he remained alone for six years, practising fearful austerities, which reduced his body to almost nothing at all.

This led him to understand that excessive fasts destroy strength and make the mind powerless instead of liberating it. So it became a question of transcending asceticism, as he had had to transcend earthly life.

And so, at the end of his ordeal, the exhausted Bodhisattva, looking like a skeleton, accepted rice cooked in milk which a young village girl offered him. Sujata, as she was called, was moved to compassion by the sight of his weakness. Then he bathed in the river. The five disciples who had been subjecting themselves to the same austerities abandoned him

Siddhartha, deciding on the life of an ascetic, removes his jewels
and cuts off his hair. Bas-relief from Barabudur, Java. Ninth
century. Musée Guimet. *Goloubew*

then, unable to accept such conduct.

Siddhartha then made for Bodhi-gaya and the tree of wisdom. While he was crossing the forest his body gave off such radiance that kingfishers and other birds were attracted and flew in wide circles around him. Peacocks joined the forest animals to accompany him in procession. The Naga king and his wife left their underground abode to come and worship him. The *devas* hung banners from the trees to show him the path.

And in this way the Bodhisattva reached the sacred fig-tree. It was the decisive moment in his career. He spread out under the tree a handful of newly mown grass and sat down, pronouncing this vow: 'Here, on this seat, may my body wither, may my skin and flesh dissolve, if I rise before I have obtained the intelligence difficult to obtain in the space of numerous *kalpas*.' Then the earth trembled six times.

However, Mara, the Buddhist demon, had been warned of the event that threatened to undermine his power, and he decided to intervene. He sent his three delightful daughters to tempt the Bodhisattva and distract him from his intention. They sang and danced before him. They were skilled in all the magic arts of desire and voluptuousness; but the Bodhisattva remained firm in his intentions and his countenance did not change, but remained as peaceful as a lotus on the calm waters of a pool, as stable as the mountains. The daughters of Mara withdrew, powerless. The demon then tried an attack with his army of devils, horrible beings, some having a thousand mouths, others deformed and with protruding stomachs; they were creatures who drank blood or devoured serpents, uttered inhuman yells, spread darkness and were armed with lances, bows and clubs. They surrounded the tree of wisdom and threatened the Bodhisattva, but their limbs became paralysed and their weapons riveted to their hands.

Then Mara risked an ultimate attempt upon Siddhartha. Riding the clouds, he threw his terrible discus, but this weapon, which was capable of cleaving a mountain in two, was powerless against the Bodhisattva: it was turned into a garland of flowers and remained suspended above his head.

Before sunset Mara had been overcome. And the still motionless Bodhisattva remained in meditation under the sacred tree. When night came, the dawn of illumination that he had sought slowly welled up in his heart. First he knew the exact condition of all beings, then the causes of their rebirths. Throughout the world and at all times he saw beings live, die and transmigrate. He remembered his own previous existences, and then understood the ineluctable chain of cause and effect. Meditating on human pain, he was enlightened about both his genesis and the means of destroying it.

When day came, the Bodhisattva had attained perfect illumination (*bodhi*), he had become a Buddha. The rays emanating from his shining body reached the boundaries of space. For seven days the Buddha remained in meditation; then for four more weeks he stayed by the tree. In the fifth week a terrible storm arose, but King Naga Mucilinda, making him a seat with the folds of his body and a canopy out of his outspread cowl, sheltered him against flood and storm.

From that time on two alternative paths were open to Buddha: he could enter Nirvana immediately or else, renouncing his own deliverance for the moment, he could stay and spread the good word. Mara exhorted him to leave this world, and Buddha himself considered that this was a wise doctrine while men were still disinclined to wisdom. Should the law be proclaimed to those who could not understand it? For one moment he hesitated. But the gods implored him in unison; Brahma in person came to beg him to preach the law, and Buddha yielded to his entreaties.

Buddha sheltering from the storm under the canopy of King Naga Mucilinda. Statue in the Khmer style of Cambodia. Twelfth century. Musée Guimet. *Eliot Elisofon (Time Inc.)*

Buddha practising as an ascetic. Gandhara style. *A.S.I.*

The preaching

But to whom should he address his preaching at first? His thoughts turned to the five disciples who had abandoned him. He went to Benares and found them there. Seeing him in the distance, the hermits said to one another: 'Here comes the *shramana* Gautama, that glutton spoiled by soft living . . . we must have nothing to do with him; we must neither go to meet him respectfully, nor get up . . . . We must not give him either a carpet, or a drink, or yet a place to set his feet.' But Buddha knew their thoughts and directed the force of his love upon them. Just as a leaf is carried away in a gale, so the hermits, overcome by all-powerful goodness, rose to give homage to the man whom they had been the first to follow.

So he preached first at Benares, in the gazelle park. According to texts, when Buddha pronounced his first sermon he 'put in motion the wheel of the law' (*dharma-chakra-pravartana*). The master's first message shows at once what the tone of primitive Buddhist doctrine is to be—entirely lucid, moderate and charitable.

'There are two extremes, O monks, which are to be avoided: a life of pleasure—this is low and ignoble, unworthy and useless and runs counter to the affairs of the spirit; and a life of fasting—this is sad, unworthy and useless. Perfection has kept its distance from these two extremes, O monks, and it has found the middle way, which leads to repose, knowledge, illumination, Nirvana . . . . And here, O monks, is the sacred truth about pain: birth, old age, sickness, death, separation from that which one loves are pain. And this is the origin of pain: it is thirst for pleasure, thirst for existence, thirst for impermanence. And here is the truth about the suppression of pain: it is the extinction of that thirst by the destruction of desire.'

And then again: 'I have come to satisfy the ignorant with wisdom. Charity, knowledge and virtue are possessions that cannot be lost. To do a little good is worth more than accomplishing works of a difficult nature . . . . The perfect man is nothing unless he pours out kindness on his fellow creatures, unless he consoles the abandoned . . . . My doctrine is a doctrine of mercy . . . . The way of salvation is open to all . . . . Destroy your passions as the elephant would trample down a reed hut; but I would have you know that it is a mistaken idea to believe that one can escape from one's passions by taking shelter in hermitages. The only remedy against evil is healthy reality.'

And so Buddha began to travel and preach, and he continued to do so for forty-four years. He covered the whole land, followed by his disciples, converting those who heard him. Many episodes in this long career of religious service have been popularised in both art and legend. Mention will be made in this volume of only some of the principal episodes and anecdotes.

The furious elephant

Devadatta, a cousin of Buddha, was his declared enemy. He made one of the royal elephants intoxicated and let it loose in the streets of the town when Buddha was going round begging alms. Terror-stricken, the town's people fled; the animal trampled down vehicles, passers-by and houses. Buddha's disciples begged him to take shelter. But he went calmly on his way. However, when a little girl blindly crossed the street, and was almost killed by the delirious animal, Buddha spoke to it in these words: 'Spare this innocent child. It is I you have been sent to attack.' As soon as the elephant caught sight of Buddha, his fury abated as if by magic, and he came to kneel at the feet of the Blessed.

The churning of the sea: devas and asuras use the body of
the snake Vasuki to churn up the sea and so extract the 'Amrita'.
Hindu miniature. Eighteenth century. *Museé Guimet*

Buddhist fresco of the genius of war. Ming. South China. *Giraudon*

The great miracle of Sravasti

King Prasenajit had organised a tournament between the Buddha and the members of a heretic sect that he was trying to convert. Sakyamuni accomplished numerous miracles in the course of this contest of miraculous powers. Two of them have remained famous. The first is known by the name of the miracle of water and fire. 'Bhagavat (the Blessed) entered into such deep meditation that his spirit was immediately set free; he disappeared from the spot where he was sitting and, throwing himself into the air towards the west, he appeared there in the four attitudes of decency, that is to say he walked, stood up, sat down and lay down. Then he reached the region of light, and no sooner had he got there than various lights radiated from his body. Some were blue, yellow, red and white, and others were the finest hues found in pure crystal. He also demonstrated numerous miracles; from the lower part of his body spurted flames, and from the upper part issued forth cold showers of rain. What he had done in the west, he also performed in the south; he repeated it at the four points of the compass.'

In the second episode the Buddha is seen sitting on a large lotus-flower with a diamond stem made up of the Naga kings; Brahma is on the right of Buddha and Indra is on his left. By a miracle of omnipotence Buddha produces an infinite number of similar lotus-flowers all over the sky with a Buddha like himself seated in the centre of each.

The conversion of Buddha's family

One by one Buddha converted his father, King Suddhodana, his son, Rahula, his cousin Ananda, who became his chosen disciple, his wife and his adopted mother, the good Mahaprajapati. Buddha also went up into the sky, where he was welcomed by his mother, together with the gods, who asked him to teach his law. When, three months later, this mission was over the Blessed came back to earth by way of a gold and silver ladder, with coral, ruby and emerald rungs. And the gods formed a procession around him.

The laborious conversion of Nanda, Buddha's half-brother, introduces a very human note, poignant and comic at one and the same time. The young man had just married the most beautiful woman in the land. The Blessed presented himself at his gate. Nanda filled the alms' bowl, but Buddha refused to take it and departed. Nanda followed him, still holding out the bowl, but receiving no word or gesture in reply. They came to the hermitage. Buddha, smiling mysteriously, had his brother's head shaved and forced him to put off his sumptuous robes and adopt a monk's habit.

Poor Nanda submitted to it; however, the charming memory of his young wife continued to haunt him. One day he tried to escape, but miraculous powers prevented him. Then Sakyamuni took him to a hill-side and there they saw an old blind monkey: 'Is your wife as beautiful as this monkey?' Buddha asked Nanda. The young husband's indignation knew no bounds, till finally the Blessed took him to the heaven of the thirty-three gods, to a superb palace inhabited by divine nymphs of incomparable beauty; of course his wife was but a monkey compared to these. The nymphs revealed to Nanda that he was destined to become their lord and master after his death.

Once back in the monastery he became the most zealous of disciples, in the hope of being born again in the heaven of the thirty-three gods. But some time later, the Buddha took him to hell, and showed him the cauldron of boiling water into which he must fall after his celestial existence was over by way of expiation for his sensual desires. These successive visions led Nanda to meditate on the doctrine, and he became a saint.

The child's offering

A little child wanted to make Buddha an offering, but had no worldly possessions. He naïvely collected some dust and, putting together his open palms, he presented it to the blessed. Moved by this gesture of faith Buddha accepted it with a smile. Later this ingenuous child was to be reborn in the shape of the great Indian emperor Asoka.

The monkey's offering

A monkey offered Buddha a bowl of honey. Overjoyed at having his present accepted, he took such a leap that he fell and killed himself instantaneously. Immediately he was reborn as the son of a Brahman.

Buddha's death

By the time he reached the age of eighty, Buddha began to feel old; he visited all the monasteries that he had founded, ordained the religious community and prepared to meet his end. He died at Kusinagara after eating some indigestible dish at the home of one of his disciples, a blacksmith by trade.

He slowly and gently expired on the banks of the river Hiranyavati, in a thicket where Ananda had prepared his couch. All around him the trees were covered in blossom. The *gandharvas* created celestial harmonies. The disciples surrounded their master in his last agony; some wept in spite of his exhortations: 'Do not say: we have no master now .... The doctrine that I have preached will be your master when I have disappeared. Listen, *bhikkus*, I beg you: all creations are impermanent, work diligently for your liberation.' Having pronounced these final words, Buddha went into meditation, then into ecstasy and finally passed into Nirvana. His body was burned on a pyre, which caught fire of its own accord and went out at the desired moment, thanks to a miraculous shower of rain. The relics of the Blessed were conserved in *stupas* (domed mounds), which arose soon afterwards on Indian soil.

Portraits and sculpture of the Buddha Gautama

In the beginning Indian artists abstained from giving their own interpretation of the features of the Blessed, who was symbolised by an empty throne or a sun wheel. When the idea was conceived of depicting him in some plastic form, they had recourse to a Greek type: Western sculptors who had settled in Bactria made him look like Apollo.

Then Indians came to portray him in their own terms, following the master's biography. Buddha had to be a monk; Bodhisattva, a prince. In both cases the same royal and divine type must be portrayed (the gods being kings of the sky, and the kings gods of the earth), but in the case of the Buddha, the signs of temporal power and opulence were removed. Both have a lenticular mark between the eyebrows (*urna*), the symbol of a luminous and radiant tuft of hair; but the Buddha has a cranial protuberance (*ushisha*), which is depicted in the shape of a turban covering a chignon. The attitudes of the body, *asanas*, express the type and degree of meditation; the gestures of the hands, *mudras*, complete this expression or indicate the completed action.

Buddha's previous lives

If, however, Sakyamuni deserved to become Buddha, it is because of all the virtues that he evinced in his earlier lives. The accounts of these lives are known as Jatakas, and they hold an important place in Buddhist mythology. These *Jatakas* also have a dogmatic value in that the deeds show, in the material world, that causal connection which according to Buddhist philosophy forms the structure of things: any event in present time can be explained by facts going farther and farther back in the past. Thus the law of *karma* is justified, by virtue of which each being, and, in particular, the Bodhisattva, becomes what he makes of himself. Here are a few examples:

At one time the Bodhisattva was a monkey-king. One day when he was sporting in a mango grove with a procession of eighty thousand subjects, archers were ordered to aim at the monkeys and kill them. The only way the poor creatures could escape was by crossing the Ganges.

The monkey-king fastened one end of a bamboo cord to the branch of a tree and the other end to his belt and then he took one gigantic leap across the river; but the cord was too short, and the only way he could make contact with the other bank was by hanging on to a tree. The eighty thousand monkeys filed across this bridge and their lives were saved.

But Devadatta, Buddha's future cousin, was among the troop of fugitives; already acting in a treacherous fashion, he pretended to stumble and suddenly fell on top of the monkey-king, breaking his spine as he did so. The heroic monkey was received by the king of Benares and died an exemplary death after giving his host some salutary advice about the way to govern his kingdom.

One of the principal Buddhist virtues is endless compassion for all creatures.

To test the charity and fairness of the king of the Sibis, Indra turned into a falcon pursuing a dove (which was itself only the metamorphosis of another god).

The dove took refuge in the king's bosom. 'Do not be afraid,' the king said, 'beautiful bird whose eye is like the flower of the *asoka* tree; I save all living beings that have recourse to my protection, even if I have to give up my kingdom and even my life itself.'

But the falcon took him at his word: 'This dove,' he said, 'is my food. By what right do you deprive me of the prey that I have exerted every effort to conquer? I am dying of hunger; you have no right to interfere in quarrels between birds of the air. If you are thinking of protecting the dove, just think of me dying of hunger; if you refuse to hand over the cherished bird to me, then give me its weight in your own flesh.' 'You are right,' the king of the Sibis replied. 'Bring me some scales!' And cutting off some flesh from his thigh, he threw it in one of the scale pans, having placed the bird in the other. The queen, ministers and servants uttered loud laments, which rose from the palace at the same time as the sound of thunder came from the gathered clouds. The very earth trembled at this act of fairness.

But the king went on cutting flesh from his legs, his arms, his chest; it made no difference—the bird was still heavier. This went on until the king was no more than a skeleton, and then he decided to surrender himself entirely, and got on to the scales.

Then the gods appeared and celestial music was heard. A shower of ambrosia fell on the king's body and completely cured it. Flowers rained down from the sky, and the *gandharvas* and the *apsaras* sang and danced. Reverting to his divine shape, Indra told the king of the Sibis that his next reincarnation would be in the body of the future Buddha.

Other Characters

Just as the *tirthamkara* of our own period had numerous predecessors in the eyes of the Jains, so in the eyes of Buddhists Gautama Buddha was preceded by various other Buddhas. The most ancient to have been handed down is the name of Dipamkara. In the course of an earlier existence our Buddha offered him flowers, and in return received from him the announcement of his own mission. The legend of this distant predecessor more or less provides a link between the two etymologies of his name—*dvipa*, island, or *dipa*, lamp—the connection being the idea of a luminous manifestation in the middle of the waters, of a diety who protects sailors, especially in the 'Islands of the South'.

The age to which we ourselves belong has known six Blesseds prior to the sage of the Sakyas: Vipasyin, Sikhin, Visvabhu, Krakuchanda, Kanakamuni, and Kasyapa. An eighth is expected, who is as yet at the stage of the Bodhisattva: Maitreya. These successive masters form the series of 'human' Buddhas (*manusi*).

The meditation Buddhas (Dhyani-Buddhas), on the other hand, are more the equivalent of metaphysical essences. They are five in number:

Vairocana, whose colour is white, has as his emblem the discus and he rides on a dragon. The Japanese Shingon sect devoted themselves to his worship.

Ratnasambhava is yellow and wears a jewel. Riding his horse, he rules the south.

Amitabha (infinite light) or Amitayus (infinite time) is red, has a lotus-flower and is escorted by a peacock. He reigns over the west, where he presides over a marvellous paradise, Sukhavati. All those who believe in him will be born again in this abode of happiness, before obtaining supreme deliverance.

Amoghasiddhi is green, the bearer of a double thunderbolt, which he carries on an eagle; his region is the north.

Aksobhya is blue; he is provided with a thunderbolt and rides an elephant; his province is the east.

The Dhyani-Bodhisattvas

From the Dhyani-Buddhas' meditation emanate Dhyani-Bodhisattvas: Samantabhadra, Vajrapani, Ratnapani, Avalokitesvara, Visvapani.

Samantabhadra, one of the most familiar members of Sakyamuni's retinue in Mahayanist texts, has the general appearance of a god of action and symbolises happiness. He is green in colour and is seen riding an elephant. His cult developed in particular in O-mei-chan and Nepal.

Vajrapani, bearer of the thunderbolt, was originally a *yakshi*, a faithful companion, Sakyamuni's replica. His importance to Mahayanist Buddhism lies in his being 'the Bodhisattva of kindly or furious countenance', the ideal in the eyes of the faithful, but a figure of terror to the impious.

Avalokitesvara, the lord endowed with complete illumination, who none the less remained here below

to save the creatures of the earth, is first and foremost
the merciful. He is also called Padmapani, and holds
a pink lotus-flower; as evidence that he originates in
Amitabha he wears this effigy in his hair. No sufferer
ever implores him in vain. As there is no shortage of
work for him in this wretched world, his thousand
arms are not too many. The *Karandavyuha* describes
his charitable peregrinations, either taking refresh-
ment to the damned in hell, converting the ogresses
(*rakshasi*) in Ceylon or preaching the law to creatures
embodied as insects and worms in Benares. So,
although his normal residence is the paradise of
Amitabha, his chosen abode is the world of suffering,
which he prefers to the peace of Nirvana.

A very strange transformation of this Bodhisattva
took place in China: as if in honour of his powers of
love, the Chinese portrayed him as a feminine type,
like the goddess Kuan-Yin (Kwannon) who carries a
child in her arms and oddly resembles the Virgin
Mary holding her Holy Son. In contrast to this concrete effigy, India sees this sympathetic saviour as a
cosmic being, who takes countless shapes:

'From his eyes come forth the sun and the moon;
from his brow, Mahesvara; from his shoulders,
Brahma and other gods; from his heart, Narayana;
from his thighs, Sarasvati; from his mouth, the winds;
from his feet, the earth; from his stomach, Varuna....
He is a lamp to the blind, a parasol for those devoured
by the heat of the sun, a stream to the thirsty; he
takes away all fear from those who are afraid of some
danger; he is a doctor to the sick; he is a father and
mother to the unhappy.'

Other Bodhisattvas

According to legend the Manjusri or Manjughosa
Bodhisattva was of Chinese origin; at least the Hindus
thought of him in the time of Itsing as living in
China, and he was a special object of worship at the
convent of Wu-t'ai-shan (*Shansi*). This name is
simply a translation of the Sanskrit *Panchasikha* or
Panchashirsha, the mountain with five summits, which
was most certainly Indian, and where a certain
Kumara-bhuta, one of whose surnames was Manjusri, would appear to have achieved sanctity. The
Svayambhu-purnana makes this Bodhisattva the patron
of grammatical knowledge and wisdom. He is portrayed in yellow, seated on a blue lion with a red jaw,
in the attitude of a teacher with a blue lotus-flower in
his hand; he often has the sword of knowledge as well
as a book by him.

Maitreya, the Buddha of the future, is still living in
the Tushita sky from which the Sakyamuni came
down in earlier times. A disciple of the latter, Kasyapa, who already possesses Nirvana, remains inside
Mount Kukkutapada until such time as he must give
the future Buddha his predecessor's robe, which has
been carefully preserved. Maitreya is portrayed in
gold and he has a great part to play.

Kshitigarbha, who is little worshipped in India, but

Tara, the *sakti* of Avalokitesvara. She was born of his tears and represents mercy. Gilt copper. Nepal. *Victoria and Albert Museum*

Matrika-devi, a Buddhist mother-goddess. Stone image from South India. Ninth century. *British Museum*

who has effigies scattered all over central Asia, plays the part of an eschatological god. He governs and supervises the six paths *(gati)* that are taken by the souls of living creatures once they have been judged: these are the six fates as accorded to man, *asura*, demon, god, animal and the damned. The paintings at Tun-huang show ten kings of hell revolving about him. This is a reflection of the mythical cosmography of Buddhism, which also appears in the inclusion of four guardians of the cardinal points, the Lokapalas, complete in their armour.

The goddesses

Just like the gods of Hinduism, the Buddhas too have their *saktis*, who take the form of goddesses and for the benefit of mankind dispense supramental knowledge *(prajna)* or compassion *(karuna)*, while the sages accompanying them furnish the path to salvation *(upaya)*.

The most highly revered is Tara, who shares the cult dedicated to Avalokitesvara, at least in Tibetan Tantrism. She originated from his tears. When red, yellow and blue she is in menacing mood; white or green she is gentle and loving: this is the same twofold nature as Siva's wife.

This sort of feminine Bodhisattva is one of those Vidya-devis or Matrika-devis (goddesses of knowledge or mother-goddesses) the list of whom includes: Bhrikuti Tara, a special form of the one mentioned above; Kurukulla, who is represented in a reddish shade, seated in a cave, with four arms, the upper pair of arms extended in a threatening gesture, and the lower pair in appeasement.

Another is Kunda, of whom the Tibetan Taranatha tells a story: 'It was lucky for the son of the tree-spirit and the beautiful Kshatriya that they chose Kunda as their patroness, since with her aid he killed the wicked queen in whose bed each night a new king of

Bengal met his death.' Kunda has either four or sixteen arms. Her kindly appearance is in contrast to her emblems, which form a threatening collection. Thunderbolt, discus, club, sword, bow, arrow, axe, trident, and so on—there is nothing missing in this military arsenal; but at the same time, for the faithful who can see it, her first pair of hands is in a teaching pose, another in that of charity, other hands hold the string of prayer beads, the gold lotus-flower, the flagon of ambrosia; and that is undoubtedly how this strange deity comes to be as propitious to those who are good as she is terrible to the wicked.

The last is Marichi, the ray of dawn, the Buddhist Ushas, who has an eye in her forehead and sometimes presents a terrible appearance with three grimacing faces and ten threatening arms. Included among the Saktis of the Manushi-Buddhas is Sarasvati, a companion of Manjusri and the goddess of instruction.

At the summit of this female pantheon Prajna holds sway; she is knowledge, corresponding to the supreme abstract male figure, Adi-Buddha, the essence of all the Buddhas.

In contrast to this serenity, Hariti should be quoted, the nurse and mother to five hundred demons. She is associated with a spirit of opulence, Panchika; her wealth is fertility.

Various other characters

In Buddhism secondary characters are also found, both in texts and iconography, who seem hideous, terrifying or ridiculous to our Western eyes, but who hold rich symbolic significance for the faithful. To take an example, one might quote: Yamantaka, Manjusri's companion, who wears a necklet of skulls; Trailokyavija, with four heads and eight threatening arms, who stands on Siva's head; Jambhala, who is outrageously corpulent and brandishes a lemon and a mangosteen.

Tribal Mythologies of Central India

Head of a woman worshipper found at Hadda (Afghanistan). Gandhara school. Fourth to fifth centuries. *Musée Guimet*

The mythology of the central Indian populations, which are not within the caste system, is as rich as it is imperfectly appreciated. As far as purely mythological studies are concerned, like all tribal literature, it simply occupies the position of a poor relation standing outside the classical tradition. Usually this literature is taken to be a mere accumulation of tales, arising more or less directly out of Brahmanic and Pouranic epics. When, as in the case of the Gond tribes, which include more than three million individuals living between Narbada, Godaveri and the eastern coast, a relatively glorious historic past can be proved, present-day political decay deals a fatal blow to the appreciation of the culture and traditions of these tribes.

The wealth and importance of tribal mythologies can be deduced from monographs in which the social organisation, religious life and economic position of a tribe are viewed simultaneously. One of the monographs that the English reader might appreciate is that which V. Elwin devotes to the Muria under the title *The Muria and their Ghotul;* this provides an excellent introduction to these mythologies by showing how alive they are today, as well as how important they are in the social and religious life of the populations concerned.

These tribal mythologies have a twofold nature: they are profoundly original and are a highly integrated part of the Indian world to which they belong. This is best shown, on the one hand, by the traditions relating to the origin of the world and of humanity and, on the other hand, by the cycle of Lingal, the hero who civilised the Gonds.

Here is the story of the creation of the world, as told by the Birhors (according to the version of S. C. Roy). This tale is characteristic of a tradition in which the creation of the world is unique and simple:

In the beginning nothing existed but the waters and a lotus with its head above water. Singbonga, the supreme spirit, lived in the lower regions. He came up to the surface of the waters by way of the hollow stem of the lotus and sat down on the lotus-flower.

Then Singbonga decided to create the earth. He ordered the tortoise to seek him out some mud at the bottom of the ocean. But the tortoise failed in this undertaking, and then the crab failed likewise. Finally, the leech dived down, swallowed some mud, surfaced and disgorged the mud into Singbonga's hand. Then, on the surface of the water, Singbonga formed a continent bordered on its four sides by four seas. Then he sowed seeds, and trees grew.

After this came the long and difficult creation of man: Singbonga created the winged horse first of all and then fashioned a clay figurine in the shape of a man. But under cover of darkness the winged horse, who was afraid of the future supremacy of the being embodied in the figurine, trampled on it before it was dry. Singbonga had to set to work again, but this time he prepared a dog as well as a man. The dog dried out first and protected the man from the jealousy of the winged horse. However, this creation was not perfect: the man had been made in one single piece, and without articulation he was incapable of sitting down or walking. Singbonga therefore made him lifeless again, gave him articulation and then brought him back to life, thus creating man in his present form.

Another tradition regarding the origin of the world and man is given by the Bison-Horn Marias who have been studied by W. Grigson:

One world had been created and destroyed by floods. A brother and sister were spared in the disaster, for they found refuge in a calabash. When the waters receded they came out. Several incidents were then introduced into the story involving Mahapurub, the supreme beings, various animals

Right: detail from Stupa I at Sanchi showing an apsara. *Goloubew*

North gate of Stupa I at Sanchi, showing recurring patterns and rich decoration typical of Indian architecture. Third century A.D. *Dept. of Archaeology, Gov. Of India*

and the brother and sister mentioned above, and finally the subject of man's food-stuffs and agricultural techniques crept in. Then the question arose of the propagation of the human species; the two children could not marry for they were brother and sister. A goddess gave them smallpox and separated them for a time. When they met again it was not as brother and sister, but as husband and wife. They then produced the first twelve boys and the first twelve girls.

This tradition is found elsewhere, for instance among the Gonds and the Saora of Orissa. V. Elwin had devoted a monograph to the latter and very many myths are recounted in it.

Other tribes have an interesting variation on the theme of the destruction of the first world that was ever created: thus the Agarias, blacksmiths scattered over central India, tell how a war with the sun brought about the destruction of the world by fire, and only one woman, who had taken refuge with her neighbours, the Gonds, managed to escape.

In all myths there are numerous references, allusions and details for which epics are responsible. The Birhors, who were mentioned above, tell the tale of the search made by Rama and Lakshmana for Sita who had been abducted by Ravana, the king of Lanka. In the course of the peregrinations, an important number of stories of a causal nature are told. In this way they provide justification for various things —the shape of the leaves of the jujube bush and the tamarind-tree, the shape of the stork's neck, and the fact that baboons have tails. At the same time, and this happens very often, kindred relationships are revealed which give the tribe a place in the history of the myth: Hanuman, the baboon, in this tale has an old Birhor as his maternal uncle.

But the five Pandavas, and sometimes their mother too, as in the case of the Gonds in the district of

Three celestial dancers carved in low relief on a pilaster at Angkor Wat. The last development of this temple came when Buddhism became the official religion of the Khmer empire in the mid-twelfth century. These dancers are in the Bayon style, which grew up after that date and is the final style of Angkor Wat
Almasy

Mandla (ex-Central Provinces), are the heroes of several adventures. An indigenous god of rain has most certainly been identified with the second of the Pandavas, the powerful Bhima: Bhima or alternatively Bhimsen, or Bhimul Pen, is god of rain, and is sometimes associated with Lingal. For instance, the Pardhans, who are bards of the Gonds throughout central India, believe that these two gods are twin brothers who emerged from eggs laid by a female vulture. Similarly, the Maria of Bastar believe that they are both responsible for rain.

Lingal is certainly the most interesting figure among the mythical heroes of the Gonds.

The first mythological cycle centred on Lingal was published in 1866, and was collected by S. Hislop in the region of Nagpur. Later on, other myths with Lingal as protagonist were discovered among the Gonds, although the same importance is not attached to him by all tribes, nor do they all see him in the same light. The Raj-Gonds, who have been mentioned earlier, have a very similar cycle to that of Nagpur which gives evidence of the hero's vitality.

The Pardhans recite a very long myth in which, starting from the creation of the world, they tell of the birth of the Gond gods and the adventures of their mother, who abandoned them in a forest. Mahadeo and his wife, Parvati, took them in and gave them nourishment. But the Gonds behaved appallingly: in the presence of Marath and Telugu gods they refused to eat the dishes Mahadeo had prepared and demanded meat and alcohol. So Mahadeo imprisoned them in a cave for twelve years. Eventually Lingal set them free with the aid of a goddess. Lingal was a younger son, who had first been driven away from home by his parents before the throne was ultimately entrusted to him by his father. He was a musician and a pious man, and with his guitar he set off to look for his gods. After a long search he found them, and they recognised him by the music he played. After he had set them free he took them to a place where they could build themselves homes. He divided them into clans and taught them the rules

of marriage. Finally, he gave them the cult of clan deities. On the way to this settlement they had to cross a river in full spate, and the youngest gods were saved only by the intervention of an animal, the monkey, with which they established close bonds of friendship and alliance. This tale of the river-crossing is very common in central India; it takes many forms, but the totem animal is usually a tortoise.

So Lingal appears as a hero who spread civilisation, and understood the language of birds and taught men techniques and rites. He was also a younger brother, and this feature is found elsewhere in other myths about him. In Bastar, among the Maria, and in the region of Betul (west of the former Central Provinces), the hostility felt for him by his elder brothers is the source of all his misfortunes. His sisters-in-law, whom he scorns, preferring the company of village girls, accuse him of misconduct in front of their husbands. Only after he has submitted to the ordeal of boiling oil can Lingal convince them of his virtue. In the opinion of V. Elwin, the character of Lingal is inseparable from the institution of the *ghotul*, the place that houses the young and unmarried, that can still be found in certain villages. In point of fact, in several tales Lingal establishes these houses and leads the dancing there. In his capacity of younger brother, Lingal is connected with the heroes of numerous myths or stories of the Santals and Mundas—stories of the Tom Thumb type—in which the heroes are both superior to their elders and the victims of their tyranny.

This incursion into tribal mythologies aims to bring out their richness, and especially to show that it is certainly much less interesting to trace the Hindu influences (such as Lingal's celibacy and austerity) than to try and replace them in their proper context; they should not be separated from the rites that are sometimes connected with them, or from the social organisation of the tribes involved. They are living mythologies and, because of this, cannot be considered merely as residue or as uninteresting evidence of traditions that they mirror and distort.

Mythology
of the Tamils

A Dravidian representation of Vishnu. *Collection C.T. Loo*

In spite of all the efforts made by the Brahmans who come from northern India to annex Tamil civilisation —efforts which they are still continuing to make—it remains profoundly original and is still on its native soil, the extreme south of the Indian peninsula. During the Middle Ages it unquestionably bore increasing traces of Brahman influence, but this was part of the general process of Sanskritisation which is the predominant feature of Indian history; but the ancient traditions not only remain alive in themselves, in texts and in folk-lore, but they are often recognisable even in the travesties that have been imposed on them.

The most ancient documents in Tamil literature, the poems in the Sangam cycle, which may date from the second or third century A.D., portray a race quite detached from religious preoccupations, a realistic people inclined towards an existential philosophy of living; they know something of the myths of northern India, but only from a distance and without seeming to believe in them. Tamil beliefs at the time of Sangam seem very different from those of Brahmanism, and, to be more precise, they seem to be of a totally different order. In fact traditions among them, even when they appear in a legendary form, are about men rather than supernatural creatures; in this instance, although myth may introduce an element of the marvellous, it really aims at constructing a concrete secular history, consisting of political and literary events presented as such. In a manner of speaking this way of thought runs counter to that of Brahmanism: instead of generalising, transposing and making sublime, the aim is to localise and keep accurate, in short to keep one's feet on the ground.

From the very beginning this is evident, even in the story of the Sangam, or literary academies of southern India: the first Sangam, we are told, lasted 4,400 years and crowned 4,449 poets; the second Sangam rewarded 3,700 poets in 3,700 years; and the third, which sat at Madurai, lasted 1,850 years and awarded prizes to 449 poets. All this seems to be of a mythical nature for, as regards the first two Sangam, there is

no means of verification, no works remain, and everything points to the fact that this is merely speculation about the political and literary history of a very distant past. We possess a few rather vague historical facts about the third or last Sangam, in particular anthologies of poems associated with it have been preserved, but the biography of their authors remains shrouded in mystery.

Mention should, however, be made of allusions to floods and to certain regions being engulfed by the waters of the ocean. For instance, the capital of the second Sangam, Kavadapuram, which is also quoted in the Sanskrit *Ramayana*, was in one of the submerged areas. Poets and commentators name geographical sites and watercourses which suffered the same fate. The problem in such cases is to decide what is history and what is myth. The striking thing, in any case, is that the Tamils go back, not to the beginning of time, but to given dates, which are relatively recent by comparison with the speculations of the Brahmans, which make one's mind reel; and it is also remarkable that they are concerned, not with the creation of the world, but with the start of their own civilisation; the circumstantial details given are quite disquieting at times, and give the impression that this is really historic and not legendary.

This question arises, for example, with regard to the great figure of Agastya. In point of fact this civilisation in the south of India is well aware of its debt to the north, the influence of which is undeniable; but tradition has personified this contribution in the form of an ascetic scholar called Agastya: he is not a god (although his image is worshipped in many places), and he is hardly a hero; above all they are intent on presenting him as a historical character who instructed the Tamils in Brahmanic spheres of knowledge. He had come, it was said, from the north, and had settled as a hermit at the top of Mount Podiyam, not far from Kodaikkanal; he was very small in stature; he would appear to have written a grammar, which is now lost, but which is said to be the source of all later Tamil grammars. His disciples

Subrahmanya, a favourite Tamil god. Tempera and water colour. South India. c. 1820. *Victoria and Albert Museum*

Kali with her foot on Siva. Her influence can be found all over India, and in Tamil country she becomes Kottavei. *Victoria and Albert Museum*

were twelve grammarians, and in addition a few doctors, for he was very knowledgeable on all subjects. One of the twelve, Tolkappiyar, seems to have been the author of the oldest Tamil grammar to be handed down, called *Tolkappiyam*; the text that we have of it seems to date from the early centuries of the Christian era, but tradition endows it with great antiquity and considers it to be in the nature of a work of revelation.

The same is true of numerous episodes in literary life at the period of the Sangam, as depicted by tradition. The great poets, such as Nakkirar, who presided over the Sangam at a given moment (unspecified), and Auveiyar, the poetess associated with a great number of moral maxims, or Tiruvalluvars, the author of a collection of moral couplets called the *Koural,* one of the greatest books of Indian wisdom, are all writers and figures of legend, and the picturesque details of their lives, which are the basis of popular culture in Tamil districts, are closely interwoven with the miraculous.

A few examples can be given. First the academy banquet at Madurai. One day the poets Kabilar, Nakkirar and Parana asked the local god of Madurai to take up residence where all the members of the academy could have a seat. The god granted them one tiny seat, which had room for only one person. The poets were astonished; but a celestial voice told them: 'This seat will recognise poets worthy of the name and will keep a place for them.' So they carried the plank to their assembly place and Nakkirar was the first to take his seat on it. Immediately the plank grew longer, and a second place appeared. Kabilar took it, and again the seat grew; Parana took his place, and so on, until all the good poets were seated.

Now when Tiruvalluvar had finished his *Koural*, which was in thirteen hundred couplets, he left for Madurai with his manuscript on his head to submit to the academy. On the way he met the good old woman Auveiyar, who asked him what was the great burden that he carried on his head; he told her that it was the sum total of virtue, silver and love; thereupon Auveiyar, with extraordinary insight, understood the meaning of the whole work, and summed it up perfectly in a single stanza. Then she decided to accompany the poet to Madurai. He himself was feeling somewhat apprehensive, for he was of humble origin and belonged to the caste of weavers. In fact he was haughtily received by the established poets of the academy. They were seated on their bench, which was then floating on the sacred pool of Madurai, and told the weaver merely to place his manuscript on the end of the plank, adding that they would soon decide what should be done with it. But then, to everyone's surprise, the bench contracted, throwing the academicians into the water, and in the end it had nothing on it but the precious manuscript. The members accepted the lesson implicit in the soaking they had received, and acknowledged the divine perfection of the work, and each of them composed a panegyric to it; this collection of stanzas now serves as a preface to the *Koural*.

However, the remote period of the Sangam is not the only time when poets were the object of a kind of golden legend. More recently, in the time of the great Sivaist and Vishnuist religious poets (between the seventh and eleventh centuries), miracles have been attributed to poet-saints; there is a profusion of biographies enriched with miraculous episodes. And the Tamil *Pouranas*, unlike the Sanskrit *Pouranas*, are usually the concern of authors whose historical existence seems likely, although the imagination has been allowed to run wild in this regard. The great Sivaist poets, Appan, Sambandan and Sundaran, have their statues in temples and, in addition, comparatively conventional effigies of them are found in great number in entrance halls everywhere: these bronze statuettes, which are rather stiff and yet have considerable grace in many cases, are fairly often found in Western museums. In short, the emphasis is always on the world of letters and the literary creator who is worshipped for his work, and this work is appreciated first and foremost for its moral teaching and for the life it recounts with many embellishments. In this respect, the other southern lands do not lag far behind: the hagiography of poets is very highly developed in the nearby Dravidian literatures, particularly in Telegur and Kannara.

Mythical creative activity continues today: relatively recent events, for instance the presence of Europeans, give rise to legends which are illustrated by popular imagery and even by paintings in temples, at Madurai or Chidambaram, for example. Here the cinema makes some contribution; mythological films, having recourse to miracles that are easy to put on the screen, are most successful of all in the Tamil part of the world.

But apart from very special aspects of Tamil mythology, account must be taken of Brahman traditions, which have become widespread. Most of the great Sanskrit texts have been translated into Tamil or adapted. Gods such as Siva and his wife, Parvati, are well known to the Tamils. However, here too it is noticeable that adaptations are often fairly free with variations, which are either somewhat exceptional or unknown elsewhere. Moreover, in spite of assimilations, which Brahmanistic centres insisted on making, one often suspects local folk-lore of being responsible for the variations, since it is to be found behind the official orthodoxy. Thus the legend of Parvati as told at Madurai has some fairly original features.

Finally, Tamil country has its favourite gods. For example, the god Murugan, who is identified with Subrahmaniyan, does not, in fact, represent quite what he does to other Hindus: here he is a predominant power in mountain districts, he is more alive, better portrayed and a favourite figure in popular imagery. He is a handsome, fresh-cheeked young man who rides a peacock; he is surrounded by fairies, daughters of the mountain. In the same pantheon there is Kottavei, the sinister sorceress, goddess of war, who feeds on carnage. It will probably suffice to say that Kottavei is none other than Kali. There is a reason for identifying the gods in this way. Kottavei has more than one feature that compares with those of Kali. Similarly, one wonders about the meaning of Kumari, the virgin, after whom Cape Comorin was named; she is worshipped by young girls, who run races on the beaches of southern India in her honour. The 'girl' Kanyakumari in the Brahmanic pantheon also gives rise to conjecture, as does Valli, 'the climbing plant', who might perhaps be called her first cousin.

Local traditions can be run to earth in every district of southern India; each sanctuary has its history; the big towns, Madurai, for example, all have their own legend explaining how they came into being; this is all illustrated in prints, particularly in holy books, in patterns on cloth and in bas-reliefs. Thus, in the Madurai legend, Princess Tadatagei, of irresistible strength, is portrayed as a redoubtable virago, unbeatable in knowledge and war; she was said to have been born with three breasts, and on the day on which she met the man in her life, her third breast fell off as had been predicted; this man was called Somasundara, but in fact he was one of Siva's avatars. She married him, and the wedding banquet proved to be an exceptional affair because of a picturesque incident involving Kundodharan, the gnome, a little chap with a round stomach, who was furious at not being invited and who appeared at the banquet with an insatiable appetite. It was useless to try to satisfy him; when the food was finished he gulped down all sorts of objects, absolutely everything he could lay hands on; the whole world was in danger, until Siva responded to urgent pleas and created the hole of abundance to appease the little man's hunger, and the River Vaigai (which runs by Madurai) to quench his thirst.

Even from this very brief sketch it is possible to conclude that the Tamils have their own mythology, besides knowing that of classical Brahmanism. They are familiar with *Maha-bharata* and *Ramayana*, like all the races in the Hindu world. For example, Kambar's version of the *Ramayana* is one of the great works of Tamil literature. For them, as for all Hindus, Sita is the model of all the feminine virtues, the perfect wife. Though they share in the national patrimony of India and honour the same moral values, yet it has to be realised that this is the result of convergence and synthesis that took place in the course of history, and that at the outset they were profoundly different.

Rubbings from stone engravings in the tombs of the U family in the province of Shantung, second century A.D. (Han period). The first register shows a meeting between two personages, one reclining and protected by a large shield, the other armed with a bow and followed by two officers. The second shows the attempt by Ching K'o to assassinate the King of Ch'in, who later became the first emperor of the Ch'in dynasty. In the third are two demons, or perhaps legendary sovereigns. To the right is Fu-Hsi, with his set-square; to the left is Nu-kua, with her compasses. Fu-Hsi, whose surname was Tsang-tsing, 'source of vegetation', was the first being to exercise sovereignty. According to an inscription beneath this engraving he set out the 'trigrams' and knotted ropes in such a way as to assure good government of the lands enclosed by the sea. The trigram was a variable pattern of three parallel lines, some unbroken – representing the male principle – and some broken – representing the female principle. In an arrangement of eight trigrams, Fu-Hsi laid down the precepts which were to govern all human relationships, including matrimony. The other figures in this scene symbolise in form and colour the essence of the diverse forms of life on earth and in the heavens. (After Chavannes (ed.) *La Sculpture sur pierre en Chine au temps des deux dynasties Han*, Pl. XXIV. Paris, 1893.)

CHINA: THE STRUGGLE FOR POWER

To speak of 'Chinese mythology' would be both ambiguous and over-ambitious. However, first and foremost, it is important to know to which China we are referring. It is quite obvious that Chinese mythology in earliest antiquity, if accessible, would be different from contemporary mythology, if such a thing exists. Not that there was at any moment of Chinese history a break that suddenly and radically altered the religious ideas and mythical notions of the entire population. The reader, however, will readily comprehend that in 3,500 years of comparatively well-known history the beliefs of the Chinese have changed, however slowly, and that it is well-nigh impossible to ignore this evolution. In any case, it is essential to deal differently with ancient and modern China for a great number of reasons. The dividing line between the two may be regarded as the Han period (second century B.C. to second century A.D.), for in this dynasty territorial conquests and long voyages provided contact with foreign cultures. This was the period in which Buddhism was introduced into China. Only ancient China will be discussed in this study.

Sources

There are two sources of information regarding the mythology of ancient China: on the one hand, inscriptions or works of art discovered by archaeologists; and, on the other, books preserved in libraries. The first constitute direct proof of the acts and ideas of the men who engraved, sculpted or drew them; so they are of very great value. However, inscriptions (on bone, tortoiseshell or ritual bronzes), which are very valuable in so many other fields, including religion, yield very little information of a mythological kind. And art work (such as bronzes or jades—used alone and in decoration—stone engravings, decorative tiling and statuettes) is relatively scarce, often

enigmatic, and serves merely to remind us that we are far from knowing everything.

The great mass of our information comes from books. Now the fact is that the books now available in libraries are not the originals. The ancient copies engraved on wooden slips that were collected in packets disappeared a long time ago, and those we have are recent editions which have come down to us through generations of different copyists, librarians and editors. It is not surprising that of all the books that were written, only a certain number have survived. Nor is it surprising that many of the latter are in poor condition: some are incomplete, others are apocryphal, later commentaries have got mixed up with the original text, and the dates of composition are not always definitive or even presumed.

Now even if by some miracle a large library dating from antiquity happened to be discovered intact, the myths known to people of that period and their forefathers would not necessarily be revealed at once. For almost all Chinese literature has been written, or rewritten, by people whom we shall call, for the sake of ease and simplicity, men of letters. Now men such as these have always displayed a tendency to rationalise and historicise myths, or, at best, to utilise them in historical schemas justifying moral or political theories. They have sought and often succeeded in effacing details that seemed shocking or irrational to them, and they even contrived to change some myths completely. Cross-checking, where possible, has shown when this has been done. However, there are very few documents that yield—at first glance—recognisable mythological information. Authors have been aware of this state of deterioration or second-hand condition of mythological legends and have therefore concentrated on historical and philological investigations, intending that what they retained, though slight in volume (for they rejected many

A further detail from the U family tombs. A man is in the coils of a gigantic serpent. Two men, possibly legendary characters, hurry to rescue him, one armed with an axe, the other with a hammer. (After Chavannes (ed.) *La Sculpture sur pierre en Chine au temps des deux dynasties* Han. Pl. XXV. Paris, 1893.)

A hollow bronze finial with two masks on each side. Fourteenth to eleventh centuries B.C.(Shang Dynasty). It consists of a *t'ao t'ieh* in the shape of a helmet above a man's face and, on the reverse (unseen), a deer above an elephant. The *t'ao t'ieh* was the mask of the ancient witch doctors and here displays the most typical features—the staring eyes, the absence of a lower jaw and the scroll decorations which symbolised thunder clouds and therefore the *yang* principle. *British Museum*

uncertain or much-worked texts), should at least be good, as a result of careful dating and classification of evidence.

Now, necessary though it may be, one must not be misled by exact scholarly dating. A student who is content to examine texts for the earliest mention of the names of mythological characters and deities will fall into the trap of sterile formalities. For the most ancient literature is not only the most rare, which is natural, but also the most arid—that is to say, the least mythological—and this is suspicious. For instance, to note that Fu-Hsi appears for the first time in the *Hsi-tzu* of the *I Ching* (end of the fifth century B.C.) is an important point in itself. But it is going too far to deduce from this that belief in Fu-Hsi dates from this relatively late period. The mere fact that there are many variations in the spelling of the name Fu-Hsi suggests that this god is more ancient still and that he must have been mentioned earlier in sources of different origins. Similarly, the legend of his birth, which conforms to the ancient pattern, and the hesitation concerning his connection with Nu-kua clearly show that this character was not 'invented' by the authors of the *Hsi-tzu*. Again the fact that Fu-Hsi is depicted on stone sculptures from the Han period certainly leads us to the conclusion that he was well known at this time, but not that he was unknown before it, for we have no stone sculptures before the Han period. But it is valuable to study the nature and the history of the *Hsi-tzu*. For it seems that this book was compiled by men of letters hostile to the Taoist school, and thus one can form the hypothesis that the position of most ancient god is perhaps conferred on Fu-Hsi for reasons of polemics, just as the trigrams (*see* caption to illustration on page 272) fit into a cosmological schema that is manifestly the opposite of that of Lao-tzu. These remarks are not intended to question the absolute antiquity of any

Protohistoric baked clay *haniwa* or tomb guardian figure.
Japan. Gowland Collection, British Museum.

Kishimo-jin, the Japanese goddess-mother of demons. Panel
painting from the shrine of Kishijoten. *National Institute of
Art Research, Tokyo*

CHINA: THE STRUGGLE FOR POWER

one particular myth of Fu-Hsi, but simply to show that this deity was probably raised to eminence by men of letters of the *Hsi-tzu* school. Consideration should be given not so much to the date of texts as to their value. The truth is that it is difficult to be objective in this field.

One point that must attract the attention of the historian of Chinese mythology concerns the geographical location of legends. Ancient China was not a state, or even a kingdom, but more of a confederation. Feudal states were much more than princely fiefs: they were lands with their own original character and they differed in their customs, their local speech, traditions and myths, in spite of a community of culture. In several of these states barbarous influence, not Chinese, was apparent. It came from autochthonous populations that were fully assimilated at a comparatively early date. This is quite evident in the case of the peripheral states, which were least involved in the federation; it is much less apparent in the case of central states, since their common culture was acquired at a very early stage and was then transmitted, propagated and developed by scribes and men of letters once the invention of writing made this possible. Thus, for example, in Han literature, Fu-Hsi is confused with another god, T'ai-hao, who was a wholly distinct entity in the time of the Warring States. Now at this period this god was worshipped, though under which name is not known exactly, in several small 'barbarous' states that were located in the province of Shantung, in eastern China. They were absorbed into the federation and, following the usual process, rapidly assimilated, though their patron T'ai-hao did not, however, survive. But we still do not know why he became confused with Fu-Hsi. Perhaps the latter was posted in the east according to the classificatory theories of the Five Elements, and the god T'ai-hao then became superfluous, being himself a native of the east, and he inevitably came under the banner of Fu-Hsi, who was so much better known.

Undoubtedly the reason for one and the same mythical character or place having several different names lies in the fact that mythological information came from various different regions (and periods), and from this we deduce that different myths were current in different parts; different, yet sufficiently similar (either from the very beginning or with the passage of time, which helped to blur individual characteristics) to allow a fusion of terminology in cases of disagreement.

Leaving this aside for the moment, the important thing is to warn the reader that what one understands by 'Chinese mythology' can only be a relatively complete, comparatively well-interpreted collection of a mass of fragments of varied origin. Because they were collected at very different dates, in different regions—thus in a variety of cultural conditions and in different social strata—these fragments are not in complete conformity with one another. But one can do no more than unravel themes or draw attention to leading ideas. Detailed reconstructions are false.

No attempt will be made in this article to draw up a complete picture of Chinese mythology, but we shall try to present some of its most characteristic elements.

The creation of the world

Chinese texts do not contain any myth about the creation of the world comparable to that of Genesis. On the other hand, there is a certain number of scholarly cosmogonic theories that are comparatively well developed: Lao-tzu, Hsi-tzu, Lieh-tzu, Huai-nan Tzu, Ling-hwun. They make use of different but extremely simplified terminology and can all be reduced to the same pattern: under the impulse of a pre-existing supreme principle, chaos (*hun-tun*), or the amorphous unformed world, divided into two active categories, the *yin* and the *yang*, and as a result of their conflicting and complementary interaction all things and all beings in the universe gradually formed and took their place, beginning with the sky (*yang*) and the earth (*yin*).

These are purely abstract theories, not myths. But it is quite probable that they are the echo or translation into philosophical language of older or more popular myths, of which, unfortunately, we know nothing.

A few odd facts may bear some relation to this. Thus the *yin* and *yang*, which in philosophical concepts are at most impersonal cosmic forces and categories of classification, may at one time have been regarded in a less abstract manner. In one passage in *Huai-nan Tzu* they seem to be spoken of as two gods (*shen*) who arose from chaos and had the task of managing earth and sky respectively.

The same thing happens in the case of chaos, which for the philosophers seems to be an invention of the mind, an essential and logical point of departure, but it is, none the less, described at times as a concrete being. For example, Chuang-tzu (fourth to third centuries B.C.), recounts in allegory form how the Emperor (that is to say the god) of the South Sea, Shu, and the Emperor of the North Sea, Hu, used to meet sometimes at the Emperor of the Centre's domain. This emperor, Hun-Tun, always treated them well. Wishing to repay him for his kindness to them, Shu and Hu said: 'All men have seven orifices—for seeing, hearing, eating and breathing—Hun-Tun alone has none. Let us try to bore some for him.' And this they did at the rate of one orifice a day. But on the seventh day Hun-Tun died. This implies that chaos unquestionably was dead as such, but the world was undoubtedly born in its place at the same moment. It is not without interest to note that the expression Shu-hu, which Chuang-tzu broke down artificially, means lightning, and this again adds a concrete touch to this re-formed fragment of myth. In certain ritual transpositions lightning is represented by burning arrows directed at a goatskin bottle, which may have represented chaos.

Other sources give more exact yet different descriptions of chaos. Thus according to the *Shan Hai Ching* ('Hill and River Classic'), an atlas of mythical regions and catalogue of demons, there was on a certain mountain of the sky, otherwise unknown, a divine bird like a yellow bag, but at the same time as red as a ball of fire, which had six feet and four wings, no face (without the seven openings), but could dance and sing (many myths that have been lost have left their trace in imitative ritual dances). This is chaos. It is also either Huang-Ti, the Yellow Emperor himself, mythical sovereign of the Centre according to certain theories (Chuang-tzu also depicts chaos as the Emperor of the Centre), or else his son. In the latter case he is a wicked son banished by the Yellow Emperor, but this is a theme unconnected with creation.

Chaos is also depicted as a long-haired dog. He has eyes, but cannot see; ears, but cannot hear; and he is without the five viscera. The details differ, but the essential feature remains, which is that chaos is a disorganised and incapable being that can be compared to a hollow sack.

The tale that comes closest to a primitive myth was found at a very late date in a post-Han work (the *San-wu li-ki*, third century A.D.): in former times, before either heaven or earth existed, chaos looked like a hen's egg. P'an-Ku was born in this egg. After eighteen thousand years chaos 'opened up'; the heavy, coarse elements, *yin*, formed the earth; by contrast the light, pure elements, *yang*, formed the sky. Every day the sky rose by ten feet. Every day the earth grew deeper by ten feet. And every day P'an-Ku found that his size had increased by ten feet, so that after eighteen thousand years P'an-Ku's body was as great as the distance between heaven and earth.

Now an even later work, from the sixth century A.D., includes different versions of the legend of P'an-Ku; on his death the different parts of his body became parts of the world. To be more precise:

(1) No indication of literary origin: his head became the four cardinal mountains, his eyes became the sun and moon, his flesh became the rivers and sea, his hair became plants.

(2) According to popular legends of the Ts'ing and Han periods: his head became the cardinal mountain of the east, his stomach became the mountain of the centre, his left arm the mountain of the south, his right arm the mountain of the north, and his feet became the cardinal mountain of the west.

(3) According to the theories of early scholars: his tears became rivers and streams, his breath became the wind, his voice thunder, his eyes lightning.

(4) According to an ancient legend: when P'an-Ku was happy the weather was fine, when he grew angry there was bad weather (as before his death).

(5) According to legends from Wu and Shu (two southern provinces): P'an-Ku and his wife are the origin of *yin* and *yang*.

At an even later date the same motif was embroidered in the following way: on the death of P'an-Ku his breath was transmuted into the wind and clouds, his voice into thunder and lightning, his left eye into the sun, his right eye into the moon, his body into the four poles and the five great mountains, his blood and humours into the rivers and streams, his nerves and veins into the strata of the earth, his skin and flesh into the fields and the soil, his hair and eyebrows into stars and planets, his teeth and bone into metals and stones, his seed and marrow into pearls and jade, his sweat into rain and swamps, the parasites upon him into men.

In total opposition to the scholarly theories of philosophers, the lack of elaboration, limited scope, and concrete, if naïve, structure of these legends point to their popular character. Even in the sixth century they seem to have been restricted to southern parts of China. It is agreed that they came in the beginning from barbarous populations, related to present-day inhabitants, who are still scattered about the same areas of the south. However, in their current form, the mythologies of these peoples do not include a legend about a primordial giant comparable to that of P'an-Ku.

If Chinese authors believed that there was no need to indicate that these collections of legends were of foreign origin, perhaps the reason is that they did not appear to them as such. Indeed, it is impossible not to be struck by some points which clearly resemble the most manifestly Chinese ideas. Thus the fact that the world does not begin until after the death of P'an-Ku, as a result of the dismembering or transformation of his body, reminds one of the legend of chaos as reported by Chuang-tzu. The operation by which the *yang* elements came to form the sky and the *yin* elements the earth resembles very closely a version related in the *Huai-nan Tzu*. But it was probably only borrowed or acquired by contamination. One wonders if the same can be said of the form of the world-egg before its separation. The same idea with its obvious symbolism is found in several primitive cultures. It is also found in one of the Chinese cosmological theories (*see below*). The fundamental theme, which is not found anywhere else in China, is that the giant gradually splits the two parts of the world and remains fastened between the two. And yet one does come across the idea that heaven and earth were gradually drawn apart (*Lun-heng*). Furthermore, by keeping heaven and earth apart by the height of his own body, P'an-Ku plays the part of a column. Later it will be seen that in fact there are columns between heaven and earth. So P'an-Ku figures as a bond, a link between heaven and earth. An ancient myth, which has been almost entirely lost, said that in primitive times there was a communication between

P'an-ku, holding in his hands the *Yang-Yin,* symbol of Heaven and Earth. According to this nineteenth-century European lithograph P'an-ku was the first man on earth. The more common idea popularly held by the Chinese, however, was that P'an-ku was born in Chaos, which resembled a hen's egg. Eighteen thousand years after his birth, Chaos opened out and the *yang,* the pure light elements, separated themselves from the *yin,* the base elements of the earth. P'an-ku steadily grew until he was tall enough to hold heaven and earth apart and his body became the various parts of the earth. British Museum.

A dragon, as portrayed on a grey earthenware roof-end tile of the Han Dynasty (206 B.C.–A.D. 200). The disc under the dragon's wing may be an allusion to the ancient myth of the dragon inhabiting the north-west of the world, whose sleep and waking determined night and day, and whose breathing regulated the seasons and the wind. *Victoria and Albert Museum*

heaven and earth, which a hero, Chung-li, received orders from the Lord on High to cut.

The 'ancient legend' quoted above, which maintains that it is fine when P'an-Ku is happy and stormy when he is angry, resembles another scrap of ancient mythology about the Flaming Dragon. It is mentioned several times in the *Shan Hai Ching,* but in somewhat inconsistent terms. But the essence of it seems to be that in the north-west desert of the world, where no sun shone, there was a huge dragon a thousand *li* long; it had a human face and its body was red. When it opened its eyes it was daylight, when it closed them it was dark. Its breath made the wind and rain. Another version was that when it panted and blew it was winter, and when it simply breathed out it was summer. Again, it did not drink, eat or breathe. However, if it did draw breath, this gave rise to wind.

Another problem arises with regard to the origin of humanity, for there are as few myths and legends about it in literary sources as there are about the creation of the world. If we exclude the amusing story of the origin of the human race from P'an-Ku's fleas (and not only is this legend very late, but it also smacks of allegory and literary elaboration) and equally if we disregard a few allusions in abstract, philosophical theories, then there is only one well-known popular legend on this subject. When heaven and earth had been 'separated', there was still no human race. Then Nu-kua shaped mankind out of yellow earth. But as this work was too fatiguing and time-consuming, she trailed a rope in the mud, removed it and created men. Noblemen and rich men were created from the yellow earth, and poor and lowly people were made from the mud-covered rope. The text with this legend in it dates from the Han Dynasty. An enigmatic phrase in the *T'ien-wen* undoubtedly refers to a similar type of legend: Nu-kua had a body, but who formed it for her? In other words, if Nu-kua is the creator of humanity, by whom was she created herself? We shall return to the subject of Nu-kua later.

The structure of the world

The Chinese have taken a far greater interest in the structure of the world than in its creation. But there too we have mainly theories and speculation, much closer, it is true, to the underlying myths than in the case of the birth of the world. We shall begin with a very brief examination of these myths.

According to late evidence (amassed in the later years of the Han Dynasty), which none the less throws light on ideas that go back to the fourth to third centuries B.C., Chinese cosmographers were divided into three schools. One of these three traditions, called *siuan-ye,* has been lost, but it is known to have claimed that the sky was not a solid body and that the sun, moon and stars moved about freely in it. Another, called *t'ien-kai* or *chou-pei* explained that the sky was

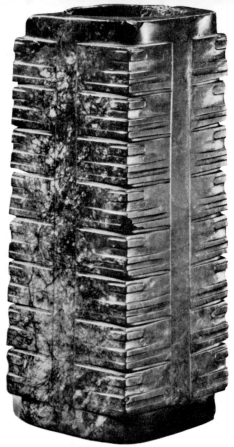

Ritual objects made of jade and used in burial. Though these examples are of the Han Dynasty (206 B.C.–A.D. 220), such ritual objects in jade were first introduced during the Shang period (about 1800–1100 B.C.) The circle with a wide centre, known as a *Huän*, is mutton fat flecked with brown in colour. Round shapes symbolise the sky, which was thought to turn. The rectangular tube, known as a *Ts'ung*, its square shape symbolising the immovable Earth, is coloured dark green and mottled grey. The symbolism of colour was as important in Chinese ritual as the symbolism of form. The material, too, had its message: jade was considered the product of both earth and water — the unified principles of *yang* and *yin. British Museum*

an upturned bowl over the earth. The sky turned on its own axis, the pole-star, which was the highest point in the sky, taking with it the stars fixed to its inside surface. The earth was a flat surface, or a truncated quadrangular pyramid, surrounded by water on its four sides, the four seas. The third theory, which probably came later than the previous one, was called *hun-t'ien* and saw the world as a hen's egg with a long vertical diameter. The sky was the inside of the shell and the stars moved across it. The earth, like the yoke, floated in the midst of the primeval ocean at the bottom of the egg (this part is not enlarged upon). It was subject to types of tide, which accounted for the seasons.

Such speculations as these are connected with traditional concepts and mythical themes that are partly recognisable.

In the first place, broadly speaking, the two last-mentioned theories are in distinct opposition. The second might possibly be related to the myth of P'an-Ku. The first, which goes farther back in time, has more varied connections. The idea of the earth being square is very ancient indeed, for it is written into the language itself. Space is defined by the four points of the compass, *yang*, but this also means 'square'. That is why the god of the sun is represented by a square mound, the capital is square and the royal domain is square, for space thus consists of squares that fit into one another (in relation to the centre of the world) or juxtaposed squares (round minor centres). The sky is round because it revolves — whereas the earth is still — and also because it is the opposite of earth, just as *yang*, odd, is the opposite of *yin*, even.

If the sky is a solid vault above the earth, it must be supported to stop it falling, just as the roof of a house is supported by columns, which is the general rule in China. There is general agreement about the existence of columns for the sky on the periphery of

earth, but there is some disagreement about the number of them (eight or four, or even only one?), and opinions as to their position differ even more radically. Only the north-west column, Mount Pu Chou, is well known. The geographical configuration of ancient China might well have given rise to a belief in the existence of very high mountains in that direction. Moreover, a sky supported by one or several columns required in addition supple chains. The term used for them is that used for the ropes that fastened the platform of a chariot to its bodywork. According to a much-used metaphor, which we have already met in the term *t'ien-kai*, the sky is compared to the platform part of a chariot (or even to a horizontal chariot wheel with the pole-star at the hub) and the earth to the body part of the chariot. Ancient ceremonial chariots were square in shape and had a round dais on top supported by a central column.

There are many possible mythical centres on earth, as many as there are social-territorial groups. It is more than probable that each local mythology claimed to have the centre of the world on its own territory. Thus in T'si country a lake on a mountain-top was worshipped as a holy place. It was called the 'Navel of the Sky'. It was probably the centre of heaven and earth for the local people, the support for the cosmic axis. But even within the domain of mythology, the symbolic cosmology (which at every moment and in every place recreates the world for religious and social reasons) must not be confused with the cosmology that seeks to offer explanations. Now the Chinese could, of course, see that even the most wondrous centre of all, the centre as defined by the king and his capital, was not at the cosmographical centre of things, since the pole-star was not exactly above it. There was some discrepancy between the axes of heaven and earth, an evident shift in position. So this is explained by a myth.

Terracotta funerary figures of the Han Dynasty (206 B.C. – A.D. 220). When a man died, terracotta replicas of the people and things that had surrounded his life were placed in his tomb, to attend him. *British Museum*

Once upon a time a horned monster, Kung Kung, ventured to fight one of the five sovereigns for the title of emperor. He was overcome, and in his rage he flung himself at Mount Pu Chou or more literally impaled it on his horns. The column of the sky was broken, the link with earth was cut. In the north-west the sky collapsed. Hence the sun, moon and stars slipped towards the north-west and the earth tilted to the south-east. Thereupon the waters spread and flowed to the south-east. Pu Chou means 'non-circular, broken'. It is also the name for a pestilential wind that blows in the north-west.

Similarly, the earth had to be upheld by eight columns. The space separating them was known, but no further details were given. They were under the earth. They were certainly best known in the circles or regions from which the *hun-t'ien* theory emerged.

Cosmographers do not explain everything. They do not emphasise the element of symbolism, which seems very important. It is often said in ancient texts that the earth bears and the sky covers or embraces, and basically this is the coupling of the earth, *yin*, feminine, and the sky, *yang*, masculine. But the references are vague, as if modestly veiled.

Another theory expressed by *Chu Tzu* is that the sky is composed of nine storeys or steps, the Nine Skies. As this does not fit in with classical theories, an attempt has been made to imply that they were nine celestial plains dividing the surface of the sky into nine zones, which corresponded to the nine 'provinces' of earth. But there is actually no possible doubt that the Nine Skies were arranged vertically, one on top of the other. Each sky was divided from the next by a gate guarded by tigers and panthers. Conversely, the earth is not without depth. Beneath are the 'yellow streams', which at one time or in certain circles were thought to be the abode of the dead. Later they came to refer to them as the Nine Streams or Ninth Streams,

probably as a counterpart to the Nine Skies, but this is not found in early texts.

At the highest point of the heavens there was a gap, *lie-k'iue,* through which lightning flashed. Beyond that gap the sky ended, there was absolutely nothing more. The same thing happened on the horizontal plane; at the edge of the cosmos there was neither sky nor earth, only a gaping void.

The sun

There is not one but ten suns, which appear in turn in the sky. They make their journey on a chariot drawn by six horse-dragons, and the charioteer is a woman, their mother. There have been fairly exact, though differing, descriptions of the journey. The chariot emerges from the Valley of Light, Yang-ku, in the far east of the world, which is bordered by a lake and a gigantic tree. The mother of the ten suns washes her children in the lake every morning. Then the sun or suns approach the tree *po*, which is also called *fu-sang* or *k'ong-sang* (hollow mulberry-tree). Nine suns remain in the lower branches of the tree, but the tenth, which is 'in operation', climbs to the topmost branch and then moves off into the sky. In the evening they reach a spot where the horses can rest and be unyoked on a mountain in the Far West, Mount Yen-Tzu. Mention is also made of a lake or river, Mong, the western counterpart of the Valley of Light in the east. Here is the tree *jo,* the counterpart of the tree *fu-sang* (one of the hypotheses regarding the meaning of these two names is 'tree of the sun' and 'tree supporting the sun'), and the sun probably returns to earth by way of this second tree. Its characteristic is red flowers, which shine by night, and are perhaps the stars. The intermediate stages of the journey, which are really just plains, springs, hillocks, correspond to the hours of the day and are hardly enumerated at all. It is not known how the sun and its

One of the ten chariots of the sun. The ten suns crossed the sky one after the other, each one drawn in a chariot by six dragon-horses and driven by their mother. Each sun represented one hour of the day, and it was an evil sign if more than one appeared in the sky at the same time. *Photo–X*

Yi, the Excellent Archer, shooting down the nine suns with a magic bow. The bodies of the three sun-ravens he has already shot down lie at his feet. Taken from *Li-sao t'u* in the Fung Ping Shan Library, University of Hong Kong.

equipage returned from the west to the east, but it is possible that there were myths about this too.

In its crude or primitive state the solar myth does not quite lend itself to the known facts. Therefore the Chinese spoke of two deities placed in the north-east and north-west corners of the world, each with the task of controlling one of the eight winds, stopping the sun and the moon and fixing the length of their course. Furthermore, it was admitted that the sun rose and set in different places, which were named according to the season. But these are later elaborations, and they no longer comply with the myth of *fu-sang*.

The sun is made of fire. It is the essence of the *yang*. In its breast is a three-footed raven—three to represent the *yang*, uneven, which is both its emblem and principal source of life. This raven is often depicted on stone sculptures in the Han period.

This is not so much one single sun myth, as can be seen at once, as a fairly heteroclite collection of mythical details of varied origin. One element at least is very ancient; from the beginning of Chinese writing the ideogram for 'east' shows a sun in a tree. Another character, which is in fact rather rare, shows a sun above a tree and means 'light'. And, finally, another depicts the sun under the tree and means 'darkness'. As for the myth of the ten suns, it has a written character or symbol that means 'dawn' and is composed of the elements 'nine' and 'sun': dawn is the moment when the nine suns stay at the foot of the tree while the tenth climbs up and moves away.

The ten suns are also connected with the following myth. Once upon a time, in a very troubled period, the ten suns all appeared together in the sky. Their excessive heat made life on earth impossible to bear. A hero, Yi the Excellent Archer, shot down the nine suns with a magic bow given him by the mythical emperor Ti-siun. The feathers from the sun-ravens

Carved stone from a tomb in Wuhang-tsen, Shantung. The Tree of Life fills the whole space with its branches. The animals and monsters towards the top represent primordial beings. Musée Guimet. *Chavannes*

flew about and fell to earth. That is why there is now only one sun.

The appearance of several suns in the sky is a sign of troubled times and especially of a change of dynasty. Historians have made note of two examples of this: two suns appeared in the sky before the victory of the Chou rulers and three before the victory of the Yin. It is clearly implied, sometimes even explicitly stated, that the sovereign is being compared or better still mythically assimilated to the sun, particularly the midday sun. The two suns at the end of the Yin Dynasty were on the one hand in the east the rising sun of the Chous, who were soon to rule, and on the other hand in the west the setting sun of the Yins, who were about to disappear. That is why, in the characteristic tales of thwarted rebellions, the disloyal minister attacks the hollow mulberry-tree, abode of the rising sun and of the sovereign about to assume power.

Finally, mention should be made of another myth connected with the sun, that of K'au-fu. He is the son of Kung Kung, the rebel, and is sometimes described as a composite animal and sometimes as a giant. He is a wind too. He wanted to journey across the sky with the sun. He overtook it in the Valley of the Setting Sun, but he was exhausted. He was so thirsty that he drained the Yellow River and the River Wei. Still his thirst was not quenched, and he hastened towards the north to drink the Great Swamp, but he died of thirst on the way. His abandoned stick became a forest. Research into the legends about this forest have yielded the information that this myth seems to derive from 'a feast of cattlemen, with a wealth of horses' (Granet).

The moon

Myths relating to the moon are similar to those concerning the sun, but they are not so well known. There is not one, but twelve moons, which follow one another at monthly intervals in the sky. At the beginning of each month the mother of moons washes her children in a lake on the western confines of the world. Like the sun the moon makes its nocturnal journey in a chariot, but the charioteer is not the mother of moons. The course it takes is not described—at least, not in the texts that have come down to us.

The twelve moons undoubtedly represent twelve lunar months, for the word *yue* refers both to the celestial body and the lunar month. This hypothesis leads to another: the Chinese do not count in weeks of seven days, but in units of ten, and the ten mythical suns may represent the ten days in the decade (the same word *je* refers both to the sun and calendar day), but the derivation is not so obvious as with the twelve moons. More generally speaking, the association of ten and twelve reminds one of the Chinese calendar system, based on the combination of ten 'trunks' and twelve 'branches', both represented by special characters or signs described as 'cyclic'. This is a very ancient system, much older than the actual texts in which the remains of solar and lunar myths were collected together, and this in turn can only lead us to believe that these myths too are of very ancient date.

The moon is made of water and is the essence of the *yin*. Like the sun it is inhabited by an animal, which is either a hare or a toad. The hare is quoted in the earliest source (the *T'ien-wen*), but this does not necessarily mean that belief in the toad in the moon is of later date. From the time of the latter Han Dynasty, in any case, the two traditions were generally accepted, and people believed in the presence of these two animals on the moon at one and the same time.

279

Heng-o on the moon. She is standing to the right of the Cassia tree, while the hare of the moon is pounding the elixir of life. Below the hare is the toad which Heng-o will become when she has swallowed the elixir. Belief in the existence of both the hare and the toad on the moon were current from early in the Han Dynasty. This bronze mirror of the T'ang Dynasty (A.D. 618–907) illustrates a variant to the usual story of Heng-o. Its pictorial style also marks an artistic transition, foreshadowing the growth in importance of painting in the Sung Dynasty. *Victoria and Albert Museum*

The mother of moons is the wife of the emperor Ti-siun. Now the same thing is said of the mother of suns, so that possibly suns and moons might have the same father; but this is not emphasised in texts. Moreover, the fact that the father is not mentioned might be a sign of a major archaism. The name 'mother of moons' is interesting. It has numerous variants, both phonetic and graphic, but one can finally show that it is closely connected with the name Chang-o or Heng-o, the moon-goddess in modern folk-lore. Modern folk-lore, then, because it has survived down to our own day, but ancient legend since it was already widespread in the Han Dynasty: Heng-o was the wife of Yi the Excellent Archer, who shot down the suns. In the course of his journeys the latter had been to the Land of the Setting Sun, to the Royal Mother of the Western Paradise, from whom he had obtained a dose of the herb of immortality which grew on her soil. On his return his wife stole it from him, swallowed it and fled to the moon, where she became the lunar toad.

The sky and stars

In the most ancient Chinese religion the sky was of great importance as the residence of the Lord on High. According to later texts the stars were the seat of a host of deities modelled on mankind who formed the Lord on High's court and administration. He himself lived in the Great Bear, in the purple Palace of Tenuity surrounded by fine gardens. The guardian of the palace was the celestial wolf, that is the star Sirius. It had vertical eyes, moved about slowly, and seemingly for amusement picked up men in its jaws and threw them into a deep gulf in obedience to the orders of the Lord on High. After this he was allowed to sleep. The men thus treated were undoubtedly dead, for it would appear that the Lord on High was the ruler of a sort of Hades.

The only relatively well-developed stellar myth that we know is that of the Cowherd and the Weaver-girl. These are two groups of three stars in the constellations of Aquila and the Lyre respectively, situated on opposite sides of the Milky Way. Every year, on the seventh day of the seventh moon, the Heavenly Weaver-girl used to leave her stellar home, cross the Milky Way (on a bridge of magpies, according to a detail undoubtedly added later, although there is an unreliable quotation to this effect in the *Huai-nan Tzu*) and go to her husband, the Cowherd. The very early origin of the myth is proved by the fact that there is already a reference to it in the *Shih-Ching*, a somewhat obscure reference, moreover, in which the partner of the Weaver-girl might well be an ox rather than a cowherd. The love-story element, which ensured the popularity of the legend and its survival down to our own times, did not emerge clearly until it appeared in an 'ancient poem' in the *Wen-siuan*, probably dating from the later Han Dynasty. The actual date of the seventh day of the seventh month is not mentioned until the third century A.D. In point of fact, during the first ten days of the seventh lunar month the two groups of stars are closest to the earth. But in order to discover this, long years of observation were necessary. The choice of the same number for the day as for the lunar month is also in conformity with Chinese custom: such dates as this indicate a time of particular symbolic intensity.

The great interest of this myth is that it links with the sky an essential feature of ancient peasant society: men and women formed two distinct and separate groups, economically and socially speaking. While women looked after the house and in the near-by gardens tended vegetables, textile-plants and mulberry-trees, men farmed the distant fields and did not return home—at least not during the fine season. But once winter had come everyone made

A bronze ritual vessel (*hu*). Middle Chou period. Eighth to sixth centuries B.C. *Musée Guimet*

for the house. Then the women would spin and weave material, which they used for bartering. But breaks in the year were provided by public festivals, in spring and autumn, when engagements and weddings were celebrated. They took place on holy ground, often by the river. The amorous and ritual gesture of crossing the river recurs in the songs of the *Shih-Ching*. In the Chou Dynasty, when these facts came to light, peasant society was patrilineal and a wife went to her husband's village. But there are numerous signs that it was not always like this, and that, at an earlier stage, society was more or less matrilocal and a man had to go and live in his wife's village. However, the legend of the Weaver-girl and the Cowherd, in its existing form, depicts the second stage, since the Weaver-girl crosses the Milky Way and goes to her husband, the Cowherd.

This myth also attracts our attention to the fact that from antiquity onwards the Milky Way was regarded as a river. It was called Han, or else Han of the Sky, Han of the Clouds, Han of the Stars or Silver Han. The word *han* primarily indicates one of the major tributaries of the Blue River. It has sometimes been thought that the name of this river was used for the Milky Way because it is the only important river in north China that, taken by and large, goes from north to south like the Milky Way. But this is not certain, for the Han does not take a north-south course until it reaches Hupei, former province of Shu, and the word *han* could also have been taken in its general sense of river. According to very explicit, but also very late, texts, the Milky Way is also compared to the Yellow River, the main river in north China. It too, and to a far greater extent than the Han, flows from north to south for a very considerable distance before its major bend. In addition, legends were collected after the Han period showing that the Milky Way could be reached either by following the Yellow River upstream or by floating on sea currents.

Sea and islands

Purely theoretically, the sea washed the world on four sides. But the north, west and south seas were beyond the limited horizon of ancient China and are therefore completely mythical. The eastern sea is certainly real, but is none the less shrouded in mystery. However, it is highly likely that in early antiquity the Chinese had no direct knowledge of this sea.

The sea is the domain of a rather curious mythological figure, Yu-ch'iang. He resides in the north or north-west. He is a wind-god, a god of the sea wind in particular, but he is not *the* wind-god, for that is a title reserved for another character, the Count of Wind. In his capacity of wind-god the *Shan Hai Ching* describes him as having a human face and the body of a bird. Two green serpents cling to his ears and two others are beneath his feet. But he is also a god of the sea. As such he has the body of a

Scroll showing the calligraphic characters of the Five Holy Mountains. The four cardinal mountains, rising in a rectangular pattern, like that of the earth itself, marked the axis or backbone of the earth. They were identified with the arms, head and feet of P'an-ku. The fifth — added later, and square like the Emperor's palace — was identified with P'an-ku's belly. Calligraphy was the basis of, and never became dissociated from the symbolism of Chinese art and myth. British Museum.

fish, but he has feet and hands too, and he rides on two dragons. His fish's body resembles a *kun*, that is to say a large northern sea-whale thousands of *li* in length. Sometimes this large *kun* grows angry. He suddenly changes into a gigantic bird, the *p'eng*, which rises from the north sea creating enormous waves. Its outspread wings darken the sky like clouds. He spends six months flying to the south sea, where finally he comes to rest. As told by Chuang-tzu this myth undoubtedly rests on a reference to the wind-system in the China Sea.

Far away to the east, in the eastern sea, there is a bottomless pit, the *kuei-hiu*, into which all the waters of the world rush headlong (or return), including the waters of rivers and seas and also the waters of the Milky Way, the celestial river, which passed through the 'Ford of Heaven'.

Above the *kuei-hiu* were five wondrous islands inhabited by Immortals bedecked with feathers and wings, and there the herbs of immortality grew and provided them with food. At first the islands were not fixed to the bed of the sea. They floated freely and were in danger of striking against the continent to the west. The Immortals found this disturbing and complained to the Emperor of Heaven. He ordered Yu-ch'iang to fasten the islands to fifteen large tortoises, three to each island. While one of them actually carried the island, the other two were to wait. They were to take it in turns, each turn lasting sixty thousand years. However, it so happened that a giant from the land of Lung-po (Count-Dragons) reached the islands in a few strides and began to fish for the tortoises. He caught six in a single attempt. The two islands, deprived of their anchor, floated off course to the North Pole and sank. In his anger the Emperor of Heaven reduced the giants to a less dangerous size, though they were still of superhuman proportions.

The search for the three remaining islands of the Immortals was to tempt many people, particularly kings or emperors who were rich and powerful enough to launch sea-going expeditions. They all failed. People who approached success saw them in the distance as clouds. As they drew near, the islands would suddenly turn upside down and appear beneath the surface of the water as reflections. If anyone was about to reach them they would float away, driven by the wind. These legends were probably fostered by visions of underwater mirages. On the other hand, it is quite well known that in humid climates there is often mist on the surface of water, which makes shores and islands seem to hover above the sea. But the great popularity of the legends about the islands of the Immortals is because they depict Taoist paradises and autonomous worlds.

Woodcut showing the God of the Southern Mountain feeding the bones of Christians to his soldiers. The mythology of ancient China persisted in vivid images into modern times. Nineteenth century. British Museum.

Earth and mountains

From the very earliest times the Chinese appear to
have attached great importance to mountains, to
which they made solemn sacrifice. They were near
heaven, rain-bearing clouds emerged from their
flanks, they were closed worlds (there was no essential difference between mountains and islands)
harbouring countless creatures and things that
possessed powers of their own. Many countries had
their sacred mountain which played the part of god
of earth. On a world-scale, four (then five) cardinal
mountains were said by the Chinese to exist, each in
one of the four corners of the earth (and in the
middle). They provided the spatial framework for
the domain of human activity, which was square
like the earth. They corresponded to the four gates
of the capital. A king had to make a tour round the
four mountains to ensure possession of his domain.
Similarly, the chief (or chiefs, as it is not known for
sure whether there was one or four such persons)
of the vassals of the four sectors of space was called
Four-Mountains. The arrival at the court of Four-
Mountains completed the tour of the four mountains
or replaced this tour whenever a new sovereign
acceded to the throne.

Of the cardinal mountains, the mountain of the
east, the T'ai Shan, received particular attention. It
is quoted in the most ancient classics, and in earliest
antiquity it was already the object and centre of an
official cult. Moreover, from the Han period at least,
it was a tenet of popular belief that after death all
souls 'returned' to a sort of Hades at the foot of T'ai
Shan. Being in the east T'ai Shan was the origin of
things and beings, source and master of life, and
consequently it came to be regarded as the master
of fate, of destiny and death. In this role the T'ai
Shan was personified by a Lord of T'ai Shan, whom
even the introduction of Buddhism and its hell never
completely succeeded in dethroning.

Beyond the cardinal mountains other mythical
mountains have been located, and these played the
part of poles or columns of the sky at the very limits
of the world. The most famous, destined to enjoy
great fortune in later folk-lore, was Kun-lun.

This mountain was in the west of the world,
farther and farther west as geographical knowledge
increased, for anything beyond it was inaccessible.
It was said to be extremely high, some said high
enough to touch the sky, and its base must have been
proportionately deep in the ground ('Where is its
base?' asks the *T'ien-wen*). The approach to it was
protected by mysterious thin water, where nothing,
not even a goose-feather, could float, or else by red
water (vermilion), which encircled the mountain
three times before returning to its source. Anyone
who drank of it obtained immortality. According to
concurrent traditions, the Kun-lun was either the
source of the Yellow River or the source of four

Monster head of litsea wood, formerly painted, with real
deer's antlers. Fourth century B.C. This underworld figure
was just beginning to be represented in Chinese art in the
fourth century. The emergence of such themes indicates the
development of Chinese mythology. Found in a tomb outside
Ch'ang Sha, Hunan. *British Museum*

Bronze mirror of the second or third century A.D. showing Hsi Wang Mu and her consort Tung Wang Kung. They are accompanied by spirit figures riding winged horses and deer. This is a representation of the Queen of the West in her early form, when she inhabited a Jade Mountain beyond Kun-lun and was the fearsome, tiger-toothed mistress of plague and disaster. *Victoria and Albert Museum*

Dragon's head. The dragon is the symbol of earth and of water, but above all it represents the fertilising power of rain. Ornamental detail of about the third century B.C., the time of the Warring States. Collection Stoclet, Brussels. *Larousse*

great rivers, including the Yellow River, which flowed in four directions (excluding north). This detail regarding the four rivers is important, for it is the firmest argument in favour of a comparison between the Kun-lun and the Sumeru of Indian mythology. The mountain itself towered up in nine superimposed steps or storeys like the sky. In its sides or summit were doors—four, nine or four hundred and forty in number according to various authors—and through them emerged the winds. For example, from the north door emerged the wind Pu Chou. Beside the doors were nine wells renowned for the purity of their water.

Kun-lun was the earthly capital of the Lord of the Sky. It was administered by a divine being who had a human face, the body and claws of a tiger and four tails. Man-eating beasts resembling four-horned goats were also found there. Another beast, with a tiger's body and nine human heads, had the task of guarding the door of light, facing the east. There were also birds, which carried out the orders of the Lord of the Sky, as well as all sorts of rare and precious plants and many divine beings (*shen*). Later descriptions came to place more and more emphasis on details of luxury and refinement to the exclusion of the more primitive and terrifying monsters. At the same time the mountain became more architectural in aspect, and under the influence of Taoism it acquired the characteristics of a paradise. But one thing remained unaltered, its essential character of cosmic mountain, column or ladder to the sky, remote in its inaccessibility.

However, the most famous character connected with Kun-lun—Hsi Wang Mu or Royal Mother of the Western Paradise—does not seem to be linked with this mountain in the earliest texts. Furthermore, she was located with reference to the Kun-lun, so she was not within the mountain itself. According to details taken from several articles in the *Shan Hai Ching*, she resided in a mountain of jade, to the north of Kun-lun, to the west of the Moving Sands (a desert on the west or north-west boundary). She had her abode in the depths of a rocky cave, where she sat on a stool with her hair flowing round her (this is the attribute of witches) and a *cheng* ornament on her head (these two details of hair and headdress indicated the female sex). She had a human face with a leopard's tail and tiger's teeth. In front of her were three green birds that went to find her food (later they were depicted as three-footed birds, like the birds of the sun). She governed the spirits of plague and calamity. Now this dread appearance and evil character of Hsi Wang Mu do not comply with later descriptions, in which she was always a goddess (a tendency in Taoism and popular religion) or a sovereign (a tendency in historical novels) of great beauty, a delicate hostess, queen of a paradise-like Kun-lun, the counterpart in the Far West of the floating isles in the Far East; she was, in addition, the possessor and dispenser of the herb of immortality. The transformation of this ogress, who was the patron of epidemics, into the guardian-goddess of the herb of immortality is rather strange. Perhaps it came about because she originally had the task of spreading malady and death, and therefore was capable of withdrawing them when she so wished. In much the same way, T'ai Shan, the master of life, became master of death.

The organisation of the world

The legends about the arrangement of the world, which are legends of heroes who brought civilisation to earth, are many and varied. Rather than draw up an uninteresting list, three particular characters will

Hsi Wang Mu, Queen of the West, in the softened form attributed to her in later times, when she was supposed to be sovereign of a delightful kingdom situated on Kun-lun itself. Her unkempt hair shows that she is a sorceress and she has beside her a phoenix—symbol of the immortality which in this role she sometimes conferred. Painting by Wu Wei (1458–1508). *British Museum*

Fu-Hsi (*right*) holding a set-square, and his consort Nu-kua (*left*) holding compasses. Both have dragon tails. Below them is Hsi Wang Mu, Queen of the West. Fu-Hsi, who was said to have been the first ruler of China (and was sometimes supposed to have reigned about 2800 B.C.) was the legendary founder of the social order and the inventor of writing. Right-hand pillar of a tomb at Pei Chai Ts'un. *Britain–China Friendship Association*

be taken—Nu-kua, Kun and Yu—and the myths relating to them discussed, though still very briefly. These three heroes had in common the fact that they regulated or tried to regulate floods. Now this word has sometimes been used in the Biblical sense. Maspero has already rightly pointed out that a 'flood' evokes the idea of sin and punishment, ideas that are totally absent in these Chinese legends. Furthermore, these were not generalised inundations covering the whole earth as were the floods described in Near Eastern and European myths, but overflowing rivers that caused partial yet catastrophic flooding. This major problem in ancient China is still not completely resolved even today. It is worth noting in this connection that in Chinese the words for 'mountain' and 'island' are practically synonymous, and that the primary meaning of the word for 'province' or 'land' is 'fluvial island', and the ideogram for it does, in fact, show a watercourse with islands emerging.

Nu-kua

Nu-kua has already appeared in this study in connection with the creation of humanity. She was a female deity, but in statues and portraits she is usually shown with a serpent's or dragon's tail, like that of a siren. This manner of portrayal was not known until the later Han Dynasty, but there is irrefutable evidence of it in both painting and sculpture. With very rare exceptions texts make no mention of this tail. Some scholars have therefore concluded that belief in Nu-kua's semi-bestial, semi-human form was a comparatively recent development, and that she was formerly depicted as an ordinary woman. This is contrary to all that we know of the evolution of Chinese mythology, which in course of time kept on humanising its characters and effacing their animal or bizarre characteristics. It is possible that the men of letters who spoke of Nu-kua in pre-Han times were

Bronze mirror of the T'ang Dynasty (A.D. 618–907) showing animals representing the four cardinal directions. Each of these directions was bounded by a sea and each marked by a mountain formed, according to beliefs of the Ch'in and Han Dynasties, of one part of P'an-ku: his head in the east, his left arm in the south, his right arm in the north, and his feet in the west. British Museum.

Bronze axe-head decorated with a *t'ao t'ieh* mask in high relief, with open mouth and protruding fangs. Although the design has become more ornamental, and a mouth has been added, the terrifying aspect of the earlier masks is still in evidence. Fourteenth to eleventh centuries B.C. (Shang Dynasty). Excavated at Anyang. *British Museum*

showing some delicacy in not drawing attention to her non-human form, especially as she was classed among the 'Three Augusts', or the first three spirits who brought civilisation to China.

Nu-kua was not alone in stone sculptures. She and Fu-Hsi were shown together, and he too had a serpent's tail. These tails intertwined, thus joining them together. In ancient references Nu-kua always seems to be alone. No mention is made of the couple Fu-Hsi-Nu-kua until the later Han Dynasty, when Nu-kua was sometimes introduced as the wife of Fu-Hsi, sometimes as his younger sister. Once Nu-kua had invented the rules of marriage and was depicted joined to Fu-Hsi, she was clearly his wife. Might she not be his sister at the same time? It has already been pointed out that Nu-kua was the creator of humanity. Later we shall see her as the heroine of a flood legend. Now we know from ethnography that among the aboriginal tribes of southern China many flood myths featured an incestuous couple, a brother and sister, who became the ancestors of the new generation of men, and Fu-Hsi and Nu-kua are sometimes associated with such couples. The former are perhaps much more ancient than written testimony suggests. But they pose many complex problems. We shall concentrate on the mythical tales concerning Nu-kua.

Once upon a time, in earliest antiquity, the four poles (extremities of the earth) were overturned, the Nine Provinces were destroyed, the sky did not completely cover (the earth), the earth no longer bore (Pu Chou, the sky), fire burned ceaselessly, water overflowed incessantly, wild beasts devoured decent people, birds of prey snatched old men and children. Then Nu-kua melted stones of five colours to repair the azure sky, she cut off the feet of a large tortoise and erected them at the four poles, she killed the Black Dragon to save the land of Chi and she took the

ashes of reeds and piled them up to stop the licentious (overflowing) waters. Once the azure sky had been repaired, once the four poles were back in place, the licentious waters driven back, the land of Chi pacified, the wild beasts killed, decent people alive and safe, the square earth able to carry and the round sky to embrace, all was then perfect.

This fragment of mythology invites numerous comments, but we shall make matters as simple as possible. Leaving aside the ills from which the world was suffering, let us proceed straight to the means Nu-kua used to remedy them.

The stones of five colours are a mystery. The five colours may possibly represent the beauty of the sky with its changing hues. But the expression 'five colours' is a cliché, which, on the one hand, is more particularly applied to the rainbow and to clouds of good omen, and, on the other hand, is often employed in the copious folk-lore of smiths and metallurgists. One wonders whether Nu-kua's stones might be different ores.

M. Granet has made a complete collection of mythical and symbolic features concerning smelters and smiths, and has shown that the alloying of metals was, on the mythical plane, yet another hierogram. There is a temptation to compare the smelting of the stones of five colours with the fact that Nu-kua is the founder (smelter) of marriage. But this does not explain either what was repaired in the sky or why and how this was done. Certain sinologists have concentrated more on the stone than on the smelting or the five colours. They have been able to show that, at least in the Han Dynasty, Nu-kua was the object of a cult as the great mediator between men and women and the goddess-provider of children. It is known that in China such cults often made use of stones, but this has no direct connection with the legend in question.

Supernatural being in armour, with his foot on a bull. He may be one of the guardians of the four corners of the universe. Glazed earthenware of the T'ang Dynasty, found in a tomb. Ceramic objects have been found even in prehistoric tombs, for their creation through the combined *yang* elements of fire and water and *yin* element of clay gave them symbolical meaning. *Victoria and Albert Museum*

The replacement or consolidation of the four poles or four extremities of the earth by the feet of a tortoise is easier, if not to explain, at least to discuss. Both in ancient and modern China people have taken a great interest in the tortoise. It seems to be a part of the universe itself because of its longevity, its usefulness as a means of divination and because of its shape, for its dorsal shell is as round as the sky and its ventral shell as square as the earth. Thus it is quite natural that its four feet should become pillars between heaven and earth. Whether because of its cosmic symbolism, its rock-like shape, its hard shell, amphibious nature, or wise and measured tread, the tortoise was regarded as a stabiliser. Steles are often placed on their pedestals in a tortoise-like position to indicate their stability and perennial quality. It has already been mentioned that the floating Isles of the Immortals, those little independent worlds, were anchored by tortoises.

The ashes of reeds that were piled up to stop the waters overflowing is rather surprising. Some commentators have thought that as reeds grow in water they were the appropriate thing for mastering the waters, either because of their aquatic nature, or because they were above water, following a principle of logic familiar to certain philosophical schools (of the Five Elements, as they were called). One explanation was that ash was sometimes used to dry things out, as in tombs.

The next question is whether the Black Dragon that she killed was Kung Kung. There is nothing to support this hypothesis. It was probably suggested because ancient mythographers wanted to connect the myths of Kung Kung and Nu-kua. It may be remembered that Kung Kung was vanquished by Chu Jung (or by other mythical figures, though it is of no importance here), and when he shook Mount Pu Chou, he caused the sky to drop and brought about flooding on earth. Nu-kua, according to certain mythographers, repaired these ravages. But in other texts this order of things is completely reversed, or else there is no connection at all between the two legends. Furthermore, any attempt to locate them, either through related cults or by studying the native lands or clans or the surnames of those who claimed these mythical characters as their ancestors, only shows that although the legends of Kung Kung and Nu-kua came from neighbouring regions (for ancient China was a small country), these areas were very different indeed.

Kun and Yu

During the reign of Yao, a mythical sovereign, there was a catastrophic flood, which lasted twenty-two years. Yao summoned Four-Mountains and asked his (or their, if there were four of them) advice. Four-Mountains suggested that they should appeal to Kun. Yao was somewhat mistrustful, but agreed to put him to the test. For nine years Kun struggled to

A mountain and a river, constant themes in Chinese religion and art. Chinese painting was intended not simply to be visually beautiful or even evocative of a mood: it was consciously symbolical, seeking to create balanced harmony from the principal and complementary elements of the earth. These were water, cloud and mist, which were symbols of the *yang* or heavenly elements; and rocks and trees, which were symbols of the *yin* or earthly elements. Mists, waterfalls, and so forth, allowed the artist to represent fruitful interpenetration of *yang* and *yin*. Painting by Tai-Hsi (1801–60). *British Museum*

master the waters by building dikes, but he was unsuccessful. He was exiled by Yao's successor, Shun, and killed on the Mount of the Feather. Then Shun gave Yu, Kun's son, the task of continuing his father's work. Instead of damming up the flooding rivers Yu hollowed out and redirected their courses. After thirteen years' continual effort he was successful, but in this time he never once returned home, even if he passed in front of his own door. Then Shun made him a gift of his empire, and he became the founder of the Hsia Dynasty.

In this form the story is interpreted as the conflict between two hydrographies, which basically resolve into two philosophical attitudes: must nature be formed (as with dams) or respectfully directed (drainage)? The tale itself is quite plausible, for the men of letters who composed it certainly intended that it should be given the above interpretation. But in order to do this they must have effaced all mythical traits. These can be reconstructed—at least in part.

Kun was not an ordinary man. He was the great-grandson of Huang-Ti, the Yellow Emperor, and he may have looked like a white horse. When his attempt to dam up the waters did not work, he went so far as to steal a certain 'Swelling Soil', the property of the Lord on High, without waiting for the necessary permission. This magic soil kept on swelling tirelessly, so Kun could have used it for building big dams. But the Lord on High was angry and had him put to death on the Mount of the Feather by Chu Jung, god of fire and master of celestial justice, the same Chu Jung as was given the task of executing Kung Kung.

An owl and a tortoise were also introduced into the myth, though how this came about is unknown. Some commentators think that these two animals advised him to build dams—to his own perdition. Others that they gave him the idea of stealing the 'Swelling Soil' or even brought it to him. Lastly, a few take it that they tore him to pieces after his execution on the Mount of the Feather.

For three years Kun's body was exposed on the Mount of the Feather without decomposing. Finally, someone (the Lord on High?) cut it open with Wu's sword. From Kun's stomach emerged his son Yu (in the shape of a horned dragon?). Kun immediately turned into a beast and threw himself into the Gulf of the Feather (or into the Yellow River). Evidence and interpretations vary greatly as to the sort of beast he became.

The general opinion is that he became a yellow bear. But one is tempted to ask what a bear would do in a waterhole. A three-footed yellow tortoise is also mentioned, as are a black or yellow fish and a yellow dragon. The location of the Mount and Gulf of the Feather is not given in detail. It is, however, known that they were on the very edge of the world. They are usually thought to have lain to the east. They are also sought in the north, near the Gate of Wild Geese.

Yu in turn was given the task of repressing the

waters, but he was better equipped than his father. He could make use of the Swelling Soil. He was aided by the Winged Dragon, who will appear again in the fight between Huang-Ti and Ch'i-You. With the Swelling Soil he stopped up the Springs of the Great Waters—as many as 233,559 have been specified. They were extremely deep and may perhaps have communicated with the underground ocean. He also used the magic soil to build the mountains at the four corners of the earth Because of their great height they could not be submerged, and thus they towered above the flood. Furthermore, their weight helped to anchor the threatened earth. As for the dragon, he traced lines on the ground with his tail to direct the waters into the river beds. The hardest task was to direct the Yellow River down to the sea. Yu had to cut through mountains to open a way. Among many others he opened up the Lung-men Pass (the Gate of the Dragons) and the Mung-men Gorge. His Cyclopean labours are recalled in many parts of China in geographical folk-lore. In this connection, one should state that other mythological characters of lesser importance or good fortune have also left their traces in legends and geographic folk-lore. Thus a certain Kiu-ling was also given the task of directing the Yellow River (his name meant 'Great Deity'—the word *ling* indicates divine or magic power—and was either a primeval god in a lost mythology or more simply a river-god who, however, seems different from the famous Count of the River). He did in fact make the Yellow River surmount the obstacle of Mount Hua or T'aihua, the cardinal mountain of the west, situated on the south bank of the river, in Shensi, before the great bend. In former times this mountain barred the course of the river and it had to meander endlessly in order to flow on to the sea. Setting his back to the mountain, Kiu-ling pushed with his hands and feet to divide it into

two. His fingerprints can still be seen in the rock. Other deities opened the way for smaller rivers.

When Yu pierced mountains and opened defiles, he either disguised himself as a bear or actually turned into one. In this connection people have inevitably thought of his father, Kun, who turned into a yellow bear after his body had been slashed open. At the age of thirty, the proper age according to the canons of Confucius, Yu was married in the land of T'u-shan, somewhere in the south. Every day his wife had to bring him food when he summoned her by beating a drum. One day when he was at work, he fell against a stone which made a noise like a drum. His wife hastened to the spot, but seeing him in the guise of a bear she fled in fear. Yu pursued her. When he was on the point of reaching her, she changed into a rock. Granet has tried to show that this legend could be an echo or transcription of male dancing: dancers disguised as bears used to stamp or skip about on stones and make the noise of thunder or the sound of a drum. Women were not admitted to these dances (they must have had others of their own) and the metamorphosis of Yu's wife may represent her death sentence for infringing this rule. But the reader must not forget that this is only a hypothesis, however solid its basis.

Now Yu's wife was pregnant. Yu begged her to give him his son. However, it is specifically stated that the rock went on growing for a full nine months. It then opened and gave birth to K'i (the name means 'to split'), who, for the first time in Chinese tradition, succeeded his father by right of heredity as king of Hsia. This miraculous birth can be compared to that of Yu himself.

In connection with Yu's great labours numerous legends have been grafted on the main tale. The two most interesting are as follows. As Yu was watching the Yellow River, a creature who was half fish, half

man suddenly emerged; this was the Count of the River who gave him a 'River Map' (*Ho-t'-u*). This map was also said to have been placed on the back of a horse (mythically speaking, horses were related to dragons—Kun, it may be remembered, was perhaps a white horse), but the beneficiary or the inventor is sometimes Yu, sometimes Fu-Hsi. This map of the river or map (design, diagram) that emerged from the river was more like a magic talisman defining the world on an ultimate algebraic formula or trigrams (which were said to have been invented by Fu-Hsi). On another occasion, when Yu was opening up the Lung-men Pass, he discovered a dark, deep cave at the back of which he came across Fu-Hsi in the form of a god with a serpent's body and human face. Fu-Hsi gave him a jade tablet one foot two inches long for measuring heaven and earth. Yu used it to level the earth and the waters. These legends seem to be of quite late origin.

Yu did not confine himself merely to mastering the flood water. He is credited with other exploits, which are obviously connected with the myth of his struggle against the waters, but may have formed part of other cycles. Thus he attacked and conquered the Mount of Clouds and Rain. He also had to give battle to Sinag-liou, minister to the rebel Kung Kung. This was a huge, nine-headed dragon, whose vomit and excrement created poisonous swamps. Yu killed it to the north of Kun-lun, and a stench arose from its spilt blood. It stopped plants growing and made animals move away. Yu tried to block up the cesspool (wrong method of damming up), but this failed three times. Then he dug out a lake (good method of canalisation), and in the middle or on the edge of it someone—Yu most certainly—built a tower. (In modern folk-lore the erection of towers or stupas for subduing wicked dragons is a frequent theme.)

If all the texts concerning Yu are taken into consideration, he emerges clearly as much more than a conqueror of waters, though this is his main function. He travelled throughout the empire and went to all parts of the world. He built the cardinal mountains (or consecrated them), not only to dominate the waters and settle the land, but also to determine direction. He inspected waters, mountains, swamps; in other words he went everywhere, even into inaccessible spots, and utilised or invented the appropriate means of transport: the boat, climbing-irons and the skiff.

As well as taking possession of the empire, Yu measured it and fixed its boundaries. He was a surveyor and geographer; in his tours of inspection he kept a level and string on his left and dividers and square to his right. He is sometimes said to have delegated two ministers to measure the world, Ta-chang and Shou-hai. The first paced out the distance between the east and west poles, the second the distance between the north and south poles. The two distances were equal—233,575 steps—for the earth was believed

to be square. It was mentioned earlier that Fu-Hsi gave Yu a jade tablet, which was probably a standard length or a gnomon, in any case a measuring-instrument of some sort. The River Map was either a geographical map or a numerical or symbolic diagram.

Knowledge or possession of the world, both of which amounted to the same thing, took material form in the Nine Cauldrons of the Hsia. Granet was able to show that here certain mythical features converge and enable us to interpret the character of Yu as that of a miner or smith. For it was in fact Yu who cast the Nine Cauldrons, the *palladia* of the dynasty. The Nine Shepherds brought him metal from the Nine Provinces by way of tribute on his accession to the throne. They also brought him the emblem of each country. These were engraved on the cauldrons. It is also claimed that geographical maps of the provinces were engraved on the same cauldrons, one province to each cauldron. However, maps or emblems, the result was the same: henceforth, one could travel anywhere without danger. And in fact it was also said (but this has no direct connection with the cauldrons) that Yu opened up the Nine Provinces and made the Nine Roads available.

Sovereigns and rebels

As this last section comes, in our scheme of things, after the organisation of the world, it might perhaps have been called the organisation of society were it not for the fact that it would be inaccurate to reduce ancient Chinese society to the chiefs and their rivals. Unfortunately, peasant or artisan society has seldom provided a subject for mythological themes. We have so far come across only one: that of the Cowherd and the Weaver-girl. The fact is, however, that the theme of sovereigns and rebels is one of the most characteristic in Chinese mythology, but it is also the most affected by reconstruction and historical theories. It has been very carefully studied by Marcel Granet.

Ch'i You and Huang-Ti

Huang-Ti is, after the Three Augusts, the first of the Five Sovereigns in traditional mythology, which was long thought of as actual history. He was adopted by the Taoists as their great patron and therefore is one of the very few gods of antiquity who has remained part of Chinese religion right down to modern times. His name is not found in earliest literature, and as it does not appear until the end of the period of the Warring States, in other words about the third century B.C., there are several convincing arguments to the effect that it was literally invented by the theorists of the school of the Five Elements. This is not quite true. The theorists undoubtedly fabricated that famous Yellow Emperor, yellow because he reigned by virtue of the earth element, but they did not create him *ex nihilo*. If certain legends concerning the Yellow Emperor give an impression of fabrication (or adaptation), others, particularly his fight against Ch'i-You, seem to come of much more ancient stock, involving an ancestor of Huang-Ti, the Yellow Emperor. Now this ancestor is known to us. He was also called Huang-Ti, but his name means August Sovereign, and he is identified with or at least goes back to the Supreme Sovereign, or Supreme Sovereign of the August Sky, the little known high god of the Yin Dynasty and of the origins of Chinese culture.

Ch'i-You was a monster, and although descriptions of him do not tally in the least, all his characteristics, even the most bizarre, are of very great importance. Here are some of them: he had sharp-pointed horns, an iron head and a brow of bronze; his hair bristled at the temples like swords or spears; he had a human body and the feet of an ox; or else he had the body of a beast and a human voice, four eyes and six arms, eight fingers and eight toes. Sometimes there seemed to be only one person involved, on other occasions Ch'i-You is said to have had eighty-one or seventy-two brothers. He ate sand, stones and iron. He invented and fabricated arms.

A more careful study of texts relating to this character shows that he was of a highly complex mythical nature, and even a brief analysis of this material would necessitate long discussion, so we shall leap straight to conclusions. In spite of his monstrous appearance he was the son, grandson or minister of Shen-nung, the ox-headed Divine Farmer, the last of the Three Augusts and predecessor of Huang-Ti. He was a god of war: his flag, a sort of comet, appeared in the sky to warn of a difficult military period. Like Huang-Ti, he was credited with the invention of the art of war and arms, and although he was vanquished, people continued to make sacrifice in times of war to him as well as to Huang-Ti. He was also quite clearly a smith or brotherhood of smiths, and, taking things to extremes, may even have been regarded as a forge himself. In addition, he was a dancer or horned jouster. He excelled in fighting with horns, which before becoming a sport seems to have been an ordeal by duel to class merits and fix ranks. His fight with Huang-Ti, of which only fragments are known, reminds one of an epic.

Ch'i-You attacked Huang-Ti (certain texts say the Yellow Emperor, others the August Sovereign) and pursued him as far as the plain of Chuo-lu in Hupei, where there was a great battle. The army of Huang-Ti included grey bears, black bears, panthers, tigers and other wild beasts. Ch'i-You's army was composed of demons. According to another tradition, Huang-Ti's army had chariots and the enemy used horsemen. Ch'i-You employed magic to produce a thick fog, and this enveloped Huang-Ti's army, but the latter's answer was to invent the compass. He also ordered his troops to blow horns to imitate the cry of the dragon. This frightful noise, which may simply have been magical, made Ch'i-You's soldiers give ground. Then Huang-Ti summoned the aid of the Winged Dragon, who made the waters rise. But Ch'i-You sent for the Count of Wind and the Master of Rain, who vanquished the Winged Dragon. In the final resort Huang-Ti brought down a girl from the skies (his own daughter, it was said), called Pa, 'Dryness', who immediately stopped the wind and rain. Then Ch'i-You was conquered and decapitated. Some say the

Winged Dragon was entrusted with the execution. Even though it had no head Ch'i You's body ran until at last it fell. That is why he had two tombs. For some unexplained reason the girl Pa could not go back up into the sky, but continued to spread drought. People suffered greatly, and Huang-Ti had to send her into exile in the north, beyond the Red Water, where she could run loose without inflicting damage. The Dragon could not get back either. He made his way underground and caused drought.

This particular myth about Ch'i-You illustrates the very general theme of the rebel. Ch'i-You possessed an outworn virtue. Minister or son (mythically and sociologically speaking, the minister — intendant or great vassal — and the son are not essentially different from one another), he represents the predecessor of Huang-Ti. The idea of a cycle is one of the bases of Chinese thought (the *yin* and the *yang* alternate). It also applies to politics and history or to historical myth. Ch'i-You possessed an ill-starred virtue. He was the rebel minister, the rival of the sovereign appointed by Heaven. His rebellion was expressed in another myth, likewise attributed to another outstanding rebel, Kung Kung: the latter mounted the 'Nine Mares' to fight the hollow mulberry-tree. The hollow mulberry-tree *(k'ong-sang)* was the abode of the rising sun. The rising sun was the future sovereign. The latter, who possessed a new virtue of good omen, could not accede to supreme rank, or make his appearance, until he had fought a victorious battle against the minister, his *alter ego*. The idea of opposition accompanies and completes that of a cycle (the *yin* is opposed to the *yang* and yet they exist only through one another). A virtue of good omen, a new virtue, can manifest itself only by opposing and succeeding to a virtue of ill omen, an outworn virtue.

Whether the victory is military or ritual, whether it takes place after a pitched battle, or a duel, sport, ceremony or competition, victory alone is not sufficient. It is of necessity sealed by the capital punishment or the banishment of the conquered. This execution is one of the basic elements of the inauguration of a new order. These pseudo-historic schemas, which are based purely on mythical data, or can be deduced from the texts of ballets or ritual, which show myth 'in action', reveal on analysis that the expulsion-execution of the rebel minister comes within the more general or ritual framework of the expulsion of the four divine monsters to the four poles (or to the four gates of the capital), where they become the guardians of the cardinal points.

JAPAN: CULTS AND CEREMONIES

The Shinto gods

The cult

Early local chronicles depict ancient Japanese society as one in which rite and ritual ceremony played an important part, with religion primarily concerned with the forces of nature, and although these ancient writings reflect the primitive and brutal, they also indicate that the early Japanese were deeply aware of their clement geographical conditions. This is particularly significant when one considers that the Japanese islands have always been the scene of natural tragedy in the form of typhoons, earthquakes and floods. One critic, Sansom, suggests: 'It may be that the naturally mild climate of Japan with its profusion of trees and flowering bushes and its fertile land interrupted by countless watercourses greatly impressed tribes arriving exhausted from the arid regions of Korea, North China and the inhospitable plains of Siberia, and a feeling of keen gratitude may thus have infiltrated the growing racial consciousness.'

This may or may not be true, but one thing is certain: the concept of major catastrophe is entirely absent from Japanese mythology as is the idea of fear-inducing divinities that are found throughout the world's myths.

Ritual was devoted mainly to acts of praise, but if the need arose it could also serve to placate or reconcile the gods. Primitive belief reveals no great workings of the mind, no tendency or ability to organise or correlate the impressions to which single individuals are always so receptive. There is not one speculative or philosophical element in this early religion; such characteristics were not to appear until contact had been established with Buddhist and Chinese ideas; in early times there was no notion of a soul, and no strict differentiation between life and death, body and spirit.

The concept of divinity

The early Japanese world was an animistic world. Both natural things and human beings were animated or permeated by a vital spirit; they possessed a sort of individual vitality. This life element in things, which distinguished them from one another in form or colour or in some other way, was thought to come 'from above' and was known as *kami* (basically 'above', 'upper part', 'up above'). Anything that had unusual power or beauty or an unusual shape was an object of worship and became *kami*. The list of *kami* is endless: mountains, rocks, torrents, rivers, trees, to quote only a few things. This primitive cult reveals a fertile but somewhat vague imagination. Deities abound, but their characters are indistinct, blurred, their powers ill-defined, and their habitat unknown. In short, although the anthropomorphic concept of divinity developed very early, the exact nature of the gods was undefined and the relationship between them is still not clear.

Religious observances

The observances connected with this primitive cult relate to the idea of growth and decline. Growth was regarded as good, decline as bad, or, alternatively, growth was life, and decline death. This attitude obviously stemmed from an agricultural way of life, and it was therefore natural that religious observances should take the form of harvest thanksgivings. But there were also preventative practices intended to avert the taint of sickness and death.

Sun and earth

The Yamato tribes were undoubtedly devoted to a sort of sun cult. Traces of this are found in their mythology, which at first had a solar bias and was largely influenced by a sun-goddess. It was not long

before pride of place was given to more modest
deities within the framework of this mythology. The
solar aspect tended to disappear, whilst the goddess
herself became an anthropomorphic-type deity of
supreme rank, with her cult-centre in the imperial
sanctuaries at Isé (near present-day Nagoya).

Early myths reveal a counterpart to the solar figure
in the form of an earth deity. The earth cult, which
at first was simply the direct cult of the soil, later
developed into the cult of Okuninushi, an anthropomorphic god who had a cult-centre at Izumo on
the west coast of Japan opposite Korea. A sort of deification of the virtue of kindliness also existed and
was embodied in the figure of Ukemochi, a food-
goddess who provided the various forms of sustenance
needed by living creatures.

Primitive history

Religious functions

In the beginning the Japanese were divided into clans,
and each clan claimed descent from one particular
god; the clan chieftain officiated over his cult. At
this time the functions of high priest and clan chieftain went together, but with the evolution of a more
complex system of government a distinction was
made between them. The task of presiding over a
specific official cult was then entrusted to certain
priests or families. Divine functions must then have
become specialised, for the mythological data furnished by ancient chronicles show that 'secret matters'
came to be entrusted to Izumo and 'public matters'
to Yamato.

The 'abstinents' or 'guardians of mourning' mentioned in chapters on Japan in ancient Chinese chronicles are an example of this sort of specialisation.
These abstinents were the predecessors of the *imi-be*
or 'guild of abstinents' who had to ensure the ritual
purity of both people and things. They were closely
connected with religious practice. The Nakatomi
family was responsible for the liturgy and empowered
to communicate with the gods on behalf of the
emperor.

In early times the priest caste was not allowed to ex-
ceed a certain number, though within these limits
any official could assume religious duties provided
that he was ritually pure, a state achieved by fasting,
lustration and other similar austerities. Then, as now,
priests combined civil duties with religious functions,
except those who served in the great national shrines.
Here it is interesting to note that the Japanese word for
government, *matsurigoto* (not government as assumed
by a single leader, but by ministers and officials),
has the literal meaning 'religious observance'.

Offences

Observances were for the most part directed towards
ritual purity. Any offence against the gods was described as *tsumi* — 'fault' or 'sin' is probably the nearest equivalent, but neither quite convey the meaning
of this expression. The object of the cult was to avoid
tsumi and, in the imperial cult, the task of preventing
tsumi was entrusted to a select group, the guild of
abstinents, the *imi-be*. The chief offence was uncleanliness. Uncleanliness meant several things. Physical
dirt was one important aspect of it, and religious
cleanliness required a clean body and clean clothes. A
basin of clear water that stood at the entrance to
Shinto shrines for rinsing hands and mouth symbolised the desire for this sort of religious cleanliness.
But impurity went beyond outward appearances and
included menstruation, sexual relations and birth,
all of which were a cause of ceremonial impurity and
had to be effaced by lustration, fasting and prayer.
A third cause of impurity was death and anything related to it: sickness and wounds. Death or contamination from death, or even the place where death
had occurred, were regarded as impure. Similarly,
there was impurity in wounds or *kega* — a term which,
it is interesting to note, also means 'defilement'. The
maladies that were the source of impurity included
sores, rashes, discharges, contact with the sick and so
on.

In matters of offence, no distinction was made
between moral stain and moral culpability. There
appears to have been no essential difference between
adultery, on the one hand, and sexual relations between husband and wife, on the other. Generally
speaking, primitive Japanese religion was lacking in
any abstract idea of morality. Sins, if this is the right
word, were states or acts that were visibly or directly
repulsive.

In the ancient cult a distinction was made between
terrestrial and celestial offences. Celestial offences
were of the type committed, for instance, by Susanowo, a turbulent male deity who ignored divisions

The Kumesu shrine at Matsue, first built in 1346 and rebuilt every twenty years according to Shinto rite. The shrines stood in enclosures with subsidiary buildings and storehouses. This one is built on stilts because of the danger of floods. *M. Sakamoto*

between rice-fields and committed other agricultural infringements. Terrestrial offences included killing or wounding, committing incest, acts of bestiality or acts affecting the well-being of individuals, though the offenders were not necessarily at fault. All these offences involved a ritual impurity or pollution, and it was the pollution that had to be effaced, not the fault that had to be expiated.

Fertility

Shinto ceremonial may have been chiefly concerned with purity, but Shinto belief centred on the idea of fertility. Rich harvests and plenty of game were of prime importance, and liturgical ritual (*norito*) of the kind recited at harvest festival in honour of all gods included expressions of thanks: 'For harvests of long-eared corn, abundant ears of corn, for things growing in the great plain, for sweet grass and bitter grass, for creatures or things living in the azure-coloured plain of the sea, large fins, narrow fins, seaweed from the deep, seaweed from the shore, clothing, brilliant material, shiny material, coarse material and fine material.' The most important ceremonies involved food: tasting the first fruits (*niname*) and divine tasting (*kanname*), both of which were performed at the imperial altar at Isé; communal tasting (*ainame*), in the course of which the emperor took his place with the gods, and with them tasted the new rice and *sake*; the great tasting (*onie*, later called *daijoe*) was a complicated form of the tasting of the first fruits celebrated after the enthronement of a new emperor as a solemn consecration of his sovereignty.

The phallic cult and its survival show even more clearly the deep interest taken in fertility. Evidence of this has survived in the form of phallic objects, most often found in rice-fields, where they served to indicate the fundamental relationship between agricultural fertility and human fertility, and sometimes at the roadside, since the symbol for the god of cross-roads was a phallus.

Sanctuaries

In primitive Shinto the cult of trees, rocks and springs was celebrated *in situ*. The objects of worship and the place in which they were found were later surrounded by pines planted to form a sacred enclosure. It was only when such objects as jewels, mirrors and swords came to be used as symbols of the gods that the need arose to house them in a comparatively permanent place. During the clan period the home of the chief was used as a shelter for the cult, and probably no distinction was made between sanctuary and residence. In fact, the sanctuary was—and is still—referred to as the *miya*, which quite simply means 'honourable house', and this expression is clearly a reference to the chief's residence. Gradually, buildings were constructed for religious observances,

and although no longer used as the dwelling of chieftain or of the head of government, they none the less retained marks of their origin as private dwellings.

Shinto sanctuaries are extremely simple, and as they are rebuilt every twenty years according to immutable rites and plans, they are in the most ancient style of Japanese architecture. They are simply wooden huts with thatched roofs, rather stylised in form, with room inside only for the altar and the priests. Private worshippers remain outside and from there present their petitions.

The cult itself consists of salutations, offerings and prayers. In early Shinto times, offerings took the form of food and drink. Later, offerings of cloth were included. This cloth was represented by bands of paper fastened to a stick known as a *gohei*. It is interesting to note that the *gohei* itself came to be regarded as sacred and was thought to be the seat of the deity and an object of worship—as it is today.

Purification

Given that *tsumi* implies 'blemish' or 'stain', one of the essential elements in the cult is purification, especially in so far as this ceremony is preparatory to the cult proper. Purification takes various forms. There is exorcism, or *harai*, practised by the priest and intended to efface the stain caused by the *tsumi*. This consists in the presentation of offerings in the form of monetary fines and the priests' pronouncement of a formula of purification. There is also *misogier* or 'washing' to efface accidental stains, such as pollution through contact with unclean things: mud, death, sickness. This is accomplished by means of ablutions, sprinkling with water or salt, or similar rites. From earliest times warm baths have served both ritual and practical purposes, and people once believed that salt placed in a little heap near the entrance to a house, on the parapet of a well, or on the ground after funeral ceremonies, had the power to purify anything that might accidentally have become sullied.

Another method of purification was by abstinence, or *imi*. Abstinence made it possible to acquire positive purity by avoiding the sources of pollution. Priests rather than laymen were in a position to practise this method. It consisted of observing certain rules forbidding various things: withdrawing from all contact with death, sickness, mourning. It also involved certain positive acts, such as partaking of certain foods prepared on a purified fire, wearing purified clothing, withdrawing from noise, dancing, singing and, in short, being away from all activity likely to produce defilement.

In contrast with the official cult, private devotions took the form of offerings placed in front of the sanctuary. The worshipper who came with a petition called the attention of the gods to his presence by clapping his hands and bowing his head. There has never been organised prayer in Shinto, or individual

prayer, unless very simple formulas can be called 'prayer'. Yet on the level of official cult liturgical orations (*norito*) constitute an important part of religious practice.

Under the auspices of public authority two types of Shinto grew up: one, the simple animistic cult of nature—and the survival of magic powers; and another, in contrast and almost independent of it, a complicated official cult closely connected with the political system and emphasising the fact that the emperor ruled by divine right and was regarded as a direct descendant of the sun-goddess herself. At one time this official cult was closely connected with nationalist ideas.

It is difficult to say exactly when Shinto became an organised religion, but there are documents to prove that in the middle of the seventh century there were more than three thousand shrines. The name *Shinto*, which means the 'way of the gods', was not used until the introduction of Buddhism, which made it necessary to distinguish between the two forms of belief. The first reference to Shinto appears under the date 585 in the *Nihongi*, or 'Chronicles of Japan', a history of the country from earliest times up to A.D. 697. There is little doubt that in the pre-Buddhist period Shinto was still a somewhat vague cult possessing neither sacred books, nor established dogma, nor moral code. But once Buddhism was introduced —in other words from the sixth century onwards— and there was contact between the two beliefs, Shinto took on a more definite shape.

The role of the gods

The idea of anthropomorphic deities probably emerged at a very early date, though it remained vague and unsystematised. But towards the middle of the Heian period (about 900) Shinto deities began to appear in the likeness of many of the personalities in the esoteric Buddhist pantheon. This new tendency in the indigenous religion, which in its early form had been totally devoid of graphic representation, was explained as *honji suijaku*, 'manifestations of the original body', a theory in which Shinto deities were regarded as local manifestations of Buddhist deities. For example, the sun-goddess, Amaterasu, became the counterpart of the Buddhist sun-god Vairocana (in Japanese: Dainichi), while, somewhat surprisingly, Hachiman, the Shinto god of war, was identified from 783 onwards with the gentle Bodhisattva Kannon and even with the Buddha Amida.

The tendency for the two systems to intermingle goes back to the Nara period. Gyogi (670–749) is reputed to have been the first to put forward this idea of fusion, which was later propagated by Ryoben (689–773). But an imperial edict dated 765 seems to show that there was not yet complete fusion at that date, for one idea expressed in it was that the Shinto gods were the protectors of the buddhas. The particular period associated with the mingling of the two cults is that which marked the rise of esoteric Shingon Buddhism, that is, the beginning of the ninth century onwards. According to an important Shingon concept the universe was divided into two parts (*ryobu*), and this concept may have sparked off the idea of a pantheon in two sections, one made up of Shinto gods and the other of Buddhist gods, who appeared both in their own shape and in the manifestation of the Shinto gods. In fact, it was the Buddhist section that was a manifestation of the Shinto. The Shingon school gave this odd alliance the name of Ryobu Shinto, or 'Shinto in two sections', while the Tendai school called it Ichijitsu Shinto, or 'Shinto of the one and only truth'. Taking Buddhist history as a whole, this type of fusion is peculiar to Japan, although wherever the great Indian religion spread similar tendencies towards syncretism can be found.

There was never complete fusion between Buddhism and Shinto, and native gods retained their own vaguely defined territory whilst the powers attributed to them varied according to the degree of Buddhist influence. Syncretism was not completely established until after the Heian period, about 1100. In 1272, for instance, the sanctuary at Yasaka, which until then had been Shinto, became a Buddhist temple under the name of Gion-ji. This twofold form of Shinto is attributed to Kukai and Saicho, though there is nothing in their writings to support this conclusion. The most that can be said is that the very catholicity of the ideas held by these great founders favoured the fusion of the two religions; in this they displayed a characteristically Japanese attitude towards religious practices.

Mythology

Japanese myths present certain obscurities. They are episodic rather than epic in nature, and there is some discrepancy involved, for they are not a co-ordinated system of legends. It is difficult to classify these myths in distinct groups, and later additions cannot always be distinguished from the original legends. However, at the beginning of the eighth century they were collected together in two important works: the *Kojiki* or 'Records of Ancient Matters', and the *Nihongi* or 'Chronicles of Japan'. These two works claim to contain legends up to their own period.

The *Kojiki* made its appearance in the year 712 and the *Nihongi* in 720, and both are products of an age primarily interested in Chinese culture, which dominated eighth-century Japan. Both volumes were written in Chinese. However—and this is particularly true of the *Kojiki*—the Chinese characters were sometimes used phonetically to reproduce Japanese sounds. These works were intended to demonstrate a politico-cultural fact, namely that the clans that called themselves the Yamato (living in the region now known as the Kyoto-Osaka) were politically and culturally superior to those in other centres. The method adopted was that of presenting a sort of official dynastic history, based on Chinese models. The compilers took the rational view of history and had a marked bias of opinion. Their treatment of the earlier periods of Japanese history was completely Chinese in approach, highly characteristic of the eighth century, and in many cases they used sophisticated ideas (which could not have been current prior to the spread of Chinese influence in the country) to interpret ancient facts. In spite of the political motives and cultural bias characteristic of these two works, and provided they are used with circumspection, they contain a mine of information about primitive Japan and are the principal sources of Japanese mythology.

The Kojiki

The *Kojiki*—or *Furu oto bumi* ('Records of Ancient Matters')—was written in the second part of the eighth century, but was not published until 712. It is the most ancient Japanese work in existence. It was begun under Emperor Temmu who, in 681, set about collecting documents of earlier periods lest they should be lost for ever. A certain Hieda no Are, who was reputed to have a prodigious memory and undoubtedly belonged to the body known as *katari-be* or 'guild of narrators', was given the task of transmitting the legends by word of mouth to a scribe, O no Yasumaro, who transcribed them. As the aim of the compilers was to glorify the sovereign and establish the claims of the dynasty on a firm basis, the legends retraced in the *Kojiki* were subject to considerable modification in the interests of national unification. And the preface reflects contemporary Chinese ideas, with which the authors were deeply imbued. They looked upon history as a basis for action and as a pattern to be copied. So the *Kojiki* was a 'selection' of legends deemed worthy of handing down to later generations as sources of useful patterns of behaviour and action applicable at the time of writing.

The Nihongi

The *Nihongi* or 'Chronicles of Japan' was published barely eight years after the *Kojiki*, in 720. Like the latter it tells the story of Japan from prehistoric times, but whereas the *Kojiki*'s narrative stopped at the year 628, the *Nihongi* continued to the year 700. Chinese influence is more marked, starting with the explanation accorded the myth of creation (involving the interplay between the *yin* and the *yang*) and going so far as to include facts boldly taken from the dynastic history of China. Although it is basically concerned with the same material as the *Kojiki*, the *Nihongi* introduces two new features. On the one hand, it reports the different variants of each mythological episode (and here we should note that these additional narratives embroider considerably on the basic accounts related in the *Kojiki*); on the other hand, it introduces a system of dates. This is arbitrary and merely reflects the author's desire to provide a Chinese-style chronology for events of Japanese history. It needs to be radically corrected in the case of the early reigns, and to a large extent the dates it quotes can be relied on only from the beginning of the sixth century.

Apart from these two main sources, there are other works dating from the same period, which make a valuable contribution to our knowledge of Japanese mythology, though they are less substantial.

The nucleus

In the beginning was chaos, like an ocean of oil or an egg, shapeless but seed-bearing. From this confusion

Izanagi and his sister Izanami, the eighth of the early Shinto couples. Izanagi is plunging his celestial spear into the ocean of chaos to create the island of Onogoro. Full colour silk scroll. Late nineteenth century. *Museum of Fine Arts, Boston*

arose a 'thing', like a reed shoot, which was regarded as a deity and given a name. Almost immediately other deities came into being and, though the number varies in different accounts, they were all of minor importance and soon disappeared. In all there were seven generations of minor deities who appeared in pairs, each pair consisting of a brother and sister: the eighth and last couple in this series acquired considerable but ephemeral importance. Its two members were Izanagi, the 'Male who invites', and his sister Izanami, the 'Female who invites'.

The creation

At the command of their predecessors, the so-called 'celestial' deities, Izanagi and Izanami went forward together over the 'Floating Bridge of Heaven' (*ama no uki hashi*) and plunged a jewel-bedecked celestial spear into the ocean of chaos which stretched beneath them. They stirred it until the liquid coagulated and thickened. Whereupon they withdrew the spear and the drops of brine that fell from it formed the island of Onogoro, the island 'that coagulates of its own accord'.

The marriage of Izanagi and Izanami

Izanagi and Izanami went down to the newly formed island and made it the 'Central Pillar' of the earth. Then Izanagi questioned his sister saying: 'How is thy body made?' To which Izanami replied: 'My body grows in all parts, except one.' Then Izanagi continued: 'My body grows also in all parts, especially one. Good were it that I should join this part of my body with that of thine which grows not. Thus shall we engender (numerous) regions.' And his young sister replied: '[In truth] it would be good.' Then the two gods, at the suggestion of the August Male, decided to make a tour round the island-pillar, Izanagi going to the left and Izanami to the right. When they met again, the young sister exclaimed upon her brother's beauty: 'Oh! what a fine man!' Then Izanagi cried 'Oh! what a beautiful woman!' But then Izanagi reproached his sister for her unthinking enthusiasm, saying: 'I am a man, and by right I must speak first. How is it that thou, a woman, didst speak first? This brings bad luck.' Then, of their union, several islands and deities were born. One of these offspring was a cripple child, or leech-child as it was known. Because of its infirmity it was abandoned on a raft of reeds, which sailed away with the current. When the two spirits saw the failure of their efforts to pro-create well they sought the advice of the heavenly spirits, who advised them to rectify the ritual error of the 'Female who invites' speaking first. Izanagi and Izanami agreed. 'Let us go round the island-pillar once again.' And so they repeated the rite, and this time the male god spoke first, rectifying the ritual error. In other versions the two gods wished to couple, but knew nothing of the art of sexual relations. They noticed a wagtail who, in the manner of the species, was shaking its head and tail violently, and by imitating the bird were able to come together.

The death of Izanami

Izanami continued to produce all sorts of gods—of the sea, waves, mountains and the eight islands of Japan. Then she gave birth to the god of fire. At his birth her lower body was so burned that she fell desperately sick; other gods arose from her vomit, urine and excrement. At last she died. Izanagi in rage and despair also fell sick, and as he crept round her couch lamenting, other deities were born of his tears. Then he seized his sword, ten hand-spans long, and cut off the head of his son, the fire-god, and from the blood so shed other spirits were born.

Izanagi in the lower world

At this point in the legend there is an important episode. Unable to contain his desire to see his dead sister-wife, Izanagi decides to visit her in the Land of Darkness, where she has built herself a castle. Izanagi tries to persuade her to return to the world above, where their work of creation is not yet complete. But she hesitates on the pretext that it is too late—although the real reason is that she has already partaken of food in the Land of Darkness. She urges her brother not to follow her and retires to her palace. But Izanagi is impatient. He breaks off a 'male' tooth from the left end of his comb, sets it alight and goes into the palace to find out why she is so long. He finds her in an advanced state of decomposition, eaten away by worms, her putrefying flesh giving off a sickening smell. In horror he turns about and flees. But she is displeased at having been discovered in such a humiliating state, and sends demons (shikome) from the Land of Darkness to pursue him. Izanagi snatches off his headdress in his flight and throws it behind him; it is immediately turned into grapes, which the demons stop to devour. The pursuit continues, and Izanagi takes the right-hand-side comb from his hair and throws it behind him; immediately the comb changes into bamboo shoots, which the demons tear up and devour. Then Izanami sends an army of fifteen hundred warriors to hound Izanagi down. But the August Male fends them off with his sword ten hand-spans long. Finally, in the pass between the Land of Light and the Land of Darkness, he finds three peaches with which he bombards his pursuers, obliging them to retire. This done, he blocks the passage with a large rock, and from opposite sides his sister and he hurl invective at one another. She threatens to kill a thousand living creatures on the Earth of Light every day; to which Izanagi replies that in that case he will cause one thousand five hundred women to bear children, and thus a balance will be established between births and deaths. At last he makes a final break with his sister, pronouncing the formula of divorce.

An ofuda, a sheet of paper folded into a lozenge shape supported in the middle by a thin stick of wood. The ofuda represents the deity whose name is written on it. This ofuda comes from the temple of the sun-goddess Amaterasu-kodaijingu at the imperial shrines at Isé, chief cult centre of Amaterasu since the first century A.D. Larousse

This legend, which demonstrates the contrasting cycles of light and darkness, birth and death, has obvious analogies with the Greek myth of Orpheus and Eurydice, and even closer ones with that of Persephone. Like Persephone, Izanami had tasted the food of the Land of Darkness and was unable to return to the Land of Light. But, unlike the Greeks, the Japanese did not take advantage of the dramatic possibilities of the situation. In the Japanese myth the situation is resolved by a compromise, just as in other episodes in Japanese mythology solutions can be found that show the same conciliatory instinct. Here we have evidence of a fundamental difference between Japanese and Greek philosophy.

Birth of the sun-goddess

After this contact with death and the infected lower world Izanagi undertakes to purify himself. To do this, he bathes in a little river in Tsukushi (Kyushu), and as he takes off his clothes and lays them on the ground a dozen spirits spring forth from his garments and jewels. In an attempt to avoid the fast upper current and the slow lower current, he dives in midstream, and at once other gods are born from the trails left by his body in the water: Amaterasu, the 'Heaven-illumining lady', is born from his left eye, and from his right eye comes the moon-god, Tsukiyomi-no-Mikoto, and Susanowo, the 'Impetuous Male', a storm-god, from his nose. Amaterasu and Susanowo will henceforth be the central characters in the legend; the moon-god rapidly disappears from the tale.

Amaterasu is brilliant and luminous, and Izanagi places under her dominion the Plain of Heaven and makes her a gift of a necklace of precious stones. Susanowo, impetuous and dark, he sets to reign over the Sea Plain. But Susanowo is inconsolable; he weeps and laments loudly and unceasingly. At the sound of his voice the mountains begin to shrink and the seas run dry. The gods do not know what to do. Then Izanagi asks Susanowo to tell him the cause of his loud grief in which he seems to take more pleasure than in his duties as master of the Sea Plain. Susanowo replies that he is grieving thus because he wants to visit his mother (Izanami) in the Land of Darkness; this is the cause of his distress. Izanagi is enraged at this impertinence and banishes him.

Union of Susanowo and the sun-goddess

Then Susanowo decides to take his leave of his sister, Amaterasu, the sun-goddess, and makes his way towards her kingdom in the skies. But his approach is accompanied by such commotion that his sister fears he may intend to encroach on her territory. And so she prepares to meet him. Over her shoulder she slings one quiver containing a thousand arrows and another with five hundred; then she seizes her bow and takes up her stand so vigorously that she sinks thigh-deep in the ground and thus stationed looks like a mighty warrior. Confronted with this formidable Amazon, Susanowo assures her that he has simply come to bid her farewell and that he has no 'equivocal intention'. To prove his good faith, he proposes that they should be joined in solemn alliance and that they should produce children. This is done at once in the following way—she accepts the sword ten hand-spans long which he gives her, breaks it into three parts, and puts them into her mouth to chew. He does the same with the jewels she offers him. From the fragments they spit out numerous gods are born.

Disappearance of the sun-goddess

In spite of all his protestations Susanowo does not improve his manners. In certain ways his behaviour worsens. He breaks down the divisions that Amaterasu has erected between the rice-fields, he fills in the irrigation ditches and befouls her home. Curiously enough, she finds excuses for him at first, attributing his actions to drunkenness. But when he flays a piebald horse and throws it over his head into the room where she is busy weaving with her retinue, so that the shuttles fly and grievously wound her maids, she gives vent to understandable anger. To show her displeasure she retires into a rocky cavern and blocks the entrance.

With the goddess shut up in the grotto, the world is plunged into darkness, and day and night cease to alternate. The myriads of spirits are greatly troubled by this turn of events; and so they assemble in the dry bed of the celestial river to take counsel and find the best means of inciting the goddess to emerge from her retreat. They set nocturnal birds near the entrance to her cave and make them sing; they hang from a tree a string of curved jewels, a mirror and offerings of white material, and in unison they recite liturgical orations (norito). The act that finally proves effective is a lascivious and provocative dance executed by the goddess Ama no Uzume. She strikes the ground hard with her heels, shows her breasts, drops her skirt and so delights the assembled gods that they burst out laughing. Stung by understandable curiosity, the sun-goddess peers out of her cave; at this the deities push the mirror up to the mouth of the cave, and the goddess, seeing a mirror for the first time, is so fascinated by her own reflection that she leaves the cave. A rope is quickly stretched out behind her to prevent her re-entering. With her emergence light again dazzles the earth and day and night begin to alternate once more.

The re-emergence of the sun-goddess marks the culminating point in the cosmogonic legend. It is difficult to say with certainty what this episode means in terms of mythological symbolism. Does it correspond to the return of the sun after some natural and lengthy perturbation, such as a mighty tempest or even a solar eclipse? The compilers

obviously took it to be the exaltation of an imperial ancestor: equally it might mean peaceful victory over the barbarians achieved by a comparatively centralised government faced with minor clans. Whatever the truth may be, this episode in the legend marks the end of any consistent narrative· hereafter there are only fragmentary episodes and incidents that lack satisfactory continuity.

Minor legends

The assembly of gods blames Susanowo for the episode of the sun's disappearance just recounted and imposes a heavy fine on him of 'a thousand tables'; as a further punishment he has his finger-nails and toenails torn out and is banished from heaven.

The food-goddess

The myth that follows next has originality and deserves attention. Susanowo, or in another version the moon-god, Tsukiyomi, is ordered by Amaterasu to go down and enter the service of the food-goddess, Ukemochi. When the god reaches her palace, the goddess welcomes him by turning her head towards the earth and vomiting boiled rice; then she turns towards the sea, into which she spills all sorts of fish, and finally she raises her face to the mountains and sends in that direction different varieties of game. All these products are presented to the divine messenger as if it were a great banquet. But he is angered by this offering from the goddess's mouth and draws his sword and kills her. On his return to heaven he recounts these events to the sun-goddess who displays extreme irritation at the thoughtless action of her messenger. In the account in which the moon-god appears, she shows her disapproval by refusing to meet him again face to face. The result is that sun and moon remain apart, the day being assigned to the one, and the night to the other. But the story does not end there. The goddess sends another messenger to the dead food-goddess. He discovers that her inanimate body has given birth to several things: an ox and horse have emerged from her head; from her forehead has come forth millet-grass; silkworms from her eyebrows; panic-grass from her eyes; rice from her stomach; corn and haricot beans from the lower parts of her body. The messenger takes these products and shows them to the sun-goddess, who extracts their seeds and gives them to another deity to sow. Then, putting the silkworms in her mouth, she unwinds the threads and thus institutes the art of silkworm culture.

Susanowo and the eight-headed serpent

The adventures of Susanowo continue. After his banishment from the sky, the Impetuous Male goes down to the land of Izumo, in the west of Japan, opposite Korea, at the mouth of the most important river, the Hi. Seeing a pair of chopsticks carried down by the current, he concludes that the upper banks must be inhabited, and he goes up river. Soon he comes across an old man with his wife and daughter, all of whom weep bitterly. In reply to Susanowo's questions the old man tells him that they are earth-spirits. For eight years a serpent with eight heads and eight tails has terrorised the countryside and it has already devoured eight of his daughters. The time has come for another to be sacrificed to it. It is a fearsome monster: its eyes are the colour of glowing embers, it has eight heads and eight tails, moss and fungus grow on its back, and flames shoot from its bloodstained belly. Susanowo offers the two old people his aid in return for the hand of their daughter. He bids them prepare a fine liquor (sake) which he pours into eight bowls placed on eight platforms surrounded by a palisade with eight openings. The serpent approaches and putting a head through each of the eight openings he drains the bowls. Each head falls into a drunken stupor, and Susanowo, drawing his sword, cuts the monster to pieces. The water of the River Hi flows red with blood. As he brings down his sword on the centre tail something chips the blade. When he cleaves the flesh to probe further he finds the famous sword (kuzanagi) 'which conquers grass', wrapped in soft material.

The Izumo cycle

Susanowo builds a great palace at Suga on the island of Izumo and marries the earth-spirit's daughter whom he has saved from the eight-headed serpent; with his wife he produces several generations of gods. Their most famous offspring is Okuninushi, Spirit Master of the Great Land (Izumo, in other words). From this point the legend mainly recounts the adventures of Okuninushi and it is obvious that a new cycle is starting. This cycle of Izumo legends, though not at variance with the group of Yamato legends, is nevertheless distinct from it. The legends about Susanowo's descendants in the land of Izumo constitute a transition between two cycles.

The hare of Inaba

Okuninushi has many brothers who are gods like himself. They are all desirous of marrying Princess Yakami, who lives at Inaba, a province not far from Izumo. They set off for Inaba taking Okuninushi with them as their servant and give him heavy burdens to carry. On the way to Inaba, they come across a hare that has been stripped of fur lying on the ground. The gods in their cruelty advise it to bathe in salt water and then to lie out on the mountainside exposed to the winds. The hare follows their advice, but as the salt water dries, the unhappy animal's skin cracks and it writhes in agony. Okuninushi arrives to find the hare lying on the mountainside and inquires the cause of its torment. The hare tells him its story: 'Finding myself on the island

of Oki, off the coast of Izumo and Inaba, I wanted to
cross to the continent, but could not find a way.
So I called together the crocodiles from the sea and
proposed a contest to see which of our two species
was the more numerous. I suggested that they should
stretch out head to tail and I would move along their
backs counting them. On reaching the last crocodile
I foolishly confessed my hoax to him, and at this he
opened his jaws and ripped off my fur.' The hare
goes on to tell how the wicked gods had then played
a trick on him, leaving him in his sad state. Overcome
with pity, Okuninushi advises him to bathe in fresh
water and to powder his body with sedge pollen.
The hare follows this advice and is restored to good
health. At this point the hare reveals that he is none
other than the hare-god of Inaba; and as reward
for this good turn he promises the hand of Princess
Yakami to Okuninushi in preference to any of his
brothers.

Adventure on Mount Tema

In their fury at failing to obtain the hand of the princess, the gods invent a plan to get rid of the Spirit
Master of the Great Land. When they reach the foot
of Mount Tema, they propose a boar-hunt; Okuninushi is to catch the boar, which they will beat down
towards the foot of the mountain. Okuninushi
agrees, but instead of sending a boar down the gods
heat a great stone and hurl it to the bottom of the
mountain. Okuninushi catches it and is fatally
burned. But his mother ascends to the sky and sends
down two spirits, a shell and a clam respectively. The
first pounds its shell to dust and the second carries
water; then, sprinkling the god, they bring him back to
life in the guise of a handsome young man. But his
trials are not yet over. The malicious gods fell a large
tree and prop up the trunk with a wedge. Then they
place Okuninushi in the gap between the trunk and
the ground and remove the wedge. Okuninushi is, of
course, crushed to death. Nevertheless he is brought
back to life again, through the renewed intervention
of his mother, who sees through the scheming of the
other gods and advises him to escape.

Okuninushi takes to his heels, and to avoid the
arrows aimed at him by the gods hastening in his
pursuit, he dives under the fork of a tree and
disappears.

The trials of Okuninushi

Okuninushi heads for the Land of Darkness to ask
advice of Susanowo, the Impetuous Male. As he nears
the palace, the Audacious Princess, daughter of
Susanowo, comes out and sees him. They exchange
looks and thus are married. The princess announces
the arrival of a young and handsome god. Susanowo,
in an apparently teasing and fatherly way, immediately calls him the 'Wicked Male from the Plains of
Reeds' and instructs him to sleep in a hut that is
actually infested with serpents. But Okuninushi's

wife gives him a scarf made of serpent's skin, which
protects him during the night. The next night
he is sent to sleep in a hut where there is a centipede
and a wasp; again his wife presents him with a protective scarf, which enables him to survive the test.
Then Susanowo aims an arrow into a meadow and
commands the exhausted Okuninushi to go and
look for it. No sooner has Okuninushi left than
Susanowo sets fire to the grass. Just when the unfortunate god is about to be consumed by flames, a
mouse appears and shows him a narrow hole in which
he can hide. This shelter saves him from the all-
devouring fire. Then the mouse brings him the arrow,
which it has rescued from the flames. Exasperated by
Okuninushi's success, Susanowo takes him to the
palace and asks him to cleanse it of vermin. The
Spirit Master of the Great Land chews some berries
from the *muku*-tree, which his wife has given him, and
a quantity of red earth, which brings bright red foam
to his mouth. Thinking that these expectorations
are merely centipedes he has masticated, Susanowo is
amused and quite happily falls asleep. Quickly
Okuninushi seizes the Impetuous Male's hair,
fastens it to the roof-beams and, taking the god's
large sword, his bow, arrows and lute, he flees with
the Audacious Princess on his back. But as he sets
off the lute brushes against the branches of a tree
and wakens Susanowo. He leaps to his feet; the beams
of the house are torn down and the palace crumbles
about his ears. In spite of the delay, he sets off in
pursuit of the Spirit Master of the Great Land, and
follows him right to the pass leading from the Land
of Darkness to the Land of Light. There, abandoning
the pursuit, he gives his somewhat tardy permission
for Okuninushi to use his sword and bow against
evil gods and to take the Audacious Princess to wife.
And this the Spirit Master of the Great Land does.

Sukuna-bikona, the dwarf

Then Okuninushi sets about building the non-celes-
tial world. A strange deity comes to his aid: a dwarf,
Sukuna-bikona, who rides the crest of waves to reach
the coast of Izumo, where Okuninushi lives. He
comes in a little boat made of bark and goose-skins.
Even his helpers do not know his name. Okuninushi
puts him on the palm of his hand to examine him,
and while he is looking at him, the little spirit jumps
up and bites his cheek. Okuninushi, displeased,
recounts this incident to the celestial gods, one of
whom recognises one of his own children from his
description of this little creature, a wicked child
who had slipped between his fingers and fallen to
earth. Nevertheless, this spirit advises Okuninushi
to treat the dwarf well. So Sukuna-bikona and Okuninushi build the world together, and for the benefit
of humanity they establish the 'method for curing
ailments' and 'so as to be rid of such calamities as
birds, beasts and crawling things, they create the
means of avoiding them and mastering them'.

Sukuna-bikona disappears from the tale when he climbs up an ear of millet, and as the stalk straightens he is projected far away into the 'eternal land'.

Division of authority

Okuninushi continues to reign over Izumo until the sun-goddess decides to send her grandson, Ninigi, to take possession of the Central Land of the Plains of Reeds (Japan) and to establish himself as sovereign. Okuninushi is pressed to hand over the land to the new lord chosen by the celestial goddess, and finally agrees. However, with due regard to the power and position of the Spirit Master of the Great Land, a form of joint government is established, according to which the divine grandson (of Yamato) will exercise power over public affairs (that is, political matters) whilst Okuninushi (of Izumo) will keep control of secret (religious) matters. Amaterasu gives Ninigi three treasures as signs of his function: a curved jewel, a mirror and the famous sword 'which conquers grass' that was found by Susanowo in the eight-headed dragon. These objects are still the three imperial symbols of sovereignty. With Ninigi the 'divine reign' on earth begins.

Light of Fire and Shade of Fire

Among the children of the divine grandson, we find two princes, Light of Fire and Shade of Fire. The story of their exchange of fortune is famous. Light of Fire, the elder brother, earned his living by fishing in the sea for broad-finned creatures and narrow-finned creatures. Shade of Fire lived on earth, catching creatures with coarse hair and creatures with soft hair. One day Shade of Fire proposed a change of fortune, the luck-of-the-sea going to him who frequented the earth and the luck-of-the-earth going to him who lived near the sea. Against his will Light of Fire agreed, and both undertook to put their new for-

tunes to the test. But the luck-of-the-sea is for the sea and the luck-of-the-mountain is for the mountain; Shade of Fire could not catch a single fish with the hook that his elder brother had given him, and, to make matters worse, he lost the hook in the sea. In vain he offered five hundred hooks in exchange, for his elder brother insisted on having his own hook back. While Shade of Fire was weeping on the seashore, a sea-spirit approached and, learning the cause of his grief, he made a boat and pushed the prince out to sea in it. Borne along by the waves, Shade of Fire soon reached a palace made of fishes' scales where the god of the sea lived, and he settled on a tree beside a well near the palace. When the handmaids of the sea-god's daughter came to draw water they saw Shade of Fire, who asked them for something to drink. They brought him water in a bowl, but instead of drinking it he brought out a precious stone he carried on him, and, putting it in his mouth, he spat it into the bowl they held out to him. The jewel stuck so firmly to the vessel that they were forced to return it to the princess just as it was. In great astonishment the princess and her father left the palace to greet Shade of Fire, for they knew that he must be a god. They received him with great ceremony. The princess married him, and Shade of Fire remained in the world of the sea for three years. But as time went by he began to think more and more of his past life, and one day he heaved a deep sigh. When he was asked the reason for this, and when he told how he had reached the palace of the sea after losing the hook his brother had given him, the god of the sea questioned all the fish to find out if one of them happened to have the hook in its throat. It was found in the gullet of the dorado and returned to Shade of Fire. The god of the sea then charged the young prince to return the hook to his brother, and offering him two jewels which commanded the waters he taught him how to use them. 'Give this hook back to your brother,' he said to him, 'and tell him this: "This hook is a large hook, a greedy hook, a poor hook, a stupid hook." Then if your brother farms on high ground, you farm the lowlands. If you do what I say, your brother will be reduced to poverty within three years. If you are attacked, use these jewels to protect yourself.'

So Shade of Fire returned to earth on the back of a crocodile. With his own hook restored, the elder brother grew poorer and poorer and finally in despair he made an attempt on Shade of Fire's life. At this, Shade of Fire followed the advice of the god of the sea and used the jewel that provoked floods. The water rose and Light of Fire came near to drowning. So close to destruction, he repented, fearing death, and then Shade of Fire used the jewel that sent the waters back, and spared his brother's life. Moved by this compassion, the elder brother swore eternal obedience to the younger.

Meanwhile, far off in the Palace of the Sea, the Princess of the Sea realised that she was expecting a child. When the moment of birth was drawing near, she told herself that it was not fitting for the child of a celestial god to be born at the bottom of the ocean, and she set off to join her husband, Shade of Fire, on earth. Here she built herself a house for her lying-in, covered it with cormorant's feathers, and withdrew into it. She forbade Shade of Fire to attempt to see her during her confinement for, when the moment arrived, like all strangers on earth, she would have to revert to her original shape. Of course, Shade of Fire was incapable of mastering his curiosity, and glancing into the house he saw his wife change into a huge crocodile, just as she was about to give birth to her child. With her secret discovered, the young woman fled towards the sea, overcome with shame, and she disappeared for ever. However, husband and wife could not forget the deep love uniting them. They were never to see one another again, and yet the princess offered eternal love, while Shade of Fire replied with a song expressing his grief: 'Till the very end of life, I shall never forget my young sister with whom I slept on the island where the wild ducks and sea-birds come to rest.'

Urashima of Mizonoe

The legend of Light of Fire and Shade of Fire is similar to the episode of Urashima of Mizunoe. Urashima had been fishing for three days and three nights without success. At last he saw a tortoise, which on capture changed into a beautiful girl. She begged him to close his eyes and led him to a marvellous island in mid-ocean, where pearls grew underfoot and jewels hung from the trees. Here, in the palace of the girl's father, a sumptuous reception was held for them until daylight yielded to darkness. Left alone together, they made love, and Urashima, madly in love with the princess, completely forgot his former life. But, three years later he was beginning to sigh for his native land, and the princess, taking pity on him in his sadness, agreed to let him go. She gave him a comb-box encrusted with precious stones and begged him never to open it, lest they should be separated for all eternity. Urashima closed his eyes, and when he opened them again he was back on his native soil. But he was unable to find his friends and family and met no-one that he knew. When he inquired what had become of his parents, he was told that there was an old legend in the village about someone called Urashima who had plunged into the sea three hundred years before and never returned. In despair he opened the box and from it arose a white mist, which floated away on the breeze. When he saw this, Urashima realised that he would never again see the princess from the sea. He turned towards the island away out at sea, and cried aloud his love for her, whilst the voice of his young wife was borne upon the breeze, begging him not to forget her. In another version, the unhappy Urashima was so grief-stricken that he ran about stamping upon the ground like a madman. And his skin, which had been so white and smooth, suddenly became wrinkled, and his shiny black hair turned completely white.

The hero of Yamato

The legends of Urashima can be compared with that of the popular hero Yamato-dake, the bold warrior of Yamato. This hero already had a reputation for boldness when his father, the sovereign, begged him punish his elder brother, who refused to be present at meals. So Yamato-dake attacked the ill-mannered son one morning when they had gone to relieve themselves, crushed him to death forthwith, wrapped the broken limbs in matting and threw them away. He was just as swift to inflict punishment upon the two Kumaso warriors, two ill-bred brothers given to idle boasts. Yamato-dake dressed up as a woman and used feminine charm to awaken their interest. The two brothers invited him to a banquet and plied him with attention. He drank with them and waited until they were completely drunk. Then, drawing the sword that he had concealed in his clothing, he slew them both. After this, in Izumo, he did not hesitate to have recourse to more debatable tricks to gain his own ends. He befriended one Izumo warrior whom he wished to conquer, and made a wooden sword. After bathing in the river with the warrior he suggested an exchange of arms. Once this was done he immediately challenged the defenceless man, who was promptly slain. Thereupon Yamato-dake set out in an easterly direction. In the course of his travels he met Princess Miyazu, to whom he was betrothed and subsequently married. Meanwhile his aunt gave him a sword and bag as he went on his way to Sagami. There the lord of the land made him undergo an ordeal by fire, much the same as that which Susanowo had imposed on Okuninushi in the burning meadow. Yamato-dake was just about to be consumed by flames when he opened the bag and found inside it a tinder with which he was able to start a counter-fire that saved him. It should be added that his mistress, Ototachibana, had accompanied him on part of the journey. There had been a tragic moment as he was crossing the sea and huge waves threatened their ship, and the princess had sacrificed herself to the sea to calm it, and, in doing so, had saved his life. Yamato-dake's career ended on the Plain of Tagi (of the Rudder), where, in spite of his unflagging spirit, his legs suddenly became as heavy as rudders and refused to carry him farther. To commemorate his death a huge mausoleum was built at Isé and public lamentation marked the death of the great hero. Yamato-dake changed into a white plover, flew into the sky and disappeared. As a result of this, his tomb was called 'Mausoleum of the White Plover'.

Conclusion

Japanese legends are primarily theogonic myths. Natural phenomena are deified, but there is no attempt to give these deifications an anthropomorphic character. The result is that a considerable number of legends are directed towards establishing a relationship between the birth of the gods and the objects or species that they represent. Moreover, creation is not the result of any external force, it is not a *prima causa,* but is produced by a sort of spontaneous act of generation, though legend does not specify the precise mechanics of the operation. A cursory survey reveals that Japanese legends are composite in nature. Their similarity to Polynesian legends is particularly striking, but universal-type legends, such as those of Izanagi's descent to the Land of Darkness, or Amaterasu's emergence from Izanagi's eye, or the adventures of Light of Fire and Shade of Fire, can be found in other mythologies.

The story of Amaterasu and Susanowo, which was referred to as the 'nucleus' of the legends, is largely solar in character and although, as in numerous other examples, the spirits are conceived as a male-female couple, the accent here falls particularly on the inherent polarity of their natures. They represent opposites: light-darkness, purity-impurity, tranquillity-turbulence. Although Amaterasu, the sun-goddess, has pride of place, her character is still vague and symbolic, whereas Susanowo is, of all the gods, the one described in greatest detail. If the solar cycle, or the Yamato cycle, seems to dominate this account of the mythology—somewhat arbitrarily—this is largely due to the political viewpoint adopted by the compilers. The tales relating to Okuninushi must be regarded as complementary to, not subordinate to, the main legend. The division of power in the myth (the temporal power going to Yamato and the religious power to Izumo) seems to imply the existence of at least two main cult-centres, in which it was possible for the two myths to evolve. There was undoubtedly a third centre at Tsukushi. It should be added that, contrary to expectation, Japanese mythology offers no evidence of dualism. One might almost say that a compromise was established in the form of separation into different spheres of interest on the part of the gods and their descendants.

Generally speaking, Japanese legends are both refined and crude, salacious and occasionally melancholic. They are never allowed to become tragic. The pervading tendency is compromise and, in spite of swaggering exploits, such as those of Susanowo and the bold warrior of Yamato, there is never the overwhelming feeling of catastrophe inherent in other mythologies. This may be due to a deep-seated harmony between the Japanese and their natural environment. If this is the case, then it is understandable that when they came to personify aspects of this much-loved natural scene, they should have placed emphasis not only on a somewhat down-to-earth functionalism, but also on such qualities as fertility, purity and beauty.

The Buddhist pantheon in Japan

In the sixth century B.C. the Buddha Sakyamuni preached the Buddhist gospel in India; from there it was introduced into central Asia, then into China at the beginning of the Christian era, and finally it would appear to have been brought to Japan in the year 538 by a Korean embassy. So it had existed for more than a millennium and had seen a gradual evolution (necessitated by internal developments as much as by foreign influence) when it ultimately reached Japan and the end of its eastward journey. There Buddhism encountered a highly distinct religious outlook founded on deep-rooted Shintoist concepts, which it was able to leave unharmed while creating a second world of religious belief alongside the original faith. The new belief had many connections with the old, but it retained its own particular field of activity, corresponding to new needs that Shintoism was unable to fulfil. As a result, Buddhism

Shaka-nyorai. He is pointing to the sky with his right hand and to the earth with his left, to show that he has taken possession of both. Gilded bronze statute of the mid-eighth century. Todaiji Temple, Nara. *Shogakkan*

became a living faith in Japan and was absorbed into individual hearts and national custom without losing its own individuality in the process. It is still there beneath almost all the doctrinal trappings, even though it built up a vast pantheon in the phases of its history. In its Japanese form this pantheon is the subject of the present study, but before we discuss it a brief account of Buddhism in general and Japanese Buddhism in particular is essential.

The Buddhist idea of the world

Buddhist doctrine is based on awareness of the pain inherent in existence: pain inherent in this present life with its instability, pain inherent in the successive existences, which transmigration imposes on living creatures after death. There is no creator to preside over this terrible mechanism: it rests entirely and uniquely on the law that each one of us is the fruit of his own earlier actions.

Beings have no origin other than their acts. The 'burden' of their acts is their only reality. Their person, which they believe to be an individual unit, is but a composite collection, giving rise to the image of an illusory 'self' endowed with independent existence. Their boundless concern for themselves, their passions, their anxiety, proceed from this illusion and it is this that causes them to be perpetually reborn, for it ensures that they commit the kind of act that holds them fast and does not set them free.

Admittedly, within transmigration itself, all conditions are not equally unhappy. If three of the six great paths or destinies to which Buddhism allocates mankind are fearful (that of rebirth in hell, or as a ghost tortured by hunger and thirst, or as an animal), and a fourth (the path of the titan) is distinctly wretched, two are considered quite happy: existence as a human being and existence as a god. But as each of these conditions lasts only for a time and is terminated at the very moment when the effect of the acts that have determined it ceases to operate, rebirth into better conditions is only a provisional remedy for pain. True happiness is something different, and consists of a state in which destinies are transcended and the mechanism of transmigration has ceased.

Enlightenment: Bodhisattva and Buddha

This state of happiness can be attained only by a process that is the reverse of that maintaining transmigration: by acquiring a clear vision of the inconsistent nature of the 'self'; by destroying the currents that are the factors of existence. After innumerable lives dedicated to this end, a day will come when the final effect of the final act of attachment will cease to be felt. Then, rather as the flame in a lamp flickers out when there is no more oil, so the living being will enter into that blessed state from which there is no rebirth: Nirvana, which some see as annihilation, nothingness, and others as immortality.

Of those who may hope to accede to this state, some

stand out because of personal sublimity or the highest possible awareness of the true nature of things, called Enlightenment *(bodhi)*. The vocation of Enlightenment is acquired after taking a solemn vow, which makes the person taking it a Being of Enlightenment (bodhisattva). His career continues until the moment when, in the course of his ultimate existence within the framework of human destiny, he effectively achieves Enlightenment: then he becomes an 'Enlightened' (buddha). Some buddhas enter Nirvana without passing on their knowledge to others; they are called 'buddhas for themselves alone'. But the greatest of the buddhas, 'perfectly and completely enlightened', work for the salvation of the world. They are referred to by the somewhat mysterious appellation of *tathagata,* which seems to mean 'those who arrived thus'; this marks the ineffable state of 'being thus', at one with the true nature of things.

For many years Buddhists had but one saviour, a buddha who is often called quite simply 'the Buddha', that is Buddha Sakyamuni, the historic founder of their religion, who was born in India in 558 B.C. and entered Nirvana in 478 B.C., after he had obtained 'Perfect, Complete, Unsurpassable Enlightenment' and preached to the world his law of deliverance.

Admittedly it was acknowledged that Sakyamuni had been preceded in unknown ages past by six other buddhas. Similarly, it was hoped that when his law eventually disappeared another saviour would come, whose name was already known, Maitreya, or 'the Friendly One'. Like Sakyamuni before him, he was as yet only a bodhisattva leading his penultimate existence in a divine paradise.

Buddhism and the Great Vehicle

At the beginning of modern times a new doctrinal tendency appeared. It stressed the need for a form of salvation that extended not only to the strongest, the most capable of resolution, but to all men — in fact, universal salvation: this was the Mahayana or 'Great Vehicle', which took this title because it claimed to 'convey' many more creatures towards Enlightenment than the former school, which was dubbed the 'Inferior Vehicle'. Not content with imagining buddhas succeeding one another in time after long intervals during which the world relapsed into darkness, this doctrine was also to promote a large number of saviours occupied in teaching human beings and also devoting themselves to their wellbeing.

Some of these saviours were buddhas, who lived and preached in realms of radiant light, towards which worshippers were invited to direct their thoughts and hopes. These buddhas were regarded as timeless beings. The most popular had his realm in the West and was known as Amitabha ('Infinite Light') or as Amitayus ('Infinite Life'). It is still not known for certain whether their activity could be prolonged indefinitely because they had postponed

Japanese wood-carving of Buddhist inspiration, showing a spirit, bearing in its right hand the lotus symbol. An important symbol for all sects of Japanese Buddhism, the Lotus of the good law came almost to be worshipped in itself among the Nichiren sect. *Bildarchiv Foto Marburg*

The fourteenth-century Kinkaku-ji temple at Kyoto. Kyoto was the centre of the religious revival which firmly established Buddhism in Japan in the ninth century. The extreme formality of the temple set against the wild natural background illustrates the constant Japanese desire to harmonise opposites. *Orion Service & Trading Co., Inc., Tokyo*

the ultimate stage in their career—entry into Nirvana —or whether the very concept of Nirvana was orientated towards the idea of permanent being. Furthermore, Sakyamuni himself did not escape this evolution. Even in the early days of Buddhism he had already begun to take on a transcendent air, which gradually became more and more pronounced. It was acknowledged that he too had been a buddha since time immemorial. His terrestrial body had been a mere phantasm emitted by his 'essential body'. His Enlightenment and Nirvana here below had been mere illusions conjured up for the edification of other members of the human race.

The other saviours were bodhisattvas who temporarily renounced the state of a buddha, sometimes when on the very brink of it, so as to remain active among men within the framework of the destinies of transmigration. In this salvation—conscious cosmos, where buddhas were like kings, they were frequently compared to watchful captains.

Tantric Buddhism

Buddhist concepts were profoundly modified for certain schools from about the second half of the eighth century onwards, in consequence of a previously latent tendency in Buddhism towards speculations included under the general heading of Tantrism (after the *tantra* or canons in which they were written down). These speculations have their roots in very ancient Indian beliefs. The latter specified that there were analogies of structure and basic identity between man as microcosm and the macrocosm itself. Man could use this common identity to modify the spiritual and material factors in the universe if he proceeded from his own person and followed appropriate ritual.

In the highly purified form of Tantrism that spread in the Far East and particularly in Japan, the universe was said to be composed of six elements (earth, fire, water, wind, space and knowledge) and was the manifestation of the body, word and thought of a principal buddha or a 'pan-buddha', called Mahavairocana, the 'Great Illuminator'. Our bodies were thought to be miniature replicas of this cosmic body; our word was identical to his word; our thought was one with his thought. Enlightenment would take place within us, 'in this our own body', as soon as the effect of mystic ritual, in which act, word and thought were brought into conjunction, had led us to the rediscovery in ourselves of that basic identity with the Buddha, which had previously existed unknown to us.

Many figures in Tantric mythology consist of formulas, meditations, forces, even personifications of passions (one of the major ideas in Tantrism being, in fact, that far from opposing the passions, one should cultivate them so as to capture and use the power they contain for spiritual purposes). These figures were sometimes terrifying in appearance, a reminder of the violence necessary to crush the obstacles that lay in the path of Enlightenment. In this category we have the *vidyaraja* or 'Kings of Science', thus named because they were the incarnation of supreme and sovereign formulas, the means to the possession and mastery of knowledge, and anyone who wished to attain to the state of Enlightenment had to have them in his possession.

The place of the gods in Buddhism

Although Buddhism invented its own cosmology to harmonise with its explanation of the world, and as a result in no way accepted the idea of a creator-god, none the less it never denied the existence of gods—who were simply creatures superior to men. That is why Buddhism welcomed local gods into its pantheon whenever it succeeded in taking root. Naturally the first that it incorporated were the gods or *deva* of India. Since they were the native gods of the birthplace of Buddhism, where Buddhist cosmology developed, they came to occupy a fundamental position in this religion.

In Buddhism gods are mere creatures in a hierarchy of transmigration, and they cannot be compared in dignity to the buddhas and bodhisattvas, who have succeeded in transcending this condition. But of all creatures condemned to live and die they are said to hold the highest positions, enjoy the longest lives and have most power at their disposal. And so Buddhism allows human beings to worship them and earn their favours. However, Buddhist god-worship had its disadvantages. It blurred many of the original native characteristics, particularly in the case of the more important gods. It often reduced them to the role of devout zealots of Buddha and his law, depicting them as primarily concerned in helping other creatures attain a state of Enlightenment. But it is interesting to observe that Indian gods and goddesses, once transported under Buddhist direction to distant lands, often tended after a period of adaptation to reassume their original identities in the minds of local believers: that is, they became once more non-Buddhist deities, frankly pagan in type, who were asked to grant wealth not deliverance.

Japanese Buddhism up to the end of the Nara period

When Buddhism was introduced into Japan at the end of the first half of the eighth century, it met with opposition from powerful conservative clans, who attempted to destroy it by force. It was finally saved by the support of a great prince, the regent Shotoku (572–624). Once he had vanquished the enemies of 'the law of Buddha', he wanted to make it the spiritual guide and temporal protector of the young Japanese state, which was just beginning to feel continental influences. For the next two centuries Buddhism continued to develop in Japan. Different

Amida Buddha, sitting on a lotus pedestal. Amida was the nearest approach to a Western god in Japanese Buddhism. The faithful, believing that the end of the world would come in A.D. 1052, looked to Amida as their only hope of salvation in the time available. Gold-lacquered wood of the fourteenth or fifteenth century. *Seattle Art Museum*

doctrines, representing the various stages in the philosophical development of the two 'vehicles', were studied in monasteries built around the successive imperial residences, particularly at Nara, the first established capital of Japan. The new religion knew its greatest triumph when a grandiose foundation was erected in Nara with affiliated monasteries in the provinces: it illustrated the doctrine of 'flowered ornamentation' (*kegon*), which regarded all phenomena as the reflection of one and the same absolute nature and imagined the cosmos to be pervaded by a refracted beam of light, which was symbolic of universal compenetration.

Meanwhile, monks tried to make the Japanese familiar with the idea of retribution and of faith in the power of salvation of buddhas, bodhisattvas and gods. A work of edification that appeared at this time has a revealing title: *Book of strange and holy things relating to the retribution of good and evil in this present life, which have now come to Japan.*

The Heian period

In the late eighth century the Nara clergy began to interfere in affairs of government. In its desire to escape this influence the court looked for another capital, which was founded in 794 as 'City of Heian' on the site of present-day Kyoto. This marked the beginning of a period of religious revival. In 804, two famous monks, Saicho and Kukai, better known by their posthumous honorary titles, Dengyo-daishi and Kobo-daishi, visited China. The first brought back the doctrine of a school founded two centuries earlier on Mount Tendai in south China, which based its worship on the Hokkekyo, or 'Lotus of the good law', an important canonical text of the Great Vehicle; this refuted the doctrine of 'flowered ornamentation'

and claimed that inanimate matter itself had in its possession the nature of Buddha, in other words a propensity towards Enlightenment. One of the preoccupations of the sect of Tendai was to bring together the teachings and religious practices that the various Buddhist schools of thought offered their worshippers at that period. This accounts for the fact that it played a large part both in spreading Amidist beliefs (*see next section*) and esoteric doctrine, which were taught to the exclusion of all else by the other great sect founded by Kukai at the same period.

This was the Shingon sect, or 'Sect of Formulas'. It took its inspiration from Tantrism and held that all creatures and things were fundamentally identical in nature to the Supreme Buddha Mahavairocana. This doctrine relied upon a largely esoteric tradition. As its name indicates, it was concerned with formulas and mystic gesture, which were the vehicles by which the adept gradually acceded to a state of union with the innermost being of things.

Thanks to the Tendai and Shingon ideal of universally accessible Enlightenment and to their efforts to propagate the law in the most remote parts of the country, Buddhism became more firmly established in Japan than it had been hitherto. These two sects brought with them many cults, images and new rites, mainly of Tantric origin, to which their very mystery imparted an aura of prestige. Moreover, they were able to develop ingenious systems, which, in the name of the principle of double truth — surface truth and absolute truth — enabled them to assimilate the *kami* or deities of ancient Japanese religion and present them as different manifestations of the buddhas, bodhisattvas and Buddhist gods; these were known as the 'Shinto biparti' (Ryobu Shinto) in the Shingon sect and the 'Shinto of the Unique Reality' (Ichijitsu Shinto) in the Tendai sect.

Emergence and development of Amidism

From the tenth century onwards, but especially from the middle of the eleventh, faith in the powers of salvation of the Buddha Amida (Amitabha), which had already developed into an independent belief in China, increased and evolved within the Tendai sect. One of the reasons for this was the existence of an ancient prediction that held that the law formerly preached by the Buddha Sakyamuni would enter a final era of decadence at the beginning of its third millennium, which in Japanese chronology was reckoned to be the year 1052. The idea gradually took shape that after that it would be impossible for the majority of mankind alone and unaided to obtain Enlightenment here below, 'in this world without Buddha'. If they wished to attain Enlightenment, they would first have to be reborn in the Pure, Blessed Land of the West (*Gokuraku-jodo*), where the Buddha Amida preached. According to a monk called Honen (1133–1212), whose fervour lent definite weight to this doctrine, the only condition imposed on those who wanted to reach this Pure Land was to repeat tirelessly the name of its buddha — Namu Amida-butsu, 'Homage to the Buddha Amida'. According to Shinran (1173–1262), the boldest of Honen's disciples, even repeated homage was not essential: the only thing that counted was the faith of the devout in the vow of salvation made by Amida. The Jodo sect, founded by Honen's worshippers, and the sect known by the name of Shin, or 'True Sect of the Pure Earth', created by Shinran's flock, raised great hopes in the average layman, who regarded it as a form of religion more in keeping with his needs and condition than earlier Buddhism with its primarily monastic ideal.

Zen and Nichiren

Two currents then emerged in opposition to Amidism. Both reacted against it and argued from the fact that the world was entering its final period of the law to justify their claim that there should be a return to the true principles of Buddhism. One of these currents was known as Zen, or 'School of Ecstasy', which, like the others, originated in China, but numbered among its Japanese representatives one highly original master, Dogen (1200–53).

Like Honen and Shinran, Dogen started off as a monk in the Tendai sect, then he became the apostle of a form of monasticism with the strictest possible methods: the practice of ecstatic concentration, the quest of Enlightenment beyond privation, discipline and careful attention to each act and to each second of daily life.

The second of these currents is associated with a fiery-spirited monk called Nichiren (1122–82), who wanted to restore to the Buddhism of the Great Vehicle — as embodied to perfection in the primitive teaching of the Tendai school and, especially, in the sacred text of the 'Lotus of the good law' — its original purity destroyed by the concerted influence of Shingon esotericism and Amidism. Nichiren reproached Amidists for their devotion to a buddha of a land that was not their own, and for their neglect of their own saviour, the Buddha Sakyamuni, whose timeless nature and infinite solicitude towards all creatures was exalted in the 'Lotus of the good law'. In spite of some grandiose views, the religion that the Nichiren sect finally offered the majority of its adherents consisted of little more than a rather militant piety in which the formula of worship addressed to the Buddha of the West was replaced by another addressed to the 'Lotus of the good law', Namu Myohorengekyo, 'Homage to the Lotus of the marvellous law'. So the 'Lotus' itself, rather than its buddha, became the object of worship that Nichiren, by his sheer energy, won back from Amida Buddhism. Undoubtedly the Zen sect did most to keep the figure of the Buddha Sakyamuni alive in Japanese religion.

Buddhism in later times and popular beliefs

After the thirteenth century Japanese Buddhism ceased to seek renewal on the doctrinal plane and survived by living on the different traditions that it had built up for itself in previous centuries: Tendai, Shingon esotericism, Pure Land, Zen and Nichiren. But popular beliefs went on developing and adding features to the legends of different figures in the Buddhist pantheon. Thus, from the fifteenth century onwards, when the development of the merchant and speculator class was accompanied by the development of the cult of gods of good fortune, a certain number of Buddhist deities who had come to be regarded by the populace as patrons of wealth acquired a second personality in this new context, and this partially submerged the old.

Principal Buddhist deities

In accordance with the distinctions outlined in the preceding section, the Japanese divide the more elevated members of the Buddhist pantheon into four main classes as follows: (1) the *nyorai* class — that is, the *tathagata* or buddhas; (2) the *bosatsu* class or bodhisattvas; (3) the *myoo* class — the *vidyā-raja* or 'Kings of Science' in Tantrism; (4) the *ten* class — the *deva* or gods.

Shaka-nyorai

Shaka-nyorai (the Buddha Sakyamuni) is worshipped in most monasteries in Japan, with the exception of those devoted to the True Sect of the Pure Land, which are of exclusively Amidist persuasion. But for the majority of believers today this buddha arouses a feeling of respect rather than true piety. Shaka seems

Shaka coming down from the mountain, emaciated by the austere exercises which he has performed in his efforts to attain Enlightenment. Drawing in ink on paper of the Kamakura period, about 1200. *Seattle Art Museum*

to them not so much a superior being from whom they might expect concrete help, or to whose statues they might pray, as a very great 'saint', the most perfect embodiment of Buddhist virtues.

There are various reasons for this attitude. We spoke earlier of the way in which Nichiren's efforts to divert his contemporaries' fervour away from the Buddha of the West towards the glorious Sakyamuni of the 'Lotus of the good law' basically resulted in the exaltation of the Lotus itself; he did not succeed in turning Shaka into a true rival to Amida in popular faith. Moreover, the Zen sect, in whose teaching Shaka plays a leading part, is by nature little inclined to look on buddhas as supernatural beings. Its Shaka is primarily a great example; prayers offered to him must be regarded as acts of gratitude. It should finally be added that since the Meiji period, the influence of primary schools has been felt throughout the country, and Japanese children are taught in their textbooks to regard Sakyamuni as the historic founder of Buddhism.

The most popular festival for the Buddha Shaka takes place throughout the land on his birthday, 8 April (formerly the eighth day of the fourth lunar month). It is celebrated in all temples, including those of the True Sect of the Pure Land, and is considered to be more in the nature of a commemoration than a true ceremony of devotion. Its correct title is Kambutsu, 'Aspersion of the Buddha', but it is known familiarly as Hanamatsuri, 'Festival of flowers'. It is celebrated by placing beneath a cupola of flowers a bronze statue of the Buddha at birth, pointing up to the sky with his right hand and down to earth with his left to signify that he is taking them under his command. In remembrance of the scented bath, which, according to legend, the sublime child was given by the gods, the statue is sprinkled with a ladle full of sweet tea, a sugary concoction simulating ambrosia. Those present take a little of this sweet tea home with them, for it is thought to be a purifying drink and also to give children the gift of good hand-writing when blended with Indian ink.

There are four main types of statue of Shaka in Japan: (1) Tanjo Shaka, Shaka as he is at birth, as described above; (2) Shussan no Shaka, Shaka emerging from the mountain emaciated by unavailing fasting, which he thought fit to impose on himself like the ascetics of his period, before attaining to the state of Enlightenment—a much-honoured theme in Zen iconography; (3) Shogaku no Shaka, Shaka after complete Enlightenment, depicted either seated or standing, making a placatory gesture with his right hand and with his left a gesture indicating the fulfilment of vows—this is the normal type of statue of Shaka used in the cult; (4) Nehan no Shaka, Shaka lying down on his entry into Nirvana, supporting his head with his right hand.

The Nichiren sect has a special statue they use in their services, composed of three parts. The central

Mask of a religious dancer of the Nara period. Such masks were used by actors in Gigaku, a form of Buddhist temple drama, which reached Japan from China and was popular in the Nara period, but died out soon afterwards. Gigaku masks were made of camphor wood. The ceremonies probably featured simple mythological stories and were accompanied by music and partly danced. Musée Guimet. *Giraudon*

Amida surrounded by his attendants and welcoming the faithful across the Ocean of Sorrows. From the tenth century the Amida Buddha gained ground in Japan at the expense of the traditional conceptions of Buddha. Instead of relying solely on their own efforts, the faithful hoped to attain Nirvana through his intervention. Part of a thirteenth-century painted scroll at Konyoji, near Kamakura.

Dainichi, the Great Illuminator or Buddha of Light, who as supreme, eternal and omnipresent Buddha was worshipped especially by the Shingon sect. He is bejewelled and is making the gesture of the 'fist of recognition'. Gilded wooden statue by the sculptor Unhei, 1175 or 1176. Eujoji, Nara. *Fujimoto Shihachi*

part consists of a table with an inscription of praise to the 'Lotus of the good law'. The left-hand section is a seated statue of the Shaka; the right-hand one is of Tahonyorai (Prabhutaratna), a buddha of ancient days who is said in the 'Lotus' to have emerged one day from ecstasy to invite Shaka to share his seat and his glory.

Yakushi-nyorai

Yakushi-nyorai (the Buddha Bhaisajy aguru) is one of the fictitious buddhas who appeared with the Great Vehicle. At the outset of his career, which was eventually to lead him to the supreme state, he is reported to have made twelve vows, including a vow to cure all sickness and to obtain for mankind the remedies it needed: hence his name, which means 'Master with remedies', and hence, too, the little medicine-jar usually seen in the left hand of statues of him. Another of his vows was to acquire a body that would gleam like beryl, so that he could light all things by his own radiance. And so the territory in which he preached, which was situated in the east—and so was symmetrically opposite to that of Amida—was called 'World of pure beryl' (Joruri-sekai).

Yakushi was already known in Japan at a very early date. Two famous temples were consecrated to him in the neighbourhood of Nara in the seventh and eighth centuries, and at the beginning of the ninth century Dengo-daishi selected his statue to be placed in the centre building of his monastery on Mount Hiyei, the centre of the Tendai sect. The Shingon and Zen sects also worship this buddha, who, on the other hand, is not venerated either by the sects of the Pure Land or the Nichiren sect. However, the popularity of the 'King of Medicines', as he is still called, goes far beyond the framework of doctrinal preference and specialisation. His sanctuaries still attract crowds of pilgrims who come to beg for cures.

Amida-nyorai

Amida-nyorai (the Buddha Amitabha), the Buddha of Infinite Light, who preaches in the Pure Land of the West, is of all the characters in the Japanese Buddhist pantheon the one who comes closest to the popular Occidental idea of God. Unlike Shaka, who belongs on a very human plane, and Yakushi, who is eventually almost on the verge of folk-lore, Amida retains a halo of profound devotion. The help required of him is almost always of a spiritual order and involves peace of mind or ultimate purpose. He is the great refuge that one thinks of in the hour of death.

For this reason, the invocation or non-invocation of Amida is, more than any other, related to the religious denomination of the worshipper: it is considered to be indispensable in sects of the Pure Land, it is frequently found in the Tendai sect, strictly prohibited in the Nichiren sect, and held in little esteem in the Zen sect. In Shingon there is one very unusual characteristic, for they, in fact, go beyond Amida, who is only a hypostasis, and address themselves to the Supreme Buddha Dainichi-nyorai (*see below*).

Of all the statues of buddhas Amida's is the one most frequently encountered in Japan. There are two main kinds. One shows the buddha seated, his hands together, making a gesture indicative of concentration with his thumbs bent: such is the famous Great Buddha of Kamakura, which dates from 1252. The other depicts him standing, making a welcoming gesture. In the latter there is a boat-shaped halo, generally behind his back: it reminds worshippers of the fact that Amida is a ferryman whose compassion leads them beyond the ocean of pain. This second type is the one in exclusive use in the cult of the True Sect of the Pure Land.

There are two more well-known types of portrait

of the Buddha of the West: the Amida-raigo, 'Amida coming to welcome', who is seen floating down on clouds and surrounded by bodhisattvas playing musical instruments to meet a worshipper whom he is to welcome to the Pure Land; and there is also the Yamagoshi-Amida, 'Amida crossing the mountains', in which one sees the saviour appearing like a bright giant behind the hills of the familiar Kyoto landscape, flooding the countryside with white radiance. Both of these were held in high esteem at the time of the development of Amidism.

The theme of the Pure Land of the West itself is equally familiar to the Japanese imagination. Many books and paintings elaborate on its paradise-like splendours. Below the celestial court, in the midst of which they depict Amida, the six destinies of transmigration are often portrayed too, particularly hell with all its tortures (*see the sections on* Jizo-bosatsu *and* Emma-o).

Dainichi-nyorai

Dainichi-nyorai (the Buddha Mahavairocana), the 'Great Illuminator', is, as we have already said, the personification of the Absolute in the form of a supreme, omnipresent buddha. In the middle of the eighth century the school of 'flowered ornamentation', which knew him by the name of Roshana, had a colossal statue in gilded bronze built to him in their great monastery in the capital. Unfortunately, this has not survived, though a mediocre reproduction, dating from the eighteenth century, the Great Buddha of Nara, is still in existence. About fifty years later, Kobodaishi reintroduced his cult into Japan, and within an entirely new framework turned him into the fundamental object of worship in the Shingon sect under the name of Dainichi-nyorai.

Thereafter, Dainichi-nyorai's image was portrayed inside two concentric figurations, or *mandara*, which represented two complementary aspects—and ultimately identical aspects—of supreme reality: the aspect of primordial reason, inherent in living beings; the aspect of terminal knowledge, 'produced by exercises', which buddhas achieve. In the first of these graphic representations, called 'the womb of great compassion' (Daihitaizo-mandara), Dainichi-nyorai, wearing a red halo and seated on a red lotus, is making his characteristic gesture of concentration with his raised fingers brought together to form a triangle with the palms of his hands. In the second graphic scheme, called 'on the diamond plane' (Kongokai-mandara), he has a white halo and is seated on a white lotus and is making the gesture known as 'fist of recognition', in which the index finger of his left hand is held clenched in the right hand. Unlike the other buddhas, who are portrayed without adornment, Dainichi-nyorai is usually draped in finery and wears a diadem after the fashion of a bodhisattva.

In the two *mandara* there are very many characters depicted round the Supreme Buddha, symbolising all the attributes and manifestations of his omnipresent reality. The most important of these are four buddhas who, with Dainichi-nyorai, form a group of five in the centre. The first, Ashuku-nyorai (the Buddha Aksobhya), who is sometimes identified with Yakushi-nyorai, corresponds to the East. The second, Hosho-nyorai (the Buddha Ratnasambhava), corresponds to the South. The third, who is none other than Amida-nyorai, corresponds to the West. The fourth, Fukujoju-nyorai (the Buddha Amoghasiddhi), who is sometimes replaced by Shaka-nyorai, corresponds to the North. These buddhas not only refer to the five orients (centre and four corners of the earth), but to the five elements (earth, water, fire, wind and space) and to the five colours and all the other classifiable categories. They also represent the five sorts of knowledge in the possession of the Supreme Buddha, which the follower of Shingon esotericism must attempt to acquire in order to accede to Enlightenment. So they are called Gochi-nyorai, the '*tathagata* of the five forms of knowledge'. Here we are no longer concerned with buddhas who, like the Shaka, the Yakushi and the Amida of the Great Vehicle, were at one time bodhisattvas and achieved Enlightenment after a long career, but with buddhas who have been buddhas since all eternity and are, in a way, hypostases of Dainichi-nyorai on the level of the organised cosmos.

Although the group of five buddhas, to whom the founder of the Shingon sect dedicated the great pagoda in the centre of his monastery on Mount Koya, remained quite outside the current of popular devotion, this is not true of Dainichi-nyorai himself, who was a very familiar figure to worshippers in this sect and also, though to a lesser degree, to those in the Tendai sect. With both sects this figure awakens a faith in nature that is somewhat difficult to define;

it is certainly much less sentimental than in Amidist faith, but there is a sort of confidence in the destiny of man in the heart of the mysterious evolution of things.

Miroku-bosatsu

Miroku-bosatsu (the Bodhisattva Maitreya) is, as we have said, a well-known character, and he had, in fact, been known since the very early days of Buddhism. He is the buddha of the future as in the earlier case of Sakyamuni and like him will one day be born again into this world to save all living beings. Miroku was known in Japan long ago and for a time was very popular. But the hope, brought by Amidism, of short-term salvation in the Pure Land of the Buddha of the West meant that the expectation of Miroku's distant coming lost its meaning for many worshippers.

Faith in Miroku remained strongest in the Shingon sect, which, with the exception of a few attempts at compromise, was always rather hostile to the idea of predominantly Amidist worship, although according to Shingon doctrine the buddhas who appear on earth are nothing but manifestations of the universal buddha, Dainichi-nyorai. Legend has it that Kobo-daishi, the founder of the sect, himself taught the importance that should be attached to this faith: going back to an ancient tradition inaugurated by Kasyapa, one of the great disciples of Sakyamuni, in the twilight of his life he went into motionless ecstasy and asked that he should be carried to the tomb in this state, where he was to remain until the future buddha should attain Enlightenment.

In the thirteenth century the Shingon sect and certain old Nara schools that were still active attempted to divert the fervent worship bestowed on the Pure Land of Amida away from the latter towards the 'Heaven of satisfied gods', where Miroku was to have his penultimate existence. But this was to no avail, and the figure of Miroku continued to lose popularity. Although the Shingon and Zen sects still worship him today, for the majority of Japanese the name of this bodhisattva brings to mind little more than a graphic figure. He was, in fact, often sculpted in the early stages of Japanese Buddhism (sixth to eighth centuries), and there are still statues of him, several of which are rightly considered to be masterpieces.

He is portrayed either as a buddha, though this is anticipating things—in which case he is called Miroku-nyorai—or as a bodhisattva, seated in the so-called 'pensive' attitude: his head bent forward on his right hand, while with his other hand he is grasping his right ankle raised above the knee of his left leg. The Shingon sect usually portrays him holding a little receptacle, a stupa, which is undoubtedly both a symbol of buddhas who have already appeared, his predecessors, and of their succession to the 'throne of Enlightenment', which he is preparing to inherit. The jovial image of the bodhisattva called 'Miroku with the large paunch', which became wide-

Sho Kannon, the 'Holy' or 'Correct' form of the compassionate bodhisattva Kannon. Although he has assumed a princely form, emphasised by his jewels and fine clothes, the position of his hands indicates that he is still the all-merciful, who grants the fulfilment of vows to all who approach him. Statue at Yahoskiji, Nara. Second half of the seventh century. *Fujimoto Shihachi*

Kannon with the horse's head. In this form he usually had eight arms and four faces with irate expressions—a typically Tantric element that crept into the Buddhist pantheon. In this form he is often spoken of as a *myoo*, or 'King of Science' rather than as a bodhisattva. Full colour silk scroll. Late nineteenth century. *Museum of Fine Arts, Boston*

spread in China fairly recently, is almost unknown in Japan. It is sometimes encountered in Zen monasteries, particularly those belonging to the branch known as Obaku, which was introduced by a Chinese master in the seventeenth century.

Kannon-bosatsu

Kannon or, to give him his full title, Kanzeon-bosatsu (the Bodhisattva Avalokitesvara) seems to be the most perfect embodiment of the ideal bodhisattva as envisaged by the Great Vehicle. Kanzeon means 'He who looks at (perceives) the voices of the world'. This bodhisattva, who is everlastingly concerned for the sufferings of men, is said to be an 'ocean of compassion'. He is the 'Great Compassionate One', 'He who looks every way'. In misfortune and peril, he is the one most frequently sought: he listens to every prayer, procures peace and safety for his worshippers, performs countless miracles to save them and assumes any shape for this purpose. A famous text in the 'Lotus of the good law'—which seems to be a later addition—praises his endless merits.

Kannon appears to have been associated with the Buddha Amida from the very beginning, and he has an image of him on his diadem. Together with the latter and another bodhisattva, by the name of Daiseishi (Mahasthama-prapta), 'He who has attained great strength', he forms a group called Amida-sanzon, 'the Venerable Triad of Amida'.

In Japan, where he was undoubtedly introduced at the same time as Buddhist faith itself, Kannon has always been the object of fervent devotion. The Amidist Tendai and Jodo sects hold him in particular esteem, seeing in him man's finest intercessor after Amida. The True Sect of the Pure Land takes the opposite view and does not worship him at all, for they think that Amida should be addressed directly, without an intermediary. The same is true of the

members of the Nichiren sect, though they have a totally different reason for their attitude; they dislike this bodhisattva's connections with the Buddha of the West and reject, as heresy—that is, as something outside the sacred text of the 'Lotus of the good law'—the chapter in it devoted to his praises. However, Kannon is highly esteemed in the Shingon and Zen sects, where his cult is totally unconnected with Amidism. Furthermore, the popularity of the 'Great Compassionate One' goes far beyond sect teachings. Prayers are addressed to him concerning not only religious life, but all fields of everyday existence. If you leaf through monastery guides and note the list of benefits that may be conferred upon those who revere his image, you find the same formulas time and time again: 'Family tranquillity', 'Cessation of calamity', 'Banishment of ills', 'Fulfilment of vows', 'Invitation to happiness'.

There are very many pictures and statues of this bodhisattva. Only a few will be mentioned here—those that are particularly well known in Japan. The first that is worthy of mention is the form known as Sho Kannon, meaning 'Holy' or 'Correct', which is a straightforward portrayal, showing Kannon with the diadem and finery that bodhisattvas normally wear in remembrance of the princely condition that Sakyamuni enjoyed before Enlightenment. The hands of the statue are either joined or are placed in one of the two attitudes indicating placation or the fulfilment of vows.

Two other types that were known in Japan at an early date are those called Juichimen, 'Of the Eleven Faces', in which this bodhisattva wears on his head a crown of smaller heads with different expressions, and Senju 'Of the Thousand Hands', in which a forest of arms forms a huge halo around his body.

The esoteric Shingon sect added three more forms to these three main ones and proclaimed that each

of the six Kannons that now went to make the group lent his aid to one of the six destinies of transmigration. One of the new Kannons to be venerated was called Nyoirin, 'With the Jewel that grants desires and the precious Wheel'; this bodhisattva is depicted with six arms, and his head is supported on one hand in a pensive and slightly nonchalant attitude. Another was called Bato, 'Horse's head', and he usually has eight arms and four faces wearing irate expressions that are overshadowed by the horse's head in the centre of his diadem. This is a reminder, among other things, of the anecdote in which Kannon transformed himself into a horse one day to save some merchants under threat of death. The highly unusual appearance of this statue with its angry countenances, together with the fact that it is often spoken of not so much as a bodhisattva but as a *myoo* or 'King of Science', shows that the character of Bato (Hayagriva), as borrowed from ancient Indian mythology, was in fact a characteristically Tantric element that had crept into the Buddhist pantheon. Bato Kannon is the form of the 'Great Compassionate One' dedicated to the salvation of animals. That is why in certain areas he is the object of very popular worship as the divine protector of beasts. The last one of the group of six Kannons, who is called Jundei, unlike the rest is almost unknown.

According to another tradition, based on the chapter about this bodhisattva, Kannon can assume no less than thirty-three different shapes and changes his identity in order to teach individuals in the most effective guise. Almost a thousand years ago this tradition gave rise to a great pilgrimage to thirty-three famous sanctuaries in the neighbourhood of the ancient capitals of Nara and Kyoto, the 'Pilgrimage to the Thirty-Three Holy Places of the Provinces of the West'. The monastery of Kiyomizu, at Kyoto, and the monastery at Hase, near Nara, which were included in this pilgrimage, are undoubtedly two of the three most popular cult-centres to Kannon in the land, the third being the monastery of Asakusa at Tokyo.

Although the character of Kannon (Kouan-yin as pronounced in Chinese) has acquired the characteristics of a feminine deity in China, the same is not true of Japan, where, in spite of the very maternal gentleness and grace he exudes, he has basically retained the nature of a bodhisattva, in other words, a masculine being in essence, though one who is usually regarded as existing on a plane where there is no question of distinction between the sexes.

The familiar portrait of Kannon in which he is seen enveloped in a large white cloak, which covers his head like a veil, is very popular in China (no doubt due to the markedly feminine air that it gives the bodhisattva) and equally widespread in Japan, though it is not normally treated as an object of worship by the Japanese. From about the fifteenth century onwards it was little more than a theme in traditional painting, a theme executed in the manner of the Chinese masters, which is particularly to the aesthetic taste of the Zen sect.

Monju and Fugen-bosatsu

Monju-bosatsu (the Bodhisattva Manjusri), 'He whose beauty charms', is the personification of supreme wisdom. So he is sometimes called 'Guide of all buddhas', 'Mother of Enlightenment'. According to tradition his residence was on Mount Wu-t'ai, in north China, which consequently became a famous place of pilgrimage.

Monju was known in Japan at quite an early date, and from the ninth century onwards it was the ambition of many monks to go to his holy mountain in China. However, this bodhisattva did not become really popular among the Japanese until the twelfth and thirteenth centuries, following the great religious crisis regarding the world's entry into the 'final period of the law'. To those who chose him as their refuge at this point, Monju appeared in his wisdom to be the best guarantor of their salvation in later existences. In contrast with the quietism of the Amidists, who were not, however, completely ignorant of this 'Guide of all buddhas', he was the embodiment of the 'holy way' of Enlightenment achieved by individual inspiration. So his cult was held in particular esteem in the ancient schools of Nara and in the Shingon and Zen sects. Today, although still very popular as a symbol of wisdom—there is a proverb that reads: 'Whenever three are assembled, there is the wisdom of Monju'—his position in Japanese religious life has diminished. However, he still has a very famous sanctuary at Ama-no-hashidate on the Sea of Japan.

Monju is usually depicted seated on a lion, holding either a book or a scroll in one hand, and a sword in the other, as the symbol of wisdom striking down the obstacles to Enlightenment. Other images show him holding a sort of sceptre with a curved end such as monks used to brandish at one time during their sermons.

Fugen-bosatsu (Bodhisattva Samantabhadra), 'He whose goodness is omnipresent', is often associated with Monju, though the former's character is nothing like as clearly defined. They are frequently seen together with the Buddha Sakyamuni, and this is known as Shakasanzon, 'the Venerable Triad of Shaka'. One explanation is that, in contrast to Monju, who is the embodiment of acquired knowledge, attainment of Enlightenment and supreme wisdom (all of which represent the outcome of the Buddhist effort to achieve deliverance), Fugen represents innate reason, the practice of exercises and concentration—that is, the point of departure and means by which the Buddhist effort towards deliverance can be made. It is also said at times that Fugen is to Monju as compassion is to wisdom.

Similarly, the complementary roles of the two bodhisattvas are reflected in their iconography by the animals they ride. Fugen is seated on an elephant, which is usually white and has six tusks, and either he has his hands joined or he holds a long lotus-stem. Monju and Fugen are sometimes depicted as two young brothers, each one bending over his mount: they then become Chigo Monju, Chigo Fugen, 'Monju and Fugen as children'.

However, Fugen's popularity in Japan really developed independently of Monju's and it came rather earlier from the historical point of view. It was primarily based on the 'Lotus of the good law', for in the last chapter of this work the bodhisattva proclaimed that he would protect all those who worshipped this sacred text. Moreover, he evinced particular solicitude for the salvation of women, who for this very reason preferred to worship his bright image. A famous tradition, which was reported for the first time at the beginning of the thirteenth century, states that Fugen appeared one day to the monk Shoku (910-1007) in the guise of a courtesan, thus showing that the 'Nature of Buddha' was present even in the most sinful women.

Another reason for Fugen's popularity at the same period was a belief in his power to prolong human life. In this connection he was given the name of Fugen Emmei, 'Fugen who prolongs life', and he was depicted in this capacity with twenty arms, resting on four elephants back to back.

Fugen is still a well-known figure in Japan. But now, like Monju, he is merely the object of a somewhat unusual cult. His statues are found most often in the monasteries of the Tendai sect, faithful to the tradition of the 'Lotus of the good law', and in those of the esoteric Shingon sect.

Jizo-bosatsu

Jizo-bosatsu (Bodhisattva Kshitigarbha) is more involved in everyday Japanese life than the other members of the Buddhist pantheon. However, he does not seem to have been very popular in the early times of Buddhism in India, where he appeared at a comparatively late date.

The name Jizo, which is said to mean 'Earth-womb', initially referred to a Tantric concept. An analagous idea is found in the name of another bodhisattva, who has since been consigned to oblivion, although he played an important part in the traditions of the Shingon sect, Kokuzo-bosatsu (Bodhisattva Akasagarbha), 'Space-womb'.

Jizo is connected with the earth element and therefore with the lower world, and he appears to have acquired his great popularity as protector of the dead in central Asia and China. Moved to compassion at the thought that this world would be 'without buddhas' from the day Shaka entered Nirvana until the coming of Miroku, this bodhisattva took a solemn oath not to attain Enlightenment himself and to remain within the pain-stricken universe of transmigrations as

Fugen, who prolongs life, one of the most important bodhisattvas. Sitting on a lotus flower, he is riding a four-headed white elephant supported in turn by many more white elephants. Fugen was revered for his understanding, which sprang from the concentration of his contemplative exercises. Coloured silk kakimono (vertical hanging scroll) of the Kamakura period, thirteenth to fourteenth centuries. Private collection, Tokyo. *M. Sakamoto*

Monju-bosatsu, personification of ultimate wisdom and Mother of Enlightenment, riding on the back of a lion and accompanied by two attendants. Print from a woodcut in the Monju shrine at Ama-no-hashidate. Collection of E. D. Saunders. *Larousse*

'fundamental vow', and although he had no connection with the Buddha of the West at the outset, in his capacity of bodhisattva of the six destinies and protector of the dead he found himself automatically associated by the Amidists with their descriptions of the world; on the one hand is the Pure Land, on the other is the dark and suffering universe consoled by Jizo.

According to a belief that seems to have grown up under the patronage of the Jodo sect from the fourteenth to fifteenth centuries, there is in hell a deserted river-bank known as Sai-no-kawara where very young children go when they die if their parents give vent to useless lamentation instead of offering prayers to help them be reborn. These poor infants spend their days using stones from the beach to build little shrines that are intended for their parents, brothers and sisters who are still in the world above and finally for themselves. But at nightfall demons come and destroy these buildings with big iron rods. Then Jizo appears to console the children and shelter them in the folds of his robe. 'In this land of darkness,' he tells them, 'I am your mother and father: think on this, and have confidence in me, morning and night.'

This belief has made this bodhisattva even more popular. It accounts for the fact that in cemeteries and in nooks along the roads there are countless stone statues of Jizo dressed in a bonnet and child's apron of red material, often with a pile of pebbles at his feet. Moreover, the prayers offered to Jizo are not only for the happiness of dead children, but also for their safety in this present life: people ask him to allow them to bring up their children to manhood without harm.

Jizo, the patron of the world of death, in fact has in his possession (like Fugen, as described above) power to prolong life. Emmei Jizo, as he is called when this favour is requested of him, is always portrayed in a seated position, holding his long stick with rings on the end in his right hand, and in his left hand, the 'Jewel that grants wishes'.

This bodhisattva is also asked to cure eye complaints, undoubtedly because as master of the land of darkness he also has power to chase darkness from the eyes of the living. At one time this consoler of the six destinies or 'ways' of transmigration and guide to the dead on their journey to the other world was also regarded as the guardian of travellers. In this capacity he seems to have been grafted on to an ancient local deity who was the protector of the open road and had crude stone statues erected to him on banks bordering roads.

'One buddha, two bodhisattvas' is a Buddhist saying. In popular Japanese faith it doubtless refers to Amida on the one hand and Kannon and Jizo on the other. Jizo is thought in Japan to be so intimately involved with human misery that many people do not think to accord him the rather awe-inspiring

long as this 'black period' lasted. To this end, like Kannon, he can assume six different shapes, relating respectively to each of the six destinies. But Jizo's connection with hell is the primary reason for the tremendous worship bestowed upon him.

We have already mentioned the ancient Indian concept relating to the existence of a form of justice in after-life and a law of retribution for man's acts. This concept developed greatly in China and mingled with old local beliefs. Thus hell was considered to be not only a place of torture for creatures born into the lowest of destinies, but also a place where each one, be he good or bad, had to be judged after death so that his new fate could be fixed (*see the section on* Emma-o).

In contrast with the infernal magistrates who were the embodiment of the stringencies of inexorable law, Jizo was the counsel for the dead and their consoler. Making use of the ancient Buddhist principle by which one could alleviate another's 'burden' by transferring to him one's own acquired virtues, Jizo struggled to obtain some mitigation of their condition. He was the light of this dark world. The most popular statue of him shows him as a gentle-faced monk with shaven head, dressed in a long robe and holding a stick with tinkling rings on one end, which put the powers of darkness to flight.

Jizo was little known in Japan before the middle of the eighth century. His cult first developed in the esoteric Shingon sect and the Tendai sect. Its most popular form was known as 'Jizo's Contribution', and for this people would come once a year and proclaim before a statue of this bodhisattva that they repented of the sins committed during the year, and then they would pray to him to banish their afflictions.

Although Jizo belonged to what might be called the 'cycle of Miroku', because of the nature of his

dignity of bodhisattva. He is often quite simply called Jizo-son, 'the Venerable Jizo'. The only two sects who do not worship him are, for the same contradictory reasons as before, the True Sect of the Pure Land and the Nichiren sect.

Fudo-myoo

Fudo-myoo (Vidyā-raja Acala) the 'Immovable' is the main figure in the group of Godaimyoo, or 'Five Great Kings of Science', whom the Shingon sect introduced into Japan in the early years of the ninth century. As we have already briefly indicated, these are personifications of mystic formulas of sovereign power. Shingon esotericism considered the 'Five Great Kings of Science' to be the 'bodies of anger' of the Five Buddhas, the counterpart of the Five Bodhisattvas who were their 'bodies of compassion'. In actual fact these terrible figures exercised their wrath only against the forces of wickedness and nothing else, and so they, too, although in a very different mode, were an expression of the buddhas' compassion. Another explanation, which some like to think more profound, is that the *myoo* are in reality irate forms adopted by the moving spirit of the worshipper himself when obstacles are encountered.

The physical appearance of these characters, especially in the Tantric pantheon, was, generally speaking, very different from that of the bodhisattvas and seemed to originate in ancient types of spirits of Indian folk-lore.

Fudo was placed in the centre of the Five Great Myoo and corresponded to the Supreme Buddha Dainichi-nyorai. Quite early in Japanese history Fudo became an object of independent worship, which survives to this day. His body is usually blue-black, although there are famous statues of a 'yellow Fudo' and 'red Fudo'. His stocky shape resembles — as a symbol of purity, it is said — that of the undeveloped adolescent. His extremely strained face, his mouth bristling with protruding teeth, and his eyes, one of which is dilated and the other contracted, speak of tremendous effort. He has a sword in his right hand and in his left a rope, symbolising the destruction of obstacles and victory over the forces of evil. He is either seated or standing on a rock that is said to be as hard as diamond and is a symbol of strength. Behind him is a halo of flame symbolising purification. All these attributes explain the nature of his 'vow', which is to give to men unshakable resolution.

Thus Fudo is regarded as a guarantor, a support in all enterprises requiring strength of purpose. He is both the patron of strength of religious purpose, particularly of the ascetic, and he also takes to witness anyone making a vow.

Moreover, his formidable strength is regarded as one of the best forms of protection that exists. People have often prayed to Fudo in the course of Japan's history to protect them against the great perils of

Aizen-myoo, the god of love. He represents love transformed into desire for Enlightenment, and guilty passions are subdued by his ferocious three-eyed face and the snarling lion which looks out from his bristling hair. Wooden statue from Nara. 1281. *Rokumei-so*

the state, natural calamity and epidemics. The talismans that bear his name or his portrait are said to afford protection against theft, accident, and fire, and he is depicted surrounded by flames, which fail to harm him.

The most famous shrine to Fudo-son, 'the Venerable Fudo', as he too is called, is at Narita, east of Tokyo, and it belongs to the Shingon sect. Apart from Shingon, he is particularly dear to the Tendai sect, which is much influenced by esoteric doctrine. But the Nichiren sect, though in principle opposed to esotericism, has also borrowed a certain number of elements from Fudo and likewise worships this very popular embodiment of strength.

Aizen-myoo

Aizen-myoo (Vidya-raja Raga) does not form part of the group of the 'Five Great Kings of Science'. His name means 'Love'. Aizen-myoo in fact represents loving passion as sublimated through esotericism; love that has conquered of itself, not through suppression, as is usually taught, but through even greater exaltation; love transformed into desire for Enlightenment.

Like most of the 'Kings of Science' Aizen looks angry. His body is red and he has eight arms: two hands hold a bow and arrow, the classic symbols of love. He has three eyes, the third being placed vertically in the middle of the forehead. He has a bristling head of hair with a lion's face in the centre. He is usually seated on a lotus.

Shingon and Tendai first developed the cult of Aizen, but he is also revered by the Nichiren sect, which borrowed him from esotericism — as it did Fudo.

In popular belief Aizen is simply regarded as the god of love, and is invoked as such by all those who have some request to make of him. In addition many people professionally connected with love as a trade offer regular prayers to him: these include prostitutes, tavern-keepers, singers and musicians.

Bishamon-ten

Bishamon-ten or, to give him his full title, Bishamon-tenno, who also goes by the name of Tamon-tenno (the god-king Vaisramana), was in Indian cosmology one of the four guardians destined to protect the four quarters of the world from the top of a huge mountain placed at the centre of the world like an axis. Buddhism adopted the 'Protectors of the world' at a very early stage and regarded them also as protectors of the law. So the cult of god-kings was always greatly honoured in Buddhist realms, which hoped to gain from it some supernatural support against their natural enemies. When Buddhism was transplanted to the borders of Turkestan, where China maintained garrisons intended for the defence of her western frontiers, the custom arose of depicting these guardian-gods as armour-clad warriors like the Chinese soldiers of the time. And thus an iconographical type came into being which is now a familiar sight in the Far East, particularly in Japan.

Faith in the four god-kings, or Shitenno, here goes back to the famous battle fought by Prince Shotuku against the anti-Buddhist clans in 587: though it began with a defeat, it immediately changed to victory after the prince had invoked the god-kings and placed their hastily sculpted images in his hair. To show his gratitude, he built a monastery in their honour, which is still in existence today in the town of Osaka, although the actual buildings have been destroyed several times. From that time onwards the Shitenno were under the patronage of the state and had to receive regular worship, which reached its height in the middle of the eighth century when, by order of the emperor, their statues were placed in each of the official religious foundations in the provinces. People prayed to them as the guarantors both of national military security and of material prosperity, particularly good harvests.

About the beginning of the ninth century the spread through Shingon and Tendai esotericism of Tantric ritual bearing on the protection of the state perceptibly undermined the official cult of the four god-kings; for this ritual invoked the even higher powers of the 'Five Great Kings of Science', especially Fudo. But, at the same time, the figure of Bishamon, guardian god-king of the North, who had from the very beginning, even in India, been regarded as the most important member of the group, began to be accorded individual worship. This stemmed from individual initiative in two great centres: Mount Kurama, to the north of the new capital of Heian, and Mount Shigi, to the south-west of Nara, near the place where Prince Shotuku had won his miraculous victory.

The monasteries in which Bishamon was worshipped taught that he procured happiness of ten

山　野　高
堂　門　沙　毘　院　剛　金

Bishamon-ten slaying a monster. Bishamon was the most important of the four guardians of the cardinal points of the universe. As defender of the axes of the world, he became identified with the stability of the royal house. Bishamon was the protector of human life against illness and demons. Print from a woodcut in the Kongo-in shrine, on Mount Koya. Collection of E. D. Saunders. *Larousse*

sorts. The tenth and highest was none other than the maturation of the 'fruits of Enlightenment', but this was not the form of happiness that retained the attention of the god's worshippers as a whole.

When he first became popular, Bishamon was primarily invoked, it would appear, as the protector of human life. He was said to be particularly good at curing sickness and routing evil demons. In India tradition turned him into the master of a sort of fearful spirit called *yaksa*, and images of him, like those of other god-kings, showed him trampling underfoot a demoniacal figure. And so he was thought to have great power over all supernatural evil beings, by whom the Japanese of the period believed themselves to be surrounded. Moreover, as the sole inheritor of the role attributed collectively to the four god-kings, he won great favour among men of war as the deity who presided over the fortunes of battle, particularly when Japan entered a period of incessant feudal skirmishing in the twelfth century.

But the quality in Bishamon that finally prevailed over all the rest was that of dispenser of wealth. This role, which actually corresponded to the first of the ten sorts of happiness Bishamon was able to dispense, was well known earlier in India, where the regent of the North is described as the possessor of fabulous treasures. It began to predominate in Japanese faith from about the fifteenth to the sixteenth centuries, a period that saw—and this was mentioned towards the end of the introduction to this study—the simultaneous development of the merchant class and the cult of gods of good fortune. It won Bishamon a place in the joyous group of the 'Seven Gods of Happiness' (*see the following two sections*).

Bishamon is considered to be a particularly vigilant protector of the worshippers of the 'Lotus of the good law'. So his main adherents are in the Tendai and Nichiren sects. Like the other god-kings he is portrayed in armour, trampling underfoot one or two demon-like creatures. He has a spear—or stick—in one hand, and in the other a precious reliquary.

Benzai-ten

Benten or, to give her complete name, Benzai-ten, Benzai-tennyo, the 'Goddess of the Gift of Eloquence', originally personified the waters of an Indian river, the Sarasvati (or 'Rich in pools'), which murmured so melodiously that it was thought to evoke the accents of speech or music. She was regarded as an important figure in Brahmanism, for she was the patron not only of language, but of wisdom, knowledge and the arts in general, and she appears to have been incorporated into the Buddhist pantheon at a fairly late date.

In Japan her cult would seem to have developed initially about the middle of the eighth century due to a famous canonical text of the Great Vehicle called the 'Supreme King of the Golden Radiance' (*Kon-*

Bishamon-ten, one of the most vigilant protectors of the worshippers of the good law, clad in armour and trampling a demon underfoot. The spear is missing from his right hand but his left hand holds the usual reliquary. Ninth-century wooden statue. *Seattle Art Museum*

komyo-saishookyo), in one chapter of which Benzai-ten promises that she will protect all those who possess this holy book and will give them, in addition to increased eloquence and wisdom—which will help them attain Enlightenment more quickly—all sorts of material advantages: freedom from calamity, cures for sickness, long life, victory, repute, riches. So this text justified the conception of Benzai-ten as one of the deities who presided over fortune. However, in her case this role was only secondary. It belonged primarily to another goddess, who also receives high praise in the 'Supreme King of the Golden Radiance': her name was Kichijo-ten (Laksmī, or Sri-devi), in other words the personification of good fortune and beauty.

In the course of the next few centuries Shingon and Tendai efforts to graft Buddhist beliefs on to old indigenous beliefs, and thus make them take root in Japanese soil, gave new impulse and a new direction to the cult of Benzai-ten. What happened was that, in her capacity of goddess of waters, she was recognised as the 'original body' of many local deities with sanctuaries, for the most part, in the midst of lakes, pools or by the sea. The first of these deities, in whom she was worshipped from the eleventh century onwards, was the *kami* of the little island of Chikubujima, on Lake Biwa, to the north-east of Kyoto. He would appear to have presided over the fertility of the soil in riverside regions. Moreover, tradition identified her with Uga-jin, a deity of mysterious origin who was also connected with the aquatic element and the fertility of the earth, as his half-human, half-animal appearance was no doubt intended to symbolise: he had a human head with a trimmed beard and the body of a white serpent.

Benzai-ten became pre-eminently a patron of riches because of her fusion with deities of this kind. Moreover, it was realised that the word *zai*, which forms the second syllable of her name and means 'talent', could be interpreted in the sense of 'wealth, material goods' by using a certain graphic device.

In the fifteenth to sixteenth centuries and thereabouts the goddess was endowed with almost all the attributes of her former rival, Kichijo-ten, who was then forgotten because she had failed to establish herself in some local shrine. Once Benzai-ten had become, like Bishamon, one of the favourite objects of worship of the merchant class, she soon joined the latter in the group of Seven Gods of Happiness.

But this does not mean that the goddess had to forego her role of deity of eloquence and music, which, even today, particularly attracts the prayers of the geisha, those 'ladies devoted to the arts', professional dancers, musicians and conversationalists combined.

Benzai-ten is depicted as a very beautiful woman, with a very white complexion and ornate garments.

Daikoku, god of happiness and wealth and closely identified with a Shinto god who was protector of monastic and imperial territory. The god is standing on sacks of rice, symbol of plenty. The mallet in his hand is a magic instrument with which he can create gold. Image from the chief shrine of Shingon, the esoteric Buddhist sect.

Eight-armed image of the goddess Benzai-ten. Wooden statuette of the thirteenth century with sixteenth-century additions. Crown and jewels of metal. In her hands she holds attributes, some of which have been lost, including the sword (whose hilt can be seen in the foremost right hand). The foremost left hand holds the 'Jewel that grants desires'. Through the crown can be seen, piled on top of her head, the white rings of the serpent-god Uga-jin. Treasure of the Shinto temple of Enoshima, Kanagawa prefecture. *Yasuda Saburo*

She is usually shown with two arms holding either a lute or those two symbols of wisdom and the realisation of vows—namely, the sword and jewel. In another type of portrait, which is also fairly widely known, she has eight arms, and in her hands she holds various objects. She generally has a tiny *torii* on her forehead (this is a sacred portico in Shintoist shrines) and over her head there is a figurine of the strange god Uga-jin· both of these signs clearly reveal the new syncretic nature of her personality.

This syncretic nature is also evident in the architecture of sanctuaries dedicated to the goddess. Some of these have the shape of a Buddhist temple, but the majority are Shintoist in style, being merely simple little wooden buildings, painted red and hermetically closed to the outside.

All these features show how the figure of Benzai-ten became associated with old local beliefs in Japanese minds. Many people in Japan would now be unable to tell you to which of their two religious universes she first belonged.

Daikoku-ten

Daikoku-ten (the god Māhākalī), the 'Great Black One', is another extremely popular deity of happiness and wealth. In the beginning there was a god known in India by the name of Māhākalī, the 'Great Time' or the 'Great Black One', who was terrifying in appearance, a destroyer reminiscent, in many respects, of Siva. Some Buddhist texts describe him as a god of war. But towards the end of the seventh century the statue of a second god, also called Māhākalī, began to appear on the porches or in the kitchens of monasteries, not only in India but in China too, and this one looked so kindly that his relationship with the earlier one was very difficult to define. He would appear to have been first and foremost a spirit that protected the soil and provided food. He saw to the material security of monastic communities and to their needs and could, moreover, make wishes come true. In exchange, offerings were made him every day at mealtimes, mainly of food. His wooden statue, holding in its hand a bag of gold, was constantly sprayed with oil, which made it black all over, and this seems to be the explanation of the name of 'Great Black One'.

At the beginning of the ninth century the founders of the Tendai and Shingon sects introduced his cult into Japan, and in keeping with his traditional role they made him the protector of the soil on which the monasteries stood and the provider of food for these communities. But the cult in question remained purely monastic and was of little interest to the ordinary worshipper.

However, this was the period in which the initial move was made that led to the god's later popularity: this was the identification of Daikoku, the 'Great

Black One', with one of the chief gods of ancient Japanese religion, Okuninushi-no-kami, the Spirit Master of the Great Land. This seems to have taken place, in the first instance, within the Shingon sect. The Chinese characters used in writing the words 'Great Land'—in local dialect Okuni—could be read as Daikoku if they were given the Chinese pronunciation brought over to Japan, thus producing the same sounds as the characters used in writing the name of the 'Great Black One'. But the connection between the two deities went far beyond a mere play on words. The Spirit Master of the Great Land during the 'Age of Gods' had been the organiser of the soil in the territory of Izumo in the west of Japan. Immediately after the fusion of ancient myths from this region with myths from the south and east at the time of nation-wide unification under a single royal house, he became the protector and patron of Japanese soil in general: so it was much to Daikoku's interest to become identified with him.

In the matter of iconography the Shingon sect was much more venturesome than the Tendai, who continued for a long time to depict the god in his classical form, holding his little bag of gold in his left hand, and sometimes a stick with a jewel in it in his right hand; but Shingon invented an entirely new graphic scheme for Daikoku which was evidence of the complete Japanisation of this character. He was portrayed in the familiar costume of the time, with loose trousers (close-fitting at the calf), a waisted tunic, a soft bonnet on his head and a big sack on his back grasped in his left hand, exactly like sacks used by peasants for carrying their loads.

About the fifteenth and sixteenth centuries, the same period as for Bishamon and Benzai-ten, Daikoku was released from existing framework of his cult and joined the ranks of the popular gods of good fortune. The riches that he was asked to grant, and the requests that he should be as liberal as possible, necessitated his having increasingly relevant attributes. So his portraits grew more and more complicated. First he was given voluminous straw packets filled with rice—usually two, but occasionally more—which appeared under his feet. Later came a 'little mallet for discovering treasures' borrowed from old folk-lore; this was placed in his right hand, which had usually been free until then.

As his images were quite different from those of other Buddhist gods, and as he had long been identified by the monks themselves with a Shintoist *kami*, Daikoku came to be regarded more and more in this light by the common people. He was soon associated with Ebisu, an old-established *kami*, who was also connected by descent with the Spirit Master of the Great Land. Ebisu had been well known for centuries on the coast in the region of the present town of Osaka, where he had his temple. There he had been associated with another god to whom the local fisherman prayed, and in the end had

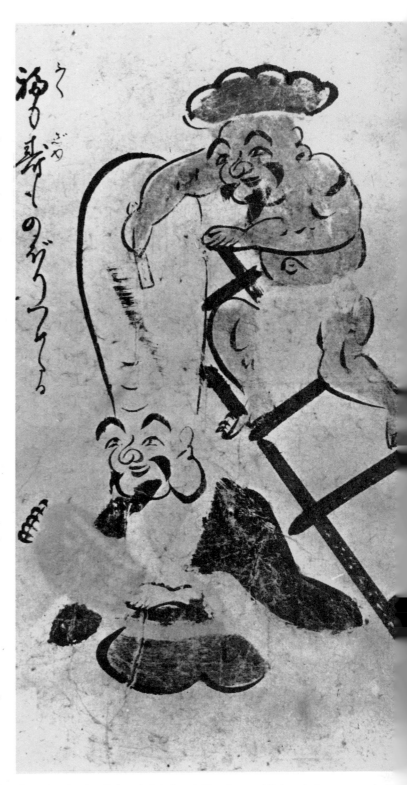

Daikoku shaving Fukurokuju's head. The star-god Fukurokuju, whose name means 'Happiness-Emoluments-Longevity', was an old man with an outsize head, one of the six gods of Chinese origin popularly added to Daikoku to form a group of seven gods of happiness. Ink and colour on paper of the Edo period—late seventeenth or eighteenth century. *Seattle Art Museum*

become patron of the very prosperous fishing industry. He had the same garb as Daikoku, and held in one hand a line and in the other a large dorado tucked under one arm. Daikoku and Ebisu became symbols of the twofold wealth of earth and sea, and were henceforth inseparable in popular worship, sometimes being called father and son (they are venerated in the great Shintoist temple at Izumo as the Spirit Master of the Great Land and his son Kotoshironushi-no-kami), sometimes brothers, and sometimes even husband and wife.

Some time previously the Tendai sect had thought up a syncretic character who was called the 'Daikoku with three faces', and who was, in fact, composed of Daikoku-ten in the centre, Benzai-ten on the left and Bishamon-ten on the right. These were the various outward forms given to the idea of bringing together the deities who presided over fortune in order to obtain the joint benefits of their several virtues.

This idea finally triumphed with the constitution of a group known as the 'Seven Gods of Happiness' (Shichifukujin), and though an attempt has been made to trace back their origin to certain Buddhist texts, in actual fact the inspiration behind them had no connection with Buddhism. The composition of this group in its definitive form, as it was fixed towards the end of the sixteenth century or beginning of the seventeenth, included in addition to Daikoku, Ebisu, Benzai-ten and Bishamon, three characters embodying the Chinese concept of well-being and long life: Hotei, a fat, jolly monk, a popular embodiment of the future Buddha Miroku, in fact a figure of Taoist rather than Buddhist inspiration; the star god Fukurokuju, literally 'Happiness-Emoluments-Longevity', an old man with an abnormally elongated cranium; and, finally, Jurojin, the 'Old Man of Long Life', who was very much like the preceding god.

These seven gods are usually portrayed rather humorously. Sometimes they are on a boat laden with precious objects, which is called the 'Treasure Ship' (Takarabune). It should be made quite clear that this group, as such, is not the object of any cult. It is more like a kind of lucky charm. In many business houses their picture is hung on the wall as a sort of good omen, especially at the New Year.

The cult of Daikoku-ten himself continues to be observed in monasteries, mainly those of the Shingon, Tendai and Nichiren sects, and it is observed by individuals too, either in its Buddhist form or, together with the cult of Ebisu, in a Shintoist form. It should be noted that almost all private people who venerate the god in this way belong to the spheres of commerce, agriculture and industry.

Shoten

Shoten, or more fully Daisho-kangiten, is a 'double-bodied' esoteric form of the elephant-headed god known in India as Vinayaka or Ganesa. Vinayaka (Binayakya in Japan) literally means 'He who overcomes'. This god is both he who overcomes obstacles and he who creates them, who impedes success, or, on the other hand, bestows it. So he has a twofold nature: partly helpful, partly devilish and evil. According to a fairly late tradition Vinayaka is the son of Mahesvara, 'the Great Lord' (Daijizaiten in Japan)—that is, Siva.

The cult of the elephant-headed god, which was subsequently to play a very important part in modern Hinduism, found its way into Buddhism at the time of major development of Tantric ideas. Following its introduction into China by the masters of esotericism, it was brought to Japan at the beginning of the ninth century by the founder of the Shingon sect. Shortly afterwards the Tendai sect in turn adopted it as one of its secret practices.

However, it was not in this simple form—in his capacity of a spirit concerned with obstacles—that Binayakya finally won popularity within Japanese religion. In this respect he remained a minor character, known only to those who practised esoteric ritual.

The form in which the god rose to eminence among the great figures of the Japanese pantheon was that embodied in a double image, showing Binayakya as man and wife embracing one another. The male partner was none other than Binayakya himself, who now appeared as a particularly violent god endowed with quasi-omnipotent strength. This terrifying god was often called Daijizaiten, 'the Great Lord', which was, of course, a name by which Siva himself was known, Daijizaiten's supposed father, from whom he might in part have borrowed his character of all-powerful god. The female deity, who can be recognised by the narrow diadem on her brow, is one of the forms adopted by the Eleven-faced Kannon (a bodhisattva) for the purpose of appeasing the male god and diverting his formidable force towards some kindly activity. Shoten or Daisho-kangiten is the name given to the form in which the god is held in the welcoming arms of this bodhisattva, and it means 'the Great and Noble God of Joy', or more probably 'the Great and Noble God in Joy'.

Esoteric sects proffer another explanation—that the male god Binayakya-Daijizaiten should be given a deeper interpretation and regarded as appearing here in his basic truth as a metamorphosis of the universal Buddha Dainichi-nyorai. The image of the two deities joyously embracing is then revealed in its total meaning: as a material representation of the union of the worshipper with the buddha who is the principle of all things. Once he has reached the supreme stage of spiritual discovery, the practitioner of esotericism will then see only one image in this double image, in these two bodies only one body with four arms and four legs.

Esoteric sects do, however, worship Shoten, the divine couple, as something else as well as a living image of the realisation of Enlightenment. They also consider him to be one of the most powerful patrons it is possible to invoke on the difficult path leading to Enlightenment; both because the prodigious energy of the god must perforce confer on anyone who can use it considerable dominion over all things, and also because the power to bring undertakings to a successful conclusion is more fundamental to Shoten, as a magnificent form of Binayakya, than to other gods.

As the cult of this god demands a high degree of initiation and an inept worshipper could run great risks as a result, it is observed in the strictest secrecy and follows rigid rules. Notably it includes rites of sprinkling and immersion in oil to which the statue of the divine couple must be subjected; this statue must of necessity be made of metal and can never be more than seven inches high. It is kept in a special shrine in monasteries, and is never under any circumstances shown to the public.

It has always been a well-known fact that Shoten ritual possesses the same sovereign power over material things as spiritual matters. In the first half of the tenth century Hoshobo, the thirteenth superior of the Tendai sect, developed a special use of it for problems regarding the protection of the state. More recently, certain monasteries under the individual patronage of this god have actively encouraged worshippers to devote special prayers to this aspect of Shoten. The two most famous monasteries are those of Matsuchiyama, in the Asakusa quarter of Tokyo, and Ikoma, near Nara, which dates from the end of the seventeenth century. In a style reminiscent of old Chinese philosophical jargon their brochures explain that the god has two bodies symbolising the happy harmony of heaven and earth, the beneficial interaction of the masculine and feminine principles, and that he is a pledge of security and health for everyone, of understanding and fecundity for married couples and of prosperity in commerce and business.

These brochures nevertheless make it clear that the form of worship devoted by laymen to this god must be equally strict and prudent. In principle it must not be expressed privately by statue worship: a simple tablet must be substituted and inscribed with his name. Moreover, this cult must be observed with pure intentions and preceded by purification rites like those for Shintoist *kami*. The booklet published by the Ikoma monastery expressly states that Shoten possesses both the compassion of a buddha and the redoubtable majesty of a *kami* and that consequently he must be treated according to the rules applicable to each of these two types of superior being.

Usually the kind of laymen who worship Shoten are, as in the case of Daikoku and Benzai-ten, merchants, speculators, gamblers, actors and geishas; they also include procurers and prostitutes, who are specially drawn to his cult by the manifestly erotic nature of this two-bodied god. The cult, as observed by these different kinds of people, often has a black side in which prudence, as prescribed by the monks,

Pagoda of the eighth-century Horiyu-ji temple one of the oldest wooden buildings in the world. The Buddhist temples, which housed groups of worshippers were far more ornate than the earlier Shinto shrines which acted merely as reliquaries, and the square construction of this pagoda recalls the four quarters of the world. *Wim Swaan*

is altogether disregarded. It becomes a sort of private counterfeit of the god's esoteric ritual in the course of which the worshipper tries to put in motion the god's irresistible powers for his personal benefit. Popular belief has it that the power and wealth thus wrongly acquired by the exercise of force on the person of Shoten later receives retribution in the form of grave misfortune and irremediable ruin. This belief and the atmosphere of secret mystery which, generally speaking, surrounds all that concerns the god explains why he is one of the few deities in the Buddhist pantheon in Japan to inspire these people with a feeling of fear.

Kishimo-jin

Karitei-mo (Mother Hariti), better known as Kishimo-jin, the 'goddess mother of demons', was according to legend a female demon who devoured children and ravaged the town of Rajagriba in India when the Buddha Sakyamuni was living there. The town's people begged him to force the ogress to desist from her horrible activities, so the Buddha concealed her youngest son beneath his alms bowl. Hariti searched heaven and earth in her despair at having lost her son, and when all proved unavailing she finally came to implore the Buddha's help. Whereupon he gave her to understand that the pain she perpetually caused others was similar to that which she was now experiencing herself. In this way he converted her; then when the ogress asked how she was to feed herself and her sons in future he promised her that an offering would henceforth be left for them every day in each of the monasteries in his community.

Once she had graduated from the ranks of evildoers to those of benefactors, the 'mother of demons' found that the previous process was reversed and she was now invoked as a protectress of childhood and bestower of children. She was depicted in art as a madonna pressing a baby to her breast with one hand and with the other holding a pomegranite, a fruit that is regarded as the symbol of maternal fecundity.

The Kishimo-jin cult, which was well known in China from the seventh century, first developed in Japan within the framework of Shingon esotericism, but it was not until it came under the patronage of the Nichiren sect that it became truly popular. The reason for this sect's particular fidelity to a former demon is that she declares in one of the chapters of the 'Lotus of the good law' that she will protect from danger all who are true to this book; now it is common knowledge that this book was considered by Nichiren himself to contain the fundamental postulates of Buddhism. There is one tradition that claims that this holy man actually benefited from her protection when a trap was laid for him in the year 1264. Belief in Kishimo-jin spread from the two great Nichiren monasteries of Kanayama, near Tokyo, and Zoshigaya (though the latter has now been absorbed by one of the capital's suburbs), and extended

in particular to eastern Japan. Very tiny infants are taken to these sanctuaries for ceremonies that will confer upon them the goddess' permanent protection. This sometimes takes the material form of little bells that are attached to their clothing and are supposed to keep all evil influence from them.

Emma-o'

Emma-o (Yama-rama), 'King Emma', was the first father of mankind according to ancient Indian tradition and the first man to die. He became king of the dead, their judge and the master of hell, before whom sinners were afraid to make an appearance, for he dictated their punishment. Buddhism recognised in this figure the deity entrusted with the enforcement of the law of retribution, and in this capacity he was incorporated into the pantheon at an early stage. Subsequently, however, the idea that the mechanics of rebirth operated automatically led even the most orthodox schools to reject the formality of a judgment on the dead as something unavailing: they then professed the belief that King Emma, once deprived of his judicial functions, appeared in hell only as a great tormentor of those reduced to the lowest condition by their own actions.

However, the idea of infernal justice was not to disappear entirely from popular belief. On the contrary it adopted a very elaborate form in Chinese Buddhism, where it mingled with old regional concepts about the underworld of death. This is the form in which it spread to Japan, where it was known from the end of the eighth century. In the tenth to eleventh centuries, it began to attract active worship as a natural complement to belief in the Pure Land of Amida.

According to the description given of death at the time, it normally began with a journey that was sometimes called the 'Journey of intermediate existence', to use an old Buddhist expression. It is described in one text as a melancholy journey across a huge deserted plain that one has to make all alone, a prey to regrets for the world above. But it was more usual for death to be announced by the apparition of infernal agents who took the victim in their charge and kept guard over him during the journey to the other world.

At the entrance to hell there was a steep mountain veiled in darkness over which the deceased tried to grope their way: this was the 'Mountain of Death' (Shide-no-yama). Farther on, they approached a great river called the 'River of Three Passages' (Mitsuse-kawa) or 'River of Three Ways' (Sanzu-no-kawa). One of these passages was a shallow ford where those who had committed minor sins crossed. The second was in the centre and consisted of a bridge made of precious materials over which good people passed. The third was a gulf with monsters and huge waves: dire sinners had to go through this. On the other side of the water was a horrible old crone called the 'Old Woman of the River of Three

Ways' (Sanzu-no-baba), and she awaited arrivals, stripped them of their clothing and hung it from the branches of a tree. Some traditions state that if she was given a coin she did not strip her victim bare and presumably that is why a few small coins were always placed in coffins.

After the 'Old Woman', the infernal guards with the ox's head and horse's head (Gozu Mezu) seized the dead and brought them into the presence of King Emma, who was a red-faced, angry-looking deity with a coarse beard. He was attired as a Chinese judge with a biretta that had a large pin through it and bore the sign for 'king' in front. In his right hand he had a tablet, the emblem of his official authority. Near by were two secretaries, the Gushojin, who consulted registers and reported to him on the good and bad acts committed by each individual. He also had a mirror, which helped him form a more definite opinion of people, for it could evoke at will the facts recounted to him; he also had a sort of staff with two accusing faces on top, known respectively as Mirume, 'the Seeing Eye', and Kagu-hana, 'the Sensitive Nose'. An erstwhile popular tradition — which is still very popular in China where it grew up — showed Emma receiving the assistance of nine other kings, each one of whom specialised in a certain type of sin. Together they were known as the 'Ten Kings' (Juo).

Once his cause had been judged, the dead man found himself sent either to one of the eight sections of hell, or to one of the other 'destinies' that between them housed all living beings in the world: phantoms, animals, titans, men and gods. Thus the endless cycle of transmigration continued for those who had been unable to set themselves free from it.

In the earlier section on Jizo there was a description of the sojourn of dead infants in the Sai-no-kawara and of the role of the kindly bodhisattva both in this abode in particular and in hell in general. Because of Jizo's benevolence and the rigorous role allocated to King Emma, it has become commonplace to regard the two characters as opposites, like kindliness and severity. This confrontation of opposites, which was well expressed in their external appearance, was also reflected in a proverb that goes like this: 'The moment for borrowing, Jizo's countenance. The moment of repayment, Emma's visage.' However, an oft-repeated dogma in Buddhist works states that Jizo and Emma in reality are one, the first being the 'original body' and superior being from which the second proceeds.

Moreover, Emma was not always thought by ordinary people to be pitiless. As lord of death he had — like Jizo — power to prolong life, indeed to send back to the light of day those who had already reached his tribunal. And so a goodly number of temples were built to him at one time: there people prayed he would show them mercy, and also that in his capacity of patron of the world of darkness

The Nio (Two Kings) who watch over the entrance of monasteries to protect them from evil influences. Their ugliness and threatening expressions are supposed to frighten away wicked demons. Wooden statues from the great gate of Todaiji at Nara. 1203. *Fujimoto Shihachi*

—once again like Jizo—he would spare them the misfortune of losing their vision of things. One of the best-known shrines in the Koishikawa quarter of Tokyo is the centre of a very touching legend on this subject: there is a tradition that the Emma worshipped there restored the sight of an old woman threatened with blindness and made her a gift of one of his own eyes for this purpose. To show her gratitude this woman kept coming regularly to the shrine to make offerings, but she was unable to bring the god anything of value because she was very poor. And so she adopted the habit of giving him the things that she liked best herself, which was a sort of vegetable called *konnyaku*. Hence the name Konnyaku Emma given to this temple, which is still famous today for its cures.

In modern Japan hell is generally thought to be a fable, and Emma is now no more than a figure in childish folk-lore, a sort of bogyman to frighten children into being good.

Marishi-ten

Marishi-ten (the goddess—or, less frequently, the god—Marici) is in Indian legend an embodiment of the ray of light that appears in the sky before the sun. Buddhist texts of Tantric inspiration on this subject explain that this light precedes the star of day in its journey across the sky and never loses sight of it although it remains invisible itself. Men are not able either to see it, know it, gain possession of it or harm it. But, on the other hand, anyone who knows its name can acquire all its marvellous powers

and become equally vulnerable himself.

Marishi-ten was brought into Japan by the esoteric movement, and was particularly highly revered in feudal times by the warrior class. It was a custom with many of them to place her image on their helmets, as a protective charm against the enemy's blows. Perhaps for this very reason, the Zen and Nichiren sects, which had numerous worshippers in military circles, also adopted her as part of their cult. Today, on the other hand, the changes in society have robbed Marishi-ten of almost all her popularity.

Marishi-ten is depicted either sitting or standing on a galloping boar or on a pack of seven boars. She herself has two, six or eight arms holding different attributes, including a bow, sword and other weapons. Her more complicated portraits usually have three heads, one of which has a boar's face. The Nichiren sect portrays her as a male god.

Ida-ten

Ida-ten is a god who protects monastic communities and is particularly worshipped by the Zen sect. This character seems to have grown out of the visions of a seventh-century Chinese monk, who claimed that he learned of Ida-ten's existence through a revelation.

Ida-ten is depicted as a handsome young man with a Chinese-type helmet and breastplate and holding a sword. A familiar Japanese saying, 'an Ida-ten race', which means a very swift race, comes from a tradition regarding this god's miraculous speed.

The Nio and Binzuru-Sonja

The Nio (Two Kings) are athletic spirits with threatening expressions who keep watch over the entrance to monasteries, from which they are supposed to repel evil influences. They are thought to possess the power of protecting children and preventing theft. Straw sandals are offered them, and when people make them a vow little balls of papier mâché are tossed upon their statues.

Binzuru-Sonja (the Venerable Pindola) is not, properly speaking, a deity at all. He was one of the sixteen great disciples of Buddha (Juroku-rakan), who lost all hope of reaching Nirvana because he thoughtlessly exhibited his supernatural powers in front of heretics—or so the saying goes. So he promised to help other creatures escape the world of pain, where he himself was condemned to remain for ever. His cult is observed in monasteries, particularly those of the Japanese Zen. However, his statue is never placed inside sanctuaries, only outside them and near the gate, because the Buddha excluded him from Nirvana. Binzuru's statues show a very old man with long eyebrows seated on a monk's high chair.

This figure is believed to have great power over illness, particularly anything affecting the eyes, and from this stems his popularity.

Ogmios, the Celtic Hercules. Though, like his classical namesake, he is clad in lion skins and wields a club, Ogmios was a god of eloquence, not of brute strength. Musée d'Aix-en-Provence. *Jean Roubier*

CELTIC LANDS: MYTH IN HISTORY

Celtic mythology is one of those subjects that is almost impossible, for a variety of reasons, to treat in general outline. First of all, it is difficult to determine the exact limit of the domain to be assigned to the Celts both in time and space. The Celts were a race rather than a nation. Their name appears for the first time in Hécatée de Milet's *Geography* about five centuries before Christ. Ethnologically speaking, central Germany appears to have been their original habitat. About the ninth century B.C. they began to invade Gaul, and successive waves continued until roughly the second century B.C.; in the sixth century B.C. they settled in the Iberian peninsula; about the fourth century B.C. they invaded Italy and seized Rome (battle of the Allia, 390 B.C.)

These Continental Celts spread through Hungary as far as Greece and Asia Minor. Celtic burial places have been discovered as far away as the Ukraine and Poland. At no time did these peoples constitute a united, coherent, homogeneous nation. They were formed of separate tribes, who were turbulent and jealous of their independence and animated by hereditary hatreds and occasional rivalries. A second group occupied the countries of northern Europe and became the insular Celts of Great Britain and Ireland. The last wandering bands of Celts went from northern Gaul to the British Isles in the first century B.C. and were called Belgians.

The result of this geographic dispersal was that the Celtic peoples disappeared at different periods, according to place and circumstance, by reason of conquest, absorption or extinction. These migrations, together with political or social antagonisms, explain the lack of unity in their religious concepts. It is probable that each tribe had its own deities; but it is not impossible that several neighbouring tribes recognised and worshipped one or several common gods. To speak of Celtic mythology is a little like speaking of African mythology. It would be nearer the truth to refer to it in the plural. Furthermore, a good proportion of the myths are still unknown to us, particularly those of Gaul.

Detail of a two-headed Celtic Hermes from the sanctuary at La Roquepertuse (Bouches-du-Rhône). Second to third centuries B.C.

The Continental Celts

It is extremely difficult to study the gods worshipped by the Gauls with any degree of accuracy. The reason for this difficulty is threefold. First of all, in the beginning Gallic religion tended to be animistic, without any pictorial illustration whatsoever. Our ancestors did not picture the natural forces that they venerated in any concrete shape; and so they left no engravings or sculptures of them. It is true that Caesar claimed to have seen 'semblances of Mercury' or, rather, semblances of a deity to whom he gave this Roman name. Raised stones or menhirs probably reminded Caesar of the square pillars that were supposed to be symbols of Hermes, the Greek Mercury; or there may have been wooden idols in Gaul.

The second reason is that there was certainly never a national religion in Gaul. Caesar, it is true, declared that all Gauls claimed to be descended from Dis Pater, which implied some common belief. Camille Jullian, the modern historian, was of the opinion that 'from the time they formed one body and went under one name, the Celts had a sovereign god, a supreme, national god, the god of the people', who can be identified with Teutates. In spite of the opinion of such an eminent authority, it seems that Gallic particularism *did* extend to religious matters. It is rare to find serious attempts at assimilation among the Celts, though in Greece, for example, the local gods of the various provinces were changed into national deities in this way. Gallic gods were usually clan or tribal gods, and their cult was limited to a restricted area. Hence their multiplicity; hence, also, the confusion reigning in the Gallic pantheon, not only because it was devoid of any sort of hierarchy, but because the deities in it remain vague and ill-defined, since none were brilliant enough to attract legends and bring them to the point of crystallisation.

Moreover, and this is the third source of difficulty, the religious tradition of the Gauls was exclusively oral. The countless verses that the Druids (from *daru-vid*—'clairvoyant, of great skill'?) taught their disciples and the victory hymns mentioned by Titus Livius died with those who had passed them on by word of mouth. All that remains are some votive and funerary inscriptions on steles and bas-reliefs (and even they date from a period when the assimilation of local deities by Roman gods had already begun), some magic formulas, and a Roman calendar engraved on bronze found at Coligny (Ain).

And so, as far as the Continental Celts are concerned, there was a mythology without myths. This is highly disappointing, for we are virtually limited to a mere list of names through the difficulties in being accurate about the character and attributes of the deities involved. However, a survey of the beliefs of the Gauls, tracing their evolution to the time of the Roman conquest, reveals a movement towards an anthropomorphic conception of their deities, which in wealth and precise detail is not to be outdone by that of the Romans.

From the mass of documents dating from the Gallo-Roman period, two groups of deities ultimately emerge, relating in varying degree if not to an unknown Celtic mythology, at least to a group of gods that is particular to the Celts. The names of the gods, the place-names and the situation of holy places give some indication of these pre-Roman deities.

It is quite obvious that the great gods of Gaul were ancient even in Caesar's time, and that the innumerable local gods whose names and portraits appear in the dedications and documents of Roman times did not suddenly come to life in the imagination and devotions of Romanised Gauls. A certain number of these gods remained intact in Gallo-Roman religion, and it is a simple matter to recognise them (since they are not to be found in the Greek and Roman pantheon) and even to recognise some archaic characteristics among them—manifestations in the form of animals or monsters, collective or trinitarian gods—that confirm their more ancient date.

In the second place, a certain number of Gallo-Roman gods or couples who emerged from the fusion of two tolerant polytheisms were the result of assimilation or association that took place in Roman times. Tacitus referred to this phenomenon as the *interpretatio romana* of indigenous gods. This could equally be defined as Celtic interpretation of Roman gods. There are certain special features by which they can be distinguished from the purely Roman gods who fulfil parallel functions and were worshipped in their own right in the three Gauls. We can learn something of the nature of the Celtic gods from these Gallo-Roman fusions by subtracting the Roman characteristics. Also, many couples were formed by the association of a Roman god and a native goddess. This rich and varied category of mixed deities is just as revealing as the previous one.

Celtic sanctuaries

Archaeological excavations in the south of France have brought to light fragments of monumental structures that were sanctuaries or perhaps temples. These remains are mainly those of open-air porticos, uprights and lintels; the decoration on them and position in which they were found tell us something about the nature of the gods worshipped there and the features of the cults.

At La Roquepertuse the remains of a third-century B.C. portico were found to be decorated with painted animals and surmounted by a large bird. Sizable pieces of sculpture were also discovered, depicting men sitting cross-legged, dressed in tunics that appeared to consist of a big rectangular scapular back and front. Could they have been priests? It seems more probable that they were gods, for the pose is that of several Gallic deities in Roman times. The lintel contains recesses intended for the display of

Megalithic remains at Carnac, north-western France, known as the Menec alignments. The significance of these rows of menhirs is unknown; though they pre-date Celtic religious practices as we know them, they are commonly found in the Celtic lands. *Roger-Viollet*

A silver-plated copper bowl of Gallic origin, showing on the outside unidentified Celtic deities. Inside the bowl can be seen the antlered god Cernunnos, Taranis with his wheel, a procession of riders with trumpets, sacrificial and hunting scenes. The finding of this bowl in a peat bog at Gundestrup, Denmark, shows how far Celtic influence had spread. *National Museum, Copenhagen*

skulls, severed heads of enemies, criminals or corpses
— no-one knows the truth of the matter. At Mouriès,
portico pillars had horses engraved on them and
were placed either vertically or horizontally: the idea
of a horse-god is out of the question, but these horses
may have been animal-demons living in an unknown
'beyond' and serving an unknown god. At Glanum
(Saint-Rémy-de-Provence) and at Saint-Blaise, lintels
with recesses again testify to the rite of displaying
skulls in or about the second century A.D. Finally, at
Entremont, in the same period, a group of several
statues conveys the impression of a funerary cult of
warriors. The severed heads are in evidence — several
have their eyes closed, others have a hand placed on
them — and human masks are engraved on stone
pillars. So the cult of some god must have been
practised in this sacred spot.

The shape of the Celtic sanctuary is equally un-
revealing about the personality of the gods. The form
is not known to us till the Gallo-Roman period, and
then it became familiar through numerous construc-
tions of non-Greek and Roman design that were built
in the three Gauls and Brittany; none has been
found in Narbonnaise. These structures have a
central plan, not rectangular: square or almost
square (Autun, and the *fana* found in the countryside), circular (Périgueux), polygonal (Alésia), even
cruciform (Chassenon). In every case, the *cella* is surrounded by a wide, covered gallery or walk intended
for processions of priests or worshippers. Very often
these sanctuaries were built near water — a spring,
marsh or well. This is the only pointer we have to the
type of gods worshipped there: they were certainly
credited with powers of healing, as dedications dating
from Gallo-Roman times amply confirm.

Naturalistic polytheism
The cult of heights and water

Heights, such as mountain summits, were held to be
divine. The 'pic du Ger' (*Garrus deus*), in the Lower
Pyrenees continued to be regarded as a god until the
end of the Roman occupation, while the other
summits gradually fell from the rank of gods to that
of divine abodes. For example, Dumias, tutelary god
of the 'Puy de Dôme', in the end became a mere
epithet attached to the 'Mercurius' whose temple and
statue were erected on that spot.

This nature worship appears more especially in the
cult of water (rivers, fountains, springs). Diva, Deva,
Devona — 'the divine' — was an appellation frequently
applied to Gallic rivers, and their present names still
testify to this: Dive, Divone, Deheune. Nemausus,
tutelary god of the citadel of Nîmes, was in spirit of
the spring there; Icaunus was the spirit of the Yonne;
Luxovious, god of the waters of Luxeuil, had Bricta
for his consort; and Nantosuelta (from *nanto*, meaning valley) was the consort of the god Sucellos. There
were numerous Gauls in Belgium who prided
themselves on the name of Rhenogenus, 'Son of the
Rhine'. Borvo, Bormo or Bormanus — 'Boiling' — god
of thermal springs, has given his name to several
French watering-places with hot springs: La Bour-
boule, Bourbonne, Bourbon-Lancy or l'Archambault.

One of the best-known deities is Epona, 'the Mule'.
She wears a diadem and draperies from the waist and
is always depicted sitting sideways on her horse. This
manner of portrayal never alters, and she is usually
flanked by a mare or foal, which she is sometimes
feeding; her symbols are a horn of plenty, a crook

and fruit. As a tutelary deity Epona would preside
over the fecundity of the soil, fertilised by the waters
(certain mythologists even claim to see in her the
exact counterpart of the fountain Hippocrène, the
'equine spring'). The cult of Epona, which enjoyed
great popularity in Gaul (indicated by the numerous
portraits of her that have been preserved), was later
imported into Italy and even into Rome. But when
the original meaning had disappeared the goddess
became the protectress of the equine race; her
portrait was put up in stables and the cavalry sections
of armies were then devoted to her cult.

The Gallic deity Rhiannon, the 'Great Queen', was
a mare-goddess.

The tree cult

Water fertilises forests, so the Gauls adored trees and
woods. Vosegus was the tutelary god of the wooded
Vosges; Arduinna was the 'Diana' of the Ardennes;
Abnoba that of the Black Forest.

In the region of the Pyrenees several Latin inscriptions tell of the tree-gods: Robur (the oak of that
name), Fagus (the beech), Tres Arbores (Three-
trees), Sex Arbores (Six-trees), Abellio (the apple-
tree); Buxenus (the box-tree).

Worshipped throughout Gaul, the oak has been
named as the supreme god of the Gauls by certain
chroniclers. 'The Druids have their sanctuaries in
oak woods,' the Elder Pliny asserts (*Natural History*,
XVI, 249), 'and they perform no sacred rite without
oak leaves. They believe that the presence of mistletoe
on a tree is indicative of the presence of the god. They
gather it with great ceremony. After sacrificing two
white bulls, a white-robed priest climbs the tree and
cuts the mistletoe with a gold sickle, and it is then
caught in a white cloth.'

The cult of this plant has left its trace in our own
customs. A number of people, either sincerely or
jokingly, think it brings good luck. This tradition is
particularly alive on the English side of the Channel.

Zoomorphic gods

In the same way, the Gauls worshipped various
animals. Horse, raven, bull and boar were sacred
animals after which were named certain towns
(Tarvisium; Lugudunum?) or tribes (Taurisci; Bran-
novices; Lugoves), and several drawings of them
have been found on coins and bas-reliefs. The raven
(Lug?) appears on the modern coat-of-arms of Lyons,
formerly Lugudunum—'Fort of Lug'. However, Lug
may refer to a Celtic god of that name, rather than a
bird. In the Ardennes, a sort of Diana mounted on a
boar was worshipped. The Helvetii around Berne
adored the goddess Artio (the name given to the
bear), and she has been proposed by some as the
equivalent of the Greek Artemis: but it is more a case
of a local deity 'with bears', as is clearly borne out by
the fact that her cult was evinced at Berne and not

elsewhere. In other parts a Mercury Artaios has come to light.

Among the zoomorphic gods we can include the serpents with rams' heads which appear on numerous monuments. They are generally associated with a god who is wringing their necks or holding them on his knee. The latter attitude seems to exclude the idea of a struggle between the god and maleficent powers symbolised by the serpents; they seem to be the god's companions rather than his adversaries. The same is true of the horned serpent who sometimes appears alongside the Gallic Mercury.

Another animal that seems to have been the object of a widespread cult is the bull. This should not be in the least surprising as this animal symbolises force and the power to beget. It has been deified in this way in other mythologies too. On the Gallo-Roman monument that was exhumed in Paris there is a bull standing near a tree. He has a crane on his head and two other cranes on his back: this is the Tarvos Trigaranos. What can be the meaning of these three cranes in association with the bull? These same birds appear on reliefs on the Arc de Triomphe at Orange and they are often found in the fabulous tales of Irish epic sagas. But the thing that is peculiar to the Gallic pantheon is the worship of a bull with three horns, of which there are numerous bronze reproductions dating from the Gallo-Roman period.

Anthropomorphic Gallo-Roman gods

Three Gallic gods

After Caesar's legions had invaded Gaul, an anthropomorphic pantheon grew up alongside the native deities of 'natural' and animal origin. The Gallo-Roman monument in Paris on one side shows the bull with three cranes, on the opposite side shows a wood-cutter god chopping down branches with his axe. This is Esus, who is mentioned by Lucan in his *Pharsalia* (I, verse 444 ff.) with two other equally sanguinary Gallic divinities:

> ... Immitis placatur sanguine diro
> Teutates, horrensque feris altaribus Esus
> Et Taranis Scythicae non mitior ara Dianae.

'The cruel Teutates appeased by gory offerings, and horrible Esus with his fierce altars, and Taranis, altar no less cruel than that of Scythian Diana.'

There is nothing in this passage to indicate that this is a Gallic triad. Taranis, 'Thundering' (in Irish *torann*), is hardly known at all except for this quotation from Lucan. He is the god of thunder, storms, the thunderbolt, and in this he is the equivalent of the Roman Jupiter, with whom he is identified in several inscriptions. Esus (compare *erus*: 'master, lord') is a sanguinary deity in Lucan, and we are told by a much later commentator that human victims were hung from trees and sacrificed in honour of this god. However, he is particularly recognisable in both Trèves and Paris in the guise of a wood-cutter — playing this part in the unknown myth to which the bull and the three cranes belong.

Teutates is endowed with more distinct features, even if they are not more clearly defined. As his name suggests (*teuta;* Gallic *touta;* Irish *tuath,* meaning 'tribe, people'), he was the 'god of the tribe'. Camille Jullian thought he recognised in him 'the chief of the gods common to all the Gauls ... their national god ... guardian, arbiter and defender of their tribes'. An arbitrary interpretation, for if Teutates had been the sum total and embodiment of all these titles, Caesar — better informed than we are — would have spoken of a single god, and not of several. The name Teutates seems to be not so much the name of an individual deity as of a general attribute that can be applied to different deities. In fact, this name is associated in inscriptions only with that of Mars (Marti Toutati), and so one interpretation only seems justified: Teutates is a Gallic god who can be equated with the Roman Mars. Thus he is above all a god of martial glory. Each Gallic tribe must have had its own Teutates, which each worshipped under a different name. For example, Alborix, 'King of the World'(?); Caturix, 'King of Combats'; Loucetius, 'Shining'; Rigisamos, 'Very royal' — all appellations that are perhaps only substitutes intended to invoke the god and yet keep his name concealed from the profane.

However, there is a risk involved in forming any hypothesis whatsoever, because the Celtic gods who, according to Lucan, demanded human sacrifices became confused with those in Roman mythology with whom they had something in common. At times their characteristics were divided up and reappeared scattered among two or three different deities.

The Gallic Mercury

In his Commentaries (*De Bello Gallico*, VI, 17) Julius Caesar listed under Roman names five main gods who were worshipped by the Gauls. 'First and foremost, Mercury is regarded as the inventor of all the useful arts, the protector of routes and travellers. They consider him all-powerful in negotiation and money matters.' Although this god may in certain ways remind one of the Roman Mercury, he has, in fact, a much wider field of action: he is pre-eminently the god of civilisation. Far from neglecting Caesar's evidence, we ought to see in this god the chief deity of the Gauls. His cult was very widespread. Called Mercury, he was adored in a dozen or more different aspects. There is a reminder of this in such place-names as Mercurey, Mercueil, Mercoeur, Mirecourt, Montmartre (Mount of Mercury). Costly statues were raised to him. One in bronze, one hundred and thirty feet high, which took Zénodore, the sculptor, ten years to complete, stood in the vast temple of

The god Esus depicted in his usual form as a woodcutter. Like Teutates and Taranis, Esus was noted for the cruelty of the sacrifices he exacted. Detail from the altar of Jupiter. Musée de Cluny, Paris. *Belzeaux*

Iron and cast bronze statue with enamelled eyes found at Bouray, near Paris, depicting an unknown god sitting cross-legged. Round his neck he wears a torque, symbol of divinity to the Gauls. His misshapen feet look like those of a pig or ox. The statue, which is of Gaulish workmanship, dates (judging from the hair style) from the middle of the first century A.D. *Musée des Antiquités Nationales*

Four horses' heads. Frieze of the third to second centuries B.C. from La Roquepertuse in southern France. These horses decorated a Celtic sanctuary and were perhaps regarded as demoniac animals in the service of some god. *Jean Roubier*

The Gallic Mercury, who bears the same emblems as his Roman counterpart—winged feet, winged helmet and caduceus. His civilising aspect was far more pronounced, however, for he was probably the chief god of the Gauls, who had assimilated the attributes of Mercury. He is accompanied on this relief from Glanum by his sacred animals the tortoise and the goat, and by one of his Gallic wives, Rosmerta, who bears a cornucopia. Musée de St-Remy-de-Provence. *Jean Roubier*

Mercury Arvernus, known as Dumiatis, which was built on the summit of the Puy de Dôme. There are very many others throughout Gaul.

Once he was assimilated with Hermes-Mercurius, the Gallic Mercury adopted his appearance and attributes. He is usually portrayed as a beardless young man with winged feet; he is normally standing (rarely seen seated), and is portrayed either naked or wearing a chlamys, with the petasus on his head and caduceus in his hand. His symbolic animals are the goat and the cock. Sometimes the horned serpent, which was mentioned earlier, is found near him. He is also often dressed in Gallic fashion. Apart from other native goddesses, the goddess Rosmerta was the consort of this Gallic Mercury.

Ogmios

In the second century the Greek rhetor Lucian devoted a short treatise to a Gallic god whom he called Ogmios. He said that he had seen him in the shape of a wrinkled and balding old man dressed in a lion-skin and holding a club. He connected him with Heracles. But the power of this Celtic Heracles was not in his physical strength. The symbol of his power was the chain that fastened his tongue to the ears of those listening to him. This Ogmios was a hero furthering the cause of civilisation; he was the god of eloquence and persuasive discourse. In Irish mythology he became the champion Ogma, whose sword relates all the exploits it accomplishes during the battle of Mag Tured; and he also becomes the god Ogma, the inventor of the oghamic alphabet. And so it seems that Ogmios is an avatar of an essentially Celtic god; as is well known, eloquence is one of the national characteristics of the Gauls: *argute loqui*.

Another Gallic Heracles is the Smertrios, who is shown in the famous monument found in Paris fighting a serpent.

The Gallic Apollo

'After Mercury,' Caesar tells us, 'they worship Apollo, Jupiter, Mars and Minerva. They think of these gods in roughly the same way as other peoples.' Apollo, the divine healer, wards off sickness and presides over health-giving springs. He is the god who disguises himself as Borvo, Bormo, Bormanus (*see above*: 'The Cult of Heights and Water'); also the god worshipped under the much-mentioned name of Grannos, 'Brilliant' (?); for example, at Grand in the Vosges, at Graheim (Württemberg) and at Aquae Granis (Aix-la-Chapelle). In the year 215, according to Dion Cassius (LXXVII, 15), the Emperor Caracalla invoked him as the equal of Asclepius or Serapis. In the Danube valley and other places this deity often bore the name of Belenos, 'Sparkling', and sometimes that of Toutiorix, 'Protector and King'. He was commonly associated with Sirona, goddess of astral nature.

Mars, depicted in Antonine style on a square buttress, Paris. A great many Gallic war-gods were assimilated to Mars, so that almost every region had slightly differing views of 'Mars'. Though the name of the original god was often preserved as a soubriquet, this deity was always represented exactly like the classical Mars. Musée de Cluny, Paris. *Jean Roubier*

Mars, Minerva, Vulcan

Mars was the god of war; but it is impossible to say whether he was the only Gallic god of war. It is probable that each small Celtic tribe had its own god of war, and when they were assimilated all these deities were given the name of Mars without further discrimination. However, original names survived, but merely as surnames. This accounts for the very many epithets — at least sixty-four — that have adhered to the name of the Gallo-Roman Mars. There is a Mars Teutates, which is the one defined by Lucan; a Mars Segomo, 'Victorious', in the valley of the Rhone and in Burgundy, whose cult reappears in Munster (Ireland) and whose name occurs again in that of the Irish hero Nia Sagamain, 'Champion of Segomo'; there is a Mars Beladon or Belatu-cadros, 'Destroyer', among the Bretons; a Mars Camulus, 'Powerful', in Auvergne, Mars associated with the god Camulus (in Ireland Cumall, father of the hero Finn); a Mars Rudianos, 'the Red', this colour being associated in the Celtic imagination with warlike activity and the world of the dead; elsewhere there is a Mars Leherennus (?), a Dunates, 'Protector of Citadels', and a Caturix, 'King of Combats'.

In spite of this widespread cult, no really typical portrait of the Gallic Mars has been handed down, nor has there been one of Apollo. Gallo-Roman artists were content to endow both with the features hallowed by Greek and Roman tradition. This is true also of Minerva.

No known Gallic goddess appears to have assumed the role of Minerva, patron of the arts. Belisama, 'Like unto the flame', a sort of vestal patron of the industries of the forge, seems to admit comparison with her. However, the Celts must have had a patron goddess of crafts similar to the Irish Bridget, for instance, who was able to integrate completely with Minerva. In the same way Vulcan replaced a Celtic blacksmith god (Gobannon in Wales), whose existence accounts for the remarkable favour shown the Roman artisan-god in the three Gauls.

The Gallic Jupiter

Jupiter does not hold the eminent position in the Gallic pantheon that he does in Rome. He is simply the personification of the bright sky and storms. The Gauls were undoubtedly referring to him when they spoke of Taranis. This Gallo-Roman Jupiter's emblem is the wheel, which is perhaps a symbol of the thunderbolt. He is often depicted on horseback, overcoming or crushing some anguished monster: symbol of the victory of heaven over earth, of light over darkness, of good over evil, and, perhaps, of civilisation over barbarism. These statues are perched on the top of pillars or columns and are found only in the Romanised parts of Gaul.

Dis Pater

Dis Pater is the name given by Caesar to a common god 'from whom all Gauls pride themselves on being descended'. Such was, in fact, the teaching of the Druids. He would appear to be a sort of Gallic Pluto, being of subterranean nature or origin. Unfortunately, we have no other reference than the brief mention left by the Latin historian, so it is difficult to identify him; but this Gallic Dis Pater may be connected in some way with the god with the mallet.

Sucellos

The 'Mighty striker' is the proposed interpretation of a somewhat enigmatic deity who appears on several monuments in the guise of a long-haired, bearded man with a thickset body clothed in a long tunic belted at the waist and either wearing tight breeches or appearing bare-legged. His appearance indicates both authority and a certain benevolence. His attributes are a mallet and a goblet or drinking vessel. If one thinks of the hammer of the Germanic god Thor, and accepts the fact that the vessel symbolises water (the principle of generative humidity), then one will be inclined to regard the god with the mallet as both a god of death and a god of fertility.

Now this same god was called Silvanus in Narbonnaise (southern Gaul), and in the area around Salzbach he is associated with the goddess Aeracura, who is depicted with a horn of plenty or a basket of fruit. He may, therefore, be a pastoral deity or a protector of crops. Indeed, he is sometimes shown with a scythe instead of a mallet, with his foot resting on a cask. His identification with Sylvain, a popular vegetation-god, is one of the most typical cases of Gallo-Roman religious fusion. One of his consorts was called Nantosuelta, a purely Celtic goddess.

343

Primitive stone figure with a Janus head from Holzgerlingen. When Celtic gods were assimilated to Roman gods the representations of the deity generally owed most to the better assured Roman tradition. *Württ. Landesmuseum, Stuttgart*

The tricephalic gods

There are in existence thirty-two effigies, most of them from the north-east of Gaul, showing a deity with three heads or three faces; these consist either of one front face and two side profiles or of two little heads attached to the main skull above the ears. About fifteen of these figures come from the area around Reims. There is also in existence a stele discovered near Trèves showing the god surmounted by the three mother-goddesses of Trèves. Another stele found at Malmaison (near Reims) shows the Tricephalus in a prominent position, this time dominating a divine couple, Mercury and Rosmerta. Thus two distinct peoples, each in its own way, would appear to have symbolised the triumph of their own god over the foreign god (or the enemy god of a neighbouring people). These images of the Tricephalus often include features connected with Mercury, and a Paris monument shows a triple-faced Mercury dressed in Gallic fashion. Rather than admit a tricephalic divine entity, there are grounds for thinking that the multiplication of heads was one of the practical ways of increasing the powerfulness of a god: the principle being that repetition equals intensity. In fact several different gods (Mercury, the god with a stag's horns, and even a goddess with stag's horns) are sometimes endowed with three faces or three heads by Gallic artists. In other cases, the person of the god is itself tripled: the Deae Matres, for example, Celtic mother-goddesses, who are sometimes anonymous and sometimes honoured under strictly local or regional names; this anonymous and collective character, and this taste for the trinity are archaisms of the Gallic religion, and not the particular characteristic of a given deity. In the same way the cross-legged, sitting position is typical of various gods, always of indigenous origin, and therefore does not indicate a specific divine personality.

'Cernunnos'

Would it be right to connect the mysterious Dis Pater with a rather strange-looking deity whose name appears in part on the famous monument discovered in Paris: .ernunnos (Cernunnos?), who usually has large antlers? This god is generally portrayed sitting cross-legged. He is sometimes grouped with two other deities; and he is often three-headed. As he generally has a horned serpent or a ram's head by him, the temptation is to see him as a chthonian deity: at Reims he is holding a purse with coins or grain falling from it in front of a stag or bull, and there is a rat portrayed on the pediment of the stele.

Dis Pater's companion (wife or sister? — we cannot be sure) is a mother-goddess who gives birth to men, animals and plants. She is also the guardian of the dwelling-place of the dead. There is some temptation to see a resemblance between this consort of the god of the underworld and the crude feminine figures

provided with necklaces and decorated belts that are found on the walls of the Neolithic caves at Petit Morin (Marne) and on the stones of some covered ways in the Seine and Oise basins, as well as on dolmenic sculptures and on the sculpted menhirs of the Aveyron and the Tarn. This goddess is most certainly the symbol of the fertile earth, the Earth Mother, similar in character to Demeter, the Cybele of Mediterranean religions. The goddess is later depicted as a robust woman wearing her hair coiled round her head beneath a low diadem. She is dressed in a tunic and coat and is seated with her knees apart and her feet together. She is raising a crook in her right hand and her left hand holds the folds of her dress, which is piled with fruit. Sometimes she has children on her lap or in her arms: in such cases she symbolises maternity and fertility.

Among lesser deities with popular cults countless *matres, matronae* or *matrae* appear on inscriptions endowed with highly varied local epithets. They are generally found in groups of three: these were the goddesses who protected the springs from which they took their names. At Nîmes there were the Matres Nemausicae, who were replaced by the god Nemausus. The cult of 'mothers' was observed in particular among the Treviri (in the region of Trèves). By classical times they are found almost only in country districts, protecting village fountains. However, they were also the protectors of townspeople and artisans. They are depicted either seated or standing, sometimes — not often — in a chariot, dressed in long robes, and their hair either falling in coils held back by a band and veil or with a middle parting separating curls. Their symbols were fruit, flowers, horns of plenty or children. They symbolise life-force and fertility and also human maternity and the creative force of nature.

In addition to countless tutelary deities there were nymphs who were worshipped as protectors of rocks and waters, and *suleviae*, who became one with the *junones*, 'who stare fixedly at their worshippers', and *proxumae*, who were types of guardian angels.

The list of warrior-goddesses is shorter: some mention should, however, be made of the Andarta of the Voconces, the Andrasta of Queen Boadicea or alternatively Nemetona, who is seen next to one or other of the Celtic Mars in groups of figures. *Tutelae, fatae* (who became known as fairies) and white ladies, all these anthropomorphic powers of Celtic folk-lore, whether kindly or malevolent, are descendants of the Mother Earth of Neolithic tribes.

In the absence of precise texts, this system that we have applied to the Gallic pantheon remains approximate and conjectural. It is necessary to emphasise this point. These Gallic gods have little individuality. They are often nothing more than epithets. There are more than twenty known epithets for Mercury's Gallic counterpart; fifteen for Apollo's; sixty-four for Mars'; twelve for Jupiter's. It is probable that the

Three mother-goddesses, one of whom holds a child. Such groups of three figures were common, and represented both human fecundity and the creative forces of nature. Musée de Châtillon-sur-Seine. *Jean Roubier*

Gauls did not have many great collective, national and universal gods before the Romans imported theirs, but they must have worshipped a considerable number of minor regional gods who resembled one another only partially in attribute and function, and became assimilated here and there with the great new arrivals.

Survival of pagan cults

Paganism has left marked traces in many places. Christian chapels may have replaced Druid or Gallo-Roman sanctuaries, but countless 'miraculous' fountains are still the object of pilgrimages, and countless 'magic' stones of superstitious rites. A statue of the Virgin is often found nestling in the hollow of some oak that was held sacred in times past. Sylphs, gnomes, will-o'-the-wisps, hobgoblins and were-wolves are just so many living souvenirs of a Celtic and even pre-Celtic past. Survivals of pagan beliefs and rites are to be found in the grasses, fires and dancing connected with Midsummer Day (24 June). Beltan's feast (1 May) commemorates the renewal of sun and life. Six months later (1 November) the cult of night and the dead (Samain's feast) celebrates the immortality of the souls of the dead; the Church turned this into All Saints' Day.

Continental and insular mythologies

There is still one utilisable source of information for Continental Celtic gods: Irish and Gallic literary texts that appeared at least half a millennium after the time of independent Gaul and the early Gallo-Roman period. For a long time experts have been aware of mythological elements in these insular epics that appear to go back to the pagan period, and may thus give us information about deities when major Celtic migrations took place. The work of M. Georges Dumézil has shown that bases of comparison can be established even between the Celtic field and the Germanic, Italian, Indian and Persian fields. The latter represent what is left of an Indo-European community, whose gods form a body corresponding to different social functions that are still perceptible in the societies that emerged from that community. Wisely handled, such indications can enlighten us as to the way the gods were organised in Celtic times. From such studies the following parallels emerge between Roman, Gallic and insular deities: Mercury, the Gallic god of the arts (Lug?), Lug Samildanach; Vulcan, the Gallic smith, Gobannon; Jupiter, Taranis, the magician Gwydyon?; Heracles, Smertrios, Ogma; Apollo, the Gallic god of healing, Diancecht, the doctor; Earth Mother, the Gallic *matres*, the Irish mother-goddesses. Furthermore, Gallic coins, studied by Marie-Louise Sjoestedt, carry portraits that seem to reflect well-known insular legends: that of the hero Cuchulainn, for example. Finally, Gallic cults of the bull remind one of the importance of this legendary animal in Irish epics. Some legends can thus be added to the one and only myth we connect with Gaul because it is portrayed there in sculpture: that of Esus and the bull with three cranes. The study of insular mythology in Christian times may, in the future, be a source of information about Gallic mythology in pagan times.

The Insular Celts: Great Britain and Ireland

The first Goidel Celts seem to have become established in Great Britain about the eighth century B.C. We still do not quite know when and how they got across to Ireland. But it is known that in the third and second centuries it was the turn of the Britons and Belgians to cross the sea. They inflicted themselves on the Goidels to the point of supplanting them and driving them back in some degree. So two groups of insular Celts emerged: the Goidelic or Irish branch, and the Breton or Briton branch (which included the Kymry of Wales and the Bretons of Armorican Britain).

Their abundant, involved mythology can be studied from several sources: (1) dedicatory and votive inscriptions; (2) Irish, Gallic or Scottish manuscripts dating from the Middle Ages,[1] but perpetuating much more ancient traditions; (3) fabulous stories and chronicles, a large part of them being Evhemerised mythical legends; (4) primitive hagiography, in which the exploits of pagan deities are attributed to Christian saints of the Celtic Church; (5) bardic tradition, which inspired Gallic, Breton and even Norman minstrels, and later the story-tellers of the *matière de Bretagne*; (6) popular tales, fables and legends.

It is worth noting that Druidism survived much later on the islands than on the Continent. Banished from Gaul by Tiberius and expelled by Claudius, the Druids took refuge in Great Britain, then in Ireland, where they survived for four centuries, reluctantly giving way to the Christian clergy. They disappeared about 560, after the abandonment of the ancient capital, Tara.

The lack of monuments decorated with figures is highly regrettable. The only ones found in any number in these lands are on the whole earlier than the Celtic settlements and go back to the Neolithic period. As in Gaul, these consist of menhirs, dolmens, alignments and cromlechs. Their only distinctive feature is the frequency of the spiral as a decorative motif in ornamental engravings on dolmenic stones. The continued cult of menhirs is particularly noticeable in Ireland, from the anepigraphic 'stone of memory' to steles bearing oghamic inscriptions or Latin inscriptions accompanied by Christian symbols. In the east of Scotland, menhirs called monuments of the Picts were copied till about the eleventh century, when the kings of Scotland had hunting scenes or battle scenes engraved upon them.

---

[1]Irish manuscripts: *Book of the Dun Cow* (whose compiler, Maelmuiré, died in 1106); *Book of Leinster* (twelfth century); *Book of Ballymote* and *Yellow Book of Leccam* (fourteenth century). Gallic manuscripts: *The Four Branches of Mabinogion* (eleventh century); *Black Book of Carmarthen* (twelfth century); *Book of Aneirin* and *Book of Taliesin* (thirteenth century); *White Book of Rhydderch* and *Red Book of Hergest*.

The insular pantheon

The major deities are common to both the Goidels of Ireland and the Britons, but they have slightly different names (as a result of phonetic evolution). However, neither their popularity nor their adventures are always identical, nor are their respective roles of equal importance.

'The tribes of Dana'

The mother of the insular Celtic pantheon is the goddess called Dana (or Donu) in Ireland, and Don in Great Britain. She is the companion of Bilé (Irish) or Beli (British), who seems to correspond to Dis Pater, from whom, Caesar informs us, the Gauls believed themselves to be descended. Their entire lineage is called Tuatha De Danann (people of the goddess Dana) in Gaelic literature, or Children of Don in documents of Gallic origin. Here is a brief list of them:

Govannon (Britain) or Goibniu (Ireland), the god of the forge, is the Vulcan of the tribe; he provides all his family and its allies with arms. He also brews the beer that confers immortality. In Ireland Goibniu is regarded as the architect of the high round towers and first Christian churches.

Lludd or Nudd, 'Llaw Ereint' (Gaul) or Nuada, 'Argetlam' (Ireland), another son of Don, has the surname 'With the silver hand' for some unknown reason. The entirely anthropomorphic explanation put forward in the Irish tale of the battle of Moytura comes too late to be quite satisfactory; no other is offered in Breton mythology. Certain characteristics of the Roman Jupiter can be found in Nuada. Lludd, according to Geoffrey of Monmouth (who connects him with a king of Brittany), had his favourite town called after him: Caer Ludd, which ultimately became London; Ludgate Hill in the City is supposed to be his tomb. It is probable that St Paul's cathedral at the top of this hill replaced a temple that was dedicated to Lludd, who was also worshipped at Lydney in Gloucestershire.

Don's third son, Amaethon, is god of agriculture.

Greater than any of those mentioned above is the god of civilisation, Gwydion, who dispenses kindness and propagates the arts. His adventures recall those of Wodan (Wotan, Odin), the Teutonic god. Both are of somewhat mysterious parentage, and both distinguish themselves in the arts of battle, eloquence and magic. Each has a consort whose name reminds one of a wheel, and it is her fate to give birth to an offspring rejected by the gods. Gwydion loses his son in exactly the same way as Wodan loses his, and they create human beings by bringing vegetation to life. However, Gwydion remained a purely regional god, known only in the counties of Wales, while Wodan enjoyed universal renown in Teutonic society.

Gwydion is the nearest equivalent to the Continental god Ogmios (*see above*) who became Ogma in

Part of the early Bronze Age monument at Stonehenge, on Salisbury Plain. Massive blocks, some of which are still standing, were arranged in two concentric circles around two horseshoe groups. It is the earliest major prehistoric monument in England (*c.* 1500 B.C.), but its function is unknown. It may have been a Druidic temple or connected with sun-worship. *Aero Pictorial Ltd.*

Ireland, champion of the De Danann at the battle of Moytura. A god of civilisation like Gwydion, Ogma is eloquent and is supposed to be the inventor of the so-called oghamic alphabet.

Arianrod ('Of the silver wheel') is the only daughter of Don, tutelary deity of the corona borealis constellation, which the Welsh called Caer Arianrod, 'Castle of Arianrod'.

Arianrod became the mother of Lleu or Llew (Welsh) by Gwydion, who forced her to yield to his embrace — an incestuous embrace if this god was in fact her brother. Lleu was given the surname 'Skilled Hand', which seems to permit an identification with the Irish god Lugh, or Lug, called Lamh-fhada, 'Long Hand'. Both Lleu and Lug are powers for good. Little is known about the Welsh god. But we know that Lug's countenance possessed such radiance that no mortal could bear to look upon him. He is the uncontested master of the arts both of peace and of war. He also bears the epithet Samholdanach (literally 'polytechnician'): he is smith, carpenter, poet, harpist, champion, historian, sorcerer. He embraces all the superior activities of the tribe. He possesses a magic lance, which advances of its own volition to strike any enemy threatening the god. His bow is the rainbow, and, in Ireland, the Milky Way was called 'Lug's Chain'; moreover, the 'Children of Don' seem to be celestial figures. For the Welsh the constellation of Cassiopeia was called Llys Don, 'Court of Don'; and Caer Gwydion, 'Castle of Gwydion' referred to the Milky Way. It seems highly probable that Arianrod herself was the moon.

The Celtic white horse cut into the hillside at Uffington, Berkshire. The cult of the horse became increasingly important to the Celts. Originally linked with the goddess Epona, the horse itself gradually assumed a godlike character, associated with fertility and the protection of the dead. *Ashmolean Museum*

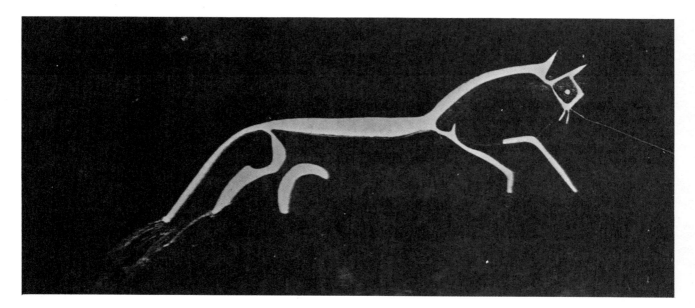

'The children of Llyr' and the sea-gods

The goddess Don is related in some vague way to the god Llyr (Welsh) or Ler, who is probably a god of the sea. His surname, Llediaith, 'Of the half-tongue' implies that his speech is very indistinct. Geoffrey of Monmouth in his *Chronicles* connects him with an ancient king of Great Britain; and later, when details undoubtedly taken from some historical event were also connected with him, he became human enough to emerge ultimately as Shakespeare's King Lear.

Ler, god of the sea, as is thought probable, has two sons, Bron (Ireland) or Bran (Wales) and Manannan (Ireland) or Manawydan (Wales), and both are more famous than their father. The Irish Bron mac Llyr is an insignificant character. But Bran ab Llyr of Great Britain is a redoubtable hero. He is an enormous giant, too big to get inside a palace or on a ship. He has to wade across the Irish Sea to fight and defeat a king and his host; when stretched across a river his body can be used as a bridge by an entire army. He possesses a magic cauldron in which the dead are brought back to life. As a harpist and musician he is the protector of the *file* and of bards. He is also king of the infernal regions and he gives battle in order to defend his magic treasures against the sons of Don when they come to deprive him of them. When wounded by a poisoned arrow he commands them to cut off his head to end his suffering, but this head continues to think and talk throughout the journey to his place of burial which takes eighty-seven years: a hill in London is his resting-place (Tower Hill?). Bran's severed head, which was buried facing south, kept the island safe from invasion until King Arthur was unwise enough to exhume it, and this made the Saxon conquest possible.

Bron (Ireland), who is unquestionably a different character from the one above, is shown as a fearless traveller sailing westward to the Land of Beyond. He is the sailor of mysterious regions. And under the name of Saint Brandan this pagan god was canonised and became the devout personage who brought Christianity to Great Britain.

The brother of the Welsh Bran, Manawydan ab Llyr, in Welsh legend is a fine husbandman and clever shoemaker. Sometimes he joins battle with the kindly gods. He built the fortress of Annoeth (Gower peninsula) of human bones.

His Irish double, Manannan mac Llyr, is a redoubtable magician. He wears a flaming helmet; his breast-plate is invulnerable; his sword never fails to slay; he has a cloak that makes him invisible. On land his steed goes like the wind; on the sea his barque follows its master's bidding without the aid of sails or oars. Sailors pray to him as 'Lord of the capes', and merchants claim that he founded their corporation. Manannan, or so legend has it, was King of the Isle of Man—where his gigantic tomb can still be seen when approaching Peel Castle. He appears to have had three legs, witness the island's coat-of-arms; three legs are depicted on it, placed like the spokes of a wheel. This god, whose surname is Barr-Find (Ireland), 'White Head', later develops into the helmsman Barin, who takes King Arthur to Avalon. In Christian hagiography he became Saint Barri, the patron of Irish fishermen, particularly those from the Isle of Man.

It would appear that these two sons of Llyr should primarily be regarded as powers of the sea, gods of waves and storms.

The Dagda

Dagda or Dagde (abbreviation of Dagodevos), 'Efficacious god', is the surname by which the god-chief Eochaid Ollathair is known. Another appellation, Ruad Ro-fhessa ('Lord of complete knowledge')

Brigantia, or Bridget. This goddess seems to have had numerous functions, particularly in Ireland, where she was the patron of Kildare, as well as protectress of poets, smiths and doctors. This relief statue of the early third century from the Roman fort at Birrens, Dumfriesshire, portrays her as the tutelary deity of the Brigantes tribe of Yorkshire. Her Roman and Oriental trappings were conventional in the reign of Severus, and the towered crown may symbolise York, the chief Roman city in the territory of the Brigantes. *National Museum of Antiquities, Scotland*

proclaims his omnipotence. The Dagda is, in fact, good at everything: he is first and foremost among magicians, a redoubtable warrior, an artisan of supreme ability. He possesses a miraculous cauldron, which can provide food for everyone in the world. He summons the seasons in turn by playing his harp. He is dressed in a hood and short tunic and has an enormous club that he draws along on wheels; as master of life and death, dispenser of plenty, the Dagda's attributes bring to mind a god like Sucellos, the 'Mighty Striker', the 'god with the hammer' as portrayed by Continental Celts. The Welsh equivalent of the Dagda seems to be Math, brother of the goddess Don.

Other gods

Morrigu Morrigan, known in Ireland as 'Queen of Ghosts', the goddess of war, appears in hideous guise to warriors departing for battle when they are about to be defeated and killed. Other cruel and sanguinary deities are probably only incarnations of this Celtic Bellona: these would include Badb, who appears in the guise of a raven, Macha, 'Battle', and Nemain, 'Panic'.

One of the Dagda's sons, Oengus (Ireland) is the Irish Cupid (whose Welsh counterpart is Dwyn or Dwynwen, 'the Saint of love'). Oengus' kisses turn into birds singing love-songs, and the music that he plays draws in his wake all who hear it.

His sister Bridget (compare the Gallic Brigantia) is a triple goddess (unless there were three sisters of the same name). She is worshipped not only by poets (whom she inspires), but also by smiths (to whom she brings wealth) and doctors (whom she helps by presiding over childbirth). As goddess of the seasons, her cult is celebrated on 1 February, the date of the Imbolc, which is the great festival of pagan purification. With the coming of Christianity Bridget became the patron saint of the town of Kildare. Perhaps she should be identified with Dana? Her equivalent is Kerridwen (Wales), who holds the 'cauldron of inspiration and knowledge'. Diancecht is the Goidelic god of health and healing, a sort of Irish Asclepius.

The Irish giant Balor, 'With the wicked eye' (or his Welsh counterpart Yspaddaden), has lowered lids and a fork is needed to raise them.

Pwyll (Wales), the ally and aid of Llyr's children in their struggle against the children of Don, has a wife called Rhiannon (from Rigantona, 'Great Queen') and a son called Pryderi, who succeeds his father as King of 'Annwn' (Breton 'Beyond'), sharing the throne with Manawydan ab Llyr in the kingdom of shades.

Castlerigg stone circle, near Keswick, Cumberland. Though many such Celtic monuments in Great Britain, and particularly in Ireland, are of a later date than those on the Continent, where the Druids were persecuted by Tiberius and Claudius, their significance is little understood. *Jack Scheerboom*

A thirteenth-century tile from Chertsey, England, showing King Mark kissing his nephew Tristan. The story of Tristan and Yseult was closely connected to the mythical elements of the Arthurian cycle. *British Museum*

Arthurian legend

Almost all the characters, gods and heroes, of Celtic mythology—more especially the Welsh versions—appear again highly Evhemerised in the tales from the medieval cycle of King Arthur, which constitutes the bulk of the *matière de Bretagne*.[1] This cycle began to take shape at the time of the Saxon invasion (450–510) and was enriched as tales from the Continent provided further inspiration.

Arthur himself, demi-god, demi-king, whose historical prototype possibly lived in the fifth or sixth century, displays various attributes and succumbs to several adventures resembling those of Gwydion, the son of Don. He is surrounded by characters who are strikingly similar to those in Gwydion's entourage in the fourth branch of the Mabinogion. His wife Gwenhwyar (Guinevere) is the daughter of the giant Ogyrvan, protector and initiator of bardism; in the early texts she was Arthur's sister before she became his wife.

Their two sons (or nephews?), Gwalchmai and Medrawt (one good, the other bad), correspond to the two deities of light (Lleu) and darkness (Dylan). Gwalchmai, 'Falcon of May', is Sir Gauvain; and Medrawt, Sir Modrer. A third brother, Gwalchaved, 'Falcon of Summer', becomes Galahad. Brandegore is undoubtedly 'Bran de Gwales', recalling the Christian

[1]The *Historia Regum Britanniae* of Geoffrey of Monmouth was completed about 1136. The heroic legends of 'Britain the Great' were turned into Arthurian romances in the twelfth and thirteenth centuries. About 1470 Sir Thomas Malory composed his *Morte d'Arthur*, translated from or inspired by French sources. The *Red Book of Hergest* (fourteenth-century manuscript) also includes some Mabinogion relating to Arthur's exploits.

Bran who brought the Holy Grail to Britain.

At least as important as the king is the powerful magician Myrddin, who is our enchanter Merlin, the holder of all knowledge, possessor of all wealth and lord of Fairyland. Uther Pendragon, or Urien, may well represent Uthr Ben, the miraculous head of Bran which lived for eighty-seven years after it was severed from his body. Lastly, Balan would be Balin, the Welsh and British god Belinus.

The mythical cycle of King Marc'h (Mark), Queen Essyllt (Yseult) and their nephew Drystan (Tristan) is likewise connected with 'Arthurian material'. A whole host of secondary characters lose their individuality and melt into the anonymous host of *korred* (dwarfs), *korriganes* (fairies) and *morganes* (female water-spirits) found in Breton folk-lore from the Armorica peninsula.

Even the most seemingly Christian element in Arthurian legend, the mystic quest of the Holy Grail, has its source in Celtic mythology. Originally it was a magic cauldron of which all the gods were envious, and they tried to steal it from one another. An old Welsh poem from the *Book of Taliesin* ('The Sack of Annwn') tells how Arthur seized the magic cauldron, but lost all but seven men in the expedition, although on setting out he had 'three times as many as would fill his ship'. The pagan cauldron changed very little when it became the Holy Grail that Joseph of Arimathaea filled with Christ's blood.

The epic myth in Ireland

The legendary beginnings of Ireland are recounted in the *Leabhar Gabhala* (*Book of Invasions, or Conquests*). Incidents that were probably taken from genuine history are mixed up with Celtic mythology, which has been Evhemerised and Christianised by successive additions of distorting elements. This collection was gradually completed and clarified by the sixteenth century: this accounts for the presence of several references to classical mythology that were introduced into the text at a late date. Here is a brief synopsis of this national legend.

After the great universal Flood the island that was to become Ireland was first inhabited by Queen Cessair, a magician (seemingly a reincarnation of Circe), and her women followers. Cessair perished with the whole of her race. About 2640 B.C. Prince Partholon from Greece landed in Ireland with twenty-four couples. At first Ireland was a smooth plain broken by three lakes and watered by nine rivers, but it was extended by Partholon and thenceforth consisted of four plains with seven new lakes. His companions increased in number: after three hundred years they numbered five thousand. But a mysterious epidemic wiped them all out at the day of Beltane's feast, 1 May, which was the tercentenary of their landing in Ireland. Their common tomb is the hill of Tallaght, near Dublin. However, about 2600, the race of the 'Sons of Nemed', whose name means 'Sacred', and who came originally from Scythia, set foot on the then deserted island— as they thought. Another troop of invaders landed about 2400, on the day of Lugnasad (1 August), the third major festival in the Celtic year. The Fir Bolg ('Belgian Men'?) formed the major part, with the addition of several other tribes such as the Gaileoin ('Gauls'?) and the Fir Dommann (Dummonni from Great Britain?). However, they united to form one race and one dominion. Finally, from the 'Isles of the West', where they studied magic, came the members of the Tuatha De Danann, who, as we have seen, were of divine descent. They brought their talismans: Nuada's sword, Lug's lance, Dagda's cauldron and Fal's 'stone of destiny', which uttered a cry when the rightful king of Ireland took his seat upon it. Each wave of invaders had to fight the race of monstrous giants that peopled Ireland in the beginning. Some had 'only one foot, one eye, one hand'; others had animals' heads, mainly goats' heads. These monsters were the Fomors (from *fo*, 'under', and *moire* or *mahr*, a female spirit whose name appears again in the word 'nightmare').

In the legend battle is joined between the Tuatha De Danann and the Fir Bolg. The first battle is fought at Moytura (Mag Tuireadh, the 'Plain of Pillars', in other words, of menhirs), near Cong in the present county of Mayo. The Tuatha De Danann are victorious. During the battle their king, Nuada, loses his right hand. This loss brings about his fall from sovereign power. The clever healer Diancecht replaces it with an articulated silver hand. Forced to yield, Nuada 'Of the silver hand' is replaced by Bress, 'Beautiful', the son of Elatha, 'Knowledgeable', king of the Fomors, and the De Danann Iriu (eponymous goddess of Ireland). The two alien races are brought together through marriage alliances. Bress weds Bridget, the daughter of Dagda, and Cian, son of Diancecht, marries Ethniu, the daughter of Balor 'With the wicked eye'. But Bress is an odious tyrant. He cripples his country with taxes and overwork; he mocks Cairbre, the son of Ogma and the greatest *file* (bard) of the De Danann. So Bress has to abdicate after seven years. Then Nuada ascends the throne again, for his own hand has been replaced on his wrist thanks to the skill and incantations of Miach, the other son of Diancecht. This occasions Miach's death, which was brought about by his own father in a fit of jealousy.

Bress, meanwhile, holds a secret council in his underwater abode. He persuades the Fomors to help him drive the De Danann from Ireland. Preparations for war last seven years, by which time Lug, the child prodigy, 'master of all the arts', born to Cian and Ethniu, has grown up. Lug organises the De Danann's means of resistance, while Goibniu forges arms for them and Diancecht produces a miraculous spring that heals wounds and brings dead warriors back to life. But spies from the Fomors come upon it and put it out of use by covering it with evil stones. After a few duels and skirmishes a great battle is joined in the northern Moytura (plain of Carrowmore, near Sligo). (The alignments at Sligo form the most important group of raised stones in existence after those at Carnac.) In the course of a fierce struggle many warriors are defeated: Indech, son of the goddess Domnu, is killed by Ogma, who is then killed in his turn. Balor 'Of the wicked eye' strikes Nuada with his fatal glance. But Lug with his magic sling puts out Balor's eyes. Reduced and demoralised, the hideous Fomors retreat and are driven back to the sea. Bress is taken prisoner and the hegemony of the giants on the island is destroyed for ever.

From now on the might of the De Danann is to decline rapidly. Two deities from the empire of the dead, Ith and Bilé, landing at the mouth of the Kenmare, interrupt the political consultations held by the victors. Mil, the son of Bilé, joins his father in Ireland, accompanied by his eight sons and their followers. Like the former invaders they appear on 1 May. Marching towards Tara, they meet three goddesses whose names are eponyms, Banba, Fodla and Eriu. Each one in turn asks the Druid Amergin, Mil's counsellor and sage, to name the island after her. Erinn is chosen as the name of the island (the genitive of Eriu) because Eriu's request is the third to be made![1] After new and bloody battles, in the last of which Manannan, the son of Llyr, 'Ocean', intervenes, the Tuatha kings are killed by the three surviving sons of Mil. A peace pact is concluded, the

[1]For the convenience of the reader we have used Ireland as a virtually definitive name; but it should be remembered that the island is referred to in mythology under several different appellations.

Tuatha surrender Erinn and withdraw to the Land of Beyond, and in return simply ask that a cult and sacrifices should be celebrated in their memory.

This is how religion would appear to have begun in Ireland.

The cycle of the Beyond

Abandoning the isle of Erinn, certain De Danann tribes withdraw beyond the western seas to a distant country called Mag Mell, 'Plain of Joy', or Tir na n-Og, 'Land of Youth'. In that land centuries are minutes, people do not grow old, the meadows are covered with everlasting flowers, and hydromel flows in the river-beds. Feasting and fighting are favourite pastimes: warriors eat and drink of fairy dishes and beverages, and their companions are women of wondrous beauty.

In the mythology of Great Britain the counterpart of this Celtic Elysium (which reminds one of the magic Land of the Hyperboreans as described by Diodorus Siculus) is Avalon, or the Isle of Apple-trees, where dead kings and heroes dwell. This concept of a land beyond the tomb, just over the horizon where the sun disappears each evening, comes naturally to island races. It explains the importance of the Druid sanctuary, the Isle of Sein (Enez Sizun, the 'Isle of Seven-Sleeps') opposite the Armorica peninsula. Perhaps we should also look upon the menhirs (or raised stones) as cenotaphs or funerary steles that were raised in honour of the great Druids or Celtic chiefs and were therefore placed on the very edge of lands haunted by the living, facing the 'Happy Plain' where the dead survive.

To return to the legend: the remainder of the Tuatha take refuge in magnificent underground dwellings, visible to the human eye in the shape of mounds. The Tuatha De Danann, who are henceforth invisible, take their new name from these new habitations: *Aes sidhe*, 'Race of Mounds'; and the Irish people continue to refer to the invisible world of fairies by an abbreviation of this name, *sidhe* or *shee*. The *ban shee* (*bean sidhe*, 'fairy-woman') of popular belief, whose appearance presages death, is only the one-time goddess of the ancient Goidel Celts. In the tales of the Ulster cycle, the *sidhe* appear to the living both in concrete reality and in dreams. They appear and disappear, though no-one knows where they come from or where they go. They can make themselves invisible and sometimes intervene in the actions of men. In the cycle of the Fenians they are in constant contact with chiefs and warriors; they take part in their banquets and their games, and even fight alongside them with white shields and bluish lances.

The Ulster heroic cycle

Apart from the mythical genealogy of the Tuatha De Danann and the no less apocryphal stories of the Milesian invasions and kings, two other great historic cycles are known in Ireland. The more interesting of the two is about the kingdom of Ulster at the time of Conchobar (Conahar: pronounced Connor). It is also the more original as it has been least altered.

The nucleus of this cycle was in existence before the second century, but the first written versions came more than nine hundred years later. The adventures of Cuchulainn (pronounced Cou-hou-linn), which form the central epic, would appear to be contemporary with the beginnings of Christianity. Tradition, in fact, puts the date of the arrival of the young king Conchobar mac Nessa at about 30 B.C.; his death is said to have taken place in A.D. 33. And the brief career of the champion of the Ulates unfolds entirely in the reign of this sovereign.

Such indications as are given in these tales of the customs of the times—dress and arms, habitation, the order regarding feasts, magic practices, usages of war (such as two-wheeled chariots, severing the heads of the vanquished enemy)—are clearly characteristic of the type of civilisation at the La Tène period. Except for the considerable religious and political role played by the Druids, the social state of Ireland at the time bears a very close resemblance to that in independent Gaul. It is also like that of Greece in the time of Homer and Rome under the Tarquins. Continental Gauls and insular Gaels are assuredly one and the same race somewhat differentiated by regional conditions.

The exploits of the champion of Ulster, the Achilles of an Irish *Iliad*, are scattered throughout seventy-six tales, each of which is rather like a theme that lends itself to countless variations. One single version of each of these tales would fill a two-thousand-page volume printed in octavo. This gives some idea of the importance of the cycle. Here is a brief summary of the labours of the hero Cuchulainn, champion of the Ulates, the knights of Ulster.

At birth Cuchulainn was given the name of Setanta. He was the son of Dechtire, King Conchobar's sister, who was married to the prophet Sualtim. But his real father was Lug 'With the long arms' (the solar myth of the Tuatha De Danann). He was brought up with the other sons of the king's vassals and warriors, who were valiant champions of the Red Branch of Ulster (an appellation that seems to refer to some militia or primitive order of knighthood). At the age of seven he killed the terrible hound belonging to Culain, the chief of the Ulster smiths. Thus he acquired the surname Cuchulainn, 'Culain's Hound', which he was later to make famous. He had prodigious strength: when anger seized him, intense heat emanated from his body and his appearance became misshapen and hideous. A short while after his first exploit he massacred three giant warriors and magicians who had defied the nobles of the Red Branch. He then went to complete his education with the witch Scatbach, 'Queen of Darkness' (an eponym for the Isle of Skye), who dwelt on Albu (Scotland) and taught Cuchulainn all she knew of magic. Before departing thence, the grateful disciple overcame Scatbach's enemy, the witch Aiffe, by whom he was to have a son. He regained Ulster with a wealth of witchcraft at his disposal and some prodigious weapons.

Now Cuchulainn was in love with the beautiful Emer (pronounced Avair), the daughter of Forgall Manach, a powerful and crafty magician who had refused him her hand in marriage and locked her up in a magic castle. His next act was to abduct his beloved after killing an entire garrison, including the fair Emer's father. Then a wearisome sequence (by modern standards) of duels and combats amply justifies the title of 'champion' attributed to Cuchulainn.

His most famous exploits were those accomplished in the course of the struggle described in the twenty tales grouped together in the *Cattle Raid of Cooley* (*Táin Bó Cúailgne*). This is the bloody history of the long war that the four other kingdoms in Ireland (the two Munsters, Leinster and Connaught) waged against Ulster at the instigation of the redoubtable queen of Connaught, the perfidious Medb (pronounced Mev; she is the Queen Mab of Shakespeare referred to in *Romeo and Juliet*). The object of this war was to ensure the possession of a magic animal, the Brown Bull of Cooley. Now, Medb was careful to commence hostilities at a time when the knights of Ulster were all paralysed by a strange periodic weakness that made them incapable of fighting or even of moving. This mysterious malady had been inflicted on them by way of punishment by the goddess Macha when they made fun of her one day. When the kingdom of Ulster seemed destined to fall into the hands of the invaders, Cuchulainn, who by reason of his divine origin had escaped the common curse, set off alone to confront the enemy band. For three whole months he fought, killing one of the enemy each day; then he fought entire groups of them and decimated them in the same way. The episodes of the raid here include a long series of duels and skirmishes in which the most diverse ruses and all kinds of witchcraft come into play. On a higher plane than that of the combatants hover two divine personages who intervene in the struggle: Lug 'With the long arms', Cuchulainn's real father, who uses a beverage and magic herbs to cure the champion's wounds each night and to give him comfort; and Morrigan, goddess of war, who helps Cuchulainn with advice, supports him with witchcraft, and even goes so far as to offer him her love, only to turn her impotent hatred upon him later.

Other tales tell us how the champion goes in a magic barque to stay in Mag Mell, 'the Plain of Joy', the Beyond of the Celtic world. There he falls in love with the goddess Fand, the abandoned wife of Manannan mac Llyr, who returns his love. Cuchulainn returns to Ulster, and (a year later) Fand keeps their rendezvous and appears before him on the river-bank. But Emer surprises them together, and, moved by the laments of Cuchulainn's wife, the goddess leaves the champion and returns to her husband, who has come to look for her.

A little later, Cuchulainn unwittingly kills his only son, young Conlach, conceived by the witch Aiffe, who has been prompted by jealousy to send him to Ireland to provoke his father to a duel. (This episode exploits the Aryan theme that is found in the Persian myth of Sohrab and Rustum and in the legend of the Teutonic Wodan.) In horror Cuchulainn succumbs to a fit of frenzied madness and from that day forth his soul is filled with deep sadness.

Thanks to the complicity of the parents and sons of those whom Cuchulainn has killed in duels, hateful

Queen Medb brings about the hero's downfall. Three witches, Callatin's daughters, who have recently visited the Orient to perfect their knowledge of evil spells, disguise themselves as three crows, and lure Cuchulainn with visions so that he follows them to the Plain of Muirthemne. They made him violate certain taboos by offering him god's flesh, which is forbidden him. Clowns ('satirists') from the Connaught court take his magic lance. Deprived of material and supernatural means of defence, the champion finds himself attacked by overwhelming numbers. Twenty omens appear to warn him of death. But his undaunted heart does not betray a trace of hesitation. He receives a fatal wound, and blood rushes from his breast. Then he is tied to a 'pillar of stone' (menhir) with his own belt, so that he may die on his feet. His black horse comes and touches him and goes away with tears in its eyes. At last Cuchulainn expires, his blood all spent, and as his sword falls it cuts off the hand of the foe who has come to sever his head and bear it away as a trophy, according to the custom of the time.

These, then, are the bare bones of the epic concerning the champion of the knights of Ulster. No mention has been made of the numerous enigmatic conversations (the meaning of which escapes us), the gnomic dialogues, the enumeration of *geasa* (taboos), the magic animals (cattle, horses, swans, ravens) and their complicated genealogy, the oft-repeated description of the frightening contortions to which Cuchulainn abandons himself when his warlike rage descends upon him. All these terrifying or grotesque details presumably have a hermetic meaning of which we have lost the key.

Cuchulainn himself—who is he? The attributes bestowed upon him and his prowess in battle appear to indicate some solar myth. Lug 'With the long arms', his divine father, is a sort of Apollo. Cuchulainn himself makes anyone who looks at him blink and close his eyes. Two horses draw his chariot; one black, the other white. The heat from his body makes water boil and snow melt. The fairy-woman who falls in love with him, the gentle Fand, is the abandoned wife of Manannan, the god of the ocean. Each of his antagonists can be identified more or less with some phenomenon of darkness or night. However, other mythologists see in Cuchulainn the glorification of a national hero, an Ulatic Roland exalted by the poetic imagination of bards. 'The myth of Cuchulainn,' M.-L. Sjoestedt writes, 'is the myth of tribal man, the exaltation of heroism as social function. In many respects, Cuchulainn appears to be the homologue on the human plane of the god-chiefs and champions.'

Pagan in its essence and development, this epic cycle of Ulster has been adapted here and there to comply with the purpose of Christian edification. So we are told that at the moment of departure for the supreme battle Cuchulainn hears the voices of angels, confesses to the true faith and receives the certainty of future salvation. Later, King Conchobar dies of grief at the news of Christ's Passion. And in the episode of the 'Phantom Wagon' Cuchulainn, who has been evoked from the dead, testifies to the truth of Christianity in the presence of the king.

The cycle of the Fenians or Ossian

This cycle is at least as important as the Ulster cycle. It developed considerably after the Saxon invasion, whereas the preceding one was already a hazy memory by then. The historic events that provide a background to the fresco take place from the year 174 (Battle of Cnucha, under Conn of the Hundred Battles) to the year 283 (Battle of Gabhra, or Gavra, under Cormac).

The tales in this cycle reveal a very different civilisation from that of the Ulates: they depict the life of nomadic hunters in the heart of primitive forests. The Fenian sagas are the appanage not of a tribe, but of a nation; and they are common to the two Goidelic countries, Ireland and Scotland. Furthermore, their tradition remains alive. An old proverb has it that if the Fenians heard that they were no longer talked about for a single day, they would rise from the dead! The Fianna (from the word *fian*, 'the band') consisted of a sort of professional chivalry instituted, it is thought, in the reign of Feradach Fechtnach (15–86) for the purpose of maintaining order in Ireland and protecting the island against invasion. The warring and hunting exploits of its members have become famous. In the third century, the period depicted in the cycle, the order of Fenians numbered a hundred and fifty officers and four thousand and fifty men. Their activities covered the whole of Ireland except for the kingdom of Ulster.

The hero, Fionn or Finn mac Cumhail, was the chief of the Fianna of Leinster, and was both a slayer of monsters and a magician. He was a poet, too, and enjoyed a pleasurable life. He was defiant and astute and was related to the Fir Bolg and the Tuatha De, as well as to Sualtim, the supposed father of Cuchulainn. In his later years he married Grainne, the daughter of Cormac, who abandoned him for the young and attractive warrior Diarmaid (Dermot).

Finn was the father of Ossian (Oisin) and, through him, the grandfather of Oscar (Osgur). His enemies were the proud Goll and his brother Conan, both sons of Morna and chiefs of the dread clan of Connaught. Apart from bravery in battle, a quality in which Finn was not lacking, the other heroes in his cycle had in common generosity, frankness and courtesy, which in his case were not altogether present. Certain commentators, such as Eugene O'Curry, have claimed that Finn's prototype is a real person, but the present tendency is to regard him as a mythical hero. His name means 'White' or 'Blond'.

The Hill of Tara, capital of the Kings of Ireland until the year 560. In the centre foreground is the Rath of the Kings. Further back are the Mound of the Hostages, the Rath of the Synods and the Banqueting Hall. *Bord Fáilte*

His father, Cumhall (or Cou), appears to be the Gallic Camulos, a name which corresponds to the Germanic Himmel, 'the Sky'. Could it be that this Finn mac Cumhall is simply an incarnation of the Breton god of the Beyond, Gwyn ab Nudd, king of the Welsh fairies? Jealousies and rivalries were already undermining the order of Fenians before Finn came into the world. Their tolls raised the population of Ireland against them; their arrogance irritated the king. Cairbre Lifechair, great-grandson of King Conn, inflicted fatal defeat upon them at Gabhra, where he lost his life.

Around this nucleus, probably inspired in part by history, a mass of miraculous episodes has crystallised, many of which unfold in mysterious lands in the midst of far-off seas. Dwarfs, giants, fairies, magicians and witches, monstrous animals, wonders of all sorts intermingle in profusion, as well as the representatives of the Tuatha De Danann. The Fenians circulate freely in the *sidhe,* underground palaces of the ancient Tuatha De, who have by now become invisible. The famous episode of the Battle of Ventry depicts their allied tribes driving back Daire Donn, the great king of the world, who has come to attack Ireland at the head of his vassals.

Ossian, the son of Finn, plays an important part in all these adventures. But his name predominates especially in the series of post-Fenian ballads in which the exploits of his father are related in the form of dialogues between Ossian and Saint Patrick, the patron saint of Ireland. At the time of the defeat of Gabhra, Ossian escaped the fate of the Fenians. The goddess-fairy Niamh (pronounced Nieve), the daughter of Manannan, saved him and took him in her glass barque to Tir na n-Og, the Celtic paradise. Ossian spent three hundred years of delightful youth there while the human world was changing shape. At length, however, he was seized with desire to see his native land, and Niamh gave him her magic steed, advising him not to set foot upon the ground. But the girth broke and the saddle slipped: Ossian fell. And when he got up again, he was nothing but a blind old man, henceforth deprived of his magic gifts.

It is a well-known fact that Ossian's supposed compositions enjoyed great popularity at the end of the eighteenth and beginning of the nineteenth centuries. Although founded on Gaelic tradition and imitated from various prose tales by unknown authors, the *Translated Poems of Ossian, son of Fingal* (which appeared from 1760 to 1763) are, in fact, the work of their so-called translator, the Scotsman James Macpherson. They aroused the enthusiasm of sensitive readers and the admiration of the most illustrious writers: Goethe, Herder, Mme de Staël, Chateaubriand, Byron and Lamartine. Napoleon read and reread Ossian. But the original names were changed and acquired poetic overtones in deference to the tastes of the period: Finn becomes Fingal; Conor becomes Caibar; Deirdre, Darthula; Conlaech, Carthon; Cuchulainn, Clessamor; Aiffe, Moina! These characters are set against romantic scenery: valleys haunted by ghosts, moonlit mountains, torrents booming over rocks, leaping fires in the evening mist. Ideas and sentiments are those of Macpherson's own contemporaries.

The great originality of Celtic religion would appear to be this strange body of spiritualist philosophers, physicians and naturalists, called Druids. Priests, divines, magicians, political counsellors, they occupied an important place in the state. According to the narrator of the *Cattle Raid of Cooley* the Ulates were forbidden to speak in front of their king, the king was forbidden to speak in front of his Druid. They held the secrets of religion and of magic science; they were the preceptors of young noblemen. But the study of this institution concerns social history and that of their doctrines, beliefs or practices is, rightly speaking, the history of religion. We are concerned only with mythology.

Now, as you have seen, we know but little of the Celtic gods; information about them is fragmentary, scattered, lacking in any semblance of order. With regard to ancient times, only the doubtless superficial assimilations reported by Greek and Latin authors are available to us; in Gallo-Roman times the Celtic surnames of local deities reveal a Gallic pantheon that is very different from that which the authors of Antiquity suggested; finally, the romantic and mythical Irish compositions of the late Middle Ages, adapted by Christian editors, are based on national heroes, magicians or sorcerers in whom it is somewhat difficult to recognise the personifications of natural or moral forces to whom the ancient Celts would conceivably have devoted a cult.

GERMANIC LANDS: THE MORTAL GODS

The domain of Germanic mythology, rich in legends and peopled with adventure-loving gods, heroes and traitors, witches and dwarfs is still something of a mystery to us, for the documents that we have at our disposal are not equally reliable. They shed no light at all on vast sectors, and contrive to contradict one another where certain others are concerned (394 and 395).

In the last few centuries before Christ the Germanic peoples must have formed a vast group, living in southern Scandinavia, the Baltic islands, Jutland and the North German plain from the Rhine to the Vistula. They spoke a common language, which died out at some unspecified date and is now extinct. Memories of their common origins and probably of joint migrations remained with them for a long time, for their original habitat was much farther to the east. There was no unity, however, for they waged frequent wars against one another. But they kept a sort of community of culture, tradition and superstition; all of the tribes, about this time, must have worshipped the same gods. No definite traces, such as written records or buildings, remain from this period, as at this time the Germanic peoples had no knowledge of either writing or architecture. We deduce the existence of this common religion from what we know of the subsequent beliefs of different branches of the Germanic group, but we cannot make any absolute assertion about it.

Certain objects belonging to prehistoric times that have been found on Germanic territory definitely testify to the existence of religious practices. Some of them, like the sun-chariot in the Copenhagen Museum, have surprising artistic quality: but no conclusion can be drawn regarding the content of the religion common to the Germanic peoples. It is almost certain that at some very early date they came from the Orient with beliefs similar to those that can be found among the Celts, Latins and Slavs who form other branches of the Indo-European family. Everyone who has studied the religion of the Germanic peoples has been struck by the analogies with the beliefs not only of Persia, Greece and Rome, but also with the faith of the Celts and ancient Slavs, as far as this can be judged.

With regard to this very early period, however, we must still be content with conjecture in spite of the confirmation afforded by comparison with the beliefs of other Indo-European peoples. The period in which the Germanic peoples retained some vivid recollection of their common origins remains beyond our knowledge; we know nothing definite about this bygone age.

The Germanic domain

The Germanic peoples made their entry into history when they came into conflict with the Romans. Before this, they had not met with any race able to write—or at least none that has left written traces of its existence. At this time the Germanic peoples were roughly divided into three major groups, two of which had already left the Baltic coasts. To the east the Goths, who came from the Vistula, had emigrated *en masse* towards the Black Sea, forming a quite separate group with its own language. To the north another group extended its frontiers as far as Scandinavia, and it, too, had its own language. Finally, the West Germans, who were probably the most numerous, spread in three directions (at least those who came into contact with the Romans did)—to the Danube and Bohemia in the south, to the Rhine in the west and, later, to the British Isles in the northwest.

Once they were scattered in this way, the Germanic peoples modified their way of life, their culture, their language and their religious concepts—often as a result of contact with the people who lived in the lands where they settled. Thus the West Germans had many contacts with the Celts, who had occupied the whole of Europe from the Elbe to the Atlantic before they themselves came on the scene. Their gods and their beliefs, which came from the same Indo-European sources, displayed remarkable similarities. During numerous migrations, wars and conquests, frequent blending took place between the myths of those races who had lived in contact with one another for many centuries and others living under quite different circumstances.

The Goths or East Germans were the first to enter the world known to history, for they were converted to Christianity—which had come from Byzantium—in the fourth century. However, we know nothing about their previous religion, for they had no written language until a translation of the Gospels was made into Gothic, and the few texts that

Sigurd and Fafnir. Rock engraving from Uppland, Sweden. At the bottom right, Sigurd is thrusting his sword through the monster Fafnir, represented as a serpent by the long band of runic inscriptions. In the centre, towards the right, is a tree with contorted branches to which Grane, Sigurd's horse, is tied. In the tree sit the two birds who will warn Sigurd of Regin's evil intentions. The figure to the left of the horse is again Sigurd. He is roasting Fafnir's heart over a fire, but, in touching the heart to see whether it is cooked, he has burnt a finger of his left hand and he is holding it to his mouth. By involuntarily tasting the monster's blood, he has learnt to understand the language of the birds. The last scene, to the left, shows Regin's forge, with the tongs, the anvil, the bellows and the hammer. We also see Regin's body, which Sigurd has just beheaded. *Swedish Travel Bureau*

mention these peoples omit to speak of their beliefs before they turned to Christianity. In the case of the West Germans, the ancestors of the Germans as we know them today and of the Anglo-Saxons, there are many sources. First of all, the ancient writers, such as Strabo, Velleius Paterculus and Pliny, give scattered references, but Caesar, in his *Gallic War,* is more explicit, and Tacitus tried to give an overall picture of Germanic religion. *Germania* by Tacitus is the most important source of information about the Germanic gods; it is certainly the earliest written source. In fact it was written at the end of the first century, probably in the year A.D. 98, that is to say, almost ten centuries before the earliest Germanic sources, which were written by poets or scholars in the tenth or twelfth centuries.

Tacitus collected a great deal of information about Germany, but it was limited to the West Germans—those nearest the Rhine. His evidence is valuable, for it makes it possible to put a date to certain stages in the evolution of the Germanic religion; and also, thanks to him, we are able to state that from this period (first century A.D.), the Germans worshipped gods in human shape and credited them with heroic adventures. It is, however, quite certain that Tacitus imagined the Germanic pantheon to be a copy of its Latin equivalent, and that he interpreted the information he had collected according to his own ideas. None the less, the fact remains that certain comparisons he drew between Germanic and Latin gods have been confirmed by the most recent studies.

Medieval sources are of two types, and they vary considerably in reliability. Christian sources, contemporary with the conversion of the barbarians, are found in great number, but are fragmentary and unreliable: their authors are not concerned to draw

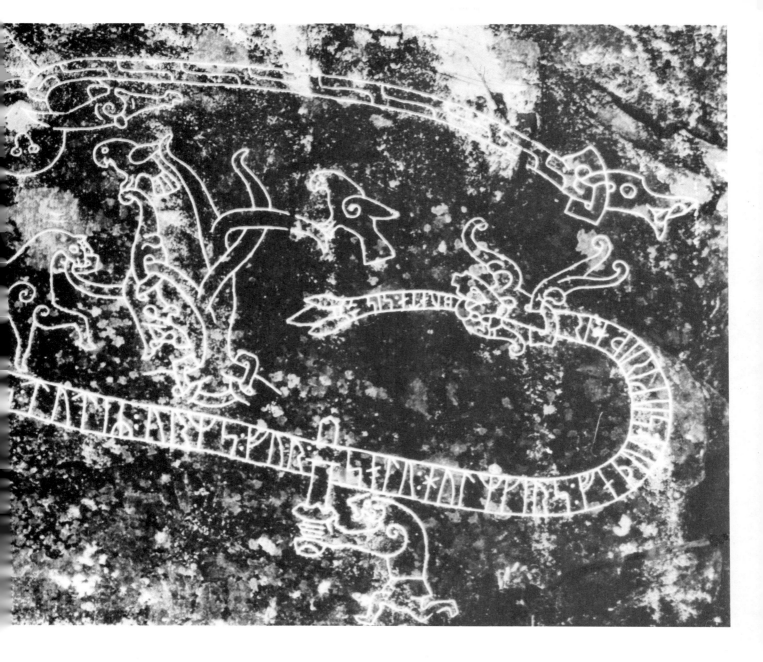

up a picture of pagan beliefs, but to point out their weaknesses. However, interesting information is to be found in the writings of Gregory, Bishop of Tours, and in the life of Saint Columban, the evangelist, who died in 615. Reference may also be made to council and papal decisions throughout the period of evangelisation, and to legal texts too, such as Salic law. The most precious and most frequently quoted Christian evidence is that of Adam of Bremen, an eleventh-century clerk, in his *Gesta Hamburgensis ecclesiae pontificum.*

It contains the only known description of a Germanic temple, at Uppsala in Sweden, though Tacitus had previously stated that the Germans did not construct temples. It is true that Adam of Bremen's account came ten centuries later and is about the North Germanic group, and it is equally true that the forms of religious life must certainly have

changed in the course of such a long period.

In actual fact, the most reliable information in our possession relates to the North Germans, those who came from Scandinavia, and this is contained in the great collection of anonymous poems called the *Edda.*

The Edda

The *Edda* is, in part, earlier in date than the introduction of Christianity into Scandinavia. Both the old and the new *Edda* are great epic compilations, which in the Germanic world hold the same place as the Homeric poems in the Greek world. About half of these poems recount the adventures of the gods. As a source of material they are richer than all the other poetic or historical texts composed in the Middle Ages in Iceland, Norway, Denmark and Sweden. Together with the *sagas,* the skalds' (or minstrels') songs, poetry, manuals and chronicles of history, this

Bronze disc partially covered with gold leaf and symbolising the sun, drawn on wheels by a horse. This so-called chariot of the sun dates back to the Bronze Age—perhaps about a thousand years B.C. National Museum, Copenhagen. *M. Hétier*

Head of the horse drawing the chariot of the sun. The spiral patterns ornamenting his eye and the solar disc symbolise the source of light. Worship of the sun was common to all the Indo-European peoples. *M. Hétier*

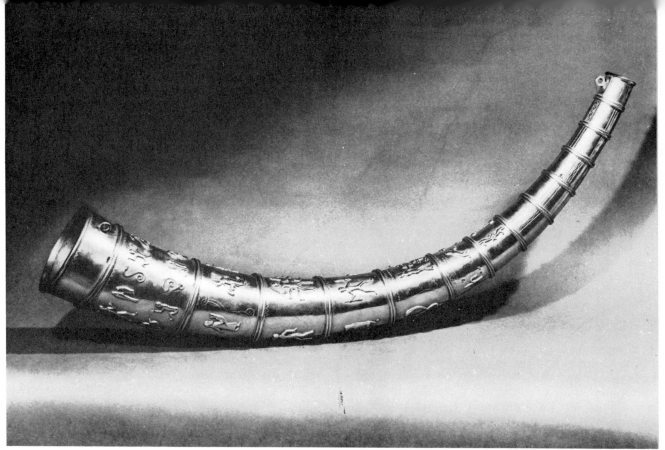

literature provides a broad and lively picture of the northern gods. There is a considerable number of them and they seem to love adventure and to be surrounded by a host of minor deities, spirits, giants and all sorts of creatures whom the Ancients would have called 'heroes' or 'demi-gods'.

Although archaeology is rarely of much help in the study of northern gods, the existence of some remarkable objects should not be forgotten, especially the gold horns found in the seventeenth century at Gallehus on the island of Seeland in Denmark. A very true copy exists in the museum at Copenhagen, taken from the design of the originals which were stolen and then lost. They are inscribed with people and animals in curious attitudes, an explanation of which has been given by the Danish scholar Axel Olrik. He managed to make out three deities—Odin in helmet and armour, Freyr holding a sceptre and a sickle and Thor with three heads. But a host of other figures are still difficult to interpret.

Scandinavian poems have been instrumental in enabling modern historians to reconstruct the Germanic pantheon, but the fact remains that all these accounts translate the beliefs of the North Germanic group at a relatively late date. This is the final form of a mythology that was shared by all Germanic races at first, and then disappeared, more quickly in evangelised German and Anglo-Saxon countries, less quickly in the Scandinavian lands, where it lingered until the tenth and eleventh centuries.

No picture of Germanic mythology can be built up without making initial use of this literature, which even after two centuries of research and comparison often requires careful interpretation. Anything concerning the gods is deliberately put in the mouths of seers, whose language is usually obscure. Dreams, prophecies and visions abound; analagous attributes are frequently lent to gods who in other respects are

A copy of one of the gold horns of Gallehus. These are decorated with figures and animals that appear to have mythological significance, but only two or three of which have been identified. *British Museum*

A detail from one of the Gallehus horns showing, in the top band, the three-headed figure which has been identified as the god Thor. British Museum.

totally dissimilar. But if the characters are sometimes badly drawn, their adventures and their battles form a coherent whole, a great drama that unfolds from earliest times until it reaches ultimate catastrophe amid fearful omens. Thus the mythology of the Germanic peoples is presented as an immense tragedy in which the epic of the gods and that of the heroes finally converge.

The creation of the world and the gods

In the poems in the *Edda* several accounts are given of the beginnings of the world and the appearance of gods, giants and men. In spite of some discrepancies a common train of thought can be found. 'In the beginning,' says the author of the *Voluspa*, 'there was neither sand, nor sea, nor salt waves, nor the earth below, nor the sky above; there was a yawning gulf and nowhere did grass grow.' This original abyss stretched from the land of ice, darkness and mist in the north called Niflheim to the land of fire in the south, known as Muspelsheim. When these elements eventually mixed, sea, earth and water emerged. To begin with rivers came from the south and flowed towards the land of ice; there they became frost-bound and died in the icy vastness. Slowly these masses of frozen river-water filled the once yawning gulf, the Ginnungagap, and then south winds came, bringing warm air which began to melt the ice. This first spring, the first trickle of water on the surface of the eternal ice, was the ancestor of every living thing, because the drops of water quickened by warm air from the south gathered to form a living body, that of the first giant: Ymir. He was the author and begetter of the giants, the human race and, to a certain degree, of the gods; but exactly how this came about—and likewise how animals were created—was not explained.

Though at first he was the only creature endowed with life, Ymir soon had a companion in the food-providing cow Audhumla, who, according to the story-tellers, arose like him from the melted ice. Thus the cow takes pride of place among animals. She becomes the ancestor of all living creatures, the symbol of fecundity, and it is interesting to note that the same thing occurs in numerous mythological tales from the Orient. Four rivers of milk flowed from Audhumla's udders; she licked the ice and grazed on the salt it contained. While Ymir was quenching his thirst with her milk and gathering strength, the cow contrived to bring forth another living creature from the warm drops that her tongue sent trickling down the frost-covered block of ice; he was called Buri. First his hair took shape, then his head, then the rest of his body. Like the giant Ymir, Buri was capable of reproduction and he created a son, Bor, who married Bestla, a giant's daughter, one of Ymir's descendants. Three gods were born of this marriage—Odin, Vili and Ve.

This is how the two races arose from the void, races that were to make the world ring with their adventures and battles: the race of giants and that of gods.

The race of giants was directly descended from Ymir, because it arose from the sweat of his body: as he was resting two living creatures, a man and a woman, took shape in the moisture beneath his left arm-pit; at the same time his joined feet gave birth to a son. This was the first generation of an immensely powerful and deliberately terrifying race that keeps on appearing in mythological tales from the north; these were the 'frost-giants' or 'ice-giants', who had human form, although their origins and powers greatly surpassed those of humanity. They appeared before the gods and threatened their empire unceasingly, for all expeditions designed to exterminate them merely saw them rise again as numerous and as strong as ever.

The sons of Bor attacked the giant Ymir and killed him. From his body gushed a huge river of blood which filled what remained of the original gulf. All the giant's descendants perished in this sea of blood, except for one of his sons, who escaped death by clinging to a fragile boat with his wife. This couple begat a new generation, and so the race of giants survived the disaster.

Meanwhile, the gods plotted against the dead giant, although he was the forefather of them all. They dragged his huge body across the abyss, and the various parts of his body then gave birth to the different elements of the world: his flowing blood made the ocean, his flesh became the firm earth, his bones were mountains and his teeth shingle. With his skull the gods created the vault of heaven, which was then supported by four dwarfs; in a fairly late poem they are given names, and these names are still used for the four cardinal points.

His brain gave birth to clouds which spread across the sky. With the ice-giant's bushy eyebrows the gods built the ramparts of their own abode, which they called the Midgard, the 'middle land'. It was, in fact, situated between the land of ice, frost and eternal silence (the Niflheim) and the Muspelsheim, the kingdom of fire and land of the burning midday sun.

Until then the sun in Muspelsheim, which was the source of all heat, had sent out countless sparks in all directions, which vanished in the icy vastness. Once the gods had fixed the vault of heaven over the world, the sun's sparks got caught in it and gave birth to the stars. The gods then decided their course and thus instituted the rhythm of the seasons, which prompted the growth of vegetation and gave rise to the sequence of days and nights. Night came first, and was followed by day; but day had to be preceded by darkness. The priority given to night, the mother of day, seems to be an essential part of a very widespread belief among northern peoples. According to Caesar the Gauls counted the hours of the day from sunset onwards, and according to Tacitus the Germans did the same.

The home of the gods

Once the world was created and organised, the labours of the gods began. It is not easy to determine who these gods were exactly. Although Scandinavian authors definitely state that Odin, the first of them, was the son of Bor, from the point at which he embarked on his eventful career he was portrayed in the company of other gods who seemed to emerge from nowhere and joined him initially to help him build the celestial abode, which was given the name of Asgard. The gods themselves were called the Aesir; the origin of this word is obscure, but it unquestionably evokes the idea of authority, arrogance, the presence of spirit and power on an intangible plane. The Germanic peoples depicted Asgard, 'the land of the Aesir', as a vast estate, which could accommodate a large race. It was an enormous enclosure with individual dwellings for the lords who lived there. It was full of fabulous riches, and was built of splendid materials, which were particularly handsome in the great council and banquet hall – the Halle.

In their palace-courtyard the gods acquired a passion for games of dice. The prominence given to these games can be explained by the fact that the different squares were associated with cosmic symbols. Numerous texts also contain proof that the Germans deliberately used games of chance as a means of divination, especially before battles, and as a way of consulting the gods. This taste for gaming on the part of the Aesir reminds one of a passage in *Germania* in which Tacitus describes the entertainments (rare though they were, he says) that the Germans enjoyed. He speaks of youths dancing in the midst of naked swords and adds: 'Dice – and this is surprising – are a serious matter for them, and they fast before playing, and are so distracted by the thought of gain and loss that when they have nothing left, in a last and final

fling they gamble their freedom and their own persons. The loser accepts voluntary slavery.'

If the account of the *Gylfaginning* is anything to go by, the gods employed the services of a giant as architect for their great fortified palace with countless rooms. He promised to build the palace in a very short space of time, and the gods in return gave their word that if the palace was actually built by the appointed day, they would hand over the sun, the moon and the goddess Freyja by way of payment. Now the giant possessed a horse that was capable of transporting incredible loads of rocks in a mere second; he accomplished his task so well that a few days before the fixed date the palace was approaching completion. The gods, who had made the bargain because they thought the giant incapable of fulfilling the conditions, grew afraid and invented the idea of a miraculous mare – a temporary disguise adopted by the god Loki – which they put in the path of the horse. The latter abandoned his work to follow it, and its master was unable to finish the building as he had promised. Furious at his defeat, the giant was about to blame the gods, but the god Thor destroyed him.

This marvellous abode was not in the land of men, but was connected to it by an immense bridge, the Bifrost, which was formed by the rainbow. The Bifrost was very strong and big enough to span the sky, and poets have praised its miraculous properties, their only fear being that it might not withstand the attack of evil spirits when they advanced against the gods, as predicted in all the Nordic prophecies.

However (to return to the story of the Aesir), once they had ordered the elements in the world and firmly established their dwelling-place, the gods turned their attention to earth. They began by raising sanctuaries in the countryside around their home, which was called Ida – a reference that would imply that the ancient Germans did in fact construct temples in spite

Northern Germanic god and goddess formed from two forked branches and probably of the first century A.D. The goddess wears her hair in a coil and the breasts have been set in separately. Found in a peat bog at Braak, Germany. The figures may represent, or be connected with, Askr and Embla, the first human beings created by Odin. *Schleswig-Holsteinisches Landesmuseum für Vor und Frühgeschichte*

of the fact that Tacitus made the opposite claim.

Then some of the gods built the first forge and made tools. 'They installed furnaces, hammered bronze, shaped smith's tongs and created tools.' But this industry was not to be their only occupation: they were merely showing the future inhabitants of the earth how to proceed. Before creating mankind they first busied themselves with dwarfs; according to one tradition, these were made from the maggots that gnawed the giant Ymir's body or, according to another story-teller, from the blood and bones of another giant in the same family. The dwarfs were given a chief, various attributes, particularly in connection with the forge, and certain of them who remained in the caves were even given human shape.

The birth of humanity

Then it was the turn of men: three gods, one of whom was Odin, were walking along the seashore and found two tree-trunks left there by the waves, and took it into their heads — the story-teller does not say why — to give them the shape and characteristics of a human couple. Out of these objects lying 'without strength of purpose', the gods created living, thinking beings: 'They had no soul, they had no senses, nor the warmth of life, nor its fresh colour; Odin gave them their soul, Hoenir their senses, Lodur life and its fresh colour.' These forefathers of the human race are called Askr and Embla in the *Edda*. The word *Ask* referring to man is not found anywhere else; it has been connected with the word *Esche,* which refers to the ash-tree, a sacred tree in German eyes. A similar idea occurs in a Greek myth quoted by Hesiod, in which the first man was made from an ash-tree. As for the woman's name, Embla, it is even more mysterious. An attempt has been made to trace it back to the same root as that from which the word 'elm' springs. The association of two different types of wood (which here represent the two sexes) recalls to mind one of the earliest devices invented by man for producing fire: a stem of hard wood is made to revolve quickly and to rub against a softer piece, producing sufficient heat to set it on fire. This device is portrayed on a Bronze Age tomb found at Kivik. The idea that the union of man and woman can be likened to this method of producing fire is a belief shared by a number of Indo-European peoples, and it is possible that the names of the first human couple in Germanic mythology owe their origin to it.

Whatever their origin may be, as men multiplied they were found places in the Midgard by the gods, and there they were entirely surrounded by water. The inhabited tracts of land were hemmed in by a round ocean and this in turn was bounded by the original abyss. The ocean was inhabited by a huge serpent, the 'serpent of the Midgard', and it was large enough to embrace in its coils all the lands known to men.

Below the world of men there was the land of the

dead, which was also the land of ice and darkness and was called the Niflheim. Only giants and dwarfs could live there, together with the dead. This furthest region was the kingdom of the goddess Hel, and the entrance was guarded by the fearful dog Garm.

This picture of three worlds placed one on top of the other recalls the Greek cosmologies so vividly that one can only suspect that it may have been taken from non-Germanic mythologies. This is all the more probable as the Scandinavian texts in which it is found appear late enough for the authors to have had some knowledge of the accounts of the ancient Greeks. What is more, there is a sort of contradiction between the world as it is described in the beginning of the Germanic genesis and what it becomes after the appearance of mankind. In fact, the Niflheim is portrayed at the outset not as an underground place, but as the land of the north, of eternal ice and long, long nights, which is never visited by the light of day. This is a description of the world that is plainly related to the real situation of the Germanic peoples, near neighbours of the icy vastness of Scandinavia. This flat world, stretching from the silent, infinite spaces of the Arctic, hemmed in and determined the universe for the Germans, to whom the midday sun has always seemed to illuminate a land foreign to their own.

But even if the descriptions of the world contain variations and perhaps even contradictions, all take into account an original tradition according to which the entire universe would appear to be a tree of fantastic size and amazing characteristics. This world-tree is Yggdrasill, an ash: the whole world lies in the shadow of its branches, it sends its roots deep down into the earth, and its topmost branches reach right up into the sky, where it is bathed in a cloud of light. This mysterious and majestic tree connects with all parts of the universe and shelters countless animals.

It is always green, although its foliage is constantly being devoured by animals of all sorts, for it draws unending strength from Urd's well. This is the Fountain of Youth, guarded by one of the Norns, the goddesses who rule the course of time and the destinies of men. The tree is therefore called the 'tree of destiny'. Miraculous dew also falls upon the tree from the sky and this too gives it perpetual life. Thus the milky, silver drops of celestial dew trickling over the leaves resemble hydromel, and poets often refer to it as the 'hydromel-tree' or 'mead-tree'.

In actual fact Yggdrasill has several roots. That which goes deep down into the fountain of Urd and is watered constantly by the Norns to keep it alive is the most poetic, but two others exist also. The first goes down to Niflheim, the land of ice, to reach the Hvergelmir fountain, from which water cascades and spreads to all the great rivers in the world. The second extends to the abode of the giants, which is eternally covered in frost, and there it reaches the fountain of

Mimir. From the very beginning the latter was set to guard it, for it is the Fountain of Wisdom. Its water is so precious that Odin agreed to lose an eye in order to be allowed to drink of it. At this price he drank of the water of knowledge, prophecy and poetry and became the patron of seers, poets and sorcerers. Through this triple origin the universal tree is connected with the three worlds—of giants, gods and men; it is also connected with the past, known to Mimir, the guardian of wisdom, and to the future, known to the Norns; they give it new life every second.

There are many animals living in the branches of the great ash-tree: at the very top a gold cock scans the horizon and has to warn the gods when their eternal enemies, the giants, prepare to attack them; an eagle surveys the whole world, and between its eyes is perched a hawk; a squirrel called Ratatosk never stops darting up and down the branches between the eagle at the top of the tree and the serpent-dragon at the foot and keeps them in a constant state of discord; a goat called Heidrun feeds on the leaves, and its milk provides food for Odin's warriors; four stags devour the foliage and even the bark of the tree, which would fail to survive were it not for the water from the magic fountain infusing new life into its veins. Finally, serpents eat away at the roots, particularly the frightening Nidhoggr, which is also described as a dragon on some occasions.

The characteristics of this tree, the way it is connected with all parts of the universe, all aspects of life, make it one of the most original creations of Nordic mythology: Scandinavians thought of the world not as being supported by a giant as in Greek mythology, but by a tree. All writers are unanimous in pointing out that the Germans held trees in particular veneration: Adam of Bremen reports that near the temple at Uppsala which he describes, there was a very high tree of unknown species with leaves that were always green. Close by its foot there was a fountain to which offerings were brought. Just as the gods assembled at the foot of Yggdrasill, the ash-tree, to dispense justice, so the chiefs of Germanic tribes held their assemblies at the foot of a tree; this custom was still observed in the thirteenth century in Frisia, where the provincial assemblies met under three great oak-trees near Aurich. Finally, it is worth noting that German architecture corresponds quite closely to this conception of the universe: Germanic peoples often support the whole framework of a building on a large tree-trunk or a high beam driven into the ground. This mode of construction may be regarded as being remotely connected with the tents used by Asian nomads, which made use of a central pillar to support the roof—much as the Nordic sky rests on the mythical ash. Among certain Germanic peoples there was a long-standing custom of raising a monument, on high ground, made out of a single tree-trunk. The Saxons called this the Irminsul or

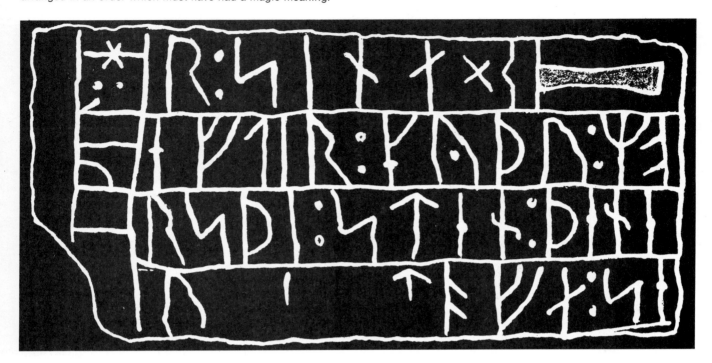

Runic inscriptions on the Hanning Stone, Denmark. Twenty-four signs have been counted, which correspond fairly closely to the letters of the Latin alphabet. These twenty-four signs are often shown divided into three groups of eight and arranged in an order which must have had a magic meaning.

'giant column', and Charlemagne on his lethal expedition into Lower Saxony destroyed one of these columns, which, the chronicler says, was the object of general worship.

But if one accepts the mythological accounts of the Germanic peoples, the world is not eternal. It is destined to founder in an immense cataclysm brought about by the giants when they eventually launch a mighty attack on the gods and their works, and the gods already greatly fear this event. Driven back into their inhospitable land of snow and frost, the giants entertain thoughts of revenge. One day they will advance in force to assault Asgard, and the seers prophesy that the gods will succumb to this attack; this will be the 'twilight of the gods'. Before the end of the world, which is written in their fate, the gods have many setbacks and adventures.

The hierarchy of the gods

The Germanic gods have always been portrayed as leading a very active life. The relationships between the gods have varied, even their attributes have altered, and it is quite certain that, varying with the period and the people under consideration, one god was more favoured than another. Thus it is impossible to draw up an exact and consistent list of Germanic gods. They are many in number, divided by conflicts and rivalries, and engaged in incessant warfare: even their power is revocable, or at least it is at the mercy of vicissitudes that never troubled the Hellenic pantheon. The idea of divine sovereignty seems to have been less firmly rooted among the Germans than among the peoples of classical antiquity. What is more, there are notable differences between the Germanic gods of the north and the west; the same major gods are found in both places, but they do not always have the same attributes, and their relationships are not the same. The divine hierarchy is greatly complicated

by the existence of two families of gods, the Aesir and Vanir, who according to legend first fought one another and then were reconciled. Other divine families exist as well, the Alfs for example, but they do not include any major gods and have only a minor role. The Aesir merit first place, for they include Odin and Thor, first among gods. There are some grounds for thinking that they preceded the others in time, since the abode of the gods is called the land of the Aesir. They were already settled there when they fought the Vanir, as we shall see later, and they allowed the Vanir to enter their abode only when they found themselves unable to repulse them.

The most recent studies propound a theory that one has great difficulty in accepting—that is that in spite of the evidence given in the poetic accounts, the Aesir were the original Germanic gods and the Vanir were a later addition to their pantheon. (This subject receives special attention from Georges Dumézil in his book *Les Dieux des Germains* (Paris, 1953).) The coexistence of Aesir and Vanir goes far back in time, and both must have been known and worshipped by the Germans in earliest times, but this fact does not make it any easier to interpret what is attributed to them in legend. In actual fact there are very many Vanir, the most frequently mentioned being Freyr, and they have far-reaching attributes. They often blend with those of certain Aesir, creating a duality that helps to make the Germanic pantheon fluctuating and varied.

However, it can be stated that four divine figures stand out incontestably in these divine races, and that they were the object of more widespread and consistent worship than the others. The great gods are primarily those whom North Germans call Odin (whose name in other parts of Germany is Wodan), Thor (called Donar elsewhere), Tyr (called Ziu by South Germans) and Freyr, who is a Vanir and is

Picture stone from Hunninge, Gotland. At the top is a battle scene recalling the German belief that to die in battle was the most glorious fate. Underneath is a ship representing the custom of sending the body of a dead man to sea in a ship, to sail towards the setting sun, and at the bottom are various mythological scenes. A.D. 700. Museum of Visby, Gotland.
Axel Poignant

often quoted alongside Njord, another member of the same family.

Before discussing their relationships and speaking of the goddesses and minor families of deities, we shall attempt to describe the characters and attributes of these great gods.

War and magic

Odin has pride of place, for he is the unquestioned chief of the entire society of gods. He is endowed with powers that surpass all others, he is the most knowledgeable, the fullest initiate into mysteries, the master of magic, of supreme science and poetry. But he is also the god of war, particularly in the West German regions, where he is called Wodan. Odin is always depicted as the patron of warriors; his first rise to eminence was as a warrior chief, and only later was he worshipped as sovereign master of the Germanic pantheon. He is the king of the gods, and his function is to be sovereign. He decides and demands, but his manifold power over other characters, whom we shall discuss later, must have had its origin in war. Wodan-Odin is first and foremost the god of battles, and he decides the fate of warriors; he also enlists them in his service in preparation for battles to come. The king of the gods is, initially, a war leader.

Since Wodan or Wode is connected in Germanic languages with the word for frenzy, the fury of battle (in modern German: *wüten*), his name reflects his warlike qualities. In the beginning Wodan was the leader of the Wild Hunt, the fantastic ride in the sky that Germans thought they heard on stormy nights — a demented gallop led by warriors who had died in battle. This mysterious and glorious troop — who trailed in their wake the memory of innumerable battles and galloped away on wild horses — had a chief, the master of passion, who breathed enthusiasm for war into the hearts of men: Wode, who became Wodan, and in the north, Odin. In so far as the figure of Wodan is connected with the Wild Hunt — the pursuit of some fantastic quarry in the company of impassioned horsemen on a night-ride that nothing can stop as it crosses the world like a hurricane — there is something disquieting about him. Here is no sovereign seated on his throne, but rather the chief of a wild horde whose thundering ride takes him across the sky leaving traces of flame. On the same stormy nights the witches also ride out on their evil pursuits, but this does not alarm the god of war, for he is also the god of magic and as such is familiar with impassioned fury. Wodan has been described as a dark horseman wearing a large flowing cloak, with a broad hat pulled down over his face, and is sometimes depicted on a white horse, sometimes on a black one. But Odin can change his appearance, and he is not always seen as this nocturnal horseman thundering through darkness and storms.

Later, when his sovereignty is more assured, he wears a brilliant breastplate and even a gold helmet;

A Valkyrie in battle. These mistresses of destiny determined a warrior's fate by entering the field of battle on horseback, deciding who was to win, and singling out those who were to perish and those who were to be gathered into Valhalla. *M. Hétier*

he has a magic spear called Gungnir. It was made by dwarfs, and they gave it the power to win eternal victory for its master; nothing can deflect it from its course once it has been hurled. When he takes his seat in Asgard he has two wolves at his side, and he throws them the food set before him, for he partakes only of drink, particularly hydromel (mead). Two ravens perched on his throne whisper to him all that is happening in the world, for one is Huginn, the mind, and the other is Munnin, or memory.

Odin's closest companion, at least in the horseman-god days of his youth, is his horse Sleipnir. He is the best horse, the swiftest, and has no less than eight feet. No obstacle can bar his path.

Valhalla

In his usual abode Wodan is surrounded by horsemen since he lives in Valhalla, where the most valiant knights who fell in battle are gathered together at his command. Valhalla is a huge hall of dazzling gold; it is sumptuously decorated, and there is no limit to the size of assembly that can be held there. The roof is not made of ordinary tiles, but of shining shields. In the evening, when the god holds banquets for his heroes, huge torches light the tables and are reflected in the armour and swords. Valhalla is so large that it has no less than five hundred and forty doors; they are so wide that each one can admit eight hundred warriors abreast.

As Wodan presides over earthly battles, he is the god to be invoked by warriors before they go into battle, and he has the right to do what he will with those who die. He chooses the best and takes them to Valhalla, where they lead the life of lords: during the day they ride and train for battle, and when evening falls they gather to feast and drink in the great hall of the castle. Not all who die under arms go to this paradise for warriors, only the most valorous and those whom the god distinguishes. Nor is Valhalla a place of eternal rest, for the heroes are not promised unending happiness; on the contrary, Wodan has gathered them round him with a view to other battles. He goes in fear of being attacked by the giants, and in order to face the great struggle at the end of time he needs all the fine swordsmen he can get. So the god allows the finest warriors to fall victim to earthly death because he will have need of them one day. Valhalla is not, therefore, a place of bliss; it is far more like a camp—of undoubted magnificence, but with the promise of renewed fighting, new exploits, and certain destruction, for it has been prophesied that the Aesir will eventually be overthrown. So, among the details given of sumptuous surroundings and royal banquets, poets often introduce a melancholy note into the descriptions of Valhalla; behind the splendour is a tragic background. Some authors have thought that this was the mark of an epoch in which Germanic paganism already sensed its approaching end. But it is also certain that nothing

seemed more enviable to the Germans than to die well—that is to say, to die fighting. These warring peoples thought it shameful to die other than under arms. 'The Cimbri and Celtiberians,' wrote Valerius Maximus, 'jumped for joy as they went to war in the belief that they would leave this world in a happy and honourable manner; in sickness, however, they would grieve at the thought of a shameful and wretched end.'

The Valkyries

Of those attending Odin some pride of place must be given to the Valkyries, who are both his messengers and his hostesses at Valhalla. They arrange the banquets and serve the warriors for whom they have prepared dishes; their special task is to bring them beer and hydromel. But these are their peaceful and domestic functions. As soon as war breaks out they change completely: with sword and armour they fly on fiery steeds, and at the god's command they enter the fray. Except to the heroes destined to die, they remain invisible. In the clamour of battle the warrior suddenly becomes aware of a brilliant Valkyrie at his side, magnificent and tragic: this is the sign that his death is approaching and Valhalla will be ready to receive him. When their mission is over and they have chosen their slain, the Valkyries gallop back to Valhalla on their magic steeds and inform the god of the arrival of new companions.

In Valhalla these men of valour still keep up their favourite occupations, and drown any thoughts of the extreme peril to which they are unceasingly exposed in sacred drinking-bouts. 'Banqueting, fermented drinks and collective drunkenness played a large part in the life of the Germanic world. And one might add a healthy part,' writes Georges Dumézil, who in this connection recalls the position occupied elsewhere by Dionysus and the Bacchic myths.

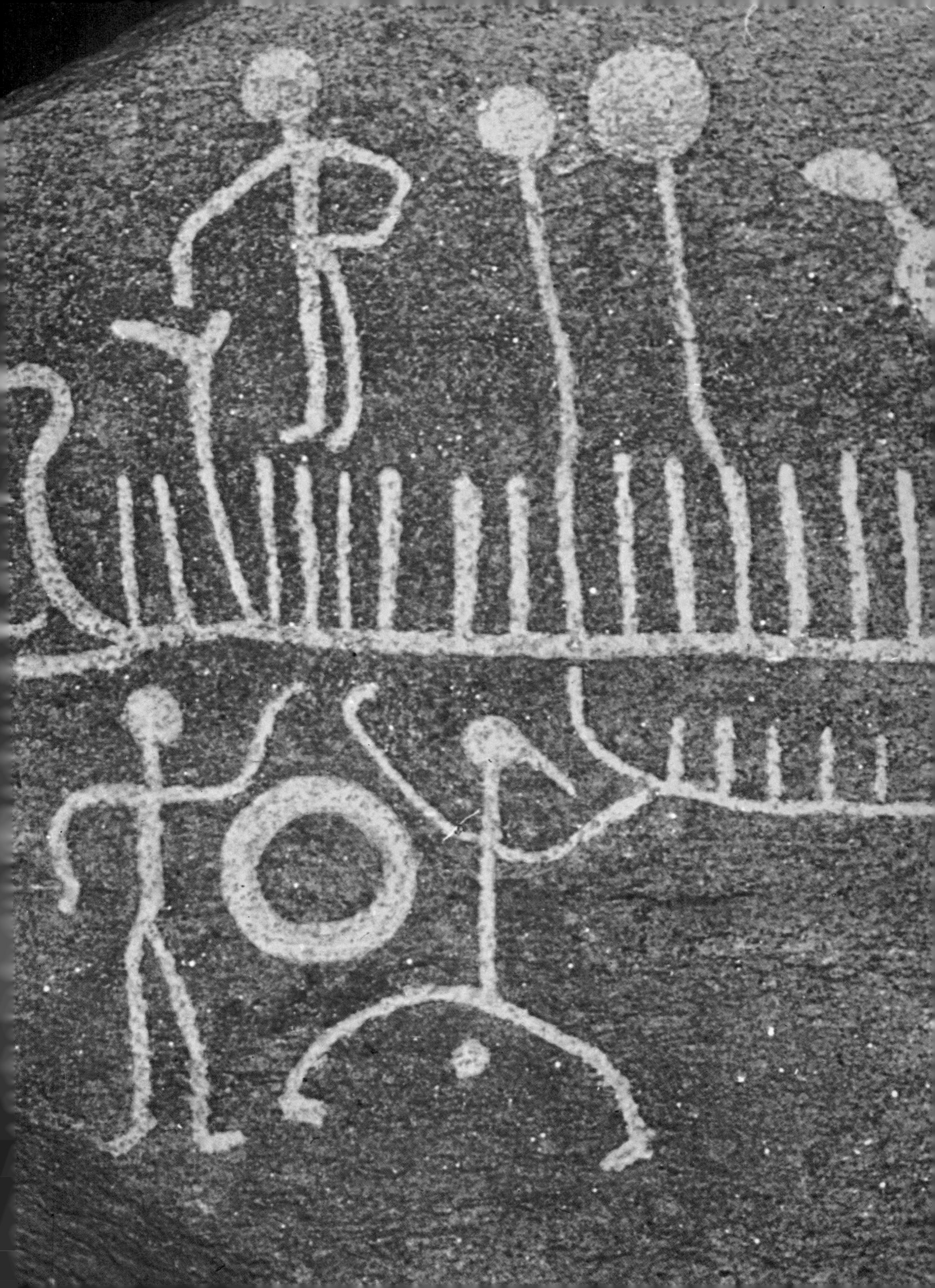

Three North American kachina dolls: lightning, a corn maiden, and snow and hail. Kachinas represented the supernatural beings who acted as intermediaries between the Pueblo people and the gods. The figures were fashioned in the form of the benefits for which the people prayed: rain, sun, fertility and rich crops. British Museum.

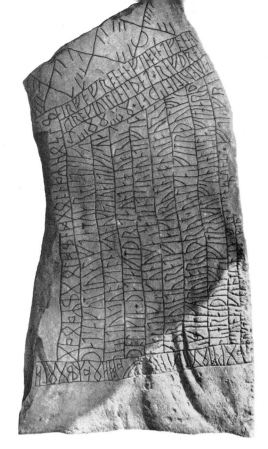

For the Germans, at least to begin with, the preparation of fermented drinks, basically hydromel and beer, was a sacred rite. Beer was offered at all solemn reunions, and the act of drinking together formed a magic bond, not only between those present, but between the men and gods invoked, and even between the living and the dead. In the preparation of the beer, its distribution and drinking, there were customs that it was sacrilege to ignore. For all important gatherings a huge quantity of liquor had to be prepared, and this was often obtained — as in Norway — by pouring each person's contribution into a large bowl; it was obligatory to continue the feasting and libations until the bowl was empty. Although beer was not, properly speaking, regarded as a magic drink, at least it made a new man of the drinker, giving him strength and valour, and, to quote an ancient Scandinavian saying, after drinking 'every man is twice the man he was'.

The Vikings indulged in a cycle of drinking parties, which occurred three times a year: at the beginning and in the middle of winter and in spring, about the date of the Christian Easter. Odin himself was regarded as responsible for fixing the date of these festivals, at which there was a banquet, then communal libation from a large bowl that marked the high spot of the festival. West Germans probably had analogous customs, since Saint Columban, the evangelist, is thought to have seen a large vat of beer that the Alamanni were preparing to offer to Wodan.

Odin as magician

But alcoholic drinks are appropriate not only to warriors, they are also the prerogative of poets and seers, who also have Odin as their patron. He is, or rather he became — for this does not entirely correspond with his savage origins — the god of poetry, wisdom and all that pertains to the spirit. His power is essentially of a spiritual order; he is more famous for depth of thought and wise counsel than for his strength. He knows and he foresees; he is familiar with magic formulas. And so this god, though originally a god of war, is also the grand master of poetry and runes, magic Germanic texts.

However, Odin's knowledge was not granted him from the very beginning; he gradually acquired it by asking questions of everyone he met. For he was a great traveller and had hundreds of opportunities to question giants, water-spirits and the spirits of the woods, elves, and all others who crossed his path. He learned most from Mimir, the guardian of the miraculous fountain into which Yggdrasill sent down one of its roots. Mimir, Odin's uncle, is a sort of water-spirit, a demon for whom all the Germanic people seem to have had the highest esteem, since his name means 'He who thinks'. The fountain whose approaches he guards is that which harbours intelligence and wisdom. Odin, in his anxiety to know everything, wished to drink of it; but Mimir would allow him to do so only if he gave him one of his eyes. Odin discovered in the waters of the fountain such secret wisdom that when Mimir was killed in the war between the Aesir and the Vanir he was able to grant him powers of survival; and his head, which the god had been at pains to embalm, still responded to the questions asked of it.

Odin also made himself master of the 'hydromel of the poets', a magic liquor that bestowed powers of prophecy. This hydromel was kept by the giant Suttung in an underground chamber guarded by his daughter Gunnlöd. Odin won his way into Suttung's underground dwelling by a trick, and there made himself so agreeable that he won the father's confidence and the daughter's love. For three nights he lay at Gunnlöd's side, and each night she allowed him to drink some hydromel. In these three draughts he emptied the pitchers and, changing himself into an eagle, flew swiftly away. Suttung also changed himself into an eagle and gave chase, but died in the attempt. A few drops that fell to earth during Odin's flight were granted to bad poets, for they were not infused with the divine spirit. Odin disgorged the rest into some large vases and dispensed it to the good poets. Of himself it was said that he 'spoke so well and beautifully that all those who heard him thought that he alone spoke the truth. He put everything into verse, as they do today in the art known as poetry.'

The hydromel of poets is shared by magicians. Poetic inspiration depends on Odin, as does knowledge of secret matters, and he is the god invoked in the only inscriptions left by Germans. They are written in runic characters on stones, a great number of which have been found in northern Germany and in Scandinavian countries. They are usually tombstones with fairly simple funerary inscriptions. Some, however, are not completely decipherable, for they display complete series of signs that do not form

Battle scene showing warriors bearing shields and axes, from a rock carving at Bohuslan, Sweden. *Kulturminnesradet, Goteborg*

Picture stone from Hablingbo, Gotland, A.D. 400. The swastika emblem in the centre is one of the most ancient and widespread of all ornamental forms. The Germans associated it with runic inscriptions because they believed it had magic properties, and its meaning was understood by the initiates of Odin. *Axel Poignant*

words and apparently have some magic significance. Odin officiated over the art of composing runic inscriptions.

Seers and magicians

Under Odin's inspiration, people who knew this art—seers, poets or priests—undertook their tasks; the god's favour was needed before an inscription served its purpose, which was to bring divine protection to those named, usually the dead. Runic inscriptions are often accompanied by magic signs, among which the swastika and Thor's hammer are frequently found; another very mysterious sign is seen rather less frequently: it consists of three interwoven horns. Those who received the breath of inspiration from Odin understood all this, for the god knew every secret: 'Odin knew where all treasures were hidden. He knew the songs that opened up the earth, mountains, rocks, funerary mounds, and he could banish all that dwelt therein by the mere use of formulas; then he would enter and take what he wished.'

The god of magicians also had the power of prophecy; he had drawn from the fountain of Mimir not only knowledge, which is of the past, but the ability to foresee the future. He now had only one eye, and yet he saw farther than anyone else, and the hypnotic power of this one eye surpassed everything. According to one legend, (*Ynglinga Saga*), Odin practised the art of prophecy: 'He was an expert in an art that afforded unrivalled power and was known as *seidhr*. He practised it himself, and that made it possible for him to prophesy the fate of men and future events, and also to confer upon men death, misfortune or sickness. Finally, as a result of this art, he could deprive a man of his reason and strength and give them to another. But this form of magic is accompanied by such effeminacy that men would be ashamed to practise it. Priestesses were taught it.'

The Germans did, in fact, listen to prophetesses and willingly followed the advice of women, who seemed to them to possess a knowledge of the mysteries of the world and of life that was far beyond the understanding of warriors. 'They go so far as to believe,' Tacitus wrote, 'that there is something divine about this sex. They listen to women's advice with docility, and regard them as oracles.' Tacitus also mentioned the nebulous and poetic Veleda, a lonely prophetess who lived up in a tower, whence she exercised her power over a vast territory.

As a magician, Odin had the power to change his appearance, and this made it possible for him to mingle frequently with mortals in their daily life: 'When he wanted to change his appearance he left his body on earth, as if asleep or dead, and became a bird or wild animal, fish or serpent.... He had a boat called Skidbladnir, in which he sailed the vast sea, and he could fold it like a handkerchief.' But the major change effected in his appearance, which was not merely a temporary disguise, ruse or amorous whim, was the facial change that came over him according to whether he was with friends or enemies: 'It must also be said that he was so handsome and noble in feature when he was amongst friends, that each one rejoiced at the sight of him. But if he was engaged on some expedition of war, then he appeared before his enemies in fearsome guise. He could change his appearance and shape at will.'

Thus Odin could travel about the world without continually attracting the attention of men, for he would take the form of a simple traveller. But he was never indifferent when there was a battle; he always took sides, and then woe betide his enemies! 'Odin was able to make his enemies blind and deaf in battle or seemingly paralysed with fear, and then their sharp weapons were no more effective than mere sticks. His men, on the contrary, went without breastplates, as wild as wolves or dogs. They bit their shields, and were as strong as bears and bulls. They killed men, and neither fire nor steel could prevail against them. This was called Berserksgangr.'

So Odin's fighters became known as Berserkir, 'warriors with bear-sarks', or shirts, as Norse story-tellers reveal. They were filled with wild, magic frenzy; they no longer quite belonged to themselves. Another being had taken possession of them; everything gave way before their animal fury. In them and through them forces were unleashed that only magic could evoke. These frenzied warriors usually were young men to whom tumult, violence and the wild desire to murder were natural. In chapter thirty-one of *Germania* Tacitus describes a society of warriors in a tribe known as the Chatti: 'As soon as they have reached manhood, they let their hair and beards grow long, and they keep this appearance, which is adopted under oath and dedicated to virtue, until they have killed one of the enemy . . . . The bravest also wear an iron ring . . . until they release themselves from it by slaying one of the enemy . . . . Their task is to be the first to join battle; they always form the front line and the mere sight of them is stupefying.' These warrior-savages scorned possessions; they were happy to accept food from others, abandoning themselves entirely to their fighting virtues, living on battle fury and the memory of it.

One race was a particular favourite of Odin's, the Volsungs. Sigi, its founder, had managed to over-come great difficulties and acquire a kingdom, and he was even regarded as one of the god's own sons, for Odin had many amorous adventures. Sigi had a son called Rerir. The latter was childless for a long time, and begged the god to give him an heir. So Odin sent an apple to his wife. After she had taken a bite of it, Rerir's wife gave birth to Volsung, who became a famous warrior. Volsung had a son called Sigmund. Now one evening when Sigmund was at a gathering of warriors in a hall built round a great tree-trunk, a stranger entered. His appearance was unprepossessing, like that of a much-travelled, solitary man, and he was almost hidden beneath a huge cloak. There was a sword in his hand, and he drove it into the tree-trunk until only the hilt was left exposed, saying that anyone who had the strength to pull it out could keep it. Then he disappeared. All those present tried to draw the sword, but to no avail. But Sigmund, the last to make the attempt, was successful. From that point onwards he had in his possession a weapon that made him invincible in battle.

But one day in later life, when Sigmund was fight-ing with his sword in his hand, he suddenly became aware of a man standing in front of him who was blind in one eye and who wore the broad hat and large cloak he associated with the man with the sword. He carried nothing but a spear, but when Sigmund made to attack him his sword broke on the wood of the spear. It was Odin himself, who had decided that

the now aged warrior must die. Sigmund expressed only one wish: that the two pieces of his sword should be kept so that they might be joined together again at some future date. Then the mended sword would make it possible for his son to accomplish glorious exploits in his turn. This son was called Sigurd; he came to be called Siegfried in later German legend, and under that name he figures in the epic of the *Nibelungen* and the Wagnerian *Ring* cycle.

Odin's strangest adventure was his voluntary self-sacrifice, a test to which he submitted so that he might be regenerated: 'For nine nights,' so an old poem recounts, 'wounded by my own lance, consecrated to Odin, consecrated myself to myself, I shall hang from the tree shaken by the winds, from the mighty tree whose roots go down men know not where.' This mighty and mysterious tree was Yggdrasill. By wound-ing himself and then hanging from the branches of the great ash-tree, the god was accomplishing a magic rite. Throughout this time of self-imposed sacrifice — nine days and nine nights — Odin waited in vain for some-one to come and alleviate his suffering. Then he directed his gaze to the ground beneath his feet and noticed some runes; he had such difficulty in picking them up and raising them to his own level that he groaned in agony. But the miraculous properties of the runes put an end to his torment; he fell to the ground completely rejuvenated, full of new strength. His sacrifice had given him back youth and vigour.

Mimir then gave Odin permission to drink once more from the fountain, and he regained wisdom and knowledge. So the god survived his own voluntary death and became again the master of the world of war and magic, mortal as were all German gods, and yet immortal, because voluntary sacrifice restored him to his prime.

Odin is a god with numerous avatars, who adopt many different disguises and have attributes of exceptional variety, and he is the central figure in the German pantheon. Certain authors have thought that for this very reason — the excessive variety of his attributes — he was in fact the late product of a mix-ture of several different traditions. But this cannot be proved, and all we know of the beliefs of the ancient Germans leads us to think that Odin-Wodan was always the sovereign god. These war-loving peoples primarily revered the god of battle, the patron of the Berserkir and of the more elegant knights of Sigurd's race, for it is an undisputed fact that both in Germanic life and culture war was a focal point of everything. All the evidence points to this. Caesar had already said that nothing counted as much as bravery to the Germans, and that they would not allow themselves to become deeply involved in agriculture lest they forgot that they were primarily men of war, and they could not become attached to anything, not even to the land they occupied, which nurtured them. In the last few centuries of paganism, certain Norsemen, such as the adventurous Vikings,

terror of the western world that had already become Christian, were probably the last to fight with the names of Odin and Thor on their lips, and the last to hope for Valhalla.

Thor-Donar against the monsters

Thor was the object of widespread worship among North Germans if the great number of place-names containing the word Thor are anything to go by. A number of proper names in Scandinavia also recall the name of the god. The Vikings in their own time said that they were 'the people of Thor'.

This god, who according to one tradition is supposed to be the son of Odin, is a warrior too; but whereas Odin was the sovereign magician who directed battles, made his enemies powerless and chose the slain for Valhalla, Thor is more like the best fighter, the most redoubtable man under arms, whose blows are invariably fatal. He is the most feared of all, for he is the strongest even among the gods. And so he exists primarily as an exterminator of giants.

He is generally described quite briefly, but we know that he is very tall, very vigorous and always carries a hammer as his particular emblem. He also has a large red beard, which some authors have interpreted as a symbol of lightning, and this certainly makes him look typically Nordic. He is often called 'the man with the red beard'. He has a terrifying voice, which resounds with striking effect; only Loki's composure remains untroubled when it makes itself heard. Sparks flash from his eyes. He is a great eater and drinker; he is easily irritated, but, on the other hand, can be a good companion. Irresistible when roused to anger, he smashes his adversaries to pieces with hammer-blows. This hammer, which will be mentioned again, is one of his three attributes, together with a magic belt, which makes him twice as strong,

Thor's hammer. Various patterns found in different places, together with a mould for casting hammers and crosses from northern Jutland. The hammer's foreshortened handle allowed it to be used as a boomerang, and it was the weapon with which Thor warded off evil spirits and which warned him of the plots of giants and demons. *National Museum, Copenhagen*

The god Thor, the great warrior, was one of the most popular Germanic gods and his worship was widespread. This bronze statuette of him holding his hammer was made in Iceland *c.* 1000. *National Museum of Iceland*

and iron gloves, with which he gets a firm grip on the hammer.

He lives in the land of the gods in his own palace called Bilskirnir: 'There are five hundred and forty rooms in the tortuous palace of Thor, and I believe there is no larger house than that of this eldest son.' He is often accompanied by a servant, called Thialfi, who also acts as his adviser. In certain texts there is some confusion between this servant of Thor and the crafty Loki, who sometimes travels with the god. The alliance between Thor, who is feared for his strength, and Loki, safe in his cunning, is a theme that has given rise to much epic treatment.

In the poetry of the skalds Thor is depicted as the son of Odin and Iord, in other words the Earth. These somewhat mysterious origins would tend to make him a sort of demi-god according to certain texts. His valour, strength and numerous adventures have often resulted in his being compared with the Greek Heracles, whose emblem is the club, a close relation of the hammer. This unique instrument of Thor's is called Mjollnir. It was forged by Sindri, a dwarf, who gave it too short a handle. In spite of this weakness the god's weapon possesses the miraculous power of returning of its own accord, like a boomerang, to the hand of the person who threw it. With it the god was able to vanquish redoubtable foes, including several giants; if he had to be without it, the best part of his power vanished.

Thor's hammer is the sign most currently found on stones bearing runic inscriptions, also in rock engravings and particularly on funerary steles intended to ensure repose for the dead. As it is still found on monuments of later date, some people have thought that it was a sign of protest against the ruling that nothing but the cross of Christ should be portrayed everywhere. The two emblems are similar, and in the saga of Haakon the Good the king was said to make the sign of the cross on the bowl containing mead (or hydromel, as it is also called) during a funeral feast; when some present protested, the valorous Sigurd explained to them that the king, in fidelity to old customs, had traced with his hands the outline of Thor's hammer.

Mjollnir also played a part in marriages, for it had the reputation of keeping evil powers away from the couple and of bringing the wife fecundity, as he governed thunder, rain, and the winds on which good crops depend.

But Thor's hammer is first and foremost the thunderbolt. When thunder growls, it is Thor-Donar's chariot, drawn by goats, rolling across the vault of heaven. When the ground is struck by lightning, the god has thrown his blazing weapon down to earth. But this god of thunder is none the less a friend to men and it is as if this crude hammer-thrower with the voice like a trumpet was a sort of good giant, brave, pugnacious and free from ill-nature. He had a reputation for terrifying evil demons, including both the monsters in Midgard and especially the fabulous serpent. More than anyone else he remained watchful of the giants' undertakings and kept an eye on all the demons who threatened the lives of gods and humans. Thor was considered a benevolent god, which perhaps accounts for the fact that so many Norsemen gave their children the god's name to place them under his protection.

Thor had adventures by the dozen, he had innumerable fights, and poets of the northern countries have told endless tales and anecdotes which throw light on this striking figure.

Thor against the giants

Thor's most worthy opponents were the giants, and he never relinquished his struggle against them; they feared him more than anyone else, for so many of them fell victim to him. Poets tell of very many expeditions that the god undertook to the land of frost or even to the land of the east, where the giants lived. Most often, Thor had some companions, of whom the most valued was Loki, a very important, godlike figure in Germanic mythology. Loki was intimate with the great gods, who came to him for advice, for there was no end to his guile, but he often rounded on his masters. He was a double-dealing and elusive character, and we shall have occasion to mention him again. One morning Thor noticed that his hammer had vanished while he was asleep. This was the most serious thing that could possibly happen to him: without his terrifying weapon he was virtually powerless. In profound anxiety he went to consult Loki, whose sharp mind was highly resourceful. Loki declared that the precious hammer 'without doubt had been snatched by some giant', and he offered to go in search of the thief. To do this he borrowed the goddess Freyja's magic cloak, which was made of feathers and enabled the wearer to fly like a bird.

Loki flew swiftly away to the land of the giants. There he had a highly opportune encounter with a giant called Thrym, and he soon made the giant confess that he had stolen the hammer and hidden it eight fathoms below the ground. He offered to return it if he could have Freyja as his wife.

On Loki's return the gods were given this message and held council, but they could not find a solution. It was necessary to recover the hammer, and so Freyja was asked to fulfil the condition. Freyja was so outraged at the suggestion that the veins in her neck became swollen and made her golden necklace break and fall to the ground in pieces. The gods got out of this predicament by resorting to a trick: Thor, they suggested, should disguise himself as the bride, wearing the goddess' clothes, veil and necklace. Thor hesitated, but in the end agreed.

So he set off for the land of the giants in disguise; Loki went with him in the guise of a maid-servant. Thrym received them in great style. During the banquet, to the giant's great astonishment, the fiancée proved to have a tremendous appetite and devoured everything that had been put aside for the women: an entire ox, eight salmon, all the spices, all of three barrels of hydromel. To allay the giant's feelings, Loki told him that the goddess had been so absorbed with the thought of her visit to the land of the giants that she had not eaten for a week. Raising his fiancée's veil to kiss her, Thrym was struck by the sparks that darted from her eyes and he leaped back. But Loki again reassured him: for the past eight nights Freyja had been so agitated that she had not slept, and that was why her eyes had such great brilliance. Then the giant decided that the ritual consecration of the marriage would take place and sent for Mjollnir and placed it on the bride's knees. Then Thor cast off his disguise, seized his hammer and struck down not only Thrym, but all his followers as well.

Thor is always portrayed as a creature full of courage and of indomitable strength; even if he happens at times to be somewhat dull-witted, and to fall into traps, in the end he wins esteem and sympathy because he is valiant and swift to avenge. He finally resolves all problems by a thunderous hammer-blow which fells monsters, traitors and hypocrites alike.

Once, however, he thought that he had been vanquished by a giant. He chanced to meet a magician, and he was ill-equipped to defend himself against such characters. So when the magician, Utgard-Loki, invited him to drain a goblet that was as deep as the ocean, and to vanquish a wretched-looking woman (who was actually Elli, 'old age', and therefore a creature whom no-one could overcome) Thor found himself powerless against the invincible magician's spells. Thor had need of opponents who fought openly; then, even if they were as high as the mountain or as hard as rock, he could inflict hammer-blows on them that would mutilate them for ever.

On learning that he had been tricked by Utgard-Loki, Thor grew furious and seized his hammer. But Utgard-Loki, the enchanter, had already disappeared, taking his castle and all that it contained with him. Thor was left alone in the midst of a grassy heath. So he was vanquished by an enchanter's tricks. All his strength was unavailing against elusive magic with its mocking spells.

The god of thunder was no more fortunate when he tried to exterminate the monster of the Midgard, for this time he was confronting not a magician, but a cosmic being more ancient than the gods themselves, who was not in any way at the mercy of fate.

Thor was still young when he decided to fight the great sea-monster whose innumerable coils embraced the lands of the earth and caused fatal storms to shatter the calm of the seas. (Here Thor was playing the part of benefactor, desiring to purge the world of

The goddess Freyja, head of the Valkyries, riding on a cat, the animal always associated with her, and blowing her horn. Freyja gathered half the warriors slain in battle to her palace, just as Odin gathered the others to Valhalla. Twelfth-century wall-painting in Schleswig cathedral. *Toni Schneiders, Bavaria*

Thor fishing for the Midgard Serpent, his eternal enemy and the monster who envelops the earth with his coils and causes terrible sea storms. Though Thor successfully hooked the serpent and almost vanquished him, the giant Hymir cut the line allowing the serpent to escape. Thor was destined to fight and never to conquer the serpent until the end of time. Carved stone, used as a doorstep in a northern Jutland church until it was identified. *National Museum, Copenhagen*

destructive forces.) So he went to a far-off land peopled with giants. He was the guest of the giant-fisherman Hymir, with whom he decided to go fishing. 'What sort of bait shall I take?' he asked the giant. 'Each man must know that for himself and make it his own business,' replied the giant rudely. But Thor was not to be put out, and, seizing one of Hymir's bulls, he chopped off its head and put it in the boat as his bait. Then he grabbed hold of the oars, which he handled so well that the giant, at first disdainful, had to admit that he was a born sailor. Then he took the boat far beyond the point at which the giant normally fished, out into the open sea where he thought he would find the serpent of the Midgard. Then he got his line ready. The serpent at once made straight for the bait; but no sooner did it feel the prick of the harpoon than it put up a furious fight. The line went taut, Thor kept his hold on it, and his two clenched fists were pulled forward and struck against the sheathing of the vessel. He started back so violently that his feet went through the bottom of the boat; then he found himself on firm ground. Balancing himself on this, he made a violent effort, pulled the serpent out of the water and succeeded in half hoisting it into the boat. It was a frightening sight, according to the Irish story-teller, for Thor shot fiery glances at the monster while the latter stared fixedly at him and spat poison. The sight was so horrible that Hymir grew afraid, and when Thor relinquished his careful watch on him for a second he seized his chance and cut the line with his knife. The serpent was freed and fell back into the water, where it vanished so quickly that Thor could not even strike it with his hammer.

And so this redoubtable monster escaped from the god, and in fact will always escape as long as the world exists; only at the end of time, on the day of total conflict when all giants and monsters attack the gods, will Thor finally discover his enemy, the serpent of the Midgard, again. On that day a lucky hammer-blow will kill the enemy; but the god himself will not long survive, just 'long enough to take nine paces', for he will have received terrible blows when the serpent lashes him with its tail.

But these stories of the end of the world are rather anticipating things; at this stage the gods, like humanity, had their entire future before them. Thor shared his fate with all the inhabitants of Asgard and, in spite of being defeated at times, he was worshipped as the god of victory. His primary characteristic was his thundering voice; he was a strong fighter and had a Gargantuan appetite. To place oneself under his protection was considered to be the finest token of victory. He was widely revered; he is to be found in most legends, for at some point or other every god needed his strong arm. A full-blooded character, his appearance in a story always has a comforting effect.

Tyr-Tiuz

The god who goes under the name of Tyr in Scandinavia is called Tiwaz or Tiuz by the North Germans, Ziu in the south, and Tiw by Anglo-Saxons; he most certainly had a place in the mythology of the early Germanic tribes. That he was one of their very first gods is beyond question, and it is equally certain that his attributes have varied and the worship bestowed on him decreased in the course of centuries. His name alone, which is often mentioned and never discussed, gave rise to very many hypotheses and comparisons. The English word Tuesday comes from the same root as the name of the god, whom Tacitus identified with the Roman Mars. The German word for Tuesday, *Dienstag*, can also be connected with the name of the god, but there is an even more definite connection with the old Norse word for an assembly of warriors, the *thing*. For naturally the relationship between a god of war and an assembly of warriors is not difficult to perceive. Outside the framework of the Germanic languages, it is significant that in Sanskrit the first supreme god is called Dyaush, in Greek Zeus and in Latin Jupiter. There is a definite relationship between all these forms, from which people have attempted to draw conclusions about the ancient attributes of the Germanic god during the early times of the mysterious and obscure religion that Germanic peoples held in common. But little progress can be made along the lines of hypotheses such as these, for one race would often transform a myth on borrowing it from another, and there is no more delicate business than that of fixing the 'filiations' between gods from one period to another.

In accounts that we have, Tyr is neither Zeus nor Mars. It is reasonable to suppose that he once had extensive attributes of which only scattered traces remain. Other figures, especially Thor, have pushed him into the background; Thor was always the example held up to fighters both in Scandinavia and in Continental Germany. But valour is also one of Tyr's virtues: 'There is another of the Aesir called Tyr. He is very intrepid and courageous and has great power of victory in battle. For this reason it is well that men of valour should pray to him.' (*Gylfaginning*, ch. 13.)

One legend at least affords proof of his exceptional energy and gives him a prominent position among the gods. This is the story of the sinister wolf Fenrir, who is to play a major part on the day of the twilight of the gods.

This giant wolf, who might well be regarded as a descendant of the original abyss, so voracious is he and capable of engulfing creatures in his mouth, is in fact one of the most vigilant enemies of the gods. One day they were informed by an oracle that Fenrir was contemplating an attack upon them, and that wisdom dictated some act of prevention on their part. The council of the gods decided not to kill him — for to spill his blood would mean sullying ground sanctified by the divine presence — but simply to chain him up. Twice they bound him with strong chains, but as soon as he stretched himself he broke them. The gods begged the dwarfs of the forge to make them indestructible fetters. So the dwarfs had recourse to magic, and instead of forging even heavier links, they presented the gods with a new kind of chain: it was nothing but a soft, silky ribbon, and yet no-one could break it. What the dwarf-magicians had done was to fuse six elements together in it: the miaowing of a cat, a woman's beard, mountain roots, a bear's sinews, fishes' breath and a bird's saliva. They had made all these ingredients into a single, supple chain that could not be destroyed.

Now that they were sure of being able to tie up the horrible Fenrir for ever, the gods sent him a challenge: each one of them, they told him, had tried to break

Deity carved in wood. National Museum, Copenhagen. *M. Hétier*

376

the chain and no-one had succeeded: so they proposed that the wolf should likewise make the attempt to prove his strength. Experience had taught the wolf to be suspicious, and so he refused this test at first, scenting a trap. However, not wanting to be called a coward, he agreed to compete if the gods would give him a pledge: one of them was to keep his hand in the wolf's mouth throughout the trial of strength, and he would crush it if the suggestion that he should break the chain proved to be a trap. The gods looked at one another in embarrassment, knowing only too well that in fact they had set a trap for the wolf, and none of them wanted to lose a hand in return. At this point Tyr quite simply stretched out his hand and put it in the wolf's mouth. Then the other gods tied up the monster with the ribbon that the dwarfs had made. Fenrir began to struggle, more and more wildly, and the gods laughed to see their enemy reduced to impotence. Only Tyr refrained from laughter, for he knew the risk he incurred. In fact as soon as the wolf realised that he had been tricked, he closed his jaws, biting off the god's hand at the wrist.

The meaning of this act of mutilation has given rise to much speculation about the part played by the god, and his place in Germanic mythology. If the god accepted voluntary and heroic mutilation, it was in order to keep his word, to respect a contract, and undoubtedly, too, to redeem by his gesture any suggestion of disloyalty in the test to which the assembled gods subjected the wolf. In so doing Tyr became the god of law, the guarantor of the validity of contracts, a being ever faithful to his word, who would accept painful sacrifice rather than go back on what he had said. So he is not only a courageous god —and therefore the guarantor of victory in battle— but a god of law, protector of contracts, the guardian of promises, oaths and pledges. This is the way modern authors interpret the figure of Tyr, which was long regarded as confused and contradictory. So Jan de Vries writes: 'In general, too much emphasis has been placed on his role as god of war, and the meaning he has for Germanic law has not been sufficiently recognised. Due account must be taken of the fact that, from the Germanic point of view, there is no contradiction between the two concepts "god of battles" and "god of law". War is not only a bloody battlefield, but a decision between two conflicting parties confirmed by precise rules of law. This is why the date of the battle and the battlefield are often fixed in advance; thus when Boiorix challenges Marius, he lets him choose the place and time. This also accounts for the fact that a battle between two armies can be replaced by a trial by duel, in which the gods make it known which side they consider to be in the right.'

The custom of trial by duel, which the Franks observed for a long time, depended on the attitude of the god of battle: when swords were crossed, the gods were always present, and they took care to see that a fair decision was reached. In the eyes of the Germans war was not outside the law; it admitted certain rules, and confrontations between warriors had to follow strict rules, as did peaceful assemblies. All important matters in Germanic cities were regulated by the *thing*, the assembly which met under arms, even if there was no question of war. When Tacitus gave his account of how these assemblies met, he emphasised the fact that they sat in arms: 'When the multitude has to come to a decision, then they take their seats in council under arms. Whether the matter be public or private, they do nothing unless they are armed. But the custom prevails that no-one takes up arms before the city has recognised their capabilities in this respect.' (*Germania,* ch. 11 and ch. 13.) If every assembly is held in arms, then, inversely, fighting is another sort of assembly, and there is no reason why one should not take literally the periphrase used by northern writers who refer to battle as being the '*thing* of swords' (*Schwerting*). Tyr is the god who fixed the rules of this assembly.

Just as Tyr sacrificed a hand to lend support by his heroic gesture to a respect for contracts, so Odin, god of wisdom, sacrificed an eye to draw knowledge from the fountain of Mimir, thus showing that nothing else was as precious to him—not even his own flesh. Georges Dumézil has shown the importance these two mutilated gods—one with only one eye and the other with one hand—acquired in Germanic faith and the light these legends throw on the constitution of Germanic societies and the spirit of their social life. Dumézil moreover states that in the fictitious history of the beginnings of ancient Rome there is also a man with one eye, Horatius Cocles, and a character with one hand, Mucius Scaevola, both of whom saved the Roman army in its fight against the Etruscans, and he establishes a very suggestive parallel between these Germanic gods and the fabulous heroes of Rome. 'It is clear that the springs of Cocles' and Scaevola's actions are the same as those of Odin's and Tyr's respectively: to lure the enemy on the one hand, and to use a pledge as a means of persuasion in a process under oath on the other; it is also clear that in both Rome and Scandinavia these actions are connected with the same mutilations under the same conditions. ...So the only natural explanation is to think that Germans and Romans alike inherited this unusual couple from their common past.'

But it is difficult to say exactly what place the Germans accorded to the god of law and war, Tyr, at least in early times. It is known, however, that he had something to do with the magic of runes, and by certain formulas and signs one could make sure the support of this guardian of oaths. It would appear that his cult was no longer widespread in historic times, except perhaps in Denmark, where numerous place-names are derived from the same root, notably in Jutland.

A fairly mysterious Latin inscription on a Roman altar has been traced back to this source too. This was discovered in England at Housesteads, not far from Hadrian's Wall. This altar dates from the third century and was raised by German soldiers serving in the Roman legions. It bears the following inscription: 'Deo Marti Thincso et duabus Alaisiagis Bede et Fimmiline et numini Augusti Germani cives Tuihanti v.s.l.m. (votum solverunt libenter merito).' The literal meaning of this inscription is as follows: 'To the god Mars Thincsus and to the Alaisiagae goddesses Beda and Fimmilina and to the majesty of Augustus the German citizens of Twenth wished to address this just homage.' The epithet *Thincsus* attached to the name of the Roman god Mars is visibly of Germanic origin, and there is a temptation to connect it with the *thing*. The god would also be called 'he who protects the assembly', that is to say the community. In that case the Germans at the Roman period would appear to have included Mars and Tiuz in one and the same act of veneration. As for the goddesses Beda and Fimmilina, they are quite unknown, for their names do not recur in any other text; the term *Alaisiagae*, which is used in reference to them both, does not bring to mind any known association either.

Facts about the god Tyr or Tiuz tend to lurk beyond the bounds of knowledge; it is none the less certain that this god is linked with the very beginnings of Germanic mythology. But this 'god of law', who was once in the front rank and was perhaps even sovereign of them all, lost his pre-eminence and became nothing more than a sort of sacred hero. This shift perhaps reflects a change in Germanic societies, which were not so much concerned with maintaining the idea of law in all its purity, as subject to the tragedy of war.

Loki

Loki is the most complex figure in Nordic mythology and his name appears more often than any other. He counts as one of the Aesir, although he does not actually belong to this family of gods. He lives with them, he is their companion and his advice is often precious to them, but he feels in no way involved in their destiny. His razor-sharp mind is always on the alert; he is quick to turn against his masters or those who think they are his masters, for no-one can claim to know him through and through.

In physique he is small, agile, with crafty eyes and a laughing face. He is handsome, has a great deal of natural charm and is very fond of the company of goddesses, who very rarely reject him. When the need arises, he knows how to remind them of this. He is not like any of the other gods, and he is not related to them. He and Odin have quite simply 'sworn to be brothers', a fact he likes to emphasise. We know little about his father, mother and brothers except their names. His father, Farbauti, would seem to be known as 'he who brings forth fire by striking'; he was also a past-master at disappearing and could vanish in an

instant. His mother, Laufia (wooded island), seems to have supplied the material for lighting fires. Originally Loki was regarded as the spirit of fire, and his name comes from the Germanic root meaning 'flame'. Popular sayings that are still in use today in Scandinavian countries frequently associate his name with phenomena connected with fire: thus in Norway when fire is heard crackling in the hearth they say that Loki is beating his children. Being as lively and brilliant as fire, he can also change his appearance easily, and he shares Odin's liking for metamorphosis. He is fond of disguising himself as a woman.

He always appears in the right place at the right time; he has luck on his side, and, like good fortune, he is quick to take to flight, to vanish and leave in the lurch the person he has misled with false advice. He knows a whole host of things and forgets none of the weaknesses of the other gods; with malignant pleasure he unveils the awkward aspect of affairs; 'in the mountain' he has a mysterious observatory where he can see without being seen; he has an insatiable curiosity; he is always active and has no fear of being found out. He is highly inventive and can always get out of a tight corner; but he is boastful with it and provoking, and he sometimes acts against his own interest for the sheer pleasure of giving a sharp answer.

He is a malicious gossip; he does not hesitate to slander and betray; he causes trouble and confusion everywhere. He tells lies, not only for the sake of the gods, but also for his own pleasure. He does not resist the temptation of trickery.

He is disloyal, he respects neither the rules of the game, nor those of battle, for he is a creature completely devoid of moral instinct. He has no sense of honour, respects nothing, turns the most sacred things to ridicule, mocks at promises and betrays his friends in the midst of danger.

Ornaments of mythological significance. 'Necklaces and rings were given me by the Father of the Armies, so that I should see into the future and understand spells. I have seen far, far, I have seen all the worlds,' says the prophetess in the *Edda*. National Museum, Budapest

The truth of the matter is that he is intimately connected with the infernal world. He is related to the giants, and he himself has engendered the most horrible monsters, of which the gods go in great fear: the great serpent of the Midgard, Fenrir the wolf and the guardian of the dead, Hel, and also Odin's magic steed, Sleipnir. Unlike the gods, Loki is quite unafraid of the ultimate catastrophe that the prophets have foretold. On the contrary, he prays for it to come about; victory will be his when the infernal powers are at last unleashed; all the proud achievements of the gods will tumble down, the emptiness of their claims will be seen, the entire universe will collapse in an indescribable hurricane, and then Loki, spirit of fire and demon of destruction, will triumph at last amid devilish laughter. There are too many things here reminiscent of Mephistopheles for the authors of poems about him not to have connected him with the Devil, particularly as presented in the medieval Christian tradition.

This many-sided, brilliant and disturbing character seems to have been created after the major gods, and he belongs exclusively to the Norse world. In the ninth and tenth centuries the skalds told the tale of his adventures in their poems. These are many and varied: all the gods have recourse to him at some point or other, he is very often summoned to their council, and even appears there without being asked; he knows the giants better than anyone else, for he has travelled about their land a great deal. He gives of his full measure in the contacts between gods and giants, for he is prompt to pass messages, to provoke conflicts, to betray those who make use of him and to sacrifice a god—or goddess—if he finds himself in a difficult position. He is often useful as a messenger, though his services are often regretted: he is only too good at blackmail, for he knows too many intimate secrets.

The goddesses themselves are not safe from his malice and deceit, as several stories show. One of these stories concerns Idun, the guardian of the miraculous golden apples that give the gods renewed youth. At one point Loki wanted to hand over these apples to a giant who had him at his mercy, and to this end he was prepared to sacrifice Idun.

On another occasion Loki's malignity was directed against Thor's wife, Sif, who had beautiful blonde hair. One day, for some unknown reason, Loki secretly cut off her lovely hair. When Thor heard of the crime, he laid his mighty hands on Loki and would have broken his bones in his frenzy. But Loki kept calm, and, although he was afraid, he began to make the god countless promises: he would make Sif a new head of hair out of pure gold and it would grow naturally just like real hair. Thor allowed himself to be pacified. Loki went to the dwarfs of the forge, the sons of Ivald, and arranged that they should not only make him a gold head of hair for Sif, but also a ship called Skidbladnir, which would make straight for its destination once it had set sail, and a spear called Gungnir, which would never stop in mid-flight. These last two tokens were intended for Odin, so that Loki could be reconciled simultaneously with Thor and his wife and with Odin.

However, his passion for gambling, which has already been mentioned in connection with Odin, got him into difficulties, and he was hard put to extricate himself. Before he left the smiths, he had a bet with a dwarf called Brokk that he and his brother Sindri, although very clever, could not forge objects comparable to those made by the sons of Ivald. Brokk and Sindri set to work at once. Then Loki disguised himself as a gadfly, which stung them incessantly in order to distract them from their task. However, the dwarfs managed to make some unbelievable objects: a ring called Draupnir, which

Gold bracteate of the fifth century, in imitation of Roman medallions, but portraying figures of Germanic mythology. In the centre and the borders are spiral patterns representing the source of light, and in the centre, a swastika, an emblem of the god of thunder, Thor. Found at Gerete, Sweden. *Antikvarisk Topografiska Arkive, Stockholm*

would keep on increasing its owner's wealth, a gold boar, which was subsequently to belong to Freyr, and, finally, Thor's famous hammer. When they were called upon to judge the issue, the gods decreed that these things were the most beautiful they had ever seen. So Loki had lost his bet, and he had to surrender to the dwarfs. He acted as if he was going to place himself in their power, but just as they were about to seize him, he vanished. He did, in fact, possess magic shoes that in a flash could carry him over lands and seas at his bidding. But the dwarfs formally complained to Thor, and he captured Loki and handed him over to them. Brokk made it known that he was going to cut off Loki's head. But the latter was not yet defeated, and, even in this extreme danger, he started a lively discussion and in the end the dwarf allowed himself to be persuaded. Then the dwarf decided that he would at least make sure that Loki could no longer continue to delude his adversaries with deceptive words, and so he sewed up his lips. He pierced them with an awl, then threaded through the holes and fastened them firmly together. But this new precaution was useless; in spite of the pain Loki managed to get the thread out of his wounds, and thus extricated himself from a wicked adventure without sustaining too much harm. There is hardly a god who has not had some quarrel with Loki; he makes no attempt to conciliate them and enjoys provoking them, as is shown in one of the poems in the *Edda* in which he heaps insults and sarcasm upon them to such an extent that the gods decide to punish him and to put him out of harm's way.

Loki, the provoker

The gods were all attending a banquet given by Aegir, the master of the seas. All the gods and goddesses were there, with the sole exception of Thor, who was away in the land of the East. There was feasting and merriment. Suddenly Loki, who had been kept away from the banquet on account of his wicked tongue, burst into the room. The sight of him silenced everyone; but he was modest and conciliatory and asked only that he should be granted the goblet that is never refused the thirsty traveller, even if he is a complete stranger. No-one answered him. Still being courteous, Loki asked if he might sit down, as the laws of hospitality dictated. The gods consulted, and in their desire to respect custom, they indicated that they were prepared to make room for him.

But once he was seated at table, Loki took the gods to task. With frightful accuracy he reminded each one of the most scandalous episodes in his career. He spared the goddesses nothing. There was not one whom he did not reproach for having betrayed her wifely duty: Idun had 'enfolded her brother's murderer in her arms', and Gefion had totally forgotten that she was the goddess of virginity. And Loki went on to boast of having himself obtained the favours of

Frankish gravestone from Niederdollendorf. About A.D. 700–800, the time of the barbarian invasions. It is inscribed with swastikas, emblems of Thor. Emblems of Thor, the god of war, and in particular his hammer, are the most common symbols found on warriors' gravestones. They were supposed to assure rest. Landesmuseum Bonn. *Deutsche Fotothek Dresden*

Engraved stone, probably a gravestone or memorial, of about A.D. 700 from Gotland, Sweden. The scenes may recount episodes from a hero's life and probably represent ritual and propitiatory ceremonies on behalf of a dead man thereby identified with the hero. The votive barque is similar to those found in ancient places of worship. *Antikvarisk Topografiska Arkive, Stockholm*

several goddesses present and proceeded to name them. He confessed his faults with wicked joy, recounted his misdeeds and complacently enumerated the wrongs he had committed against each and every one of them. Not one of them could stand up to him; he knew too much and was too quick at repartee. Odin himself lost countenance in the face of this flood of hurtful mockery pouring from the intruder's lips. At this point Sif approached him and offered him a bowl of hydromel, asking him to desist from this quarrel. His reply was further hurtful comment, and he asserted that he had held the wife of Thor himself, happy and unresisting, in his arms.

No sooner had her name been pronounced than uproar broke loose; the god of storms was on his way back and soon entered the hall, a terrible, brilliant figure commanding silence. Loki flew into a passion and attempted to outface him; but Thor brandished his hammer and seemed about to crush the insulting creature's skull. Loki recoiled in fear and left the hall, still uttering insults and curses: 'There will never be another banquet like this,' he told Aegir, 'for soon this palace, and all those in it, will be the victims of flames.'

Such audacity could not go unpunished; the gods decided to capture Loki. At first he escaped them by disguising himself as a salmon, but he was caught in a waterfall, taken prisoner and carefully bound with the entrails of his own son, Narvi. He was to remain the prisoner of the gods till the end of the world, the day of his great revenge. Then he would come to the fore, mobilising all the powers of evil and destruction.

Although there are very many poems and stories about Loki, we are given no indication of any cult accorded him, and it is therefore possible that he was created by Scandinavian poets in the last few centuries of paganism. However, there are analogies with other legends, particularly some from the Caucasus, which make us think that he was a genuinely ancient mythological figure; furthermore, he is intimately connected with the tales of the lives of other gods. But his two-sided nature, his intimacy with both demons and gods, his evident resemblance to Lucifer, pose more than one problem. The existence of such a figure as this serves at least to show that the Germans gave their gods characteristics like those of human beings, and even subjected them to a similar condition of life, since the gods tolerate and utilise this diabolical creature who is planning their downfall.

Loki's sworn enemy is Heimdall, another god. He is one of the most important of the Aesir, but we know very little about him. Scandinavian poets usually allude to him only briefly, mentioning his power and beauty. He is tall and as comely as a young prince, his teeth are of pure gold and he rides a steed with a flashing mane.

He is a god of light, as his name itself suggests, for it probably means 'he who darts bright beams'. Furthermore, his usual position is near to the rain-bow, the great bridge called Bifrost, leading to the abode of the gods. There he mounts guard; he is the sentinel whose task is to announce to the Aesir the enemy's approach. For this purpose he has a trumpet that can be heard throughout the world and this will resound on the day of the ultimate attack on the gods by the giants. Some experts have sought to establish a relationship between this god and the 'axis of the sky', a pivot supporting the sky which traversed the nine legendary worlds, and thus invites comparison with Heimdall, who was reputed to have nine mothers.

One thing, however, is certain, and that is the fact that Heimdall is Loki's enemy. The latter likes to make fun of him, he laughs at this watchman who remains for days and in all weathers with his eyes fixed on the gate of the gods. When Heimdall gets the chance, he seeks revenge for this sort of talk. One day Loki stole Freyja's necklace and hid it far out to sea on a reef. Disguising himself as a seal, Heimdall managed to reach the reef; but Loki also took the shape of a seal and laid in wait for him; after a long struggle Heimdall succeeded in getting the jewel back and he returned it to the goddess.

There is constant conflict between Heimdall and Loki, whether it comes out into the open or not, and as a result is has been construed as a symbol of the struggle between darkness and light. This secular battle eventually ends on the day of the twilight of the gods: Heimdall fells Loki with a mortal blow, but he too is slain by his adversary.

Balder

This god is the son of Odin and Frigg, a goddess, and so he belongs to a race of the great Aesir. His name does not appear very often, but the episode with which he is connected is at the very heart of the drama of the world, and the figure of this god is quite

unlike any other. He was known to Western Germanic peoples but he was most worshipped in Scandinavia under the name of Baldr.

This is the portrait painted of Balder by the story-teller Snorre Sturlasson: 'The second son of Odin is Balder, and there is much good to be said of him. He is the finest, and all praise him. He is so handsome in appearance and so brilliant that he gives off light, and he carries a white wildflower with which his own fair lashes have been compared; as it is the whitest flower of all, this will give you some idea of the beauty of both his hair and body. He is the wisest of the Aesir, the most clever in speech and the kindest. But there is one condition attached to him: none of his judgments can be realised. He lives in an abode that is called "Widely Brilliant" and is in the sky. Nothing impure can exist in this spot.' So this god of light, purity and beauty belongs to a sort of Eden, which is surprising, coming, as it does, in the midst of the battles and dramas that surround the Germanic gods throughout their lives. Balder is also a very upright judge and 'all those who have recourse to him in quarrels of law find themselves reconciled'. It is also said that none of Balder's wishes are realised; he is the absolute incarnation of beauty, justice and gentleness, and all he asks is to be able to spread harmony and joy, but he hardly ever succeeds; it is as though he were the survivor of some golden age and is now an outcast in a world no longer his own. One day perhaps the world of Balder will be realised, but for the present he is condemned to die—as the following dramatic story goes to show.

He had had a long, smooth and happy life, like that of an innocent child, a creature without malice, passions or faults; but one day he had 'grave dreams, which threatened his life'. He confided his anxiety to the gods, who decided that Balder in his goodness should be safeguarded from all danger; he had never

harmed a single being, and it was therefore right and proper that all should pledge to do him no wrong. 'Frigg—his mother—received pledges that fire would do him no harm, nor would water, nor any sort of metal, stone, earth, wood, sickness, animal, bird, or venomous serpent.' Then the gods thought of an unusual sport to test the firm assurances given by the elements and the animals. This was to tempt fate. But the gods had a great passion for gaming and gambling, and Balder himself seems to have consented to this test. One of them threw stones at him to see if they wounded him, another struck him with a sword and a stick: but nothing harmed him.

But the unwise gods and Balder, in his innocence, had counted without the vigilant Loki, who was an exasperated witness of his invulnerability: 'When Loki, the son of Laufia, saw that, that displeased him.' Loki the destroyer was most unwilling to admit that a god might exist who was impervious to wounds and insults, however pure he might be.

He disguised himself as an old woman and went to Frigg and persuaded her to talk; thus he learned that not every creature had sworn to do Balder no harm; there was one exception, a modest exception, of course, and seemingly inoffensive, but it was still a chink in the god's protective armour. 'There is a young shoot,' Frigg rashly told the supposed old woman, 'growing to the east of Valhalla called *Mistiltein* (mistletoe shoot); she seemed too young to be asked for her oath.'

Loki went and gathered a piece of mistletoe and then made his way to the *thing* where the gods were sporting with Balder.

Then he went up to Hoder, another of Odin's sons, who was not taking part in the sport because he was blind. Loki said to him: 'Join in like the others, attack him, I will tell you where he is.' As Hoder could not see, and was naïve enough to follow this advice,

affected as he was by the thrill of the sport, he threw the little mistletoe twig at Balder.

'The dart pierced Balder, who dropped down dead. This was the greatest misfortune ever to befall gods and men. When Balder had fallen, all the Aesir were speechless and incapable of raising him up.... When they attempted to speak, they first dissolved into tears, so that they were unable to express their grief to one another in words.'

They decided to give him a solemn and formal funeral: they took his body down to the sea and built the pyre on a barque which had belonged to the dead god. Then they placed the body on it to burn it. The god's horse, in full harness, was also placed on the the pyre and consumed by the flames. Almost all the gods were there, and the assembly even included giants from the land of ice and from the mountains. But even before the funeral, Frigg, Balder's mother, had given some thought to finding her son again: she asked if there was any god willing to go down to the kingdom of Hel (the kingdom of the dead) to attempt to buy him back. Since he did not die in battle, Balder was not in Valhalla, but among the dead, guarded by the goddess Hel. Frigg promised to confer her favours on anyone who was prepared to attempt this journey. Hermod, another of Odin's sons, was willing, and without further ado he leaped upon Sleipnir, his father's steed.

He rode for nine whole days before reaching the river bordering the land of the dead. There the guardian of the bridge told him that Balder had crossed the day before with five hundred men. Hermod went on his way and found himself at the iron gate that barred the way to Hel's kingdom. Sleipnir took a fantastic leap over the gate and carried brave Hermod right into the land of the dead. There he saw his brother Balder on a seat of honour in a vast hall. As it was late he allowed a night to go by before he approached Hel. But the next day he immediately informed the goddess of the mission he had undertaken for the Aesir, and he begged that Balder should be allowed to return with him to Asgard. Hel proved to be understanding: 'If everything in the world, living and dead, mourns him, he shall return to the Aesir; but he shall stay with Hel if anyone refuses and will not weep.'

As soon as they learned of this reply, the Aesir sent messengers all over the world to beg all creatures to deliver Balder from the kingdom of death by weeping for him. All wept, men and animals, earth and stones, trees and all metals too. The messengers were filled with joy at the successful accomplishment of their mission and were already on their way back to the abode of the gods when they noticed a giant-witch in a cave who went by the name of Thokk. They asked her to weep too, but she refused to shed a single tear. 'Neither in his life nor after his death did Balder render me the least service,' she said. 'Let Hel keep what she has.' But, says the story-teller, it is generally supposed that this was Loki himself, who had found a way of making Balder's misfortune irremediable by adopting this disguise.

Once Balder was dead, the world knew no more true happiness, perfect justice or ever-kindly beauty. Granted, Loki's malice did not hold triumphant sway, for he was bound hand and foot by the gods after committing too much evil; but he was not dead, and everything in the world became a mixture of pure and impure, joy and tears, beauty and ugliness, life and death. From then on the world would degenerate till the fatal moment of its dissolution.

After the great catastrophe there would be a rebirth. The earth would emerge anew from the ocean; the sons of the dead gods would return to the land of the Aesir; the earth would be fertile and beautiful: this was to be the return of Balder.

The Vanir

The Aesir and Vanir

There is another race as well as the Aesir in the abode of the gods. These gods are called Vanir. The difference between the two groups is not described anywhere in any detail. But they are very different in origin, and some idea of them can be obtained by examining their principal representatives. Odin and Thor are the most outstanding of the Aesir; the three most typical Vanir are Njord, Freyr and Freyja. All three are first and foremost dispensers of wealth and plenty; they are the patrons of fecundity and the pleasures of the earth; thus, Freyja is the goddess of love, of endless rebirth, and Freyr is the god of peace and prosperity. They love rich lands that bear good harvests. Njord lives in the sea, which is also a source of life, and he enriches fishermen and sailors. We know that the Aesir were concerned with a different order of things: human prosperity did not occupy them a great deal; they scorned gold, which was powerless against witchcraft; they lived for fighting, adventure and magic.

The Vanir form a more homogeneous group than the Aesir, since they all favour fecundity, prosperity and peaceful and fruitful relationships among men. They come of another order of inspiration, emerge from a contrary mythical tradition. For a long time historians were inclined to regard this duality as a sign that Germanic gods had a twofold origin. Since the Aesir belonged in their own right to a race of warriors, the Vanir would appear to have been initially the deities of a race of farmers and merchants, who were settled in Scandinavia before the Germans came, though they subsequently surrendered to them.

More recent interpreters of northern mythology think that the two families of gods represent two opposing but integral aspects of one and the same thing, and that the history of the two divine races, which were at first hostile to one another and then allied, goes back farther than the Germanic peoples, farther even than the dispersal of their ancestors, back to an Indo-European source.

Whatever meaning should be attributed to these myths, Scandinavian authors lay great emphasis on the fact that the gods belonged to two families, which first waged bloody war on one another before they were eventually reconciled and presided together over the destinies of the world. This good feeling among the gods, who came to share the same home, is clearly shown by Adam of Bremen in his description of the temple at Uppsala:

'In this temple, decorated entirely in gold, the people worship the statues of three gods, Thor the powerful, seated in the middle, with Wodan on his right and Fricco (that is to say Freyr) on his left. The meaning of these gods is as follows: Thor is master of the atmosphere and governs thunder and the thunderbolt, wind and rain, fine weather and the harvest; Wodan, that is to say fury, directs wars and gives man courage to fight his foes; the third is Fricco, who procures peace and voluptuousness for mortals.'

Hence three great gods of different origins, two Aesir and a Vanir, are closely associated in the cult devoted to them; this union is something more than a relatively recent, temporary alliance: it corresponds to an ancient theological structure. To be more specific, a very definite parallel with this Scandinavian triad has been found in Vedic tradition. War between two families of gods, then reconciliation and close union in a sort of sharing of divine omnipotence, is not an invention peculiar to Germanic mythology; other Indo-European peoples have left accounts of the same type. However, this episode in the life of the gods holds a very large place in Scandinavian tales; story-tellers are very fond of it.

So, according to legend, the Vanir were a pacific race and favoured wealth. One day, for some unspecified reason, they sent one of their magicians to the Aesir. She was called Gullveig. This very clever witch had accumulated great wealth and knew how to make men desirous of growing rich. Perhaps she had been sent to the warlike Aesir for this very reason, for the Vanir may have thought that if they acquired a great passion for gold they would be less aggressive. As it happened, Gullveig was such a great success with the Aesir that they wanted to force her secrets from her; when she refused to reveal them, they had her burned. But this was to no avail, for she rose again from the ashes; then the Aesir inflicted horrible punishments upon her. The Vanir demanded reparation for these outrages upon the witch, and requested either a large sum of money or else admission to their abode with the same rank as the gods. The Aesir held council, and preferred to settle the matter by war.

Great Mother giving birth to the gods from every joint. At the foot of the illustration Quetzalcoatl emerges from the womb into the world. The idea of sacrifice and pain is represented by the blood-red centre panel and the borders of blood-stained knives. The four winds are shown in the corner panels and the four rains in the side panels. From a copy of the *Codex Borgia* (folio 32) in the British Museum. Fifteenth-century original manuscript in the Vatican Library, Rome.

Wooden stem-post of a Viking ship, carved in the form of a bird's head. Found in Belgium, by the River Scheldt. Probably eighth century A.D. *British Museum*

A picture stone from Gotland showing a sun-symbol surrounded by fabulous animals. The sun was associated with Odin, and is found on many runic stones and gravestones. A.D. 400. Museum of Visby, Gotland. *Axel Poignant*

There followed a long and difficult war. Contrary to expectation, the Aesir were incapable of reducing the peaceable Vanir to subjection: 'Odin marched with his army against the Vanir, but they resisted and defended their country, and each side carried off alternate victories. Each army laid waste the other's land.... When at last they were weary, they held conference, concluded a peace and exchanged hostages. The Vanir surrendered their most distinguished men: Njord, who was rich, and his son Freyr; and the Aesir gave in exchange someone called Hoenir, whom, they said, was well equipped to be a chief.'

Thus a new race appears in Asgard, destined to furnish some outstanding figures in the society of gods: Njord, his daughter Freyja, who teaches the Aesir magic, and his son Freyr.

Even apart from this close relationship Njord and Freyr would deservedly be associated with one another, for tradition attributes to them similar functions: both dispense wealth; they guarantee agreements, particularly oaths; they favour the spread of wealth, particularly by navigation. This last-mentioned characteristic is more particularly Njord's province, for he is master of the winds and calms the sea. He is invoked when sailing or fishing is involved. He is so rich that he can give those who serve him territories and treasures.

Njord had his residence by the sea at Noatun. He was nearly always there, but his wife Skadi did not like living there. She would appear to have married Njord when in actual fact it was Balder she wanted for a husband. And so she was far from whole-hearted in her affection for her husband, and she preferred the mountains of her childhood to the seaside. At first Njord, wishing to be conciliatory, followed his wife to the land that she loved, but he soon returned to the shore: 'The song of the swan seems gentler to me than the howling of wolves.' But Skadi, who was obliged to follow her husband for a while, replied: 'Can I sleep soundly on the lord of the sea's couch, where the shrill pipings of birds interferes with my rest; every morning I am wakened by the seagull.' However, the two of them appear to have found a compromise: they would spend nine nights in the mountain, then three by the sea. It is not even certain that Skadi made this concession, for she loved her native mountains so much that she never tired of travelling about them in her snowshoes, with her bow in her hand; she always returned weighed down with game.

Freyr, the principal god of the Vanir, was the son of this ill-matched couple: he was worshipped in Scandinavia as an equal of the great gods of the Aesir; he was celebrated in many ways. Though less maritime than Njord, he was just as generous. Prosperity came to those who sacrificed to him.

Like the other major gods, Freyr had marvellous servants and talismans at his disposal. His horse knew no obstacle. His sword moved in the air of its own accord; unfortunately he was to lose it in the course of battle. He also had at his disposal the golden boar, brilliantly created by the dwarfs Brokk and Sindri, which could draw a chariot as fast as any galloping horse and was so bright that it lit up the night. His ship, Skidbladnir, always made straight for port; it was big enough to hold all the Aesir; it also folded up, and when the crossing was over, the god could take it away in his pocket.

Freyr is noted for his love for Gerd. One day, when he was sitting on Odin's throne, from which everything could be seen, he noticed in the land of giants an exceptionally beautiful girl called Gerd, the daughter of Gymir. He fell passionately in love, but he was overcome with sadness too, for he had no idea how to win this beautiful creature. Seeing him in this state, his friend Skirnir offered to go and request the far-away princess' hand in marriage. All he begged of Freyr was that he would lend him his sword, for it traversed the air of its own accord, and he also requested his horse, which would not recoil before the red flames conjured up by magicians.

Thus armed, Skirnir set off through the dark night, past shining rocks, towards the land of the giants. The home of Gerd's father, a giant, was well protected: fierce dogs were fastened to the gate; a shepherd-watchman kept an eye on all the approaches; the walls were surrounded by flames. But Skirnir passed right in front of the agitated dogs, he paid no attention to the cries of the shepherd, who tried to stop him, and leaped over the curtain of flame. Thus he got inside. Gerd was attracted by the commotion and hastened to meet him. Immediately he disclosed the purpose of his mission, at the same time offering her eleven apples of pure gold and the ring Draupnir, which had belonged to Odin. But she refused these gifts. In fury Skirnir brandished his sword and threatened her with spells: he said he would engrave very powerful runes on a magic wand in his possession which would bring about her downfall; she would lead a lonely life far away from any other creature and would fade away 'like a thistle in the depths of ice'. Then Gerd grew afraid and yielded, offering Skirnir a bowl of mead in token of reconciliation. She also promised to meet the god who was in love with her some nine nights later in a sacred wood. When Skirnir took back this reply, Freyr's heart was filled with joy once again; however, he thought it a long time to wait: 'How long one night is, how long two nights seem! How shall I ever contain myself in patience for three nights?'

There the story of the god of happiness stops; story-tellers have left no mention of the other adventures he must have had. He must have had some unsuccessful battles, for when the great combat eventually took place between the gods and the giants he no longer had his invincible sword, and was one of the first to be slain. This is the fate of a peaceful god in the midst of warriors.

Minor gods
Hoenir

In addition to the great gods, who are equally well known in Western and Southern Germany, Scandinavian legend makes mention of many other less important figures—probably with more limited cults.

Thus Hoenir, who was recommended to the Vanir as being 'well equipped to be a chief', was renowned for his strength, boldness and beauty rather than his wisdom; when Odin sent him to the Vanir, he was careful to send the clever Mimir with him, the guardian of the fountain of knowledge. Hoenir had nevertheless played a part in the creation of men, for he had given them a soul.

Hoenir usually accompanied Odin and Loki when they rode about the world. He knew how to help Odin with the magic disguises he so often used. But like anyone who owes the better part of his powers to another, he was often a subordinate, executing missions rather than taking the initiative himself. But his name was frequently mentioned, since he was often in the company of the great.

Bragi

The god of poetry did not appear quite so often; he intervened, for instance, in the great quarrel that Loki provoked, for it was he who refused to salute the intruder. This poet was master of the divine ceremonies and he was a late creation of the Scandinavian imagination. A very famous skald lived in the ninth century called Bragi Boddason, and he was the inventor of a celebrated type of stanza. It seems probable that he was deified after his death. He is bound to be one of Odin's emanations, since poetry was an attribute of the principal god, who taught men the art of song and clever rhythms. Bragi was the patron of the skalds; his conversation was distinguished by its nobility and ease. Legend also has it that he had runes engraved on his tongue: this is a way of saying that he was very clever at composing and reciting poems. He was the chief poet at the court of the gods, and he was given Idun in marriage—the goddess who guarded the golden apples. Thus poetry was identified with the source of eternal youth.

Vidar and Vali

These are two more divine figures of secondary rank who were certainly late creations by poets and never became the object of a true cult.

Vidar was another of Odin's sons, and as he rarely spoke in council he was called 'the silent Ase'. However, although his opinion was rarely voiced, no great heed was paid to it. He was even said to be rather slow-witted. But he was valiant, and he would play a particular part in the twilight of the gods: after killing Fenrir, the wolf, whom even Odin could not vanquish, he would survive to become one of the gods of the regenerated world.

Figures, possibly of magical significance, incised on the bone of an aurochs, or wild ox. Scandinavian Stone Age. *National Museum, Copenhagen*

In the same way Vali, who was yet another son of Odin, hardly appears except in the battle at the end of time, and it seems as though they may both have been thought up to avenge the ancient gods destined for destruction. Vali was also anxious to avenge the death of Balder; he was so preoccupied by this thought that he never found time to wash his hands or comb his hair.

Ull

Ull was a different type of god and probably had different origins, for there is evidence of his cult throughout a vast region in Scandinavia. Very many place-names remind one of him in the central provinces of Sweden and Norway. He was certainly a very ancient deity, whom some experts have tried to link up with Tyr, although there is no evidence of this connection. His name means 'Magnificent'. He was a handsome hunter travelling about the woods on snowshoes, the forerunners of skis. He liked running across vast expanses of ice and shooting game with his arrows. This solitary upright man had such nobility and majesty that at one time the Aesir appear to have called on him to replace Odin in his majestic functions. The latter, who was too fond of amorous adventures, had, in fact, been accused of employing unworthy measures to overcome the resistance of a girl he desired. The assembly of the gods passed judgment on him and decreed that he had proved himself unworthy, and banished him. In his absence Ull was unanimously voted the master of the community of gods. But this Nordic Cincinnatus' reign lasted only ten years: then Odin reappeared and chased him from Asgard. Ull took refuge in Sweden, that is to say towards the north, and in these parts he acquired the reputation of a powerful magician: he possessed a bone on which he had engraved magic formulas that were so effective that he could sail the sea in it.

The goddesses

The wives of the Germanic gods always remain in the background, which is somewhat surprising when you think of the heed Germans paid to the advice of women, and the importance attached to priestesses in the observation of the cults. There were very many goddesses, but in the majority of cases they have left behind nothing but their names. They have also often been confused with one another, as if there was nothing personal about their attributes, the essential thing about them being their wifely function. Literature has undoubtedly concentrated on the men; the skalds recited their poems after the warriors had feasted, and their listeners were more eager to listen to tales of fine sword-play and miraculous fighting than love intrigues.

The chief goddess is called Frija (in Old Norse the name is Frigg) and is often confused with Freyja. The name Frija means 'beloved' or 'wife'. Romans associated her with Venus, and the Germans accepted this interpretation, since they translated the word for Friday (*Veneris dies*) by 'Frija's day', or in modern German, *Freitag*. It seems that all ancient Western Germans worshipped this goddess, but we know nothing about her attributes; she was probably regarded as Wodan's wife.

On the other hand Frigg was involved in several adventures as far as Scandinavians were concerned. She was Odin's wife, and she had a share in his wisdom and knowledge of the future. At times she refused to accept her husband's friends; sometimes she protected warriors who were seeking to harm him. In the conflicts that arose, she occasionally had the upper hand when her ruses prevailed over the master's will. She was not completely faithful either; out of coquetry or self-interest, she was capable of granting her favours to other gods. However, men prayed to her to protect their marriages and to bless

them with offspring. She knew the future of mankind, but did not reveal it to anyone. When provoked by Loki, Odin once replied: 'Idiot, how can you claim to know fate? Only Frigg knows the future, but she discloses it to no-one.'

Freyja

The origins of Freyja are different, because she came from the land of the Vanir with her brother Freyr. In many cases, however, she has been confused with Frigg-Frija, for she has often been quoted as the wife of Odin.

She even accompanied the god on to the battlefield, for she had the right to bring back to her palace the Folkvang, half the warriors who died in battle. Just like Odin in Valhalla, she welcomed dead heroes and accorded them places in the great banqueting-hall. Sometimes she even waited on the guests at Valhalla as a Valkyrie. In fact she held pride of place among the Valkyries.

Like Frigg, Freyja loved adornments and jewels. Not far from her palace there was a cave inhabited by four dwarfs who were very clever goldsmiths; one day she noticed that the dwarfs had a gold necklace which she badly wanted, and so she offered them a great weight of gold in payment for it. The dwarfs, who were the masters of metals, did not want gold, but asked for another form of payment: in return for the necklace the goddess was to spend a night with each of them. She agreed and was given the necklace. But Loki had heard all about it, and, traitor that he was, he reported it to Odin; the latter then ordered Loki to recover the ill-gotten necklace from the goddess. This he did by disguising himself as various animals. But Freyja guessed who had stolen the necklace and finally prevailed upon Odin to return it to her.

As she was very beautiful, Freyja was often pursued by suitors, particularly by giants. In this way Thrym, who had stolen Thor's hammer, claimed her as his wife. So did the giant-architect who built the abode of the gods, before he was killed by Thor, who by his action saved the goddess from a humiliating fate.

Gefion

However, several different goddesses are sometimes credited with the same adventures, and in this way Freyja comes to be identified with another divine person: Gefion, 'the donor'. She, too, was one of the objects of Loki's attacks at the famous banquet. She protected virginity and also bestowed fertility. Special honour was accorded her on the Danish island of Seeland, which she was associated with in a particular legend. An ancient king of Sweden, Gylfi, had received so much pleasure from the sight of Gefion exercising her magic that he gave her a king-dom: as much land as she could mark off in one day with a plough drawn by four oxen. But Gefion had sons whom she disguised as oxen, and this increased their strength a hundredfold. They had such a strong hold on the plough that they tore away the entire depth of the earth and dragged it right to the sea: this gave rise to the island of Seeland, and in Sweden they still point out the huge hole from which masses of earth were excavated that went to form this island; the hole is Lake Mälar.

Nerthus

A special place among the goddesses must be made for Nerthus, whom the ancestors of present-day Germans worshipped, and who is mentioned by Tacitus in chapter forty of the *Germania*. With reference to a group of small races living in the south of Denmark, he writes: 'None of these peoples have any distinctive feature, except that they all observe the cult of Nerthus, that is to say the Earth Mother; they believe that she intervenes in the affairs of men and moves about among the different races. On an island in the ocean there is a sacred wood, and there a consecrated chariot can be seen covered with a veil; only the priest has the right to touch it. He knows when the goddess is present in the sanctuary and accompanies her respectfully. Her chariot is always drawn by heifers.'

During these festivals no war was allowed to break out; peace and tranquillity reigned, for Nerthus was goddess of fecundity and wealth. Later, the chariot and the deity herself were washed in a lake, and Tacitus adds: 'Slaves perform this service, and immediately the lake swallows them up. This gives rise to a mysterious terror, a holy ignorance of the nature of a secret which only those who are about to perish can understand.' This cult of the food-producing earth, together with the frightening rites described by Tacitus, was a peculiar characteristic of West Germans. In Scandinavia, Njord, the master of the sea, plays a similar role; Nerthus and Njord are two forms of one and the same function, deification

Austrian chariot bearing a bronze female figure surrounded by attendants—some on horseback carrying shields—and mythological animals. Hallstatt culture. *Graz Museum*

of the food-giving element. Nerthus is a goddess, Njord is a god; probably some ancient deity from which both are derived was endowed with both sexes; it would also personify fertility in some concrete way. We have no knowledge of such a figure, but its existence is quite plausible.

Hel

It was a goddess, also, who guarded the kingdom of the dead, at least as far as the Scandinavians were concerned, and she was called Hel. She lived underground, in the land of shades, which in many ways was like the Orcus of the Ancients, but it must not be thought of as a place of torture and punishment like the Christian hell. Hel, therefore, was not an evil deity, and she is never quoted as the daughter of the diabolical Loki until after certain late texts make their appearance, undoubtedly under the influence of the Christian faith. Niflheim was given her as her abode by Odin himself, and he also gave her power over nine different worlds, so that she could determine where everyone should dwell. She looked rather strange, for half of her face was normal and the other half was entirely black. But, even though she could look terrifying, the palace where she lived resembled the palace of the gods; she allocated a place to each newcomer, and the dead led a communal life which seemed very peaceful. When Balder, the god who was murdered, made his appearance, he was received with due honour, in a huge hall decorated in gold, where serving women hastily prepared a banquet. When the question arose of whether or not Balder would return to earth, Hel was neither cruel nor unjust. But the fact remains that this goddess, who does not seem to have had her own cult, must have been created by poets; the way in which she is portrayed reminds one of a queen of the shades.

Men and spirits

The Germans believed that the earth was peopled with innumerable beings who could not be counted as gods but were nevertheless superhuman by nature. They regarded all the elements as possessing spirits, who constantly intervened, not only in the lives of men, but also in the lives of the gods. These particular beliefs survived long after evangelisation, and the demi-gods, figures of quite secondary importance, still lived on in popular superstitions long after the great gods had been forgotten.

In all Germanic countries the souls of the dead were feared; they were thought capable of evil. The spirits of the dead were said to come frequently to take their revenge on the living for injustices they had suffered. On occasion they would come disguised as animals; and so the mice that devoured the cruel Bishop Hatto in one particular legend, after he had refused to lend help to the poor people of Mainz, were none other than the spirits of his victims.

In certain countries they thought that the souls of the dead congregated far from civilisation—on wastelands and islands. And thus large bands of ghosts, who were in reality the souls of the dead, sometimes rode desperately across the countryside. This is what legend refers to as the Wild Hunt, led by Wode, the spirit of fury (one of Wodan's forebears). The Wild Hunt crossed the sky at a fantastic gallop on stormy nights. A poet, Bürger, described it in the famous ballad *Lenore*.

West Germans believed that the favourite abode of the souls of the dead was in the west, where the sun dipped down into the sea. Some tribes went so far as to nominate Great Britain as the isle of the dead. In this connection Procopius, the historian, recounts that on the coast facing Great Britain there were many villages whose inhabitants did not pay the

Franks any tribute, though they were officially under their jurisdiction. But, in return, they were said to have the painful task of embarking the dead souls for their journey across the sea.

Even the souls of the living were declared capable of parting from their bodies to lead a semi-independent life. However, the Germans did not make a clear distinction between what we call body and soul in Christian terms. For us, the soul is completely impalpable and immaterial, whereas the Germans imagined in each person the existence of a sort of double, a second 'self', which could separate from the first to exercise corporeal functions, speak, move, act and appear in human or sometimes animal form. Scandinavians referred to this double, a man's shadow, as *fylgia,* which, roughly translated, means 'the second' or 'the one following'. The time when the double was most likely to disappear from the body of the man it inhabited was during sleep; then it would act just as it pleased, but the sleeping man was usually aware of its actions in his dreams. Thus the 'self' of dreams took on a quasi-corporeal existence. However, this double shared the fate of the man's body and did not survive his death. Wounds received by one of them were immediately felt by the other.

These beliefs went down particularly well with Norsemen; their lands have been, and still are, prolific in ghosts; the idea of men having doubles is very widespread. In legend the *fylgjir* (plural of *fylgia*) acquired a more and more independent existence, and then they became demoniac creatures who had nothing at all to do with humanity. If the necessity arose, spirits of ancestors could take this shape. In one particular saga about the chiefs who converted Scandinavia to Christianity a story is told of a man called Thedrandi, Icelandic by birth, who, one clear night, heard a knock at the door of his house. Although he had been warned never to step outside if this happened, he crossed the threshold with his sword in his hand. Then he saw nine women, dressed in black, with naked swords, riding from the north on dark horses. When he turned to the south he saw nine women in pale clothing riding on white horses. He wanted to hurry back quickly into the house, but it was too late: the black women had reached him and fatally wounded him. He was later found in the throes of death; he recounted what he had seen, and his contemporaries interpreted this tragic event in the following way: all these women were protective spirits, *fylgjir* of this particular race; the black ones were those who remained true to paganism; the white, those who leaned towards Christianity. Thus the pagan *fylgjir,* before becoming converted, had demanded a final sacrifice, which proved fatal for the unfortunate Icelander.

Norns and Valkyries

Certain other spirits intervening in the lives of men have a more obvious connection with the sphere of the gods, but they escape this sphere too, in a way, for they are the instrument of fate. These are women, renowned for their wisdom, their insight and their knowledge of magic.

In Germanic legend the mistresses of human destiny were the three spinners called the Norns. They had knowledge of ancestral precepts and timeless customs: so they were able to tell what was each man's allotted span of life. They held the gods themselves in their power, for they, too, were in the grip of fate. They came from the fountain of Urd, the source of life from which the great ash-tree drew its strength. This is how a poet describes them: 'From the fountain near to the tree come three women full of knowledge. One is called Urd, the second Verdandi; they hew through the woods. Skuld is the third. They have shaped destinies, they have selected

for the children of men their manly destinies.' According to another text, they were apparently 'swift on their snowshoes', which might be regarded as symbolic of the flight of time. The fact remains that they go to the same fountainhead, that of Urd—that is to say, Fate. In the beginning there was perhaps only one deity of time and destiny. Later three of them appeared, because three is a magic number, perhaps also because the Ancients had three fates (Parcae) who played the same part. Story-tellers credit each with a particular province: Urd knows the past, Verdandi the present, and Skuld the future.

They undoubtedly sent the fairies who were seen at the cradle of a newborn child in fairy stories, and their mission was to make him gifts or weave evil spells over him which weighed upon him all his life. The Scandinavian legend about Norna-Gesta tells how three women, endowed with the gift of prophecy, appeared at the birth of this hero. The first two predicted valour and happiness for him, but the third flew into a passion because she had been jostled by those present: ' I have decided that he will cease to live on the day when the candle beside him ceases to burn.' Immediately the candle was seized and extinguished and the mother was advised never to light it again. That is why the child was called Norna-Gesta, that is to say, 'the guest, the protégé of the Norns'.

The Valkyries also decided man's fate; but they were concerned only with warriors. On the battlefield they helped one or other leader to victory, they indicated the fighters who were to die and chose those who were to become Odin's companions in Valhalla. All Germans believed in their existence, but gave them different names. Thus those who lived in Germany, as we know it today, usually called them Idisi. The name that prevailed, Valkyrie, quite clearly means 'She who choses warriors'. Belief in magic horsewomen sent from heaven was very

widespread. It even seems to have been current in Normandy, for it was condemned by an assembly of bishops at Rouen: 'From which one can infer,' says one of the early historians of northern mythology, 'that these journeys happened frequently in Normandy, and that when Norwegians settled in this province, they could not bring themselves to renounce this belief, although they had embraced the Christian faith.'

The Valkyries are sometimes depicted by poets as virgins with swan's plumage, capable of flying through the air. These gracious creatures sometimes settled on lakes and pools near isolated forests. If a man managed to steal their feathers, they became his slaves. A reminder of this belief is found in the *Song of the Nibelungen,* the great epic poem of medieval Germany. Fierce Hagen was looking for a place to cross the Danube when he suddenly heard a faint splashing in a nearby pool. Creeping to the bank he caught sight of two girls bathing and there was swan's plumage close by. Immediately he seized it and would not give it back until the bathers had told him the fate that the future had in store for the army of the Burgundians marching towards the land of the Huns.

Brynhild, the Valkyrie who is the heroine of the musical drama by Richard Wagner, aroused Wodan's anger because she allowed a man to catch her unawares. One day, so the story goes, she flew from Valhalla with eight of her sisters. Down on earth they took off their plumage. King Agnar appeared, stole it and hid it beneath an oak. From then on the Valkyries' fate was in his hands, and he made them help him in a war against Hjalmgunnar. Now the latter was one of Wodan's favourites, and he had decided to give him the victory. Angered by the fact that Brynhild was thwarting his wishes, he punished her. He pricked her with a magic sword, sent her into a deep sleep and shut her up in a castle surrounded by flames, where she ceased to be a Valkyrie and could lead only an earthly life. She should have no husband unless a dauntless hero dared to ride through the flames that kept her cut off from the world. This hero came and was called Sigurd, the Siegfried of modern Germans.

Elves and dwarfs

Everything in nature was inhabited by a spirit, who was attached to some element, some form of life or vegetation. There were two major classes of such spirits: some were small, smaller than men, and these were elves and dwarfs. The others were very large: they were giants.

Elves, in the ancient usage of Germanic languages, was the name given to creatures associated with natural life, who were supposed to reside in water, woods or on mountains. Various different pictures have been painted of their relationship with humanity. English poetry of the Middle Ages portrays them as ethereal and luminous, full of gentleness and kindness. The Germans went in fear of them, and in the old Danish ballad from which the German poet Goethe took the idea for his *Erlkönig* their princess mortally wounds the knight who will not follow her.

They lived in a society, like men, with kings who had complete sovereignty over them. They loved gambling and dancing. They often spent whole nights tripping round in never-ending circles until they were interrupted by the crowing of the cock; then they vanished, for they were afraid of daylight and human eyes. Any man who allowed himself to be fascinated at night on some deserted heath by the beauty of their young women, and accepted their invitation to join the dance, met his doom. But usually there was no-one to witness their dancing: in the morning all that could be seen was the faint trace of their footsteps in the damp grass.

Dwarfs are the same class of creatures as elves, but they come in a special category. They usually lived underground; they were intelligent and industrious, rather than handsome; many were, in fact, deformed; their pale faces were framed by long beards. These dwarfs had the gift of prophecy. Dwarfs, says the poet of the *Edda*, were formed 'in the powder of the earth, as worms appear in a corpse... In the very beginning, they were nothing but worms, but at the command of the gods they were given their share of human reason and they acquired a human figure, but they lived underground and amongst rocks.'

Miners were the most likely to come into contact with dwarfs, for the latter were masters of metals. Sometimes in underground galleries dwarfs wore miners' clothing—the leather apron—and carried their effects: lantern, sledge-hammer and ordinary hammer. If a miner came across a dwarf it meant that he was near a good seam, for dwarfs were more subtle and knowledgeable than men, and they worked only where the earth's treasures were hidden. One of

these treasure troves is famous in German epic poetry; it was in the possession of King Nibelung and was guarded by a dwarf called Alberich. Siegfried, the hero of the *Song of the Nibelungen,* gained possession of it after he had overcome Alberich and extracted a vow of loyalty from him.

The dwarfs had another treasure mentioned in Scandinavian poetry. Its guardian, a dwarf called Andvari, could turn into a fish and live in water. But one day Loki took him captive with the aid of a magic net and would set him free only in exchange for his treasure. The dwarf had to accept this bargain and hand over all his gold. However, he tried to conceal one ring in his hand, but Loki saw it and demanded that it should be handed over too. This magic ring could go on creating wealth indefinitely. As he surrendered it to Loki Andvari put a curse on it: it was to cause the downfall of all its successive owners. And this prophecy came true: later, Fafnir, a giant who had killed his father to get possession of the magic ring, disguised himself as a dragon in order to defend his treasure, but to no avail, for he fell victim to Sigurd's sword, and once Sigurd himself got possession of the ring and the treasure he soon met his death.

The dwarfs were very clever goldsmiths and incomparable metal-workers. Both the weapons of the gods and the goddesses' ornaments came from their forges. Thanks to them Thor acquired his hammer; Freyr his magic ship and gold boar; Sif her gold hair; Freyja her golden necklace; and Odin his spear, called Gungnir, which never faltered in flight. Odin also had a ring called Draupnir, which, like Andvari's ring, had the power to multiply indefinitely the wealth of its wearer.

Some dwarfs liked the society of men, and these were called kobolds. They looked rather elderly, wore hoods and liked to seek shelter in stables or cellars. They could make themselves useful to people who gave them shelter, for they knew how to chop wood, carry water, curry horses, and remove dung. And so it was a blessing when a house gave shelter to a kobold.

Water-sprites, who were closely related to elves, lived in streams, rivers and at the bottom of the sea. In German tradition there were sprites of both sexes, and they often appeared in human guise; for example, the Wassermann, water-man, and the Nixe, the undine. When they became visible it usually meant death for anyone who encountered them; and this is what happened to youths who fell for the charms of undines. They liked to sit in the sun on river banks combing their long gold tresses; if they fell in love with a mortal, they dragged him down to the watery depths. But there were also some innocent mermaids who were sad at not being able to enjoy the company of men—like the one in the story by Hans Anderson.

There were also dwarfs living in the forests, and they were simply called 'woodmen' or 'women of the woods'. They had hairy bodies that seemed to be

393

covered with something like moss, and their skin was as wrinkled as ancient bark. But they were thought to be obliging and to know the virtues of simple folk.

In the open country dwarfs often disguised themselves as animals; when people saw crops waving in the breeze, they said that it was the 'wolf of the corn' or the 'barley dog' scampering through. In his flight from the harvesters, the wolf or dog took refuge in the corner left till the last, and he was hidden in the last sheaf. Then, according to regional custom, they either performed the gesture of killing him with the scythe, or else they brought him back in triumph, raising the last sheaf higher than all the others; even in the nineteenth century the feast to mark the completion of the harvest was still known as the 'kill-dog' in countries with Frankish traditions. Belief in dwarfs was the most popular of all and remained alive for a long time. 'In Iceland,' wrote a traveller in the eighteenth century, 'the good people point out rocks and hills where they maintain there are crowds of little underground men with the tiniest and most pleasing figures.'

Giants

Giants are also inferior spirits; they are essentially the same as dwarfs, from whom they differ in size. They came into being before the gods themselves, and were therefore the first living creatures on earth. In physique and appearance they retained the rawness and brutality of the time when the world was rising from the abyss and the ice. Various names were used in reference to them; one of those in use in Scandinavian countries also passed into other languages: that of troll.

The giants resembled dwarfs in that they were found throughout the world of nature. Theirs was the domain of heavy storm-clouds, snow and hail, and all the large-scale phenomena that caught the imagination, such as hurricanes, volcanic tremors, earthquakes and snowstorms.

Being close to the gods, and having arrived on earth before them, the giants were highly displeased when they were driven back into the inhospitable regions of the 'land of the east' or 'land of ice'. They enjoyed obstructing the masters of Asgard in their undertakings. Thor, the god of thunder, often had to fight them.

There were also sea-giants. The most famous of them, Aegir, 'master of the sea', liked to welcome gods who came to make merry in his sea palace. No torches were needed to light the great hall there, for it was decorated with gold, which imparted a brilliant light. Of course the master of the sea had collected all the sunken treasure from shipwrecks. Mimir, the sage, was another sea-giant frequently consulted by Odin. His province included inland streams, pools and lakes. His realm did not stretch as far as the sea. But Mimir lived in such close communion with the gods, and rendered them so many favours, that he could be

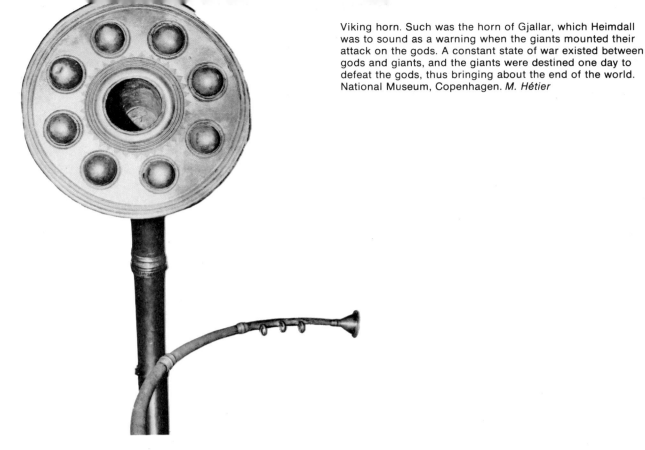

Viking horn. Such was the horn of Gjallar, which Heimdall was to sound as a warning when the giants mounted their attack on the gods. A constant state of war existed between gods and giants, and the giants were destined one day to defeat the gods, thus bringing about the end of the world. National Museum, Copenhagen. *M. Hétier*

regarded as one of them. In fact, of them all, water-sprites, at least water-giants, were the most friendly towards the gods.

The fire-giants were rarely referred to, and very little is known about them. However, Logi must be included among them; he is the giant who appeared in the course of Thor's journey to the magician Utgard-Loki. Logi did in fact beat Loki in an eating contest, and the reason for this is that Logi was the personification of flame, and a flame's appetite increases the more it consumes. Giants were able to disguise themselves; they often made use of this in conflicts against the gods. The great serpent of the Midgard and the wolf Fenrir were, in fact, giants in disguise, and they were the implacable enemies of the Aesir. But the best-known example of metamorphosis is that of the giant Fafnir, who became a dragon the better to guard his treasure. In almost all legends the giants got the worst of it; but everyone knew that they were planning their revenge, and that the rule of the gods was not destined to last for ever.

The twilight of .the gods

The Germans did not believe that the world was eternal or that their gods were immortal. Like mankind, Germanic gods had to submit to fate: their lives had begun on a given day and were destined to end on a certain day. Their existence was under constant threat, and it was so essential for them to keep on the alert that one of them, Heimdall, had the task of watching out for the arrival of the enemy and sounding the alarm. Asgard looked rather like a camp; the gods held themselves in constant readiness for war, and they knew that the hour would come when they would all have to enter the fray. And all the prophets said that in spite of the precautions taken, and the martial prowess of the gods, in spite of Thor and the countless soldiers from Valhalla, the Aesir would be defeated in the end. They would take the world with them in their downfall, for they were its protectors and its support. This battle, which was to precede the end of the world, was called the *ragnarok* by Icelandic story-tellers, meaning 'the fatal destiny of the gods'; later, about the twelfth century, Norse poets modified this slightly and changed it into *ragnarokkr*, (*rokkr* signifying 'darkness, twilight'). This is how the expression 'twilight of the gods' came into being.

In the *Voluspa* ('What the Prophetess says'), one of the oldest and strangest pieces in the *Edda,* the poet evoked all the events leading up to the downfall of the gods and the destruction of the world. If this account by the 'prophetess' is to be believed, then everything was related to the history of the gods, and the major episodes that brought fame to them individually were part of a vast dramatic whole. Of course, the fate of the gods was sealed, and none of them was destined to escape the inevitable; yet there were reasons for the storm that broke over the gods' abode; their downfall was the result of their own behaviour.

At the very beginning came the fight between the Aesir and the Vanir and any attempt at an interpretation of Germanic mythology rests largely on the meaning attributed to this early event. Without going so far as to see a meaning in all the episodes in the immense and varied epic of the gods of the north, there can be no doubt that their existence and power could be maintained only at the price of continual conflict. The world that they ruled was divided, full of mysterious and frightening forces; even after the reconciliation with the Vanir, the danger became no less acute. All northern writers have tended to give the impression of an immense, permanent tragedy, in which nothing remained; everything was destined to destruction or at least to constant, radical change.

The witch called Gullveig, the maker of gold, scattered the first seeds of discord in a world where relative tranquillity had prevailed since the defeat of the giants, now banished to the land of ice in the east. Whatever else, the enemies of the world were not at its very gates, and gods and men alike could live in peace and plenty. The gods were busy building palaces, raising altars, working precious metals and enjoying games of draughts in the courtyards at Asgard. But they took too much interest in Gullveig; they too wanted to amass piles of gold, and in order to make her surrender her secrets they tortured her. In doing this they committed the crime that started the first war. This was the basic sin that gave rise to all the others, and from henceforth war was to reign throughout the world. From that moment onwards the Valkyries flew about the universe from one battle to another. Furthermore, the gods several times broke their word to the giants. So people ceased to believe that oaths were sacred; men could not be expected to keep their word, or giants to refrain from violence. This first war was the start of an era in which the world grew divided and corrupt, ruled by force and treachery, and pervaded by perjury and crime. This world could not last; the gods themselves had shaken it to its very foundations, for they had tempted the hand of Fate.

Although they took precautions, like chaining up Loki and Fenrir, the wolf, the signs of impending catastrophe were on the increase. Fenrir fathered a litter of wolves on a giantess, and one of these sons was bold enough to give chase to the sun and snatch it between his jaws. 'The sun went black and the summers too', for the sky deprived of sunlight was always as grey and cold as in winter, filled with whirling snows that had drifted from the four points of the horizon. On earth everything was about to collapse, nothing was sacred any more, murder was paramount. 'Brothers fight and slay one another, children deny their own ancestry; the world is wicked and adultery prevails; this is the age of swords, of the battle-axe that cleaves shields; this is the age of wind, of wolf, until the very day when the world shall be no more.'

In the opposing camps, gods on the one side and giants on the other, the heralds sounded the alarm: 'In the gods' camp the gold-crested cock crows to call the heroes to arms; beneath the earth in Hel's palace, the other cock, the red one, crows and, near to the underworld, Garm, the wolf, howls, breaks loose and disappears.' Whilst 'everything is in ferment in the giants' camp', Heimdall, the watchman, sounds his horn. The trunk of Yggdrasill is racked with trembling, this oldest of trees is shaken by the giant's reawakening; the earth trembles, the mountains open, and the dwarfs who live there wander forth in despair.

The combatants assemble and make their way to the battlefield. A ship approaches from the west with ghosts on board: the giant Hrym, with raised shield,

Rock carving from Bohuslan, Sweden. It shows a man attacking a serpent with a hammer, and may represent the final conflict between Thor and his old enemy the serpent of the Midgard. *Claes Claesson*

is at the helm. His vessel is borne on a giant wave crested by the serpent of the Midgard as he swims. Driven by uncurbed anger, the monster strikes the waves with his endless tail and surges forward furiously. From the north Loki's ship approaches; he is accompanied by Fenrir with flame darting from his eyes and nostrils; his mouth hangs wide open and drips blood; his upper jaw touches the sky; his lower one brushes the sea. To the south appears Surt 'of burning heat', the chief of the fire-giants; around him flames leap from the furrowed earth. At his approach rocks shatter and men choke. The sky is all furnace, and when the sons of fire spur their horses across the rainbow-bridge between the earth and the abode of the gods, the bridge goes up in flames and collapses.

The chosen field for this great battle is near Valhalla, and each side of it is a thousand leagues long. There gods and giants slay one another in boundless confusion. Odin races forward at the head of the warriors pouring through the gates of Valhalla; the Valkyries on their shining horses fly round him in a swarm. The god makes straight for Fenrir; but the monster's mouth is so wide that it swallows up the master of the gods in one snap of the jaws. So Odin is the first victim of the slaughter. He is immediately avenged by his son Vidar. The latter puts his foot on the monster's lower jaw and clamps it to the ground; his left hand raises the upper jaw and with his right he pierces Fenrir with a sword so long that it reaches right down to his heart. Freyr, the god of dazzling light, is killed by Surt, the fire-giant. Thor seeks his old enemy, the serpent of the Midgard, who approaches him spitting so much poison that the air and the sea are befouled. Thor brings down his hammer on the monster's head with a mighty blow, and it falls back crushed and dying; but the god has suffered too much in the conflict; he has breathed in

so much poison that his strength leaves him. He attempts to move away: at the ninth step he falls, dying, to the ground. Loki meanwhile seeks and kills the handsome Heimdall; but he himself is slain by his adversary.

Thus the great gods die, in unimaginable torment, in a great onrush of storms and cataclysms. Mankind perishes with them, for the earth has become uninhabitable; no life can survive on it. Gigantic fires, earthquakes and tidal waves sweep the human race off the surface of the earth. Only bare rock remains. Stars are by now falling from the sky and disappearing into the abyss; the sun has vanished; the earth is unrecognisable. It will soon be swallowed up in the waves, for the oceans are overflowing everywhere. Once again a yawning gulf opens up on all sides. Nothing is left of all that had form and life.

But at once a new world rises from the void. 'Look,' says the prophetess, 'the earth for the second time emerges from the waves, green and fresh; foam shows white on the waterfalls; the eagle hovers high in the air and feeds on fishes on the rocks.' The twilight of the gods is nothing more than an episode, the end of a world that is to be succeeded by another. Decadence is followed by regeneration; where the old world foundered, a new earth emerges from the waters. The dramatic and bloody lives of the combatants are over; there is a renewal of peace and happiness from which new beings will benefit. The earth is a sort of Eden. 'The fields bear crops though no seed has been planted.' The meadows are green, birds circle above, fishes disport in the waters. The cycle of life starts again; in a new world a new life is begun.

A new generation of gods appears; at first they meet near the former abode of the Aesir 'to meditate on the great things and the old runes of the princes of the council'. So they do not turn their backs on the former masters of the world: they hold consultations in order to avoid their mistakes; and those members of the ancient Aesir who had no share in the quarrels or crimes of the old gods survive the wreck. These peaceful members of the ancient family will be the ones to renew the world. At their head is Loki's unfortunate victim, Balder, the brilliant god, previously beloved of all upright hearts. After his long sojourn in the kingdom of the shades, he comes back to life with all his beauty and kindliness, accompanied by his brother Hoder, and then takes his seat, as Odin did formerly, in the centre of the divine council. Even if Odin himself is gone for ever, his sons return, namely Vidar and Vali, and two of his brothers, Vili and Ve, whose names were quoted in the description of the way the world began. The valorous Hoenir also comes back to life and makes a study of the runes engraved on magic wands so that he may know the future and tell everyone that the great era is beginning. Two of Thor's sons, Magni and Modi, complete this divine council. 'That which was bad becomes better; Hoder and Balder take up residence in the castle of victory and the gods are joyful.'

Balder is the master of this resurrection of the world and the gods; whereas in the former reign of violence and war 'none of his judgments were realised', now he is the lord of the new world, where his word will be law. The great catastrophe has purged the world of ancient evils; storm has swept the sky clean; the horizon is pure. As in the very early days, men and gods can begin their history again, they can rebuild what was spoiled by passion and corrupted by violence and desire for gold. The new gods have but to return to the old days, to go back to the source of things. They will rediscover the good and the true, which too much drama made them forget. 'Once again miraculous tables of gold will be found in the meadows, and these in ancient times used to be the property of the gods.'

Whatever the truth may be with regard to these 'tables of gold', of which nothing is known, it is certain that according to the prophetess, a happy and worthy future opened up before the world on the day after the great conflagration. Like the phoenix the whole world, which had seemed to rock, woke up more beautiful and more pure than ever. The senseless war between cosmic forces, the sudden disclosure of natural and supernatural weapons, the insane use made by mankind of its knowledge and its magic, had brought about the collapse of the world, the darkening of the sun, the end of celestial harmony, the destruction of all life on earth. But this universal twilight lasted no longer than the space of a single night; in the morning, the sun shone anew, the grass was young, the animals disported themselves in all the elements; men found hope again and went back to their work under the protection of celestial powers. For some men had survived the universal explosion; the seeds of future man were enclosed in Yggdrasill's

A ship's grave set amongst pine-trees at Gnisnüre, Sweden. The old practice of ship burial was recalled in later times by screening off the grave of a great warrior or chieftain with standing stones in the form of a ship. *Axel Poignant*

Man's head, from the chariot discovered at Oseberg. Despite his foolishness, man had a happier destiny than the gods. He was to survive into the new and peaceful world after the Twilight of the Gods. *Universitetets Oldsaksamling, Oslo*

own tree-trunk against which flame, fire and darkness could do nothing. Men who escaped the disaster had only the morning dew to keep them alive in its shelter. The earth would be peopled by their descendants.

For the new world, unlike the old, was not under threat of catastrophe; the forces of evil and destruction had fled, no-one was now planning the end of the world, there were no more monsters or giants to forge weapons of ultimate destruction, no-one was now concerned to unhinge the world: 'The black dragon has fled far away and the shining serpent has left the depths of the pit.'

The prophetess' last vision is of a world dedicated to beauty, wealth and the happiness brought by peace: 'I see a hall, as bright as the sun and covered in gold; it is at Gimle: there the valorous nations will live, they will live in joy for as long as one can foresee.'

Those who survive the great drama, the just and peaceful men like Balder, face an infinite future of happiness and prosperity, the New Age of the world.

The great Germanic myths are therefore the history of a drama of world dimensions. The gods lead warriors' lives, dedicated to a tragic end. These sombre, gory imaginings acquired a great hold over the souls of men. Nordic paganism had a very long life. Evangelisation from the Occident crept slowly northward. In Denmark King Harold Bluetooth was converted in about 965, as shown in Ielling's beautiful monument; it depicts Christ surrounded by runic inscriptions and decorative pagan figures. In Norway energetic converted chieftains brought the people round to the idea of Christianity about the year 1000. For centuries before that time Anglo-Saxon and German princes had been receiving baptism. And yet, to people's infinite surprise, we have seen, in modern Germany, the resurgence of neo-paganism, fostered by the most tragic war-myths of the Germanic tradition. This neo-paganism, too, has known its twilight of the gods in the form of a conflagration that may remind one of the 'tale of the prophetess'. But the prophetess also says that after dire catastrophe the world rises anew, happy and peaceful, and that it will remain so into the most distant future.

Seated statuette found near Prishtina, in Serbia, and bearing markings on the belly similar to those on the he-goat found far away in Poland (see picture on page 412). *Prishtina Museum*

SLAV COUNTRIES: FOLK-LORE OF THE FORESTS

The origins of the Slavs are unknown and must perhaps remain hidden for ever in the dark night of time. However, our increasing knowledge of linguistic principles leads us to the reasonable assumption that the separation of the Slavs from the main body of Indo-European peoples must have taken place at a very early and remote date—in the second millennium before Christ.

If there was a Balto-Slav community, what were its geographical limits? This question has been raised by several experts and is still being discussed today, as are questions regarding the maturation and changes in the material, spiritual and social civilisation of these peoples.

Thus the study of their system of beliefs and religious practices is of particular interest. Long periods of their history are largely outside our knowledge, and what little we know is due entirely to archaeology, which is constantly reaping the benefit of new discoveries. This is the principal source of our knowledge, enabling us to make what interpretation we can of ancient Slavonic cults and beliefs.

Towards the end of ancient times a very few written texts relating to the religious life of the Slavs made their appearance. The Middle Ages provided a more abundant harvest, but its fruits were not evenly spread over the different areas occupied by these peoples. The interpretation of these texts, as of archaeological finds, requires the aid of folk-lore. Admittedly folk-lore does not go back to earliest times, but it occasionally represents what is left of a more ancient social consciousness. The 'facts' of folk-lore must be handled with extreme care: through the ages layers of inconsistent elements have settled one on top of another. Here again linguistics may come to our rescue and shed light on different manifestations of the religious cult, faith and magic.

And yet, in spite of the help afforded by these particular tools, we have at our disposal only fragmentary facts, which are inadequate when we need to know the truth about the religious history of the Slavs and about its evolution during the time that these peoples began to emerge from their infancy and settle in clearly differentiated societies, which they were to build into independent states in the course of the Middle Ages.

The beliefs of the ancient Slavs would appear to have served primarily to express the needs of agricultural populations, reflecting them in terms of imagery. It has been established that in the Bronze Age and the first Iron Age (the Hallstatt period), that is to say from about 1700 B.C. to about 450 B.C., the sun was an object of worship—as was fire, too, no doubt—and it was thought to be a manifestation of the mysterious power that granted life and heat and produced fine crops, but could also on occasion manifest its anger in the form of drought, thunder and lightning or destructive fires.

The existence of this type of solar cult is clearly proved by the solar symbols found on Slav ceramics; it would also seem possible that the figures of swans or other aquatic creatures bore some connection with it too. The Slavs also worshipped the vital force of the Earth Mother, symbolised by pictures of draught animals, such as oxen. At the end of this period circles of stones appeared here and there—and there seems to be no doubt whatsoever that they were connected with some cult—for example, those found on Mount Radunia and Mount Slez (present-day Sobotka) in Silesia. However, no completely satisfactory explanation can be given of their function.

It is not possible at this point to go into detail regarding the most ancient forms of religious life, particularly magic, though there is some interesting evidence in this field. We shall restrict ourselves to manifestations of organised religion in the form of well-developed cults and mythological expression; it might, however, be worth recalling one fact — namely, that Herodotus in his *History* (IX, 105) was already in a position to refer to certain customs peculiar to the Neuri, which were either contemporary with the author himself or somewhat before his time. In fact, this race is more and more frequently connected with the primitive Slav community: 'These Neuri seem to be sorcerers. In fact Scythians and Hellenes living in Scythia relate that there is a custom among the Neuri whereby once a year everyone changes into a wolf for several days, then returns to his original shape. For my own part, indeed, I do not believe these fables; however, that is what they state, even under oath . . . .' The theme of the werewolf became an integral part of Slav belief about this time and was to survive right down to our own age in Russian and Polish folk-lore.

Disintegration of Slav family communities of the patriarchal type probably began in the fifth to fourth centuries B.C. and took the form of deep-rooted social changes that continued into the early centuries of the Christian era. Both spiritual culture and production techniques were affected by Celtic influence at an early stage, and later by the influence of the provinces of the Roman Empire. From these regions came many frequently valuable imports, including statuettes of Hellenistic and Roman gods. We know hardly anything about the welcome their cults received, even from eminent members of Slav tribes, but it is impossible to minimise the role they played during this period in the religious evolution of the Slavs. It can at any rate he presumed that these cults made Slavs acquainted with the forces of nature in personified form, thus preparing the way for identical, but this time autochthonous, attempts at systematising beliefs.

The first important piece of written evidence about Slav religion does not appear until the sixth century. It was composed by Procopius of Caesarea (*De Bellis*, VII, 14–29): 'They [the Slavs] in fact regard one god, the creator of lightning, as the master of the world; they sacrifice oxen and other animals to him. They know nothing of fate and allot it no part in human life. But when they are in danger of death, whether in sickness or war, they swear on their oath that, if they are spared, they will sacrifice to the god for saving them, and if they escape they do as they promised and are then convinced that they have bought their safety. They also worship rivers, nymphs and other spirits, and make offerings to them all, and they make vows and predictions at their sacrifices . . . .'

This description points to the preponderant role played by the god of thunder: he is the god who is found at the dawn of the Middle Ages among numerous Slav races in the guise of the sun-god. Some scholars suspect Procopius of concealing the true aspects of Slav mythology beneath a layer of Hellenism.

This heritage of beliefs and religious practices was the fruit of long maturation imposed on the Slavs

Rock carving from Lake Onega, U.S.S.R. These rock carvings and paintings are connected with fertility magic and sympathetic magic and usually feature animals. The few men that are represented often wear a mask. 5000–1500 B.C. *Ravgonukae*

Three-headed god, carved in stone. Found on the Dalmatian coast. Little is known of the early beliefs of the Slavs beyond the fact that with the migrations of the fourth century A.D. they had spread from their original homeland, between the Oder and the middle Dnieper, southwards to the Balkans, westward to the Elbe and eastwards to the upper Dnieper. National Museum, Belgrade. *M. Hétier*

when they were obliged to assume their proper part in the evolution of Europe. The fourth century saw the beginning of the series of migrations that were to take them from their original habitat between the Oder and middle reaches of the Dnieper as far as the Balkans, the territories between the Oder and the Elbe, and also towards the upper Dnieper. In addition to the two groups that existed previously, the western and the eastern, there was also a third group, that of the southern Slavs. They remained united for many centuries, as their languages retained a remarkable degree of uniformity, and there were many common features in their cultural, material, spiritual and social patrimony.

Once the era of migrations was over, the dispersal of these tribes over vast tracts of central and eastern Europe made profound changes in their common religion inevitable. The southern Slavs found themselves almost immediately under the influence of the Christian religion, and so they were the first to take this particular step forward in their evolution. Then the others in turn accepted the new faith during the ninth to twelfth centuries. This change coincided with an important social and political evolution, which was to exercise a profound influence on men's minds, moulding them to face the needs of the era opening up before them.

The building of the new social order, the laying of the first foundations for the new states, were necessarily reflected in changes in pagan religion. It is not easy to distinguish what in the cultural heritage of the Slavs on the threshold of this new epoch constituted their legacy from ancient times (in which the proto-Slav community flourished) and what was the recent result of the social upheavals of the seventh to tenth centuries. We should be inclined to presume that the characteristic tendency of the Slav pantheon to move towards anthropomorphism (personification of the

forces of nature) must date from the early Middle Ages; the origins were certainly ancient, based on the cult of ancestors, characteristic of all Indo-European tribes, and on the idea that the forces of nature possessed a life of their own. But apart from a god of thunder and a little-known demonology, we know hardly anything about their religion in ancient times. The ninth to twelfth centuries are quite a different matter. As a result of much information given by autochthonous and foreign chroniclers, mainly during the period of conflict between paganism and Christianity, the Slav gods emerged from anonymity and revealed certain features, which by then had taken on a distinctly mythological colouring.

Medieval observers of Slav paganism were well aware that it was emerging from what was, on the whole, a fairly primitive form and was evolving towards more structural forms. A curious Russian text called *The Way in which Pagans acclaimed Idols* (ninth to twelfth centuries) has this to say about eastern Slavs: 'And these very people have begun to the ancestors), to Perun, their god, whereas formerly sacrifice to the Rod and to the Rozanitsa (deities of they sacrificed to vampires and *bereguini* [nymphs].'

There is little or no point in looking for the history of the gods and their great deeds in these texts; they were not a subject for popular poetry, and Christian witnesses, who were of necessity hostile, were not at pains to hand them on. Thus the Slav gods remain lost in dense cloud, only occasionally broken by a passing flash of lightning or a piercing ray of sunshine. Slav mythology is neither narrative nor anecdotal, it is more like a catalogue of supernatural powers; the music of poetry is heard only in popular beliefs on the borderline between folk-lore and demonology, and these have survived almost to our own day. However, the contribution of Slav religious history to the history of comparative religion seems not entirely

negligible: it reveals, perhaps more clearly than others, modes of thought in which the religious element is most closely welded to the social element.

Gods and men

The solar cult, which had its origin in earliest times, continued to hold the central place in the religion of the Slav peoples during the early Middle Ages, as can be seen from one of the principal names given to their god by great numbers of both eastern and western Slavs: Svarog, god of the sun and fire, with its derivative Svarozits (Svarozic). This theory is confirmed by traces of archaeological evidence that we mentioned earlier and by analogies with the religions of other Indo-European peoples; and in the last resort much support for it is found in folk-lore. At harvest ceremonies, as an Arabic text from the ninth century indicates, a handful of corn was thrown up in the air to call forth the protection of the gods. In Poland they were accustomed to raise their hand towards the sun when they swore an oath, and this practice continued till the end of the Middle Ages. Not long ago, the Polish, Ukrainian or Bulgarian peasant greeted the rise of the solar star with a deep bow or a special prayer.

However, we find ourselves faced with considerable difficulty when it comes to making a closer examination of the character and extent of this cult. Two pieces of evidence exist to prove that the deity of sun and fire possessed the attributes of a supreme or principal god, but these two reports are six hundred years apart. One of them is given by Procopius of Caesarea, whom we quoted earlier, and it dates from the middle of the sixth century; the other is given by Helmoldus of Bosau, in Holstein, and comes from the second half of the twelfth century. Speaking of the Slavs Helmoldus states '... they do not deny that there is among the multiform godheads to whom they attribute plains and woods, sorrows and joys, one god in the heavens ruling over the others. They hold that he, the all-powerful one, looks after heavenly matters only; that the others, discharging the duties assigned to them in obedience to him, proceeded from his blood; and that one excels another in the measure that he is nearer to this god of gods ....'

Belief in this god was the result of a combination of concepts expressing admiration, fear and love for some closely related phenomena involving the sky, the sun and fire. This symbolic unity, however, covered various vague functions that are difficult to differentiate, especially where powers were shared among several deities whose fields of activity more or less overlapped. And equally, different names might be used in different regions with reference to this unity.

The name of Svarozits comes down to us from the two farthest corners of the area inhabited by the Slavs. The first comes from the frontier separating the Poles and the Veleti: we know that in the beginning of the eleventh century Svarozits was the god of the Veleti and that a temple had been dedicated to him at Radogoszcz (Rethra), the capital with the three peaks and the three gates of the Redarii (Thietmar, VI, 17); we also know that a hundred years later in this same temple, in the midst of other 'demons', a god called Radogost held sway. This name seems to be one of the local variations on Svarozits, or else a regional adjunct to his name, which would appear to have been in use in the time of Adam of Bremen, who mentioned it in his work (II, 21).

In his own town Radogost possessed a wooden temple that rested on animals' horns; the external walls were decorated with sculptures of the gods and the interior was filled with statues of them; a number of them were in armour; insignia (*vexilla*) were kept in the temple and a horse was stabled there. Bishop Burkhardt of Halberstadt rode it when he waged a victorious campaign against the Veleti in 1068.

Svarozits was also known in Russia; he was worshipped there as master of fire, especially the fire used to dry grain. But Svarog was also worshipped and was identified with Hephaestus, according to a clearly intelligible twelfth-century translation of a Byzantine text, just as his son Dazbog was identified with Helius. As Svarozits is a patronymic name for Svarog, this would appear to be a case of divine genealogy, and perhaps of complete identification between Svarozits and Dazbog. The meaning of the two words is uncertain: Svarog may be etymologically connected with the Polish word *swarzye* ('to quarrel, get angry'), and certain scholars have connected this idea of impatience, anger with a god of fire; others see the name as stemming from the Indo-European root *svar*, which has been preserved in Sanskrit, and is none other than 'light', 'sky', 'sun'. Dazbog's name

Oak-tree used for cult practices into which are set boar's tusks. Divinities of nature were generally worshipped out of doors, in a clearing around a special tree, such as this one, or round trees which had an odd natural shape or were very old. Such practices continued into the fourteenth century. (After *Istoria kultury drevnei Rusi* Vol. II, p. 54.)

can also be explained as meaning 'dispenser of wealth' and this also has a bearing on the concepts that formed around the solar cult. There is definite proof of the presence of Dazbog in Russia, though Serbian traces of him are less reliable. In Poland the only proof that he eventually became known there is the surname Dadzbog, frequently found among the nobility of Mazovia in the fifteenth and sixteenth centuries.

In fact Svarog, Svarozits, and Dazbog seem to complete the very short list of individual gods known to all Slavs. Each country must now be studied separately if any further additions are to be made to the list.

Perun, god of the thunderbolt

There is one god who has a perfectly sumptuous cult and appears in Kiev in Russia. This is Perun, and his principal worshippers consist of princes and their entourage. He was invoked at the taking of an oath, but his functions were not defined until the sixteenth century, when Polish historians undoubtedly deduced them from Perun's name, *piorun,* 'the thunderbolt'. This, however, seems a highly probable deduction and poses an important problem for religious historians. It would seem that the cult of Perun might well mask or overlap that of the Norse god Thor, Lord of the Storm and Master of Lightning. As proof of his Scandinavian origin, details of certain rites performed before Perun are quoted, such as placing arms at his feet, and there were special imprecations hurled at anyone who broke a vow. This would indicate that the entire cult was imported from the Varangians. It would probably be more accurate to presume that all these practices — that were to some extent foreign — had encountered an autochthonous cult of the thunderbolt in Russia, and had embellished it with the characteristics proper to the god of

knights and Varangian merchants.

The cult of the thunderbolt was known to Serbs in the Balkans as well (although the actual name of the god involved is unknown), but there it was already Christian in form and in fact crystallised around the character of Saint Elias; in Poland there are no definite traces, and the only proof that exists is in toponymy. But the Lithuanians also had a god of the thunderbolt called Perkunas; and this fact opens up new perspectives for historians to debate. Perun may well be identified with the thunderbolt, but Perkunas more probably derives from the archaic Indo-European name for oak (cf. Latin *quercus*). This tree, which has a special attraction for the thunderbolt, was often dedicated to gods of lightning. The Norse god Thor's mother was called Fiorgynn; and this brings us to common mythological sources, going back to earliest antiquity, from which Slav, Baltic and Germanic beliefs stemmed.

The Russian dynasty was so assiduous in its attentions towards the god of the oak and the thunderbolt that it might be suspected of harbouring political designs beneath its devotions: when Slav rulers were building their great states, they needed to create in their subjects the feeling of belonging to one and the same ethnic and cultural body. Nothing could have contributed better to this end than a common ideological current or at least pre-eminence accorded certain cults. In the most ancient Russian chronicle, *The Record of the Years*, recorded at the end of the eleventh century but based on earlier documents — the part devoted to Saint Vladimir's life, for instance, is based on a source dating from the first half of the eleventh century — this fact is mentioned with a great wealth of detail: 'and Vladimir began to reign alone at Kiev. And he placed the idols on the hill outside the palace: Perun carved out of wood with a silver head and gold moustache. And Khors, and Dazbog, and Stribog and Semargl and Mokos. People made them offerings, calling them gods; sons and daughters were brought and sacrificed to demons. So they sullied the earth with their sacrifices, and the Russian earth and this hill were covered in blood. But God in his mercy did not wish for the death of sinners, and on that hill there stands today the Church of Saint Basil of which we shall speak again later. But to return to the above: Vladimir then put his uncle Dobrynia in Novgorod. And when Dobrynia arrived at Novgorod he raised an idol to Perun on the banks of the river Volkhov; the people of Novgorod made sacrifices to him as well as to their own god . . . .'

Although we know of sporadic cases of human sacrifice in other Slav territories, historians with their suspicious minds have been led to remark that the whole passage seems to be a pure paraphrase of Psalms (CVI, 36–38) used by the pious scribe to paint the crime of paganism in the blackest possible colours.

Once again archaeology brings us back to actual

An eleventh-century cult object, in the form of a small horse, found in the excavations at Opole in Silesia. The tenth and eleventh centuries saw a strengthening of Slav religious practices as part of the effort of the border peoples to withstand the political and cultural domination of the Christian world and the Empire. *Archaeological Museum, Opole*

physical reality: near Novgorod, on the banks of Lake Ilmen in the neighbourhood of Perynia (which reminds one of the name of Perun, god of the thunderbolt), a circle of stones was found in a complicated pattern of eight-lobed leaves, and this was surrounded by a deep ditch thirty-eight yards in diameter. In the centre of this circle traces of a stone pedestal were also found; archaeologists are inclined to the belief that a statue once stood here, but that it disappeared shortly after its erection, when the old religion had to give way to the new in 988.

Minor Russian gods

In the old Russian chronicle that was mentioned above, some information is found, though it is not uniformly reliable, regarding treaties concluded between Russia and Byzantium. In 907 it is said that Oleg and his men were required to swear on oath 'according to the Russian law', and that they 'swore on their swords and on Perun their god, and on Volos, god of cattle, and peace was thus confirmed'. The same thing happened in 917. One Czech tradition, as late in date as the sixteenth century, also referred to a god called Veles, who was no doubt identical with Volos. There are certain indications that this god of cattle was probably the god of prosperity and perhaps also of commerce; Ibn Fadlan states that idols were erected at market-places; this would explain why Volos had no place in the pantheon that Vladimir erected in front of his palace, for his choice rested more on the warrior-gods.

The catalogue quoted above of gods worshipped at Kiev before the arrival of Christianity presents problems of exegesis: besides Perun and Dazbog, whom we have just discussed, Khors is mentioned, and he also appears in the *Geste of Prince Igor;* but these references tell us nothing about his functions or his origin. The name may be Slav; others believe it to

be of Turkish origin, which is probably closer to the truth, bearing in mind Vladimir's apparent plan to assemble at Kiev representatives of different cults observed by his subjects and soldiers.

As for Stribog, the best one can do is quote from the same *Geste of Prince Igor*, in which the winds are regarded as the grandsons of Stribog; some scholars think that the Russians are being apostrophised at this point, and that therefore no reference to the winds is intended. However, there is not much proof of this, even if the etymology of this word—which would be the onomatopoeic root *stri,* expressing the creaking produced by the wind—is acceptable.

Even less is known about Semargl or, as certain manuscripts put it, Sem and Rgl. According to etymology the first name—if one admits that there were two—would appear to have some connection with the family (*siemia,* family) and the second with barley (*roż,* old word for barley). But other experts include Semargl among foreign gods and simply attribute this name to the fertile imagination of the chronicler, whose account of paganism and Vladimir's baptism did not appear until the end of the eleventh century, so he cannot have known very much about the earlier cults of pagan Russian society.

On the other hand, Mokos' existence is well substantiated: she is a female deity quoted in several sources and also represented in popular folk-lore (as Mokusa); she is said to wander during Lent disguised as a woman, visiting houses, worrying woolspinners, guarding and fleecing sheep herself; at night strands of fleece are laid beside stoves for her. Linguists are inclined to think that her name comes from a Finnish surname, which would indicate that it had been borrowed at some period from that race.

Some isolated references can be given in addition to the preceding meagre information; these are scattered about in a few homilies and Russian literary works dating from the Middle Ages. Thus, in various regions of Slav territory, and in particular in Russia and the Balkans, a demoniacal creature was known to man and went by the name of Troian. The remarkable *Peregrination of the Mother of God in the midst of Suffering*, dating from the twelfth century, says: 'They forgot God and believed in that which God created for our use; and they called all this by the name of gods: the sun and the moon, earth and water, quadrupeds and reptiles . . . (and they made) the gods Troian, Khors, Veles, Perun; they believed in evil spirits and even to this day remain in a guilty state of dark unenlightenment.'

In the Balkans Troian was regarded as a god of night with wax wings (like Icarus); the most likely theory is that Troian was simply the Divus Traianus, the Roman emperor Trajan, whose official cult seemingly influenced the Slavs in Dacia.

To this list should be added Pereplut, whom people worshipped by drinking from a horn; some linguists think this name refers to the goddess of changing fortune.

It has been rightly remarked that it is very difficult — with the exception of the sun-fire entity — to define any internal relationships whatsoever between these obscure characters in the Russian pantheon. A reasonable number of characteristic features seem to indicate that there was not a long interval between the dawn of these cults and their eclipse. The few deities that there were coincided with the emergence of related social needs and appeared as and when the great political organisms were being elaborated with Russia and Kiev at the head. So it is not surprising that certain features of these gods, and some of their names, mirror foreign influences adapted to local needs.

Temples and sacred images

Although we know little enough about the gods themselves, archaeology has taught us a little more about their cults. Apart from the discoveries at Perynia, near Novgorod, excavations at Vschstiz, on the banks of the Desna, in a *gorod* (fortified enclosure), led to the discovery of a holy place, semicircular in shape and bounded by ten wooden pillars; at the foot of these pillars ceramic vases were laid out, and in the centre of the semicircle were traces of a brazier. Some sacrificial traces were also found near the remains of forge fires in a fortified enclosure at Pskov; beside the pillars were small hearths, and horses' bones and ceramic vases were found there.

Of the various sculpted figures of gods that have been found, the most famous has been known now for something approaching one hundred years; this is the *Swiatowid*, which was rescued from the River Zbruch and given this name because it had four faces crowning a stone pillar — a characteristic way of depicting Svantevit, as is well known from twelfth-century literary descriptions of the Island of Rügen.

It is a superb monument and, in fact, the four sculpted faces constitute four cycles which probably refer to four distinct deities: two male and two female. Although two other figures somewhat similar to the *Swiatowid* found in the River Zbruch were discovered near Kamenets-Podolski in 1850, and although there are other polycephalic specimens in existence in southern Russia which have been known for a long time, it is still a moot point as to whether or not they belong to the Slav pantheon; in the course of the Middle Ages these regions saw frequent migrations of nomadic Turkish tribes.

The gods of pagan Russia came to a sudden end in 988. Prince Vladimir decided to be baptised and returned to Kiev and 'gave the command to overthrow the idols, to break these and those, to cast them into the flames. As for Perun, he had him fastened to the tail of a horse and dragged across the slope through Borytchevo right to the stream. He positioned twelve men to hit him with sticks, not that wood could feel anything, but as a way of mocking the Devil, who deceived men in this particular shape; let him therefore pay for his crime. Lord, thou art great and thy works are marvellous: worshipped by the people yesterday, and today put to shame! As the statue was dragged through the stream towards the Dnieper, the infidels shed tears upon it, for they had not yet received holy baptism. And when they had dragged it they threw it in the Dnieper. And Vladimir said to his officers: "If he should stop, push him far from the banks, until he is over the rapids, then you can abandon him." So they carried out his commands. When they released him, he went over the rapids and the wind cast him up on the lower bank and the bank was called Perun's bank; and it has this name even to this day.'

At Novgorod the precinct dedicated to Perun was destroyed in a similar way and his statue cast into the river to the accompaniment of beating. In the morning a peasant on his way to market saw it floating near to the bank. He pushed it away with a stick and shouted: 'You, old Perun, you have had enough to eat and drink, now float away from here, be gone!'

Little is known about the cult of gods in Poland in the early Middle Ages; as was the case in Bohemia, the rapid victory of Christianity effaced even the traces of organised cults. However, there can be little doubt that the same efforts to develop certain rites were made on Polish soil as in Russia. Cults were adapted to fit into the emerging political structure and given a political role or at least one connected with the apparatus of power. We have references to attempts of this sort undertaken on Polish territory. We know, for example, that Mount Slez-Sobotka, which towers in solitary state in the middle of the fertile plain of lower Silesia, was the centre of a pagan cult towards the end of the tenth century. 'It was the object,' Thietmar, Bishop of Merseburg (VII, 59) writes, 'of great veneration on the part of all local

Two sides of a carved stone pillar surmounted, it is thought, by a representation of the god Svantevit. This pillar, almost nine feet high, is called the *Swiatowid* because it bears a face on each of its four sides—two of male and two of female deities. It is uncertain whether this unique monument, which was fished out of the River Zbrucz in 1848 at Liczkowce, is in fact of Slav origin, even though the figure bears in its right hand the horn associated with Svantevit; it may be connected with Turkish nomadic tribes which passed through the area in the Middle Ages. *Archaeological Museum, Cracow*

people because of its size and purpose, for iniquitous mysteries were celebrated there....' It was in fact an important feature in the social life of the Slenzanes, one of the many little regional states of that period. Archaeological traces of a cult-centre of the ninth century were also discovered at the top of Lysaya (Bare Mountain), later called Mount of the Holy Cross, in the central mountains of Poland. Later in the twelfth century, the Bishop of Wroclaw had to set about destroying cult-centres near to Jawor. Wooden images of old gods were still kept there. Heads of oak statues have been preserved down to present times. One was recently discovered in the bed of the River Warta—eloquent illustration of the system of liquidating gods mentioned above and one certainly applied to ancient cults.

In Bohemia paganism left even fewer traces; in fact, the only reliable written source gives the name of a god called Zelu, but this dates from the fourteenth century. Some experts have thought that they could detect a mythological element in the most ancient legends surrounding the origins of the Premyslid Dynasty, but there has been no confirmation of this supposition.

On the other hand, Pomeranian and Polabian paganism reached a high level of religious organisation, and many scholars think that foreign influences, particularly Norse, played some part in it. This problem seems to be quite complex. One might attempt to resolve it by referring to the fact that small Pomeranian and western Slav states were subject to rapid change in their political institutions from the tenth to the twelfth centuries. The sovereigns of these countries also sought to strengthen their states by somewhat deceptive ideology, and thus they tried at times to impart a fresh impulse to pagan religion. We had an eloquent example of this at Kiev before the final choice was made in favour of Christian religion. Elsewhere attempts were made to develop a hierarchy of priests around the cult of the main regional god, as was the case with the Polabian Slavs and also, during the eleventh century, with the people of western Pomerania, who were, of course, baptised by Boleslas the Valiant in the year 1000, but returned to paganism as soon as they managed to shake off the Polish yoke. The most favourable and effective solution to political problems both internal and external, at a time when pressure from neighbouring Christian states was increasing, consisted of conversion under conditions of independence for these pagan races. And this the Slovene and Croatian princes managed to bring about at the end of the eighth century; then Bulgarian, Moravian and Serbian princes achieved the same object, together with the rulers of Bohemia, in the ninth century; in the tenth century, and for the second time, the princes of Bohemia, the Hungarians and the Russians, and in the north the Scandinavian sovereigns followed suit. But for the smaller states between the Elbe and the

Head carved in oak and found in the lake at Jankowo, in the Mogilno district of Poland. This may have formed part of a larger statue of a god of the kind often destroyed in the medieval struggle between Christianity and paganism. *Archaeological Museum, Poznan*

Stone idol wearing a headdress similar to that of the *Swiatowid*, found at Novgorod. Historical Museum, Novgorod. (After *Istoria kultury drevnei Rusi* Vol II, p. 71, 1951.)

Oder the acceptance of Christian faith was synonymous with national destruction. After the great revolt of Veleti and Obotrites in 973, which ended in their victory, the threat of liquidation that hung over their political existence was dispelled for two centuries. Then, in answer to the exigencies of the times, there began an era of ardent attempts to construct a new society and individual states that could measure up to the strength of the political units round about: the Germanic empire, Denmark, and Poland. Their influence put a brake on normal historic development and made the efforts of western Slavs to create more important states quite useless; in the course of the twelfth century they obtained the political surrender of the whole of the Polabian and Pomeranian region. The decisive role played by the empire in this trial of strength opened the way to the Germanisation of autochthonous populations and to German colonisation in these territories.

Paganism had a twofold mission to fulfil under these conditions: not only did it guarantee the survival of ancestral customs, but it was also to reinforce resistance against the enemy by developing original cults so that they might effectively rival Christianity. In the course of these attempts elements were borrowed here and there from neighbouring tribes. For instance, on the Island of Rügen (the Slav Rana) the population had to contribute a tithe towards their principal god. But the main lines laid down in these cults remained the same as for their forebears.

Svantevit

Christian observers have left us detailed descriptions of the political and religious life on this island situated near the southern shores of the Baltic, and these include well-documented evidence regarding the cult of Svantevit, 'Strong lord', whose role became so exalted that he was made sovereign of the little state of the Rani. The college of priests apparently exercised quasi-theocratic powers there. In actual fact, we also know of the existence of a little group of lords who elected the princes and then had to pay heed to their desires. The cult of Svantevit reminds one of a supreme, and in reality, unique deity and this would fit in with the need for a concentration of power; it is possible that the name of Svantevit, like that of similar supreme deities, concealed the ancient concept of Svarog-Svarozits.

The centre of this cult was in the north-east of Rügen, at Arkona, on one of the wooded peninsulas with steep cliffs dropping right down to the sea. Saxo Grammaticus (XIV, 39) left us a vivid description of the temple and rites celebrated there: 'the centre of the castrum was a square on which you could see a wooden temple of great beauty, famous not only for the magnificence of the service, but also for the statue it contained. The external precincts of the temple attracted the eye because of various very primitive sculptures and paintings. Only one entrance was

Two clay statuettes of horses. These ritual objects were found near Mikulvice, Moravia, Fourth–fifth centuries A.D. *Brno Institute, Czechoslovakia*

open to passers-by. The temple itself was inside two enclosures. The outside one consisted of walls with a red roof; the inside one was simply composed of four pillars, and instead of walls there were hangings, and only the roof and a few transverse beams were the same as in the external precinct. In the temple stood an enormous statue, taller than any human form, with four heads and necks, which lent it a somewhat terrifying appearance. Two looked ahead, and two behind, one faced the right and another the left. The moustache was shaven, and the hair cut in deliberate imitation of the style usually affected by the Rani. In its right hand it held a horn, fashioned in a variety of precious metals, which the officiating priest filled each year with wine, so that he could predict from the drink the harvest to come. The left hand was supported against its side as if the arm were bent. The robe on the statue fell to its calves, which were of a different wood, and at the knee was a join that you would fail to see unless you looked very closely. The feet were at ground level, for the pedestal was buried in the earth. To one side you could see the bit, saddle and various insignia; a sword of extraordinary size increased the wonder of it all, and the admirable work on sheath and hilt enhanced the intrinsic value of the silver. The ceremony unfolded in the following manner: the day before the festival the priest, whose long moustache and flowing locks made him stand out from the rest of his uniformly dressed compatriots, swept the temple with the greatest care, and he alone was allowed to go into it, although he had to take care not to breathe in it.

Each time he wanted to draw breath he ran to the exit so that no human breath should touch the god and thereby sully him. The next day, when the assembled people were waiting at the gates, he took the bowl from the statue's hand and scrutinised it attentively to see if any of the liquid he had poured in

had disappeared. If some had gone he predicted a bad harvest and advised the people to keep the new crop for future times. But if the bowl was still full, he predicted abundant harvests to come; on this basis he decided whether the dispensation of provisions should be liberal or strict. Then he poured the old wine at the foot of the statue in sacrifice, and filled the bowl with new wine, and having revered the idol as if he had given it drink, in solemn prayer he invoked total prosperity for himself, then for the land; on behalf of his fellow-citizens he called for increased wealth and new victories. After the prayer he tilted the bowl to his lips and emptied it at one gulp, and then, having filled it again with wine, he replaced it in the statue's right hand. An offering of honey-bread was also brought (like the Continental *pain d'épice*), which was circular in shape and almost as tall as a man. The priest placed it between himself and the people, and asked if it could be seen from the back of the crowd. When they had confirmed this, he expressed the wish that those who could see it should be unable to perceive it again the following year; but it was not death that he was thus invoking for himself or his fellow-citizens, but more plentiful crops to come. Then he greeted those present as if this greeting were from the god himself, and having counselled them to remain faithful to him and to observe the festival diligently, he promised victories on earth and sea as the surest recompense for their diligence. The rest of the day was set aside for wild rejoicing; the people consumed the dishes consecrated to the god till they could eat no more, for these offerings satisfied their own gluttony. It was customary on this day of festivity to eschew temperance, and it would have been thought a sin to observe it. Everyone, man or woman, once a year voluntarily offered a piece of ground in honour of the idol. A third of the arms and booty captured from the enemy too was

410

Cult stone found at Leczno, near Danzig. The horse shown on this stone, like other such objects, may once have symbolised the forces supposed to be incarnated in the animal. But gradually the objects came to be accorded a cult in their own right. *National Archaeological Museum, Warsaw*

dedicated to it, as if its help had led them to victory. Three hundred horses and their riders were also regarded as belonging to the god; they gave the priest all the booty they had won in battle or by trickery. They made all sorts of insignia and ornaments for the temple out of this booty, which they then put in closed coffers where, in addition to some quantity of coins, there were precious materials rotten with age. There were many other gifts there donated collectively or by private persons, which had been brought, to the accompaniment of vows, by people with some favour to ask. And this idol to which all Slavs paid such heed was also visited by neighbouring kings, who brought gifts (Christian kings at that, like the Danish Sven). This god also had other temples in different places, which were ruled by priests of lesser importance and dignity. He also had his own white horse and it was sinful to pull a hair from its mane or tail. Only the priest dared to feed the horse and ride it, lest the prestige of the divine steed be lowered, as would have happened if any further use had been made of it. According to the beliefs of the Rani, Svantevit (for this was the god's name) went to war riding this horse against enemies of his faith, and this was proved by the fact that although the horse was shut up all night in the stable, in the morning it often appeared out of breath and spattered with mud, as if it had had a long way to travel on returning from some expedition. They also foretold the future with the aid of this horse in the following way: when they had decided to wage war on some land, the priests laid three rows of spears in front of the temple: in each row there were two spears in the shape of a cross, with the spearhead buried in the ground, and the rows were equidistant from one another. In the course of preparations for the expedition, the priest offered up a solemn prayer, then brought the horse from the antichamber of the temple, holding it by the halter, and if on entering these rows the horse put his right foot first, instead of his left, that was regarded as a good omen for war; if, on the other hand, although it might only happen once, he put his left foot first instead of the right, they abandoned their plan to invade the foreign land . . . .'

The end of the reign of Svantevit, god of war and fate, was brought about by a foreign hand; the Danish king Valdemar, with the aid of the princes of western Pomerania, conquered Arkona in 1168; he overthrew the statue and ordered ropes to be fastened round its neck so that it could be led away for burning. Archaeological research has led to the discovery of the site of the temple and made it possible to determine its size (20 metres square).

Another god called Yarovit (which perhaps means 'Severe lord') was worshipped at Wolgast and Havelberg; a shield was kept in his temple and was brought out in war to obtain victory; his festivals were celebrated with much pomp. On this same island of Rügen at Gardziec (Gartz) a god called Ruievit was worshipped, and he had seven faces carved out of oak. There were also two gods called Porevit and Porenut, whose names, though greatly deformed, have come down to us not only through Saxo Grammaticus, whom we have already quoted, but also through one of the Icelandic sagas of the thirteenth century. In western Pomerania a three-headed god called Triglav was in command—undoubtedly another version of the old principal deity, Svarog-Svarozits. According to Herbordus (II, 32) (Saint Otto, Bishop of Bamberg's hagiographer and a missionary to Pomerania), Boleslas the Wrymouth commanded Triglav's temple at Szczecin, one of the four in the town, to be built, 'with marvellous care and skill. It had sculptures within and without and from the walls projected images of men, birds and beasts, the appearance of which was so natural that they might have been thought to be living and breathing. Now there was a three-headed image which had its three heads on one body and was called Triglav . . . . There was also there a large and shady oak-tree with a delightful fountain underneath, which the simple-minded people regarded as rendered sacred by the presence of a certain god, and treated with great veneration.'

In another important urban centre at Wolin, there was a small statuette of Triglav, but it was made of gold; when danger threatened it at Christian hands, the priests entrusted it to a widow, who hid it in the hollow of a tree. According to these priests, the three heads of Triglav symbolised his dominion over three realms: the sky, the earth and the places underground; the statue's eyes were blindfolded, a sign that this god was so good that he did not wish to look upon the malice of men.

So, just when paganism was being liquidated elsewhere, Christianity found organised local cults throughout Polabian communities. They have

He-goat carved in wood. Figure of the tenth or eleventh century found on the island of Lednica, near Gniezno. *Archaeological Museum, Poznan*

bequeathed us the names of various deities, but we do not have as many written commentaries about all of them as we do about Arkona, Szczecin or Wolin. Some of these names have been quite simply invented by German clerks who could not speak Slav, and therefore mistook terms referring to concepts for proper names, such as that of judgment or law (*prawo*) for the god Prowe at Oldenbourg (Stargard). Some of these names seem plausible, such as those of the goddesses Zywa and Pogoda given by Helmoldus (as Siwa and Podaga) and repeated by John Dlugosz in his *History of Poland* written in the fifteenth century. In the appeal launched by Bishop Adelgot in 1108 in favour of a crusade against the Slavs, or rather in the stylistic exercise on this topic, a god called Pripegal is mentioned, who is said to thirst for Christian blood and is compared in this text with Priapus.

'Men and Spirits'

The gods themselves were cast into the rivers Dnieper and Volkhov, their ashes mingled with those of the city of Arkona, but it is possible that they left something behind within the ranks of the Slav peoples. One of the curious and peculiar characteristics of the world of religious concepts known to Russian Slavs in the Middle Ages was 'double faith': the concurrent existence of Christian notions and pagan beliefs. The Church struggled against the latter without much success, occasionally allowing itself to be affected by the influence of popular mentality, especially by certain outward forms of magic. Let us leave aside this aspect of religious life covering, as it does, a huge field with a great psychological and social bearing and restrict ourselves to a brief reference to certain aspects of demonology as conveyed in historical sources and in the information provided by ethnography. In spite of a considerable number of itinerant themes common to the whole of Europe, an analysis of this material makes it possible to isolate from this strange world certain features and personifications that are more peculiarly Slav.

At one extreme are the witches, sometimes, though less often, the sorcerers, and they regard humankind with malevolence. For a long period and in spite of persecution by the Church seers had enjoyed popular esteem in Russia, and in the ninth century they even headed popular revolts against the social and religious order in process of consolidation; and so sorcerers should be regarded, so to speak, as negative replicas of these seers, as is proved by all the archaic vocabulary relating to this field, which forms part of the common proto-Slav background. In later folk-lore witches turn into birds and in this guise quench their thirst on human blood. The souls of the dead might return as vampires; so people defended themselves against them by disinterring the dead and either burning them or thrusting a wedge of alder wood

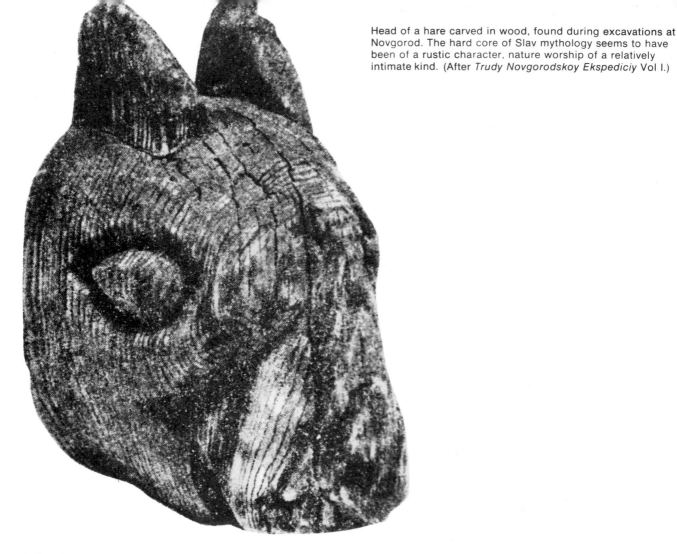

Head of a hare carved in wood, found during excavations at Novgorod. The hard core of Slav mythology seems to have been of a rustic character, nature worship of a relatively intimate kind. (After *Trudy Novgorodskoy Ekspediciy* Vol I.)

right through them. Other demi-demons hostile to men inhabited the wind and the clouds.

On the other hand, a general sense of friendship, not only among Russian Slavs, but also among the western and southern branches of their family, extended to the familiar little demons, who were either the souls of their forebears or, alternatively, domestic spirits. They were given offerings and food, and people prayed to them. In Russia they were called *khoromozitel*, then *domovoi, domovik;* in medieval Poland, *uboze,* to which reference is made in a fifteenth-century sermon as well as in popular beliefs.

Demons from the souls of people who met a premature death, especially those of unmarried girls unacquainted with pleasure, or those who died under tragic circumstances, envied the living their continued existence in this world of joy and sunshine. The expression that all Slavs used for this type of spirit was *nav*, and it is found at the three extremes of the Slav world: in Russia, Bulgaria and Slovenia.

In the fifteenth century John Dlugosz, a venerable canon from Cracow, applied his zeal to rebuilding the Polish pantheon in the likeness of Greek and Roman gods with the aid of a series of archaic expressions and old patronyms. Unfortunately, he drew more readily from his own imagination than from the mythological data concerning the ancient Polish people. After critical analysis of his text there is very little left of his list of gods on which one can rely; of those who may survive the test, there is Nyia, whom Dlugosz calls 'the Polish Pluto'; in all probability Nyia

had more modest beginnings, rather similar to those of the *nav* in other Slav communities; in other words, he was a spirit of deceased souls. Also forming part of this group were the spirits of girls who died before marriage, and they were embodied in the *rusalki* (undines). In the Balkans this name was taken from *pascha rosarum*, the Rosalia, an ancient festival of the dead, but it also covered autochthonous beliefs, including, in Russia, belief in nymphs of a similar type called the *bereguini* (from *bereg*, river-bank) and, in Poland, the *boginki*, snatchers of newborn babes, who left their own deformed offspring behind instead (*odmience*, changed ones). Water-spirits (*topielce*) and undines dwelt in the lakes, and even in the nineteenth century on the shores of the lakes of Augustow people sacrificed chickens to them.

The spirits of the forest did not originate in the bodies of men; however, on occasion they knew how to assume human shape, or to disguise themselves as werewolves; they were more like woodland fauna, and would appear before travellers only to lead them astray, for they actually reigned beneath the foliage. Spirits called *vila* dwelt among Slav tribes in the south, and the fact that their name is mentioned in Russian homilies is some proof of their existence, though no further details are given. They were beautiful naked girls who charmed shepherds and young boys, sometimes appearing as swans or falcons, horses or wolves. Sometimes they lived in woods, mountains or clouds, and brought forth rain and hail or whirlwinds, but they were also helpful to man.

413

An anthropomorphic creature, the *poludnitsa-przypoludnica,* who is familiar to Czech, Lusatian, Slovak, Polish and Russian ethnologists, wanders—like the *daemon meridianus* found all over Europe—through the fields in summer, occasionally killing men and appearing in the whirling gusts of wind that come before storms.

Another mythological type that is equally well known across the length and breadth of Europe is that of the spirits of human fatality, and Russians, Croats and Slovenes provide best proof of their existence. In Russia, they are called Rod and Rozanitsa; in Croatia Rodienitsa. These are deities connected with the birth of man. Even in twelfth-century Russia it was forbidden to offer them honey, bread or cheese. The Czechs called these spirits *sudicki,* literally demons of fortune, of that which is destined and meted out to man (*soud,* judgment). Human fate (*dola*) was likewise embodied in the figure of a pro-

tective spirit who might none the less prove to be negligent or hostile on occasion. He had his preferences—for example, for commerce or agriculture—and if the career that a man chose went against fortune's own inclinations the result was not a happy one. The *dola* appeared in the guise of a man or woman, god, cat or mouse.

The Slavs were interested in natural phenomena and gave pride of place to the concept of fertility. It was entitled to embodiment in demonological form: the *spor.* This spirit watched over the growth of corn in the fields and of cattle in the stable; every family sought its presence among them. Death appeared to men as a woman dressed in white; they sought to trick her and sometimes succeeded in duping her. For the Slav, the outside world—sky, fire, earth, water, clouds, rainbow (dragon drinking water), quadrupeds, reptiles (serpent, spirit of the hearth)—provided substance for demonological beliefs, which

A small gold figure of a bull, perhaps excavated from a barrow. The Slavs found evidence for their demonological beliefs in the natural world around them. *S.C.R.*

Phallic divinity of the twelfth century found in a well in the fort of Leczyca, central Poland. Fertility was one of the chief aspects of nature worshipped by the Slavs. *Archaeological Museum, Lodz*

had their roots deep in the archaic night of time, though in some instances they have remained current down to our own time. Their cult was celebrated in the open air around trees that were either particularly old or had some peculiarity of shape; prayers were offered to them in wooded groves at the foot of great boulders. The invocations were accompanied by public ritual—banquets, prophecies and offerings—for instance, the first crop was offered to ensure a plentiful harvest. Even in the fourteenth century, in the valley of the Isonzo, the Slovene population worshipped a tree and the spring at its foot, just as their brothers at Szczecin had done two hundred years earlier.

It would appear that they were more willing to renounce gods who were personified as idols than the worship of trees, sacred woods, springs, stones and hills.

If the Slavs seem not to have quite such a rich mythological imagination as other races, the fault does not lie entirely with the somewhat late and fragmentary evidence at our disposal; their pantheon was set up quite late, and it enjoyed favourable conditions for development for only a short time; it represented the cult of nature rather than Manichean tradition. The latter found expression in the personification of lesser spirits, which retained their connection with magic and peopled the Slav household. There too, however, embodiments of the different manifestations of nature had precedence over other sources of belief; vegetation-demons were the most numerous, and the attitude of the people towards them was more often expressed in a confident faith in their help than in fear. Perhaps it is permissible to repeat here the opinion of an expert: 'People like to use shortened versions of their names when praying to their gods: the Slav rose to face his god filled not so much with compunction as with childish love, somewhat tinged with flattery . . . .'

Nature worship fitted in best with his particular inclinations, allied, as it was to a pan-demonism *sui generis* and a highly developed knowledge of magic, but he was equally capable of organising more advanced cults as social and political exigencies became clear. When these latter were taken from him and replaced by a thousand times more powerful pantheon, being of Christian origin, he kept for his own daily use the great realm of magic, and enriched it with new additions; he carefully preserved the practices of his ancestors, finding in them a means of satisfying his deep psychic needs, both individual and family, and even social needs arising out of rural life.

Carved stone statue from the Ketrzyn district. Though
nominally controlled by the Teutonic Order, little impression
was made on the underlying culture in the Baltic lands other
than in eastern Prussia. The old cults persisted in the remote
districts. in some places until the Reformation. Masurian
Museum at Olsztyn, Poland. *M. Kaczyriski*

BALTIC LANDS: NATURE WORSHIP

Medieval Balts were divided into three main groups: the first occupied Prussia, the second Lithuania, and the third Latvia. In fact these groups were composed of smaller tribes, and the ethnic character of certain of these tribes was transitional between the three main groups.

In the west the Prussians reached as far as the mouth of the Vistula and were separated from the Poles by the wooded plateaus of their lakelands; the south-east limit of their habitat, a country called Yatvingia (or Sudovia), adjoined Russian territory. To the east of the Prussians, beyond the Niemen, was the land of the Lithuanians and the related tribes of the Samogitians; farther to the north, beyond the western Dvina, the Latvian colony began, and it stretched in a northerly direction to the rivers Sede and Aa, on whose farther banks were Finno–Ugrian races, their nearest neighbours being the Estonians.

The origins of Baltic races are lost in the night of time. Certain linguists presume that together with their neighbours they formed a Balto-Slav community. Archaeology has supplied information indicating that the settlement of Balto-Slav, if not just Baltic, races on the south-east shores of the Baltic Sea was noted way back in the Bronze Age—from about 1300 B.C. Written sources dating from the first century A.D. contain the earliest information concerning these tribes, and these increase in number in the course of the early Middle Ages. It seems that the Prussians did not cross the course of the Pasleka (Passarge) in a westerly direction until the sixth century, and then they reached the Vistula and occupied territories that had previously belonged to the Slavs. At the beginning of the Middle Ages there were more important changes in the eastern frontiers of Baltic races.

The latter showed great strength and energy, and wherever it was possible tried to organise political entities similar to those being formed by their neighbours. However, they were overtaken in this race by Russian and Polish states, which had great power even in the tenth century. This fact put a brake on their efforts to create their own state. Finally, in the twelfth and thirteenth centuries, when the Prussians had succeeded in bringing their social and political schemes to maturity, they were wiped out by the Teutonic Order, which obtained the complete submission of these regions between 1233 and 1285, devastating the whole of Prussian territory with fire and slaughter.

However, even in the fifteenth century the Prussian population outnumbered the German element. In the fifteenth and sixteenth centuries we notice a sharp decline in the use of the original Prussian language, the last traces of which are recorded in the seventeenth century. The decay of Prussian customs, which came about as the rural population became more and more profoundly Christian, would appear to have played an important part in the loss of the original language spoken by the Prussian population. Prussian nobles rapidly assumed the new faith after their defeat and frequently made this gesture to ensure their right of entry as lay lords of the State of the Order. (The country districts, for their part, had to be satisfied with somewhat negligent evangelical activity on the part of the Teutonic bishops, with the exception of the bishopric of Warmia, and only German was spoken—not the native tongue.) But pagan ceremonies as well as animal sacrifices persisted in Prussia till the sixteenth century; paganism hidden away in villages and forests did not receive the death-blow until the Reformation.

A similar fate dogged the Latvian group for a number of centuries, for it was not able to create its own monarchy; and in the beginning of the thirteenth century it was subdued by the German missionary

Folk burial monuments made of painted wood. From the Klaipeda region, Stankiskai. (After Alsekaité Gimbutiené. *Die Bestattung in Hitauen in der vorgeschichtlichen Zeit*, Tübingen, 1946.)

states (those of the bishops and the Knights of the Sword, who shortly after joined the Teutonic Order). So the Latvian population turned Christian quite early, but the change went no deeper in their case than in that of the Prussians. It merely enabled them to keep their autochthonous beliefs in a form suited to the new conditions and also—because the Germanic colonists were more isolated in this region in the heart of the autochthonous rural population—to carry out a rescue operation for the Latvian language in the country areas under the domination of the German lords.

On the other hand, the Lithuanians had already created their own state half-way through the thirteenth century, and in the course of the fourteenth century it became highly dynamic, both expanding towards Russian territories and acquiring a strong monarchy under the aegis of a regular dynasty. In the year 1385 the Grand Duchy of Lithuania concluded a treaty of union with the kingdom of Poland, and in the following year accepted the Roman form of the Christian faith for the Lithuanian people, though in the east huge tracts of land were inhabited by Orthodox Russian populations.

Whereas the Lithuanian nobility was quite quickly converted, and particularly in the sixteenth century was subject to quasi-complete influence from Poland, the rural population remained faithful to their ancestral beliefs and language. Remnants of the ancient faith still survived to quite a large extent throughout the sixteenth century.

The late evangelisation of the Balts aroused in scholars the hope that they might have left clearer traces of pre-Christian beliefs than their neighbours, for they were the last pagans in Europe. This hope had already been expressed in the course of the Renaissance, when some interest was shown in the past history of the original Prussians, who had almost completely disappeared at that time, and also in the past history of the Latvians, Lithuanians and minor ethnic groups that still inhabited vast regions of Lithuania, Samogitia and Livonia. Unfortunately, it can be proved that our main sixteenth-century informants, both the German and Polish 'authorities' on the subject of early Prussian and Lithuanian paganism, allowed themselves to be carried away by their imagination as far as the religion of the Balts was concerned, and by inventions of their own inspired by Greek and Roman antiquity. The verification of Latvian beliefs brought better results. In the same way some valuable information was provided by the folk-lore of these tribes. But the imposing mythology, particularly of the Lithuanians, that was evolved during the Romantic period had to be set aside for good, and a much more modest image of the Baltic pantheon accepted. It fits in much more accurately with the slower rhythm of the social evolution of these peoples compared with that of the Slavs and Scandinavians.

Early Prussian gods

During the Middle Ages all the Baltic peoples were agricultural and so the cult of nature was observed everywhere and attracted the attention of Christians in foreign countries. According to the chronicler of the Teutonic Order, Peter of Dusburg (*c.* 1326), the Prussians did not know of God and worshipped the sun, moon, stars, thunder, birds, quadrupeds and even toads. So, although nature worship is the common property of many peoples, the Balts none the less differed from their Norse neighbours in their tendency towards zoolatry. Traces of these cults vanished soonest among Prussians, who were converted from the thirteenth century onwards, though not very effectively converted perhaps. However, in Latvia and in Samogitia certain features, such as the cult of serpents, persisted in native custom right up to the nineteenth century.

There is eloquent proof of the cult of fire. In Nadrovia, a Prussian province situated in the Pregola (Pregel) basin in the neighbourhood of Romowe, a perpetual flame was kept burning under the aegis of a priest called Criwe.

The sacred woods, fields, lakes and rivers were thought to be the dwelling-places of gods and demons; no trees were cut there, no grass scythed, no fish were caught and no water drunk. People had to avoid the river-banks, and all these places were carefully guarded against intruders, particularly foreigners.

Faith in an after-life was expressed not only by a highly developed ritual of cremation, but also by offerings to the shades of ancestors made in the cemeteries of the different clans, especially in autumn after the harvest. Even in the second quarter of the fifteenth century, the Bishop of Sambia, Bishop Michael, forbade the celebration of pagan burials, meetings in woods and forests at the foot of tombs, the organisation of solemn meals and sacrifices as well as the invocation of demons; and the punishment for infringement of his law was a whipping and fine. The souls of the dead visited homes, and they could, as the Polish chronicler Master Vincent explains (beginning of the thirteenth century), be changed into animals. Another thirteenth-century text quotes a widespread belief among Prussians that during cremation priests could see the dead man rise on horseback, armed and surrounded by other spirits, and fly up from the pyre on which his own body was burning towards heaven and the other world.

The sylvan and aquatic worlds were also full of spirits, and no doubt, as in Lithuania, they were given one and the same name — vele. Little dwarfs and gnomes (kaukis) were also familiar figures who protected the home, and there were also protective goddesses, laume; in the province of Natangia the mountain Laumygarbis was dedicated to them.

It is highly probable that in Prussia there were equally familiar deities who protected different objects and property, in other words protectors of the domestic hearth, cattle, horses, gardens, corn, roads, rivers and fish. In the 1547 Catechism there is a list of superstitions connected with the cult of trees, rivers, serpents, stones, Perkunas, Zempat (master of the earth) in his capacity of defender of cattle, and Laukosargas as guardian of the fields and corn; then follows a list of the collective gods worshipped — deivai, goddesses, kaukai, aitvarai, all kinds of demons, gnomes and winged spirits.

Some of them were perhaps the object of considerable local worship. In the thirteenth century there is a reference to Kurke (Curche), an agricultural deity who took the shape of the last sheaf to be cut in the cornfield and was the object of a special cult. This name is connected with the expression kurke referring to the grain-weevil, a parasite found in corn. During the harvest it would find a treacherous hiding-place in the last ears of grain. Then during the ensuing ceremonies an effort would be made to appease this demon, who could turn into a protective, kindly deity. We know of two other names, thanks to an account written by the Bishop of Warmia and dated 1418; these are Patoll and Natrimpe, but we still do not know what they mean. Prussian toponymy, as well as the 1547 Catechism already quoted, contains evidence of the cult of Perkunas, god of the thunderbolt, who is a familiar figure in sources relating to Lithuania.

This world, which is supernatural in its characteristics, invaded everyday life (certainly on feast-days and festivals) and political and economic life too by reason of its rites and prophecies. As for sacrifices, there is reliable information to show that animal sacrifices were offered to the gods: goats, oxen, trout and horses — all of which, if possible, had to be black in colour. Human sacrifice was also known to exist: lots were drawn for captured warriors. The gods took a third of the spoils of war — which was offered to the gods in the course of a public banquet (snike) accompanied by gaming and dancing and the consumption of hydromel. Church edicts were particularly vehement in their condemnation of such practices as these but as late as 1520, when enemy vessels chartered by the town of Danzig made their appearance on the rivers of Sambia, the local authorities allowed the Prussians to sacrifice a black ox to ward off the enemy. During the ceremony two barrels of beer were drunk. The vessels departed, true enough, for ghosts appeared before the eyes of the crews; but with them all the fish disappeared, and the offerer of the sacrifice then confessed that he had forgotten to make an exception in the case of the fish; to make reparation an extra sacrifice was offered of a black trout.

We know nothing about Prussian temples, except for the place of shelter where the perpetual fire burned. A priest known as Criwe, who has already been mentioned, summoned assemblies at Romowe not only of Prussian tribes, but also of other Baltic peoples, and he seems to have had a certain influence. The actual name Criwe undoubtedly comes from the bent stick carried by this representative of the high caste of sacrificial priests. Many Prussian chiefs are thought to have enjoyed sacred functions as well as political office; this is illustrated by the Russian chronicle of Volhynia in 1245, which refers to the chief of Yatvingia, Skomond, as 'an illustrious magician and a prophet'. As for the lesser intermediaries between gods and men, the treaty concluded in 1249 between the converted and the Teutonic Order speaks of 'tulissons' and 'ligassons' who composed hymns celebrating the deaths of illustrious men.

Sources are as silent on the subject of the iconography of the gods as they are about temples. However, Prussian archaeology has brought to light on Prussian territory granite statues representing human figures, horn in hand and wearing a cone-shaped headdress. The strangest thing is that these stone statues look rather like other statues found in the Ukraine and even in central Asia. The size of these statues and the substance of which they are made make it impossible for them to have been imported, but so far no satisfactory explanation has been forthcoming as to how they originated in Prussia or which peoples owned them.

Lithuanian gods

The Lithuanian people, like their cousins the Prussians, remained faithful to the old beliefs for a long time. The first attempted baptism, in 1251, of the Duke Mindavgas (Mendog or Mindvog), who was subsequently crowned king, has been described by a Russian chronicler who did not approve of his Catholicism: 'Mindvog's baptism was hypocritical.

He continued to sacrifice to his gods secretly, to the first among them, Nonadey, and to Telavel, and to Diviriks, and to the hare-god, Meiden. When Mindvog was riding through the fields and a hare ran across his path, he would keep away from the undergrowth and take care not to break a single branch. And he sacrificed to his gods, and burned the bodies of the dead, and openly practised his paganism.'

After the final conversion of Lithuania, which the Grand Duke Iogailos (Jagellon) accomplished in 1385, paganism persisted among the ordinary people for two more centuries; the fact that the Polish priests working among the peasants were completely ignorant of the Lithuanian language favoured the continuation of the pagan faith.

An examination of the evidence of religious beliefs in Lithuania clearly reveals certain differences between it and the original Indo-European or Balto-Slav models which we know from the religious systems of the Slavs and other peoples of central and eastern Europe. Though it may not be surprising that the forces of nature rarely achieved full personification, we are bound to feel some surprise, in view of the slow pace at which the various social groups consolidated and were welded to the governing group, to find a slightly richer mythology, which moreover shows clear traces of foreign influence.

There is not a great deal of information on the subject of Lithuanian beliefs, it is true; a few valuable pieces of evidence from Russia in the thirteenth century, random scraps of information from the fifteenth century, and the treatise on the Lithuanian faith by Jacques Laskowski, which appeared about 1570 and provided abundant, picturesque, and yet confusing details that lent the author's personal touch to the whole subject. This completes the list of main sources of information.

It seems that pride of place among the individualised nature-gods was given to Perkunas, whose name is connected with the original Indo-European name for the oak (Latin *quercus*). In the preceding study of the role played by Perun in Slav and particularly in Russian mythology the reader's attention was drawn to the connection between the latter and Perkunas. Now one need only add that in Lithuania Perkunas was not only the tutelary deity of the heavens and the thunderbolt, but also of martial expeditions. On such occasions as these he gave Lithuanians his help by controlling nature—he would, for instance, make watercourses freeze up.

The list previously quoted of Duke Mindavgas' gods has in first place the name Nonadey, which has defeated all scholarly attempts at interpretation. On the other hand, the second name, Telavel, appears at an early stage—in the thirteenth century—in a myth worthy of attention: he was the celestial smith who forged the sun and put it in the skies. In the fifteenth century the missionary Jerome of Prague, 'having ventured into the heart of Lithuania—according to his own account—found a race that served the sun and observed the cult of an iron hammer of extraordinary size. When he asked the priests the meaning of this cult, they replied: at one time the sun was not seen for several months, for a very powerful king had captured it and imprisoned it in the most impregnable fortress. Later the signs of the zodiac helped the sun, breaking down the tower with a very large hammer; they freed the sun and gave it back to mankind; so this instrument is worthy of worship, for it gave light back to men.'

Even if we count the signs of the zodiac as one of the embellishments supplied by the scholarly Master Jerome, we must recognise the fact that this particular myth continued to enjoy popularity for several centuries. The centre of the solar cult in Slav countries was the sun itself; here, it is replaced by this smith-god. This leads us to the assumption that these are branches of Finnish belief. A smith called Ilmarinen (in Finnish, Kalevala) was also responsible for forging the sun. The iron hammers worshipped by Lithuanians may have corresponded to the thunderbolts with which the kindly gods used to break the grip of snow and ice in the spring. In modern Lithuanian folk-lore yet another idea of the sun appears (in Lithuanian the sun is feminine in gender: *saule*), and this is the concept of the sun as a young mother.

The idea of the deification of the rainbow appears in the name Diviriks, for it can be taken to mean 'divine rods', which was a common metaphor for the rainbow. Meiden, the hare-god, undoubtedly refers to the deity of forests and animals (*medinis*, wooded, sylvan). A goddess called Zvoruna is also known to have existed, and thirteenth-century Russian sources attribute the meaning 'bitch' to the name; the dog referred to would seem to be a hunter, which turned into a protector of animals and of the hunt itself. These names had faded into oblivion by the sixteenth century, although the habit persisted of addressing familiar spirits similar in type to the Roman *indigitamenta*.

These deities were the protectors of different phenomena connected with the home, fields, forests, agricultural development and hunting. Many of them lived in woods, trees and streams; they would freeze if the everlasting sacred flame went out.

Foreign observers have always stressed the fire-cult in Lithuania. The high altar in the Church of Saint Stanislas in the castle of Wilno (Vilna) was built in 1387 on the spot 'where they had burned the flame in the erroneous faith that it was eternal'. The fire that burned on the summit of the hill overlooking the River Niewiaza was regarded as the most sacred object in Samogitia; water was used to extinguish it in 1434, and the ashes were thrown into the river so that pagans would be unable to revive the flame. Priests were appointed to attend to these hearths, and they uttered their prophecies before the flames. Jerome of Prague stated that 'friends sought advice about those who were ill; they would draw near to the fire during the night, and in the morning they would assert that they had seen the shadow of the sick person near the sacred fire; as it warmed itself the shadow gave signs that were interpreted to mean the preservation of life or the approach of death'.

Apart from the sites of sacred fire, no mention has been made of any temples in Lithuania. Rites were celebrated in the open air, in sacred forests (alkas) that man had not sullied with his activities, at the foot of trees, especially oaks, near springs and large erratic blocks, worshipped as cult-centres. But priests were not the only ones who officiated at sacrifices; the Duke of Trakai (Troki), Kestutis (Kiefstut), personally slaughtered a red ox outside the tent of Louis of Anjou, king of Hungary, in Volhynia in 1351 and plunged his hands into the beast's blood crying: 'Cast thy glance upon this horned beast, O lord, and upon us.' Human sacrifice was also made of prisoners of war.

The cult of ancestors had been more effectively destroyed by the activities of the Roman Church in Lithuania than in Orthodox Belorussia. However, reminders of the cult occur in popular Lithuanian songs, in the form of traditions relating to the kingdom of the dead (vela)—a world shrouded in grey mist and cold—and these were extended to include forests. The service for the vela began with weeping over the corpse; then the deceased was reproached for abandoning his own kin. Even as late as the nineteenth century lamentations (rauda) took the form of a short piece of poetic prose, such as this of the wife bewailing her husband: 'O thou, my ploughman, my reaper, the sons of man are busy in the meadows, their scythes in their hands, and my child's sickle is eaten away with rust.' This also reveals traces of the cult of the vela, which Christianity could not destroy. We find again in the words of the widow beseeching her dead parents-in-law: 'O, take hold of the white hands of my husband. O, stand him before the gates of the vela. O, open the gates of the vela, for we are the first, we are more cunning. O, open the gates of the vela. O, seat him on the bench of the vela, in the row for which he is destined.'

The drama of death found another mythological form which accounts for the custom of cremation. This myth was extensively developed, but it too seems to have been borrowed from the Finns. It is worth quoting it direct from the thirteenth-century Russian text:

'Sovi was a man. When he had captured a wild pig he removed nine spleens from it and gave them to his sons to roast; the latter ate them. And he grew terribly angry with them and was tempted to go down to hell. He failed to pass through the eight gates, and it was only through the ninth that he accomplished his purpose, with the aid of the son (who showed him the way). When the other brothers irritably reproached the latter, he gently disengaged himself and said

beseechingly: "I shall go and find my father again." And he went down to hell. When the father had supped in his company he made a bed for him and buried him in the earth. The next day, when he had risen, the father asked him if he had rested well, but he groaned: "Oh! Worms and reptiles have eaten me." On the second day, the father gave him supper, then put him in a hollow tree and made his bed there. The next day he asked him (the same thing), but the son replied: "Countless bees and mosquitoes have stung me. Oh! I have slept badly!" The following day the father made a huge pyre, and threw his son into the brazier; the next day he asked if he had rested well; the latter replied: "I slept as peacefully as an infant in its cradle."'

In Lithuania there was much pomp surrounding the cremation of the dead. The remains of the Great Duke Algirdas (Olgierd), who died at the end of May 1377, were burned along with eighteen saddle-horses. His body was clad in a robe of purple brocade and an overmantle studded with pearls and precious stones clasped with a gold and silver belt.

In Lithuanian households they worshipped spirits of the hearth, which assumed the shape of serpents. 'Each peasant,' so Master Jerome recounts, 'in some corner of his house had a serpent asleep on some hay, which he fed (on milk) and to which he made offerings.' Lithuanian people shared with the whole of Europe a belief in demons, witches (lauma, deiva, ragana) and werewolves. They also believed in the fairies of fate (laima) who appear in a popular song of modern times first written down in the last century: 'Harken, harken to these marvels! The pool froze in summer, no horse could be watered there, no bucket washed, but one day laima brought forth the sun....'

The last active phase of belief, which was described in 1570, testifies to the disintegration of the ancient system under foreign influence. Beneath this influence, if one seeks below the surface, the characteristics of the ancient system can still be traced throughout that vast world peopled by little demons: here we find Aitvaras, who was known to the Prussians—a brave little demon who brought good fortune to the master of the house, he would find shelter behind the big stove in the cottage or barn; food used to be left for him: flour, corn, hay, milk. Another spirit called Pusait, who lived in the woods, used to hide under lilac-bushes and was attended by little dwarfs (kaukis) whom he would send to the Lithuanians to bring him bread, beer and cooked dishes. Only when the Jesuit missionaries intensified their attempts at evangelisation at the end of the sixteenth and the beginning of the seventeenth century did they finally rout the last of the Lithuanian demons, who had till then lain low in Samogitia.

As far as the major gods are concerned, it is stated that they did not form a definite pantheon. Before the Lithuanian monarchy could apply itself to the task of bringing order to bear on the hosts of deities of all kinds, Christianity had caught up with it. Even in the thirteenth century Christianity seemed the best weapon against religious disunity, and by 1386 it had brought the results expected by the Lithuanian state.

Latvian gods

The Latvians were converted at the beginning of the thirteenth century, but obstinately held to the customs and language of their ancestors, in spite of the pressures of foreign rule. The progress of the Church was greater and swifter along the coastal strip and on the shores of the Dvina (Davgas), but in the centre and towards the east the remains of paganism persisted until the seventeenth century, to the great astonishment of Catholic and Protestant clergy.

Missionaries found no major gods there. But an old man questioned in 1606 by Jesuits—who asked him how many gods there were—replied: 'There are different gods according to the diversity of people, places and needs. We have one god who reigns over the heavens, we have yet another who rules earth; the latter, who is the greatest on earth, has other gods of lesser importance at his command. We have one god who gives us fish; another game; we have one god for corn, for the fields, for gardens, for cattle—that is to say, for horses, cows and other domestic animals. The sacrifices made to them differ too: to some the offerings are larger, to others smaller, according to the rank of the gods concerned, and all these offerings are made to certain trees and certain woods. These trees are said to be sacred. To the god of horses—who is called Deving Usching—each person offers two pieces of earth and two loaves of bread, and throws a piece of bacon on to the fire. To Moschel, the god of cows, butter, milk and cheese are offered, and if a cow falls ill, someone rapidly makes an offering to the trees, and it gets better. To the god of fields and corn, the Deving Cerklicing, at certain times they sacrifice a black ox in the woods, or a black chicken or a black piglet and some barrels of beer, a little more, a little less, according to circumstance and the degree to which this god Cerklicing has helped them.'

The deities who accompanied the Latvians from the cradle to the grave had highly specialised functions: Laima, the one destined by fate, presided over childbirth; Delka cradled the newborn child; different gods were in charge of flowers, fish, languor, wealth, rivers, wells, gardens, fields, wind and forest. There were the patrons of huntsmen, fishermen, sailors. Their names are a simple combination of the word *mate* (mother, wife) and their activity: Laukamat (mother of the field), Mezamat (mother of the wood), Lopemat (mother of cattle), Jurasmat (mother of the sea), Darzamat (mother of the garden), Vejamat (mother of the wind).

They had to make sure of the good will of all these little gods by means of offerings left on stones partially hidden in the earth. These rites were observed under oak-trees for men, lime-trees for women, but they could equally take the form of collective sacrifices. At crossroads a goat used to be sacrificed in honour of wolves, as protection against the anger of the woodman—or god of woods: Mezavirs or Mezadevs. On feast-days in October and November it was a good thing to leave food in the spot where one bathed (*pirts*), which was carefully swept out for the occasion, or else in the barn; this was left for the souls of the dead and one uttered the words: 'We have served you according to our means, leave us in peace till the new year.' In the courtyard or on the threshold the Latvian would arrange 'an extra place' (*atameschenes viete*), and there on a little flat stone he would throw the remains of meals and drinks, for the familiar spirit who lived under the earth.

Linguistic analysis has shown that several of these gods' names are not really Latvian in origin; it would seem that, in order to translate archaic, autochthonous phenomena, foreign terms were sometimes borrowed and used, such as this Deving Usching from the Russian *usien*, which, moreover, was in itself of obscure (Finnish) origin, or Moschel, which seems to be a diminutive of Mary.

Popular songs in our own time still speak, if concisely, of sons of god and daughters of the sun, but it is difficult to attach a mythological meaning to these traces of poetry, though one must concede that Latvian song (*zinge, dzisma*) retained a much more apparent tendency to personify nature than did Lithuanian song.

Thus in Baltic myth the characteristics of a world possessing a divine hierarchy are rarely conferred on the whole field of supernatural powers. For the most part they are merely shapeless and anonymous incarnations of the forces of nature; deities with limited and temporary powers, which elsewhere—in Greece, for example—were in some cases promoted to the rank of major gods, or else, as in Rome, lived for a long time with the latter in the *indigitamenta* of the pontiffs.

So one can deduce from this the importance that the study of Baltic beliefs could have for the history of comparative religion; to us they seem like the primitive phase, in which the transparently obvious meaning of divine names, and the functional names applied to forces which man regarded as supernatural not only prevented a fusion of different divine functions, but also stopped mythological anecdotes forming. Attempts to create a hierarchy— for example, in the case of the eminent position held by Perkunas—were balked by Christianity; the latter, in Baltic countries as elsewhere, absorbed and triumphed over gods more easily than it suppressed and overcame demons, minor gods and spirits dwelling in nature and in the home.

FINLAND-UGRIA: MAGIC ANIMALS

It is difficult to obtain a clear idea of Uralian mythology in the period when the Uralian peoples still formed a unit. They must have begun to disperse about the beginning of the fourth millennium before Christ. The Samoyeds seem to have separated from the parent stem about this time. A thousand years later the Ugrians (ancestors of the Hungarians, Voguls and Ostiaks) in their turn left the other Finno-Ugrian peoples, who continued to disintegrate slowly and were still doing so in the centuries immediately preceding our own era.

Moreover, as the testimony left by Uralian languages is of late date, we have only very brief information about the mythological past of these tribes. The evidence provided by foreign observers is not entirely trustworthy, and even this is meagre and usually comparatively recent. Furthermore, the Uralians maintained more or less constant contact with many other peoples: Indo-Europeans and Turks, for example. Directly or by the intervention of certain tribes, they were aware even in very early times of beliefs current among peoples far distant from themselves, and they either appropriated or adapted these. And so it is not surprising that each race of Uralian origin developed its own more or less composite mythology. From now on we must try to reconstruct the original mythological concepts by means of comparison and with the aid of linguistics, archaeology and other sciences.

There is no study in existence at present that treats all the various mythologies of the Uralian-speaking peoples. Researchers have been able to do little better than outline a few partial hypotheses here and there on some particular aspect of this mythology.

However, by isolating what appear to be the most ancient features of the beliefs of all these peoples, whose languages go back to the original Uralian, the following essential points can be determined:

The Uralians must have had some knowledge of Shamanism. Evidence taken from the Samoyeds, Lapps, ancient Finns, Voguls, Ostiaks and even the ancient Hungarians all points quite positively to this fact. All these peoples believed in the power of sorcerers, who followed certain procedures and performed certain rites in order to enter into communication with spirits from both heaven and hell. These sorcerers were perhaps recruited from those of privileged lineage and were invested with supernatural powers. They could leave their own bodies and fly up into the sky or down below the earth. They could also be embodied in different animals: birds, serpents or magic stags, for example. They could hide inside sea-monsters. They were able to discover the cause of illness and effect a cure by acting on the evil spirit responsible. They interpreted the wishes of the spirits of the dead and also of the various demons present in nature. They were seers, and their particular province was occult knowledge, which made them invincible or invulnerable.

The instrument used by the shaman was a sacred drum decorated with cabalistic signs, which he struck with a sort of beater in the shape of a spoon. The officiant himself finally fell into a trance in a state of virtually total catalepsy, though he usually obtained this effect by swallowing toadstools.

Shamanism is not native to the Uralians. It is found in analogous if not identical guise among other peoples, more particularly throughout Siberia, notably the Tungus and Kets (Ostiaks of the Yenisei).

The sorcerers had their own hierarchy. They were not all equal in power. Only recently the Tavguis Samoyeds and those of Yenisei made distinction between three grades of sorcerer. Only those of the highest grade used the drum and knew how to raise or detect spirits.

Uralian mythology must have reflected the concepts that animated Shamanism.

As far as one can reconstruct the basic outline, the principal myths dealt with the following subjects.

First there was the myth regarding or explaining the creation of the world. The traditions that have come down to us basically describe the creation of the firm earth, and these mythical accounts of the creation of this earth, which is the abode of men and animals, presume that men and at least some animals were already in existence, as well as certain spirits. In essence the Finnish myth is simply this: there was water everywhere, and an eagle flew over it looking out for a dry spot to lay its eggs. Suddenly it caught sight of the knee of the sorcerer Vainamoinen protruding above the water. The bird took it to be a strip of firm earth and laid its egg there. She then sat on the egg. But the magician sleeping in the water woke up because he felt his knee burning. He stirred. He moved his leg and caused the half-hatched eagle's egg to fall into the water. It broke and the yolk formed the moon and the sun, and the pieces of shell made the firm earth and the stars.

The Samoyed Yuraks in their account tell of the supreme god, Num, who wondered one day if any part of the earth were visible, although he could see only water. He sent several birds in succession to explore the watery depths until one of them, a diver-bird, returned with a small fragment from the bottom in its beak. Num made a floating island of it, which he slowly consolidated and extended in ways that vary from one account to another. The Voguls and Ostiaks have a similar tale which included elements of obviously later date. In short, what emerges from all these legends is that the creation is not conceived to be the very beginning of the universe. The appearance of the firm earth is the first thing to be described. But a limitless stretch of water, sometimes with overlying fog and mist, precedes the earth. The creation of birds is not mentioned separately; they exist at the same time as their creator and help him in his work. As for human beings, we do not know how Uralians imagined them to have come about, for accounts vary in this respect. Usually it is a question of a man and a woman who beget children after various episodes involving certain animals and relatively evil spirits.

These various discrepancies and gaps are indubitably due to the incomplete traditions handed down to us, and perhaps also to the fact that Uralians never succeeded in developing a homogeneous concept of creation. The uninitiated must have had quite a different concept of it from that held by sorcerers who had occult knowledge.

Whatever the variation of detail, creation is not shown to have been achieved all at once. Another very widespread myth recalls a time when the universe was plunged in darkness because neither sun nor moon nor stars as yet shone in the sky. That is when a hero, whose description varies from one tradition to another, comes 'to deliver' the sun, the moon and the stars in order to put them in their familiar places. This 'liberation' is depicted as a perilous enterprise, rather like that of Prometheus or the labours of Heracles. The hero who brings liberation, and who is often a very tiny person, surmounts the difficulties in the way of his mission. He gets the stars of light back from a monster who has concealed them in his body, or goes for them to a mountain, or under water or underground. Pursued by evil spirits from whom he has snatched the stars, the hero frees himself from them by various magic devices. He throws them a

drop of liquid, which becomes an impenetrable sea or river, he drops a stone, which becomes an enormous mountain (often quoted as the Ural mountains). This myth is often combined with tales explaining eclipses of the sun or moon. In such cases there is said to be a monster who has devoured the sun or moon and these stars of light must be won back from him. This monster is often conceived as a giant, an incarnation of the North, land of darkness and cold.

There is a third mythical cycle related to the above, and this tells of the conflict with the evil power living in the North, a power depicted either in the guise of a woman (in Finnish tradition) or a wicked giant (by the Samoyed Yuraks). This deity of the North (and of the land of dark and cold) has a magic instrument on which the prosperity of men depends. An expedition sets off to gain possession of this talisman, for the ownership of it is at the root of agriculture, or, more generally speaking, of abundance. In Finnish tradition the talisman in question was given the name of *sampo* (this is the form in which it figures in the *Kalevala* of Elias Lonnrot). Naturally the deity of the North, in whatever form he is depicted, reacts to his aggressors, and this gives rise to fabulous battles the outcome of which varies from instance to instance.

As the mythical motifs become interlaced and are superimposed on one another, it is difficult to discern what springs from any one particular cycle. The Finnish *sampo* has often been associated with the concept of the column supporting the universe. It seems apparent that the Uralians believed that the sky was supported by columns or a single column. This supposition arises from the fact that cult-centres both among Samoyeds and Lapps are generally situated on heights, even on mountains. Otherwise the cult took place in sacred woods containing the Tree of Life, which may have been a symbol for the column supporting the firmament. The Finnish explorer T. Lehtisalo has commented on a sacred mountain-top in the Urals that bears the name of *minis'ei*, meaning in Samoyed Yurak, 'the bearer', and he points out that Samoyeds think that upright stones and mountain-peaks are supports for the universe.

Similarly, experts in Lapp history have pointed out that these nomads worshipped isolated stones pointing up to the sky, and so placed them in order that they might support the world. But it must be recognised that Lapp terminology is of Norse origin and that they might have acquired this concept of the column supporting the world from Germanic peoples. One has only to recall the Irminsul column destroyed by Charlemagne during the war against the Saxons at Eresburg in 772.

It would appear that the 'column' supporting the universe was thought to be the pivot round which the earth turned, and this accounted for changes in the position of the stars at different times of the day and night. There were mythical stories to explain the origin of this: it had been built by a prodigiously clever smith, and it had to be kept in a good state of repair, otherwise the universe might collapse and the firmament fall and crush the surface of the earth. The pole-star was presumed to be the top of the sacred column. The sky revolved around this star.

T. Lehtisalo, the Finnish explorer, has reported that the Samoyed Yuraks, amongst whom he lived, look on the central pole in their tents (*simsi*) as an emblem of this same column supporting the universe, and the shamans made it the object of certain rites, especially after the death of one of the tent's inhabitants. Certain ceremonies are performed in which the ascent to heavenly regions takes place *via* this column, and at such times the hole in the top of the tent represents the opening in the firmament through which the enchanter can reach the sky to go and look for the spirits that dwell there. It is worth noting in passing that the Samoyeds, for example, imagine the sky to be a series of stratified layers. The 'seven skies' are frequently mentioned in magic chants, and mythical heroes take wing to the 'seventh sky'.

In the esoteric knowledge of the shamans the pole-star must have represented a pivot round which the firmament revolved. Popular traditions reflect this idea here and there. The constellations were located by reference to the position of the pole-star, which was thought to be fixed.

The vault of heaven reached its highest point in the precincts of this star. Then it got lower and lower in concentric circles until it touched the earth on the horizon. Certain accounts claim that it was not always so. In the beginning of things there was a time when the sky was not very high up above the heads of men. It was no higher than the top of the tent or hut in which men lived. It was easy to communicate with the sky or celestial deities through the opening left in the top of the tent. This was an advantageous situation, which made it easier to obtain the favour of kindly spirits. But according to certain legends it would appear that one day a woman complained that smoke or mist had got into the hut unnecessarily, and this angered the spirits on high, who then sent a giant or some other mythical creature to lift the sky and raise it to its present height. This memorable event marked the point at which men found it necessary to have spirits or sorcerers to intercede between themselves and celestial deities.

On the far horizon the sky met the earth and it was so low that only birds and tiny creatures had room to stand beneath this ceiling that would have crushed men of normal height. Tradition, particularly Finnish tradition, imagined these dwarfs to be like pygmies who hunted birds with bows and arrows.

The lands on the edge of the horizon, especially to the south, were those to which birds migrated in autumn to return only when spring reappeared. It was thought that birds of passage took the majestic path across the sky from south-east to north-west, in other words the Milky Way.

But other explanations of this corridor of stars were preferred. People thought they could make out the trunk and branches of a huge tree that had fallen across the sky. It was said to have been a giant oak, which had grown so tall that it cut off the light of the sun, moon and stars. The clouds had ceased to move in celestial space because they got caught in the branches of the monstrous tree. At this point a tiny creature emerging from the sea or from under the earth was said to have approached the trunk and to have struck it with a gold or copper hatchet. The tree fell, obstructing a whole portion of the sky but leaving the sun, moon and stars clear, and they began to follow their courses once more and the clouds were also able to move about again in the sky.

Most accounts make no mention of the origin of this tree. In popular Finnish poetry, where this tree is called *iso tammi*, 'the great oak', it is said to have been planted by three girls, three fiancées. And it was felled, according to the same tradition, by a sort of Tom Thumb who emerged from the sea, a tiny, black figure, strong enough, however, to chop down the tree with a single stroke of his little axe.

An analogous myth has left ethnologists in some perplexity. It refers to another monstrous animal, ox or giant stag, which, according to certain versions, was also struck down by a tiny man who suddenly emerged from the sea. This is the Finnish legend of the 'great ox' (*iso harka*). Some attempt has been made to see in this an allusion to the Great Bear, or even to the aurora borealis, which would mean that it was an etiological myth. But we do not know whether it really goes so far back in time or whether the Uralians knew of it, for it may have been a late legend peculiar to the Finns.

Other tales thought to relate to celestial phenomena include those of hunting the great stag, or the magic reindeer or the magic elk. A particularly skilful hunter set off in pursuit of an animal of enormous proportions, which fled after raiding and destroying men's herds. The hunter caught up with it, but at the last moment it reared up and escaped. The hunter has been taken to be a personification of the pole-star, and the stag or elk of the Great Bear.

People have in fact interpreted this constellation as representing one of the cervine species, for, according to legend, elks, stags or reindeer (it varied according to the region) originally had six feet so they could run very quickly, so quickly, indeed, that they could easily escape hunters. Several tales tell how the animal in question fell to the ground and lost two of its feet, so that huntsmen were then able to overtake it and kill it.

Speaking generally, constellations were regarded as animals that had been taken up to the sky, and the elk was a particular favourite, for among certain Uralian-speaking peoples it seems to have been the object of special worship.

The Pleiades also seem to have captured the imagination of Uralian-speaking peoples. The Voguls regarded them as a monstrous elk that had taken refuge high up in the sky in order to escape a pursuing hunter who wanted to cut off two of its feet.

This same hunter left the marks of his skis in the sky, and this is the Milky Way—the path followed by migratory birds. In other versions the Milky Way is formed by the tracks of game fleeing from the celestial hunter.

The sky as such was the abode of certain deities. All peoples of Finno-Ugrian or Uralian tongue have a sky-god in the historical period: Num in the case of the Samoyed Yuraks, Torum for the Voguls, Jumala for the Finns. It seems that this deity was not unique in the beginning, but had others around him who were usually depicted as his children and descendants, mostly sons and grandsons. These celestial deities dwelt in a place of light. Samoyed legend goes so far as to specify that the sky-god is made of fire, so the sight of him is more than human eyes can bear. There may be some confirmation of this tradition if, as certain theorists propose, one must ultimately regard the name of the Finnish sky-god Jumala as a radical word, originally meaning 'brightness, light'. Uralians would appear to have thought of sky-gods as beings of light inhabiting the firmament among the bright stars.

It is probable that this myth was associated with the sun cult. In fact rites were performed facing the east; similarly the bodies of the dead were made to face the east, in other words pointing towards the rising sun.

The moon cult bequeathed a legend of a 'man in the moon' to many traditions. The tale is the same almost everywhere: a thief, either man or woman, was disturbed by moonlight. In order to put out this round light, he tried to paint over the disc, but remained stuck there; and on bright, moonlit nights his shape is still visible, outlined against the moon.

Other spirits also make their home in their sky in addition to the official sky-gods: these are the spirits of thunder, who are particularly irritable. Yuraks imagine the sound of thunder to be the noise made by these spirits fighting the 'bull of the North' ('bull' here refers to a male reindeer or elk). Samoyeds believed that these thundering creatures had only a single hand, one leg and one eye.

The concept of thunder was undoubtedly modified by other concepts acquired from foreign sources. Finns and, generally speaking, western Finno-Ugrians imagined the god of thunder to be an old man dressed in blue who pursued the evil spirits engendered by suffocating heat. The god of thunder shot his arrows at the enemies he met. These arrows fell to earth and became stones; the discovery of these stones brought protection to their owner. But throughout western Finno-Ugrian territory the cult of the Norse god Thor seems to have impinged on ancestral traditions of thunder, and the symbol of the god of thunder became the hammer he used to strike his adversaries.

On the confines of earth there was a great whirl-pool, which swallowed up any fishermen who were unwise enough to draw near. This great whirlpool was the gulf that led to the underwater empire of the spirit of the waters. This spirit lived among its own kind in a mountain on the sea-bed. This is often portrayed as a veritable town where everything happens just as on earth, but the creatures there differ from human beings in ways that vary from one tradition to another.

Naturally spirits also haunted the waters of lakes and rivers. Sometimes, in certain dark lakes or darker stretches of rivers, tradition went so far as to stipulate the existence of two beds. If a fisherman did not take certain precautions, then the fish escaped through holes of varying sizes to the lower bed.

Communication between earth and hell took place on the confines of earth or through caves in certain mountains. The way into the underground world was usually found at the mouth of a river that gave into the ocean of ice. To get there one had to follow the river downstream. When the shaman or mythical hero reached the lower world he found that the river-water flowed back against the stream. This was an attempt to explain why streams never ceased to flow. Their source was nothing more nor less than the spot at which the water emerged from the subterranean world to flow again through the world of the living. The lower land was dark. It was lit only by the moon. But a more ancient tradition inferred that the dead took a spare sun and moon with them to hell, which indicates that hell had no light of its own. On house-shaped tombs a sun and moon were depicted for the dead person's use—to light his way where there was nothing but darkness.

In the underworld some earthly conditions were reversed. Infernal beings walked with their feet in the air, and turned to the left instead of to the right. In other respects Uralians must have imagined that infernal life proceeded under the same conditions as terrestrial life. Everything happened in the same way. The subterranean empire was usually ruled by a fairly powerful deity who governed the dead and, more especially, the vast numbers of spirits living underground. They were the spirits that caused sickness and death. Even so, the decisions of life and death were not taken by underground spirits, however powerful. The sky-god decided the duration of human life. That is why man could defend himself against sickness by subjugating the bad spirits or conciliating them, but he was forced to submit to the sovereign word and death-sentence of the celestial god.

The Yuraks thought that the 'support' or 'bearer' of the earth was to be found in hell. He was an old man who held the world in his hand. But he had grown tired and his hand trembled, and this threatened the balance of the earth. It moved and swayed, which was perhaps a way of accounting for earthquakes. To obtain some relief the old man summoned two men (usually brothers) and he changed one into a prop or 'foot' of the universe, while the other became the 'weight' of the earth. And so the world was saved from downfall and destruction. Another version (again of Yurak origin) takes into account a famous shaman who seems to have gone up into the sky to Num. The latter sent him below earth to Nga, god of death and hell, and he married the latter's daughter. His function was then to hold the earth in his hand, and he was called 'the Old Man of the Earth'.

Once the dead had followed the course of the river as far as the opening in the great whirlpool they finally reached the empire of the dead. There they crossed several watercourses (generally three), guided by a bird. They had to surmount different obstacles, the nature of which varied from one tradition to another, before they came to their place of residence. We do not know whether this was assigned to them or who was responsible. It is impossible to disentangle the pristine version from the details imposed by later foreign traditions. However, there is little reason for presuming that there was any sort of judgment or rite of admission. On the other hand, recently noted superstitions lead one to think that people may have imagined the abode of the dead to be under the cemetery where the actual tombs were. These, as far as one can make out from the discoveries of ethnologists, must have consisted of quite vast abodes built in relatively close imitation of human dwellings. It is possible that people believed that the dead continued to live a life very like the one they had known on earth under the very soil where their tombs had been raised. As far as one can tell from the rites observed in modern times, the cemeteries of the dead were quite close to the clan's dwellings. Each clan had its own cemeteries. Thus the dead were still with their families and could continue in after-life the existence they had known on earth.

However, as far as we know, this was not eternal. After a comparatively brief period there was a second death. This could be immediate if the deceased person ceased to receive sacrifices of food from the living, on whom it was incumbent to perform this duty. This premature death in after-life brought individual or collective misfortune on those left on earth. But even at best those who had gone down to the underworld faded away completely in the end. According to certain traditions they were then born again and were reincarnated in their grandchildren.

Underground spirits

The dead were not the only inhabitants of the underground world. There were giants and all sorts of spirits of various sizes and degrees of vileness who lived in the lower regions. However, it is difficult to determine whether all these spirits were in separate categories. The Yuraks believed in hairy giants who lived under the earth and under trees, and there were other giants who could be differentiated from the first type because they fed on resin from larch-trees, which seem to have been sacred trees. These giants were empowered to cut themselves in two, or even to tear off their own limbs one by one, so that they could either feed on them themselves or give them as food to men they wanted to destroy. Then they would make themselves whole again. The giants would subject shamans to the same treatment when they went underground to seek the cause of sicknesses so that they could cure the sick on earth. A shaman to whom this happened felt no pain, perhaps a mere prick or twinge on the tip of his nose. Then he too made himself whole again.

So the underground regions were the seat of spirits who set sickness and calamity loose upon men and animals. To withstand their maltreatment or find a remedy for the ills they brought about, one had to go and visit them so as to make them take action and learn how they acted on their victims. When the shaman returned from his exploration, or in other words when he came out of his trance, he brought back what was needed to cure or preserve the person or animal in danger. He knew the cause of the ailment, and he acted accordingly, either making the required propitiatory sacrifice or observing the preservation rites that were known to him. In order to accomplish his mission, the shaman changed into a bird, serpent or other such animal that could with its speed get through every gap and escape the traps set by evil spirits.

These ideas of the underworld were much enriched or modified in course of time by ideas acquired from foreign traditions. The *manala* of the Finns (land beneath earth) was identified with the *tuonela* 'land of death', which was evidently of foreign origin as it had a Germanic name. At this stage well-known elements from the mythology of peoples of classical antiquity also appeared: the dead had to be conducted to the fatal river. Once they had reached the bank, they had to ask a sort of boatman to take them across; this function was often performed by the daughter of the god of the underworld.

As far as one can judge by comparing accounts that have come down to us, the Uralians do not seem to have introduced the idea of the last judgment into the conditions attending death. Death is not so much a change of state as a transfer to a different place. Earthly living conditions prevail, but the other way about, as it were, in a more sombre setting reminiscent of a photographic negative. There is no discrimination between the dead according to whether they were good or bad in life. There is hardly any mention of it except in a few scattered tales, and even here it is probably a late addition. Knowledge of good and evil appears to have played no part in the mythology of the Uralians; on the contrary, the important thing in their eyes was efficacy. Any one myth would serve to demonstrate the efficacy or lack of efficacy of a mode of procedure, attitude or manner of behaviour. Almost all ancient tales found among the Uralian peoples tend to show that there are two sorts of conduct: that which leads to failure and brings sickness and death and that which allows one to triumph over evil spirits and the vicissitudes of life. This attitude may reflect the mentality of a nation of hunters and fishermen whose lives depended on successful hunting or fishing expeditions.

This same mentality may have coloured the foreign myths that were borrowed later. There is evidence of these myths almost everywhere, though they have been adapted in various ways.

There is the myth of the blacksmith who made himself a 'bride'. In Finnish legend there is the mythical character Ilmarinen (whose name seems to have come from *ilma* 'sky, air') who one day by chance, it appears, forged a woman in gold, but was disappointed when he laid her on his couch, for she was cold and lifeless. Samoyed tradition speaks of it as a wooden doll on which work had only just begun. The sister of the sculptor did not wait for him to finish his work; she hacked it to pieces and hid it beneath some refuse. Then she gave herself to her brother and a son and daughter were born of this union.

Another myth concerns an animal — seagull, fish or deer — which was chased and caught only to escape again and reveal itself as a girl of dazzling beauty who had been changed into an animal by a spell and could regain her human shape only if she married a human being.

The enchanter (who for the Finns was the famous Vainamoinen) was also depicted as the inventor of the ancient musical instrument, the zither. He made it of different things, usually including fishbone, the bones of animals, a skin, and hair or hide. Then he began to play and the whole of nature was filled with delight.

Wild animals grew tame, the elements ceased to rage, harmony reigned over all at the sound of this music. This is the myth of Orpheus transposed to a Uralian setting.

Several exploits, or rather 'labours', undertaken by this enchanter are described. Once he found himself in difficulty just as he was putting the last touch to a boat or some other object. He realised that he lacked three magic words; to complete his work and make it valid he had to utter the three words come what may. The enchanter, who was obviously nothing more nor less than a typical shaman, fell into a trance. Then he entered the body of a monster, living or dead, and there he was able to seize the lost words. Then by a trick, the nature of which varies in different versions, he freed himself from the monster's entrails and returned to earth, where he completed his work. This tale, which reminds one of Jonah and the whale, perhaps came late, but it is very widespread and is adapted to local tradition.

This tradition, which in time became a composite thing, welded together elements from different sources so that it is now impossible to determine the autochthonous part of it. Sometimes one even has occasion to wonder whether historical events were incorporated to any degree.

A Finnish tale with a legendary air about it describes an expedition attempted in the North by a group placed under the direction, if not the command, of Vainamoinen, the enchanter. Their aim was to gain possession of a mysterious object, called *sampo* in Finnish (that is the form of the word used by Elias Lonnrot in the *Kalevala*). This instrument would seem to have 'ground out' prosperity. Possession of it ensured an abundance of everything. This expedition took place in a strange country where everything acquired miraculous proportions and shapes: 'Gate of gold,' says the popular Finnish song, which speaks of this land as 'place of darkness'. The *sampo* was buried deep under a mountain. It was defended by a rich and powerful people governed, according to the Finns, by the 'Woman of the North', who was a terrifying enchantress.

The Samoyed Yuraks believed in a huntsman, Vylkka, who went to the giants in the North to get them to improve hunting conditions, for the Samoyeds had 'lost their luck' and were in danger of dying of hunger for lack of game. After many episodes he returned to his native land, where he found that his reindeer had increased to ten thousand and that he had succeeded in bringing back good luck to Samoyed hunters. The theme is the same: a hero sets off on a perilous expedition to ensure the survival of his own people. This expedition takes him to the heart of the North and brings him to grips with strange beings, some of whom are friends and others enemies. With the help of the former he succeeds in getting out of the toils of the latter. After surmounting all dangers he returns home glorious, powerful, honoured and naturally provided with one or several wives, whom he has deserved or bought by his prowess.

One legend about the origin of the bear, widespread in regions occupied by the Voguls and Ostiaks, has been compared with the myth of Prometheus. According to this tradition the bear was the son of the sky-god. At first he lived in the firmament, but he was seized with an irresistible desire to go down and see what was happening on earth, which he could just see behind cloud, sometimes covered in a white carpet of snow, and sometimes completely green. Weary of his requests, the sky-god allowed him to go down, fastened to the end of a chain. Once on earth the bear nearly died because he did not know how to hunt. So his father, the god, put a bow and arrow into his hands. He also taught him how to make a fire so that he would not die of cold. But at the same time he forbade him to attack animals friendly to men or men of good conscience. Nor did he have permission to touch the corpse of a man or animal. On the contrary, his mission in his capacity of son of the sky-god was to see that honesty and justice reigned among men. He was instructed to punish the wicked, perjurers, liars and rogues. That is why but a short time ago, as Lehtisalo recounts, Samoyed Yuraks swore by the hair of a bear's head when they had to take oaths. It did not take the bear long to forget the words pronounced by his father. He was not afraid to attack men. So they killed him, and from that moment on men had the right to kill the bear. At the same time they took possession of fire and the bear's bow and arrow. From that time onwards men knew how to shoot with the bow and they had knowledge of fire.

In certain tales the bear made a girl captive and forced her to be his wife. They had a son whose fate varied according to different versions of the tale. Some experts have regarded this as a reflection of the totemism that dominated the religious concepts of the Uralians.

The same concept reappears in one of the myths of which Hungarians have a somewhat obscure recollection. This is the myth describing the origin of the dynasty of conquering chiefs who led the Hungarians into the lands of the Danube where they settled at the end of the ninth century. Queen Emesu had a dream. In her dream she saw a goshawk approach and fertilise her. Then from her breast flowed a broad river of fire. Then she gave birth to a boy, who was given the name of Almus, which means 'Born of the dream'. Almus was a chief, the ancestor of Arpad the conqueror and all his line.

However characteristic this account, it is by no means certain that it reflects Uralian tradition. There are grounds for wondering whether in fact it was not more probably inspired by Turkish tradition, since we know that this legend may go back to the time when the Hungarians were living in contact with the Turks. They were probably part of a federation of tribes, with the Turkish tribes holding a dominant position, and it is probable that they attempted to account for the divine or supernatural nature of their chiefs by shaping a legend analogous to that which later appeared in the *Secret History of the Mongols* on the subject of Genghis Khan. Similar legends have been piously transmitted by popular tradition in more than one Turkish or Mongol tribe.

The thing that really shows the difficulty one has in determining the authenticity of tradition is the plight of Hungarian historians confronted with the legend that goes by the name of the Wondrous Hind (*Csodas-zarvas*), as reported by Hungarian chroniclers. This legend concerns Hunor and Mogor (theorists have sought to link the latter name with the word Magyar — the Mongoloid race now predominant in Hungary), who were the progenitors of the Hungarians. On one occasion when they were hunting together they caught sight of a fleeing hind. They hunted it down, but by a miracle it escaped them and they searched for it in vain. They did not find it, but they did discover a plain that was just right for raising cattle, so they then took leave of their father and went to settle in this new land.

This tale clearly recalls the hunt for the great stag or elk that was mentioned earlier. Several Hungarian specialists have advanced the theory that once again this is a case of reflected totemism, basing their assumption on the fact that the mother of Hunor and Mogor was sometimes given a name, Enech, which seems identical (in its ancient form) with the modern Hungarian word for heifer, *uno*. The Hungarians seem to have descended from a female deer. A confirmation of this interpretation of their beliefs is the fact that the word in question was an early acquisition from the Turks. Now we know that traces of totemism seem to have been preserved in Turkish communities. However, one may well wonder to what degree true Uralian tradition became confused with a tradition of Turkish origin that infiltrated later on. The magic hind escapes its pursuers just as the great stag or magic elk or reindeer escapes in the Uralian myth.

It is just as difficult to see anything other than acquisition in the various elements that go to make the legend of the Flood. Accounts of the Flood have been found among Samoyed, Vogul and Ostiak tribes. They refer to a tidal wave of water or fire which covered all habitable lands. Men and their animals escaped by taking to boats, and they waited on mountain-tops for the waters or flames to recede. The analogy with Biblical tradition is so striking that one is justified in wondering whether it is not quite simply a transposition of the latter.

On the other hand there can be no doubt about the Nordic origin of a myth found among the Karelians about the god Rauni and his wife, whose union ensures the fecundity of nature, for in this myth a reflection can be seen of the legend of Freyr, Norse god of fecundity. Even the name of the divinity, Rauni, is merely a Finnish adaptation of an ancient form of this Germanic god's name. So what we have here is the myth of Freyr and Freyja.

An analogous myth concerns a certain Sampsa Pellervoinen, who is deity of the sowing-season, and this myth also comes to light through Finnish accounts. This god was asleep while nature went on strike. The 'Boy Winter' was sent to wake him up, but he did not stir. Then the 'Boy Summer' arrived and succeeded in rousing him from his lethargy. In other versions this same god, after committing incest with his sister, fled to the dark North, where different people came in turn to look for him.

All these tales remind one of well-known myths in the world of classical antiquity, and the versions found either on Finnish or Lapp territory or among other peoples of Uralian tongue give the impression that they became implanted at a relatively early date.

Recently collected tales of the Uralian-speaking peoples deal with numerous themes found throughout the entire world. Specialists in popular tradition, notably those of Finland, Estonia and the Scandinavian countries, have patiently sifted the different variants of these tales, and they have been at pains to compare them with analogous tales discovered elsewhere.

All that we know of the past of the Uralians and all the monuments that we possess of their ancient folk-tradition indicates that the mythology of the Uralian-speaking peoples has always included features found equally in the folk-tradition of other peoples, some of whom lived a great distance from them. That is why this study was prefaced by the remark that it is impossible to define a distinct Uralian mythology. If such a mythology ever existed we are in no position to track it down. That which has been handed down to us bears the imprint of so many different influences that at most we can pick out the myths that seem to have been shared by the different Uralian peoples. But we cannot tell whether this common property was furnished by Uralian tradition alone or whether it is more a case of parallel adaptation of traditions introduced among different Uralian peoples after their separation.

The Uralians did not live in isolation. However remote the regions that they inhabited, none the less they maintained relatively close contact with other peoples, particularly the peoples of ancient Siberia, those of central Asia, and finally and especially those who in the the very early days occupied the territory between the Carpathians and the Urals—that is to say, the peoples of the Russian steppe. Now we know that these were Indo-Europeans, especially northern Persians, and there is every reason to suppose that these contacts between Uralians and peoples of Indo-European tradition resulted in the exchange of ideas and religious concepts.

At a later date—possibly about the beginning of the Christian era—these exchanges developed considerably and the entire field of Uralian folk-lore felt the profound effects of this. The Lapps and Finns had lived in constant contact with Germanic tribes, particularly Norsemen, and they borrowed countless mythical and religious elements from them, even ideas pertaining to magic. Moreover, Russian influence prevailed in territories occupied by the Mordvins, the Cheremiss, the Permiaks, the Voguls, Ostiaks and, later still, the Samoyeds. The spread of Christianity helped transform folk-tradition, without, however, effacing all trace of the pagan past. In certain sectors, those for instance of the Samoyeds, the Voguls, the Ostiaks or even the Finns of Karelia, it has been possible to detect a sort of transmutation of Christian ideas into pagan-type myths. The saints of the Christian Church were changed into deities of pagan inspiration to such an extent that researchers may have been mistaken about the origin of cults arising out of these reshaped traditions. And so Uralian tradition, which was stronger than imported tradition, gained the upper hand in the end and remodelled the myths it had absorbed. It is only in very recent times that the active formation of myths has ceased.

This process can be explained by the century-long backwardness of most Uralian-speaking peoples in their intellectual, technical and social evolution. But then they made up for this backwardness at such a rate that the mythology of the Uralian-speaking peoples soon became a collection of traditions that had fallen irredeemably into disuse. From that point it belonged to archives and books.

So although we cannot imagine what original Uralian mythology was like, we can state that Uralian tradition knew how to appropriate the elements it borrowed from its foreign counterparts. However, this assimilation never took the form of integration into a systematic collection of ideas. When we speak of Uralian mythology we are referring not to coherent systems of mythical concepts, but to isolated myths, comparatively reliable evidence of which can be found from tribe to tribe. We do not come across homogeneity anywhere at all.

This disparity, which sometimes even reaches the proportions of dissonance, is perhaps the result of the composite character of Uralian traditions. Too many elements came from outside, which were never welded together, and so simply coexisted. Traditions may also have diverged at the very beginning, some being of a popular nature, while others were the prerogative of a certain élite. In time the profane tradition and the esoteric tradition of the shamans may have affected one another. Finally, the accounts that have come down to us are the product of purely oral tradition. From one story-teller to another the tradition varied and changed, and as Uralian peoples lived in scattered little communities no synthesis was possible. For all these reasons Uralian mythology resolves itself into separate mythological traditions, none of which is really homogeneous.

SIBERIA: THE THREE WORLDS

The huge territory of Siberia was divided between three or four main population groups before Russian infiltration. In the west, Finno-Ugrians (Ostiaks, Voguls) spread from European Russia and settled in the Ob basin, where they became neighbours of the Samoyeds who lived farther north. In the south, Turko-Mongol races (Altaic peoples, Khakass, Tuvin, Buryats) inhabited the Altai, the Minusinsk basin, the Sayan mountains and the region around Lake Baikal. One part of this group, the Yakuts, settled along the middle reaches of the Lena and also pushed out to the north-west and north-east. Another race that was linguistically close to the Turko-Mongols, the Tungus, was scattered right across Siberia, eventually meeting up with the Ugrians in the west and the Chukchi in the north-east. Another group is thought to go even farther back in the time and is known by the name of Paleo-Siberian: this includes the Yenisei river people, the Gilyaks of Amur, Kamchadals, Koryak, Chukchi and Yukaghir from the north-east, who are not actually related except for the last four mentioned, who go by the name of Paleo-Arctic. The one and only small group of Eskimos in Siberia lives on the coastal strip of the Bering Strait, the others inhabiting Alaska, northern Canada, Greenland and Labrador. Chukchi-Koryak-Kamchadal and Eskimo mythologies have certain things in common and will, to a certain extent, be treated together.

The creation of the universe

The universe, as described by the Siberian peoples, may be compared to a large and almost symmetrical egg divided vertically. On the far horizon the jaws of heaven clash with those of earth, thus producing winds. There are three registers altogether: upper, middle and lower 'earths'. Between the world above and the world below, which is often a mere reflection of the former and, like it, is composed of an equal number of layers or floors, the earth proper seems to be a thin surface, described as oblong, square or octagonal. The axis of the universe, birch-tree, larch or golden oak as the case may be, connects the three separate registers and goes through the earth at its centre or 'navel' and through the sky at the point of the pole star, which is also called the navel or hub of the sky. Its branches span the different spheres, and its roots go down into the nether world. The ancient earth-goddess dwells in the tree itself or by its roots, and the souls of unborn children inhabit its branches like frail birds, while the Sun and Moon take their seats near the top.

This vertical division is a characteristic feature of Turko-Mongol races, but it does not always, or even obligatorily, involve a strict order of superimposition; around the Tungus *dunda* are scattered spheres, seas, stars. Nor does this exclude other images. Beside the world tree another transverse axis joins top and bottom; this is a vast river in the view of the Ob river people and those of the Yenisei, and a little river in the eyes of the Tungus people, who believe that it has its source in the sky and ends in the lower world. So contact between the regions of life and death is established upstream and downstream. Two beings were required to accomplish the task of creation. The demiurge had a collaborator, his future enemy and rival, in the shape of his brother or, occasionally, his wife. This dualism is highly apparent in the creation myth common to Turko-Mongols and Finno-Ugrians, and is also perceptible

Samoyed shaman, beating his magic drum while travelling to
the world of the dead, generally thought of as underground.
He is riding on a bear, which is sometimes considered a god,
but more often an intermediary with the underworld, whose
god Erlik sometimes takes his form. (After Prokofieva.)

in the myths of some other peoples. The very business of creation seems like a competition: 'Since you claim you are stronger than I am,' Num said to Nga, 'organise the earth.' The sky was already in existence, as was the primordial ocean. A bird—duck or diver, who was either sent down by the demiurge and his partner or was an actual incarnation of these two beings—went down into the ocean depths and brought back sand or mud in its beak. From this arose the earth. Doh, the great shaman of the Yenisei river people, went about things in the same way when he grew tired of flying over the waves and wanted islands to rest on. In other versions earth arose from spittle or a bubble bursting on the surface of the water; this theme of the progressive growth of continents is also found in Tungus mythology. In the Vogul myth Num-torem's collaborator strengthens the unsteady earth by passing a belt with silver buttons around it (Urals).

Each of the two demiurges, Num and Nga, Ulgan and Erlik, the great Burkhan and the great Cholmus, made his own contribution, fashioning his own concept of nature, creating his own animals and eventually mankind, but at the same time their respective achievements tended to clash. Under the influence of Christian, Moslem and Buddhist ethics, and perhaps traces of ancient Mazdaism, the protagonists became more clearly outlined and evolved into a god and a devil, incarnations of good and evil. This devil was often confused with the first man, who was also the first to die, and thus became the king of the Land of Beyond. The creator was never concerned with the deceased. They never went to his heaven. The Kamchadals have a myth in which the creator's son, the ancestor of the human species, was the first to open the way to the lower world and to offer the living the example of death; so there was a direct relationship between humanity and the master of the lower world. The Amur races depict the couple Khadau and Mamaldi either as the first human couple, parents of the first shaman or shamans themselves, who became the masters of the underworld, *buni*, or else as actual creators. Mamaldi created the continent of Asia and the island of Sakhalin before she was killed by her husband, and here the fundamental antagonism between the two demiurges re-emerges. However, Khadau's wife continued to quicken the souls of future shamans who were forged, in the first instance, by her husband. We do not know whether the Yeniseian Khosadam, the wife of the high god Eç, who was driven out of the sky for being unfaithful to her husband with the Moon, took part in creation, but she appears as a devourer of souls rather than a sovereign of the dead. The name 'father' given to Erlik by Altaic peoples is undoubtedly indicative of something more than mere respect intended to disarm him. Erlik is both the first man and the elder brother of the creator; he acquired his present ter-

rifying appearance largely on contact with the Buddhist Yama.

In his appointment of the universe, the great god rather groped his way, in an empirical fashion. He created wicked and dangerous creatures, then killed them off. He claimed that mankind would graze like cattle, then realised his mistake. He handed over the sun and moon to the devil, and his aides had to plot to get them back. Other sources, on the other hand, state that there were too many suns and moons, and a hero had to shoot them down with arrows. They rarely specify exactly how the great god created man, whether by sculpture or modelling, or whether he procreated him; but it would seem more likely that man descended collaterally with him. The emergence of human beings on earth sometimes seems accidental: 'they were there', without explanation of their origin and source— either from lack of thought or lack of interest.

Shamanism is sometimes depicted as a divine achievement: the great god expressly wished to give men a protector against illness and chose the eagle as their ancestor or original shaman. Shamanism is often attributed to the devil, and the diver, a demoniacal bird, is said to be the shaman's aide. There again, man is often quoted as having educated himself in the relevant arts. There is a story about a Tungus who grew tired of waiting for divine help, and so one day he made implements and set to work: 'Do as you know best' was all the great god told him. The Samoyed story is that their shaman was repulsed by Num and so went down to Nga to obtain his daughter's hand and the promise that he would 'free' the souls of the sick in future if shamans performed correctly. The growing powers of the shaman overshadowed the great god in the end, and the latter challenged him to competitions that culminated in the shaman's defeat and the diminution of his powers—to humanity's great loss. Other heroes took their stand against a cruel or indifferent divinity. A very ancient myth that the Khakass and Samoyeds had in common and their neighbours the Tunguses adopted told how a man temporarily succeeded in overcoming or cheating the great god and death who had banded together against the living.

Sky gods

In the highest of skies (which were placed one on top of another) dwelt the supreme god—a benevolent rather than actively beneficent figure. Once his creation was finished he simply surveyed its functioning from afar, or even lost interest in it: 'If they prosper, let them grow, if they die may they perish!' and had only the slightest contact with men through an intermediary. Ulgan seems more accessible than Kudai, but even the shaman guided by a spirit and bearing a sacrifice does not quite reach him, and has to hand his victim over to the messenger, who conveys the supreme god's wishes. There are no graphic images of the creator, and he is not always given cult-worship. His concern for human beings is on the collective scale, not with the individual. His sons, daughters and servants were put in charge of groups and individual people.

The presence of the supreme god is the essential guarantee of order and balance in the universe. Num or Torum (Ugrian) or Eç, in the case of the Yenisei people, make regular journeys over the earth to check the mechanism of creation; in other mythologies the sky-god never seems to leave the upper airs. The Vogul Num is somewhat reminiscent of Odin. His abode in the seventh sky contains the water of life and magic appliances. The sun and moon are his eyes, and with them he can see everything visible and concealed. However, the image of the sky-god, modified by the great religions of Europe and Asia, generally stays rather vague, and its actual importance is hard to define. His name gives us no indication: he is vaguely referred to as the lord, light, the eyes of the world, the power on high, and these different appellations are often of foreign origin, Iranian in the case of Kudai, Greek in the case of Num, which comes from *nom*, 'law', a term adopted by Mongols and Sogdians. Buga, in Tungusic, which is etymologically related to *bog*, the Russian for 'god', belongs to a family with derivatives not only in Indo-Aryan languages, but also in Mongol and Far Eastern languages. In Tungusic he refers both to the universe in general and its celestial representative(s) and to the territory or holy place of some clan together with the female spirit who rules it. There were eventually several expressions that referred to one and the same deity, just as occasionally one single word would be applied to an entire category of beings: there are whole series of *kudai*, *torem*, *erlik* and *nga*. This last term is not even exclusively applicable to spirits of the underworld: it refers to the creator himself in the view of the Samoyeds on the Yenisei. Khovaki or Savaki is a name used by the Tunguses in the north-east for the creator; in Transbaikalia it refers to the spirits who protect the shaman.

The family and servants of the great god constitute the celestial pantheon with its relatively distinct hierarchy. Connections between the various sections do not always exist, and when they do they are often quite loose; for instance, the upper regions are not the prerogative of kindly spirits. In Yakut myth the third sky is inhabited by a great god, Ulu Tojon, the stranger or white creator. He governs the wicked *abaasy*, who populate not only the lower world, but the north-eastern part of the universe. He would also appear to be a master of thunder, who donated fire to mankind and one of their three souls, and shamans also claim to be descended from him. In the

The 'path of Ulgan'. This is the path followed by the Altai shaman when he approaches the great god Ulgan. From bottom to top are the sacrificial tent, with a fire lit before it; the horse being sacrificed and three libation bowls for the three chief deities which the shaman will meet; the victim's skin hung on a peg and the sacred birch with its nine tapty, or degrees. The shaman meets the first deity, who is standing in front of his home, and then passes the nine 'stations', which correspond to the nine tapty of the birch. Then he crosses three regions, the first covered with white sand, the second with blue sand, and the third—which is beyond the clouds. He eventually arrives before Ulgan and offers him the soul of the sacrificed horse through the god's messenger, with whom the shaman actually deals. The god is shown with rays of light spreading out all about him. (After Uno Harva.)

mythology of the Buryats, there are fifty-four kindly *tengri* in the west opposite forty-five wicked *tengri* in the east — rather an unusual orientation — with a vast number of offspring and *qat* of lesser rank. They are not all worshipped, and in the minds of the people only the main names or categories linger on. Esege Malan presides somewhat vaguely over the western sky; Erlik, king of the dead, comes from the east. The *qat* dwell on high mountain-peaks, and the *ukhan qat* govern the waters below. The warrior-princes of the stars, especially Mars and Venus, and the seven Old Men of the Great Bear, help mankind and livestock to multiply. Here the importance of Mars and Venus overshadows that of the Sun and Moon.

The Sun and Moon, who are independent deities or else mere instruments in the hands of the high god, may be either husband and wife, brothers or one the parent of the other (the Sun often being female and the Moon generally male), and are complementary to one another in Siberia, rather than opposites. The Sun, who is worshipped rather more and is always regarded as beneficent in these cold countries, communicates with vegetation spirits *via* his rays of long gold hair with their life-giving powers. The Moon takes the Sun's place during its long absences and marks the passing of time. Both — though the Moon to a lesser degree — have powers of healing, indeed of bringing back life. The Moon is more directly connected with human souls, which it takes to women who want children; it succours and eventually welcomes back these souls in the role of kindly guardian, or else snatches them away and destroys them when its mood is that of evil magician. As 'Sun of the dead' it lights the lower world, and the deceased go back up to the Moon prior to their reincarnation.

Earth gods

Above is the blue sky, a male principle, and below the black earth, also known as the golden surface, the female principle. The cult of Mother Earth existed among huntsmen as well as farmers and cattle-raisers. At a very early date, the Mongols worshipped the goddess Atugan. However, in this pastoral race under one central military authority the male element was to predominate — at least in the official religion. Genghis Khan worshipped Sky and Earth, and the combination proved to be his strength, though his successors prayed only to 'the Eternal', Tengri. Where there was a goddess, she never adopted a warlike attitude.

The connections between the great goddess and great god are never very clear except occasionally in Ugro-Samoyed mythology; although at a late date there was an attempt to reconcile the two separate cults. The wife of the creator must, in the same way,

have been confused at times with the earth deity. She does not live in the sky — at most she goes there sometimes and the Samoyeds say that the rainbow shows where she has passed by; and she does not live with the high god. The Vogul goddess Joli-torem would appear to be a sister of the creator; without taking an active part in his work, she would seem to have directed it to some extent; but in contrast, the devilish Khosadam of the Yenisei people, the malevolent ex-wife of Eç, is not an earth-goddess and pursues a single-minded course of destruction. Instead of the two antithetic principles, Sky and Hell, the mythology of the Ent-Samoyeds stages a triad: Sky and Earth together gave birth to the god of evil and death, Todote; but this is an isolated example. The source of all life is the Great Mother. She possesses the strength and substance of nature (*musun, djol, iab, kut*), and there is a tiny bit of this in each creature, animal, plant and even in certain objects. According to their own activities, different races worship the goddess as a presider over game, over growing grass, food for cattle, the plants useful to man or cereals. She also presides over births and looks after health. In each of these roles she has in course of time acquired a special personality, which ultimately achieved independence. Thus separate deities parted from the central trunk, represented by the Mother. In the mythology of the Yakuts she split into three goddesses: of earth, cattle and children. Itchita, who chose to live in the most beautiful of the white beech-trees, acquired a host of tiny servants, spirits of grass and trees, and keeps the black spirits of sickness away from men. Ynakhsyt protects cattle and is offered the first dairy produce in the spring. Ajysyt is the goddess of children and helps women in childbirth, constantly laughing and swaying back and forth, a movement that creates or encourages life.

Runic inscriptions made by the ancient Turks of Orkhon (seventh to eighth century) mention Umai as one of the most powerful deities. This 'Mother of cradles', 'rich mother of the sixty golden tresses' has survived down to our own time among Turkish peoples and is called Umai, Ymai or Mai. In number and colour her tresses, like the gold threads of the sun's rays, symbolise productive force, an idea heightened by the epithet 'rich', which is often attached to her name. Her essential function, which is 'to increase older and younger brothers and sisters' and to look after cradles, is clearly shown in her very name, which means 'matrix' or 'placenta'. Mongols, who use the term *umai*, but do not recognise this goddess, for their part worship a fire queen, Mother Ot, 'born when Sky and Earth separated', and she is most often invoked at marriage ceremonies. Her radiance 'goes right up to the 99 *tengri* . . . traverses the 77 layers of Mother Atugan', her kindly warmth produces and maintains existence. Ot and Umai were certainly one single deity in the beginning. The Khakass praise Ymai for warming the earth and the 'white

435

Koryak drawings. The first picture shows Kala, an evil spirit, intercepting a sacrifice being sent to the gods. Below, the shaman is seen beating his drum beside a dying man. Above, the supreme god and his wife, with souls all around them. The second picture again shows a shaman beating his drum, but this time the sacrifice reaches the gods, who all have haloes around their heads. (After Jochelson.)

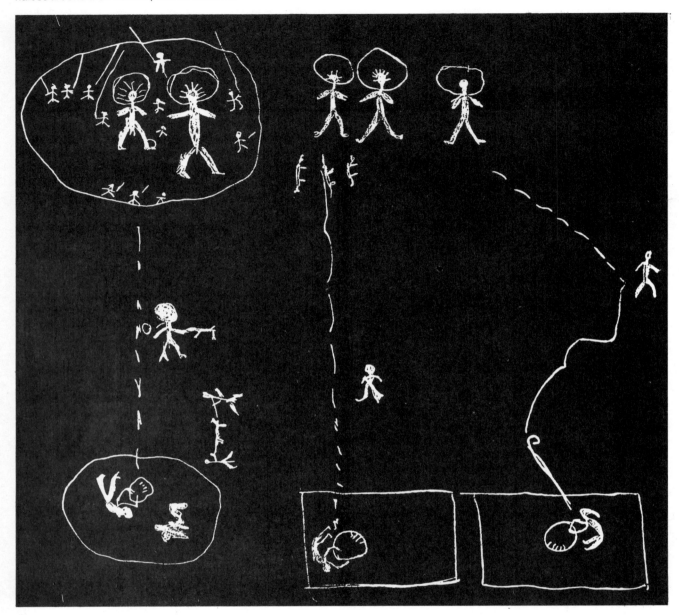

clouds', a role which is definitely that of a fire-god. The Mongols continued to associate Ymai with fire, but for the Turks the goddess acquired a more patently maternal function. With other Siberian peoples the spirit of the hearth and home is always female too. Her presence dictates the rules whereby the mistress of the house should regularly provide food for the 'ancestress', and they forbid any contact that may sully or prove harmful to her; if the flame should go out, the life of the family would be extinguished with it. On the other hand, 'wild' fire lit in the forests is the abode of a male spirit. The precautions to be taken with regard to him are the same, the fire 'man' punishes those who insult him and endows those who 'feed' him.

Umai reappears in another form in Tungus mythology. In Tungus dialects there is a group of words with the same etymology: *ome*, 'matrix'; *omo*, 'nest, den'; *omi*, 'soul', or to be more accurate, souls

that wait reincarnation and meanwhile in the form of fledglings inhabit the Tree (or the two trees) of Life that each clan possesses. The *mama* decides where these *omi* are to go and is called Umysa, Umisi, etc. Umai at this point becomes divided into the different clan *mamas*. Even in Altai, although the population as a whole worships Umai, each particular family possesses its *amagandar* or *orokannar*, protectresses who alone can ensure a happy release by their very presence.

Similarly, the great earth-goddess resolves into local spirits. Every small Tungus group, widely scattered as they are, builds up its own microcosm with its world tree, its mythical river, its village for the dead, its earth-mistress, whose jurisdiction is restricted to clan territory. Beneath the sacred stone, the old *dunne musun* keeps the skins of all the forest animals. The shaman goes to her as suppliant or robber, and equally beseeches the *bugadi musun*, an enormous female elk, accompanied by her tribe of wild beasts. These two 'mistresses' obviously represent the human aspect and animal aspect of one and the same person. The primitive vision of the earth as a female animal is seen in drawings in which the middle world is depicted as an elk or eight-footed female reindeer, and in the epithets 'hairy' or 'fur-covered', which are applied to earth. The Orochi say also that the forests are her fur and animals her parasites. The *ie-kyl*, 'animal mother', with whom the lives of Yakut and Tungus shamans are closely connected, is an avatar of this old earth. In the view of the Gold tribes, the mother of shamanistic spirits is identified with the great mistress of nature; with the Yakuts and Tunguses there is separation and specialisation, but the relationship is discernible. To unearth the secrets of the universe, the shaman must participate in original twofold nature, and so the *ie-kyl* creates a double animal for him, who will help him throughout his life.

There are other avatars too, the 'guardians of the roads', who keep watch over all the essential points of the universe and guide the shamans and, sometimes, heroes in their perilous journeys throughout the worlds. The folk-lore of all these peoples mention these clever counsellors who point out the right path and the ways of escaping danger.

Master-spirits

The combination of earth and water was worshipped by ancient Turks and modern Altaic peoples and given the name of Jar-Sub. In the widest sense, Jar-Sub refers to the universe, which, in the case of the Altaic race, is ruled over by seventeen lords of continents and seas; in its narrowest acceptation it means 'native land', in other words the native soil, whether vast or otherwise, inhabited by certain master-spirits.

His mountain, his forest, the waterways on his territory and the spirits who govern them, who are really present close by, are the things that interest the huntsman, fisherman and cattleman in an immediate and perceptible manner. Once outside the immediate circle of his own activities man is confronted by the spirits of neighbouring, alien territories, who must *a priori* be hostile. Different categories of spirits watch over either a fixed zone or a particular species. They are given the inclusive name of 'master-spirits', a title most often conferred upon them by the Turko-Mongols, Tunguses and Gilyaks. The Samoyeds have 'mothers' who created species (fox, fish, reindeer) that they watch over, as in the case of *Illibem berti* or *paduri*, who is the ruler of both domestic and wild reindeer. In other mythologies the 'masters' are connected not so much with a species as a given spot. The spirit of the 'rich dark forest', the joyous Baj Bajaniai, beloved of the Yakuts,

'gives' furry animals and certain birds. In the beliefs of the Buryat and the Altaic peoples, the forest *azi* is confused with the mountain *azi* when the latter's abode is wooded. The *azi's* cattle is represented by wild game. They do not allow it to be destroyed thoughtlessly, but they will surrender it under certain conditions and gamble it away among themselves or with bold hunters who venture into their caves. These spirits are neither good nor bad, and with their families lead a similar existence to men, going about on skis, singing, dancing, quarrelling, waging war. They like to receive as offerings the products they do not have themselves (alcohol, tea, tobacco) and also eloquence, musical talent and individual merit. It is necessary to conciliate them, but to attract their attention too much has either happy or fatal consequences. Curious and avid for human company, the *azi* reward those who have pleased them, but they also capture human souls on occasion, robbing them of reason and life. Anyone who falls in love with the 'mistresses' with long red hair and sagging breasts who live in the mountains is granted either prosperity or death, either sent back laden with rich treasures or kept for ever in the bowels of the mountains. Each seemingly accidental death means a summons from supernatural sources. The Gilyaks believe that those who die by drowning go to live with the master of water, while the victims of bears or tigers go to the mountain *yz*. Gilyak master-spirits actually appear as bears and tigers. Once they are back home, the spirit shakes his animal-skin, hangs it up and assumes human shape again. The mountain is in itself another world, as is the sky, sea, and hell, and each has its own supernatural inhabitants; to set foot there is almost the equivalent of a journey to the Beyond. The dead who become deified and are then classed as *yz* acquire more importance in the eyes of their own kin than the deities themselves, who are more remote, and these unfailing reinforcements of chosen recruits periodically give a new lease of life to a cult that is not, as in the case of the Ugrians of the Ob, dedicated to distant ancestors.

In Altai, master-spirits are already human in shape, but their Gilyak equivalents have not yet quite lost trace of their animal beginnings. The process of anthropomorphism is complete when the orc is reduced to the role of aide to an anthropomorphic god of the sea and the bear to the role of 'dog' belonging to the god of the mountain. Throughout Siberia the bear is known and revered in various capacities, if not as a deity, at least as an intermediary or temporary incarnation of a deity. Once he has been put to death he is used as a messenger to convey prayers to the beings on whom he depends. In spite of his celestial origin—according to Finno-Ugrian tradition he came down from the skies in a silver cradle—he also makes communication possible with the underworld. He is the mount the Samoyed shaman uses to descend to the lower regions, and just as the earth-goddess sometimes assumes the shape of a reindeer or elk, so the god of hell (Erlik, for example) occasionally appears in the guise of a bear.

Water and the underworld

Although water is classed with earth in the old combination of the Jar-Sub, water both belongs to and clashes with all the different spheres for which it provides a channel of communication. It is a complex element, both productive and cunning, proceeding from heaven and hell, and it is divided into two categories — flowing waters and dormant waters. The sea, which is meaningful only for those who live along the coasts of the Okhotsk and Bering Seas, is identified with a vast river in Turko-Mongol mythologies, which allude to its source and mouth. In the north, the Arctic with its deserted or well-nigh deserted shores evokes only desolation and death. Its dark islands are the sojourn of the deceased or of monsters. The Ob and Yenisei, according to Ugro-Samoyeds and Yenesei-dwellers, flow into enormous icy gulfs ruled over by terrible gods who devour human souls. Thus these river-dwellers regard the north and the lower stretches as the direction of death, and two alternatives are open to the shaman setting out for hell: to go to an orifice — for instance, at the great fork known as the navel of the earth — or to set sail on the river that will lead him to the village of the dead.

Master-spirits govern rivers and streams. Their temperament and the feelings they inspire distinguish them from their colleagues of the mountains and forests and there is often hidden hostility between these representatives of the liquid element and those of the hard soil. The water-spirit is a disturbing creature who is rarely illustrated and often seems malevolent, being more jealous of his fishes than the master of the forest is of his game. The same term, *kul*, is used in Ostiak and Vogul to refer to 'demon' and 'water-spirit'; the Selkup Samoyeds regard the latter as the god of the lower world who inflicts sickness on men. Dormant waters are even more dangerous, and communicate directly with the lower world. Pools, lakes, and marshes are simply orifices through which devilish creatures emerge, and aquatic birds — divers, swans — share the infernal nature of these waters. On the surface and at the edges are many hairy monsters, with claws and long tusks, and only one eye, one arm and one leg. Their infirmity seems to be the very condition of their strength, for they gain in supernatural power what they appear to lose in physical qualities. They sometimes seek matrimonial relationships with humans;

more often they enter into conflict with them, and this is not to their advantage. There is a sign used to indicate their affinity with the lower world: the presence of iron. The inhabitants of the lower regions are either partly or entirely composed of iron — for example, the black Chebeldei, whose noses are eighteen metres long, and the Yakut *abaasy*, including the son of the chief, who is a cyclops with one eye 'like a frozen lake' and has hair, lashes and seven enormous teeth of iron.

There is a two-way traffic through the different regions. In addition to shamans, some privileged individuals go to see the spirits and the dead, who dwell on the mountains, in the sky (moon) and at the bottom of water, as well as in the underworld. A hero may meet his dead parents, then bring them back to their village whether they will or no, and, if need be, kill them in order to do so: having been killed in the other world, they then find themselves alive again in this one. The barriers between life and death, both of which are temporary, remain fluid. The processes of resurrection and metamorphosis (flagellation, shaking) are often the same: it is a question of returning to an earlier state or appearance, there is nothing radical or definitive about the change. Even external intervention does not always seem necessary; the reanimation takes place as though automatically. One dies 'a little', temporarily or for good. With the same ease as he changes skin, dies or goes back to the mythical period of the *tylgund*, the Gilyak 'moves' from one world to another, and suddenly decides that he and his kin will become men or *milk* (devils), as the case may be, in one of the four regions of sky, mountain, sea or underworld.

Where does the 'middle earth' finish and the chthonian world begin? The domain of the earth-goddess is in principle limited to the surface: even if she lives beneath the roots, she looks upwards towards light and life. But every death is a preparation for rebirth, there is gestation in the bowels of the earth. It is difficult to determine where the goddess' influence ceases and where the truly infernal areas begin. The seventeen sections of the Jar-Sub seem to be conceived both on the surface and in depth. The division of earth into seventy-seven or eighty-one superimposed layers, over which reigns Mother Earth or subordinate *atugan*, certainly constitutes in Mongol mythology a late and artificial creation, which can be ascribed to the influence of the ninety-nine *tengri*, but it helps us understand this indetermination regarding levels and attributes. The sovereign of the lower world who is 'somewhere down below' has difficulty in coexisting on equal terms with the earth-goddess. As the female image recedes, so the importance and prestige increase of this almost invariably male character, chief of the spirits of the underworld, judge of the dead, both feared and worshipped by the living.

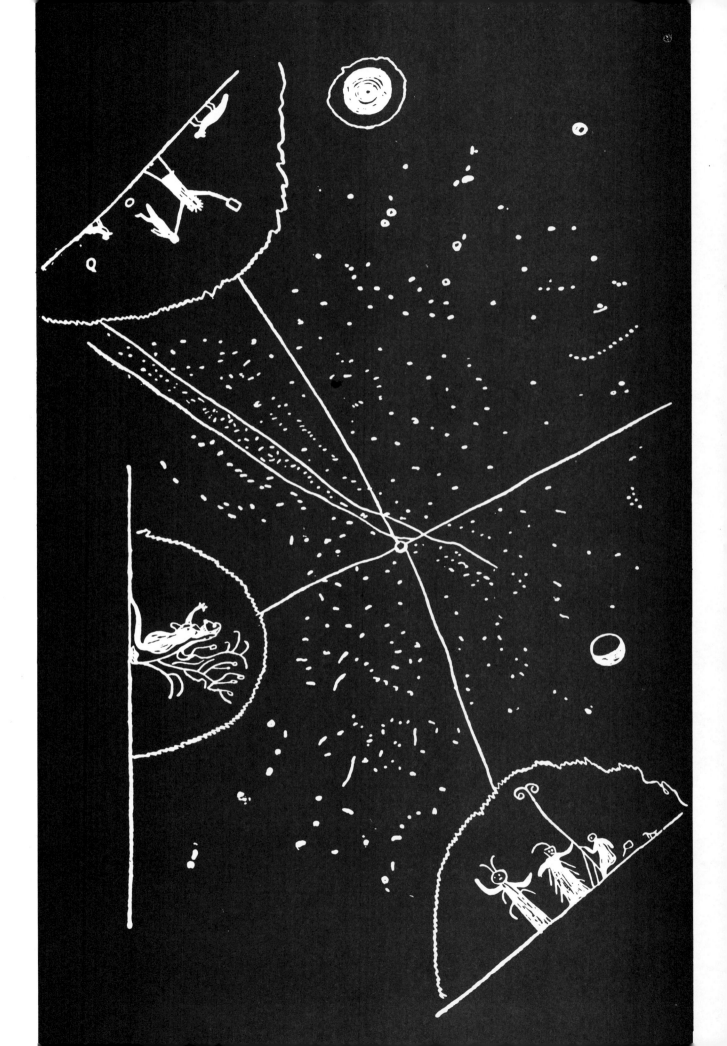

Wooden dance mask from Alaska consisting of two faces and two human hands and incorporating elements of the various animals hunted by the Eskimos, webbed feet, a whiskered snout and furry tails, together with a harpoon. The mask is painted with green, red and white. *American Museum of Natural History*

ESKIMO LANDS: MAN AGAINST NATURE

The characteristic feature of Eskimo religious thought is its anthropomorphic view of the universe. Deities, stars and natural phenomena have their origin in human adventures, often of an anecdotal nature and full of prosaic details. The Eskimos have given relatively little thought to the birth and elaboration of the world. The earth is depicted as a tent resting on pegs, with a cover over it—the vault of heaven—which was slashed by a knife in four different places to allow the north, south, east and west winds to escape. Beyond is another world, the sky, which resembles the earth. According to a fairly general belief, the earth tilted at one time, and its former occupants now live underneath.

Creation

There is no true creation myth in Eskimo mythology, except in Alaska, where the function of the demiurge is ascribed to the Crow Father. If one takes into account the fact that the Crow cycle is characteristic of Paleo-Arctic Siberians and is also part of the mythology of American Indians of the north-east coast, whereas on Eskimo territory it is known only to Alaskans, then the logical conclusion is that in the case of the last mentioned it is of foreign origin. Nevertheless, it is firmly established in Alaska. In the most complete version, the story tells of a creature called Tulungusaq who first came to life in the midst of darkness in a dead, silver sky. But another being was already in existence prior to him, the Swallow. She shows him clay soil just hardening at the bottom of a great abyss; and so he disguises himself as a crow with artificial wings covered with feathers attached to his body and a beak growing from a convenient protuberance on his brow. This is the disguise he uses to change into a bird, but he is always in a position to abandon this mask. All vegetation springs from fragments of clay which the crow buries in soil

on earth (earlier, in the sky, he seemingly went about things in the same way). With the same material he fashions animals and men. However, the emergence of the first four men, if not due to a sort of spontaneous generation, seems none the less independent of a governing will. The Crow himself is astounded to see creatures emerge from husks, and so he fashions women for them, then other human beings to people the earth more quickly. However, the day comes when the earth, like the sky, is no longer large enough for its inhabitants: the latter make it bigger by throwing into the sea pieces of a gigantic monster which change into islands and weld themselves to the coasts.

With the aid of the Swallow the Crow endows the world with light. Days and nights had previously run into one another, and time did not exist. In all tales there is some mention of this primordial darkness in which the first men lived until the day when the Crow—in some versions the Hare—procured sun and moon for them. 'Light came because the word of the Hare who wanted it was stronger than that of the Fox who was afraid of it,' states a Netsilik legend. As part of his task as a culture-hero, the Crow teaches men how to build houses and boats and how to hunt and fish, and, once his task is over, he returns to the sky to produce stars in like fashion. In some versions, he quarrels with the Eskimos, who kill too much game for his liking, and first tries to exterminate them, then robs them of the sun. His elder brother later succeeds in getting the solar star from him and returning it to mankind, but he has not strength enough to make his way back to the sky, and so his descendants never learn how to remove their masks and have to stay on earth as mere crows. It is very interesting to rediscover here a theme that was characteristic of the Finno-Ugrians and Turko-Mongols—namely, a conflict between two brother creators who quarrel over

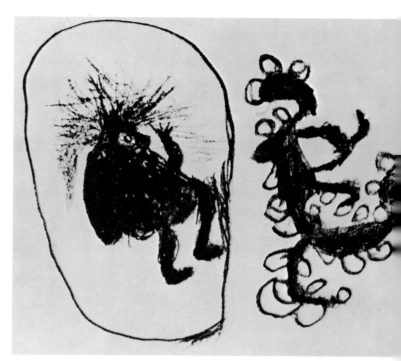

the sun, each thwarting the other's attempts at world organisation. In much the same way a bird is here introduced, demiurge (Crow) or messenger and help-mate (Swallow), just as the diver appeared in Siberian mythology.

The mythology of the Paleo-Arctic Siberians has retained little of this Great Crow, whose derided descendants were brought low and became mere birds, and in their tales of him they depict him simply in a repulsive or comic aspect, as a caricature. In particular Koryak and Kamchadal cycles, which are almost exclusively devoted to Kutq, present the Crow as a glutton, an obscene cheat, whose tricks finally backfire against himself. His history and that of his family include whole series of misadventures, and he is systematically ridiculed. With the Eskimos this attitude of intentional—even ritual—irreverence is considerably modified.

The sea-goddess

The goddess of sea-creatures has different names in different regions; we shall refer to her by her most popular name—Sedna. Her story, with its main episode about the severed fingers that produce sea-mammals, has many variants. Most tales mention her refusal to marry, or her freakish union with an animal or even an object. In the course of a voyage or escape she was said to have been cast out of a boat, usually by her own father, who cut her fingers off one by one to make her let go, and then she sank to the bottom of the sea where she now dwells and keeps strict guard over all that lives there. So she belongs both to the category of transgressors and to that of the persecuted from which deities are, from preference, recruited, not only by Eskimos, but by many other races too. One of the expressions used in reference to her is highly significant: 'She who did not wish to marry.' Now society rejects the single person, the celibate, as abnormal. Usually Sedna married in the end, but made a bad match. Her monstrous unions, according to certain sources, produced several races on earth.

It is, of course, true that Sedna feels no kindliness towards humanity. However, she acts neither arbitrarily nor directly: she never moves about of her own free will, and is, as it were, rooted to her stone dwelling. Her sinister appearance would kill any ordinary man; only a shaman can withstand the sight of her. Huge, voracious and impotent, with a wild temper, she keeps watch—using her one (left) eye—over the sea-mammals swimming beneath her lamp in the large pond that contains every species. Where her right eye should be, there is black hair; the sins of men rain down, like excrement, on her tangled black tresses. Her companions and help-mates are a dwarf—often her father, sometimes a child—and an armless woman with whom she shares her husband, a sea-scorpion. Sedna's father also has only one eye and one arm; with his right hand,

The spirit of a dead man who became a helper of the shaman, with two dead animals. After Rasmussen.

which has only three fingers, he seizes the dying; in fact his appearance usually heralds death.

Sedna punishes human beings indirectly, but effectively: she withholds wild game, thus bringing about famine. Human beings arouse her displeasure by infringing her rules, particularly by having miscarriages and secret abortions. The fault lies not in the act, but in the secrecy. An impure woman affects those around her. A hunter thus contaminated, or equally one who, for his own part, does not observe the rules properly, and does not kill as he should, endangers animals, and Sedna's reaction to this is something more than resentment: she experiences actual physical pain in the places where the sea-mammals separate from her body. According to certain sources she also controlled wild game on earth; others attribute this function to her father or other spirits, but information on this subject is still vague and contradictory. This goddess in her apparent paralysis never leaves her own element, the sea, and it is difficult to see what influence she might have on terrestrial fauna. Sedna is even said to hate reindeer. In the language of spirits and shamans seals are called 'gifts' (of Sedna), caribous are the 'fleas of the earth'; their pelts must be cured and their meat eaten at different times. The Mother of Caribous was an old woman, who created them out of bits taken from her undergarments and brought them to life by magic words. Later the two mothers of animals were able to fuse into one single purveyor of game, known as the 'Great Dish of Meat', that highly important meat of which the Eskimo diet is almost exclusively composed.

It was a period of hunger that brought about the emergence of the first angekkok. To save starving humanity, a man decided to go to the mother of sea-creatures, so he 'dived' through the ground and made

his way to the 'abode of sustenance' and brought back game to feed mankind. Now, whenever famine threatens, angekkoks (Eskimo conjurers) follow the same course. There are many obstacles. On the sea-bed are moving boulders. The more famous the shaman, the easier his path. At the goddess's gate a Cerberus—sometimes her dog-husband—mounts guard, then farther on Sedna's father tries to get to grips with the intruder. When he comes to the goddess herself, the angekkok sometimes uses violence, sometimes gentleness. He untangles and cleanses her hair, which teems with men's malodorous sins, he calms her with apologies and pledges, but he also manages to capture her with the aid of a hook and brings her up to the surface of the water, releasing her only on certain conditions. In order to free the animals that she refuses to hand over, he sometimes repeats the original gesture of cutting off the goddess' fingers.

Sedna's kingdom, which goes by the name of Adlivun, is also used as a sojourn, at least of a temporary kind, for the souls of the dead, a sort of purgatory where the deceased stop to be purified before they go on to a more pleasant spot, the Land of the Moon, for instance, to which only a few privileged people and those who die a violent death accede immediately.

In Alaska Sedna disappears and is replaced by the moon-god. On the other side of the Bering Strait the Chukchi have a powerful Mother of Walruses and a story about a girl whose fingers were cut off but they make no connection between the two. On the other hand, it appears that the two deities of sea and moon became fused in their mythology into one Woman of the Sea, who went to live in the moon. The Eskimos keep the two great deities quite separate and unconnected.

443

The moon-god

All Eskimos have a moon-god, but in Alaska, where Sedna is unknown, he reigns in solitary state as uncontested master. His sister, the sun-goddess, plays a much smaller part and is not greatly concerned with the affairs of men. Like Sedna they are of human origin. They too are cast out by society after committing the greatest criminal act of all, incest, he deliberately and she involuntarily. When she recognises her nocturnal visitor as her own brother, she cuts off her breasts and throws them in his face: 'Eat them, since you love me so!' Revolving round her tent she slowly rises up into the air, pursued by her brother. Their two torches turn into sun and moon, though it was believed that these existed before this time, and the god and goddess simply took possession of them.

The man in the moon has wider powers than Sedna, but he uses them less ferociously. He directs natural phenomena: tides, storms, eclipses, earthquakes, falling snow, and he also has at his disposition all game and wild fowl. In his abode, like Sedna's, there is a great pool for sea-mammals, and, in addition, pigeon-holes for filing away the souls of terrestrial animals. He tells the orphan who has taken refuge with him not to forget to make offerings to him in future when there is a scarcity of game, for he controls everything: 'I mean the whale, the white whale, walrus, caribou, every animal in the world.' Again like Sedna, he keeps watch over the behaviour of the human race. Impurities go up to him, instead of down to her, not in the form of dirt, but as pungent smoke, which hurts his eyes and angers him. Into the jars of water—miniature seas—held out to him by suppliants Alignak drops their future prey if the water is clear—in other words, if they have a clear conscience. When hunting is bad, the Alaskan shaman does not dive down to Sedna, like his colleague from Canada or Greenland—he goes up to the moon. He does not meet the same obstacles, but he is accompanied by his subordinate spirits, the *Tunrat*, in this none the less perilous voyage.

Although redoubtable and at times irascible, the spirit of the moon evinces no particular malevolence towards men. Iglulik Eskimos say that he wards off Sedna's anger (the two coexist in this mythology), which is by far the more terrifying, by inflicting moderate punishment upon himself. His powers are naturally less in Canada and Greenland, where Sedna's presence restricts them to some degree. He is admired as an exemplary huntsman, whose gifts and luck one would like to share.

There is general proof of his powers of fertilisation. He cures sterility in women, whereas Sedna seems by comparison hostile to the idea of reproduction; pregnant Iglulik women are strictly forbidden to touch any part of the seal, the goddess' animal. The spirit of the moon sometimes carries off women to his home and makes them fertile, then sends them back to earth. If they die in childbirth they go straight back to the Land of the Moon without submitting to the purgatory of Sedna's Adlivun. On the other hand, although childless women pray to the moon, those who fear pregnancy must avoid contact with moonbeams.

The spirit of the moon again appears in the guise of protector of the disinherited. He gives the persecuted their revenge in the form of physical strength—one of the most coveted advantages—if they 'weep' to obtain it. He makes the child-who-could-not-grow vomit up the impurities he has swallowed and turns him into a prodigious fighter. He welcomes—or rather, abducts—the orphan so that he will not suffer harsh treatment: at the same time, he steals his stepmother's soul and gives it to the orphan that he may destroy it. For the moon-god's powers of attraction are strong, and he acts on creatures and seas alike, for their well-being or destruction. The lone traveller, the woman who goes to draw water by night, or the hunter staring at the moon's disc suddenly finds the star approaching. In a flash a man is there, with his sledge and four black-headed dogs harnessed to it, and they carry away to the sky anyone, whether he consents or exhibits fear. When he disembarks on the Land of the Moon, the guest goes into the double house where the moon-god and sun-goddess live alongside one another, but in their separate quarters. Intense brilliance and heat come from the part occupied by the sun-goddess. Beyond, in a great village, the souls of the dead engage in different sports, and come to welcome the living stranger; others rest on a bench in the spirit of the moon's abode. The spirit of the moon hospitably offers food, but the living stranger is rightly afraid lest he may not be able to return to his own kind again if he accepts, and he goes in particular fear of the strange and ferocious companion of the spirit of the moon who is armed with a curved knife, called the *ulu*, with which she will slit open his stomach and then devour his entrails once she has made him laugh. And so he prefers to take flight, and to return to earth, where he must without fail tell of his adventure or else the spirit of the moon will withhold his soul and his life. But the sojourn of the dead in the Land of Day on the moon seems so pleasant that those who have hopes of reaching it directly hardly fear death. Suicide is a temptation which the spirit of the moon encourages. Up above, the elect live a life of hunting and endless sport, and never experience cold or hunger as they await reincarnation, which is likewise the task of the spirit of the moon. During the periods when he disappears from the sky, he is busy taking back souls to earth so that they may commence a new life, sometimes initially in the guise of animals.

Pinga, Asiaq and Sila

Among Caribou Eskimos, the moon-god is subordinate to another deity, the mysterious Pinga, who

Issitoq, or the Giant Eye, a spirit which helps the shaman and whose special task it is to hunt out those who have infringed the rules. Such infractions are punished by Sedna, who causes famine by withholding the hunter's prey. After Rasmussen.

Nartoq, a spirit with a huge stomach, which the shaman succeeds in taming. After Rasmussen.

replaces the moon-god in certain of his functions. 'The one on high' seems to be the celestial counterpart of Sedna, 'The one below'. As guardian of earthly game, particularly caribous, it would seem that she should live on earth. Perhaps this was the case at one time, but her origins are unknown, nor do we know how she got up there or where exactly she resides. Her character remains equally vague. Pinga directs hunting, and does not allow men to massacre too many caribous. She watches over the souls of the living, and sick people pray to her; she confides the dead to the care of the moon-god, who on her instructions brings them back to earth to begin a new cycle of existence, and on occasion she provides helpful spirits for the angekkoks, but does not, it would appear, follow human behaviour with the same strict or severe attention as do the spirit of the moon and Sedna.

A third female spirit, Asiaq, governs, at least to some extent, the atmosphere and weather. She is of human origin, and her fate, like that of Sedna and the spirits of the moon and the sun, is somewhat out of the normal run. Like them she enters into an odd alliance. She did not, however, refuse to marry, but as no-one wanted her, left her village and travelled the world in search of a husband. Finally, she stole a child that he might become her husband, and from then onwards lived in retirement with him. She produced rain by shaking out a pelt dipped in urine (thunder, on the other hand, was the result of two pelts rubbing together). Shamans go to Asiaq to obtain good weather, which nowadays she no longer 'fabricates' of her own accord as she did at one time. In very recent traditions Pinga and Asiaq are regarded as male. This process of bestowing masculinity on its characters is very common in mythology in general.

After 'The one below' and 'The one above' we come to Sila, 'That which is outside everywhere'.

445

Slia-Sila-Hila-Hla is not the name of a deity: it means 'air, weather', and also 'sense, reason'. This force is personified when one couples the word *sila* with the title *inua*, 'master'. The Iglulik give the 'master of the air', *silap inua*, the personal name of Nartsuk. He was the son of a giant who witnessed his own parents' murder and then flew up into the air changed into a spirit. But his role seems quite limited here, and nowhere else is there any allusion to the origins of the *silap inua*, whose human outline remains extremely vague. Moreover, the character itself holds less interest than the notions it contains. He is the air, not the sky; movement, not wind; the very breath of life, but not merely physical life; he is clear-sighted energy, activating intelligence, the powerful fluid circulating 'all round' and also within each individual; to be deprived of *sila* is the same as being deprived of sense, and at the same time, it is the equivalent of acting contrary to morals, since reason is no longer there to guide behaviour. In its anthropomorphic form this life-principle became the *silap inua*, which was shortened to *sila*. Sometimes he is thought to be extremely terrifying, sometimes benevolent, and in the latter case he will dispense part of his own *sila*-substance to a sick man to revive him or to the angekkok postulant to allow him to realise himself fully. So the candidate to shamanism will 'exhibit himself' to attract Sila's attention and compassion. However, among Caribou Eskimos he will also 'show himself' to Pinga and Sila is identified locally with the latter. Moreover, in the Hudson Bay area, Hila is feminine. He also functions, on occasion, simply as Sedna's agent. The plural *hilap inue* is a collective name for a category of air-spirits with no specifically determined function. So these 'controllers' of the *sila-hila* seem as varied as they are vague: one might regard Sila as a sort of incomplete deity, a power that remains abstract, beside other deities who are only too human—to the point of being prosaic.

Inuat and Tungat

'God', 'goddess' and 'spirit' are, in fact, only very approximate translations of the Eskimo terms *inua* and *tungak*. *Inua*, third person of the possessive of *inuk*, 'man', literally means 'his man' and requires an object. One is the *inua* of something or someone; it is the double with the human face hidden within an animal, element or natural phenomenon; it is the operative intelligence determining the functioning of a thing or person. At the time of the Great Crow, it was the belief of Paleo-Arctic people and Alaskans that living creatures had a twofold nature, and could without difficulty assume human or animal form by changing a mask and clothing. This is no longer the case, forms have become fixed. But, deep within an animal, there still crouches 'his' man, which is invisible to the uninitiated, but is represented on masks. For instance, in a whale's stomach there is a young woman who maintains the lamp-life. After the death

of an animal, the *inuat* depart from it, but continue to exist, shades who must be regularly propitiated. From being a twofold individual, the *inua* has developed into the idea of a possessor, a master. The great spirits—Sedna, the spirit of the moon, Sila—are, respectively, the *inuat* of the sea, the moon-star, the air. The *inuat* are not connected in any way with kindliness or maleficence, nor is there any sort of hierarchical order amongst them. From the *inua* of the salmon to that of the moon, from 'double' to 'master', the distance is great, but the title quite simply evokes primordial anthropomorphism which is seen even in the details of a landscape.

There are other spirits too in the world of nature, of various origins, though they are all more or less connected with monsters, and they go by the names of *tug'ny'gat*, *tungat*, *tungrat* and *tunrat* among western Eskimos—terms which, by metathesis, have become *tornat* and *torngrat* in the eastern parts of Eskimo territory. Their appearance varies as much as their origin; moreover, they grow larger or smaller, or change shape at will. These spirits of places, of the disembodied dead, of ancient animals and various monsters are connected with a distinct spot (mountain, cliff, lake) or they are errant, dangerous and even terrifyingly (though rarely systematically) evil, and are in each and every case possessors of some of the secrets and powers of the universe. The shaman meets them in his dreams or ecstasies and copies on masks their twisted features—half human, half animal—thus tapping the potential force and knowledge that they represent. They sometimes appear of their own accord to reply to his questions, to help him see the invisible, and fly up in the air. Hence the name *tungalik*, 'he who has *tungat*', which is the local way of referring to the angekkok. Without them he would be unable to communicate with the supernatural. Some consult him, protect him, and others obey him in doglike fashion. Thus *tungat* and *inuat* appear as two very different categories, though they are not necessarily completely separate. The spirit of the moon may be given the title of *inua* or *tungak* according to the speaker's intention—one referring to his human origin and the other emphasising his powerful nature. *Tungak* is closer to the notion of 'divinity'. Above the *tungat*—though not necessarily at their head—is a super-*tungak*. In Alaska, the wisest of the wise, Tungrangayak, is depicted with his body covered in circles or eyes with which he can see everything: 'My whole body is nothing but eyes . . . I look in every direction.' In Labrador, Torngarsoak has the appearance of an enormous white bear; he lives in caves and rules over wild game. In Greenland there is a gigantic creature—half man, half seal—who is known as Tornarsuk or Tornatik and 'comes from the sea' to reveal to the angekkok the cause of maladies. Missionaries in search of the supreme being—and Eskimos desirous of granting their wishes—have turned not to Sila, but to Tornarsuk, more suited to identification with the Christian God.

Two Eskimo spirits attacking a third one, who is trying to make off with a child's soul. After Rasmussen.

Pendant of painted wood from Alaska, depicting the Eskimo Lord of the Whales. Whales, like all other sea mammals, are the province of the Moon, who can withhold them from mankind if they do not send him offerings. *Smithsonian Institution, U.S. National Museum*

Nujalik, the hairy woman, who is the patroness of hunting for animals on land. After Rasmussen.

Kigatilik, a terrifying spirit with huge fangs, who puts the shaman to flight. Eskimo drawing. After Rasmussen.

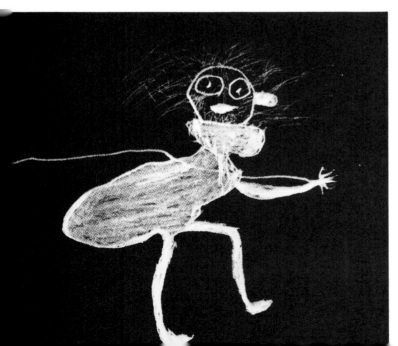

Sioux chief wearing his feathered headdress. On horseback
and armed with a hatchet, he is surrounded by men with
guns and powder-horns. Though horses were introduced only
by the Spanish, they were quickly incorporated into Indian
myths and daily life. When the Indians first heard gunfire
they took it for the thunder of Manitou, the Great Spirit.
Painting on buffalo skin. *Musée de l'Homme*

NORTH AMERICA: SPIRITS OF GOOD AND EVIL

About the middle of the sixteenth century, when the first Europeans began to settle on Indian territory in North America, there were more than 2,000 independent Indian tribes living there, frequently in a state of war. Modes of life of the tribes varied according to natural resources available. Salmon fishing, especially on the north-east coast of the Pacific, caribou hunting in the sub-Arctic zone of Canada, stag hunting in forest regions and buffalo hunting in the Great Plains stretching from the Mississippi to the Rocky Mountains were the main sources of food. Where climate permitted, maize was grown—for example, by the Iroquois tribes in the east, in the area of the Great Lakes, and to an even greater extent by the Pueblo tribes in the lower Colorado valleys of the south-west. Where there were no other means of subsistence, wild crops were gathered, as in the case of the Menomini, who lived to the west of the Iroquois group and gathered wild rice, and the Salish tribes on the Columbia-Fraser plateau, who collected mountain berries; south of this plateau in the semi-desert of the Great Basin the Shoshon Indians dug up edible roots; in southern California the Indians were even worse off and lived mainly on acorns.

The basic economy dictated the type of habitat in each case: permanent villages for farmers, tents for the semi-nomadic hunters who followed migratory game (in the course of the seventeenth century great numbers of horses brought in by the Spaniards furnished fresh incentive for the raiding Indians of the plains). From the linguistic point of view the tribes belonged to different families; those found in the Great Lakes were the Algonquins, Sioux and Iroquois. Social structure, together with the institutions and ritual involved, likewise produced distinct types. There were priests on the one hand, and also magicians or medicine-men more or less independent of the former, who claimed to have powers of healing, of producing rain and of guaranteeing the success of individual and collective enterprises.

The major part of some three hundred surviving tribes has been gradually confined to 'reserves' in the past century. Those peoples who were not farmers have seen great changes in their way of life; the last buffalo have gone; agricultural crops have mostly replaced natural crops. Social behaviour, moreover, has been modified by the increasing influence of white civilisation; little by little Indians have become citizens of the United States. Cross-breeding has taken place among autochthonous tribes and with white men.

So traditional Indian mythology originally grew up within a framework that has now been discarded. There have been very few additions to ancestral ideas: the relative importance of the creator has been emphasised, sometimes as a result of the influence of Christian preaching; occasionally local Indian prophets predicting the return of the dead and the re-establishment of an hegemony have instituted ceremonial dances in preparation for this return (Ghost Dance); finally, the cult of Peyotl has spread from Mexico.

In its most classical form North American mythology reveals common basic traits that lie beyond the seeming disparities of regional variations. The principal common denominator is the very active role assigned a body of protective or evil spirits; by comparison, the creator of the universe remains in the background, particularly as far as human fate is concerned. The majority of protective spirits are mythical animals or the like, but they also include the sun (worshipped by the huntsmen of the plains and by farmers, such as the ancient Natchez from Louisiana), stars (Nebraskan Pawnee mythology was enriched by astral folk-lore), thunder or 'thunder-

Painted wooden raven-head mask, opened to show the face of the sun-god. From Bilchoola, on the north-western coast of America. As the mask represents the hero-ancestor, the wearing of it signifies the assumption of divinity. The raven was the totem for most of the hunting tribes of the north-western coast. *Linden Museum, Stuttgart*

Indian sculpture from Alaska, showing a priest with a knife and offering bowl. Antithetic ideas of creation and destruction exist throughout North American mythology, and propitiatory sacrifices to the gods of hunting and agriculture were commonplace. *Bildarchiv Foto Marburg*

birds', gods of maize, spirits of mountains, rivers or such minerals as flint, which was used for arrow-heads. In contrast with these protectors, there are also giant monsters, such as the Kwakiuktl cannibals from the north-west coast of the Pacific or the Algonquin horned water-serpent. Tiny creatures who are waggish rather than wicked are believed by Indians to haunt woods and pools. The spirits of the dead are in principle to be feared, for they come to steal men's souls and to inflict death unless the medicine-man intervenes. In actual fact, all supernatural beings possess ambivalent powers, since protectors kill men's enemies and evil spirits accord their patronage to certain privileged people (members of certain bodies or medicine-men).

Protective spirits and the creator of the cosmos usually reside in celestial worlds or on mountain-tops. Monsters inhabit underground worlds and the depths of the sea. The land of the dead is sometimes thought to be in the sky at the end of the Milky Way, sometimes, though more rarely, underground (in that case it is occasionally associated with the creator). So Indians regard the universe as a series of worlds one above the other, with the world of men in the centre. For instance, the Bella-Coola tribe on the shores of British Columbia believes that there are five worlds; in the second of these, immediately above our own, a House of Myths contains the main gods.

Another fundamental feature of Indian thought is the link between the different worlds or cosmic sectors and the six points of space: the cardinal points, zenith ('the top') and nadir ('the bottom').

A sacred colour is associated with each sector or direction: The Zuñi tribe in New Mexico and several other Pueblo societies think of the north as yellow, the west as blue, the south as red, the east as white, the zenith as multicoloured and the nadir as black.

Each sector, each real or mythical mountain on the human horizon is associated with various animal, vegetable and mineral species, and farmers also associated them with the six varieties of maize, each of which is given symbolically one of the six colours of space. Animals, plants and minerals, the source of material prosperity, are thought to be under the domination of protective spirits, who grant them to men when the appropriate rites are performed.

Indian mythology can be studied from different points of view, and initially as an etiological account: the myths recount and justify the origins of the cosmos, the earth and men, of techniques and institutions; the latter in so far as they jointly affect moral, social and ritual rites and taboos. In most traditions the universe is described as having passed through an initial phase in which the populations consisted of animals and occasionally of seemingly anthropomorphic creatures who behaved like men, but at the same time played the part of demiurges and 'transformers'. Bella-Coola Indians account for this lack of differentiation between the animal and the human by saying that men were created in heaven and at the command of the creator chose the form in which they would inhabit the world – for example, as a raven, eagle, grizzly bear or brown bear.

The major hero varies according to the individual regions and their geographical and cultural divisions: he is a raven in Alaska and in the northern part of the north-west Pacific coast (there are affinities with Siberian myths here); he is a blue jay farther south, a coyote (prairie-wolf) on the Columbia–Fraser plateau and in the plains, a rabbit in the Great Basin and in the south-east, a hare in certain eastern communities. In other tribes there are mythological figures – such as Manibozho in the legends of the Algonquins, Glooskap in the tales of the Penobscot people of the north-east, and Wiyot in some communities of central California. (Anthropologically speaking, American Indians belong to the Asiatic race. They came from Asia across the Bering Strait in successive migrations. Definite cultural affinities have been noted between Siberian traditions and northwest Indian traditions; both, for instance, recount the adventure-cycle of the Raven setting the world to order.)

The first step taken by these mythical animals or analogous heroes was to bring order into the cosmos; they gained possession of fire, wind, rain and snow by dint of petty thefts cunningly carried out in a variety of supernatural places, the main one being the House of the Sun; they made mountains rise on soil that was once flat, they formed gulfs and riverbeds. Once upon a time, when the world was first inhabited, according to a Bella-Coola myth, there were no rivers to be seen, for they were imprisoned in a cave called Nusmatliwaix. The approach to this cave was barred by a huge rock. The rivers were not the only prisoners; the cave contained all the river-

Wooden deer mask from Eastern Florida. Most Indian tribes believed, not that their ancestors created the world, but that, taking the form of an animal, they totally reorganised it, laying down the social order. Hence the importance of these masks, which represent the ancestor's animal form. *University Museum, Philadelphia*

451

dwellers too. The Eagle was the first to try to break this barrier, but without success. Then the Raven succeeded. Since that time the river Bella-Coola has followed its present course.[1]

The animals who brought civilisation to the world were divided into peoples, and the tale of their rivalries is known to man; ultimately they decided to institute death, so as to avoid over-population and famine. Myths show them to be wise and intelligent, engaged in a systematic struggle against monsters, but at the same time cruel, egotistical, licentious, covetous and greedy. They liked to dupe those around them. However, on many occasions they showed such stupidity that they themselves fell into greater traps than those they set for others. When the Rabbit was journeying about the world, according to the Koasati Indians in the south-east, he met a troop of ducks swimming in a pool. So he went towards them with a rope about his waist, dived to reach them, and then fastened all their feet together. When he had done this, he surfaced in the midst of them, and the ducks flew off with the Rabbit dangling between them. The grandmother of the Rabbit had just finished wiping a pot and had put it on the ground when they flew over. The Rabbit called out to his grandmother and she saw him. When he was immediately overhead she hurled the pot and broke the rope, and the Rabbit fell to earth.[2]

Finally, this first mythical universe was destroyed, either by fire or flood, at the instigation of monsters. According to the Alaskan Githwan tribes, for instance, the Frog-woman or Volcano-woman (alternatively known as the Metal-woman because she benefited men by giving them copper) destroyed the world by fire. These are ambivalent attitudes, beneficent and maleficent, as has already been pointed out, and they are illustrated by other traditions in which a culture-hero is responsible for the Flood, although his intention may have been to palliate the action of the monsters. The Algonquin Manibozho, for instance, decided to produce a flood to extinguish a fire lit by his adversaries. Manibozho himself took refuge on a mountainside with a few animals. When the waters began to recede he ordered the musk-rat to dive down for some mud so that he could form the earth and men. He taught the latter the techniques necessary for survival; he established social institutions; he prescribed ceremonial ritual. Coyote and other culture-heroes did the same. There is proof of this in a Crow myth (found among the Sioux tribes in Montana), which also shows how prim-

itive mythology absorbed later elements. In this legend Coyote is described as having invented horses, although the only domestic animal the Indians had before the arrival of the Spaniards was the dog.

One character, who must have been the Old Coyote-man, made a boat. When he had finished it, it began to rain, and all the mountains were covered by water. When the waters receded, this boat ran aground on a high mountain. Two ducks made their way towards it; there was nowhere else to settle. Coyote asked them to dive down and find earth. One duck dived three times, but did not come back to the surface. So the Old Coyote-man told the other duck to bring him back mud in its beak. At the fourth attempt the duck returned with mud in its beak. Then Coyote scattered it about him and it became the earth. He traced out rivers and bays, made mountains and hills. From the mud he brought forth buffalo and horses; out of this mud he also created other animals. From leaves he made tepees (tents) and from mud he brought forth men. Also from mud he fashioned a wife for himself. The Old Coyote-man and his wife made arrows and all the things that men are wont to use. He told men to have sexual relations and in nine months they would have children. When they grew in number Coyote divided them into different tribes and settled them in a circle. He left one tribe in the middle and made the others its enemies. This central tribe was known as the Crow tribe. He instituted a dance to be executed over every enemy that was slain.

Other peoples, either in the western plains or in the south-west (Pueblos and the Navajo, their neighbours) believe that men were created in the fourth earth-womb. They were without light and warmth, and some had tails and black skins. Then mythical characters, with the aid of animals, gave them their present appearance and brought them up to the surface of the earth. The maize-gods, particularly Maize Mother, were connected with this ascent. The 'emergence' was followed by long peregrinations, each tribe being taken to its ordained habitat by supernatural beings. According to the Keresan Pueblos of New Mexico, for instance, the bowels of the earth contained four worlds, one on top of the other: the lowest was white, then red, blue and yellow. Iyatiku, 'Mother of Men' (and, as we shall see, Maize Mother), created a fir-tree, which acted as a ladder to the red world. Then she asked the Woodpecker to peck a hole through the thick layer of rock that barred the way to the world above that. Mankind stayed for four years in the blue world; the same procedure was used for the next two stages: a tree formed a ladder and the Woodpecker made a hole. Finally, the Badger and Old Man Whirlwind helped bring about the emergence. The place where men emerged though was too sacred for habitation; Iyatiku ordered them to emigrate south. Before she returned to the white world below she gave mankind an ear of

[1]Th. McIlwraith, *The Bella-Coola Indians*, Toronto, 1948, vol. 1. p. 342
[2]J. R. Swanton, *Myths and Tales of the Southeastern Indians*, Bulletin No. 88, Bureau of American Ethnology, Washington, 1929, p. 208

maize: 'This is my heart,' she said. 'It will be your food, and the sap from it will be like milk from my breast.'

Like the Indians who claim to have been created after the Flood (such as the Crow tribe quoted above), any tribe that associates its own beginnings with the emergence always claims to have held the place of honour in that arrival upon earth. It ascended first, it emerged at a central point. Myths of this type invariably add that other men remained prisoner in the bowels of the earth; Maize Mother and the mythical dead went to join them there. (These dead jointly represent the qualities of the ancestors and of protective spirits who are embodied in ceremonial masks—the Pueblo Kachinas—and they return at intervals to visit the living and assure them of good maize harvests.)

There are many incidents connected with the peregrinations that started at the point of emergence. The Pueblo Zuñi tell of the tragic death by drowning of the children of the first men. There is also in Pueblo mythology a story about a girl (who in myth is confused with foam) who went to collect pine-cones in the mountains and was fertilised by the Sun: twins, the little gods of war, were the offspring of this union. They left their mother and made their way towards the dawn to convince the Sun that he was their father. They had to pass several tests set by the Sun before he recognised them as his sons and gave them bows, arrows and javelins for killing monsters.

From the etiological point of view, myths are the justification and experience of the strictest prohibitions, particularly incest. In one fairly widespread story the Sun and Moon are quoted as two characters of different sexes; they desired one another, coupled, then learned that they were brother and sister. The sister was filled with shame and fled. Her brother pursued her into the sky, where they became the day star and the night star. Among the Indians of North America systems of relationship, the organisation of alliances and reciprocal agreements of the social, family and religious sub-groups all spring from the blood-ties between each of these separate units and some mythical hero. The image of the hero, who is the ancestor of his line, is sculpted on ceremonial masks, and in British Columbia it is also found on totem-poles erected in front of the chieftains' dwellings.

The great American ethnologist Boas was the first to realise the close relationship that exists between a given society, its way of life, its culture and its mythology: myths in fact reflect the material, social and religious image of the society in which they developed. But for the Indians mythology has another implication apart from its etiological function—it is a living reality: it is the guarantee of stability, security and the tribe's future prosperity, and to this end the major episodes in mythology are periodically staged as ritual drama. Costumed and masked actors bring the mythical past to life in songs and dances for the benefit of those who live in the present. The most important Algonquin ceremonies are called Midewiwin (or Great Medicine Dance) and depict the hero Manibozho's anguish on seeing his brother killed by monsters; then follow songs and dances instituted by supernatural beings for the inauguration of the lost brother as chief of the dead; and thus Manibozho is consoled. Even today the Algonquins believe that the celebration of Midewiwin has the immediate effect of safeguarding the health of all members of the tribe and ensuring wealth and group survival. The Pueblos in the south-west have Kachina dances that are performed each season from one solstice to another, and do rather more than simply recall the fact that the Maize Mother bestowed food-giving ears of maize upon their ancestors. Indeed, those members of confraternities who wear the Kachina masks and have ears of maize in their belts are the incarnation of the ancestors and the gods: thanks to their actual presence the maize will continue to grow.

The power attributed to mythical beings has a direct bearing on the medicine-man's magic; the protective spirits from whom the latter derives his authority are usually traditional heroes: Raven, Eagle, mythological characters who were the first to possess this ambivalent power to kill and cure. When the world began, in the words of a myth belonging to the Takelmas Indians in Oregon, a powerful mountain, the Old Rock-woman, was given the task of fighting the sorcerers (that is, evil spirits who sent sickness). She was given appropriate tools: a pot for boiling her enemies' hearts, a poker for stirring the heart in the pot. She was taught the necessary songs. Having put a sorcerer to death, she asked two other mountains (twin peaks) to join her. The two peaks executed a war-dance with one of the sorcerer's severed arms, then bowed to one another.

In fact, when an Indian medicine-man acquires or exercises his powers, the mythical protectors are a positive reality to him. They first appear to him to bestow upon him the privileged gift in a dream or vision bordering on a trance: 'In a dream,' related a Yuma medicine-man from Arizona, 'I was called to the mountain Awikwame. I reached it in four strides. I saw the shelter. In the shelter were two men, both unnaturally tall; they were certainly spirits . . . .' The tale goes on to tell how the protective spirit taught his chosen pupil the correct procedure for obtaining the desired cure. Now this demonstration, which is frequently given the future medicine-man, is still the same as that given the early ancestors. A man was dying of exhaustion, according to a Winnebago myth, and, seeking solitude, he made for a mountain-top. Animals appeared before him and began to nurse him. The Raven began. He cried: 'E-he-a, E-he-a', and gave a remedy. Then came the Wolf. He prowled round the sick man howling and spitting out magic remedies. The man was

Two totem poles from Haida Indian settlements. The totem pole is a form of heraldry, indicating the owner's lineage, and sometimes forms a memorial to the dead. The detail on the left, showing a head, comes from the Museum für Völkerkunde, Hamburg. *Bildarchiv Foto Marburg.* The free-standing pole on the right tells the story of Yetl the raven. Yetl himself appears at the top disguised as a chief with a ceremonial hat and staff. Beneath this he appears at intervals with his beak flattened to indicate it is broken. Nineteenth century. *British Museum*

Painted wooden raven-head mask from Bilchoola, on the north-western coast of America. This mask would have been used in one of the periodic ritual ceremonies commemorating the myth of the hero-ancestor and reaffirming the social order which he laid down for the tribe. *Linden Museum, Stuttgart*

Carved Indian pipe-head. Pipe-smoking was a ceremonial activity, and tobacco was grown only for this purpose. Whenever the council of each self-contained tribe met (and the meetings might last for several days) smoking and passing of the pipe was an important symbolical custom, and each member brought his pipe and pouch. *Bildarchiv Foto Marburg*

almost cured; he was already much better. The Tortoise then began to exercise her powers, crying as she did so: 'Ahi, ahi, ahi, ahi, ahi', and she moved round the man and made him drink an infusion. At that point he was almost entirely cured. Then all the animals who had cured him said to him: 'Man, even so will you cure your fellows.' They gave him all the magic remedies he needed.

So myths may be regarded as etiological and typical, an image of the society that produces them, active in so far as ritual and the practices of medicine-men give them a physical reality; but they must also be envisaged by the ethnologist from various other points of view. First of all, their possible connection with actual tribal history must be considered. For example, the Arikara and Pawnee Indians, who originally farmed in Louisiana, are known to have moved up the Missouri valley and made their way north and west towards the plains. Once they had settled in the plains they became hunters. This is reflected in the myths about their emergence, which tell of their migrations on earth towards the west or north; other myths depict heroes who are anxious to save their people from famine, and so, thanks to protective spirits, they are married on the mountainside to both the Maize Mother and the Buffalo-woman. The Sun Dance, the most important piece of ritual for the Indians of the plains, is in fact intended to ensure successful hunting together with fruitful crops.

Mythology and ritual may also reflect a fusion between two tribes that is based on historical reality. Cushing, the ethnographer, describes an example of this with regard to the name of Zuñi clowns. It is a custom among the Zuñi Indians, as in many other societies, for actors with grotesque masks to parody priests when the most sacred rites are being celebrated (in this particular case, they are in contrast to the Kachinas). These priests, say the Zuñi Indians, are Koyemshis, ancestral children who were drowned shortly after the emergence, and who are also known by the name of Ahlashiwe, in other words 'Old Stones'. Now the term Ahlashiwe also applies to a kind of fetish-stone from the west. So the Koyemshis would seem to represent the survival of foreign gods belonging to the Salado race, which originally came from the west and fused with Zuñi tribes.

Finally, as Claude Lévi-Strauss has been able to show, students of North American mythology should now use the method of structural anthropology. To study the structure of myths is to study the thought-structure behind them. North American mythology follows symmetrically constructed patterns in which protectors are contrasted with monsters, heaven with earth, the living with the dead, male with female, 'nature' (hunting, wild crops and raw food) with 'culture' (maize-farming, cooked food and prepared food-stuffs). Aware of these contrasts, North American mythology attempts ultimately to mediate between them by using a dialectic process of

Top: A storage box showing a beaver in the centre, a bear beneath and two ravens in the bottom corners. They are all totem emblems of northern tribes and are connected with the legendary past of the tribe's ancestors. Haida Indian. National Museum of Canada. *Art Institute of Chicago*

Above: A carved wooden figure of a killer whale. The enemy of the Northwest Coast fishermen, the terrifying figure of the killer whale features in many of their legends. Kwakiutl Indian. *Taylor Museum, Colorado Springs*

Left: Woven shirt with a bear design. The totem animals were often displayed in this distinctive style, with limbs outstretched in frog fashion and with faces or eyes marking the joints. Tlingit Indian. *Museum of the American Indian*

The cult-objects of the North American Indians derived from simple natural objects. The shell, inlaid with turquoises, was worn as an amulet in the winter solstice ceremony. The feathered prayer-sticks recall that many spirits, including the Great Spirit, took the form of birds, and that an eagle's feather stained red was the image of the breath of life. The double-headed serpent staff of the Zuñi Indians demonstrates that even their natural enemies had a place in Indian ritual and magic. *British Museum*

homology. Indian thought in fact replaces two terms that are irreconcilable with two equivalent terms that may admit of another as intermediary. 'After which, one of the two polar terms and the intermediary term are in turn replaced by a new triad, and so on.'

The fundamental antithesis is between life and death; it can be transposed by interpreting the first term as agriculture (source of life) and the second as war (source of death). A 'mediatory notion' between agriculture and war can be found in the idea of a scalp, since a scalp is 'the harvest of war'; that is why, in myths, scalps produce dew.

Another example of mediation between life and death appears in the enigmatic personality of the two culture-heroes, Coyote and Raven. These creatures feed on carrion; they come half-way between animals that prey on others (for they feed on flesh) and herbivorous animals (for they do not kill what they eat). Now there is an homologous association between animals of prey and herbivorous animals on the one hand, and hunting and agriculture on the other, and, by extension, war and agriculture. Now let us once again compare life and death and war and agriculture: we see that Coyote and Raven are ultimately mediators between life and death and that their simultaneously destructive and beneficent character and

function are reflections of the duality they exist to surmount.

The search for a formula of mediation between life and death is more immediately comprehensible in those myths in which a human being rises again from death: for instance, a man gives up his own life in order to submit to ordeals in the land of the dead, and when he triumphs over them his much-lamented wife is allowed to return to the world above and he himself is given the personal right to reincarnation. In a variant of this myth, warriors sacrifice their lives, not to save a wife, but for the sake of tribal prosperity. According to another variant a young man who has no parents risks his life to bring back the daughter of a chieftain who has died of love for him; in this case the ordeals over which he triumphs are no longer set in the world of the dead, but in the house in which his beloved died.

Finally, it is impossible to understand a North American myth, and all the variants involved, without taking into account the geographical and cultural context and re-establishing the structural pattern according to which it was built. But this is true of any myth; so the mythology of North American Indians does not constitute a special case in the exercise of mythical thought. It conforms to rule.

Double set of sacrificial steps at Tenayuca. These pyramidal structures symbolise the theocratic and mythological hierarchy of the Aztecs, which sought to place gods and men in a formal relationship of power and obligations, each individual, even gods, dependent on all the others. *Raul Flores Guerrero*

CENTRAL AMERICA: GODS OF SACRIFICE

The first missionaries received an impression of bloodshed, violence and stupefying excesses, and these characteristics may well account for the events that marked Mexico's history. At a time when the whole of Europe was ablaze with the pyres lit by the great Inquisition in their fight against heresy, the representatives of the faith found their way to this country where blood flowed freely, where the gods were so exigent that they were described by no name other than *este demonio*; a land in which Xochipilli, the young god of beauty, love and youth, the Flower Prince, was depicted with a death's-head contorted into the most hideous of smiles, and where even to-day children play with puppets called 'dead-mariachi', the 'dead-peasant' and sometimes 'dead-dead man'. So they were faced with an entirely different conception of the world, and an 'alien' religious universe.

Of all the various races in Central America, two have left a deeper impression than the rest, though for different reasons: the Mayas and Aztecs. The Maya empire was highly 'civilised' and ancient, and it had evolved and reached a stage of development that might be described as too perfect, though even before the arrival of the Spaniards it had already begun to decline. The Aztecs, on the other hand, were a young race in mid-development and had to face up to the terrible impact of the Conquest almost alone. And so there is a sort of arbitrary tendency—with some historical basis, though in actual fact quite unjust—to take as a permanent image of the Aztecs what they were at the very moment when all their values were overthrown, disregarding the fact that their development was incomplete. To give only one example, their written language, which in the beginning was nothing more than a collection of simple markings (figurative, toponymic or genealogical), undoubtedly would have evolved to form an alphabet in time.

Monument III from Cozumel. It shows a ball-player worshipping the sun god who is suspended from the jaws of a beast of prey. A.D. 600–800. Museum für Völkerkunde, Berlin. *Walter Steinkopf*

The Aztecs

Ceremonial axe in the form of a helmeted man. Totonac style. Human sacrifices were made in a variety of ways. Beheading was perhaps the most humane; others included flaying, killing with arrows, burning and tearing out of the heart. *Musée de l'Homme*

The Aztecs, then, were a people whose development was cut short, and their religion is only a rough attempt to synthesise various cultural trends, an unresolved contest between the gods of a huge pantheon: on the one hand, ancient gods of conquered lands, gods of the earth, fertility and rain and agrarian gods; and, on the other hand, young, victorious, violent solar deities and warrior-gods.

The history of the Aztec tribe is no mystery: they were a small, wandering race driven from all fertile lands and treated as 'barbarians' by other tribes until they achieved a sort of supremacy by dint of violence, faith and, indeed, treachery. Though not long established on the Gulf of Mexico (1325), the 'people of the Sun' had succeeded in forming not so much an empire as a confederation under its leadership. Although the gods proper to the Aztecs — primarily Huitzilopochtli, who guided them in their wanderings — dominated their daily life, other gods, conquered or half-forgotten, found their way into the pantheon and were given constant worship (a part of the sacred enclosure of Tenochtitlan was kept for the least important of them). And perhaps one cause of the extreme religious repression the Aztecs were made to suffer was the refusal of Jesus Christ to enter this pantheon as the nine hundred and ninety-ninth god.

However, this seeming chaos in divine affairs was not chaos at all. On the contrary, this universe had its own definite structure, and the inter-relationships between gods followed a distinct trend. Hence the extraordinary number of myths, for they were attempts to construct and explain.

At the time of the Conquest there was a clear and discernible line of evolution which came to an abrupt end. The Mexican clergy, which was an immense and all-powerful body (it is thought that the number of persons dedicated solely to the cults was as high as 5,000, and the 'emperor' himself simply represented the highest point in the theocracy), was engaged in an attempt to unify the religion, to introduce order and a hierarchy, and to attain a sort of syncretism. Conquered or 'specialised' gods were gradually becoming absorbed as aspects of more powerful gods.

This tendency was developed to its limits by Nezahualcoyotl, king of Texcoco, who raised a tower to the 'abstraction'. He built a nine-storey temple (like the nine heavens, or nine stages in the journey of the soul before it found eternal repose) dedicated to the 'unknown god, creator of all things', whom he called Tloquenahuaque, 'He who is very near'; or Ipalnemoani, 'He by whom we live'. There were no statues in this temple: the supreme god, conceived in this way, was impossible to depict. But this was a step taken by an individual, a search for a god who was the 'first cause', though Nezahualcoyotl himself did not dare refute his people's divine pantheon. These gods simply took their place on the great pyramid at

Stone mask representing Xipe Totec. Life, to the Aztecs, had to proceed from death. By wearing the skin of a sacrificial victim the priest symbolised the rebirth of vegetation in the spring. Xipe Totec thus came to be seen as a god of spring and flowers. Aztec, probably fourteenth century. *British Museum*

The Five World Regions. The four cardinal points were associated with the four sons of Ometecuhtli who created the world: Xipe Totec, Camaxtli, Quetzalcoatl and Huitzilopochtli. They were also connected with the four 'Suns' which preceded our own world and which all ended in destruction. The fifth and central region is that of the present world and represents instability, for it will end in earthquakes. Xiuhtecuhtli presides over it. Codex Féjerváry-Mayer. Mixtec, probably before 1350. *Liverpool Museum*

lower levels. Monotheism is completely foreign to the Aztec concept of the world. For instance, according to one of the creation legends (reported by Torquemada) the original goddess, Omeciuatl, would appear to have given birth to a sacrificial knife made of obsidian, *tecpatl*; this knife fell upon the northern plains (from which the Aztecs came) and as it fell gave birth to 1,600, in other words countless, gods. So polytheism is written into the very beginnings of Mexican myth.

Curiously enough, according to other creation legends gods and men were the sons of an original divine couple: Ometecuhtli and Omeciuatl, 'the Lord and Lady of Duality', also known as Tonacatecuhtli and Tonacacihuatl, 'Lord and Lady of our Flesh'. But this first couple who created the other living beings always had a limited cult. They seem, moreover, to have lost their importance about the thirteenth century, at the time of Nahuatl domination. These gods of creation gave birth to four sons, whom they instructed to create the world, other gods and, lastly, men. These four 'active' gods were red Tezcatlipoca, also known as Xipe Totec and Camaxtli; black Tezcatlipoca (always called Tezcatlipoca); white Tezcatlipoca: Quetzalcoatl; blue Tezcatlipoca: Huitzilopochtli. Each of these gods represented a time, a space, a collection of beliefs connected with a cardinal point, a colour, an order of the universe.

Thus one of the most striking characteristics of Mexican religion is this form of 'rationalism', everything, every event being the manifestation of a god, the recollection of a moment in his history, the expression of his will. There are no natural phenomena, only gods closely dependent on one another in their dealings with men. This dependence is reciprocal: it is this that gives the Aztec race the idea of its involvement and responsibility. It is a chosen race, elected to help the sun in his task, which is to allow the world to continue. If the predestined race did not perform its duty, if it no longer gave the god his nourishment—blood—the world would stop.

Each myth has been handed down in different versions depending on date, region and transcription; in fact, there must have been a considerable gap between religion as we know it (as the priests taught it in the *calmecacs*), and as lived by the lower classes, the *macehuali*, especially outside towns where ancient deities counted for more than the young gods and philosophic theories; Tlaloc, god of rain, or ancient goddesses of fertility, earth and maize, must have known greater favour than Tezcatlipoca or Huitzilopochtli, the sun-gods, young gods of violence and missionaries of the 'Aztec vocation'. Moreover, the conquerors saw on the great *teocalli* in Mexico twin temples: the temple of Tlaloc and the temple of Huitzilopochtli. And Huitzilopochtli, war-god and chief god of the Aztecs, was the son of Coatlicue, the ancient earth-goddess. Similarly,

two priests were at the head of the sacerdotal hierarchy: the grand priests of Huitzilopochtli and Tlaloc.

Thus the religion of Anahuac in Central Mexico presents a certain number of highly particular characteristics, some of which defy definition: fundamental and limitless polytheism, a concept of history and the world in terms of 'conflict' (male powers fighting against female powers, Tezcatlipoca against Quetzalcoatl, nocturnal against diurnal powers, the sun against the moon and stars, good against evil; a deep-seated idea of human responsibility, leading ultimately to extraordinary sacrifices and self-sacrifice, and also to the use of a great number of 'recipes' (most gods were magicians, *necromanticos y hechiceros*; men can try to change the course of things by magic practices); total pessimism—for, as we shall see, the world is condemned, and gods, like men, are mortal—leading to well-nigh complete submission to the 'Book of Destiny'.

The most significant myths in Mexican cosmological thought are, by definition, creation myths, because they allow one to grasp the Mexican notion of the world as something eternally threatened, and reveal the concept of mankind as being in a state of eternal reprieve. Most documents we have—illustrated codices from before Cortez's arrival, commentaries in the Nahuatl language and Latin script, works of the early missionaries, great works like the famous Aztec Calendar—make mention of a myth known as the legend of the four suns, which has come down to us in several different versions. (The version followed here goes by the name of the *Legenda de los Soles*.)

There were four eras known as 'suns' before our own: all ended in cataclysm. The first sun, *nahui ocelotl*, 'four tiger', lasted 676 years. The inhabitants of earth perished, devoured by tigers, on the day that bore the date 'four tiger'. 'Then the Sun disappeared . . . .'

Chicomecoatl, the maize goddess. She was sometimes called 'Seven Snakes' or identified with Tonacacihuatl, the goddess who, with Tonacatecuhtli, formed the first divine couple, whose four sons created the world, the other gods and men. *Bildarchiv Foto Marburg*

The goddess Chalchiuhtlicue, wife of Tlaloc. She was goddess of running water and streams, and was invoked for the protection of new-born children, marriages and chaste love. Granite terminal from Central Mexico. *Philadelphia Museum of Art.*

Calendar stone found near the main temple enclosure at Tenochtitlan. The Aztec calendar set out the mathematical formulas according to which the whole universe was organised and which governed the actions of men and gods alike. Priests spent much time studying the calendar. Carved after 1502 just before the downfall of the Aztecs. *National Museum of Anthropology, Mexico*

Another sun followed with the name *nahui ehecatl*, 'four wind'. Mankind was swept away by terrible winds, and the survivors changed into monkeys. This era lasted 364 years.

Then came the sun *nahui quiahuitl*, 'four rain'. A fearful shower of fire destroyed beings and things after 312 years. Men were transformed into birds.

The last sun, *nahui atl*, 'four water', lasted 676 years, at the end of which time men became fish. The flood destroyed the world and only one man and one woman survived.

The sun that is now ours goes by the name of *nahui ollin*, 'four earthquake'. 'This, our own, is that of those who are alive today . . . .'

The first sun was ruled by Tezcatlipoca, god of the north, of cold and darkness, who often disguised himself as a tiger; the second depended on Quetzalcoatl, god of the west and witchcraft; the third on Tlaloc as god of the south and fire; the fourth on Chalchihuitlicue, goddess of the east and water. As for our own sun, it is the sun of the centre (five is the number of the centre and of instability); it is dedicated to Xiuhtecuhtli, the fire-god, and will end in earthquakes.

The order of suns is not the same in every text. Dr Caso preferred to adopt a different order: sun of water, sun of fire, sun of wind, sun of tiger. The tigers eat the creatures—giants—who inhabit it. Many tales or traditions affirm the presence of giants in the 'steps' of the empire (Tlaxcala traditions, for example, report fights between Indians and giants who were known as *quinametzin*). This version of the myth contains the idea of evolution, the earth being peopled each time with more perfect creatures: fish, birds, monkeys, giants. There seems to be the same progression in the basic food connected with each species: the last-mentioned had *cencocopi* or *teocentli*, an early species of maize, and even men had no knowledge of agriculture.

In fact, the Aztecs, the trustees of maize-farming, evinced the greatest scorn for 'savages', barbarians in the north, 'redskins', tribes of nomadic huntsmen and gatherers of wild crops, as the Aztecs themselves had been some two hundred years earlier. But these races did not have *nahual*—that is to say, the 'spirit'.

This tradition may be compared with that of modern Huichol tribes, who have the same ethnic and linguistic origins, and have remained very close to the Aztecs—that is to say, to what the Aztecs were at the time of the Conquest. They believe that Majakuagy, their culture-hero, fought against the barbarians, taught his race the principles of government and invented agriculture for them, especially maize-farming, which is divine in essence.

If these worlds were destroyed, the reason is that they were imperfect. And this is a very important Aztec concept: basic pessimism. Our world too will end, as the previous worlds ended, in a terrible cataclysm. Determinism of this kind forces men, even at that level, the level of creation, never to relax their attention. Every new day, every new century is a divine triumph, and therefore a human triumph, and only sacrifice can prolong the life of mankind.

Quiche Indians have a comparable myth: the gods created four races in turn, all of them imperfect, before they came to our own. It was only maize, a noble substance, that finally brought them success in the creation of mankind and won from men the worship that was their due. So Aztec pessimism is on two planes: our world will end—it will end because it is imperfect. Our sun is no more complete than the previous ones, our human race will also be destroyed, when the gods decide to 'terminate the contract' that binds them to us.

This solar myth contains one particular idea that is fundamental to Aztec thought: the extraordinary importance of numbers, each one connected to a particular god, to a colour, to a point in space, to joint influences—good or bad. The suns (of which there were four) all terminated on a date bearing the number 4 (an unlucky number). They each lasted a fixed number of years, which always had some connection with the number 13 (that of time itself, that which represents the completion of the temporal series) and the number 52, the Aztec century, *xiuhmolpilli*, the 'ligature of the years'. The first sun lasted 676 years, or 13×52; the second 364 years, or 13×28 or 52×7; the third 312 years, or 13×24 or 52×6; the fourth 676 years, again 13×52. The first and last suns were thus the most 'perfect' since they contained only two numbers.

Every act, every event, every destiny was ruled by the Divine Calendar, the 'Book of Destiny', *tonalamatl*. As each century, each year, each month, each week, each day belonged to a god and thus participated in a certain universal order, human destiny was the meeting-point of these forces, and individual liberty the synthesis of these dependent parts. The notion of *tonal*, which simply referred to destiny at the outset, gradually came to be translated by the actual word 'soul', the idea of 'destiny'—in the sense of future—being replaced by that of 'individuality'. Upon the birth of a child, or before an important event, the priests consulted the great book and abstracted portents from it. Even before he had a name, a child was known by the day of his birth. (For instance, the Chimalpopoca codex refers to the great Toltec god in these words *Ce Acatl Quetzalcoatl*, 'One-reed Quetzalcoatl'.) Even the name of the newborn babe was taken from the joint influence affecting his birth, and it in turn influenced his life. Cuauhtemoc 'the falling eagle' (the sinking sun), was the name given to the last Aztec emperor.

The Calendar was extraordinarily complicated

and a large part of the clergy was engaged in its study and teaching. Here we shall simply quote the main lines it followed. Each day was referred to by one of these twenty signs:

1. *cipactli*, aquatic monster
2. *eecatl*, wind
3. *calli*, house
4. *cuetzepalin*, lizard
5. *coatl*, serpent
6. *miquiztli*, death
7. *mazatl*, stag
8. *tochtli*, rabbit
9. *atl*, water
10. *itzcuintli*, dog
11. *ozomatli*, monkey
12. *malinalli*, grass
13. *acatl*, reed
14. *ocelotl*, jaguar
15. *quauhtli*, eagle
16. *cozcaquautli*, vulture
17. *olin*, quaking
18. *tecpatl*, flint
19. *quiauitl*, rain
20. *xochitl*, flower

So each day has a name and a number. But there are only thirteen of these numbers, with the result that the day '13 acatl' is followed by the day '1 ocelotl'. This period of thirteen days is the Aztec week. To find the same combination of day and date, one has to wait $13 \times 20 = 260$ days. This is the *tonalpohualli*, written in special books called *tonalamatl* and interpreted by seers known as *tonalpouhque*.

The years bear the name of one of the following four signs: *acatl, tecpatl, calli, tochtli*. These are called 'year-bearers'. These signs too are linked with the numbers 1 to 13. Before the same sign is found again with the same number one has to wait $4 \times 13 = 52$ years. This period is the Aztec century, the *xiuhmolpilli*. The world always ran its greatest risk at the end of such a period. Was this century to be the last? All fires were extinguished, a huge and silent procession was formed, led by the priests and followed by the entire population, and it made its way to the spot named *cerro de la Estrella,* near Ixtapalapz. If at midnight the planet Yohualtecutli crossed the firmament, the fires were relit, and the final cataclysm was postponed by 52 years.

The computation of days according to the Divine Calendar was complicated by other systems. There was the civil year composed of 18 months, 20 days and 5 extra days without signs, ill-omened days called *nemontemi*: the Venusian year was composed of 584 solar days. After 65 Venusian years the three calendars – divine, solar, Venusian – once again indicated the same date. This lapse of time was called *cehueutiliztli* 'an old age' and represented the longest stretch of time to be studied by Mexican *tonalpouhques*.

As each sign belonged to a god and to a particular point in space (for example, the four year-bearers had these connections: Acatl with the east, Tecpatl

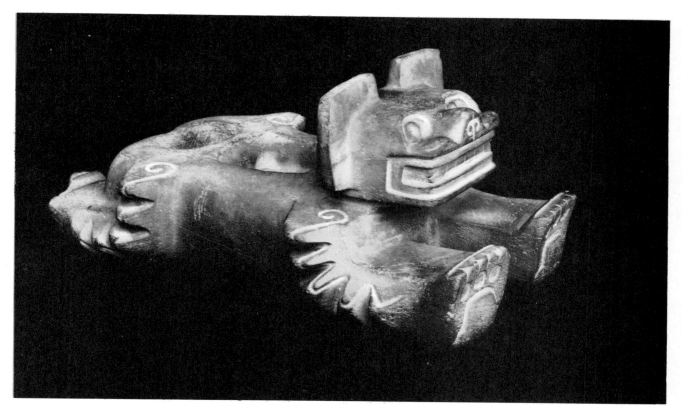

with the north; Calli with the west; Tochtli with the south), the destiny of each man was played out at a well-defined point in space and time.

Thus the destiny of mankind depended on divine will, but even more on the order in the universe. The rising, setting and reappearance of the Sun symbolised death and the rebirth of all things, just as the emergence, waxing and waning of the Moon (or birth, youth and death) symbolised endless periodic change, the rhythm of life. Aztec myths all attempted to explain the cosmos. The tribe, in its ceaseless wish for triumph, identified itself with the victorious Sun. The Aztecs were called the 'people of the Sun'. The story of the Sun, of its fight against the powers of darkness, is both divine history and the archetype of human adventure. Thus, for instance, Quetzalcoatl, the culture-god, had to undergo a frightful ordeal and fight against Tezcatlipoca, the supreme god of night. In the same way the historical Quetzalcoatl, the priest-king of Tula and mythical hero, was driven from his town by Tezcatlipoca's clergy. The 'ball-game', a rite that is of importance throughout Mexico, is the dramatic recreation of this combat.

All the great gods of the Aztec pantheon, both the tribal gods and those they won over, have a solar aspect and *are* the Sun in one of its attributes.

Tonatiuh, an ancient god with a somewhat less active cult than others, is the Sun itself. He is depicted in the centre of the Aztec Calendar, with protruding tongue, demanding human blood to sustain him.

Tezcatlipoca is, one might say, the anti-sun, the god of night and the evil powers then set free, the god of darkness, the Sun conquered and gloom victorious.

Quetzalcoatl represents the setting Sun, the Sun that has won its victory and is returning to the west. He is a white, bearded man, not as a sort of prefiguration but because he was old, wise, 'white'.

Huitzilopochtli is the brilliant, victorious Sun at the zenith. He is a young war-god, the special god of the

Onyx offering bowl in the form of an ocelot or jaguar. Teotihuacan culture, about A.D. 600. The jaguar was one of several gods previously worshipped in Mexico that the Aztecs incorporated into their own mythology. The jaguar and eagle were first to offer their own sacrifice so that the Sun could move. *British Museum*

Quetzalcoatl in the shape of Ehecatl, god of the wind, seated on his shrine—a temple on top of a pyramid. It was as Quetzalcoatl-Ehecatl that he supervised the sacrifice of all of the gods, so that at the creation of the fifth world the Sun would not be extinguished. The pyramid here is similar to the flight of steps on which victims were sacrificed. *Rijksmuseum voor Volkenkunde, Leiden*

Xochipilli, who, though prince of flowers and god of beauty, love, happiness and youth and god of music and dancing, was always represented as a dead man, his face grimacing with a horrible smile. *National Museum of Anthropology, Mexico*

Ceremonial axe representing Xolotl, the planet Venus. He is portrayed with a dog's head, one of the forms he assumed when attempting to avoid sacrificing himself for the sake of the Sun. Xolotl became the mythological twin of Quetzalcoatl. *Xalapa Museum*

Xipe Totec (Our Lord the Flayed One) dressed in the skin of a human offering. The marks on the back caused by flaying, and the gash in the breast through which the bleeding heart was torn out, have been sewn up. Stone carving, A.D. 1507. *Museum of the American Indian*

Aztecs. One could continue to give examples. If the gods were not all sons of one and the same divine couple, then their kinship would spring from their connection with this solar hierophany.

After several fruitless attempts the world, our sun, was finally created. But nothing existed, there was no life since there was no sunshine. The gods were in a dilemma. They met together at Teotihuacan and asked one another: 'Who will have the task of lighting the world?' One god responded to their appeal: Teccuciztecatl, 'He of the sea-shell'. The other gods refused to reply, for 'all were afraid and excused themselves'. A little god, Nanahuatzin, whom no-one thought much of, was appointed: 'Be the one to give light, you pimply little god.' The two gods then began to do penance for four days. Next they made offerings. Everything that Teccuciztecatl offered was of definite value: precious feathers from the quetzalli bird, fine stone flints, scarified needles of red coral; 'and the copal that he offered was very good'. Nanahuatzin, for his part, offered only green reeds, in bundles of three, maguey thorns stained with his own blood, and, 'instead of copal, he offered the scabs from his spots'.

Shortly before midnight the two gods, one magnificently apparelled, the other dressed in paper garments made from the bark of trees, were brought before the *teotxcalli*, where the sacred fire had been burning for four days. Teccuciztecatl went forward, then drew back, and four times hesitated to enter the blaze. Nanahuatzin, on the other hand, threw himself straight into it. After them an eagle was the first to enter the fire, and this made its plumes black for ever. Then came a tiger, 'which did not burn and only scorched', and from that time on its coat had black and white stripes. (The two great companies of Aztec warriors are known to have been those of the eagle-knights and tiger-knights or

jaguar-knights. This clearly involved a recreation of the myth.)

In another version, translated from sixteenth-century Spanish, the pimply little god is described in this way:

'Nanahuatzin, as he was poor, had nothing to offer, but he sacrificed in his small way, and offered what he could, however slight . . . . Then Nanahuatzin went into the fire by magic art, in which he was very knowledgeable . . . and was chosen to be the Sun . . . .'

To continue in the words of Sahagún: 'First came forth the Sun, and after him, the Moon.' These were the gods reborn in the form of stars. But they both shone with equal brilliance. To punish Teccuciztecatl for his cowardice, one of the gods threw a rabbit at the Moon's face: that is why there are dark patches over it today, in which Mexicans think that they can make out the shape of a rabbit.

But the two stars stayed motionless in the sky. They were dead. Then the gods decided to make sacrifice of themselves and to die, so that the Sun might live. Only one tried to escape: Xolotl. He fled and changed first of all into a double ear of maize, then into a double maguey plant (*mexolotl*), then into a fish (*axolotl*). Finally, he was captured, thus completing the sacrifice of the gods. (Xolotl, who was also the doublet of Quetzalcoatl, became the god of monsters, twins and double ears of grain. First and foremost he was the god of magicians because of his ability to change shape.)

Nanahuatzin, the god who died and rose again, is another one whose name has the same etymology as Quetzalcoatl. The story of this pustulous little god, who was either leprous or syphilitic and was ignored by everyone before he became the Sun, is a prefiguration of the history of the Aztec race and the victory of the poor, wandering, little tribe over its powerful neighbours.

But this myth has another meaning: it is the victory of the male principle, the Sun, over the female principle, the Moon. The name Teccuciztecatl comes from *tecciztli*, the sea-shell, which is the symbol of both the Moon and the female organ. Although one is dealing here with a god, the Moon is none the less regarded as a female principle, connected with vegetation, fertility and water. All vegetation goddesses wear a nasal ornament in the shape of a moon, called *yacameztli* (literally: 'nose moon'). This sex symbolism recurs in the choice of animal thrown by a god in the Moon's face: a rabbit. The Centzon totochtin, '400 rabbits', are deities of drunkenness and licentiousness.

It would therefore seem that the extraordinary importance of human sacrifice does not spring from purposeless cruelty, but from the most terrible of necessities: that of feeding the Sun. Each sacrifice is a continuation of the divine sacrifice. The statement that 'Mexico bathed in a river of blood' is justified. There are countless examples. At the festivals held to commemorate the foundation of the great Teocalli in Mexico the canals in the city flowed swift with blood.

This absolute obligation to feed the Sun lies behind many institutions at the basis of the social structure. The holy war, *xochiyaoyotl*, the 'flowered war', which the gods demanded, sprang from the necessity to find victims at a time when the country was relatively peaceful. Similarly, the two orders of warrior-knights, as representatives of the Sun, knew for what purpose they had been created and looked on their mission as a privilege: namely, to nourish the Sun, first by taking prisoners, then by dying themselves on the sacrificial stone. After death the most coveted fate of all was theirs: they became eagles, 'companions of the Sun', and they accompanied him in his journey to the zenith. There is a story about Tlahuicole which illustrates this idea: this brave Tlaxcaltec

warrior had been taken prisoner. So great was his fame that the Emperor offered him the command of an army in his war against the Tarascs and heaped honours upon him. But on his return from this campaign, Tlahuicole requested that he might die by gladiatory sacrifice, a privilege granted brave warriors, for he was asking his enemies: ' . . . to put an end to his unhappy days, for in living he considered himself to be dishonoured and by dying he would win the honour his whole life had procured for him, and that it would be best to put him to death . . . .' (Torquemada)

After his death the Aztecs celebrated for eight days with feasting and dancing '*por ser de persona tan singular y eminente*'. Moreover, we know that any warrior who took a man prisoner wept with him, calling him 'my son'.

One of the historical reasons behind the terrible collapse of Mexico in her fight against the Spaniards perhaps lies in this situation: that the Spaniards were seeking to kill as many of the enemy as possible, whereas the Aztecs wanted as many prisoners as possible to offer to their gods.

So there was neither scorn nor hatred for prisoners condemned to death; rather, the Aztecs treated the prisoners with respect and fraternity. The gods were very close to men and made in their image. So an offering of human blood was the only one worthy of them. Some animal sacrifices were made too. But these were always animals associated with the Sun legend, such as the quail, and so they were human 'substitutes' in a way. According to certain traditions Quetzalcoatl went down to hell after the destruction of the last sun with his twin brother, Xolotl, as his companion, in an attempt to steal the bones of earlier men and thus create our own human race. But Mictlantecutli, the 'Lord of the Sojourn of the Dead', was furious and sent quails to pursue them.

Just as human life stops when the blood ceases to flow, and this 'precious water' is at an end, so the world would cease to exist if the Sun were deprived of his sustenance, *tlaxcaltizitli*, and if there were no further offerings of blood. Because these beings and substances were identified with one another, man-god and blood-water, they gave birth to rites to which the term 'sympathetic magic' may truly be applied. For example, in honour of Xipe Totec, 'Our Lord, the Flayed One', the god of vegetation and its renewal, a prisoner was shot to death with arrows; his blood was allowed to seep slowly to the ground, to 'water' it, and mythically it acted as rain. Similarly, young children were sacrificed to Tlaloc, god of rain; as they walked to meet their death, they had to weep; their tears actually *were* rain. This same idea is taken to it utmost limit in the ritual cremation of the body of the human sacrifice, which is a veritable communion rite.

Quetzalcoatl, the supreme culture-god, who was the first to introduce a certain moral concern into religion, always betrayed the greatest aversion to human sacrifice:

'When Quetzalcoatl was alive, demons tried to trick him several times, so that he would make human sacrifice and kill men. But he never yielded or consented, for he loved his vassals well . . . .'

Animals were the only form of living sacrifice he would make to the gods—snakes, turkeys, butterflies, all of which were symbolic and had a divine, solar significance. But above all he offered his own blood.

However, the real significance of all this was not the suppression of human sacrifice, but the fact that it was made spiritual. It was not human blood, but one's own blood that counted in the eyes of gods. In the myth about the birth of the Sun we saw how Nanahuatzin, whose name came from the same root as Quetzalcoatl, first offered maguey thorns stained with his own blood, then sacrificed his own life by throwing himself into the flames. In another myth Quetzalcoatl succeeded in stealing the bones of the dead and sprayed them with his own blood in order to create a new human race. Thorns used for scarifying the flesh are often evident in manuscript illustrations of this god.

Similarly, although the warrior caste may have attempted to take more and more prisoners to offer the gods, especially Huitzilopochtli, the priests, on the contrary, followed Quetzalcoatl's example— for he was the sacerdotal archetype—and made more and more personal sacrifices, which took the form of scarifications and pierced tongues and ears. There were countless types of human sacrifice: flaying, decapitation, by the use of bow and arrow—and each one had its own symbolic significance and was related to a particular god (flaying, for example, was connected solely with Xipe Totec, and the priest who stepped into the victim's skin thus represented the renewal of vegetation in the spring). The two most common forms of sacrifice consisted of taking the living heart from the victim or of burning him to death. In the first case the prisoner was placed on his back on the sacrificial stone, the *techatl*; the priest, armed with the sacrificial knife, *tecpatl*, opened up the victim's chest, took the heart, and raised this gory object known as the 'precious tuna (fruit of the cochineal cactus) of the eagle'. This, for instance, was the fate of the young men who, for one whole year, had been privileged to represent or, to be more exact, had 'been' Tezcatlipoca. The second of the two main forms of sacrifice seems to have been confined to Xiuhtecuhtli, god of fire, who also went by the name of Huehueteotl, 'the old god', and it appears to have been intended to indicate his rebirth, the renewal of nature, death followed by life. In the myth recounted earlier we first saw the two leading gods throw themselves into the flames, seeking death in order to be reborn. Then the other gods sacrificed themselves in turn, dying at the hand of Quetzalcoatl–Eecatl or Quetzalcoatl–Xolotl, depending on the text, in order to provide food for the Sun, and move him to action. In both cases death was the condition of life: death-birth and death-food.

The myths that have been briefly told above have given us some idea, first, of the birth of the world, the human races that preceded the present one, then the present world and the present sun, going from the general to the particular; now we come to the birth of the Aztec Sun, Huitzilopochtli, chosen god of a chosen race.

He was the Sun at its height, a victorious sun who struck down his enemies with his *xiuhcoatl*, 'fire-serpent'. He is described by chroniclers in this way: 'He was another Heracles, who was extremely robust, of great strength and warlike humour, a great destroyer of races and killer of men . . . .'

He had a miraculous birth. In the Coatepec sierra, or 'serpent mountain' lived a woman called Coatlicue, 'serpent-petticoated', who was the mother of the Centzon Huitznahua the '400 southerners' and their sister, Coyolxauhqui. One day when Coatlicue was doing penance in a ravine, she received a ball of feathers in her bosom and became pregnant. This filled her sons with fury: 'Who has made you pregnant? Who has brought this infamy and shame upon us?'

Their sister, Coyolxauhqui, urged them to put their mother to death. But the child within her gave Coatlicue comfort. And when the warriors arrived, Huitzilopochtli stepped forth from his mother's womb clad in armour and killed his sister and then his brothers in spite of their supplications.

Thus Huitzilopochtli, tribal god of the Aztecs, and eponymous god of Mexico–Tenochtitlan, embarked on a massacre as soon as his life began, and this mark of bloodshed is imprinted on the history of his race. The story of his birth is an illustration of one of the oldest myths in the world: the Sun's fight against the powers of darkness. Huitzilopochtli is the conquering Sun in his finest hour. He was the son of an ancient earth-goddess, brother of 400 (in other words, countless) southern stars, and of darkness (most intent on killing him). His success in battle was due to his *xiuhcoatl*. Historically speaking, one can possibly regard the birth of Huitzilopochtli as the reflection of the merciless struggle imposed on the Mexican tribe by their 'elder brothers', the peoples installed on the plateaus of central Mexico before their advent.

The part played by the serpent in the cosmological thought of the Nahua tribe is extensive, and it would be impossible to list its various symbolic meanings. Initially it represented chthonian forces. Huitzilopochtli was the son of the 'serpent-petticoated' woman. On the Aztec Calendar there is a serpent entwined round the central motif, and *cipactli*, a monster, part serpent, part crocodile, supports the world on its back. The serpent is also a synonym for strength and skill. Huitzilopochtli's flaming brand, which, as we have seen, won him victory, was a serpent. Similarly, the culture-god who gave the Toltecs the secret of weaving, embroidery, working with gold, was called Quetzalcoatl, the 'precious serpent-bird'. In the cosmology of Huichol Indians, who are, as we have seen, very close to the Aztecs, the serpent plays an essential part. In fact everything is serpent: human footsteps, floating ribbons, rivers, rain, lightning and processions. The sea surrounding the world is the largest serpent; it has two heads, and the sun has to pass through its open jaws when day turns to night. But for the Huichol tribe the serpent is also the symbol of skill, for it can walk the earth without feet and swim without fins. The markings on its back are so beautiful that a Huichol woman cannot take up a piece of embroidery without envisaging a serpent. Similarly Aztec merchants, *pochteca*, never travelled without first making sure that the day of their departure was one bearing the *coatl* sign. The twins belonging to Xolotl, who symbolised the miraculous, are still referred to as *coatl*, serpent (in modern Mexican: *coate*); and the name Quetzalcoatl may be translated as 'precious twin'.

As a water creature the serpent was also the actual symbol of water. Tlaloc, the god of rain, was represented by a mask composed of serpents. It may also have been a sexual symbol. But its mythological function does not end there. In esoteric religious language serpent means 'grief'.

So there was real 'participation' between men, gods and certain privileged creatures, such as the serpent. At the centre of all Mexican religious ideas there was the notion that human or divine nature was fluid. Gukumatz, the Quiche god-hero, became in turn a serpent, eagle, tiger, blood-clot; the only common denominator in these metamorphoses was the concept of some living thing. Similarly, all Aztec gods changed according to circumstance and the demands of the

Stone figure of Xiuhtecuhtli, the god of fire, to whom the present sun, the fifth one, is dedicated. *Museum of the American Indian*

Xiuhtecuhtli as Huehueceotl, the 'Old God'. As Huehueceotl, Xiuhtecuhtli was offered an endless stream of human sacrifice, for only blood was worthy of a great god. Vatican Codex. *Raul Flores Guerrero*

Xiuhcoatl, the fire serpent, which was the weapon with which Huitzilopochtli massacred his sister and brothers immediately after his birth. Xiuhcoatl was, therefore, the symbol of the victorious Sun which demanded sacrifice. Monumental stone statue. *National Museum of Anthropology, Mexico*

Colossal statue of Coatlicue, 'she whose skirt is made of serpents', an ancient goddess of the earth and of maize, who gave birth to the fully armed Huitzilopochtli, god of war and storms. Coatlicue fed on human bodies. Her hands ended in claws and her necklace was made of human hands and hearts. *National Museum of Anthropology, Mexico*

Turquoise mosaic pectoral ornament in the form of a double-headed serpent. The serpent symbolised many things in Aztec mythology, but particularly strength (through Xiuhcoatl) and skill and ingenuity (through Quetzalcoatl). Mexican, fourteenth to fifteenth centuries. *British Museum*

moment. Tezcatlipoca adopted various disguises to deceive Quetzalcoatl. (His very name, the 'smoking mirror' that sees into the future, is indicative of his potentialities as a magician-god.)

In fact, these gods were not involved in real transformations: they simply possessed the ability to *be* several creatures at one and the same time. We have already had an example of one and the same god appearing several times in the same myth in different forms, under different names or 'doublets'. Quetzalcoatl uttered these words to his *nahual* as he went down to hell: 'Go and tell them that I shall come and leave them.' And the *nahual* then cried: 'I shall come and leave them.'

So there was a sort of dialogue between the same god in two different forms. Another name for Tlaloc was the 'sorcerer-prince', Nahualpilli.

Few problems have proved as controversial as Nahualism. The term is usually taken to refer to the ability of certain predestined beings to change into animals with a more or less avowed intent. *Nahual* was primarily a reference to the animal that protected each individual, then to the sorcerer who possessed the gift of changing into an animal. Some writers (Brinton, for instance, in the wake of Brasseur of Bourbourg) have attempted to define Nahualism as a sort of anti-religion, an Indian national movement against authority and Christianity. In point of fact, a belief in certain protective animals rightly or wrongly identified with a sort of individual totemism was common to the whole of America. So it was not 'magic' in the sense of negative religion, but the manifestation of ideas current before the Conquest. For instance, Jacinto de la Serna and Ponce tell the story of an old woman who came to the door of a convent to complain of the treatment she had received at the hands of two priests. When the latter showed their astonishment and protested their innocence, she said: 'But I was that bat, and now I am exhausted.' She was referring to the fact that the previous day the two priests had struck at a bat to drive it away. Several other tales go to show that a man and some animal, his *nahual*, have the same identity. There is in existence a very curious figure, which was found in an oratory, and it depicts an animal, half eagle, half tiger, bearing these words: 'Our Lord and Virgin Mary, who are those whom the plebeians, the sick and ill, those who work in the fields and on the mountain call tiger and eagle....'

Similarly, in Mexico today northern tribes identify the Virgin Mary with the 'young eagle-mother', goddess of the upper regions. Myths are full of these transformations. Xolotl was depicted as a dog. Gods often took the form of their 'disfraz', their *nahual*. The Cihuateteo, women who died in childbirth and became deities, returned to earth in terrible shapes to terrorise human beings. In the original ball-game Tezcatlipoca confronted Quetzalcoatl as a tiger. This is not so much a religion 'wrong side out' as total consubstantiality. What counted was life, and the vehicle through which it passed, blood, the precious water. The intoxicating drink, *pulque,* so popular with the gods, was also called 'blood'.

It seems practically impossible to distinguish between magic and religion in Mexico. In so far as there was never one single, complete official religion, but only an overlapping and mingling of various elements, it would be quite impossible for religion to become completely magical. In the pre-Conquest period the great gods (and their rites) of defeated pantheons were adopted by the conquerors; each time this gave rise to a sprinkling of rites, which, although they had rather fallen into disuse and were losing their deeper meaning, were still observed by the conservative element in the clergy and population.

One may ask what common factor there is underlying belief in a sect of sorcerers, who could turn into animals in order to do evil, inflict illness and steal life and, on the other hand, the gods' initial ability to undergo transformation. There is the same conviction that all beings are drawn along in a single flux. If it is true to say that Nahualism existed as a sect, like all forms of Mexican witchcraft it came from an excess of energy that no civilisation—be it our own or those that preceded it—could dam up.

Each man had his *nahual,* an animal that protected him and was of the same substance as himself, and made its presence known in various ways (such as by leaving footsteps in sand) that could be divined; man's destiny, too, was regulated by the Divine Calendar, the *tonalamatl. Tonal* originally meant 'warmth, sunlight', and then gradually came to mean 'destiny, luck', and ultimately 'that which is proper to man'. Today certain Indians use *I tonal* or *I nahual* indiscriminately to refer to the spirit that protects the individual, his spiritual principle. It thus becomes his 'soul', a soul that is much freer than our own, for it

Tlazolteotl, eater of filth and goddess of unbridled sexuality, in the act of childbirth. Despite her own character, she was unusual among Aztec deities in expecting humans to follow a moral code and she received confessions of sexual wrong-doing. Aztec statue of aplite set with garnets. *Dumbarton Oaks, Washington (Robt. Woods Bliss Coll.)*

can be carried off, or snatched away, or it can leave the body and then re-enter it.

It is interesting to consider how the Aztec soul reacted to the revelation of Christianity. As we have already seen, monotheism was inconceivable to Tenochca Indians; their all-powerful and omnipresent religion was practically devoid of ethical notions. The type of life in the next world was decided not by a man's merits in this life but by the manner of death that terminated it: warriors who died in battle became Quauteca, 'companions of the eagle', and went to the eastern paradise, Tonatiuhichan. Those who met death by drowning or certain illnesses connected with water, like leprosy, went to Tlalocan, Tlaloc's paradise. The rest, who had not been chosen by any one particular god, went to Mictlan, where they underwent numerous ordeals before attaining final repose and dissolution after some four years. So the fate of souls was fixed not by the sanction of human merit, but by divine dispensation.

The gods themselves made no demands on their worshippers except that they should provide them with blood—that is, food—and that they show courage in battle. Only two of them betrayed any ethical preoccupation: Quetzalcoatl, as we have mentioned several times, and the goddess Tlazolteotl, the goddess of uncleanliness. She was an ancient earth-goddess connected with fertility and carnal love. Her cult included confession of sexual sins and the name of the month dedicated to her—and to other earth-goddesses—*ochpaniztli*, meant 'clean sweep'.

Thus there was to be a clash of two totally conflicting concepts once the Conquest was over, and many surviving ancient rites were thought by the newcomers to be heresies. As the gods were so close to men, attempts were made to reach them by various hallucinatory processes, such as the use of intoxicating drinks, toadstools or peyotl (a cactus). This hypostatic communion with the deity was regarded as true black-mass ritual. In fact the use of peyotl was taken to Mexico and later to the southern United States by Chichimec nomads and it is still an object of a cult. And far from being a question of 'witchcraft', it

is so much part of the cult that among contemporary tribes of northern huntsmen bad medicine-men and evil sorcerers are said to drink the 'plant hostile to peyotl'. (Jimson–Weed.)

Thus new gods were relatively easily accepted by the Aztecs. And in the course of time beliefs and rites were superimposed on one another in the most extraordinary fashion, and missionaries struggled in vain against them. The national shrine of the Virgin in Mexico is exactly where that of Tonantzin, 'Our revered mother', used to be. As the gods changed their shapes and names at will, they could easily be 'debaptised' and change into Jesus Christ or one of the saints. In former times Cihuacoatl came back to earth to weep at the crossroads, for she had abandoned her infant's cradle in the market, and in it there was a sacrificial knife. In this day and age, the Llorona, 'She who weeps', is said to haunt markets, clasping to her heart an empty cradle or the body of a child. And when Quetzalcoatl was driven from his kingdom by Texcatlipoca he set off eastwards promising his people that he would return. (The arrival of Cortez is known to have been regarded as the return of the awaited god by the *tonalpouhques*, and he was welcomed in a manner befitting a god.)

So we may state in conclusion that military and religious defeat came to the Aztecs just when they were trying to realise their ideal of making Mexico *Cem Anhuac tenochca tlalpan*, 'the world, tenochca earth', and the emperor *Cem Anahuax tlatoani*, 'the king of the world'. Their defeat had been announced by the most terrifying omens, with the result that the beginning of hostilities against the Spanish was accompanied by the deepest pessimism. Religion, which had been their strength, was to bring about their downfall. Mexican pessimism, which might be described as active pessimism, had led them to supremacy and was now to take them to disaster. It was as if the gods had attempted to create an increasingly perfect human race, and undergone the same evolution themselves; then, since everything was ultimately destined to dissolution, had simply accepted death for themselves.

The Mayas

Knowledge of pre-Columbian Mexican mythology owes a great deal to the Mayas: they are the only people to have left us sacred texts that we can decipher with relative certainty. Other races, such as the Toltecs, Chichimecs and Mixtecs, for example, must have thought just as intensely about religious matters, but their thinking is less accessible to us. Our main source of information about Mayan mythology is the 'Book of Advice' (*Popol-Vuh*), a work compiled in Quiché dialect (the Quiché are a separate branch of the Mayan race) shortly after the Spanish conquest and written in Latin script. We also have annals of the Cakchiquels (neighbours of the Quiché tribes) and a collection of chronicles known by the name of *Chilan Balam*, dealing with the history of Yucatan. But the others cannot compare with the *Popol-Vuh* in the introduction it affords to the mythical thought of the Mayas. It is not a simple matter to interpret the work: it is, in fact, dated many centuries after the Mayan empire fell (for it was at its height between A.D. 300 and 900) and so must have been based on tradition, with no guarantee of freedom from distortion. It is also possible that its editor did not entirely resist the influence of the pervading Christian environment, and he may have taken a 'Biblical' line, simply in a spirit of compliance. Furthermore, the *Popol-Vuh* presents authentic myths and historical traditions in an almost inextricable form. Given a certain legend, we can never be absolutely sure which is its correct domain. In point of fact, the distinction between myth and reality, which is so evident to us, is not always meaningful in Mayan thought: myth was to them a 'category' of historical thought, for history itself emerged through a mythical schema that was in a way the 'philosophy' of this history and impelled it in its particular direction. The composition of the book is highly complex in itself, and it is full of contradictions, anachronisms and repetition, which cannot all be put down to the compiler's maladroit treatment of the material, for they were inherent in the religious and cosmogonic thought of the Mayan tradition. For these reasons the picture one obtains of Mayan mythology is rather

Stele D at Quiriga, a Mayan monument carved from a single block of stone. The front and back are carved in elaborate relief showing a human figure wearing ceremonial dress and carrying the ceremonial axe and buckler. The sides are devoted to calendrical inscriptions. *British Museum*

473

vague and largely artificial; but, in spite of all these limitations, the content of *Popol-Vuh* is none the less of considerable interest and constitutes a virtually unique document about the mode of thought that we term 'mythical'.

In the first place, creation appears as an organisation, a 'classification': the 'Book of Advice' says: 'Great is the recital, the history of the time when all the corners of the sky and the earth were completed, and quadrangulation, its measure, the four points, the measuring of the corners, the measuring of the lines, in heaven, on earth, at the four angles, in the four corners.' The universe consisted of three quadrilaterals placed one on top of another. The first one was the sky, the middle one was earth, and the third was the underworld. 'Spiritual' powers coexisted in the original chaos; they separated at the moment of creation. Each of the corners of the world was marked by a boundary in a particular colour: these boundaries were red, white, black and yellow, and each had a chieftain or 'regent'. Four of these 'regents' were called Tzakol, Bitol, Alom and Qaholom (or Cajolom) — uncertainty of phonetic transcription that has come via the Spanish accounts for variations found in modern authors. Then in addition to these four regents first came Tepeu and Gukumatz, 'powers of the sky', then another god called Cabaguil, or 'Heart of the sky'. These gods are all solar by nature; they were the light that floated upon the water.

These seven gods formed a council and between them arose the 'word', which was the creative act: the result of this was creation, the manifestation of the council's agreement. This first creation consisted essentially of plant life. But this vegetation-type creation was not satisfactory to the gods who fashioned it; they wanted to produce living beings. That is how animals came into existence, and birds, serpents and 'mountain-spirits', and these creatures

The Great Plaza at Tikal. This is the largest known Mayan ceremonial centre and perhaps the earliest in use from A.D. 200–900. The picture shows Temples II, III and IV seen from Temple I, surrounded by the ever-encroaching rain forest. *British Museum*

A penitent kneeling before a priest and mutilating his tongue by passing a rope of thorns through it. Lintel 24 from House G at the Maya ceremonial centre at Menché (Yaxchilan), Guatemala. Seventh–eighth centuries A.D. *British Museum*

474

Two folios from a copy of the *Codex Cospiano*, a Mexican religious manuscript. They show the second group of 13-day periods within the 260-day magical calendar known as the Tonalpouhalli. The small dark figure repeated in many of the compartments is a dual personality: Tecpatl, representing

penance, when he stands on the right, and Iztli, one of the Nine Lords of the Night, when he stands on the left. The top and bottom rows of figures represent the Fates Above And Below of the days in the smaller squares between them. *British Museum*

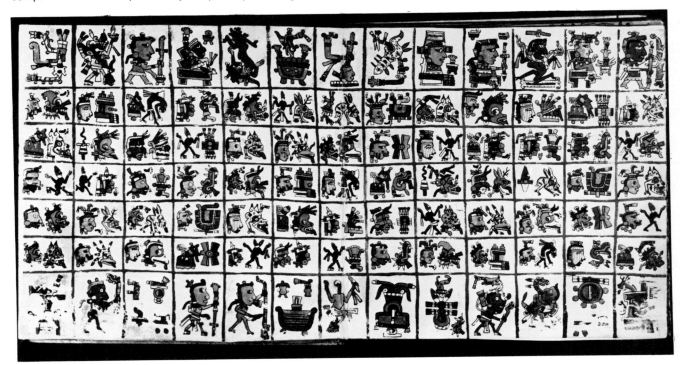

were given to earth that they might 'guard' the plants; to each was assigned an abode; each was given his own tongue. The gods' intention was that these animals should pay them homage: 'Speak, pray to us,' said the gods; but the animals could not speak like men; they simply cackled, they simply roared, they simply croaked. When the 'Fashioners' heard their ineffectual speech, they conferred together: 'They were unable to say our names.' 'Not good,' the 'Begetters' said, and they went on: 'Now you will be changed. Your flesh will be pounded beneath the tooth; let this be done, let this be your burden.'

Thereupon they continued their series of attempts to create mankind. The first attempt failed; then the gods fashioned men out of damp mud, but these creatures changed back into mud with the action of the water. The third creation was more subtle. The four primordial 'regents' changed their names. They became Ixpiyacoc, Ixmucane, Hunahpu guch and Hunahpu utiu, and were joined by 'fabricating gods' called Ajtzak and Ajbit. It would appear that the new names adopted by the four original 'regents' resulted in each of them becoming two distinct beings, so that thirteen gods presided over this third creation. Moreover, this moment marked the appearance of a female deity with the double name Chirakan-Ixmucane, who provided a partial link with one of the gods of creation.

These deities made a fresh attempt to create men, sculpting them out of wood. They were animated puppets: 'They lived, they begat, they made daughters, they made sons, these puppets, these wooden structures. They had neither spirit nor wisdom, and no recollection of their constructors, of their creators. . . . They remembered nothing of the spirits of the sky; that is why they came to nothing . . . .' The gods put an end to this rough-hewn race by a great flood,

but death did not come of its own accord; it was brought them by 'demons': Xecotcovach devoured their eyes, Camalotz cut off their heads, Cotzbalam devoured their flesh and Tucumbalam pounded their sinews and bones. Then for the first time the god of death made his appearance. There is a curious episode that occurred at the time of this flood, involving a revolt on the part of creatures and things against this human race that was incapable of paying homage to the gods; now that their masters had had a curse put upon them, they inflicted on men the treatment they had received themselves. The dogs the men had not fed devoured them, millstones crushed them, pots burned them, hearthstones pursued them. It was said that this race did not entirely perish: it was driven into the forest and survived in the form of monkeys.

Suddenly, at this point in the 'history', the 'Book of Advice' interrupts its 'genesis' and inserts a legendary cycle involving the twins, a couple found in many other American mythologies. There are many legends belonging to this cycle, some of which are obviously intended to explain rites that were still observed in the historical period. 'At that time,' says the 'Book of Advice', 'there was nothing but dim light on the surface of the earth, there was no sun . . . .' But a giant, called Gukup Cakix, pretended to be both sun and moon. This was not true; Gukup Cakix was but a vain, cruel and clumsy creature. Two real deities, two brothers, Hunahpu and Ixbalanque, decided to put an end to the giant's pretence. They made their way to the spot where Gukup Cakix usually went to eat fruit and laid in wait for him; then with their blowpipe they inflicted an illness upon him. First Gukup fell, but he was not dead; when Hunahpu hurled himself upon him, Gukup severed his arm, then returned home to his wife, Chimalmat, and his two children called Zipacna

Chichen Itza was founded during the New Empire (c. A.D. 900). Although its temples were built by the Toltecs they also show Mayan and Tula influences.

Below: The entrance to the Temple of the Warriors. The figure in the centre is a chac-mool, a reclining figure with bent knees and head turned to one side such as is usually found at a Mayan temple door. He has a receptacle on his knees, presumably to receive offerings. *M. Hétier*

Right: A standard bearer representing a deity. *Almasy*

Bottom: The altar in the Temple of the Warriors. The pillars are covered with symbolic figures. *Roger-Viollet*

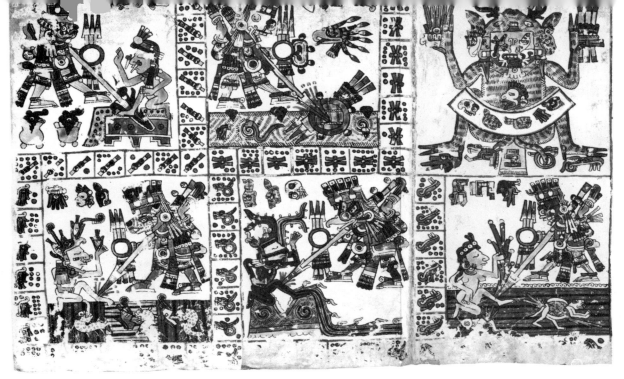

Details of the Mayan calendar, part of the fifteenth-century *Codex Borgia*. Venus here is Tlauixcalpantecuhtli, the Great Lord of the House of the Dawn. The two upper sections show *(left)* that on these days Venus is a danger to Princes and *right)* the days when Venus destroys warriors. The lower sections show the days when *(left)* crops are in danger; when all things to do with mountains are threatened *(centre)* and the days when Venus is inimical to women and the creatures of the great waters *(right)*. The figure in the remaining section is Camaxtli, a god of fate, with the twenty day signs attached to various parts of his body. *Biblioteca Apostolica Vaticana*

Intricate bas-relief at the Temple of the Nuns, at the Mayan city of Uxmal in Yucatan. Elaborate buildings were erected in Yucatan with the aid of Toltec mercenaries about 1050, but they flourished for only about a century and a half. *Mexican Government Tourism Department*

Jade plaque found near Puerto Barrientos, Guatemala. It is the oldest contemporarily dated Mayan object and it is from this that archaeologists date Mayan history. The obverse (left) shows the planet Venus represented as a god in the ceremonial dress of the warriors and priests. The reverse (right) shows a number of glyphs which give a date according to the ancient Mayan calendar, totalling 94,537 days from the beginning of the Mayan era, and probably corresponding to 320 A.D. *National Museum of Ethnology, Leiden*

The Burial Chamber in the pyramid of the Temple of the
Inscriptions at Palenque. *Instituto Nacional de Antropologia.
Mexico*

A worshipper kneeling before a double-headed serpent deity. Lintel 25 from House G at the Maya ceremonial centre at Menché (Yaxchilan), Guatemala. Seventh–eighth centuries A.D. The Mayas venerated animals because they showed the gods where they could find the materials from which they would create mankind. *British Museum*

Mayan sculpture from the Temple of the Soothsayer at Uxmal, Yucatan. This figure is sometimes known as the Venus of Yucatan. *G. Strouvé*

and Caprakan. The twins, however, sought out their grandparents, two white-haired old people, who were none other than two of the primeval deities. With their help Gukup and his wife were punished; both died and Hunahpu retrieved his arm. Only the two sons of the giant remained. The elder, Zipacna, was bathing in a river, when 'four hundred youths' passed, all carrying an enormous tree, which they intended for the central pillar of their house. Zipacna summoned them and asked them what they were doing. When he heard their reply he offered to carry the beam himself; this he did. The young people asked him to come back the next day to help them again; but they plotted together, for they thought it 'scandalous' that a single man should do the work of several. They planned to dig a large hole and make the giant go down into it and then they would bury him. But Zipacna was not to be taken in; when he was asked to dig the hole, he did so, but in such a way that he arranged an outlet, and when the youths thought that they had buried him, he got away. The young people spent four days celebrating their supposed victory. When they were quite drunk Zipacna reappeared and massacred them. And the young ones were changed into stars, the constellation known as the Pleiades. The twins determined to avenge them, and tricked Zipacna by using a wooden crayfish as a lure, and then they buried him alive.

After this the twins also put to death Zipacna's brother Capakran, a spirit of mountains and earthquakes. They had to make him eat a bird that had received ritual consecration by anointment with white earth, and this accursed food brought about the last giant's death.

The twins had countless adventures; they seem like demiurges whose acts affected the world. Their sphere of activity covered both the world of earth and the world below; they were the creators of magic —their acts being repeated in the echoing gestures of the sorcerer by the process known as 'sympathy'. They presided over the ball-game, which is not so much a game as a rite of cosmic significance.

Finally, the time for the fourth creation arrived, and this produced the present humans. Materials for making men came from plants, especially maize, the best food-producing grain. But the animals had to show the gods where these precious plants grew. First of all there were twice two men, who took possession of the world at the command of the gods. The number, four, corresponded to the 'four corners' of the world; it appeared to express a harmony between the human and the cosmic. Then the gods created four women, the companions of the four primordial men.

After the Mayan race became decadent its mythology absorbed many legends and beliefs brought by the conquerors, and in return it provided the new syncretism (which arose from the mingling of races and migrations) with some of its own original elements. Mayan mythology lived on in some tribes and continued to furnish the vital structure for human thought. It is also inscribed and may one day be deciphered from the countless monuments of Mayan culture that survive in the Mexican provinces of Campeche, Quintana Roo and Yucatan.

The ruins of Macchu Pichu, the ancient fortress city of the Incas. Set high up on a precipitous mountain peak, it was built of huge blocks of stone without cement. Macchu Pichu may well have marked the mountain about sixty leagues from Cuzco where the Children of the Sun were said to have been created—or alternatively the mountain on which they alone escaped the waters of the Flood. *Jerry Frank*

Colour plate. Top: Large mask from Iquitos. Eighth or ninth century. Nazca. *Holford*

Bottom: Ceremonial vessel in the form of a dove. The bead held in its beak represents seed. Twelfth to thirteenth century. Chimu. *Holford*

Chimu ceremonial knife representing a divinity, probably
Nayn-Lap. Found in the Ilimo district of the department of
Lambayeque. *Holford*

SOUTH AMERICA: CREATION AND DESTRUCTION

There are gaps in our knowledge of South American mythology in spite of a wealth of documentation, which covers almost four centuries. The major gaps unfortunately occur in the mythology of the highest civilisations that continent has produced, particularly that of the Inca and Chibcha civilisations. Unfortunately, these gaps will not now be closed, mainly owing to the lack of interest on the the part of Europeans. Our regret is all the greater now that archaeology leads us to suppose that the culture of ancient Peru embraced an extremely varied supernatural world and mythical epics full of dramatic incident. Ceramics produced by the Mochica civilisation, which came a thousand years earlier than its Inca counterpart, are decorated with motifs inspired by legends of gods and heroes. It is not possible to interpret the scenes painted or shown in relief on the sides of vases in very many cases. This can be done only when the scenes illustrate oral traditions written down by the Spaniards after the Conquest or myths found among the modern Indians of Amazonia, who have kept part of Andean folk-lore alive.

Whenever South American Indian myths are under survey, the tradition is to classify the motifs according to the cultural areas in which they were transcribed. We have, however, preferred to give an overall picture in this present instance, without taking into account the very different levels of civilisation achieved by different indigenous societies, and our reason for this lies in the similarities, one might even say the complete identity between certain categories of myths regardless of the regions from which they came. With very few exceptions the collection of Inca myths that has been handed down is found equally among other South American tribes from Guiana to Tierra del Fuego.

In the strictly religious sphere one wonders if one should venture to compare the nature-gods wor-shipped by the Incas in their temples with the anonymous spirits that magicians from Amazonia or the Guianas conjure up in their huts. There is a considerable difference between supernatural beings as envisaged by the clergy of a refined civilisation and those whose anger 'savages' endeavour to appease; but the contrast between Inca religion and that of so-called 'primitive' South American tribes is less decisive when one turns to other manifestations of their religious life. Beliefs of the majority of Inca subjects might well be confused with a rather crude animism, even 'animatism' to some degree, since they were always concerned to endow with individual personality the obscure and mysterious forces that apparently dwelt in certain objects.

Peruvians gave the name of *huaca* to any object or phenomenon in which they saw some supernatural manifestation. *Huacas* were mountains, rivers, lakes or simply rocks with strange shapes. In spite of four centuries of Christianity Quechua and Aymara Indians from Peru and Bolivia continue to make offerings to spirits they feel are all around them intervening in their daily life. Magicians hold nocturnal seances to summon them and converse with them.

The folk-lore of Amazonian tribes from Guiana is full of tales reflecting the way these Indians imagine the spirit world. Spirits are usually human in shape. Their true nature is betrayed only by some detail of appearance, such as a painted face, a physical deformity or a mania. For instance, the toad-spirit swallows any pots and jars he may happen to come across.

Some groups of spirits are repugnant or frightening in appearance: they are hairy with prominent, arched eyebrows and are either entirely deprived of articulated movement or else clamped together in twos like Siamese twins. Many of them are skeletons or skulls. Spirits frequently appear in the shape of a

friend or parent. However, some peculiarity always gives them away: no toes, for example. Whistling or creaking is noticeable when a spirit approaches. Those who ignore these peculiarities expose themselves to accidents and misadventures, and such incidents form the theme of countless stories and legends.

Certain spirits are happy in the company of men, and they are kindly and helpful. To anyone who lends them his aid they bring good fortune in hunting and fishing. Others marry ordinary mortals, but they make touchy and nervous partners. The slightest disregard for etiquette, a violation of the least taboo makes them discontented and provokes them to flight. There are myths that tell of men's voyages to the land of spirits and what they saw there.

Between these almost undifferentiated spirits and the gods proper there is a category of supernatural beings with more sharply drawn personalities, who might be termed 'demons'. They hold limited powers and have a fairly rudimentary cult.

Each animal species comes under the protection of one of these demons, to whom Indians give such names as 'Father of peccaries', 'Father of caymans', 'Father of monkeys'. The demon in each case looks like a huge specimen of the species he rules, but he is capable of taking human shape whenever he wishes.

The 'fathers' or 'mothers' of animals are not against their 'sons' being killed to provide food for men, but they inflict pitiless punishment on the hunter or fisherman who destroys for pleasure and not to satisfy his needs. Among Peruvian Indians this belief took the form of worship accorded certain groups of stars in which they thought they could see the image of a celestial animal guarding or protecting his earthly counterparts. The constellation that we know as Lyra, for instance, was a llama followed by its spouse and little one. Shepherds prayed to them that their flocks might prosper. Similarly, a certain number of stars in the constellation of Scorpio formed the outline of a feline in the sky and this not only figured in mythology, but also played a part in the cult.

A certain number of these demons embody natural elements or phenomena and deserve to be termed gods though they are not the objects of a true cult. The Incas are known to have accorded pride of place to the Sun, Inti, the ancestor of their dynasty. Though promoted to the rank of national god, this celestial sovereignty depended on the terrestrial power of the Inca and adoration of him became confused with the homage due to the latter. There are traces of a solar cult among forest Indians, particularly the Guarani and Carib tribes. Otherwise the Sun and Moon are simple mythological characters who are not credited with influence over human fate. These two stars in their anthropomorphic form are, on the contrary, the heroes of adventures which form an important part of their mythology.

An aerial view of Macchu Pichu showing the temple ruins. *Rapho*

After Inti, 'Thunder' was the second deity in the hierarchy—the Incas' master of the thunderbolt, hail and rain. He traversed celestial space armed with a club and sling, and the noise they made when he used them was heard as the rumbling of the storm. People thought they saw his shape in the sky, outlined by the stars of the Great Bear, near a 'river', the Milky Way, from which he drew water to spill upon the earth.

The Guarani Indians of Paraguay and Brazil envisage thunder as a human being who, seated on a wooden trough, noisily crosses the sky. Lightning is the reflection of his labret (a resin-stalk sunk in his lower lip). This god is called Tupan and he is the deity whom missionaries associated with the Christian God. Several Guiana and Amazonian tribes attribute thunder to fantastic birds beating their wings during storms (the thunder-bird of North American mythologies.) Earth Mother, to whom the Inca peasants prayed to make their fields and their flocks fertile, is still the main pagan deity worshipped by their descendants. They have no definite ideas about her personality, but are happy to associate her with the Holy Virgin. Only one Amazonian tribe gives the earth anthropomorphic form and that is the Jivaro tribe. Their magicians use tobacco juice to reach a state of intoxication in which Earth appears to them in a vision and they can converse with her.

All tribes refer the origins of the world and human institutions to an august personage whose character and functions are not always clearly defined. Sometimes he is a creator or great ancestor who retires to some universe once he has accomplished his terrestrial mission; sometimes he is a sort of kindly but capricious spirit who lingers on the earth he has created to change its physiognomy and initiate men into the techniques and usages that will enable them to subsist and live in society. In this capacity he

assumes the role of a culture-hero. Sometimes the creator, the ancestor, the culture-hero and the transformer are one and the same person; sometimes they share the burden and are then presented as members of one and the same family. Finally, culture-hero or heroes are occasionally animals endowed with reason.

Around these supernatural beings crystallised the explorations of the enigmas, great and small, that nature inflicts on men. Their adventures and actions constitute mythical cycles that are at one and the same time cosmogonies, natural histories and tribal annals.

In the long list of creators and transformers in South American mythology, several sorts emerge. Some are conceived as grandiose characters wrapped in mystery, others are hardly respectable magicians. Witoto Indians in eastern Colombia have a metaphysical idea of the creator. He was born of the 'word', that is to say of incantations and myths possessing magic powers that existed before all else. He was responsible for passing on these formulas to men, thus making rites and ceremonies specially effective. He is also an incarnation of vegetation, but, in spite of his great might, men do not address him in prayer.

Here is the tale of creation as told by the Chibcha Indians of Colombia. When it was dark, before anything in the world existed, light was enclosed in something big, which the Muiscas called 'Chiminagua'. This thing called Chiminagua—by which they mean 'god'—rose to become bright and to free the light that was in it. Then with the emergence of this light things began to be created. First of all this god brought to life black birds and, as soon as they had taken shape, he ordered them to fly over the world spreading vapour with their beaks, and this vapour was pure and brilliant light. When the birds had obeyed, the whole world became bright and full of light as it is today. Indians regard this god as the omnipotent

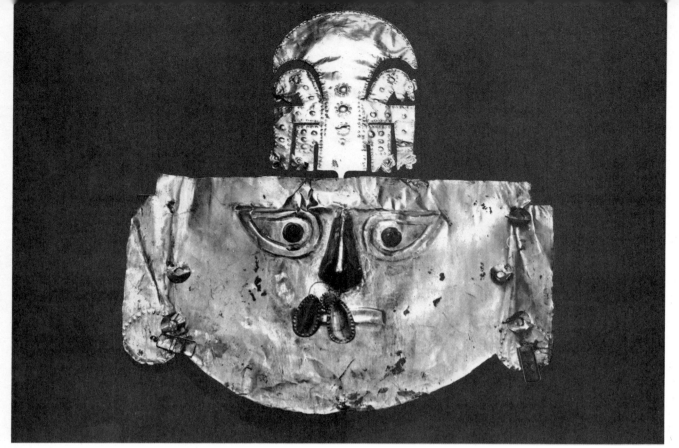

Early Peruvian gold objects from the collection of Señor Mujica Gallo. *Michael Holford*

Above: A funerary mask such as were placed over the faces of mummies. It has emerald eyes set in turquoises and above the head is a crest with animal-god designs. Chimu period, twelfth—thirteenth centuries A.D.

Left: a sacred puma with a human face depicted on its tongue. The tiny ear-pendants are in the form of ceremonial axes; the body is covered with a double-headed serpent design and forms a pouch into which the faithful may have put cocoa. Probably the original regalia of the priests included a puma or jaguar skin which was replaced by a gold replica as the people grew prosperous. Mochica period, fourth—ninth centuries A.D.

Below: Golden plate of the Chimu period. In the centre is the earth-goddess holding maize, yucca and sweet potatoes and around her are several figures carrying the same cereals. The whole probably represents a calendar for sowing and harvesting.

Stirrup vessels of the Mochica culture A.D. 1–900. These funerary ceramics were intended to contain the liquid needed by the dead in the subterranean after-life. The liquid was poured through the curved neck at the top and the base was often painted with zoomorphic or anthropomorphic figures.
Above: A seated figure dressed as a deer and carrying a club.
Right: A feline deity, flanked by snakes. *British Museum*
Below: A vessel in the form of a head with huge fangs rising from a vegetable body.

master of all things and consider him to be fundamentally good. He created all there is in the world, and it is this that fills him and makes him so beautiful.

Some tribes ascribe the origin of things to a common mother. At the top of the celestial hierarchy Chamacoco Indians place the goddess Eschetewuarha who, as wife of the Great Spirit, dominated it and ruled over the world. She is the mother of birds (clouds) who spread rain. Chipibo Indians in Ucayali believe that the world and its contents are the work of a celestial woman, who is undoubtedly a personification of the sun. Sometimes creation is the work of a mythical animal—for example, the scarab according to the Lengua Indians and a falcon in the mythology of the Okaina Indians.

The creator may be confused with another mythological character, the transformer or culture-hero. The latter is characterised by his immoderate liking for metamorphoses. The series of changes that he brings about in the world obscures his role as creator. Myths depict him as a prophet travelling the earth to complete the work of creation and to teach men the arts and usages proper to civilised life.

The culture-hero is rarely conceived to be a solitary being. He is usually flanked by a companion, the 'Deceiver', a muddle-headed and stupid person who opposes him and corrupts all he creates. He often plays the part of the 'Rogue' or 'Trickster' in North American mythology. Most South American tribes tell of the adventures of twins who are either true culture-heroes or the sons and successors of a culture-hero. Carib Indians in British Guiana make Makunaima either the creator of heaven, men and animals, or a simple transformer who, together with his brother, gave beasts their present shape, caused the deluge, and, as a victim of often unfortunate enterprises, would have perished many times over had his brother not brought him back to life.

Tuminikar, the culture-hero of the Wapishana and the Taruma Indians in Guiana, is essentially good and wise, but his brother Duid is an idler who constantly plays tricks on him. He is behind all the annoyances and worries inflicted on men. The twins are often identified with the Sun and Moon.

One of the most widely found myths in South America is one that has many variations, but tells the tale of the adventures of the twin sons of the culture-hero or creator whose wife was devoured by one or more jaguars (or some other monster). The twins were found in their mother's womb by the Mother of the Jaguars (or other monster) and she adopted them. They showed that they were supernatural by the speed of their growth and their skill in all they did. A bird or some other creature revealed to them the jaguars' crime. They sought their revenge by ambushing the jaguars and exterminating them. Then they set off in search of their father, but before they found him they had several unhappy adventures, which they brought on themselves by picking quarrels with the spirits of forests and waters. The more stupid twin was killed and torn to pieces. But his brother collected the pieces, blew upon them to bring him back to life and then took vengeance on the murderer.

They also underwent several ordeals, including having to pass between rocks that clashed together and crushed whatever lay between. One of the brothers failed to get through and perished, but the other escaped danger and brought him back to life. Finally, the twins found their father again and remained with him.

According to Indian mythology from Tierra del Fuego nature is the work of Kenos, the first man and great ancestor, sent by the supreme being to bring order into the world. Kenos created the present human race by using peat to fashion male and female organs, which gave birth to the first Onas. Kenos taught them to speak and instructed them in the rules by which society is governed. In the end he flew up to the sky where he became a constellation. His function as cultivator and fashioner of the world was taken over by two brothers, who gave the Onas their essential pieces of equipment. However, they modified the laws laid down by Kenos. They robbed men of their powers to rise again after brief sleep.

The elder brother, who was less intelligent than the younger, wanted men to be given food without having to work for it, but his more circumspect brother was opposed to this, claiming that the harder things are to obtain, the greater the joy one has from them. The twins made nights shorter, for they had previously been too long; they taught men to make fire, to hunt seals and to extract oil from fish.

Bacairi Indians regard the twins Keri and Kame as the benefactors and creators of the human species. They stole from a vulture the sun and moon, which were feather balls. They introduced sleep by stealing a lizard's eyelids—the lizard being 'master of sleep'.

Viracocha, the supreme being of the Incas, is, as far as we can tell from the badly transcribed and obscure myths about him, creator, culture-hero and transformer all in one. He is manifest in several successive creations, but, once he has peopled the earth, he abandons his role of creator and changes into a culture-hero. He gives men laws, and enjoins men to obey them. He travels about the Andes with a mysterious companion in whom we recognise the 'Deceiver' who opposes the culture-hero. When Viracocha created good men, Taguacipa made them bad. If Viracocha raised mountains, the 'Deceiver' changed them into plains. After many adventures, which account for nature's peculiarities, Viracocha came to the sea and, throwing his cloak on the waves, he embarked on it and disappeared over the horizon. Thus he conformed to the myths of most culture-heroes who depart in the direction of the setting sun once their task is completed and go and live in the land of the dead. The creator and cultivator is rarely promoted in Indian tribes to the rank of the great god or supreme being. The Incas may not have relegated him to some distant empyrean, but this is because he belonged to a pantheon in which other gods had a clearly defined place and role.

Dualism is a familiar aspect of the myth of the culture-hero Bochica, who was known to the Chibcha Indians. Their hero came from the east, and travelled the earth, after he had created all things, to impose severe laws on mankind. He disappeared in the west leaving his footprint on a rock. He was followed by a woman, Chie, whose teaching contradicted his own. She urged men to rejoice and make merry. So Bochica punished her by turning her into an owl. Then, in spite, Chie helped Chibchachum flood the plain of Bogota. Bochica appeared on a rainbow and threw his gold stick at Tequendama, splitting the mountain in two and thus enabling the waters to flow away. Chibchachum was given the task of carrying the earth on his back. Each time he moved it from one shoulder to another there was an earthquake.

The supreme god of the Tierra del Fuego Indians (Ona, Yaghan and Alakaluf) does not seem to have been a deified culture-hero. These Indians, who were among the most primitive in South America, thought of him as a spirit who neither ate nor drank and who lived in the celestial vault beyond the stars. He was usually invoked by such epithets as 'the strong', 'the highest', 'the sky-dweller' or 'the father'. He created the world, but it was refashioned by the culture-hero and the ancestors. This god can hardly be called a creator, but he was the guardian of morality. If men sinned against him, his anger was expressed by inflicting sickness and death.

The origin of mankind

The appearance of the first men on earth is the subject of many myths, which by their central theme

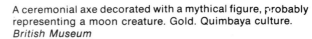
A ceremonial axe decorated with a mythical figure, probably representing a moon creature. Gold. Quimbaya culture. *British Museum*

reveal two opposing concepts. According to the first of these, the first men came from the sky or an underworld. It is the belief of Mosetene Indians that Dohit, their culture-hero, fashioned the first men from clay. Bacairi Indians believe that Keri and Kame changed reeds into men. In Chibcha mythology the Sun and Moon fashioned the first man with clay, while using reeds for the first woman.

Many myths deal with failures on the part of the creator. The culture-hero of the Taulipua Indians had fashioned the first men in wax, but when he saw that it melted in the sun, he used clay that the sun dried out. Chocoan Indians say that their culture-hero carved the first men from wood. No sooner had these men left the sculptor's hand than they departed for the next world, where they were destined to live for ever. Now the culture-hero cut his finger while working, so he put wood aside and fashioned men out of clay, thus depriving them of immortality.

Successive creations did not always derive from a poor choice of material. The creator was sometimes forced to destroy or change the creatures he produced because of crimes they committed or because of their unworthy conduct. Before sculpting in stone the ancestors of all nations of men, Viracocha, the great god of the Incas, had already fashioned from clay or carved from rocks one human race which he had to destroy 'because they had transgressed his precepts'. Chocoan Indians likewise speak of a race of men that was destroyed because it was addicted to cannibalism, then of a second generation of human beings who were changed into animals, and finally a third version of mankind whom the culture-hero fashioned from clay.

Myths of other tribes deal not with the creation of men, but with the causes and circumstances of their migration, and they sometimes state their place of origin as being below earth, sometimes in the sky.

As a sample of the myths in this category, we shall analyse the version given by the Mundurucu Indians, who were discovered by the companion of the creator when he pursued an armadillo and found himself being dragged by it to a lower world. The creator created the cotton-plant in order to make a rope of its fibres. He pushed it through a hole that connected the underworld to the land of men. The latter were thus able to reach the surface of our earth. The cord broke before all the men could climb through. A great many remained underground and each day receive a visit from the Sun.

The ancestors of the Caraja likewise emigrated from a world below our own. They left it in spite of the exhortations of a chieftain who predicted that on earth their fate would be death, whereas they enjoyed immortality in their native land.

The members of all Inca communities thought that their original dwelling-place was a cave, mountain or lake. The spot at which their ancestors emerged was regarded as sacred. These myths flatly contradict that of Viracocha's creation; accordingly, to bring the two versions into line, they invented the idea of Viracocha's sending the first men he had sculpted from stone across the world by subterranean paths until they eventually emerged from caves, lakes or rivers.

The Warrau Indians of the Orinoco River held that their ancestors dwelt in the sky, whence they descended to earth by means of a rope to steal game. The Toba Indians of the Gran Chaco thought that women had come from the sky. At night they used to slide down a rope to rob men of fish they had caught. A falcon cut the rope and the women were forced to stay on earth as company for the men.

The peoples of the Peruvian coast recounted to the Spaniards that men had arisen from three eggs, one of gold, another of silver and the third of copper. Caduveo Indians of the Gran Chaco also thought that they had come from eggs hatched by a gigantic bird.

The origin of cultivated plants

Many myths tell how men acquired cultivated plants. According to a certain number of versions the culture-hero made men a gift of them. He had seemingly stolen them from some animal who was their owner. This is the way in which one of the twins in Bacairi mythology stole manioc from a stag that had got it from a fish. Aguara-Tunpa, the fox-god of the Chiriguano Indians, devised a trick to get hold of the husks of the carob-tree, which the viscacha (a native rodent) had appropriated. The Aymara Indians in Bolivia have clung to the idea that it was the fox who was invited into the sky and brought back with him grains of maize. Spirits are sometimes the possessors of useful plants and they have the monopoly of them until a day comes when someone — man or animal — steals a few grains from them. Some myths stipulate a close connection between cultivated plants and the human body. Sometimes there is a mysterious being

487

who, when beaten, drops around him fruit or tubers; sometimes it is a man or woman who, when killed and buried, changes into useful plants. A particularly famous version of this myth was found on the coast of Peru in the sixteenth century. In the beginning the man and woman created by Pachacamac had nothing to eat. The man died of hunger. One day the woman, who was gathering wild fruit, accused the Sun of letting her pine away. The Sun made her fertile. The god Pachacamac killed the child that was born from her womb and cut it to pieces. He planted the teeth, which were transformed into ears of maize, the bones, which became manioc roots, and the flesh, which produced gourds and other vegetables. The culture-hero of the Caingua Indians demanded that his body should be dragged across the fields after his death. From his sexual organs sprang maize-stalks and beans, and from his head, gourds. The ashes of a human being or fabulous animal often became plants, as in the case of the cannibal woman, burned by the Toba Indians, who changed into tobacco leaves.

According to the tradition of some tribes in Guiana (especially the Carib tribes), cultivated plants all come from one and the same tree, the American equivalent of the Tree of Life. This endless source of food was discovered by the agouti (a rodent), who kept it secret. But his paunch aroused the suspicions of Makunaima (one of the divine twins) and he had him watched—to no avail. After several adventures his brother Manape eventually found the tree. Makunaima then decided to pull it down in spite of the agouti's opposition, for he warned the god that such a volume of water would spill from the trunk that the world would be submerged. Makunaima overruled this and thereby brought about a flood. After the miraculous tree had fallen, its plants spread over the earth.

According to the Cuna version of the same myth, at the top of the tree there was not only earth and plants but also every kind of fish and animal. Every time the sun-god tried to cut the tree, the animals came to lick the wounds he inflicted on the wood to cure them. Clouds (creepers) kept the tree up, and there it remained until a squirrel attacked the creepers with a golden axe. Before it fell the sun-god spread gold and silver nets to catch everything at the top of the tree.

The origin of fire

Indians are very conscious of the effects of the acquisition of fire on the human condition. Before they came into possession of this element, men were no more than animals. Fire is never thought of as something created. It had always existed, but was the property of an animal—occasionally a spirit—which kept jealous watch over it and refused to share it with men. So it had to be stolen. The culture-hero or a kindly animal accepts the challenge. Usually the master of fire and the thief belong to an animal species associated with this element because of some peculiarity of physique. For example, the red, bald head of the vulture, the humming-bird's brilliant plumage, the black mark on the rabbit's throat, the jaguar's colours seem to have marked out these animals for a part in the story of the conquest of fire.

In the versions (the Guarani version in particular) in which the vulture appears as the master of fire, the culture-hero changes into the rotting carcass of some animal in order to gain his ends. The vulture throws him into the fire, but the hero then reverts back to his normal shape, scatters the glowing embers, picks one up and flees. This exploit is often attributed to the toad, which can swallow embers. When the jaguar was the sole owner of fire, he used to eat roast meat. Then, when it was stolen from him by the rabbit and the toad, he had to be content with raw meat. Sometimes the owner of fire was said to make an

A pottery stirrup vase with figures painted and in relief representing three maize deities. The importance of the crops is emphasised in the myths by the difficulty with which the first seeds were obtained. Mochica culture. *British Museum*

attempt to deprive the thief of his loot by evoking heavy rains, but birds stopped the water touching the brand by spreading their wings over it.

Some tribes in Guiana believe that fire is a substance that certain creatures—usually women—drew from the orifices in their bodies. The culture-hero managed to direct this element into certain types of wood.

The origin of death

In the view of many Indians, men would not have to undergo death if the culture-hero (or chance) had decided otherwise. Long, long ago, the Onas, weary with age, had abandoned themselves to sleep, and when they awoke they persuaded the culture-hero, Kenos, to wash them. Thus rejuvenated, they began life all over again. One of the twins terminated these rejuvenations and made death final. There is another story about death that makes its point rather more dramatically: there was a great magician who wanted to make the Chipewya Indians immortal. He advised them to give amicable greeting to a stranger who would come and visit them. Unfortunately for them, the Indians turned aside from a man carrying a basket full of rotting flesh, taking him for Death, but gave an affectionate welcome to Death itself in the guise of a pleasing young man. Peruvian Indians, at least those in the Huarochiri region, regarded death as an accident provoked by a thoughtless gesture. Long ago, when a man died his soul would return after five days. For unexplained reasons one soul returned to its body a day late. The dead man's wife in her impatience reproached him bitterly and went so far as to beat him. The soul took offence and departed for ever and from that time death was irremediable.

In several Amazon tribes there is a tradition that men could have died and been born again alternately if they had obeyed a command they were given or understood more fully a message from the culture-hero or some other person. For instance, according to Cashinawa Indians the father of the culture-hero had advised them to listen well when he rose up into the sky and shouted 'Change! change!' Unfortunately his son mistook this for 'Finish! finish!' This error meant that men could not renew their bodies as do serpents and lizards.

Astral myths

Celestial phenomena and the constellations occupy a privileged position in the etiological myths of South America. The special interest Indians took in the sun and moon has led several scholars to interpret the main themes in their mythology in purely astronomical terms. Explanations of this nature really pertain only to a limited number of themes.

In their endeavour to account for the different phases of the moon, various tribes made the latter a man who grew fat or thin according to the way women fed him. In Bacairi cosmology and that of other Indians, the Moon was first nibbled, then swallowed by animals, lizard or armadillo.

As for the shadows on the moon, the usual explanation takes the form of an—often incestuous—love story. A young man (the Moon) visited his sister (the Sun) one night, but left her before dawn. So that she might recognise her lover the girl scratched his cheeks or rubbed juniper juice, which could not be washed off, on his face. Ashamed at being unmasked, the young man went up into the sky, where one can still see his scars.

There is a widespread belief among South American Indians that eclipses are caused by a celestial feline that occasionally springs at the moon to devour it. The Incas were known to have attempted to frighten the monster on such occasions by making the greatest possible noise. Elsewhere, particularly in the case of the Bacairi Indians, eclipses are attributed to huge bats hiding the sky with their wings. Constellations in the night sky are shaped like creatures or objects that figure in myths—where some account is given of their presence in the firmament. In the eyes of several Carib tribes certain stars in the Great Bear or Orion depict a human leg. This would appear to have been lost by someone in circumstances that are described at length but vary in detail.

The Southern Cross is an enormous nandou pursued by two young men (alpha and beta of Centaur) and by their dog (alpha and beta of the Cross). The Milky Way was composed of the ashes of a celestial tree. In the Gran Chaco, the Three Marys (the three stars of Orion's belt) are three old women who escaped the world-wide fire.

Many tribes know of the story of a star (usually Venus) who fell in love with a poor and ugly young man. She came to him on earth and took care of him. She had power to increase crops. In some versions

the star-woman, who did not wish to be seen by her husband's family, hid in a gourd or jar, but was discovered by his mother. The star decided to return home and take the young man with her, but he could not stand the intense cold in the sky, for stars, say these Indians, were 'fires of ice'. Toba Indians think that they can see mortars in the sky in which the star-woman pounded carobs for her husband's meals.

The rainbow is a celestial serpent. It was first known to men as a small earthworm, and then it ate so much it grew to gigantic proportions. In the end men had to kill it because it was demanding human hearts to satisfy its appetite. Birds came and dipped in its blood and their plumage took on the vivid colours of the rainbow.

Indians make a distinction between the Sun, which is envisaged as a human being, and warmth or light, which radiates and can be identified with such things as the ara parrot's diadem of feathers or any other brilliant adornment. Chipewya Indians think of the Sun as a dark-skinned man with a feather crown. The Sun was originally a cannibal and was killed by a man he was about to devour. The murderer took his feather diadem, but it did not fit him. So the world was plunged into darkness until the youngest son of the Sun raised on high the feather headdress and took his father's place. Similarly, the sun-god of the Guarayu Indians lived in a land lit by birds. The creator, in the opinion of Chibcha Indians, first sent the sun into the world and then light-bringing birds. According to the cosmogony of the Bororo Indians, the sun is a piece of incandescent metal borne across the sky by spirits. Bacairi and Caraja tribes describe the dawn, the sun and the moon as tufts of feathers driven hither and thither by vultures on the wing, until one day the divine twins succeeded in getting hold of them.

The sun's journey has also provided material for myths. Caraja Indians say that at one time the Sun used to flash so quickly across the sky that no-one could complete any task. The help of the culture-hero was sought by a young girl who could not see to pick up her dead wood, and he went and broke the Sun's leg, so forcing him to make his journey more slowly.

In the adventures attributed to the Sun and Moon, the latter is always the weakest. Whereas the Sun triumphs over every danger and obstacle, the Moon is unsuccessful and is slain and quartered. The Sun puts the pieces together again and brings him back to life, exactly as in the myth about the twins in which one of the brothers is identified with the moon.

The destruction of the world

Four times cataclysms descended on the world destroying all—or almost all—living creatures. The first was a world-wide fire. This varies from tribe to tribe, but the explanation of it is that it was started either by the fall of a heavenly body or by a deliberate act on the part of the creator or culture-hero. The Apapocuva–Guarani Indians are convinced that this cataclysm, which took place at the beginning of time, will be repeated on the day that the creator removes the supporting struts from under the earth. The earth will catch fire, and everlasting night will descend upon the world. Then the creator will release the blue tiger to devour men.

After the fire had devastated the earth, it was repeopled by a man and a woman who had escaped the general conflagration by taking refuge in a hole. Vegetation covered the surface of the earth once more, either because spirits came to man's aid, or because he found seeds or shoots scattered by the fire, or because he used some magic device to make the ashes of a tree germinate.

After the 'Great Fire' came the 'Long Night'. Men could not leave their homes. The majority died of hunger. The Araucanians say that the world was plunged into darkness because two mythical characters—the twins—stole the sun and imprisoned it in

a vase. The birds could not find any more food, so they offered the twins women on condition that they freed the sun. But the twins refused. Happily for humanity, the partridge upset the vase and the sun was able to shine again.

During the 'Long Night' domestic objects staged a rebellion. Weary of being used by men, mortars, pestles and pots turned against them and sought to kill them. In North Peru there is a fresco in a temple dating from the Mochica period that depicts the rebellion of household objects. This episode was known to ancient Peruvians, and several modern tribes on the eastern slopes of the Andes are still familiar with it.

No collection of myths is complete without the tale of the destruction of mankind following a flood caused by heavy rain, swelling rivers or tidal waves. This disaster is often attributed in Peru to the culture-hero's anger and displeasure with the men he created because they did not obey his laws or offended him in some other way. Pariaca, for instance, drowned the people of Huarochiri in Peru for being inhospitable to him. The Yaghan Indians made the Moon responsible for the Flood. She caused a tidal wave by way of revenge for the blows she received when men discovered the secret of feminine mysteries.

Sometimes an animal is involved — for instance, a water-serpent, who is wounded by some careless human and makes a river overflow. Some trivial incident is often the cause of the catastrophe. The Witoto tribes say that the master of calabashes cut off the tail of a beautiful parrot, and the bird's owner had his revenge by flooding the world. We have seen that Carib Indians in Guiana and Cuna tribes in Panama connect the Flood theme with the myth of the Tree of Life. The most unusual version is that of the Araucanian Indians: two serpents, Kaimai and Tren-tren, made the waters of the sea rise, simply to prove to one another how great their magic powers were.

The theme of Noah's Ark is not often found in South America. The Spanish chronicler who noted down the Inca version of the Flood refers to a 'box' in which a man and a woman managed to escape. According to the Chiriguano Indians the world was repeopled by a little girl and a boy who were placed by Indians in a calabash. In other tribes the couple or family who survived the Flood set sail on a raft or in a canoe or managed to climb a mountain or get to the top of a tree. The mountain is sometimes said to have increased in height as the waters rose. As in the Bible story, the survivors of the cataclysm received a warning when the waters were receding from an animal, generally a bird, often a mammal.

Many casual episodes are linked with the story of the Flood. For instance, those who have taken refuge at the top of a tree are attacked by various fish — a sword-fish even tries to cut down the tree. Certain animals' features are explained by accidents that befell them at the time of the disaster. The fox's tail trailed in the water and became black; terrified people were changed into howling monkeys; those who could not get down from the tree were changed into ants, monkeys or frogs. A theme widely found in North America about water-birds that built the world is associated with the Flood by Caingue and Aré Indians. Various water-birds went to look for earth and dropped it into the sea until it was full.

After the Flood the earth was repeopled by the descendants of the couple or couples who escaped the world-wide destruction. According to a tradition among the Canari Indians in Ecuador, two youths found refuge on the Huanyan cerro, which had risen above the waters. Every day these two survivors of the Flood went to look for their food in the forest, but whenever they returned to their hut they invariably found a copious meal served. One of the brothers took up his position near the house to solve the mystery and saw two parrots that changed into young girls. They managed to catch one of the bird-girls. She was the ancestor of all Canari Indians.

OCEANIA: SOCIETY AND TRADITION

Although it may be difficult to decide what myth is, and to isolate it from the various forms of oral literature (invocations and chants, legends, folk stories and sayings), it is easy to recognise a mythological turn of mind whose specific function is acknowledged to be mythological by completely different peoples. It is possible to give a precise definition of this function: it is, according to C. Lévi-Strauss, to provide members of a society with a logical pattern whereby they may overcome the grievous contradiction that arises between their beliefs and their practical experience. This is revealed most clearly in traditions that are intended to account for the origin of the world, the existence of living creatures and culture: since they bring into play the strongest possible contrasts between metaphysical, cosmological and moral principles, they afford a perfect example of this type of dialectic.

For this reason it seems preferable not to confine oneself to similarities of theme or character, although, of course, they exist in considerable number in the myths culled from very different parts of Oceania, but rather to take each cultural area and inquire into the meaning of the correlations and conflicts between the principal elements in the mythical drama. In fact, Oceania includes several large heterogeneous civilisations (Polynesia, Melanesia, Micronesia, and Australia) with affinities that can be attributed to very early migrations and are of the greatest possible interest for the historian or linguist, though they make it impossible to treat mythology as a single reality. In this sphere, attempts at generalisation seem all the more dangerous, as the complete heterogeneity of cultures is further enhanced by local peculiarities arising from the insular character of the majority of peoples concerned. One might go so far as to say that each of these societies strives to imagine, at mythological level, its own solution when confronted with universal problems. So one and the same myth comes to appear in different versions in the various 'cantons' of individual cultural areas and in various social classes or ritual brotherhoods. Furthermore, the same text may be regarded as mythological in one village and historical in the next. So the wisest course is to study in turn the myths of origin found in the four great cultural communities of Oceania, and to refer, in conclusion, to any common characteristics that may have arisen during the analysis.

Polynesia

In this huge area there have been migrations—at least two successive waves of them—and varying degrees of fusion between invaders and autochthonous populations, which, together with the immense distance between archipelagos, have bought about variations that make each individual group quite distinctive. However, though the political systems, technical achievements or plastic arts may be in sharp contrast in different societies, it seems that mythological thought, on the contrary, reveals at its deepest level a homogeneity that one would not find in Melanesia or Australia. There are, of course, differences, particularly between the three great cultural centres for the region (New Zealand, eastern Polynesia with Raiatea and the Hawaiian Islands), but they are better described as modulations of a common theme.

The most serious difficulty lies in the choice of Polynesian texts for analysis, and there are two reasons for this. Firstly, the oral literature, which has been collected systematically among these races for more than a hundred and fifty years, has now reached very considerable proportions; secondly and more especially, indigenous thought makes no distinction between myths and historical chronicles, and uses the same word to refer to both (for instance, in Maori it is *korero*). It should be added that the constant need felt by victors and ruling classes to justify their own powers has led to increasing fusion between the two categories. In such cases myth, which is often constructed in retrospect for political ends or for prestige, is merely the humus from which the genealogical trees grow. In other cases, according to the priests (*tohunga*), myth is the mnemotechnic instrument co-ordinating certain ritual formulas (*karakia*). So objective criticism of the documents relating to indigenous commentaries and to the practical use of myths would provide a wealth of information, but it would not fall within the framework of this study. Myths will here be considered from the point of view of their context, and we shall make a comparison between the different societies. Viewed from this angle, it is quite evident that two great bodies of belief must take first place: the first attempts to account for the beginning of the world and living beings; the second describes the original conditions of life and, to be precise, the development of culture (techniques, social rules and values).

Origin of the world and life

True myths of origin are of two types. The first, which has been called evolutionist or genealogical, regards the appearance of primitive chaos either as the outcome of successive transformations of matter (the latter itself resulting from mutation in the void) or as the final stage in a long parthenogenetic filiation, with the metaphysical entities (void, thought, space) and the elements of the tangible world engendering one another in turn. This concept, which is remarkable for its extreme abstraction, prevailed in the Cook Islands and Hawaiian Islands.

The other type of cosmogony propounds the theory that some impersonal first being, usually called Io, created cosmic substance from its own breath. The most remarkable feature that emerges from typological comparison of this kind is the coexistence of the two versions in the majority of archipelagos (for example, New Zealand, Society Islands, the Marquesas Islands and Samoa).

One attempted explanation of this situation is that myths of the first type were of popular origin, whereas the second sort were connected with the dogma of the sacerdotal class. However, this is unimportant: what matters is that whatever their relative age and authenticity, the two systems were accepted by one and the same civilisation at a certain period, and one has, indeed, to think of them as coexisting. There is one other factor that justifies this course of procedure: when we come to consider the personal gods and living creatures who appeared later, only one official explanation is offered. By comparison it then becomes possible to make out the common denominator of the two earlier concepts: both express nostalgia for a primordial unity

that would appear to have been destroyed as life blossomed forth. In both cases chaos is depicted as one undifferentiated substance; both metamorphoses and parthenogenetic birth theories are exclusive, and the intervention of the creator is not inconsistent with this hermetic identity, since Io is usually defined as 'soul of the world', in other words both the subject and object of creation.

Then there follows an episode that gives the first hint of the never-ending flow of contradictions that is to come. From the heart of chaos itself arose the principle of sexual differentiation, which magnetised cosmic matter: thus, from the union of Papa and Rangi, female Earth and male Sky, came forth Life. But as soon as they gave birth to living creatures, these were condemned to eternal imprisonment between the bodies of their parents, who never relaxed their close embrace. Light and darkness were unknown as long as Sky lay with Earth. The first individual gods in the Polynesian pantheon were also produced by this couple, and they held a council to discuss how they should free latent Life. Tu, who later became god of war, suggested that they should destroy Papa and Rangi, while Tane, god of forests and birds, proposed separation without violence. The other brothers favoured the latter solution, with the exception of Tawhiri, lord of winds and tempests, who was opposed to any change in the existing situation. So Tane separated his parents, and, using his own body as a pillar, kept them apart. Light then made its appearance in the world. But Tawhiri took refuge with his father and sent an army of winds to attack his brothers, who took to flight. Tu, however, held out against him, and from that point there was constant war between them. Tu attempted next to chastise his brothers for their defection in the struggle against Tawhiri, and conquered them. Later, after an eventful war, Tu himself was conquered by Tane, who drove him from the sky and sent him into exile on earth. Finally, Tane created the first woman, Hine, out of sand and clay, and coupled with her. Then one day Hine learned that her husband was also her father, and, filled with shame, she fled to the underworld and became its queen—Hine-Nui-Te-Po (Great Lady of the Night). The first act of incest, from which mankind originated, brought Death into the world, and from that time forth Hine-Nui-Te-Po worked unceasingly to attract the living to her kingdom.

What is the meaning of this myth? When compared with the preceding descriptions of chaos, it seems manifestly dialectic in structure. If the tale is divided into elementary sequences, an unbroken chain of postulates emerges—these postulates being explicitly propounded, then neutralised. It is correct to say that the whole field of Polynesian (especially Maori) metaphysics is dominated by the antinomy Day–Night, with its modal accompaniments Sky–Earth and Life–Death, and this makes the logical

493

function of the myth quite clear. Thus the coupling of Sky and Earth, which imprisoned latent Life, expresses the initial situation in a 'philosophy' free from contradiction, but condemned to immobility. With the separation of Sky and Earth and the emergence of Light, the fundamental contrast or opposition noted earlier appears for the first time and is immediately neutralised (Tane's mediation, which ensures a link between the two elements of the couple). The following combat is marked by the defeat of the gods who favoured a middle course in the matter of their parents' separation, while Tawhiri and Tu are condemned to eternal conflict which produces neither victor nor vanquished. This represents an irreducible antagonism between two extremist demands for permanence, one within, the other outside of the Sky—Earth opposition, which neither party will agree to assume. In fact, Tawhiri, by his hostility to any change, seeks in vain to perpetuate the original immobility, while Tu's will to destruction, which would put an end to procreation by means of the first parents, expresses a dream of a life without beginning or end.

Tane's later victory over Tu ends in the former's installation in the sky and the latter's permanent banishment to earth. So Tane abandons his role of mediator, and the opposition that was previously neutralised is then reaffirmed with new vigour. Finally, the union of Tane and Hine, celestial god and creature moulded from clay, represents a second attempt at conciliation, which fails with Hine's flight to the underworld.

So it can be seen that the whole tale is constructed as a dialectic apparatus intended to study thoroughly, then to resolve, the different modalities in a basic metaphysical contradiction. The trend of mythical thought is to progress from disjunction to logical conjunction and to draw from each opposition or contrast the necessary energy to accomplish the next stage. It thereby tends constantly towards a state of rest that would reinstate primitive unity. This is the solution sought in the final union of Tane and Hine, which reproduces the initial fusion of Sky and Earth. But this is an incestuous union, which means that any hope of going back in time is a mere delusion. It is quite useless for the god to make Hine his wife: she is still his creature, and by her very existence proclaims that the distinction between Sky and Earth has been irrevocable since life emerged. Moreover, with the entry of Death into the world, the contradiction, which was temporarily counteracted by the act of incest, arises again in a new form, and provides an impulse towards other mythical developments (in particular, the Maui cycle).

This interpretation, which corresponds more or less to the version found in New Zealand, should now be compared with the variants found in the other archipelagos. Although it is not possible to enter into great detail here, it will be quite adequate

Ancestral panel from a Maori ceremonial meeting house in New Zealand. Among the rituals performed here were those designed to thank the gods for the produce of the sea, which was then shared out, just as Maui thanked the gods for the islands he fished out of the sea. *Dominion Museum*

Tu, war-god throughout Polynesia. Son of Papa and Rangi, the Sky and the Earth, Tu proposed to kill them, but was overruled by his brother Tane, who merely separated them. Tu, victorious in an ensuing quarrel, punished his brothers, but was in turn exiled to earth. Tu was responsible for the existence of a constant state of war. Wooden statue from Hawaii. *Peabody Museum of Salem*

to describe certain local differences. For example, in the islands of Samoa the creation of earth and of the first woman is attributed to Tangaroa, who then couples with Hine. At first sight this tale is in manifest contradiction to the Maori schema, for Tangaroa is usually defined as god of the sea and thus the violent contrasts and oppositions would cease to be pertinent. But the two versions are easily reconciled on a more careful analysis: in fact, the Samoans, unlike other Polynesian races, look on Tangaroa as a celestial deity, and even go so far as to say in their myth that he created the earth by taking several rocks from the sky and throwing them into space. This variant deserves our attention, because, far from invalidating the previous hypotheses, it presents additional oppositions, thanks to the exceptional nature of the celestial function assumed by Tangaroa. (The only other place it is found is Tonga, but there it is in precisely the same context and has the same result.)

As for the myths of Tahitian origin, the substitutes they propose for the characters and circumstances in the cosmic drama throw even more glaring light on the structure revealed by the Maori document. For instance, in the exposition of the initial situation, the coupling of Papa and Rangi is replaced in this tale by a primordial egg, which Ta'aroa (Tahitian name for Tangaroa) breaks into halves that then become earth and sky. Furthermore, the functions attributed to Tane in New Zealand are here bestowed upon Ta'aroa in the early period. Then, when the latter confines himself to the role of mediator, they devolve upon Tane, who is invested with the celestial character necessary to the interplay of oppositions.

Finally, the creation of Hine and her marriage poses another problem; in several myths from the Society and Marquesas Islands, the creator and husband of Hine is Tiki (or Ti'i, according to the

linguistic group), not Tane. Tiki requires some further explanation. For a long time experts thought him to be either the first man, or an evil spirit invoked by sorcerers. Recent research, in which ritual and marriage chants have been examined, has now established that this character represents virility. Now Tiki was created by Tane to serve as his artisan and messenger — or such is the explanation in eastern Polynesia. In other words, his intervention in the Hine sequence does not alter its meaning; Tiki is intended by his phallic nature to ensure communication between the sexes, and he proclaims the importance of the mediation that Tane wished to effect between the celestial and terrestrial poles.

The preceding study has been deliberately restricted to the more explicit myths of origin. However, it allows a glimpse of the complexity of Polynesian mythical thought, as well as the variety of logical processes brought into operation to formulate certain philosophical problems. But, in fact, almost all oral literature, either by allusion to the subject in the first few lines of chants or by implication in maxims and proverbs, refers to the formation of the world and the creation of mankind. This only emphasises how useless it would have been, within the framework of this chapter, to have attempted even a brief analysis of the Polynesian pantheon.

The origin of culture

Of all Polynesian heroes, Maui is undoubtedly the most famous. He is the central character in a vast cycle containing several dozen legends in a coherent order. He has a thousand and one adventures, which are still told today to amuse children, and these were annexed to the scholarly ideology of the sacerdotal class in some archipelagos, while in others they formed a body of folk wisdom. These sociological considerations would suffice to justify the lasting interest of specialists in this character. But the essential thing is that all Polynesians credit him, more or less directly, with the invention of their principal techniques and the institution of certain values. Furthermore, the fundamental ambivalence of his activity has attracted attention over a long period: though he is a culture-hero, Maui is also a 'trickster', and thereby arouses laughter or indignation. In different societies there are differing versions of the myth, which favour either the first or the second of these aspects. In the Hawaiian Islands, for example, the emphasis is placed on the hero's social nonconformism, whereas the inhabitants of the Tuamotu and Marquesas Islands stress his erotic exploits, and in the Society Islands there is a sublimated idea of him pertaining to a hierarchy of social statutes.

First of all, we shall outline a version found in New Zealand, which seems particularly homogeneous and complete. The birth of Maui is presented as an accident. His mother was delivered before her time, and,

Right: Bark painting of a culture-hero. Australia. British Museum.

Below: A bark painting giving graphic expression to the central story of the Wawilak myth belonging to Eastern Arnhem Land. Basically the story is that of two Wawilak sisters who led their children out of the southern inland to the Liaalaomir totemic hole. The elder sister profaned the pool and as a punishment the women and their children were swallowed by Yurlungger, a python.

The story cannot be 'read' from the painting but the sisters and the water-hole occur in several places. There is a snake coiled around the two sisters and a child. The light dots indicate rain, representing the flood that followed the python's despatch of the sisters.

The artist who painted this owned the right to express the myth. He accompanied his work on each section with the appropriate ritual and song. *Poignant*

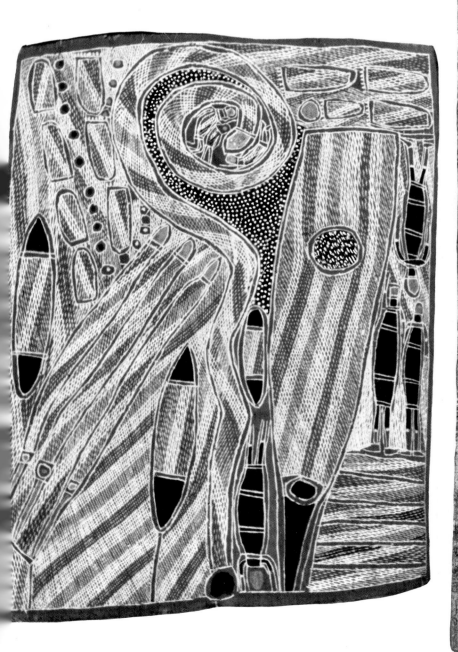

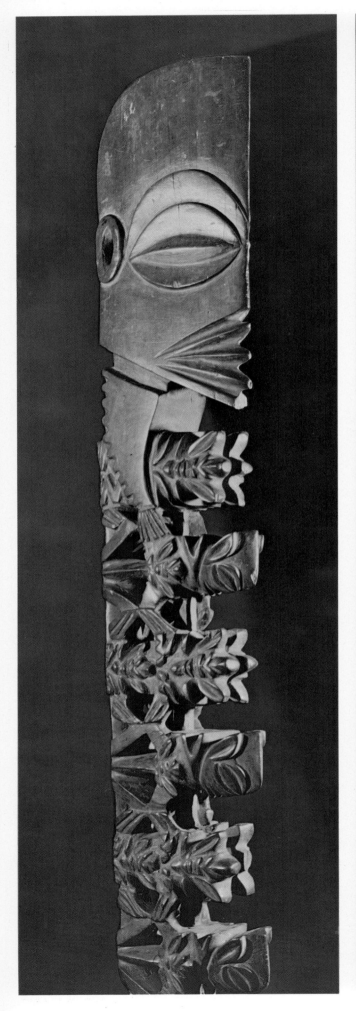

Maui, most famous of Polynesian heroes. A descendant of the Sun, he was at first rejected by his human mother and was doomed to betrayal by the gods. He lengthened the days by maiming the Sun, but failed to win immortality for human beings. Panel from a tribal meeting house. *Hamburg Museum*

Opposite (left): Rarotongan staff-god.

Opposite (right): A malanggan. New Ireland. British Museum.

fearing the evil propensities of miscarriage, threw her offspring into the ocean. The child, though half dead, was saved by his ancestor the Sun, who took him to his kingdom. He stayed there till he reached adolescence and received a divine education. When he later returned to earth, he sought out his mother and revealed his identity, and in spite of incessant quarrels with his elder brothers, he decided to live among men. His first adventures in magic (particularly metamorphoses) filled his father with wonder, and he attempted to give him his blessing, but committed some ritual error. From that time forth the hero was in danger of eventual and inevitable betrayal at the hands of the gods. None the less, he commenced the cycle of his prodigious 'labours'. He went to the far end of the world and gained possession of the jaw of his divine ancestress Muri-Ranga and made it into an invincible weapon. Then he decided to lengthen the duration of the day, for it was not long enough for human activity. So he hid by the gate from which the Sun emerged every morning and attacked the god with the magic jaw-bone, which he used as a club; maimed by this attack, the Sun could then move only slowly in his orbit. As for the secret of fire, which men did not yet have in their possession, Maui obtained it by a combination of trickery and force from his ancestress Mahuika, who ruled on the edge of the chthonian world.

One day when he was out fishing, he quarrelled with his brother-in-law Irawaru, who refused to share the catch. To punish him for his selfishness, Maui changed him into a dog, thus creating one of the two species of domestic mammal known in Polynesia. Finally, the hero thought that he was ready for his most difficult task: to bring men immortality. So he went down to the underworld and found Hine-Nui-Te-Po asleep there—this goddess was thought to be his ancestress. Bidding his friends the birds be silent, he undressed and, slipping between her legs, tried to force his way right inside the goddess to inflict defeat on Death. But one of the birds burst out laughing at the strange spectacle of Maui half engulfed in the giantess. She immediately awoke and killed the hero. This failure sealed the fate of mankind, and it lost for ever the benefit of a second life.

On reading this tale, one aspect immediately seems to merit our consideration: Maui's activities are accompanied by incessant comings and goings between gods and men. This very obvious factor suggests the lines on which an analysis should be conducted. As this myth professes to be an explanation of the origin of civilisation, before any hypothesis is established one should know more about the stage humanity had reached at the time of the hero's birth. The answer is given in three contradictory versions, each formulated with extreme clarity. First of all, man is still floating between nature and

culture: he eats his food raw, 'like the beasts', as the myth puts it, and, according to a Hawaiian version, which credits Maui with raising the sky, he is a four-legged creature; he is barred from any sort of regular work by the shortness of the day, and is quite unaware of certain essential techniques. Secondly, though mortal because of the original act of incest, he can return to life after banishment to darkness. Finally, if one draws the logical conclusion from the origin-myths studied above, man must be regarded as a true mixture of celestial and chthonian elements as a result of the union of Tane and Hine. This is the initial situation that Maui must transform so that the human condition may be established in specific detail; this task consists of overcoming three contradictions. If one goes back over the myth with this in mind, the different elementary sequences reveal their meaning.

The hero's miraculous birth, which gives some indication of his fate, is the first sign of the Polynesian attitude to his adventures. Born of human parents, he must fully assume the triple contradiction imposed on humanity; but his exposure to the sea, which breaks his ties with his own kin, immediately frees him from the specifically human and changes him into a neutral agent equally removed from gods, men and animals. This is the truly crucial moment in his life, when he becomes an empty sign with endless potentialities awaiting polarisation. At this point his adoption by the Sun orientates him in a celestial direction, but he refuses this a little later. The following sequence, his return to earth, closes the first half of the story by bringing it round full circle: it is a return to the initial situation, for Maui will henceforth be the victim of human ambiguities as a result of his decision to return to earth. The ceremony of benediction, which confirms his new status, is far from redundant, for it introduces a motive into the system: by giving death precedence over life—in advance, as it were—the father's ritual fault destroys the constantly threatened equilibrium which the hero now incarnates. All his later exploits are a dramatic bid to defy the ill luck that appears at this moment. As for the capture of Muri-Ranga's jaw, it represents the supreme desecration that Polynesians inflicted on their vanquished foes. As an attempt to remedy the preceding imbalance, this episode is the opposite and counterpart to that of the benediction. Corresponding to the basically beneficent ritual, which is, however, to cause Maui's eventual downfall, is set the most scandalous impiety, which will make him invincible for a long time to come.

The next three 'labours' (capture of the Sun, discovery of fire, metamorphosis of Irawaru) symbolise the victory of culture over the natural state: the beginning of productive work, the discovery of fire, and the prohibition of incest. Since C. Lévi-Strauss's research on the subject, it has been accepted that the one universally attested rule found throughout

the ages, the prohibition of incest, must be regarded as the supreme rule, that by which man, freeing himself from biological slavery, becomes fully man. Furthermore, this author has shown that the function of this rule was not so much to prevent certain marriages as to ensure a rational distribution of women within the social group. Now it should be noted in this connection that the name Irawaru actually refers to incest in Maori. If we take this into joint consideration with the fact that in all primitive civilisations the sharing out of food and the sharing out of women are regarded as two facets of one and the same institution (barter), on which the cohesion of society depends, then the meaning of Maui's quarrel with his brother-in-law becomes clear. As sanction of the refusal to share, the treatment inflicted on Irawaru symbolically inaugurates the prohibition of incest.

With the final sequence, the logical motivation in the myth reaches its height in a desperate attempt to reabsorb all the contradictions in the human condition. One feels an immediate need to envisage several levels in the analysis of this episode. One is struck first of all by the symmetry and similarity between Maui's death and his birth. The hero's adventures do, in fact, seem sandwiched between two obstetric accidents: he is born after abnormal emergence from his mother's womb and dies trying to force his way into Hine's womb. It seems certain that this particular concept of the quest for immortality is a recurrence of the universal theme of *regressus ad uterum*, just as it is probable that, on the ritual plane, it refers to initiatory tests by which the neophyte enters a new life. But an interpretation of this sort by no means exhausts the various meanings of this sequence, for comparison with other mythical events immediately reveals that several pertinent traits have been left out. In particular, no account has been taken of the origin of death, which is hardly justifiable under the circumstances. In essentials there is a curious symmetry between the present episode and Tane's incest with Hine, when regarded as an explanation of the origin of death. So it follows that the attempt to conquer death must be considered, at least provisionally, as a second act of incest aimed at cancelling out the consequences of the first. In so far as it is the coupling of two identical beings (of the same blood), who behave as if they were different by nature, incest does indeed afford a means of overcoming the dilemma between identity and dissimilarity. Now this may, in fact, be the precise meaning that one should attribute to Maui's final exploit.

In mythical times, humanity is defined as mortal, though able to enjoy the advantage of a second life. Thus it is torn between the chthonian and celestial poles; and it is this human fate that the hero fully assumes on his return to earth. Hine, on the other hand, is of univocal determination: she is chthonian and possesses immortality. So the contrast between the two protagonists is that of the simple opposed to the complex, the one against the manifold. Their confrontation denotes the destruction of a mode of thought that is forced to give way to the antithetic. So the unwonted union that Maui attempted is seen to represent the promotion of this opposition. The recompense is peace and permanence; this is amply indicated by the search for immortality evoked in the tale. As for the hero's death, it sheds light on all beliefs relative to culture and shows that our hypothesis regarding a second act of incest is not groundless. If, in fact, this hypothesis is admitted, then the final punishment is invested with significance: it gives precedence to the cultural order that Maui attempted to ignore by committing incest with his ancestress. The fact that this dramatic attempt of his was in vain indicates that Maoris believe that mankind possesses only one means of facing up to its contradictions—culture. Finally, it should be noted that all the characters in the myth, whether their attitude be one of hostility or collaboration, are either closely or distantly related. This must undoubtedly be regarded as an affirmation that the development of culture finds its instruments and limitations in connections between kinsmen.

It is now possible to work out why all the various known versions attribute a disturbing ambiguity to Maui's conduct. Why is this culture-hero a 'trickster'? The preceding analysis has given an implicit answer to this question by showing that the two aspects are not contradictory, but complementary. Maui is able to bring culture to mankind simply because he enjoys the status of trickster. The hero's successive sojourns in the sky, on earth and in the world below, like his incessant movement between gods and men, suggest that his activity is basically outside the scope of one particular universe. This activity may be reduced to the never-ending pursuit of man's reconciliation with himself. Such observations as these are prompted by the demands of logic, but several of the hero's characteristics, which at first sight seem ill-matched, are in accordance with these requirements: the shame attached to the circumstances of his birth, the solitude inflicted upon him by his mother's abandonment of him, his trickster's nonconformism with which he boldly defies gods and men. Of course it is possible to regard these things as manifestations of the personal whims of Maori storytellers, but these whims do not operate arbitrarily; proof of this lies in the fact that different aspects of Maui converge. The main concern throughout many seemingly subordinate motions and episodes is to put the hero in a position to accomplish his mission of mediation.

Let us now compare the different versions of the myth. One point claims immediate attention: legends found outside New Zealand are silent on the subject of Maui's death. A lacuna of this importance deserves a more serious explanation than those that merely

state that the Maoris possess overwhelming intellectual superiority over the other Polynesian races. It is true that research on the subject is not yet at an end, but one significant correlation can already be indicated: in the versions in which the final sequence is omitted there is no allusion whatsoever to immortality. So it follows that, although truncated, the myth may still be placed in the structural context discovered in the Maori document. And, in fact, it is a simple matter to show that the variants involving different exploits on the part of the hero do come within the framework of this schema. This is the case with the traditions of the Hawaiian, Cook and Samoan Islands, which claim that Maui raised the sky. Whatever the circumstances of this act, the enterprise always has the effect of completing the attempt of the cosmogonic gods to make the world more habitable. It is an attack upon a problem which is quite clearly outlined: once the sky has been separated from the earth by Tane, it continues to rest on flowers and bushes, forcing men to make their way about on all fours like animals. This type of identification between animals and men, expressly formulated by natives, affords proof that the hero's task is to make the domain of nature retract and culture advance.

The same is true of the tale of fishing for lands told in the Hawaiian and Tuamotu Islands. The story, which is part of cosmogonic belief, shows how Maui wins a twofold victory for culture. Once he has overcome the persistent hostility of his brothers, who represent mankind in its natural state, he decides to go fishing, using the magic jaw-bone as a hook, and from the depths of the ocean he brings up one or several islands. This exploit, which delivers up new lands to Polynesian colonisation, also goes to show that fishermen cannot divide their catch without first offering thanks to the gods with appropriate ceremony.

The extraordinary fame enjoyed by the Maui chronicle, and its influence, which spreads beyond the Polynesian area and can frequently be detected in Melanesia and Micronesia, must not make us overlook the popularity of several other heroes. In sharp contrast to Maui, there is, first and foremost, Tahaki. He is handsome and strong, will not stoop to make use of trickery and, from the Hawaiian Islands to New Zealand, is the prototype of the respected chieftain. Some experts, impressed by him as a bold sailor, have tried to discover a historical basis for this aristocrat; but in actual fact a careful analysis shows that this character belongs not so much to the category of myth as of fairytale. That is why he has no true place in this study.

Melanesia

Geographically, Melanesia consists of three principal regions: New Guinea, a ring of volcanic archipelagos (Solomon Islands, New Hebrides, New Caledonia) and, somewhat remote from the rest, the Fiji Islands. But the mere idea of Melanesia poses a problem for anyone more particularly concerned with human realities. In sharp contrast to the mythology of Polynesia, what strikes one here is a stupendous heterogeneity, though the actual land area involved is only one-fifth of that of Polynesia. In what must perforce be called the 'Melanesian universe', physical anthropology, linguistics and sociology carve out their respective empires, which clash or overlap, but whose boundaries never coincide.

For the sake of convenience, three major cultural entities can be marked out, but any attempt at definition would only reveal our comparative ignorance. The first consists of the Negritos in central New Guinea. Very little is known of this extremely humble race, which is probably the only autochthonous one in this region. At most, one can risk a few suppositions as a result of one or two studies on the subject of the Negrillos in central Malaya (Semang). The second group, which goes by the name of Papuan, settled in large numbers in New Guinea and several of the Solomon Islands—seemingly as the result of very early migrations. In this connection, we should point out that the classification adopted must not be taken too rigidly: in fact, the term 'Papuan' covers some highly dissimilar idioms. So it is not surprising to find that information about societies included under this heading is not always consistent. The third and now largest group in the region, though it was the last to arrive, consists of Melanesians as such, and this group is typified by a much more highly developed culture and the use of Malayo-Polynesian languages. They have settled on most islands and are better known than any other race; a considerable number of their myths has already been collected.

The originality of the last two groups is seen in the main outline of their mythological structures. Thus Papuan legends place particular emphasis on ghosts and on the theme of sex. Melanesians seem to consider ogres and cannibals as essential mythical characters. But the most significant difference is in the field of cosmogonic ideas: alike in the belief that the world has always existed, Papuans state that in the mythical dawn of time it had already adopted its definitive form, whereas Melanesians say that the intervention of supernatural beings was still necessary to furnish it and complete its resources. However, both groups are equally concerned to economise on true creator-gods, and this brings these two concepts into violent contrast with Polynesian traditions.

The creation

As will now be obvious to readers, Melanesian material will provide the most important contribution to

Malanggan carving from New Ireland. This fetish has a fearsome head at either end and is covered with symbolic markings. *British Museum*

501

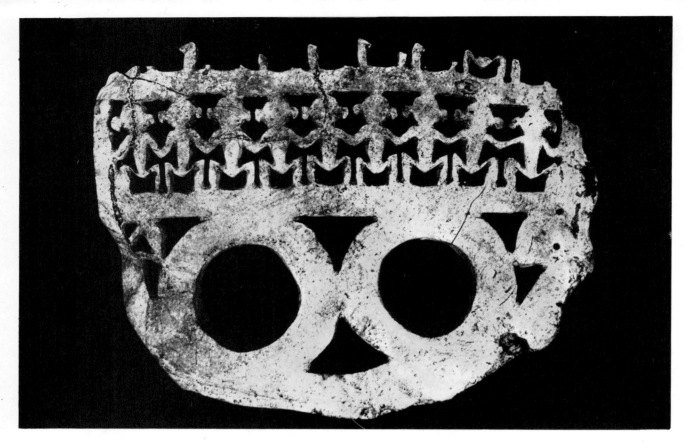

Tridacna carving from the Solomon Islands, used to seal the gable ends of model huts where the dead chiefs' skulls were kept. The figures represent the spirits of ancestors. *Museum für Völkerkunde, Basel*

Mask depicting a good spirit and worn during ritual dances to ward off typhoons. Much Melanesian mythology concerns the cruelty of nature and the role of gods and spirits in tempering it. Thus the sun never stopped beating down until intervention of Qat. *Hamburg Museum*

this section, the available Papuan myths being brought in only for the purposes of cross-checking when the need arises.

As, in their view, the world is a first principle, Melanesians describe it, prior to the emergence of supernatural beings and men, as a desert totally devoid of familiar landscapes. Matter is sterile, bathed in cruel, perpetual light, with no seasons to provide variety; furthermore, the ocean has no tides. So everything combines to make this mythical period a reign of utter stagnation until a spirit is eventually born who will organise the universe. In the view held in the Banks Islands, this event is heralded by a rock dividing to permit the emergence of Qat, the central character in Banks Islands mythology.

Qat, who is a spirit (*vui*), not a god, creates various living things (such as trees and pigs). To create the human species he carves the bodies of three men and three women from a tree; then he fashions them with care and hides them for three days in the shade of a clump of trees. Finally, he imbues them with life by dancing and beating a drum in front of them. However, another powerful spirit, Marawa, notices Qat's exploits and decides to imitate him. So Marawa, in turn, fabricates human beings by the same process. But when his creatures begin to move, he buries them under leaves and branches in a hole he has dug in the forest. After seven days he takes them from the ditch, but finds them in a state of inertia and decomposition. Marawa's unfortunate enterprise is responsible for making man a mortal being.

Later, at the request of his brothers, who are tired of everlasting daylight in the world, Qat brings to men the gift of darkness. His work is completed when he inaugurates the rhythm of the seasons and endows the ocean with tides and the earth with regular rainfall.

Before we look for the meaning of this myth, it

Statuette used in magic rain-making rites. This figure is carved, like the first human beings, out of a single piece of wood and its function reflects the typical preoccupations of an agricultural people. New Caledonia. *Museum für Völkerkunde, Basel*

should be emphasised that the Melanesians are first and foremost a race of farmers whose thoughts and acts are ruled by the agrarian calendar, as can be seen from the different types of magic connected with rain and crops. It is easy to see the mark of such ideas in the story of Qat. It may even seem to have been entirely conceived to establish the primacy of agriculture. In fact, the many interventions on the part of the two *vui* result in the replacement of the principle of permanence by that of periodic change, and the latter is, of course, of capital importance to men who are inclined to identify the notion of life with the crop-cycle on their plantations. Once one realises that Qat's brothers, who ask for the establishment of a regular succession of days and nights, have the names of plants, it is impossible to be in any further doubt as to the correct interpretation. As for the creation of man, it represents complete identification with the vegetable kingdom; in fact, doubly so, since the ancestors of humanity owe their very substance to a tree and die through burial in the earth and among branches.

Very similar themes are found in most regions peopled by Melanesians. For instance, in a myth found in the New Hebrides the origin of agriculture springs from rivalry between Day and Night. Tortali, master of the sun and spirit of day, had taken a mortal, Avin, to wife. She lived a happy, idle life in a wondrous garden, which constantly provided her with the richest of food. One evening, in defiance of all the warnings she had been given she took advantage of her husband's absence and gave herself to Ul, master of the moon and spirit of night. On his return, Tortali learned of her adultery and drove Avin from the garden. Ever after, women had to work to get their food from the earth, while their bodies had to submit to the menstrual cycle. It is, of course, true that the idea of punishment coupled

with that of agricultural activity introduces a new note, but the primary factor is the aforementioned combination of the idea of agriculture and the negation of permanence. This is stressed by the inability of Day to maintain his authority in the face of Night's powers of seduction, and by the mention of the periodic cycle that is a feature of feminine existence.

As far as the origin and nature of the human species are concerned, the other known legends can be reduced to the same structure. This is true of another version of the story of Qat that is told in the Banks Islands: the creator does not sculpt his human beings from the wood of trees, but fashions man from clay and woman from plaited fronds of sago-palm. The suggestion implicit in these symbols is that mankind contains in its very substance the fundamental harmony between the earth and the vegetable kingdom. Much farther north the inhabitants of Saa in the Solomon Islands believe that their ancestors sprang spontaneously from sugar-cane when, one day, two buds burst open and a man and a woman emerged. The meaning of this image is perfectly clear.

As for the Melanesians in New Britain, they have a myth that tallies with the two versions in the Banks Islands in several respects. Some first being, who is not given a name, draws the shape of two human figures on the ground, lets his own blood fall upon them, then covers them with leaves, thus creating the two great culture-heroes To-Kabinana and To-Karvuvu. The latter gather coconuts and dash them to pieces upon the ground; four women emerge and become their wives. The fate of humanity lies in this union of the earth and fruits from which it sprang. Finally, the emergence of death, which is still regarded here as a contingent phenomenon that could have been avoided by certain precautions, also has its place in this system of beliefs, which, in itself, explains man's daily experience as part of a continual cycle. Death is present as a potential in the world of men because of some mistake (as in the example already quoted from the Banks Islands) or malevolence (New Hebrides), and as such it is still dependent on human initiative. In the sequence of mythical time, men are radically different from spirits and have a status far removed from anything associated with them today because it is conditioned by ambiguity. For instance, throughout the whole region of Melanesia, and even in several Papuan groups, men are credited with the ability to grow young again at will and thus to avoid death. There is the widest agreement on this point, in spite of variations of detail: when they reach old age, men slough their skins, as snakes do, and enjoy renewed youth. A woman retains this power of regeneration until she returns home one day in the shape of a beautiful girl and is not recognised by her own children. Then, in despair, she dons her old skin and can never be rejuvenated again. This type of tale, which is found in numerous archipelagos, is better understood when

Painting on a sago leaf from a ceremonial house in New
Guinea. The painting represents two cockatoos. According to
the myth current in the Banks Islands, the first woman was
made of a sago leaf, and given as wife to a man made of clay.
Museum für Völkerkunde, Basel

compared with two remarkable variants on the same theme.

The first, which comes from the Admiralty Islands, is about a grandmother and her grandson; the latter refuses to believe in her change of shape and wants to marry his own ancestress, who assumes her former appearance again to avoid incest. The second is a story told in the Banks Islands, and it depicts death as a solution invented by Qat to put an end to quarrels arising out of avarice and greed. Men had multiplied indefinitely and become so numerous that younger generations were driven to poverty by the egotism of their elders; so death became necessary to prevent monopoly and to ensure the equal division of wealth. In other words, in both these cases immortality was regarded as the source of disorder: by hindering the proper functioning of matrimonial and economic rules it finally brought one generation into conflict with another.

However, one must actually go farther into the matter than these indigenous interpretations permit; and then, quite apart from the circumstantial framework of the tale, it will become apparent that this form of immortality contains its own logical condemnation. The situation that Qat abolishes stems from an untenable contradiction: the repeated reprieves bestowed on mankind by constant rejuvenation are an aspiration to permanence, but at the same time permanence is negated by the process of sexual reproduction. And so native thought is here momentarily fixed as it swings sadly between a quest already abandoned and a new choice yet to be made. The acceptance of death, which is but the counterpart of sexual reproduction, breaks the deadlock: the individual renounces his own permanence to ensure the permanence of his race.

So it would appear that the different myths we have studied, whether they tell of the origin of night and the seasons, the creation of man or the fatality of death, refer to a major schism in Melanesian philosophy. Their function is to suggest a means of transcending the opposition between permanence and change. As in several other agricultural societies (for example, the North American Zuñi), the solution seems to have been modelled on the predominant techno-economic activity.

However, the presence of the same mythological structure in a great number of Melanesian populations must not be allowed to obscure the fact that Fiji is an important exception. In this group of islands, where the influence of Polynesian culture has long been a matter for observation and comment, it was traditionally held that mankind had emerged from a bird's egg hatched by the divine serpent Ndegei. This is a very similar concept to that held in Polynesia, which depicts human nature as ambivalent as a result of man's twofold chthonian and celestial origin: in this case Ndegei personifies infernal powers and the vital principles of the soil.

The origin of culture

The fact that there are no creator-gods in Melanesian mythology explains why the origin of culture is usually attributed to characters who have already played an essential part in the organisation of the cosmos: Takaro and Mueragbuto in the New Hebrides; Qat and Marawa in the Banks Islands; To-Kabinana and To-Karvuvu in New Britain and New Guinea. The most obvious connection is the fact that they appear in pairs; together they form a couple, and are depicted as such in the legends of the different regions and invoked thus in people's prayers. Their attributes and activities are in direct contrast, and at the same time counter-balance each other. Thus, for instance, Qat, who is the giver of life in the material world, has as his counterpart Marawa, who brings death to mankind, and, similarly, To-Kabinana and To-Karvuvu represent the two alternatives implicit in human destiny. Furthermore, whenever the two heroes are endowed with definite qualities, the one is a model of kindness and intelligence and the other embodies wickedness and stupidity. Finally, in certain ritual formulas their image is interpreted as the contrast between right and left. What is the meaning of this dualism? It would appear that the union between these two supernatural characters is far more important than their antagonism, and is an expression of the means by which man assumes his destiny—that is to say, the acceptance of restraint. Their opposition to one another never culminates in static neutrality; its content is strictly dynamic. Marawa, for example, does not put into practice a negation of life, but simply adds death to Qat's own achievements, replacing eternity by a process bounded by a beginning and an end. Moreover, the myth that tells of the many quarrels between these two characters also emphasises their collaboration (Marawa helps Qat in desperate situations) and shows that they hold complementary functions. In this connection there is a most revealing tale from New Britain about the origin of fishing with bait. To-Kabinana made wooden figures that looked like the main types of edible fish and put them in the water to attract others towards the bank. To-Karvuvu, as usual, was not to be outdone, and he so shaped his bait that sharks appeared in shoals. When the sharks had devoured most of the other fish, fishing became difficult and offered only small hauls.

If the perpetual rivalry between the twins has any meaning other than an obsession with failure and frustration, then it can only express their allegiance to a never-ending, common task: the quest for equilibrium between men and also between man and his natural surroundings. Here, in fact, the debilitating dream of the endless growth of wealth must be rejected, and man must anticipate scarcity and become dependent on his techniques of production, both victor and prisoner of matter.

A very similar lesson is illustrated in a myth from
the New Hebrides about a taboo placed on coconuts.
A spirit called Takaro had forbidden the eating of
coconuts, but his rival, who was known as Mueragbuto, lost no time in violating the taboo. Takaro
punished him for his greed by making him eat coconuts until he died of over-eating. The remarkable
thing about transgressing this taboo is that death is
inflicted through a surfeit of food. Now it is just such
consequences as these that people wish to avoid
when the taboo on coconuts is enforced today: even
now, in many societies, the chieftain periodically
forbids villagers to gather nuts in certain coconut
groves so as to build up reserves as an insurance
against lean times.

Finally, the culture-hero couple possesses one very
obvious characteristic which makes its functions in
mythology more comprehensible: most legends
grant the couple the status of mediator. If we go
rather deeper than the couple's quarrels and their
circumstances, which vary according to region and
to the techniques or values they reveal to men—construction of hut dwellings, institution of matrimonial

groups—then we see that the consistent behaviour of
the two protagonists, evolving as they do between
supernatural beings and mortals, in fact confirms
an underlying unity. In this connection natives on
the Banks Islands believe that Qat is present at different times in a lone cloud floating between heaven
and earth, in a ray of sunshine piercing the mist or
in the smoke from volcanoes. So there is nothing
arbitrary in the fact that tradition makes them the
authors of culture, they are culture itself (conciliation of antimonies, link between life and death), and
the achievements with which they are credited simply make this idea more intelligible to the uninitiated.
When eventually we come to areas in which these
two enemy-associates are unknown (Papuan zone in
New Britain, Admiralty Islands), we find that here
the myths actually furnish us with significant counter-
proof, for they ascribe the same attributes to the semi-
divine serpent who has pride of place in these parts.
But, as his status has to be made more explicit, they
also turn this mythical creature into a spokesman for
the dead, and the holder of an important phallic
function (mediation between the sexes).

Micronesia

Micronesia is a collection of tiny, scattered islands, which can be roughly divided into five archipelagos: the Gilbert, Marshall, Mariana, Caroline, and Pelew groups. The local peoples, who number about 100,000, seem to the anthropologist to be a comparatively homogeneous combination of three elements—Polynesian, Melanesian and Indonesian—and to the linguist as part of the Malayo-Polynesian family. As they had long been well off the major trade routes, and, in general, had been neglected by ethnographers, very little was known about them until the Second World War. So the mythological material that has been collected is very slight, and it is to be feared that inquiries undertaken since 1945 may prove to have come too late to save certain major traditions from oblivion.

There are in the majority of myths striking resemblances to themes we have come to connect with Polynesia and Melanesia. Some features, on the other hand, are typically Micronesian: flight achieved by means of mock birds endowed with magical properties or by wickerwork baskets; prominence given to the siren and the crocodile, the latter probably linked with totemic beliefs. However, the originality and interest of this oral literature lies in the ordering and combination of local and borrowed elements.

Origin of the world and life

We must make special reference to the cosmogonies of the Gilbert Islands, which are an echo of the Polynesian type: primordial night coinciding with the coupling of Sky and Earth; then separation of the two elements accompanied by the emergence of light. This schema, which is readily recognisable, is made more complicated by the intervention of a deity, Nareau, who will be mentioned again later. As for detailed variations from Polynesian tradition, they might provide sociology with some useful data, but they would require closer analysis than can be attempted here.

In other archipelogos, particularly the Caroline and Pelew Islands, explanations of the origin of the world can basically be reduced to one single concept, which totally ignores the principle of creation *ab nihilo*. A rock is given as the matrix of the universe, and it is said to exist prior to any natural or supernatural operation. It is often associated with an endless stretch of original sea, and it produces the first gods, who construct the world. In the central Caroline Islands the eldest god, Solal, plants on the primordial rock a tree or mast, which he proceeds to climb, stopping half-way to create the earth, depicted as a plane surface, then continuing his ascent to the top, where he places the sky. This is to be the kingdom of Aluelop, while Solal, his brother or creator (it varies from version to version), becomes the master of the lower world, an underwater domain with the original rock at its centre.

Similarly, in the Pelew Islands, the god Tpereakl

Carved ornament from the gable-end of a New Guinea ceremonial house. These huge houses (sometimes forty feet high) are the meeting place of the men and are barred to women. The gable-end depicts a human face with staring eyes, dilated nostrils and protruding tongue, similar to the Gorgon heads of ancient Greece. *Moeschlin and Baur*

and the goddess Latmikaik, who arose from a wave-beaten rock, are said to share the governing of the world and to be the origin of all life. Tpereakl took up his abode in the sky, and Latmikaik at the bottom of the seas, where she gave birth to two sons, called 'First in the Sky' and 'First in the Lower World', and also produced shoals of fish. Shortly after, the fishes built a gigantic tower, which rose from the ocean and became the earth. Mankind would appear to be the result of the matings of certain gods and fishes.

Our attention is immediately held by two features, which in all the six known versions of the myth quoted above are developed with considerable emphasis. First there is the dualism that typifies the organisation of the world and the attributes of the first gods: the celestial world is in direct contrast to the 'lower world', which lies underwater and is also chthonian by nature, whereas the domain of earth is but a no-man's-land between the two. Of course there are deities and terrestrial spirits in the myths of this region, but they play a minor part and are somewhat flat characters. Indeed the pantheon of Ifaluk himself (central Carolines) is no exception to this, though he expressly entrusts the sovereignty of earth to the goddess Audjal. The second consistent feature is the way things expand vertically, as though the genesis of the universe started in the lower world and developed from there. This concept, which underlines the notions of high and low, must certainly be compared with the opposition between the sky and the lower world. The installation of the three cosmic planes, whether the work of fishes or of the god of the deep, is depicted as the construction of a tower or climbing of a tree, and thus it takes place along a world axis that will later be used as a channel for the introduction of culture and natural calamities into the world of men.

The meaning of these various images becomes clear when one considers the indigenous concept of the origin of mankind: man is begotten of the powers of the lower world alone, and has nothing in his make-up that predisposes him to play the role of mediator between the two extreme planes of the cosmic structure, as was the case in Polynesia. His nature is irrevocably defined as subject to chthonian and underwater gods; even tribal and clan chieftains, whose authority he recognises in his daily life, are supposed to have been installed on earth by the first spirits. A myth from Ponape Island in the Carolines provides indirect confirmation of this interpretation. Unlike other insular peoples, these islanders seem to believe that the human race was the offspring of a marriage between water and plants. Here truly chthonian functions are substituted for underwater protagonists, though the schema remains intact. It may be that techno-economic factors are partly responsible for this particular version:

whereas fishing and sailing seem to be the predominating activities in the neighbouring islands, on Ponape all the magic richness of seed-time and harvest bears witness to the primacy of agriculture, as can be seen from the luxuriant vegetation and a more varied diet than is found elsewhere.

However, this univocal determination of the human species, expressed so forcefully in these different tales, does not save native philosophy from one major contradiction. Since the Micronesian ascribes the origin of all life to the lower world, he thus identifies himself with fishes and plants and thereby deprives himself of the right to make comparison with natural phenomena when explaining the basis of man's originality. Now the fact that man is different from the rest of nature is proved not only by his actual experience, but also by his deep emotional conviction, indicated in the myths that justify depilation and tattooing on the grounds that he needs to be quite distinct from animals. So the question is to discover what the celestial world represents in this system. Empyrean and lower world are endowed with complementary functions, and the gods and spirits who dwell there have the same origin and collaborate closely in the maintenance of cosmic order. For instance, tidal waves, cyclones and tempests are, in the view of the inhabitants of the Carolines, works of collaboration between the powers on high and those below (Aluelop and Solal). But, this being the case, it is odd that the decision should always be taken by the god of the sky, while the lower world confines itself to supplying the necessary energy and matter for the explosion of the cataclysm. This factor testifies to the significance of the relationship between the celestial deities and men: the latter receive from the former their rules of conduct and a system of values they must respect. The powers above have the task of supervising and sanctioning human activities, and so they are the ones to bring to earth the foundations of culture, and their intervention is always in the nature of a verdict. Even the occurrence of death is far from being an unintelligible natural fatality and is primed with ethical intention. Humanity in its initial state was immortal, and was accumulating endless wealth and power when Aluelop realised this and took umbrage. So death was sent to earth as a permanent threat and insuperable barrier.

Similarly, a myth from the Pelew Islands tells how light was introduced into the world by Iegad to force men to work and to prevent spirits from helping them, since the latter can operate only in darkness.

In comparison with the lower world, which is conceived as the storehouse of energy from which life and natural phenomena proceed, the empyrean in these examples represents the source of culture and death. To be more precise, it is the kingdom of the normative. At this point the contradiction inherent in the Micronesian's appointed place in the world scheme can be clearly defined: man has deep roots in the lower world (thanks to his very beginnings and his biological needs), but he knows himself to be divorced from animals and spirits alike by a celestial decree which forces him to respect certain values. This discord between what is and what must be, accounts, as one might say in the language of Western philosophy, for the feeling of transcendence. Such a statement makes it necessary to track down the occasional influence of Christian thought on this mythology. It is incontestable that a good part of the material collected in the Gilbert Islands by Arthur Grimble bears the marks of missionary teachings; the coming of death following the tasting of the forbidden fruits of the Tree of Knowledge and the curse put on the works of the flesh constitute obvious plagiarism of the Bible story. But the fact that there is plagiarism throws into greater relief the originality of concurrent myths that have quite different structure and details. Finally, both the culture-hero Olofad's ascent to heaven and also levitation as practised by magicians—which symbolise man's dreams of overcoming the antinomy between the world on high and that below—reveal the realisation of a need for transcendence that owes nothing to the West.

The origin of culture

An examination of the myths that tell of the establishment of civilisation leads one immediately to put those of the Gilbert Islands in a category of their own. In fact, they bear witness to two distinct and separate currents of inspiration. The first, which bears a striking resemblance to Polynesian traditions, gives pride of place to the culture-hero Bue, whose exploits, for the most part, are identical with those of Maui. The second concerns Nareau, a character sometimes defined as the creator-god already quoted (Lord Spider, first of all beings), sometimes as the latter's son. At all events, it should be noted that Nareau appears in these tales in the guise of a spider or lone cloud floating in the void, and this sort of image is widespread in Melanesia (personifications of Qat and Marawa). The most comprehensive body of beliefs found here is concerned with the origin of fire. The capture of a ray of sunshine symbolises the theft of fire from the sky; it is first driven away by the lord of the sea and the lower world, then brought to earth, where there is strong opposition to it before it is finally adopted. It would appear to be the same dialectic of above and below as that revealed earlier in the documents from the Carolines and Pelews: culture is sent by celestial powers and rejected by chthonian powers, which represent the natural kingdom, and men regard it as an external violation against which they must defend themselves.

In all myths from the Caroline and Pelew Islands telling of the acquisition of techniques and basic values, initiative is clearly divided between a celestial deity and a trickster hero. Thus in the central Carolines the god Lugeilan, son of Aluelop (assuredly another name for the god known as Luk on the island of Ponape), is said to have come down from the sky to teach men for the first time. He brought with him the arts of tattooing and hairdressing, and taught men to exploit the possibilities of the coconut-palm. One of his brothers, who was also a sky-god, was regarded as the instructor of carpenters and canoe-builders. It should be noted that, in this region, the first stage of the development of culture is ascribed to celestial powers alone, who are also held responsible for the phenomenon of death. In this respect certain beliefs relative to the purpose of tattooing may throw light on the Micronesian concept of culture. This art, with its different motifs varying from island to island, was presented to men by Lugeilan as a means of ensuring immortality. Made mortal by a transcendent decision—which separated them irrevocably from the gods—men then obtained for themselves some hope of survival that was denied all other species. This privilege is an ultimate recourse against the fate to which their biological status condemns them: the individual can escape death only by identifying himself with the works that constitute the cultural patrimony of the group.

The second stage in the development of civilisation corresponds in these myths to the adventures of the very popular hero Olofad. Son of the god Lugeilan and a mortal woman, he was already adult when he emerged miraculously from his mother's skull. After playing some abominable tricks on men, he went up to the sky and waged a long and eventful war against the gods. He was finally put to death by his opponents and then resuscitated by his father, who allowed him to make his home in his palace in the sky. From that time forth Olofad divided his time between sky and earth, joining men in their dances and songs and transmitting Lugeilan's instructions to them. In the course of one of these visits he brought the secret of fire down from the sky.

With the intervention of Olofad there appears on the part of indigenous thought an effort to overcome the basic antinomy between the world above and the world below that is inherent in the mythical origins of mankind. Torn between two contradictory allegiances—his allegiance to the world below proclaimed by his biological nature, and the other implied in his adoption of values imposed by celestial powers—the Carolines islander makes the culture-hero his agent and mediator. Olofad's twofold nature makes him suited to this part, and now, with the introduction of fire, he can complete the work of civilisation and impart to it previously unknown harmlessness.

Statuette of polished wood representing an almost featureless human figure. From the island of Nukunono, Micronesia. Musée de l'Homme. *Pasquino*

Kihe-Wahine, patron-goddess of demons and lizards in Hawaii. In Samoa lizards were thought to be incarnations of Tangaroa. *Walter Steinkopf.*

Limewood spatula used for preparing betel, from New Guinea. The figure forming the handle is an ancestor image. The body is decorated with tattoo patterns which were said to have been invented by the gods. Buffalo Museum of Science, New York. *Simmons*

Australia

There were some five hundred aboriginal tribes in Australia when it was annexed by Britain in 1788 and they formed an estimated population of some 300,000. This number may appear surprisingly low at first, but one must take into account the naturally adverse conditions as well as the extremely rudimentary mode of life in these societies. The Australian aborigines had no knowledge of agriculture or pottery and no domestic animals except the dingo; they lived a nomadic life, hunting and gathering wild crops. But the fact that they all endured hardship must not be allowed to create the impression that Australian societies were completely homogeneous: from one end of the continent to the other there were the most varied types of social organisation (systems of exogamic 'halves', with sections and sub-sections) and rules of kinship. The variety is so striking that one can go so far as to say, especially after the fine work recently devoted to the northern tribes, that ethnological thought would have developed quite differently if the inhabitants of Arnhem Land had been studied prior to those of central Australia. Under these conditions it is not astonishing that several rival concepts intermingle or clash in the mythological material, which, moreover, has not been put together consistently from region to region. Better knowledge of early migrations and their original starting-point, of the part played by the Tasmanians—a negroid population which has been extinct for many years—and of Melanesian influence would undoubtedly provide the key to the problem, but we must at present resort to hypotheses in most cases.

However, two very evident characteristics emerge from all Australian myths and make it possible to distinguish them from other traditions of Oceania. First, there is the association of myth and ritual that is closer than one usually finds elsewhere. Not only does the myth of origin form the object of the 'revelation' that enables various cycles of initiation to come into being, but in addition it is relived by those taking part in certain ceremonies, the ritual being nothing more nor less than myth in action (the Kunapipi cult in Arnhem Land, for example). The second unusual feature is connected with the presence of totemism, whose ideology has often altered the most ancient myths, while at the same time finding expression in specific images.

Origin of the world and life

The origin of the world is rarely explained, and the sky and earth are regarded as having existed from all eternity. The Aranda in central Australia are an exception, for they tell how the earth slowly emerged from an endless sea.

On the other hand, the origins of man, of animal and vegetable species and of different types of landscapes have given rise to many myths that are rich in implication. To grasp its complete meaning it is best

Carved wooden figure of a sacred being. The style of these figures derives from grave posts, and they are exhibited to postulants and used in dancing. This one represents Laindjung. His face is white with foam as he has just emerged from the sea, and he wears a chin ornament. Twentieth century. *Australian Institute of Anatomy*

to place this oral literature in the basic context of indigenous thought that identifies human life with that of animals and plants. That is why the same fertility rites are used to make game more plentiful and to prepare women for maternity. As for myth itself, it is, according to informants, a 'means of giving life' to individuals and to the group by connecting them with the Dreamtime—a mythical period that is everlastingly present and is the source of all life. If one were to draw up a schema one could differentiate between two interpretations that have often coexisted in one and the same tribe: the first, which is probably the more archaic, attributes the creation of living beings to celestial heroes, whereas the second quotes it as the work of totemic ancestors.

The sky-hero known by the names of Baiame, Daramulun or Nurundere seems to be the central figure in the beliefs of eastern Australia, where he was generally associated with puberty rites and the initiation of medicine-men. He was regarded as the 'Father of all things', dwelling in the sky in a place filled with fresh water and quartz crystals, the magic instruments of the medicine-men. Several tales depict him as the master of life and death, who was asked to cure the sick. Between procreation—which was beyond the bounds of human initiative, since the biological facts of conception were not known—and death, which was always thought to come from supernatural causes, the celestial hero was the expression of a dialectic that was fully revealed in the function of the medicine-man. In the stereotype mystic dreams that decide the medicine-man's vocation or 'enthronement', he sees himself put to death by the celestial being and carried off on the Rainbow Serpent's back to the empyrean, where Daramulun brings him back to life and transmits magic powers to him. The symbolism of these imaginary ordeals, which are strictly codified by tradition, is very clear: the medicine-man candidate makes his departure from natural or normal life through death, thus leaving a realm of ignorance to accede to a higher life. The status that society attributes to the medicine-man thus clearly represents a transcendence of the contradiction inherent in the human condition as defined in myth: men's lives, in spite of the supernatural interventions, which stand out as landmarks, are of necessity far removed from religion for the most part, but they are enclosed within the framework of two transcendent events, procreation and death. It would appear that indigenous thought attempted to overcome this intrinsic antinomy by imagining a privileged human type to whom society would entrust the task of effecting a reconciliation. The celestial hero would then appear as the source of contradiction and, at the same time, as the sovereign power capable of integrating this contradiction. Among the Aranda tribes in central Australia there was a similar cult of a primordial celestial hero who was regarded as a master of initiation. The body of myth devoted to him shows him to have been alive

Bark painting in the traditional cross-hatched style, showing pelicans and baramundi fish. Bark paintings are made for use in instruction, to illustrate part of a myth. They are also associated with the ritual used in purification and increase ceremonies and the objects and animals depicted are always of totemic significance. *Axel Poignant*

Left: Carved wooden housepost. New Zealand. British Museum.

Below: A jade tiki from New Zealand. The tiki has the form of a small distorted human figure, is believed to have magical properties, and is worn as an amulet. British Museum.

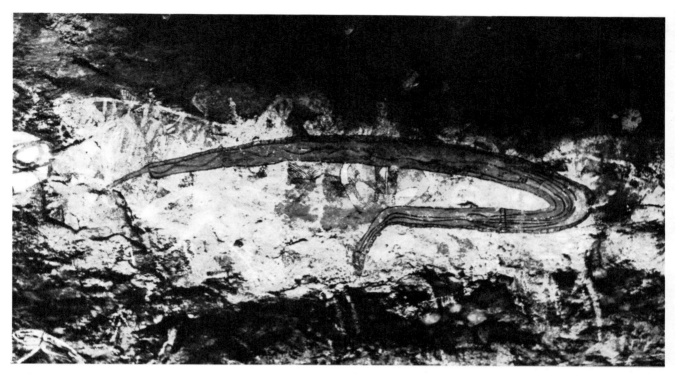

prior to the Dreamtime, and this would seem to confirm the general opinion that this type of belief is genuinely archaic. Moreover, one other piece of information that has been handed down suggests some ancient ideological conflict: it is said that this hero used to go back and forth between the sky and earth by way of a high mountain, which he then razed to the ground to prevent the totemic ancestors who came into being in the Dreamtime from escaping their condition. But, in actual fact, he was more honoured as a sort of cultural instructor who established religious ceremonies, and his activities as creator took second place.

With the emergence of the theme of the death and resurrection of the medicine-man, the celestial hero was recognised as the agent for regeneration, who ensured the survival of the group on a symbolic plane by means of a dialectic of permanence and change. There is a similar structure in the Djanggawul cycle, which developed in the north-east of Arnhem Land. The Djanggawuls were two sisters and a brother whose celestial origin was clear – at least in the case of the women, since they were regarded as the daughters of the female Sun. These mythical creatures came from a distant and somewhat vague land that lay to the north-east of the continent of Australia. In the course of their journey by canoe to Arnhem Land, they stopped off at the island of Bralku, the kingdom of primordial spirits and sojourn of the dead. After they reached the east coast of Arnhem Land, they crossed the region from east to west, following a tortuous itinerary and creating the ancestors of the various human groups. They also gave the countryside its present contours and vegetation, leaving behind them in fixed spots the sacred objects that even today are the focus for the most important ceremonies.

The cult connected with the myth has a remarkable characteristic – it is restricted to the exogamic 'half' only, Dua, while the opposite 'half', Jiritja, elaborated his more important ritual around different mythical beings, though he still recognised the Djanggawuls as his distant ancestors. This may, perhaps, be an indication of the ceremonial precedence taken by the first 'half' over the second. Many factors, such as their westward-bound journey and the red plumes they wore, symbolising the sun's rays, enable us to recognise the Djanggawuls as solar deities, as R. M. Berndt has pointed out. As far as the events reported in this cycle of legends and songs are concerned, they all refer back to the single theme of fertility. As the aborigines of this region were well aware of the part played by the sex act in procreation, impressive erotic symbolism was used to explain the origin of things. Thus the three gods brought forth springs and trees in Arnhem Land by planting magic sticks (*rangga*) in the soil, and their phallic function is clearly indicated by informants. In addition, the region was initially peopled by the Djanggawul sisters, who had many confinements, which marked the successive stages of their journey. All these details prove that this society was profoundly preoccupied by the idea of satisfying sexual needs and also by the need for food. The close association of the two in myth was indicative of a collective will to survive.

Finally, analysis of the evidence reveals that life, in all its manifestations, was conceived as a cyclic phenomenon in imitation of the apparent movement of the sun. This, for instance, is the meaning of the canoe crossing with its beating of paddles, which produced the regular rhythm of the tides. The rhythm of the seasons, on the other hand, was symbolised by the formation of black and yellow clouds, characteristic of the rainy season, which came from afar to guide the gods on their way. Moreover, the same theme seems to reappear at each stage of the journey,

Bark painting from Yirrkalla depicting scenes from the Djanggawul myth. The top panel shows the two sisters, Miralaidj and Bildjiwuraroju, standing by a spring and, next to them, a portrait of the artist. The second panel shows the sisters giving birth to the first aborigines. The third panel shows, on the left, eight sacred *rangga* emblems, which the Djanggawul planted in the earth to make trees; in the middle are the sisters with their brother, and on the right the rising and the setting sun. The last panel repeats the theme of the second. Twentieth century. *Art Gallery of N.S.W.*

whenever the Daughters of the Sun retire into their sacred cabin.

In the case of races who constructed their entire concept of the world around totemic ancestors, the myths of origin have an entirely different structure. Experts have pointed out that, in this case, one is dealing with lay ideology and not a religious system. So it is natural that this oral literature, which is primarily sociological in function, should grant some precedence to explanations of the origin of culture and somewhat neglect cosmological subjects.

Generally, myths of this type tell of the migrations of culture-heroes, who are regarded as the first ancestors of the group (eastern region of the Great Desert). These creatures, who cannot really be said to have attained the status of 'men', emerged from the ground at the beginning of the Dreamtime and created waterholes wherever they went, and these subsequently became cult-centres. At the end of their voyage, when they had taught men the principal techniques and social rules, they sank back into the earth and disappeared for ever. They are not creators, and although one may attribute to them the origin of a small part of mankind, one does so in a way that implies no supernatural powers: they coupled with women who were living in the region before their arrival. The circumstances of such tales as these bring out the chthonian status of totemic heroes, and this characteristic enables one to apprehend the significance of their journey, which is recounted in profuse detail. The minute description of their itinerary, which relied on actual topographical details, was ever present in the collective memory of various riverside tribes, each of which jealously guarded exact knowledge of the section nearest its normal habitat.

Alongside this totemic type of ancestor, who played the part of master of the soil, one should quote another mythical personage, whose cult was quite widespread in Northern Territory: the Great Mother. Like the Djanggawul sisters in Arnhem Land, she is a goddess of fertility, but seems to differ from them in her chthonian nature. She too had a long journey across country, but this did not follow the sun's trajectory; it more closely resembles the voyages of totemic heroes with their probable echoes of early migrations.

The origin of culture

The myths that recount the origins of techniques and institutions are generally quite explicit, thanks to ritual manifestations closely associated with them. Thus, for instance, ceremonies of initiation enable one to decipher the meaning of events that happened in the Dreamtime (engulfment by a divine serpent, the rivalry between male and female powers for the possession of sacred objects).

Like totemic ancestors in most regions of Australia, the Wati-Kutjara (Two-men), who are the culture-

Bark painting from Yirrkalla depicting the rain-makers Wuluwaid (the male figure) and Bunbulama (the female figure), holding *tjurungas*. Above them is the rainbow and about them the falling rain. The rainbow-serpent is the messenger of the supreme deity, who lives in a sky full of fresh water. Twentieth century. *Collection of C. P. Mountford, Adelaide*

A *tjurunga*, or sacred tablet. These represent the individual's totem and are kept in sanctuaries. They play an important part in ceremonies, especially initiation ceremonies, and the uninitiated are forbidden to look at them. The designs often had mythological significance and this one is decorated with sun and rainbow patterns. Musée de l'Homme. *Larousse*

Cave painting from the Wellington Range, Western Arnhem Land. It shows a ritual tribal fight or *makarata*. Candidates for initiation submitted themselves to this trial by ordeal in order to be accepted as full members of the tribe.
Axel Poignant

Bark painting consisting of a *maraiin* or sacred pattern, from Cape Stewart, Arnhem Land. It resembles the body designs on men participating in sacred rituals, painted from their shoulders down to their knees. The V-shaped space corresponds to the man's neck and chest. *Maraiin* rituals are generally concerned with fecundity. Twentieth century.
Art Gallery of New South Wales

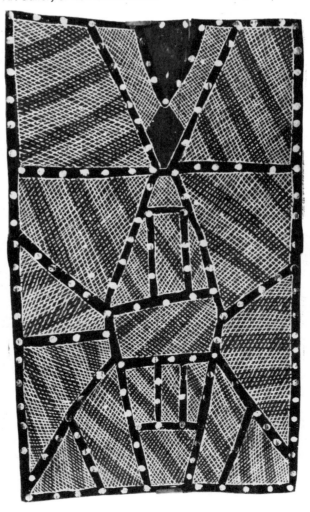

heroes of the Western Desert, created many ceremonial instruments (particularly decorated boards and *tjurungas*), and gave them to men, who have guarded them jealously ever since as a means of remaining in contact with the 'Dreaming'. Going on their way, the two brothers circumcised and cicatrised one another. Then the elder gave his sister in marriage to the younger. This last-mentioned episode is of great interest, because it reveals a function of such operations that is often overlooked: they discharge reciprocal obligations that lie behind the exchange of women among allied groups. Observers have made particular note of the fact that the novice acceded through these rites to a new life, but they have failed to appreciate the rule in numerous dualist societies, by which the adults in one 'half' must initiate the young in the opposite 'half'. As ritual co-operation is superimposed on matrimonial exchange in order to unite the two groups, to disobey a rule of this kind would be the equivalent of incest. If one admits, as some evidence suggests, that circumcision symbolises the cutting of the umbilical cord of a child at birth, one can imagine what role is played here by the Wati-Kutjara: this is a question of the symbolic abolition of the cord that attaches the heroes to one and the same mother, so as to permit the marriage of the younger with the elder's sister.

In the Djanggawul cycle of Arnhem Land, there is an example of the use of similar themes to express different functions. Once they had given birth to a multitude of human beings, the Daughters of the Sun lost their sacred objects for ever (matting, wickerwork), for they were stolen by their brother

Bark painting showing the baramundi fish, which once, according to an Arnhem Land myth, lived at Kaitjouga, a few miles inland from Blue Mud Bay. The track which he left behind him on his journey to the sea is now a large river. The fish continued south from Maitjouga along the coast, towards Yurakosi. From there he went inland again, creating another river. *Larousse*

and male children. Then they had to submit to the removal of the clitoris, and from that time the separation of the sexes was irrevocably established, accompanied by a division of labour that reserved for men the privilege of religious activities. At once our attention is drawn here to a fact that probably sums up the historic evolution of this society: initially, in the field of ritual, women had precedence, and this was not taken from them by men for some considerable time. The two goddesses seem to have given birth to the various species of living things without their brother's intervention, and his presence seems to be a later addition intended to make the tale conform to present-day knowledge.

Certain basic features are found in all the societies we have studied. First, there is the constant concern that the ideal on which men must base their thoughts and acts should be situated in the most distant past, usually at the beginning of the world: one must always imitate as faithfully as possible the great culture-heroes and the first ancestors. The total absence of eschatology, which is quite in accordance with the development of the many Messianisms that arose in defiance of European colonisation, has largely contributed to the acceptance of the idea that 'primitive' societies were pledged to a repetitive history. Such a statement must be viewed with prudence, for the examination of myths and their variants shows that the past, which gives these societies their *raison d'être,* is periodically reconstructed in view of political fluctuations. None the less, it is true to say that the various traditions that have been studied express a radical rejection of change, dramatically illustrated in the fight between Tawhiri and his brothers in Polynesian cosmogonies.

Similarly, the recurrence of the theme of original incest is worthy of attention: in fact, the context suggests in each case that the regulation of sexual relationships is conceived to be the primary basis of culture — it is the respect in which man differs from the animal kingdom.

When we come to consider the ambivalence of these culture-heroes, who are both the benefactors of humanity and tricksters, we are forced to the conclusion that it corresponds to a function recognised in these mythologies: Australia is no exception in offering the example of a simpleton and a sage who institute culture while engaging on droll adventures. Apart from differences of detail, myth always ascribes to this character the role of mediator between gods and men. But one must go even farther, and consider whether this ambiguous creature may possibly symbolise the imaginary solution to a very real conflict deep within the social structure. It can, in fact, be observed that Polynesian societies, which eventually deprive Maui of his trickster's grin to make him a pious and chivalrous hero, are the only ones in which a lasting balance has been established between political power and religious authority.

Finally, if Polynesian navigators believe that night marks the beginning of the world, whilst Melanesian farmers regard life as a conquest won from eternal day, may not some coherence be found, in spite of the apparent contradictions, if one applies the logic of myth and reflects on the basic techno-economic activities involved?

Three female figures making gestures of adoration. Dogon sculpture on the shutter of a granary. The zig-zag patterns behind the figures and in the border around the panel represent the pattern followed by the creator as he passed from east to west and from north to south during the formation of the world. Musée de l'Homme. *Giraudon*

AFRICA: MAGIC AND SYMBOLISM

In recent years, the ideas of African religion generally accepted by Europeans have been strongly criticised. It is true that one still comes across such terms as fetishism, animism, manism or totemism; and these terms are certainly applicable to certain aspects of these religions. Animism, for example, can be applied to the cult of spirits, or totemism to archaic alliances between clan chieftains and animals; but they do not exhaust the entire wealth of African religions. A reaction set in with Father Schmidt, who brought to light the importance of the supreme being in Negrillo mythology, and replaced the former evolutionistic schema—development from fetishism or animism to polytheism—with a contrary schema based on the idea of a progressive decadence from primitive monotheism, which was just as arbitrary as the first.

Some revision, of course, is badly needed, but it must take as its starting-point the findings of the school of Griaule, not those of Father Schmidt and his followers. In former days ethnologists described African religions from the peasant point of view, and we can rightly comprehend the implication of this only by asking ourselves if we should gain an accurate and complete definition of Roman Catholicism by questioning none but the peasant population and describing their acts alone. Griaule and his successors have gone beyond such ideas as these (which are not so much thoughts as such, as beliefs in action) and shown how refined the beliefs of the priest class are; and one finds almost everywhere, on closer acquaintance with initiation ceremonies, the existence of a twofold knowledge—'surface knowledge' and 'profound knowledge' (these are the very terms of Bambara initiates).

But the type of research that aims at an understanding of 'profound knowledge' is only just beginning. And it is difficult as yet to give a definitive picture of African mythologies. The documents at our disposal are incomplete and are far from indisputable in the case of many tribes (many tales that are given as fables or fairy stories being, in fact, nothing more nor less than exoteric versions of deeper myths). The secret law protecting this profound knowledge usually forces us to extract the forbidden myths indirectly from the study of symbols and mystic correspondences, or to deduce their nature by patiently reflecting on the features of material culture, the way rooms are arranged in houses, the design of a musical instrument, certain modes of stereotyped behaviour, or the sequences in agricultural, artisan or religious ritual. And it will no doubt be obvious that this dangerous method, fraught with risk of error, demands on the part of researchers a great deal of patience, critical acumen and active sympathy with the very spirit of the people concerned.

Finally, one must add that disagreements between priests or rivalry between religious brotherhoods have at times produced distortions of the original tales. It is difficult to choose between the great number of variants of one and the same myth which have sprung from these interpretations. The most we can do is to draw up an initial balance-sheet of African mythologies, which must be regarded as provisional.

Mythologies, in the plural, and not mythology; for there are many quite different races in Black Africa. And although continual migrations throughout the course of history have sometimes caused these peoples to intermingle in the same territories, and although a whole series of adoptions of gods, myths, and symbols has contrived to blur the boundaries between religions, we feel that the best method of approaching the study of these mythologies is still that of taking certain cultural, linguistic or ethnic areas and treating them in turn.

Pygmies, Bushmen, Hottentots

Anthropological criteria (small stature) and ethnological criteria (hunting and gathering of wild crops) amply indicate that the Pygmies of the equatorial forest are a race apart. The disciples of Father Schmidt took them as their starting-point when they formed the theory of primitive monotheism, which had, they thought, been quite unadulterated at one time and was incorporated in a cult that included prayers and offerings of first fruits. But the Pygmies live in close association with the Bantu, and as they often borrow the name of the latter's supreme god, we must leave in abeyance this problem of primitive monotheism, since our present knowledge is not adequate to its solution. All that we can say is that the god of the Pygmies, unlike that of the Bantu, is above all the lord of forest and game, that he was perhaps first thought to exist in the guise of an animal, but that he is now considered to be a sky-god.

This supreme god, Khonvum, appears as one who directs or controls celestial phenomena. When the sun dies, he collects broken pieces of stars in his sack and tosses armfuls of them at the sun, so it can rise again the next morning in its original splendour. But he still retains his original character of 'Great Huntsman', with his bow made of two welded serpents that assumes visible form as the rainbow. He makes contact with men by the intermediary of either a real animal, the chameleon, or an imaginary animal who appears in dreams—the elephant Gor, whose powerful voice gives rise to thunder. Below Khonvum there is a whole series of monsters, whose stories are told when people gather together in the evening—stories such as that of the ogre Ngoogunogumbar, who swallows children, or the dwarf Ogrigwabibikwa, who changes into a reptile. It should be added that the area over which the Pygmies spread before being pushed back into the heart of the forests was considerably larger than their present habitat, and that there are grounds for regarding the myths of gnomes, sprites and little sylvan spirits that one comes across all over Africa as inspired by the first meeting between the Negroes and Pygmies.

The Bushmen also have a supreme being, whose name varies from tribe to tribe, and may be Kaang, Khu or Kho, or Thora, but he has no cult. Thora has an adversary, Gauna or Gawa, leader of the spirits of the dead, who dwell in the sky and are at the same time the wicked spirits of wind, hurricane, storm, lightning and thunder. One may well wonder what these great gods represent. Gawa is the supreme god of the Damara tribes and, in consequence, his disguising himself as a wicked deity possibly expresses the ethnic contrast between Bushmen and Damaras. Kaang himself, according to one expert, Baumann, is not so much a supreme being as a primordial character endowed with magic power, who would appear to have become a creator under the influence of the Bantu.

However, the special characteristic of the Bushmen's mythology is the existence of animal-spirits, such as the Praying Mantis, I Kaggen, married to Hyrax (*Hyrax capensis*), or the Antelope or Porcupine, heroes of dozens of adventures that explain various celestial phenomena. It is difficult to trace a line of demarcation between Kaggen and Cagn, who is, moreover, confused with Kaang, and this accounts for the way in which Baumann interprets the Bushmen's supreme being. Cagn is a 'magician', who plays tricks and whose strength lies in one particular tooth; birds are his messengers or emissaries. He was eaten by the ogre Kwaihemm, who then vomited him up. On another occasion he was attacked by the Thornbush-men, who killed him; ants ate his body, leaving only the bones, but his bones joined together again and Cagn came back to life. One of his daughters married some serpents, who were also men and thus became Cagn's subjects. All these adventures and many others, such as that of the creation of the moon from an old shoe, are recounted during the rites of initiation for young boys. So they may be considered as explanations of these rites, and the swallowing of Cagn, his death and resurrection may be regarded as the symbolic expression of the death and resurrection of the boys during their initiation, which is presided over by a priest disguised as an animal. A similar explanation may be accorded the marriage to serpents, which reflects an ancient matrimonial association between a group of praying-mantis-men and a group of serpent-women.

The Damaras are the remaining members of a little-known race whose civilisation has a place somewhere between that of the Bushmen and that of the Hottentots. Their supreme god and creator of the world, Gamab, is actually also known to the Bushmen by the name of Gauna (demoted to an evil deity) and to the Hottentots by the name of Gaunab, who is yet another adversary of the supreme being. Gamab lives in an upper sky, beyond the sky of stars, and with his arrows he kills certain chosen human beings, who instead of staying on earth as ghosts, take a difficult path over the abyss and up to Gamab. They live with him in the form of old men and women, Gamagu or Gamati, in the shade of the celestial tree, feeding on human flesh (this accounts for the fact that shortly after the burial of the dead there is little more than bones left in the tomb), and thus they have no need to hunt in order to live, or to procreate children, for the spirits of children come to the abode in the sky to make the Gamagu and Gamati happy.

The Hottentots have a higher level of technical civilisation. They are often regarded as a cross between the Hamites from the north-east, a pastoral people, and the Bushmen. Their mythology seems to reflect this twofold origin: their supreme god, Tsui-Goab, who is by nature a great priest or sorcerer, seems to belong to the immigrants, and the national hero, Heitsi-Eibib, a name derived from Heigib, 'the great tree' (which reminds one of the Bushmen's Hise, spirit of the bush), who teaches men how to hunt, seemingly belongs to the second of the two ethnic groups that constitute the Hottentot race. Tsui-Goab, whose cult is celebrated when the Pleiades appear, lives in the Red Sky; he commands storms, sends rain for the crops and speaks with the voice of thunder. His name means 'Wounded knee', and he has an adversary who lives in the Black Sky, and who has of late been identified with the Bushmen's Gauna or Gaunab, chief of the dead; Tsui-Goab kills Gaunab in the end, but he is first wounded in the knee in the course of a fight, and thereafter he has a limp. Heitsi-Eibib, who is the second great character in Hottentot mythology, was the offspring of a cow who ate some special grass and conceived the hero in this way. As first ancestor, spirit of the bush, culture-hero of huntsmen, he appears as a sort of magician who performs miracles, dies and comes to life again (with the result that some mythologists associate him with the Moon) and is victorious in his fights against monsters. However, if he is to be associated with the Moon, then he must also be connected with the origin of death. For it was the Moon who sent Leprosy to men with the announcement that they would be born again and be immortal. But Leprosy did not convey this message of life; she cheated the Moon and instead brought mankind word of death.

Bantu tribes of the south and east

A divining bowl for the detection of witches, from the Bavenda of northern Transvaal, South Africa. The bowl is filled with water and movements of seeds floating on the surface and touching various symbols carved on the bowl are observed. *British Museum*

Ethnologists have rightly emphasised the importance of the cult of royal or family ancestors in Bantu tribes. But although the ancestors, who are the intermediaries between mortals and the supreme god, play a large part in ritual, they have not, however, eliminated other manifestations of holiness in belief and myth.

The predominant figure in Kaffir mythology (Zulu and Xhosa) is that of Unkulunkulu, 'the Very old', who is not only the image of the first man, ancestor of the human race, but is also the image of the demiurge, in so far as he is the son of Unvelingange, 'He who pre-exists', and is delegated powers of creation by the supreme being. He arose from a bed of reeds, and therefore from the ground, Mother Earth, and seems to have been the creator of the customs and techniques typical of Kaffir civilisation. But although he is a culture-hero, and consequently a benefactor of humanity, he is also indirectly responsible for death. He said to the Chameleon: 'Go! Go and tell men that they will not suffer death.' But the slow and lazy Chameleon lingered on the way; so Unkulunkulu grew angry and sent a second messenger to men, the Lizard, to tell men that death would come. When the Chameleon got there, the Lizard had already been before him, and that is why men are now mortal. This myth is found among many other Bantu tribes, such as the Basuto or Baranga, and is well known by the name of 'perverted message'. It is connected with the idea that the Chameleon was supposed to be one of the first living creatures; he is said to have made his appearance before the earth emerged completely from the primordial waters, and since he had to learn to walk in the mud he acquired this slow movement which caused the coming of death.

Southern Bantu tribes have a supreme being who is conceived as a creator, though his image is not equally clear in all tribes. The work of one specialist, Junod, has brought to our notice the god revered by the Baranga tribe, who goes by the name of Tilo, the sky, and is present in rain or storms, speaking with the voice of thunder. In addition, he is connected with all that is mysterious in the universe, such as children's convulsions and the birth of twins (called 'sons of the Sky'). They also have a cunning, mystifying hero, who often appears in animal guise and gives rise to a special cycle of humorous tales. Stayt, a scholar who has produced work on the Bavenda tribe, has made known to us one of these mystifying heroes, Sankhambi. There is a Sesuto tale that tells of a monster that used to devour humans; eventually the only person left on earth was an old woman who had gone into hiding, and who, without the aid of man, gave birth to a child bedecked with amulets, to whom she gave the name of the god Lituolone. On the very day he was born, the child attained adult stature. He asked his mother where other men were, and,

being told of the monster Kammapa, he took hold of a knife and prepared to fight it. He was swallowed by the fabulous animal, and this allowed him to tear the beast's entrails to pieces and bring forth from its stomach thousands of human beings. However, men were not grateful to him; they were afraid of the might of this creature born only of woman, who had never known childish sport. They decided to get rid of him by throwing him into a ditch, or, alternatively, by making him fall into a fire, or by poisoning him. But his cunning always got him out of difficulty. There are several such heroes throughout this region: the Zulu tribes have Hlanganu, the Bapedi tribes have Huveane and the Subiya tribes have Séédimwé. These tricksters set mythologists many problems. For instance, the Bushmen's supreme god, Huvé, is close to the Basuto Huveane, and one wonders what link there is between the crafty demiurge and the supreme god. Sometimes they tend to become confused; on the other hand, they sometimes appear as opposites, and then one catches a glimpse of the conflict between two mythologies, that of the invaders and that of the autochthonous race. However, all these hoaxers have a certain number of common characteristics: miraculous birth, rapid growth, fight against ogres or monsters, need to defend themselves against the hostility of their family or race, miracle-working power that links them with the supreme creator or at least gives them the appearance of culture-heroes.

One cannot find a link between the Bantu and another race, the Hereros, who are nomadic Hamites, but they have borrowed the Bantu deity Ndyambi-Karunga, a composite deity that includes a sky-god borrowed from West Africans and an earth-god borrowed from Angola peasants. However, this deity has been pushed into the background of mythology by the figure of Mukuru, the first man, who is connected with the Nilotic peoples or Zulus. The present Herero tribe chieftains are incarnations of Mukuru and are supposed to be continuing his work of bringing civilisation to men. The two names, Ndyambi and Karunga, are found in different forms in numerous Bantu tribes, perhaps as a result of the influence of Christian missionaries who looked for African names to describe the Christian God. We know of a Ndyambi, a Nzambi and Nzame. Karunga or Kalunga refers to all that is mysterious or terrible, whether it be the depths of the ocean or the lower

Stone statue of a Bakongo chief making a ritual gesture, from the Congo. The position of the chief in relation to his people reflected the spiritual order in the same way as the myths reflect it, and like all human actions and family relationships can be interpreted symbolically. Musées Royaux d'Art et d'Histoire, Brussels. *A.C.L.*

world, kingdom of the dead. But Ovambo tribes think of him as someone who sends rain, makes crops grow, and punishes any infraction of traditional custom. The Hereros even give him a wife, Mufifi, but there is controversy on this point.

In Uganda, Hamite shepherds mingled with autochthonous farmers. They did not fuse together, but rather formed stratified societies, with one layer of masters, cattle-raisers (Bahima), and one layer of serfs, peasants (Bahera). There is in the mythology of this region a reflection of this ethnic composition. Among Baziba tribes, for instance, the Bahima section worships Wamara, whose mother is Nyante, the preexisting universe, whose father is unknown. Wamara had four sons, to whom he distributed the different divisions of reality: Kagoro, mythical hero; Mugasha, god of water; Kazoba, god of the sun and moon, whose son Hangi supported the celestial vault; and, finally, Ryangombe, who was god of cattle. This is the beginning of a very complex cosmogony with a wealth of different adventures, such as that of Mugasha's love for Kagoro's sister, the conflict between the two brothers, and Mugasha's leg wound. These Bahima deities take precedence over the Bahera deities, chthonian gods relegated to the rank of terrestrial spirits or genii.

In the northern part of south-east Africa, the Masai have a supreme god, Ngai, who is associated with the sky and rain. Two of his hypostases take the form of clouds and fight one another, one being black and good, the other red and wicked. There is also an earth-goddess, Neiterogob.

In the beginning, there was only one man on earth, and he was called Kintu; the daughter of the Sky saw him and fell in love with him, and persuaded her father to make him her husband. Kintu was summoned to the sky, and such were the magic powers of the daughter of the Sky that he emerged successful from the ordeals imposed on him by the great god. He then returned to earth with his divine companion, who brought to him as her dowry domestic animals and useful plants. As he bade them farewell, the great god advised the newly-weds not to return to the sky. He feared that they might have incurred the anger of one of his sons, Death, who had not been informed of the marriage, as he had been absent at the time. On his way to earth, Kintu realised that he had forgotten to bring grain for his poultry. In spite of his wife's supplications, he went back up to the sky. By then the god of death was there. He followed in the man's footsteps as he returned to earth, hid near his home and killed all the children who were eventually born to Kintu and the daughter of the Sky.

There are analogous myths in Madagascar. They form one of the variants of an almost universal belief in a visit made by the first men to the sky, and consequently in the existence of a path between the earth and the world above that was ultimately destroyed by human wrong-doing.

The Congo group

Bantu tribes may have varying ways of life, but there are many characteristics common to all their mythologies—first and foremost belief in a supreme god, Nzambi or Nzame. Undoubtedly, Christian influence played its part, and this creator-god replaced or drove out the ancient deities, then reduced them to the rank of demiurges, or enemies of the supreme god, or even simple spirits of the forest. As evidence of this, the existence of a root-word, *mba* or *mbi*, is quoted, which refers to creative activity and is found in the names of some of these spirits or demiurges—for example, Yangombi and Kombu. This suggests that they were at one time true creator-gods. In the Congo basin one also finds Nzakomba, Djakomba and Mbomba.

Nzame created the first man, Fam, who was intended to be master of all things; but he grew vain and revolted against Nzame and destroyed the earth. Fam was then buried in a hole. Nzame created the second man, Sekume, the ancestor of the present race. Sekume made himself a wife from a tree, Mbongwe. But Fam was not dead, and from his hole he inflicted misfortune on mankind. Then Nzame came down to earth; in the course of his journeys he fell in love with a pretty girl called Mboya, and had a son by her, who took the name of Bingo. But husband and wife were jealous of one another, and quarrelled over the child's affection. In a moment of anger Nzame flung Bingo from the heights of the vault of heaven. Bingo was found by an old man called Otoyom, who brought him up. His mother searched for him in vain, and she is still wandering the world, unable to find him. His father too was filled with remorse and wanted him back, but Otoyom was a great sorcerer, and at the last moment he always managed to rescue Bingo from Nzame's grasp by hiding him either in the depths of a cave or in the hollow of a tree. Once he had grown up, Bingo

Male ancestor-cult figure. It would be mounted on the cylindrical bark box in which the ancestor's bones are kept. Fang tribe, Gabon. British Museum.

Bakota head made of wood covered with copper. The eyelids are shown sewn together, presumably as a sign of death. Such heads are placed on top of byeri boxes, or reliquaries for the dead of the family. Byeri boxes play an important part in ritual and in daily life, being a link between men and the supreme god and between families and the political leaders. Musée de l'Homme. *Giraudon*

became the culture-hero, the teacher, of humanity. This collection of tales, which we have borrowed from Fan (Pahouin) mythology, shows a remarkable sense of history.

The idea of a cycle of creation seen at various stages, or of several creations, is found among many races in the same area. A myth from the lower Congo tells how the Sun quarrelled with the Moon one day and threw mud at her to dim her brilliance; but during this quarrel a flood ravaged the earth. When the flood was over, the supreme god was forced to create a new race of men, for the old race had changed into monkeys.

Another idea—that of the son of the supreme god as culture-hero—is also found throughout the Congo basin in different forms. The Nyokon tribes in the Cameroons, for instance, think of Nyiko, the divinatory spider, as the first son of the supreme god, Nyokon. When Nyiko became the lover of his mother (Mfam) his father drove him away. However, this child, driven from the sky like Bingo, retained the secrets known to his father and could therefore communicate them to men by his powers of divination. Of course it is not possible to explain all the elements of civilisation by reference to these fallen sons. And the legends explaining the origin of different elements vary enormously, especially as the Bantu tribes in the Congo had a monarchy and thought each king made his own contribution to the development of humanity. So the Shongo tribes maintain that the eponymous hero Woto or Oto introduced fire, circumcision and ordeal by poison; Nyimi Longa organised the four ministries; Minga Bengale taught men how to make nets for hunting; and Mantchu-Muchangu instructed them in the art of making clothing from bark. Sometimes these inventions led to some ruthless dealings. For instance, in the Bakuba or Bushongo tribes the god Bumba was

said to have appeared in a dream to a man called Kerikeri and taught him how to make fire. Kerikeri kept the secret to himself and charged men a high price for the embers they needed to cook their food. The king's daughter, Mushanga, wanted to know his secret, and so she made Kerikeri fall in love with her; when night came, she told all the villagers to put out their fires. When Kerikeri came to her, she remained frigid. 'What is the matter? Don't you love me?' 'How can I think of loving when I am shivering with cold!' So Kerikeri was forced to light a fire in front of her and so reveal his secret. 'Did you think that I, the daughter of a king, loved you for yourself alone? Your secret was all I wanted to know, and now that your fires is lit you can go and find a slave-girl to put it out.' Thus the art of lighting fires passed from a simple mortal to the royal family.

Woman thus plays an important part in mythology. But her role is ambiguous. Sometimes she divulges the secret of fire. In other myths she is involved in the discovery of masks, but then men take possession of them, and finally women are barred from their use altogether. Finally, woman is often responsible for bringing death to the world. The Lolo (Lele) tribes in the western Congo tell a story about a god offering the first men a choice of two packets, one containing pearls, knives and jewels, and the other immortality. Women, in their vanity, immediately seized the first packet and the gift of immortality was lost. The Baluba tribes believe the first men to have been immortal; when they grew old, they changed their skin just as snakes do, and were thus rejuvenated. But they had to make this change in secret; eventually an old woman was surprised by a curious neighbour as she was changing her skin, and death came into the world.

The Negroes on Lake Kivu thought that men did, in fact, die and were buried, but came back to life again afterwards. Then, on one occasion, when an

old woman was emerging slowly from her tomb, one
of her daughters-in-law fell upon her and rained
blows on her head shouting: 'Die, for what is dead
must stay dead.' But women are not the only creatures
responsible for the appearance of death in Congolese
mythology. We also find the previously mentioned
theme of the 'perverted message' and in addition the
theme of divine punishment. The Bakongo tribes
tell how Nzambi created a man and a woman who
had a child. 'He may die,' the god told them, 'but do
not bury him. Await my return.' However, the parents
did not have faith in the divine promise, and when
the child died they put his body in the ground.
Nzambi punished them for their disobedience by
making death the inevitable end of men.

A similar story, told by the Bambala tribes, concerns
the punishment of pride. Men wanted to know about
the moon; they drove a large stake into the ground
and a man climbed up it, holding another stake in
his hand, which he fastened to the end of the first one;
on this he fastened a third, and so on, until the tower
collapsed; and with it perished primitive man.

Bantu mythology must not be regarded as fixed
and unchanging. It is moulded on the events of history, and it has even managed to find a place within
its framework for the phenomenon of colonisation.
According to a story told by the Fan tribes, the supreme god dwelt in the centre of Africa with his three
sons, the White Man, the Black Man and the Gorilla.
But the Black Man and the Gorilla disobeyed the
supreme god, so he withdrew to the west coast with
his white son and bestowed all his wealth upon him.
The Gorilla retired to the depths of the forest; and
the poor, ignorant black people followed the sun in
its course until they came to the coastal regions of
Africa. There they found the descendants of the
White Man, who poisoned them slowly (the reference
is to malaria), and finally they died on the seashore,
regretfully dreaming of the time when they were
united with the supreme god and were happy.

The Nilotic tribes

Nilotic culture is related both to Paleo-Negritic culture and to that known as Hamitic. It had produced stratified mythology in keeping with different status and functions of invader and invaded.

The Shilluk tribes have a creator-god, Juck, whom they inherited from non-Shilluks. Juck fashioned the world, but does not direct it. Although he is the supreme being, he is also impersonal might: 'he is present to a greater or lesser degree in all things'. So he is both one and many, creator and cosmic energy. Beside him there is Nyikang, the ancestor god of the Shilluks. The two gods coexist, as do the vanquished race and the victorious race; but Nyikang is the indispensable intermediary between men and Juck, who can be reached only through him, and thus coexistence goes hand in hand with domination. Some believe that Omara, the first man, came down from the sky, and Nyikang was his grandson; others think that Nyikang was the descendant of the first cow created by the supreme god, who produced this deity in conjunction with the river. Finally, there are others who believe him to be the son of a crocodile mother.

In any case, so the myth goes, Nyikang quarrelled with his half-brother about who was to succeed to their father's throne and fled after losing the battle, taking with him the insignia of royalty. When he reached the land that was to become the Shilluk kingdom, he created the subjects of his new realm by changing wild animals into men. Alternatively, it is said that he fished men out of the water with his fishing-line or that he brought them out of a calabash. According to Westermann, he is a god of agriculture and rain; in one legend he is shown to be in conflict with the Sun. But he is also his people's first king, and as culture-hero he institutes marriage between brothers and sisters, totemism and ritual murder of the king every seven years. Nyikang was supposed to have strangled himself, or to have disappeared in a whirlwind. But he is not dead, for he continues to live in his successors. The object of the enthronement ritual in these tribes is to put the new king on the seat of power formerly occupied by Nyikang. For when Nyikang dies, all Shilluks will disappear with him. No better expression could be given to the idea that he represents the whole of the nation, territory or state, and also the cosmos—in so far as he is the distributor of rain—closely connected in his physical being with social organisation.

An analogous stratification is found in the beliefs of the Dinka tribes. There is a supreme being, Nyalitch (or Nyalic), creator of the world, lord of spirits, who lives in the sky whence he sends rain to men. And there are the two divine ancestors, Deng and Aywil. Deng (Rain) is also regarded as a celestial creator, quite distinct from Nyalitch, though he is also an emanation or projecton of him. Deng, on contact with Paleo-Negritic tribes, adopted the role of ancestor of the Dinkas, and disappeared—but did not die—in the course of a violent storm. Aywil seems to be the founder of Dinka religion: before he came, men worshipped the divinity through mediums in a state of trance; Aywil learned to worship him without the help of these intermediaries. He preached that people had to pray to the supreme god through his son Deng and his mother Abuk, and these were the only intercessors. But the first man, Diing, opposed the new law, and there was a fight which terminated in an agreement: Aywil and his sons were to have the sky and the rain, while Diing and his sons took the food-producing earth.

The Dog appears throughout the region of the upper Nile and the neighbouring areas as a culture-hero. He was responsible for bringing fire to mankind. Previously, fire had belonged to the Serpent, the Rainbow or the sky-gods. But the Dog ran towards the hearth, burned his tail, threw himself howling into the bush and set light to the dry grass, where men had only to come and gather the flames. But he later had his revenge on men who do not respect him. A legend from Uganda tells how the supreme god entrusted him with the task of bringing immortality to the living, but when the latter laughed he declared: 'All men will die, only the Moon will come to life again.'

Sudanese mythologies

The Volta basin and Upper Niger

Two great civilisations intermingle in this area, the civilisation known as Paleo–Negritic, based on the cult of the earth, and the neo-Sudanese civilisation with its divine kings, such as those in Mali or Ghana. Islam unfurled her banners overhead, but paganism persisted in some areas, and even the races that embraced Islam have kept many of their ancient beliefs.

Dogon mythology has become much more familiar since Griaule made his findings known. The supreme god Amma created Earth and married her; but the clitoris of Earth, represented as a nest of termites, rose against the divine phallus, and Amma had to cut it out before taking possession of his wife. Yurugu was the child of this union. He was to introduce disorder into the world. But once again Amma fertilised Earth with rain, and from this new relationship was born twins, a male and a female, Nommo, who were to become the model for future creations. Nommo respectfully covered his mother's bare body

A wooden dance headdress from the Sudan with stylised antelope horns and two small human figures It was used in the dances performed by the men of the Bambara tribe in dances which re-enacted the mythological origin of agriculture. British Museum.

with a fibre skirt, but Yurugu, as an only child desirous of finding his female counterpart, cast aside her covering and committed the first act of incest, from which emerged the wicked spirits of the bush. But Earth had thus become impure, and this impurity was marked by the first appearance of menstrual blood. Amma left her, and continued the work of creation alone. To begin with, he fashioned the first eight ancestors, four males and four females, who fertilised themselves and gave birth to eighty descendants, from whom were to spring the populations of the world. Later, Nommo sent to men the first smith, who sailed down the rainbow in the ark, which contained a copy of all living creatures, minerals and techniques; the smith is the culture-hero of the Dogons, since he brought them in the primordial ark the foundation of all social institutions.

The Kurumba water-spirit, Domfe, resembles the Dogon Nommo, and he comes down to earth with rain and wind and the first food-bearing seeds. The culture-hero of the Gurunsi, like that of the Dogons, is the first smith, sent by the spirit of the waters. The Mossi, who came from the east, encroached on these indigenous populations and brought with them the idea of divine kingship. In the beginning the god of the sky created four brothers and divided his terrestrial kingdom among them. The eldest chose a spot where there was iron and became the first smith; the second chose a place where oxen were passing and became the first Fulani; the third brother's share was a site full of bales and donkeys, and he was the first merchant; the youngest inherited a magnificent palace, and he was the first king, the leader of the earth. The elder brothers came to do the youngest homage, and from their collaboration arose the organisation of the Mossi state.

The Bambara tribes, like the Dogons, believe in a continuous creation, in which things emerge in succession from the 'Voice of the Void' in whirlwinds and words that spiral upwards. The primordial spirit dropped upon the earth the globule that became Pemba and the water that became Faro. Pemba, founder of the wood family, moulded the first woman out of earth, and she gave birth to plants and animals. Pemba wished to govern the world, which was still in chaos, and so he asked his wife, Musso Koroni, to plant him in the soil. So he became the king of all the trees, the *balanza*, and he required all women to make love to him. Musso Koroni, who had sustained injuries in the course of her early sexual encounters with the thorns on the tree, was jealous, and from then on she travelled the world circumcising and excising and introducing disorder and evil wherever she went. Meanwhile, Pemba, who had instituted blood sacrifice, increased his strength each day with all the blood spilled over him. Faro could not accept this increasing power, for it was he, indeed, who gave creatures life by means of water. He fought the *balanza*, uprooted it and then carried on the work of creation, reorganising the universe, ordering it according to the wisdom of his word, classifying living creatures, giving starving humanity agriculture and placing spirits everywhere as his representatives and intermediaries. Even today he continues his work, returning every fourth century to the centre point to control the harmonious progress of things.

The Songhoi worship both Zins (Moslem jinns), who were the first creatures of the supreme god on earth and shared the waters, earths and winds, and the Holeys, who were created either before men or immediately after them. The Holeys shared the different races that came either from Egypt or Hausaland and were man-eaters or masters of the soil. On their arrival the Zins were all-powerful, and Songhoi mythology is essentially the tale of their fight against the Holeys. Faran, the son of a fisherman, who taught him the techniques of fishing, and a spirit-woman, who revealed to him the art of magic, triumphed in single combat over the blind Zin Zinkibaru, the master of fishes, who had taken captive a family of Holeys known as Toru. So the Torus were able to obtain precedence over all the other Holeys and also over the Zins, whom they likewise reduced to slavery. Then Dongo emerged from their ranks and became the spirit of thunder and master of the sky, and he taught Faran the initiation rites, by means of which the cult of the Holeys could develop, though they were separated from one another and each was responsible for his own section of reality.

The Fulani (Peuls) regard themselves as distinct from Negroes; however, a spirit of the waters introduced the cow to them, and so they became cattle-raisers. The story tells how a monkey-smith took this cow and tied it up near the cave where he was working. The Fulani, passing by, stroked the animal and drew milk from it. He asked for the smith's beast, and in

A dance mask worn during ceremonies performed to ward off sorcerers. Dahomey. *Larousse*

Opposite:
An ivory statuette used in the Benin cult of Oromila, the spirit of divination and the Benin equivalent of the Yoruba Ifa. Nineteenth century. British Museum.

Wooden Dogon sculpture representing the development of man in the form of Nommo. Musée de l Homme. *Giraudon*

Dogon antelope mask painted on stone. The virtue of a mask does not reside solely in being worn. Masks and representations of masks are significant and powerful objects in themselves, for they *are* the world and its system. Musée de l'Homme. *Giraudon*

return cut off the monkey's tail, shaved him and turned him into a man. For his part, the smith circumcised the first Fulani. Their blood flowed and intermingled. A close alliance was henceforth to unite the Fulani shepherds and the artisan-smiths, an alliance known as *seninku*, which was cemented by a law forbidding them to spill one another's blood or to intermarry (since marriage involved bloodshed), and by the ritual exchange of jokes or insults every time they met.

Central and Eastern Sudan

The principal figures in central Sudanese mythology are heroes who are the ancestors of clans or ethnic groups. Nzeanzo, for instance, became the corn-god of the Bachama and Batta tribes. Tsoede was beloved of the Nupe people. In the eastern Sudan, on the other hand, this position is held by a jester-god, who is often regarded as a culture-hero.

During one of his journeys, Edigé, the king of Igara, made love to the daughter of a local chieftain and had by her a child, Tsoede, to whom he gave his ring and a 'charm' before continuing on his way. The child grew to manhood, and when he was thirty years old his uncle sent him to be the king of Igara's slave, in accordance with laws of his chieftaincy. The king recognised his son, but the latter aroused the jealousy of his half-brothers; and so his father helped him to flee, first bestowing upon him the royal insignia. Tsoede managed to escape his half-brothers. Then he seized the chieftaincy by killing his maternal uncle, and finally he conquered the land that became the Nupe kingdom. At the same time he gave his subjects their first knowledge of techniques—the techniques of the smithy and of canoe construction—the first social institutions (for example, the institution of matrimony) and religious institutions (such as human sacrifice or the fertility cult). Nzeanzo, 'the boy who is not a boy' since his mother came down

Dogon sculpture of a horse-rider carrying a spear and representing Nommo, the 'mentor of the world' and the mythical fount of all Dogon culture. All events and objects in the world symbolise aspects of Nommo. Totemic shrine of Orosongo. Marcel Griaule Collection. *Larousse*

from the sky and he himself emerged from her thigh, in Batta religion dethroned the sky-god, the latter being a more or less forgotten supreme being. Mythology tells of his fight against his uncle, the god of death, and makes him both a deity who brings rain and fertility and a culture-hero who teaches men metallurgy and medicine.

The various tribes of the Sara family tell how the god of the sky, Nuba, entrusted fruit-bearing seeds to Su and sent him down a bamboo-shoot to take them to men; once he reached earth, he was to beat a drum so that Nuba might draw up the bamboo. But half-way there, Su decided to taste the peas; clumsily, he dropped some peas, and these struck the drum-skin. Nuba drew up the bamboo and Su fell heavily to the ground and broke his leg. Another version found in the same Sara family tells how the supreme god, Wantu Su, had a nephew, Wantu, to whom he gave a drum containing a little of all that he had in the sky so that Wantu might give this to men; he was to slip down a rope and beat a drum to announce his arrival on earth. In this version it is a crow who struck the resonant drum-skin in the course of the descent, and as the drum fell and broke, men, fishes and plants were scattered far and wide in the newly created world.

The Banda tribes believe that the supreme god has two sons: Ngakola, who breathed life into the first man fashioned by his father, and Tere, who was given the task of taking down to earth animals and the seeds of plants. Here again Tere struck the warning drum too soon. The contents of baskets were scattered on the ground, the life-giving water spilt out of its divine container, and the birds flew away. Tere ran after them, and the animals that he managed to catch be-

came the ancestors of domestic animals and those that escaped the ancestors of wild animals; the same thing happened with plants.

Throughout the eastern Sudan one finds a mischievous deity who likes fun, though he also brings the gift of civilisation to men. Half animal, half human, he is the counterpart of Tere, whose legend appears above. The Manja tribes call him Bele, the Zande tribes Tule; the Mangbetu refer to him as Azapane and the Babua as Mba. To go back to Tere and the Banda tribes' legends about him, this hero succeeded in reaching the sky by dint of subterfuge, but he played such wicked tricks on the supreme being that the latter felt like sending him away. In the end Tere obtained his pardon, and stayed in the sky in the shape of the constellation of the Southern Cross. The Zande hero, Tule, is the subject of amusing fables, which are told when people gather together in the evenings. He is said to have given water to men by stealing it from an old woman who had hidden it, and he gave them fire too, albeit involuntarily, as a result of a visit to the smith-gods. His bark loin-cloth accidentally caught fire, and as he fled in fear through the bush he begged fire to leave him and settle in the trees; from that time forth this was the abode of fire, and by rubbing together the sticks from trees men could produce sparks for their own use. Tule is connected with the trap-door spider, who is given the name of Ananse by both this race and the Ashantis. The Manja tribes also have a hero called Seto, who is brought back to life in the form of the trap-door spider. Tere, according to the Bandas, is finally changed into the constellation of Orion. This means that virtually throughout this cultural area the jester-god has three forms — human, animal, celestial.

The West African seaboard

Olokun, shown with a lizard in each hand and with mudfish legs, as god of the sea and of the Benin River, of water and of riches. He was always depicted as male in Benin, but is sometimes asexual or bisexual elsewhere. Sixteenth or seventeenth century Benin bronze. *Rijksmuseum voor Volkenkunde, Leiden*

The religion of West Africans has often been described as polytheism, even when animism was particularly fashionable among ethnologists. This will convey some idea of the importance of mythology in the area. We shall take as our main examples the Ashanti, Fon and Yoruba tribes.

The Ashanti have a sky-god, Nyame (or Nana Nyankopon), who sends farmers rain, and a mother-goddess representing the earth, Asase Ya, who is regarded as the former's wife. She had four children, from whom are descended all the *abosoms*, deities of waters or trees, who today number several hundred. The most famous of them is Tano, who was perhaps a god of thunder initially, for he dances with the axe, which is the symbol of the thunderbolt; but he is now known as a river-god. In Ghana there is a story about Tano which tells how in spite of being a younger brother, he deprived Nyame's elder son, Bia, of his inheritance by practising a deception on their blind father. In this way he came into fraudulent possession of the rich land of Ghana, leaving Bia nothing but arid stretches of the Ivory Coast. However, the most interesting personage in the whole of this mythology is Ananse, the Spider, whose task it was to prepare the substance of the first men for Nyame to infuse life into. Disguising himself as a bird, he created the sun, the moon and the stars (unknown to his master), and also instituted the alternation of day and night.

The Abure tribes believe that the Spider acts as intercessor between Nyame and mankind; he takes their complaints to the supreme being. As a result of his intervention, when there was no time to rest between hard tasks in the fields, Nyame created night and sleep; when night in turn seemed oppressively black, the moon was created to lighten the darkness; when day was too cold, Nyame created the sun; but when the sun's hot rays burned everything, the Spider prevailed upon Nyame to send rain to extinguish the bush fires. However, as the rain continued and fire gave way to flood, on Ananse's request Nyame set the boundaries of oceans and rivers; on the sixth day Nyame himself came down to earth, and to placate men who were complaining of the heat even during the rainy season, he promised to send the harmattan, a drying wind. Then he returned to the sky as quickly as possible to avoid having to listen to further complaints from his subjects.

In most of these tales Ananse appears as a cunning, roguish creature, and even succeeds in marrying Nyame's daughter; but he so tries his father-in-law's patience that the latter is finally obliged to punish him. He is also regarded as the first king and plays the part of culture-hero, bringing mankind cereals to sow and the hoe for use on the land. So this is a very complex and rich figure, who can be placed alongside the jester-gods already described.

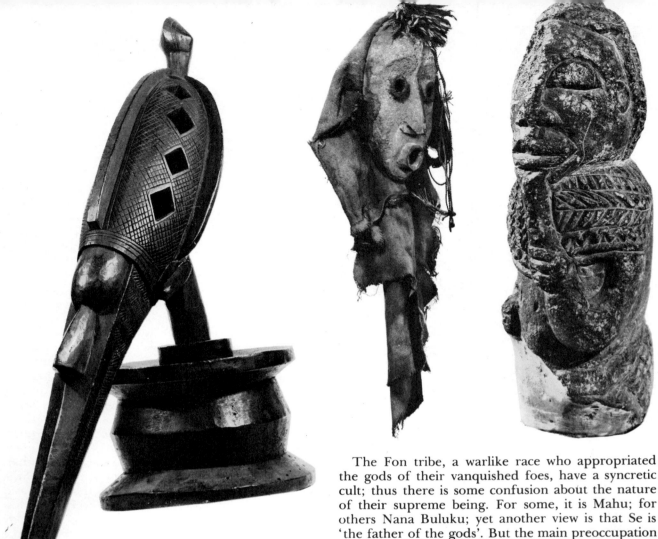

Fetish of blackened wood in two pieces. The upper represents a human head in which the features have been reduced to a nose and forehead, topped by an elaborate cap. The whole revolves upon a stout rod in the circular stand below. It was used by the Nalou-speaking people of Guinea. British Museum.

Wooden mask of the Dan people, Ivory Coast. This mask punishes those who infringe the laws and customs of the community by its own power, and offerings are made to the mask as such. Dan masks do not portray people or objects and do not represent deities or spirits; but they always depict a human face and are a development of an earlier type of mask representing deified ancestry. *Rijksmuseum voor Volkenkunde, Leiden*

Anthropomorphic stone statuette of the Kissi people in Guinea. Spirits are thought to enter into human shape not only in cult statues, but even in live humans during rituals. Life itself is a symbol and human beings enact mythological situations. Musée de l'Homme. *Giraudon*

The Fon tribe, a warlike race who appropriated the gods of their vanquished foes, have a syncretic cult; thus there is some confusion about the nature of their supreme being. For some, it is Mahu; for others Nana Buluku; yet another view is that Se is 'the father of the gods'. But the main preoccupation of the tribes of Dahomey is not so much with this supreme being, as with the cult dedicated to the masters of the various divisions of nature, known as the Vodu. The two main gods are Mahu and Lisa, the twin children of Nana Buluku; Mahu represents the female principle—the earth, the moon and fertility; and Lisa the male principle—the sky, the sun and power. The idea of twins is a neat way of expressing the balance maintained between sky and earth, day and night, work and rest, or, alternatively, the coexistence and complementary nature of opposites. This divine couple had a son, Dan, who represents the movement of life in the universe. And although he also is a twin, he stands for unity in the world. 'Dan is life and Mahu thought,' the Dahomeans say. Dan adopts different shapes, the best known of which is Dan Ayido Hwedo, the Rainbow, which encircles the world in order to integrate its various parts, and is symbolised by a serpent biting his own tail. However, this recognition of the dynamic unity of the universe does not prevent the Fons distinguishing between the various sections of reality, each section being headed by a great Vodu. But Vodu act only at Dan's instigation and that is why altars to the gods are very often decorated with symbols of Dan. The Vodu consist of four great families—the families of sky-gods, of thunder-gods, of earth-gods and of gods of fate, as well as the all-important family of ancestors, particularly royal ancestors. These families include notably Sagbata, the earth-god, who inflicted small-pox on mankind to punish the human race; Xevioso, thunder-god, who appears as a ram ejecting an axe

from its mouth; Gun, god of iron; and the sea Vodu, such as Avlekete or Agbe. Apart from being god of iron, Gun plays the part of the culture-hero in his capacity of eldest son of Mahu and Lisa. But in the 'twin' or twofold concept of the universe, which is the main characteristic of Fon thought, he is also Xevioso's twin, and as the latter with his thunderbolt is responsible for sending rainstorms to fertilise the earth, the lives of men depend on this comple-mentary, twofold activity, technical activity marching alongside the creative activity of the cosmos itself.

At the head of the Yoruba pantheon is Olorun, the supreme being, who is not, however, an object of cult worship. In the beginning he reigned on high; below there was nothing but the primordial waters — Olokun, the sea. Together they gave birth to two sons, Obtala, the elder, and Odudua, the younger. Olorun gave the elder a little earth and a chicken with five toes and asked him to descend upon the waters to fashion the earth. But on the way Obtala drank some palm-wine, which went to his head, and he fell asleep. Olorun then sent Odudua with these words: 'Your elder brother got drunk on the way down. Go, take the sand and the five-toed chicken and fabricate the earth on top of Olokun.' Odudua threw down the handful of earth, the chicken scratched it, scattered it over the sea, and so created the earth.

Another myth quotes Obtala as the master of the sky and Odudua as Earth Mother. The sky covered the Earth, and from this union was born the second couple, Aganju (dry land) and Yemaja (wet land). Their son, Orungan, yielded to his desire for his own mother, who could not avoid his embrace, and from their sinful love came forth the sixteen great gods of the divine pantheon, who shared the various spheres of reality and the different human activities: Dada, Schango, Ogun, Ochossi and Schankpannan.

Each of these gods has his own cycle of legends. For instance, Schango is depicted as the king of Oyo, who particularly loved war and triumphed over his foes with the aid of his magic thunderbolt. But in the end his subjects grew tired of his demands, and his two generals, Mokwa and Timi, were deputed to approach him and ask him to renounce the throne. 'I am a great magician,' he replied. 'No-one can compel me, but I am tired of life.' Then he took a rope and went to hang himself in the forest. But when people went into the wood to seek the body, Schango had dis-appeared; he had gone down into the earth and had become Orischa, that is to say, a deity. Mokwa, explaining to the crowd the meaning of Schango's dis-appearance, instituted the first Schango priesthood.

Schango had three wives, Oya, Oschun and Oba. Oya, who was his chief wife, stole the secret of his 'magic' from him, and that is why she shared his power and personified violent rainstorms; after the death or disappearance of her husband, she turned into the river Niger. Oschun, who was also a river-goddess, was Schango's favourite, and he won her from his brother, Ogun, the god of iron and smiths. She made certain of his love, so she said, by her culinary secrets. And so Oba was neglected, and one day she asked Oschun how she should set about making herself worthy of affection. Oschun told her to cut off her ear and put it to cook in the soup. So Oba cut off her own ear and cooked it in order to gain her husband's favour. But when Schango found a fragment of human flesh on his plate he grew angry and sent Oba away. She turned into a river, and even today, where the Oba and Oschun rivers meet, they are both highly agitated – as if an everlasting quarrel raged between them.

The reader must not be surprised to discover discrepancies between some of these myths. These

Cult figure dedicated to Schango, one of the sixteen main gods and the great king of Oyo among the Yoruba. She wears on her head the double-headed axe which is the symbol of thunder and Schango's magic weapon, by virtue of which he is able to conquer all enemies. *Larousse*

Two Yoruba Eschu figures. Statuettes of Eschu, who like the priests of the cult are messengers between the gods and men, have their hair shaven except for a piece which rises up at the back of the head—the hairstyle worn also by the Ilari, the King's messengers. The statuettes are often hung around with strings of cowrie shells, with which Eschu can read the future. Bastide Collection. *Larousse*

nature-gods are also clan ancestors, and the differences between legends are the result of competition between the clans to extol their own founders at the expense of the others, and this means that each band of worshippers has its own version of the beginnings of the world or the genealogies of the Orischas. For each Orischa has his own brotherhood. But above the priests who direct them there are divinatory priests called Babalawo.

Maupoil's book about geomancy on the Slave Coast provides a completely new collection of myths, which are connected with the different manifestations of fate, with the way in which the half-nuts fall from the necklace of Ifa (Yoruba) or Fa (Fon). However, it must not be imagined that these tales constitute a mythology distinct from the first; for they have two meanings and can be translated from one mythology to the other, although the relevant system of correspondences, which is part of the esoteric knowledge of the Babalawo, is still largely a mystery to us. Whatever the truth may be regarding this obscure point, the two systems are connected to one another by the legends about the origin of divination: the cult of Ifa or Fa is closely connected to that of Eschu (Yoruba) or Legba (Fon). Of course Eschu and Legba can be identified with one another, but the Yoruba have laid particular stress on the malicious nature of their deity, and this provides a link with those jester-gods we have so often mentioned, whereas the Fons seem to have placed the emphasis on the phallic character of their god. But Eschu and Legba are slaves of the gods, or servants, or messengers, and consequently they are the indispensable intermediaries between gods and humanity. That is why the first sacrifices are made to them, as a preliminary to all ceremonies, so that they may open the way between the sacred and the profane; and that is why they bring 'the word' from gods to men. In

Fetish hut in Abomey, Dahomey. The symmetry of the design reflects the 'twin' concept of the universe characteristic of Fon thought. The symbols themselves are a curious mixture of elements assimilated in the course of time, from primitive weapons of the original warrior people to a rifle, and from wild animals to a Christian cross. *Almasy*

Fetishes in a forest hut between Enugu and Nsukka, Nigeria. They are painted with symbolical designs. Though the ancient symbols are retained, they often come to correspond to new social realities. This fetish hut is close beside a modern road. *Almasy*

other words they are the very founders of divination.

At one time men became forgetful and no longer worshipped their deities, and so the Orischas sent their messenger to earth so that men would begin to make offerings to the gods again. He sought out Orungan: 'The gods are hungry.' 'The sixteen gods must have something to satisfy them,' Orungan told him. 'I know of something suitable. It is a big thing made up of sixteen palm-nuts. When you have succeeded in getting sixteen palm-nuts and you know what they mean, you will be able to reconquer men.' Eschu went and collected the nuts and learned their meanings, and that is how he founded the religion of Ifa; for Ifa, son of a supreme god, had been changed into a palm-tree, and the nuts that convey the divine word are none other than the children of the miraculous palm-tree. But there are somewhat different myths, which tell of the conflict between the Babalawo and the other priests dedicated to the cult of the Orischas. Eschu is sometimes regarded as the slave of an old man, Ifa, to whom he is forced to surrender the art of divination; sometimes it is Ifa who possesses this art first, but his slave Eschu, who is dying of hunger on his master's doorstep, rebels when he sees Ifa receiving princely gifts from those consulting him. By trickery or lies Eschu prevents the inquirers from reaching the old man; so the latter is forced to confide some part of his knowledge to his servant; he keeps the nuts for himself, but allows Eschu to read the future in cowrie-shells.

We should, on examination, find the mythologies of all coastal peoples from Guinea to Nigeria as well developed as those quoted above. The three examples given here are, however, enough to convey an idea of their abundant wealth.

Oya, mother goddess of the Niger, who shared the power of her consort Schango, because she had stolen the secret of magic from him. She is depicted here in her good aspect as goddess of water and fertility. The double-headed axe on her head, symbol of Schango, is studded with copper nails, denoting Schango's copper palace, from which lightning flashes across the sky. Wooden head of a Yoruba ceremonial dance staff, K. van der Horst Collection, National Museum *of Ethnology, Leiden*

The meaning and function of African mythology

It is fully apparent from the indications we have given that African mythologies as we know them today have arisen from different beginnings and passed through various phases. Written into the very tales they tell is the encounter between Paleo-Negritos and the new arrivals, and the stories also reflect historical realities of alliances and conflicts, feudal systems and great monarchies. It has been impossible to indicate more than a few of the variants, but, of course, legends do unquestionably change from region to region, and from one religious body to the next. However, these temporal or geographical variations are matched by no great change in the meaning of myth in African life and thought. Frobenius had some presentiment of this when he wrote: 'In the Yoruba tribes, there is a unity between mythological creation and the individual facets and totemic organic bases of society . . . there is *conformity* between social concepts and religious concepts, both of which reveal here a common basis, an indissoluble unity, a unity that proceeds from their very roots and has no equivalent.' Now this is where we must be extremely careful: for we are not here concerned with the classical concept that relates myth to rite, which establishes religious ceremonies as a copy of mythical archetypes, and furthers the cause of religion by continuing or miming these archetypal patterns.

With the classical concept we remain in one and the same domain, the domain of religion. But in Africa it seems as if the whole of human life is contained within the mythical framework, as if the difference between the sacred and the profane no longer existed. Mythology provides man with models or patterns on which he must base his conduct, from the gesture of sowing seeds to the act of love, from house-building to the touch of the fingers on the musical skin of the drum.

This aspect of African mythology emerges most clearly from the works of Griaule, who has shed considerable light on the subject. We shall return to this point later. But to grasp its originality we must first contrast it with another mythology, that which Leenhardt studied in New Caledonia and which might perhaps provide a definition of another mythological area. Canak mythology is not so much a process of thought as a way of life; rather than a system of symbols, it is a collection of acts of participation, between man and nature, woman and the totem, between money and liana-creeper, as if individuals were indissociable from things and were still one with society and the cosmos. African mythology, on the other hand, though it includes participation, establishes a 'distance' between levels of reality; there is not confusion, but rather *mimesis* between the

mythical, the cosmic, the sociological and the individual. Everything happens as if the world were divided into watertight compartments, but these compartments correspond, they are 'analogical' to one another. And so mythology provides us with a pass key and enables us to move from one to the other. The world of participation (for participation certainly continues to exist as an ontological, existential substructure), the foundation of these analogies, correspondences or communications, gives way to systems of symbols.

In the Dogon tribes, according to Griaule, 'as, indeed, in other Sudanese tribes, everything can be regarded as symbol. One fact, in any case, is certain, that among this population every thing (object, creature, situation or act) that has been studied up to now has proved to be to some extent a symbol. And this arises out of the system of classification itself. Because one element in a "family" has a fixed place in a given series, its essential role can be summed up in the symbolic relationships it has with the other elements in the series, with the eponymous element, and via the latter with the rest of the family, which is itself hinged to the universal function. So one must expect correspondences, and the first—the simplest to understand—will apply to elements occupying the same rank in the twenty-two series that go to form a family. But these internal correspondences presume the existence of others, external ones, with similarly placed elements belonging to other families. All these additional links, on the one hand, mean that symbol and symbolised are reversible . . . and, on the other hand, that a symbolised thing has numerous symbols, and, inversely, the symbol is valid for a wide range of symbolised objects.'

And it may well be that not all peasants are capable of giving the symbolic meaning of their gestures, although they obey the law of the system, just as

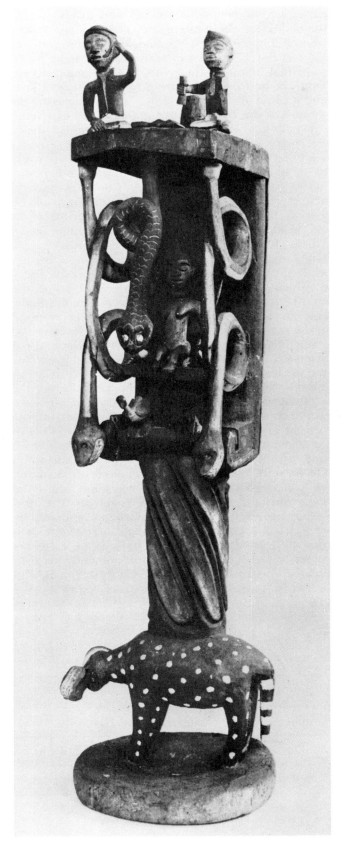

Protective statuette of the Bambara people, Sudanese Republic. Bambara mythology is particularly thorough in assigning to every known aspect of life its ritual place in the spiritual world, much of this being expressed in a symbolism of agriculture. *Segy Gallery, New York*

Loango sculpture with spirits in the form of men, animals and snakes. Snakes have an important part in the African mythologies. They are the source of life, fertility symbol, rainbow symbol, intermediary with ancestors, or totem, depending on the tribe. Douai Museum. *Luquet*

Roman Catholic peasants would be incapable of communicating to an observer the principles of Roman Catholic theology; and this, of course, explains why knowledge of African religion has been superficial almost down to our own time. But in his very recent studies Zahan has shown in connection with the Bambaras how this apprenticeship in symbolic language is carried out in societies of initiation, by extremely ingenious pedagogic methods and in such a way that societies of children progress until they become societies of adults or 'wise men'.

It is possible to give only a few illustrations of this idea here, starting with the Dogons. The plan of the house is, on the one hand, Nommo in human guise, and man lying on his right side in the position of procreation. The village, and each of its districts, is the projection of creation on the ground. Cultivated fields, starting with the three great archaic fields in which the ancestors touched the earth, are laid out in a spiral pattern, which is a copy of the movement of creation and puts them in a theoretic order; similarly the peasant works in zigzag fashion, east-to-west and west-to-east, all the while progressing from north to south so that his work may go forward in the very steps of world movement. Of course, every mythical pattern is repeated in a series of instruments, things, institutions or gestures, which diversify it. For instance, the ark piloted by the smith-instructor which came down from heaven to earth is reproduced in the Niger fishermen's canoes, the weaver's shuttle, the tool-box, the anvil, the sledge-hammer and screen belonging to the smith, the grain loft, the seats in the house, the drum, and the harp-lute.

Generally speaking, the world is divided into twenty-two categories of beings which closely correspond, element for element; there are twenty-two species of insects, twenty-two species of animals,

binding the agricultural and the conjugal act. But the couple lie beneath a shroud, and this is because the bed is also the tomb of the ancestor Lébé, who is himself a hypostasis of Nommo, and is a reminder of the fact that before it can germinate the female seed must first be put in the ground. Thus one proceeds from the gesture of the sower to the gesture of love, and it could also be represented in this way: from the gesture of the Dogon potter to that of the merchant, everything is epiphany, revelation of the myths of the gods.

Similarly, Mme Dieterlen has indicated in her study of the Bambara universe a system in which everything has its place and its part to play, from stars to useful objects, from the spirit to waste matter. Agricultural work is initiated by the nocturnal wanderings of an old woman who follows the mythical itinerary of Musso Koroni. The straws used in basketwork symbolise order and Faro's classification of beings, while the interlacing spiral of straw follows the vibra-tions of cosmic creation. There is identity between the seed of creation, the seed of crops and man's body. Human life spans seven ages, which correspond to the seven skies, the seven earths, seven waters and seven stages in the growth of millet. There is also a 'science of bands' from which traditional garments are made, and each one reveals an aspect of meta-physics, a fragment of Bambara myth. Thus the white band represents Faro, the bright one; the kayo band reproduces the Rainbow; the Sirakele band the descent of Faro from the seventh part of the sky to the seventh part of earth; the baguni nyama, which is made up of twenty-two squares of indigo and white alternatively, represents creation in its total harmony, whilst its separation into two registers recalls the 'twin' duality. Another band represents the des-perate journey of Musso Koroni when abandoned by her husband. One could go on and on giving exam-ples: the chieftain's seat in its various elements represents the ancestor's skeleton and thus helps to maintain the strength of his successor. D. Zahan, who in studying this subject was struck more by the

twenty-two species of plants; man is divided into twenty-two parts, and so on. Naturally, social or-ganisation is no exception to this rule: paternal lineage represents Amma, origin of all things; mat-ernal lineage is Mammo, combined creation. The reader may remember that Amma's creation was compromised by Yurugu, and similarly when a child is separated from its mother it finds itself, like Yurugu, in an incestuous situation with regard to her. So he seeks a mother-substitute in his mat-ernal uncle's wife, whom he calls his 'wife', and with whom he may even have sexual relations. But as he cannot give his nephew his wife, in the end the uncle gives him his daughter. Thus, the rules of kinship and marriage also emerge from mythical patterns. Once they are married, man lies on the right side and woman on the left; a shroud is spread over the couple and under the bed they place seeds that are sown in spring. In their union, the man is the replica of the water-spirit who makes fertilising rain fall upon the earth, and woman is the seed, thus

The Fali concept of the world and social institutions

Human body	head	chest	stomach	right arm	left arm	legs
Family	patriarch	father	maternal uncle	paternal uncle	1st wife	2nd wife
Edible grain	red millet	water melon	millet in season	haricot beans	ground-nut	wild melon
Wild mammals	hippotragine antelope	buffalo	boar	waterbuck	Buffon's kob	reedbuck
Birds	marabou	hawk	vulture	kite	hornbill	raven

variants of the myths than by their conformity, does not connect the organisation of Bambara initiation societies with cosmogony, but he throws light on the whole system of symbols, of analogous relationships, which, in these societies, link animals, plants, various parts of the human body, the divisions of the cosmos, stages of knowledge, etc. He succeeds in showing how the neophyte in passing from one society to the next gives all the bones of his body in turn that they may be integrated into the cosmos and how, in exchange, he receives from this same cosmos, shred by shred, his other nature, which permits him to declare himself identical with the universe. However, is this not to suggest that myth may be regarded as the mirror in which these analogies and symbols are reflected, if, indeed, they do not have their actual foundation there?

In a study that appeared recently, Lebeuf showed how the mythology of another Sudanese population, the Fali, dictates their concept of the world and social institutions. The world arose from two eggs, one a toad's egg and the other a tortoise's egg, which turned in opposite directions while their insides went round the opposite way from their outsides. From these two eggs stemmed the first division of the universe, which was a binary division.

Subsequently, the first smith came down from the sky on a bean-stalk with a chest that broke along its diagonals as it fell, thus forming four triangles, and he introduced into this binary division—consisting of wild earth and human earth—a new quaternary division, which meant that the animals, plants and things contained in the chest were scattered in the four directions of space. And as there were twelve such living things, the quaternary division extended to form various series, all with twelve elements in them. These various series of twelve corresponded closely to one another in accordance with a schema suggested in the following table; it will be seen that such diverse elements as social considerations and human anatomy alike have a place in it:

These staggered divisions explain and justify the whole of Fali life. Humanity is divided into two clans, those of the Tortoise and the Toad, linked by inter-marriage. The houses produce the primordial eggs and project at ground-level the mythical geography, first binary, then quaternary. But as the world is endowed with two contrasting movements, which are then repeated in the opposite directions, the house 'turns' in the same way, one clan's dwellings being put round the opposite way to another's. As the eggs contained an inside and an outside that moved round, so the masculine and feminine parts of the house also turn in opposite directions: the head or father of the family ensures the continuity of the general movement of the universe in his own home by day through his ordered passage from one task to another, and by night by joining each of his four wives in turn and coupling with them in a complete four-day cycle; meanwhile the wives keep the opposite gyratory movement going, from the bed-room to the granary, from the granary to the kit-chen. All the rules of kinship and all the matrimonial alliances likewise repeat or echo the various moments of myth, with the result that human existence down to its slightest detail falls within a mythical system, and the actions of men both at home and outside continue and maintain the order and progress of the world.

The three examples that we have just given were all taken from peoples in the Sudan. And the reader may have wondered if the importance of mythical models and symbolic thought is typical of only one of the cultural areas studied in this section. This impression perhaps receives a measure of confirmation when one reads the works of ethnologists who have taken an interest in the mythologies of other cultural areas and sees that they have left the myths somewhat suspended in the void. However, we think that these characteristics do extend to other areas, and a whole series of facts enables us to support this statement. First the monarchies of the divine kings serve simply to inscribe the laws of mythical creation on phenomenal reality. The few examples of myths

sexual organ	thighs	anus	nose	ears	eyes
3rd wife	4th wife	eldest son	eldest daughter	other sons	other daughters
spring millet	white peas	red peas	black sesame	white sesame	other sesame
long-eared fox	oribi antelope	gazelle	species of monkey	hares and rabbits	palm-rat
swan	owl	falcon	dove	wader-bird	crowned crane

Wooden corded mask of the Dogon people representing the first dead ancestor. Death is never forgotten in Dogon society. In each family the husband and wife sleep under the funerary blanket, and their bed symbolises the tomb of the ancestor Lébé, essential spirit of Nommo, the founder of the Dogon civilisation. Marcel Griaule Collection. *Musée de l'Homme*

about the beginnings of kingship that we quoted earlier already make this point: perhaps we may be permitted to elaborate on the Fon example (Mercier). The king is compared to Dan Ayido Hwedo, the celestial serpent, for he is the support of society, just as the rainbow is the support of the world; and he is also the principle of sociological life, just as Dan is the principle of cosmic life. Like Dan, the rainbow, the king changes colour, that is to say he never dies, but is born again in his successor. And just as Dan is the father of fecundity, the king is the father of his kingdom's wealth. The twin-like duality that we noted at the basis of Dahomean mythology is also found in the political organisation in the form of double monarchy. There is only one king, but there are two courts, two series of officers who correspond to one another, two rituals in honour of the royal ancestors, two sets of palaces—those of the queen mothers and the men kings; all of which finally amounts to the fact that the government of society is but a copy of the government of the universe and that the mythical pattern of twins is reflected both in the world of the Vodu and in the world of the living. In the same cultural area the work of Frobenius, followed by that of Denett, has brought to light the fact that in Yoruba tribes a quadripartite structure is applied to the universe, with its four cardinal points, related to the four great gods (the east related to Schango, the north to Obtala, the south to Odudua, the west to Ifa), and its four days of the week—Odjoawo, day of secrecy and therefore of Ifa-Eschu; Odjo-Ofun, day of Ogun, of the smithy and war; Odjo-Jakuta, day of Schango, who sends his thunderbolt and gives rain; Odje-Osche, day devoted to Obtala. And the sixteen Orischas who emerged from Yemaja's stomach correspond both to a quadripartite system to the second power, and also, as we have already said, to the sixteen figures of divination represented by the palm-nuts. And this led Frobenius to the following conclusion: 'What we have here is therefore a system that, on one of its two main tracks, unites east and west like the sun in orbit, and following the second track unites north and south; a system that also encircles the world in an east-to-north direction. Eschu's bonnet...the four faces that decorate the boards of Ifa, the contents of sectioned chests correspond exactly to one another. So we are not confronted with facts that have been brought together by chance, but by a systematised whole, a vast concept of the world.' This concept enables us to explain the arrangement of details in social and political life with its left side and its right side suggested by the main markings of the boards of Ifa. There are ministers of the right and ministers of the left at the court of the kings; there is a domain of light and a domain of shade in the construction of houses, the planning of towns, with Eschu's altar at the entrance, as intermediary god. But this lateral arrangement must not make us forget the division into four, which is more fundamental still. The

Ancestor figurines of the Kaka tribe, Cameroon. Their zig-zag legs, concave faces, round eyes and pointed chins are typical. Milwaukee Public Museum.

political council is composed of four chiefs: Iyalode, mother-priestess; Oba, divine king; Balagun, general; and Bashun, chief minister.

It is possible to sense in the Atlantic coastal area the existence of similar phenomena to those that have been more clearly expounded in the section on the Sudan; but there is the possibility of encountering an insurmountable obstacle when we come to the Bantu world. Research in this direction is only just beginning. The Baluba and Lulua (Tiarko Fourche and H. Morlighem) divide the world into four planes—sky, earth, the abode of good spirits and that of bad spirits—and these four planes form a cross with their meeting-point in the centre, each of them having the same cruciform pattern. The creator is positioned at the crossroads of the celestial plane. Similarly in the family, the husband lives in the centre house and his four wives reside at the ends of the arms of the cross. In council, the lord is seated on his throne in the centre of the mat, and at the four ends are the lord of the throne, the lord of friendship, the war chief and the spokesman.

Magic societies attached to clans meet at hidden crossroads in the bush. The grand master stands in the centre, while his four dignitaries are stationed at the entrances to the four paths, but not equidistant from the centre point. Another mythical idea is introduced here, that of the great current of life that flows through the universe and which is depicted by the image of the coiled python (cycles of life) that curves round in spirals; as a result of this concept the four dignitaries, instead of being equidistant from the centre point, are, according to their place in the hierarchy, on appropriate spirals at an ever-increasing distance from the centre at the crossroads.

Balandier has made a study in Gabon of the political aspect of the Bwiti secret society, incidentally showing that by their construction the place of worship and

Wooden club used in dances in the cult of the Yoruba thunder-god Schango. The double-headed axe represents thunder. Like other nature gods, Schango is also considered a clan ancestor, who showed his strength by his love of war and his wisdom by his knowledge of magic. Museum für Völkerkunde, Hamburg. *Bildarchiv Foto Marburg*

A carved wooden mask representing an antelope. Guro tribe, Ivory Coast. The antelope was of great significance to the hunting tribes of Africa and is frequently represented on their ritual masks. British Museum.

Funerary head in pottery, which appears to be more a portrait than a symbol. Ashanti people, Ghana. Mythology in the European sense of stories is highly developed among the Ashanti and is peopled by hundreds of gods. *Rijksmuseum voor Volkenkunde, Leiden*

musical instruments are reminders of the symbolic wealth of the society's myths. Finally, young researchers are beginning to take an interest in the esoteric teachings of the initiation ceremonies among Bantu tribes in South Africa. This means that for the whole of Black Africa we can now affirm the primordial importance of the myth both as epistemology, the basis of an entire theory of what we shall call 'symbolic' knowledge, and as the basis of family, social, political, even economic structures (the latter by way of techniques), which are nothing more nor less than exemplifications of mythical patterns.

Surely, then, there is a possibility that we should find ourselves confronted with fixed systems, immobilising men and societies in a mimesis of primordial divine gestures? The answer to this can be found in the explanations given above. We have observed that creation always takes place in stages, that the culture-hero, for instance, shoulders the task of ordering reality that originally belonged to the supreme being. Thus myth is caught up in the movement of life and the sequence of time. Encounters between invaders and autochthonous populations, constant migrations involving encounters with ancient gods of the earth (masters of the soil), then struggles between cities for country-wide leadership, or between religious brotherhoods desirous of consolidating their powers—all these factors leave their mark on the different variants, later additions and distortions. Sometimes it is possible to follow these changes in historical documents, as in the case of the Fon or Yoruba tribes, whose development is reflected in travellers' tales that span the different periods. However, the observer is immediately impressed by the desire to shape the new to the same pattern as the old. The many legends that explain the tenuous alliances in Sudan are quite contradictory; yet they all conform to the same desire to account for the alliance on the grounds of a twin relationship— in other words, to integrate the new facts arising out of the people's historical development (whether it be an encounter between different ethnic groups or contacts between castes) into the framework of traditional metaphysics or mythology. It also happens that mythology orientates historical explanations in its own particular direction, as if the events of history could never be anything but a translation of the ancient gestures of the gods in the flux of time. For instance, tribal wars are a continuation of the quarrel we mentioned in connection with Oschun, between Schango and Ogun, and they are in a way taken over by the respective religious bodies connected with these gods; Sagbata inflicting smallpox on men because they would not worship him is an expression of the revolt of earth against newcomers who have a sky mythology. But this last example makes us realise that although history may, on the one hand, follow the current of myth, on the other hand it may send it off in new directions at the risk of distorting it. In such a case myth gets farther and farther away from ecological, sociological and temporal realities. It is no longer the ontological foundation, it becomes an 'explanation', which will follow changes in substructure. In short, it becomes an ideology.

Funerary statue of the Bakoto, Congo. Wood, covered with
yellow and red copper and brass leaf. The human face
resembles a mask. It is set on a stalk-like neck which opens
out into a diamond shape representing the whole body. The
copper is elaborately worked in patterns whose symbolism is
unclear. Vérité Collection, Paris. *Giraudon*

Bronze head of a spirit from Benin, West Africa. Issuing from
the eyes and nostrils are snakes which are devouring frogs.
The snakes signify great strength in the magical sense. The
four ibis on the head are also associated with magical power,
probably connected with medicine as they are similar to those
found on medicine staffs. The crown of the head is decorated
with scrolls such as are frequently found on bracelets worn
as amulets. British Museum.

Carved bedstead from Madagascar depicting hunters with spear, club, and gun and a great variety of animals. The Madagascans explain the multiplicity of animal life by the competitive creative efforts of Andriamanitra and Andrianahary. The creatures of the one constantly try to destroy the creatures of the other. *Musée de l'Homme*

Madagascar

Madagascar stands at a crossroads between the races — and influences — of Indonesia, Melanesia and southern Africa, and in this respect its position is recognised as unique.

The Madagascan pantheon is headed by a supreme god, perhaps the Indonesian god. Father Dubois has, however, written that 'Madagascans do not have the same fear of Zanahary, their supreme god, as they have of the spirits of the dead.' And the ancestors, who are still worshipped regularly, appear to be intermediaries endowed with the power to take prayers up to him, for, according to a proverb: 'Man becomes dizzy if he goes up towards him.' However, there is not one Zanahary only, for liturgical texts actually differentiate between Zanahary above and those below, male and female Zanahary, Zanahary of the north, south, east and west. Indeed, the supreme god, Zanaharibe, is only the highest Zanahary in the hierarchy, the head of all the rest (such as Andrianahoabo, the lord on high, who sometimes comes down from the sky on a silver chain, or Andrianamboatena, the master of earth, to quote only the most powerful). The Earth–Sky couple has given rise to an important collection of myths. Sometimes the Sky (female) and the Earth (male) are regarded as a husband and wife who disagree and want to part. 'I am like red pepper,' says the Sky, 'and you are like eyes; now you know that red pepper and eyes must never come together'; and in spite of Earth's supplications the Sky goes up above. Earth and Sky are sometimes shown as two brothers who quarrelled over which one was the elder. 'I am the elder,' said Earth, 'for I am the ancestor of all living creatures who take their food from me.' 'No,' replied the Sky, 'for I am above you, I am over you.' However, the two opponents were soon divided by war, with Earth bringing up troops to attack the Sky, and the Sky bombarding Earth with stones or rain. But the two Zanahary stopped the combatants in mid-battle. That is why the Earth, which was on its way up, is now dented to form mountains and valleys, though it was flat in the beginning; it also accounts for lakes, which were formed when the Sky spat on its victim. In this agonistic framework, which seems particularly important in Madagascan mythology, the myth about the origin of fire can also be included. Once upon a time, the Sun sent Flames to Earth to protect it, and above Earth, Thunder ruled in uncontested glory. Thunder and Flames began to fight, and in order to defeat the Flames, Thunder had to call upon his old friends, the Clouds; the Clouds burst into heavy rain, and the Flames were vanquished; some hid in the depths of mountains, whence they occasionally emerge as volcanoes, others hid in stones and in tree-trunks, and that is why men may today produce fire by striking flint or rubbing together two pieces of dry wood.

The creation of man appears in various forms, according to the different races on this large island. Sometimes the Zanahary are said to have fashioned him, sharing the work between them. Rampanohitaolana first set out the bones; then Rampanaohozatra bound these bones together with sinews; Rampanaonofo clad the skeleton in flesh; Rampanahoditra enveloped the result in skin; Rampanaora pumped red blood into the body, in other words gave it life; and Rampamelombelona gave it breath, in other words a soul. At one time, according to another legend, the sky was inhabited by Andriamanitra, who was good, and Andrianahary, who was bad. When they grew tired of being always in the same place, they created the earth, then the first human couple. Then they quarrelled (still the same agonistic theme). 'Let us work separately,' said the first. 'Each of us will do his best to invent different things.' The first made domestic animals, the second made wild animals; the first made the hive with honey, the second made wasps' nests. Andrianahary in fury cried: 'You are the first, and I am only the second. But I shall give the things I have made greater power, and they will spoil yours.' So Andriamanitra was forced to invent new plants as remedies or magical cures for all the ills created by his younger brother.

Alongside these myths, there is the theme that men were created from wooden statues sculpted by one god and brought to life by another, a theme that may, of course, be found occasionally in Africa, but occurs particularly frequently in Indonesia. Naturally enough, in Madagascar this theme became identified with that of the fight between Sky and Earth, between the Zanahary on high and the one below. The Zanahary below fashioned statues of wood and clay, which he did not succeed in bringing to life, so the one above gave them breath to make them live. But they quarrelled over the new creation, and so the Zanahary above made a point of continually taking from the living a measure of that life he had given them: this was the origin of death. The Zanahary below took back his possession, the body; and the one above took his, the breath of life.

Sometimes the creation of man does not proceed from the great gods, but from an intermediary divinity. Zanahary, king of the sky, and his wife, Andriamanitra, were said to have a son, Razanajanahary. Since Razanajanahary was bored, Zanahary summoned a creature called Rangidimaola (which means 'He who was not made by the supreme god'; this is in many mythologies the way the intermediary deity is described—a jester-god, in many cases) to be his son's companion. Unfortunately, Rangidimaola became so vain and offensive that Zanahary flung him from the heights of heaven down to the earth below. But Razanajanahary did not forget his former playmate; he came to see him and, though he could not obtain his father's pardon for him, he brought his friend three small pieces of wood, which Rangidimaola sculpted to look like men and to which Razanajanahary then gave life.

One explanation of death, as we have seen, lay in the conflict between the two Zanahary, above and below. But there are other explanations too—for instance, that it was the result of a free choice made by man. It would seem that the supreme god said to the first couple: 'You must accept death, but choose between the death of the moon or the death of the banana-tree. If you choose the first you will have no children, but you will come back to life like the moon who disappears and reappears. If you make the second choice, you will perish for ever like the banana-tree, but you will have many offspring.' Men preferred to attain immortality through their children.

There is in other regions of Madagascar a curious character who was not fashioned by the gods, but he reappears under the name of Zatavu. Zatavu was regarded as a great magician, and in his pride he asked the supreme god for his daughter's hand in marriage. His rise to the sky with its different episodes (he jumped from the top of the gable, he sat on the silver throne of the supreme god, etc.) reminds one of an Indonesian cycle. But the girl whose hand Zatavu won by his own cunning decided to put her husband to the test: she asked him to bring her his mother's liver. To begin with, Zatavu tried hard to deceive her, bringing her a calf's liver, then a cow's liver; but in the end he killed his mother. Then his wife fled: 'Since you are capable of killing your mother when driven by desire, you are also capable of killing your own child. You might even kill me.' One of the most famous episodes in the Zatavu cycle concerns the origin of rice. The daughter of the supreme god, who was used to rice, the celestial food, could not get used to either manioc or maize on earth. She went and asked her father for a little rice, but he refused. But the girl's mother took pity on her and gave a cock and a hen rice to eat and sent them to her daughter as a present. When the animals were killed, the grains of rice were taken from their stomachs and sown in the soil. The supreme god then sent hail to destroy the growing crop, but it did no good; rice had entered the lives of men.

Beneath Zanahary and the demi-gods or intermediary gods, there is a whole series of creatures, spirits of the dead, who are the objects of cults or legends. The Vazimba, for example. These are dead natives who used to live on the island before the arrival of the Merina and are worshipped by the invaders, either in holy places or at their stone tombs. There is a story about a Vazimba woman who had two daughters, Rasoalao and Ravola, to whom she bequeathed her wealth before she died, making the elder and stronger, Rasoalao, the gift of wild animals and the younger, Ravola, who was frail and shy, a present of tame animals; so people pray to the former before going hunting, and cattle-rearing is the province of the latter. Then there are the ancestors, Razana, of whom it is plainly said: 'They have gone to be gods.' Lastly we must mention the undines, Zazavavindrano: these water-maidens are the subject of some of the most charming tales in Madagascan mythology; they waylay a man, draw him into the water, and marry him. Sometimes a fisherman catches one of them and makes her his wife. In all cases, a taboo is placed on the marriage (salt usually being the thing that is taboo) and if the man happens to violate it, the undine disappears for ever.

The names of the gods vary according to ethnic groups or regions. Zatavu, to whom these words are attributed: 'I created my body, I was not created by God', is known elsewhere as Ratovoana, 'He who created himself', and he has also been compared with Ratuvuantani, the young adolescent in Sakalava myth. In spite of these differences, throughout the island there is very great unity of theme and inspiration. Perhaps this mythology could be described as one of battles for prestige, rivalries between brothers, between powers of heaven and earth, husbands and wives, magicians and benefactors, all of which tend towards the establishment of rank, hierarchy and privilege. Nevertheless they always leave a place for the vanquished in some sector of the sacred and, consequently, in men's prayers.

SUGGESTIONS FOR FURTHER READING

The preceding pages have presented an introduction to the mythologies of the world. The extent of our knowledge varies from region to region, and where the more advanced and sophisticated societies have left a wealth of information the author has the more rewarding though not always the simpler task. Many books have been written, and continue to be written, about the meaning of the Greek myths, for instance, and the stories surrounding the Hindu pantheon; archaeologists, historians, and specialists in comparative religion all make some contribution to their interpretation. With the primitive societies, and with those whose remains and records are scanty and difficult to decipher, the main contribution comes from the anthropologist and the ethnologist, and their task is made easier as conditions of travel improve. The farthest parts of the world are yielding information now, though there are still places where the researcher is not welcomed.

It is largely true that a detailed examination of the myths of even a single region would require as many pages as this one book encompasses. It does, however, show the vast range and diversity of the subject, and it is the publishers' hope that readers will be led to explore in greater detail this fascinating world which contains the explanation of so much of man's behaviour and so many of his fears; his superstitions and taboos; his very instincts—myth is often an attempt to articulate these—and some of the beliefs which, while seeming recent in time, are as old as man himself.

GENERAL

Everyman Dictionary of Non-Classical Mythology. J. M. Dent & Sons, Ltd., London, & E. P. Dutton, New York, 1952.

Frazer, Sir James. *The Golden Bough.* 1 vol. ed. Macmillan & Co. Ltd., London, & St. Martin's Press, New York, 1922.

Funk & Wagnalls'. *Standard Dictionary of Folklore, Mythology and Legend.* 2 vols. The Mayflower Publishing Co., London, & Funk & Wagnalls, New York, 1951.

Graves, Robert. *The White Goddess.* Faber & Faber, London, 1948.

Harvey, Sir Paul. *The Oxford Companion to Classical Literature.* Oxford Univ. Press, 1937.

MacCulloch, John A. & Gray, Louis H. *The Mythology of all Races.* 13 vols. Cooper Square Pubs. Inc., New York, 1922.

The Oxford Classical Dictionary. Oxford Univ. Press, 1949.

Smith, G. C. *Man and his Gods.* Jonathan Cape, London, 1953.

PREHISTORY

Clark, Grahame. *World Prehistory. An Outline.* Cambridge Univ. Press, 1961.

Howells, W. W. *The Heathens.* V. Gollancz, London, 1959.

James, E. O. *Prehistoric Religions.* Thames & Hudson, London, 1957.
The Origin of Religions. Unicorn Press, London, 1937.
The Origins of Sacrifice. John Murray, London, 1933.
The Cult of the Mother Goddess. Thames & Hudson, London, 1959.

Maringer, Johannes. *The Gods of Prehistoric Man.* Weidenfeld & Nicolson, London, 1960.

EGYPT

Aldred, Cyril. *The Egyptians.* Thames & Hudson, London, 1961.

Cerny, J. *Ancient Egyptian Religion.* Hutchinson, London, 1952.

Glanville, S. R. K. *The Legacy of Egypt.* Oxford Univ. Press, 1942.

Mercer, S. A. B. *The Religion of Ancient Egypt.* Luzac & Co., London, 1950.

Wainwright, G. A. *The Sky Religion in Egypt.* Oxford Univ. Press, 1938.

Egyptian Mythology (in *The Mythology of all Races,* see GENERAL).

EMPIRES OF THE ANCIENT NEAR EAST

Cottrell, Leonard. *The Land of Shiran.* Souvenir Press, London, 1965.

Drioton, Etienne. *The Religion of the Ancient East.* Burns & Oates, London, 1959.

Finegan, Jack. *Light from the Ancient Past.* Oxford Univ. Press & Princeton Univ. Press, 1946.

Hooke, Samuel H. *Myth, Ritual, and Kingship.* Clarendon Press, Oxford, 1958.
Babylonian and Assyrian Religion. Hutchinson, London, 1953.

James, E. O. *Myth and Ritual in the Ancient Near East.* Thames & Hudson, London, 1958.
The Ancient Gods. Weidenfeld & Nicolson, London, 1960.

Kramer, Samuel Noah. *History begins at Sumer.* Thames & Hudson, London, 1958.

Parrot, André. *Sumer.* Thames & Hudson, London, 1960.

Sandars, N. K. (trans.) *The Epic of Gilgamesh.* Penguin Books, Harmondsworth, 1960.

WESTERN SEMITIC LANDS

Driver, G. R. *Canaanite Myths and Legends.* T. & T. Clark, Edinburgh, 1956.

Epstein, Isidore. *Judaism: a historical presentation.* Penguin Books, Harmondsworth, 1959.

Gray, John. *The Canaanites.* Thames & Hudson, London, 1964.

Harden, D. B. *The Phoenicians.* Thames & Hudson, London, 1962.

Pritchard, J. B. *Ancient Near Eastern Texts relating to the Old Testament.* Oxford Univ. Press & Princeton Univ. Press, 1955.

Semitic Mythology (in *The Mythology of all Races*).

GREECE

Cook, A. B. *Zeus.* Cambridge Univ. Press, 1940.

Cottrell, Leonard. *The Bull of Minos.* Evans Bros., London, 1954.

Graves, Robert. *The Greek Myths.* 2 vols. Penguin Books, Harmondsworth, 1948.

Kerényi, C. *The Gods of the Greeks.* Thames & Hudson, London, 1951.
The Heroes of the Greeks. Thames & Hudson, London, 1959.

Mylonas, G. *Eleusis and the Eleusinian Mysteries.* Routledge, Kegan Paul, London, 1962.

Otto, Walter F. *The Homeric Gods.* Thames & Hudson, London, 1955.

Greek and Roman Mythology (in *The Mythology of all Races*).

ROME

Bloch, Raymond. *The Origins of Rome.* Thames & Hudson, London, 1960.

Grant, Michael. *Myths of the Greeks and Romans.* Weidenfeld & Nicolson, London, 1962.
The Roman World. Weidenfeld & Nicolson, London, 1960.

Rose, H. J. *Ancient Roman Religion.* Hutchinson, London, 1949.

Rostovtzeff, M. *Rome.* Oxford Univ. Press, 1960.

Warner, Rex. *Men and Gods.* Penguin Books, Harmondsworth, 1952.

Greek and Roman Mythology (in *The Mythology of all Races*).

PERSIA

Duchesse-Guillemin, J. (trans.) *The Hymns of Zarathustra.* Allen & Unwin, London, 1952.

Ghirshman, Roman. *Persia, from the Origins to Alexander the Great.* Thames and Hudson, London, 1964.
Iran. The Parthians and Sassanians. Thames & Hudson, London, 1962.

Henning, W. B. *Zoroaster.* Oxford Univ. Press, 1951.

Vermaseren, M. J. *Mithras, the secret God.* Methuen, London, 1963.

Wales, H. G. Q. *The Mountain of God.* Bernard Quaritch, London, 1953.

Widengren, G. *Mani and Manichaeism.* Weidenfeld & Nicolson, London, 1965.

Zaehner, R. C. *The Rise and Fall of Zoroastrianism.* Weidenfeld & Nicolson, London, 1961.

Armenian and *Iranian Mythology* (in *The Mythology of all Races*).

INDIA

Bouquet, A. C. *Hinduism.* Hutchinson, London, 1947.

The Buddhist Scriptures, (trans. by Edward Conze) Penguin Classics, Harmondsworth, 1959.

Elwin, Verrier. *The Myths of Middle India.* Oxford Univ. Press, 1949.
The Tribal Myths of Orissa. Oxford Univ. Press, 1954.

Humphreys, Christmas. *Buddhism.* Penguin Books, Harmondsworth, 1951.

Jaini, Jagnanderlal. *Outlines of Jainism.* Cambridge Univ. Press, 1940.

Weber, Max. *The Religion of India.* Allen & Unwin, London, 1958.

Indian Mythology (in *The Mythology of all Races*).

CHINA

Birch, C. *Chinese Myths and Fantasies Retold.* Oxford Univ. Press, 1961.

Harvey, E. D. *The Mind of China.* Yale Univ. Press, 1933.

Watson, William. *China.* Thames & Hudson, London, 1961.

Werner, E. T. C. *Myths and Legends of China.* Harrap, London, 1922.

Chinese and *Indo-Chinese Mythology* (in *The Mythology of all Races*).

JAPAN

Anesaki, Mahasaru. *History of Japanese Religion*. Kegan Paul, London, 1930.

Aston, W. G. *Nihongi: Chronicles of Japan*. Allen & Unwin, London, & Oxford Univ. Press, New York, 1956.

Kidder, J. Edward. *Japan*. Thames & Hudson, London, 1959.

McAlpine, H. & W. *Japanese Tales and Legends*. Oxford Univ. Press, 1958.

Watts, Alan W. *The Way of Zen*. Thames & Hudson, London, 1957.

Japanese Mythology (in *The Mythology of all Races*).

CELTIC LANDS

Anderson, Flavia. *The Ancient Secret: In Search of the Holy Grail*. V. Gollancz, London, 1953.

Branston, Brian. *The Lost Gods of England*. Thames & Hudson, London, 1958.

Jones, T. & G. (trans.) *The Mabinogion*. J. M. Dent & Sons, Ltd., London, & E. P. Dutton, New York, 1963

MacNeill, F. M. *The Silver Bough*. Wm. MacLellan, Glasgow, 1957.

Sjoestedt, Marie Louise. *Gods and Heroes of the Celts*. Methuen, London, 1949.

Yeats, W. B. *Mythologies*. Macmillan, London, 1959.

Celtic Mythology (in *The Mythology of all Races*).

GERMANIC LANDS

Branston, Brian. *The Gods of the North*. Thames & Hudson, London, 1955.

Ellis Davidson, H. R. *Gods and Myths of Northern Europe*. Penguin Books, Harmondsworth, 1964.

Jones, G. *Eirik the Red, and other Icelandic Sagas*. Oxford Univ. Press, 1961.

Oxenstierna, E. G. *The Norsemen*. Weidenfeld & Nicolson, London, 1965. Picard, B. L. *Tales of the Norse Gods and Heroes*. Oxford Univ. Press, 1954.

Turville-Petrie, E. G. O. *Myth and Religion in the North*. Weidenfeld & Nicolson, London, 1964

Vries, J. de *Heroic Song and Heroic Legend*. Oxford Univ. Press, 1964.

Eddic Mythology (in *The Mythology of all Races*).

SLAV COUNTRIES

Chadwick, N. K. *Russian Heroic Poetry*. Cambridge Univ. Press, 1932.

Ćurčija-Prodanović, Nada. *Yugoslav Folk-Tales*. Oxford Univ. Press, 1957.

Downing, C. *Russian Tales and Legends*. Oxford Univ. Press, 1956.

Talbot Rice, T. *The Scythians*. Thames & Hudson, London, 1957.

Slavic Mythology (in *The Mythology of all Races*).

BALTIC LANDS

Cambridge History of Poland. 2 vols. Cambridge Univ. Press, 1950.

Gimbutas, M. *The Balts*. Thames & Hudson, London, 1963.

North European Mythology (in *The Mythology of all Races*).

FINLAND-UGRIA

Kirby, W. F. (trans.) *The Kalevala*. 2 vols. J. M. Dent & Sons, Ltd., London, & E. P. Dutton, New York, 1962.

Vorren, O. & Manker, E. *Lapp life and Customs*. Oxford Univ. Press, 1962.

Finno-Ugric and Siberian Mythology (in *The Mythology of all Races*).

SIBERIA

Finno-Ugric and Siberian Mythology (in *The Mythology of all Races*).

ESKIMO LANDS

Carpenter, E. *Eskimo*. Oxford Univ. Press & Toronto Univ. Press, 1959.

Coccola, R. de, and King, P. *Ayorama*. Oxford Univ. Press & Toronto Univ. Press, 1955.

Judson, K. B. *Myths and Legends of Alaska*. Chicago Univ. Press, 1911.

Rasmussen, Knud. *The People of the Polar North*. Kegan Paul, London, 1908.

NORTH AMERICA

Burland, Cottie. *North American Indian Mythology*. Paul Hamlyn, London, 1965.

Clark, E. E. *Indian Legends of the Pacific North-West*. Cambridge Univ. Press, 1958.

La Farge, Oliver. *A Pictorial History of the American Indian*. Spring Books, London, 1962.

Macmillan, C. *Glooskap's Country*. Oxford Univ. Press, 1956.

Martin, Paul Sidney. *Indians before Columbus*. Chicago Univ. Press, 1947.

Palmer, Wm. Rees. *Why the North Star stands still*. Bailey Bros. & Swinfen, London, 1957.

Spence, Lewis. *Myths and Legends of the North American Indians*. Harrap, London, 1914.

North American Mythology (in *The Mythology of all Races*).

CENTRAL AMERICA

Goetz, D. and Morley, S. G. *Popul Vuh* (Trans. from the Spanish of Adrián Recinos). Wm. Hodge, London, 1951.

Morley, S. G. *The Ancient Maya*. Oxford Univ. Press, 1946.

Nicholson, Irene. *Firefly in the Night*. Faber & Faber, London, 1959.

Peterson, Frederick. *Ancient Mexico*. Allen & Unwin, London, 1959

Séjourné, Laurette. *Burning Water*. Thames & Hudson, London, 1957.

Thompson, J. E. *The Rise and Fall of Maya Civilisation*. Oklahoma Univ. Press, 1956.

Vaillant, G. C. *The Aztecs of Mexico*. Penguin Books, Harmondsworth, 1952.

Von Hagen, Victor W. *The Ancient Sun Kingdoms*. Thames & Hudson, London, 1962.

Latin-American Mythology (in *The Mythology of all Races*).

SOUTH AMERICA

Bushnell, G. M. S. *The Ancient Peoples of the Andes*. Penguin Books, Harmondsworth, 1949.

Flornoy, Bertrand. *Inca Adventure*. Allen & Unwin, London, 1956.

Leicht, Hermann. *Pre-Inca Art and Culture*. MacGibbon & Kee, London, 1960.

Mason, John Alden. *The Ancient Civilisations of Peru*. Penguin Books, Harmondsworth, 1957

Von Hagen, Victor W. *The Desert Kingdoms of Peru*. Weidenfeld & Nicolson, London, 1965.

Latin-American Mythology (in *The Mythology of all Races*).

OCEANIA

Berndt, R. M. *Djanggawul*. Routledge, Kegan Paul, London, 1952. *Kunapipi*. F. W. Cheshire. Melbourne, 1951

Heyerdahl, Thor. *Aku-Aku*. Allen & Unwin, London, 1958.

McConnell, Ursula. *Myths of the Munkan*. Cambridge Univ. Press, 1957.

Mead, Margaret. *Coming of age in Samoa*. Jonathan Cape, London, 1929.

Métraux, André. *Easter Island*. André Deutsch, London, 1957.

Paxton, P. *Bush and Billabong*. Alliance Press, London, 1945.

Reed, Alexander. *Legends of Rotorua*. Bailey Bros. & Swinfen, London, 1958.

Ward, Russell. *The Australian Legend*. Oxford Univ. Press, 1958.

Oceanic Mythology (in *The Mythology of all Races*).

AFRICA

Abrahamsson, H. *The Origin of Death*. Kegan Paul, London, 1952.

Fuja, A. *Fourteen Hundred Cowries*. Oxford Univ. Press, 1962.

Gorer, Geoffrey. *Africa Dances*. John Lehmann, London, 1949.

Parrinder, G. *West African Religions*. Epworth Press, London, 1949. *African Traditional Religions*. Hutchinson, London, 1954.

Rattray, R. S. *Religion and Art in Ashanti*. Oxford Univ. Press, 1927.

Wingfield, R. J. *The Story of Old Ghana, Melle, and Songhai*. Oxford Univ. Press, 1957.

Yoruba Folk Tales. Longmans, Green & Co., London, 1949.

African Mythology (in *The Mythology of all Races*).

INDEX

Index to Illustrations